This is a study of Colombia during the final century of Spanish rule, spanning the years between the accession of the Bourbon dynasty to the Spanish throne in 1700 and the collapse of Spain's colonial authority in 1810. Based on extensive research in Spanish and Colombian archives, it gives a full account of the region's economic and political development during a distinctive period in Spanish American history when the Bourbon monarchy strove to rebuild Spain's power by rationalizing the institutions and expanding the economy of its empire. Colombia (then known as New Granada) was one of the first of Spain's American dominions affected by Bourbon reformism, and the interactions of new policies with existing economic structures, established forms of government, and entrenched political practices are central themes in this book.

To gauge the impact of Bourbon imperialism, the study focuses first on the context within which colonial government functioned, sketching the salient features of its development from the sixteenth century, charting the regional components of economy and society during the eighteenth century, and tracing the trajectory and economic influence of the gold mining industry that underpinned its commerce. The book then analyzes the influence of Spanish imperialism on the region's economic and political development by examining the origins and effects of Bourbon policies designed to revitalize Spanish exploitation of the region's resources and to assert authority over its peoples. In so doing, it offers a general reassessment of the impact of Spanish imperialism on the region's economy. These findings are matched by a detailed depiction of political and ideological developments during the eighteenth century, showing the interplay of institutional reform and intellectual innovation with rebellion and sedition, mapping shifts in creole political thinking and assessing their implications for the stability of the colonial order. Finally, the book turns from the functioning of the colonial order to a close examination of the context and causes of its collapse, showing, by way of conclusion, how external events interacted with internal pressures to bring about the fall of the colonial regime and the emergence of a movement for political emancipation.

D1552916

CAMBRIDGE LATIN AMERICAN STUDIES

GENERAL EDITOR
SIMON COLLIER

ADVISORY COMMITTEE
MALCOLM DEAS, STUART SCHWARTZ, ARTURO VALENZUELA

75

COLOMBIA BEFORE INDEPENDENCE

For a list of other books in the
Cambridge Latin American Studies series,
please see page 400

COLOMBIA BEFORE INDEPENDENCE

ECONOMY, SOCIETY, AND POLITICS UNDER BOURBON RULE

ANTHONY McFARLANE

CAMBRIDGE
UNIVERSITY PRESS

PUBLISHED BY THE PRESS SYNDICATE OF THE UNIVERSITY OF CAMBRIDGE
The Pitt Building, Trumpington Street, Cambridge, United Kingdom

CAMBRIDGE UNIVERSITY PRESS
The Edinburgh Building, Cambridge CB2 2RU, UK
40 West 20th Street, New York NY 10011–4211, USA
477 Williamstown Road, Port Melbourne, VIC 3207, Australia
Ruiz de Alarcón 13, 28014 Madrid, Spain
Dock House, The Waterfront, Cape Town 8001, South Africa

http://www.cambridge.org

First published 1993
First paperback edition 2002

A catalogue record for this book is available from the British Library

Library of Congress Cataloguing in Publication data
McFarlane, Anthony, 1946–
Colombia before independence: economy, society, and politics
under Bourbon rule / Anthony McFarlane.
p.   cm. – (Cambridge Latin American studies: 75)
Includes bibliographical references.
ISBN 0 521 41641 8
1. Colombia – History – to 1810.   2. Spain – History – Bourbons, 1700–
3. Colombia – Commerce – Spain.   4. Spain – Commerce – Colombia.
I. Title.   II. Series.
F2272.M4   1993
986.1′01–dc20   92-42299   CIP

ISBN 0 521 41641 8 hardback
ISBN 0 521 89449 2 paperback

For Angela

Contents

PART V   CRISIS IN THE COLONIAL ORDER

Tables and illustrations

Tables

Figures

Maps

Acknowledgments

My work on Colombia has benefited over the years from help and advice given by a number of people, whom I now take the opportunity to thank. Professor John Lynch provided invaluable guidance during my first years of research, enabling me to develop an interest in Spanish American colonial history and, under his supervision, to complete the doctoral thesis that started my work in Colombian history. I also benefited from his support while I was Research Fellow at the University of London's Institute of Latin American Studies, and from the friendship and interest of Professor David Rock, then a colleague at the Institute.

Friends and fellow historians in Spain and Colombia have done much to make my periods of archival research fruitful and agreeable. Particular thanks go to Hermes and Gilma Tovar, historians at the Universidad Nacional in Bogotá, for the generosity and friendship that they have shown over the years and that I have much enjoyed in Bogotá, Seville, and Sigüenza. My other great debt in Colombia is to Margarita Garrido and the late German Colmenares. Their invitations to teach at the Universidad del Valle in Cali enabled me to benefit from their expertise in Colombian history, while simultaneously enjoying the tremendous hospitality that they and their families have unstintingly offered. The staff of archives in Colombia and Spain have been unfailingly courteous and helpful. I am particularly grateful to Señora Pilar Moreno de Angel and to Dr. Jorge Palacios who, as directors of the Archivo Nacional in Bogotá, did much to expedite my research by providing the assistance of the archive's microfilming service.

I would also like to extend my thanks to those who have given me help during the writing of this book. Simon Collier encouraged me to proceed and gave gentle but timely reminders of the need to finish. At the University of Warwick, Rachel Parkin, Rebecca Earle, and especially Caroline Williams have contributed to the task of constructing and presenting the tables in the text, help that I very much appreciate. My colleague Dr. Guy Thomson patiently read a draft of the book and made encouraging comments, and Professor John TePaske very kindly allowed me to refer to the data from the royal treasury in New Granada, which he and Professor Alvaro Jara have compiled from records in the Archivo General de Indias. Financial help from the Ford Foundation's Foreign Fellowship Program helped me to start research in Colombia, and subsequent grants from the University of Warwick, the British Academy, and the Banco de España have at crucial intervals provided the means to sustain and to extend my interest in Colombian history.

Money and measures

castellano: a weight of gold worth approximately 2 silver pesos, depending on the assayed value of the gold

peso de oro: 2 silver pesos

marco: a weight of gold valued at 136 silver pesos

doblón: a gold coin worth 4 silver pesos

peso: a silver coin worth 8 reales

real: 34 maravedis

carga: 260 pounds

quintal: 100 pounds

tercio: 100 pounds

fanega: 110 pounds

arroba: 25 pounds

libra: 1 pound

Abbreviations

Archives

AGI	Archivo General de Indias, Seville
AHNM	Archivo Histórico Nacional, Madrid
AHNC	Archivo Histórico Nacional de Colombia
ACC	Archivo Central del Cauca, Popayán
AHA	Archivo Histórico de Antioquia, Medellín
ACM	Archivo del Cabildo, Medellín
BNC	Biblioteca Nacional de Colombia, Bogotá
BL	British Library, London

Journals

ACHSC	*Anuario Colombiano de Historia Social y de la Cultura*
AEA	*Anuario de Estudios Americanos*
BHA	*Boletín de Historia y Antigüedades*
HAHR	*Hispanic American Historical Review*
JLAS	*Journal of Latin American Studies*

Introduction

This is a history of Colombia during the last century of Spanish rule, when
the territory of the modern republic of Colombia stood at the heart of the
Spanish Viceroyalty of New Granada. Based largely on research in Spanish
and Colombian archives, it is primarily designed as a contribution to the
historiography of Spanish America during the period of Bourbon rule
between 1700 and 1810. However, as there is no general history of
Colombia during this period, the present study also aims at a synthesis,
combining the results of archival research with the evidence and inter-
pretations found in the specialized works of other historians of colonial
Colombia.

The choice of region and period covered by this study are easily explained. Apart from its intrinsic interest, Colombia, or New Granada as it
was called during the period of Spanish rule, is a region that deserves more
attention from historians of Spanish America. For, although it was a
colony of second rank that did not compare in size or wealth to the
viceroyalties of Peru and New Spain, New Granada was independent of
the great colonial economic systems that focused around silver mining in
the older viceroyalties, and stands as a separate and distinctive territory
with a character of its own. From the sixteenth century, the country had
its own mining sector, its own connection to the system of Spanish
Atlantic trade, and an increasingly distinctive society in which the Indian
population was largely replaced by people of mixed race. During the
eighteenth century, New Granada also became the core of the first new
viceroyalty created since the sixteenth century, and saw one of the greatest
popular rebellions of the late colonial period. Then, during the early
nineteenth century, it became a major theater for political experimenta-
tion and conflict following the break with Spain in 1810, and, after 1819,
provided Bolívar with a base for launching wars of liberation against the
remaining bastions of royalist control in the continent.

The period covered here, between 1700 and 1810, is of special interest,
since it encompasses a distinctive phase in the history of Spain and its
empire, delimited by two major political conjunctures. Opening with the
crisis triggered by the accession of the Bourbon dynasty to the Spanish

throne in 1700, and closing with another crisis caused by its collapse in 1810, this was a period when the Bourbon monarchy sought to rebuild Spain's control over its empire, both politically and economically. Indeed, it is said that resurgent Spanish imperialism became so forceful in the later eighteenth century that it constituted a veritable "second conquest of America," and was so disruptive of established interests that it prepared the conditions for the movements that later led to Spanish American independence.[1]

Our general picture of Spanish American history in the eighteenth century is, then, of colonial regions exposed to a burgeoning Bourbon imperialism, which, by rationalizing the colonial political and economic system in disregard of colonial interests, created a context for the eventual collapse of imperial authority. Does New Granada fit into this picture? We know this was a region that, like others in Spanish America, was directly affected by Bourbon policies designed to change traditional economic and political relations with the parent power; we also know that Bourbon colonial reform generated political tension and resistance, most notably during the Comunero rebellion of 1781. Indeed, historians of colonial Colombia invariably assume that economic and political change during the period of Bourbon rule created tensions that prepared the way to independence, either by inducing or by exacerbating strains in the country's social and political fabric.[2] But how, precisely, was late colonial Colombia affected by the revival of Spanish imperialism during the eighteenth century? Did Bourbon administrative reform transform the colonial order in New Granada, giving Madrid tighter control over the territory's government and forcing its people to contribute a larger share of their resources to metropolitan needs? Did Bourbon economic reform change the character of the colony's economy, making it contribute more to Spain to the disadvantage of colonial interests? And what, precisely, were the repercussions of Bourbon policies on political attitudes and behavior in the colony? How did colonials react to new metropolitan demands, and what was the character of their response? Can we detect in colonial political behavior any alteration in political culture involving new ideas and principles, perhaps signaling the emergence of a proto-national consciousness that would later surface in the movements for independence?

In addressing these questions, this book will show that, throughout the eighteenth century, the Bourbon monarchy's efforts to tighten Spain's control over New Granada and to enhance exploitation of the region's

1. The best statement of this position is John Lynch, *The Spanish American Revolutions, 1808–1826* (2nd ed., London, 1986), chap. I.
2. This argument is forcefully put by Indalecio Liévano Aguirre, *Los grandes conflictos sociales y económicos de nuestra historia* (3rd ed., Bogotá, 1968).

resources were constantly beset by difficulties. At the start of the century, Bourbon ministers found that the colony's government and commerce were in considerable disarray. Under Hapsburg rule the region had been thoroughly hispanicized, but lax government, characterized by corrupt practices and the collusion of Spanish officials with provincial interests, had seriously undermined Madrid's ability to enforce its will. New Granada's economic ties to Spain had also become very tenuous. Trade through the Spanish monopoly had done little to develop exports other than gold, and during the transition from Hapsburg to Bourbon rule a substantial share of New Granada's small markets for European imports was being taken by foreign interlopers through contraband. New Granada was, moreover, a large, diverse, and loosely integrated territory, where the division of power among provincial governments impeded the imposition of a central command from Spain, and where geographic realities inhibited the construction of clear lines of commerce and communication with Spain.

To bring the colony back under closer Spanish control was, however, beyond the capacity of early Bourbon governments. For although reform started early in New Granada, it proceeded fitfully and was inefficiently applied. Pragmatic reactions to general problems of colonial commerce and defense were followed by reversals of policy and long periods of inaction. The first experiment with viceregal government was short-lived, and the accompanying reform of the colonial commercial system did little to change the colony's economic relations with the metropolitan power. The reestablishment and consolidation of the viceregency at mid-century gave the crown a more solid authority in New Granada, and the simultaneous reform of the commercial system brought a steadier flow of transatlantic trade. However, neither Spanish viceroys nor Spanish merchants substantially altered the position of the colony within the empire. The viceroys gave royal authority a stronger image, but New Granadan government continued to be dominated by a small, conservative colonial establishment in which long-serving officials colluded with local interests in order to enjoy the prerogatives and perquisites of office. New Granada's commercial development was also dominated by vested interests, which, bred in the restrictive practices of Spanish commercial monopoly, sought not to expand commerce but rather to sustain their hold over the existing channels of trade.

During the reign of Charles III, Spanish policy toward New Granada was for the first time shaped within a coherent strategy for controlling the colonies and harnessing their economic and fiscal potential. However, as soon as Madrid made a concerted effort to strengthen the colonial state in New Granada, it encountered a powerful reaction in defense of local autonomy. That reaction, embodied in the Comunero rebellion of 1781, not only revealed the continuing weaknesses of colonial government, but deflected Madrid from the wholehearted pursuit of plans for restructuring New Granada's administration. And, if rebellion blunted the edge of Bourbon political reform, the Caroline program for imperial economic reform, built around the concept of *comercio libre*, or freer trade within the empire, also failed to transform New Granada into a productive satellite of Spain. Trade with the metropolis expanded, but long-standing obstacles to commercializing and controlling New Granada's resources meant that the regime of *comercio libre* had a limited impact on both the character of colonial commerce and the organization of the region's economic life.

It seems, then, that the picture of late colonial Colombia as a society where metropolitan exploitation and oppression induced major economic changes and generated irreparable political rifts is substantially flawed. In fact, the forces of political change derived more from demonstrations of Spain's debility than from displays of its authority. First, the dissemination by Spanish functionaries of ideas for social and economic improvement, of the kind that Bourbon "Enlightened Despotism" introduced to advance the development of the Spanish nation, combined with the rise of republicanism in North America and Europe to induce a change in the cultural values and political outlook of New Granada's small educated creole minority. At the end of the eighteenth century, Bourbon policy accentuated creole resentment toward colonial government by excluding creoles from positions of power and influence that they felt their birth and education gave them the right to share. At the same time, the transmission of new economic and political ideas through colonial officials, books, and newspapers gave educated creoles tools for criticizing the colonial regime and for developing a new assertiveness. The principles of contemporary science and political economy also encouraged them to identify and classify the character and resources of their land, and this in turn enabled creoles to perceive their country in a new light. Through discussion and exchange of information, they gradually came to conceive of a community with an identity and interests that transcended the narrow, localized boundaries of New Granada's distinctive regions. But if an alternative to Spanish rule was first imagined among New Granada's small creole intelligentsia, the supersession of the colonial order only became possible when metropolitan power collapsed at its center. In the end, it was imperial crisis, rather than reactions against Bourbon absolutism or the foresight of enlightened "precursors," that created the conditions for political emancipation in Colombia.

These observations and arguments, which form the main threads of this book, are elaborated in detail in five separate sections. Part I depicts the contours of New Granada's economy and society during the colonial period. In characterizing the country's social and economic structures, some

Colombian historians have emphasized variations in modes of production. Luis Nieto Areta, for example, distinguishes between "colonial" and "anticolonial" sectors, associated with different patterns of colonization and land tenure. More recently, Salomón Kalmanovitz has analyzed the colonial economy in terms of the social relations that developed between settlers and Indians, landowners and mestizo peasants, and slaveowners and slaves.[3] These are valuable interpretative and explanatory approaches, but for the purpose of this analysis, which focuses on New Granada's place within the Spanish empire, I prefer a different approach, one closer to that used by Ospina Vásquez in his economic history of Colombia.[4] This method characterizes the colonial economy by region, starting from the assumption that each region had its own peculiar structure, based in the history of Spanish and native interaction after the conquest and shaped by local variations in geography, climate, resources, and access to the circuits of overseas trade. Thus, the chapters in Part I depict New Granada's social and economic development during the eighteenth century by outlining the pattern of regions underlying administrative divisions, plotting the provincial contours of economic and social life, and tracing trends in the production of gold, the territory's most valuable commercial commodity.

This portrait of the forms and dynamics of colonial Colombia's economy is complemented, in Part II, by a detailed account of the territory's overseas commerce. This has three parts. The first is an analysis of Bourbon commercial policies and their effects on movements of shipping and trade during the eighteenth century; the second shows how the expansion of commerce affected the exploitation of resources and the development of the territory's economy; a final chapter in this section analyzes the character, evolution, and influence of the mercantile community that handled the territory's overseas trade, focusing especially on the peninsular merchants who dominated trade in Cartagena de Indias, New Granada's leading port.

These essays in the economic history of eighteenth-century New Granada are followed by an account of the territory's administrative and political history during the late colonial period. Part III examines the principal stages in the evolution of Spanish administrative and fiscal policies during the eighteenth century, from the first experiment with viceregal government in 1719–23, through the permanent re-establishment of the Viceroyalty of New Granada in 1739, to the "revolution in government" planned by Charles III's ministers during the 1770s and 1780s. Discussion of policy change and its institutional and financial implications is paral-

3. Luis Nieto Arteta, *Economía y cultura en la historia de Colombia* (6th ed., Bogotá, 1975), chap. 1; Salomón Kalmanovitz, *Economía y nación: Una breve historia de Colombia* (2nd ed., Bogotá, 1986), Part I.

4. Luis Ospina Vásquez, *Industria y protección en Colombia, 1810–1930* (Medellín, 1955).

leled, in Part IV, by analysis of the structures of government, the characteristics of colonial political culture, and the political repercussions of changes in the institutions and ideology of the Hispanic monarchy during the later eighteenth century.

Part Five concludes the study by examining the effects of international war and metropolitan crisis on New Granada's economic and political life at the turn of the century, and by explaining the conditions that made a movement for self-government possible during the years of imperial crisis from 1808 to 1810. A brief epilogue then suggests how the underlying structures of society and economy set down under Spanish rule continued to shape the country's development for at least the first half-century of its existence as an independent republic.

Before proceeding, a word of definition. When referring to eighteenth-century Colombia, I prefer to use the Spanish name "New Granada" instead of the rather cumbersome and anachronistic "colonial Colombia." In fact, New Granada was a title that was attached to several administrative entities of different scale and purpose during the period of Spanish rule. When first established by Gonzalo Jiménez de Quesada in the mid-sixteenth century, the *Nuevo Reino de Granada* encompassed the Chibcha lands he had conquered, and did not initially extend far beyond the hinterlands of Santa Fe de Bogotá and Tunja. The name then took on a wider meaning following the establishment of the audiencia of New Granada and the archdiocese of New Granada during the mid-sixteenth century. The audiencia's jurisdiction embraced central and northern Colombia, whereas the southern half of the country, in the huge province of Popayán, came within the jurisdiction of the audiencia of Quito. The archdiocese, on the other hand, linked New Granada to the dioceses of Popayán, Santa Marta, Cartagena, and Mérida. Finally, during the eighteenth century, New Granada became associated with the much larger political entity of the Viceroyalty of New Granada, which incorporated a huge area in its jurisdiction, embracing the audiencias of Quito and New Granada and the captaincy-general of Venezuela. To avoid confusion, the reader should note that my use of the term New Granada follows the usage common among Colombian historians, and refers only to the territory of modern Colombia.

1

Foundations

To trace the origins of the Spanish colonial society that later became the Republic of Colombia, we must return to the opening decades of the sixteenth century, when Spaniards ranged along the coast between Cabo de la Vela and the Isthmus of Panama, searching for gold and slaves. [1] Experiments in permanent settlement on these mainland shores started early. Alonso de Ojeda founded the first colony in Colombian territory at San Sebastián de Urabá in 1510, after his raids in the Cartagena region had been repelled by belligerent local tribes. Further Indian hostility, again provoked by Spanish slaving raids, forced another move west, to Darién, where the Spaniards founded a new base at Santa María de la Antigua. Again, the colony was short-lived. Stricken by disease, the local Indians became incapable of supporting the Europeans' parasitic community, and in 1524 Santa María de la Antigua was abandoned. Yet again, the Spaniards moved west, this time to Panama, which, as Castilla del Oro ("Golden Castile"), became a fresh focus for Spanish activity. [2] Then, in 1526, other Spaniards created another, quite distinct base in Colombian territory, at the eastern end of the Caribbean coast: by founding Santa Marta, they opened what was to become a crucial frontier for conquest in Colombia's interior.

Initially, Santa Marta saw the same kind of destructive exploitation that the Spaniards practiced in Castilla del Oro. Indian communities were looted for gold, provisions, and slaves; if they mounted resistance, they were burned out of their homes and fields. These scorched-earth tactics soon depopulated the area and, as surviving Indians fled to the neighboring Sierra Nevada mountains, Spanish settlement dwindled. Santa Marta remained, however, and became a platform for expeditions into the interior, beginning in the early 1530s with forays beyond the Sierra Nevada in search of fresh sources of plunder. [3] In the same decade, the Spaniards

1. The best source of information on these early years, on which this account is based, is Carl O. Sauer, *The Early Spanish Main* (Berkeley & Los Angeles, 1966), pp. 104–19, 161–77.
2. Ibid., pp. 218–37, 247–82. Also Mario Góngora, *Los grupos de conquistadores en Tierra Firme, 1509–1530* (Santiago de Chile, 1962), pp. 16–38.
3. Juan Friede, "La conquista del territorio y el poblamiento," in *Manual de historia de Colombia* (2nd

obtained another permanent foothold on the coast, when in 1533, Pedro de Heredia founded the town of Cartagena de Indias. This settlement soon attracted hundreds of adventurers and rapidly extended its influence westward to the Sinú River and the Urabá area, and southwest into the lower reaches of the Cauca and San Jorge rivers. Gold found in the Indian tombs of the Sinú acted like a magnet, pulling in Spaniards to plunder the area in callous disregard of Indian life and culture. Eventually, Spanish looting gave way to a more systematic exploitation of the land and its peoples. During the 1540s, stock raising was established in the vicinity of Cartagena, and surviving Indians were gathered in encomiendas to provide the tributes required to sustain the invaders' settlements. Like Santa Marta, Cartagena launched expeditions inland, questing into the interior for fresh sources of Indian gold.[4] Thus, during the 1520s and 1530s, Spaniards had laid the foundations of one important region in Colombia's colonial society: that of the Caribbean coast, focused on Cartagena and Santa Marta.

By establishing bases on the Caribbean littoral, Spaniards not only put down permanent roots on the Colombian coast; they had also created stations from which to conquer and colonize the Colombian interior. After years of reconnaissance, raiding, and small-scale settlement on the Caribbean shoreline, penetration into Colombia's interior was finally achieved in the late 1530s and early 1540s, after Pizarro's discovery of Peru. At first, his conquest of the Inca state threatened to undermine Spanish activity in Colombia, as the promise of rich rewards lured Spaniards to Peru. But Pizarro's achievement also spurred Spaniards to search for new civilizations in the lands between the Caribbean and Peru; within a decade of the Peruvian conquest, bands of European adventurers entered the Colombian interior and created the "Kingdom of New Granada."

Patterns of conquest

Spanish conquerors entered Colombia's interior by several routes. One led from the south, emanating from the zones of conquest opened by Pizarro in the Inca realms of Peru and Quito. This movement was spearheaded by expeditions under the command of Sebastián de Belalcázar, who led his men from Quito into the Cauca Valley. In 1536, Belalcázar established Cali and Popayán, bases from which Spanish settlers were subsequently to carry on a prolonged and violent struggle against the surrounding Indian communities. He then launched expeditions northward, in search of the

ed., Bogotá, 1982), vol. I, pp. 130–6. On the history of Santa Marta later in the sixteenth century and during the seventeenth century, see Trinidad Miranda Vásquez, *La Gobernación de Santa Marta, 1570–1670* (Seville, 1976).

4. Carmen Gómez Pérez, *Pedro de Heredia y Cartagena de Indias* (Seville, 1984), especially pp. 1–91.

legendary El Dorado. One of these northerly *entradas* followed the course of the River Cauca into the western and central cordilleras of the Colombian Andes; this prepared the way for the creation of a chain of settlements linking the Cauca Valley to Spanish settlements in the gold-rich lands of Antioquia during the late 1530s and early 1540s. The other *entrada* was along the Magdalena River toward the Eastern Cordillera. In 1538, Belalcázar entered the lands of the Chibchas, only to find that other expeditions, from Santa Marta and Venezuela, had arrived before him.[5]

The first expedition to find the land of the Chibchas arrived in 1537, sent from Santa Marta under the command of Gonzalo Jiménez de Quesada; it was shortly followed by Belalcázar's *entrada* from the south, and by an expedition led by Nicolás de Federman that entered the Colombian highlands through Venezuela.[6] After reaching a compromise with the other leaders, Jiménez de Quesada took control of the Chibcha region. He established the *Nuevo Reino de Granada* and, in mid-1539, founded the city of Santa Fe de Bogotá as its capital. Bogotá then became a new focus for conquest and colonization within Colombia, as conquering expeditions fanned out into neighboring regions. To the north, Spanish settlement extended to Vélez, Tunja, and Pamplona; westward, Spaniards crossed the River Magdalena, founding towns at Ibagué, Mariquita, and Honda. Eastward, they moved down the slopes of the Andes to the fringes of the Llanos, establishing strongholds at Medina de las Torres, Santiago de las Atalayas, and San Juan de los Llanos. To the south, they forged a way through the Quindío Mountains, thus opening contact with the nascent settlements of the Cauca region, an area that in turn communicated with the conquest zones in Quito.[7] By the end of the sixteenth century, two streams of exploration and conquest had converged in the mountainous heartlands of Colombia. With the discovery of these lands, rich in gold and Indians, came the exploration, occupation, and exploitation of the surrounding areas, filling the space that lay between Spanish bases in the Caribbean and Spanish realms of conquest in the Inca Empire. A new and distinctive network of Spanish colonization, formed from the scattered archipelago of settlements that Spaniards created in the lands stretching southward from the Caribbean coast deep into the interior, now came into existence.

This web of incipient urban centers, from which the Spaniards sought to dominate the surrounding countryside, did not immediately constitute

5. Silvia Padilla, M. L. López Arellano, and A. González, *La encomienda en Popayán: Tres Estudios* (Seville, 197), pp. 1–19.

6. Juan Friede, *Invasión al país de los chibchas, conquista del Nuevo Reino de Granada y fundación de Santa Fe de Bogotá* (Bogotá, 1966); an excellent recent summary is Jorge Orlando Melo, *Historia de Colombia: La Dominación Española* (2nd ed., Bogotá, 1978), vol. I, pp. 145–55.

7. Melo, *Historia*, pp. 125–44.

a coherent colonial dominion. Before the arrival of the Spaniards, there
was no indigenous state with a command comparable to the Aztec and
Inca empires. Consequently, the conquerors of the northern Andes could
not appropriate a powerful indigenous tributary empire, as Cortés and
Pizarro had in Mexico and Peru. Instead, Spanish conquest and settlement
divided Colombian territory into distinctive and often competing regions
of colonization, each associated with the radius of action of the groups that
had conquered them. In the north, the *gobiernos* of Cartagena and Santa
Marta were two such regions; in the center of the country, the *Nuevo Reino
de Granada* stood apart as another distinctive entity; finally, most of
southern and western Colombia came into the huge *Gobernación de Popayán*, which formed a region separate from the *Nuevo Reino*. Indeed, for
some years it seemed that Popayán would become independent of both
Peru to the south, and New Granada to the north. When Antioquia
became a separate province in 1563, this possibility disappeared, but
Popayán remained a society that was in many ways separate and different
from New Granada. It was a region where conquest was much slower than
in the *Nuevo Reino,* because the prolonged resistance of Indian nations in
the Central Cordillera prevented Spanish settlers from exploiting resources
of land and labor in the manner of the encomenderos in New Granada.[8]
For most of the colonial period, the province of Popayán came within the
jurisdiction of the audiencia of Quito, rather than the audiencia of New
Granada. Postconquest Colombia was, then, a fragmented entity, geographically, socially, and administratively. Spanish settlements were widely dispersed and each tended to become a distinctive cell, whose inhabitants sought to mark off their own territory from competitors in order to
monopolize its resources. This tendency toward the creation of autonomous local units was, moreover, accentuated by the difficulties of communication over long distances and rugged terrain.

Environment and settlement

The geographical context within which Spanish colonial society took
shape in Colombia is readily appreciated by glancing at Map 1.1, which
shows the main contours of the territory's topography. Over a thousand
kilometers separate Cartagena on the Caribbean coast from Pasto on the
borders of Ecuador, and between these points lie several distinctive physical and climatic regions. At the heart of the territory lie a great body of
mountains, formed by the northernmost extension of the Andes. From a
single chain in the south, the intruding mountains fan out into three
cordilleras that drive high, almost parallel wedges through the center of

8. German Colmenares, *Historia económica y social de Colombia, vol. II: Popayán, una sociedad esclavista,
1680–1800* (Bogotá, 1979), pp. 11–22.

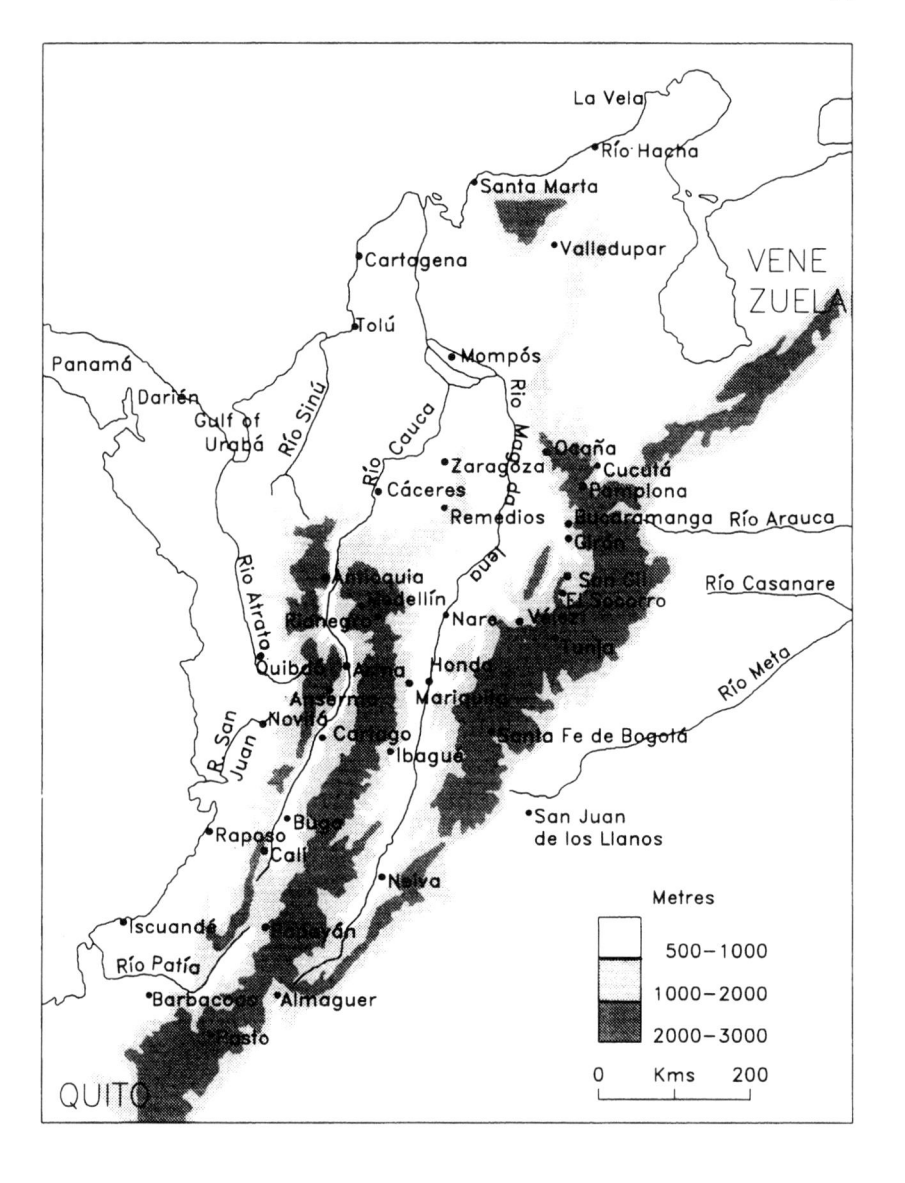

Map 1.1. New Granada: Relief.

the country, separated by the deep longitudinal corridors cut by the courses of the Cauca and Magdalena rivers. The cordilleras reach impressive heights, averaging 6,000 feet in the west, 9,000 feet in the center, and nearly 10,000 in the east, with many peaks of over 14,000 feet. The rest of the country falls into three great lowland tracts, flanking the mountain core. One lies to the west, on the Pacific coast, where the rivers of the Western Cordillera drain toward the ocean through a rugged lowland strip, mostly covered by dense rainforests. Another lies east of the Andean core, where the high peaks and intermontane basins of the Eastern Cordillera slope down into another, much larger lowland region. Here, the massive, rolling plains of the Colombian Llanos are formed around the many rivers that flow from the Eastern Cordillera into the headwaters of the Orinoco and the Amazon. Finally, in the north of the country lies another great lowland region, broken only by a final, isolated outcrop of high mountains in the Sierra Nevada of Santa Marta. This is the Caribbean coastal plain, a huge area traversed by several great river systems that flow from the cordilleras toward the sea.

Proximity to the equator means that most of the territory is tropical, but changes in altitude bring sharp regional and local variations in climate. Four main climatic zones stand out. The first, and most extensive, is the tropical lowland, which the Spaniards called *tierra caliente,* or hot country: this may be defined as including all areas at altitudes below about 3,000 feet, with an annual mean temperature greater than 24°C. Some of the tropical lowland areas supported substantial native populations at the time of conquest. Notable examples are the fertile pockets of land along the coastal fringe between Santa Marta and the Sinú River, and the tracts of *tierra caliente* in the central reaches of the Cauca and Magdalena valleys, where soils were fertile and rainfall moderate. But most of the tropical lowlands were very sparsely populated both before and after the arrival of the Spaniards. On the western coast, bordering the Pacific, the high temperatures of *tierra caliente* were combined with heavy rainfall and the poor, swampy soils of the region were covered by a dense layer of primeval forest. In the east, the Llanos offered equally few inducements to settle. The seasonally flooding grassland and forests of the plains were unsuitable for arable farming, and supported only nomadic groups of hunters and gatherers. These, then, were regions that tempted very few Spanish settlers, most of whom preferred mountainous zones where altitude alleviates the heat of the tropics and where large native populations were found on fertile lands.

One such zone was found in the climatic zone of *tierra templada,* or warm country, where the land rises to between 3,000 and 6,000 feet and the mean temperature falls to about 17.5°C. There, on the temperate slopes and valleys of the cordilleras where cereals and root crops could be supplemented by sugar, tobacco, and cotton, Spaniards found well-peopled, fertile lands. The other climatic zone that drew Spaniards was the colder country, called *tierra fría,* which lies between 6,000 and 9,000 feet. Here, especially in the Eastern Cordillera around Bogotá and Tunja, and in the southern highlands around Pasto, Spaniards found an environment that was ideal for a mixed agriculture of maize, potatoes, and European cereals such as wheat and barley. Beyond that, above 9,000 feet, lay other zones which, like the Indians, Spaniards largely neglected. These were the much colder and largely uncultivable lands of the *páramo*, mist-shrouded moorlands that merge into the lower limits of the snowline at 13,000 to 14,000 feet. It was, then, in the *tierra fría* and *tierra templada* of the mountainous interior, amidst the cordilleras and on the slopes of the Magdalena and Cauca rivers, that Spaniards located most of their colonial settlements. In these settings, they not only found an environment amenable to Europeans but also encountered large and advanced Indian societies. Upon this basis, colonial society put down its firmest foundations.

Indigenous societies at the time of conquest

Invading Spaniards encountered many different native cultures within the territory of modern Colombia. None survived the encounter intact, and some disappeared completely. In Colombia, as in other parts of the Americas, contact with Europeans seems to have been deadliest for Indians in tropical lowland regions. When Spaniards first arrived on the Caribbean shoreline in the early sixteenth century, the coastal hinterland was populated by several distinctive groups, most of whom were to disappear in the onslaught of war, disease, and exploitation. The Tairona people, who inhabited the slopes of the Sierra Nevada and its neighboring plains in the Guajira Peninsula, were the most developed of these cultures. They lived in nucleated, densely populated settlements and subsisted by cultivating maize, yucca, chile peppers, and other vegetables; the Tairona also cultivated cotton to provide material for clothing, and were probably the most technically advanced people in preconquest Colombia. They employed irrigation in their agriculture, were expert in ceramics and gold working, and, though they built mainly in wood, used stone for public buildings and for the elaborate causeways that linked their settlements.[9] West of the Tairona region, the Spaniards encountered other groups whom they were also to overcome. The most striking of these coastal societies was the Sinú people, who occupied the middle reaches of the Sinú River and its neighboring plains. Like the Tairona, they lived in stratified communities with permanent systems of leadership, used irrigation in their agriculture, and created fine metal artifacts from gold obtained through trade with tribes in the interior.[10] Between the Tairona at the eastern end of Colombia's

9. Gerardo Reichel-Dolmatoff, *Datos históricos-culturales sobre los tribus de la antigua Gobernación de Santa Marta* (Bogotá, 1951).

10. B. LeRoy Gordon, *Human Geography and Ecology in the Sinú Country of Colombia* (Berkeley, California, 1957).

Foundations

Caribbean littoral and the Sinú in the west, there were smaller native groupings with their own distinctive languages and forms of social organization. They, too, were generally sedentary agriculturalists living from maize and yucca, the two great tropical staples, supplemented with abundant fish and game found in the coastal area. The Caribbean littoral was, then, relatively heavily populated prior to the conquest and its arc of settlements, stretching along the coast and inland along the major rivers, was to act first as a barrier, then as a springboard to Spanish invasion.[11]

The mountainous Andean interior was the main target for such invasion. There the Spaniards found flourishing indigenous cultures, particularly in the high basins of the Eastern Cordillera. During the evolution of maize farming in the distant past, the intermontane basins, narrow valleys, and cool highland plateaus had attracted migration from the riverine settlements of the coastal lowlands. Because maize requires a particular pattern of seasonal distribution of temperature and rainfall for its most productive cultivation, native farmers had spread inland, moving along the valleys of the Magdalena and Cauca rivers and onto the mountain slopes in search of the optimal combination of physical and meteorological factors. The benign terrain and climate of the Eastern Cordillera's high basins provided just such a combination, and the Indians who settled this area developed relatively dense concentrations of population based on an intensive and varied agriculture. In the region formed by the upper drainage of the rivers Bogotá and Sogamoso, situated between 8,000 and 9,000 feet, a vibrant native civilization was emerging at the time of the European invasions. There, tribal groups had come together within the two loose federations of the Chibcha "kingdoms," supporting a hierarchy of chieftains, warriors, and priests, and conducting an active and intensive exchange of agricultural products, textiles, salt, and gold, both between themselves and with Indian groups in other regions of the country.[12]

To the west and southwest, in the Cauca Valley and Central Cordillera, there were many other Indian groupings whose origins, cultures, and relationships are still far from being fully understood. None of these groups was comparable to the Chibchas in social and political complexity, but taken together they formed a very significant element of the preconquest population in Colombian territory. The majority of these Indian groups lived in agricultural communities based on maize farming supplemented by hunting and fishing, with specialized artisan production of cotton textiles, an active commerce, and remarkable skills in gold and

11. For a summary account of the coastal peoples, see Melo, *Historia*, pp. 44–8.

12. Detailed accounts of Chibcha economy and society are found in Guillermo Hernández Rodríguez, *De los Chibchas a la Colonia y a la República* (Bogotá, 1978), pp. 22–199, and in A. L. Kroeber, "The Chibcha" in Julian H. Steward (ed.), *Handbook of South American Indians*, 7 vols. (New York, 1963), vol. 2, pp. 887–909.

metal working, especially among the Quimbaya people. Social and political institutions varied considerably, but many were large, relatively complex communities, with thousands of inhabitants organized under hereditary leaderships and systems of tribute. There is no certainty regarding the origin of these groups. Some historians believe that these peoples were of Carib origin, because of the apparently widespread practice of ritual cannibalism reported by Spaniards. Others, using evidence of linguistic patterns, maintain that they were descended from Chibcha peoples who had fused with groups of other origins. Whatever their provenance, when faced with Spanish invasion these distinctive, often competing cultures were to mount a fierce and prolonged resistance to the Spanish invaders.[13]

In the Magdalena Valley and its surrounding slopes, the Spaniards encountered numerous other Indian societies, most of them probably the descendants of Caribs who had migrated inland along the great river and its tributaries. Such peoples – the Sondaguas, the Carares, the Muzo, the Colima, and the Pijaos – were sedentary agriculturalists. They subsisted from maize and yucca cultivation, lived in tribal communities organized in extended families without any high degree of specialization or hierarchy, and often occupied territories that were only roughly demarcated from those of their neighbors. To the south, in the upper reaches of the Magdalena, this pattern varied. There, the peoples known as the Timaná, the Yalcones, and the Páez lived in larger, more stratified communities based on maize and potato cultivation, and with cultural and linguistic characteristics that suggest an ancient affiliation with Chibcha rather than Carib culture. Still farther south, in the highland areas where modern Colombia borders with Ecuador, there were other Indian groupings, some of possible Carib origins, others distantly related to the Chibchas, and all of whom again represented distinctive cultures. Of these, the Pastos and the Quillancingas were probably the largest.[14] These groups had an advanced agriculture, based on cultivation of maize and potatoes, and some were to survive as substantial peasant populations after the Spanish conquest.

Native societies were quickly and severely depleted in the century after the conquest. It is impossible to gauge precisely the scale and pace of the decline, because estimates of the Indian population at the time of the conquest vary widely. Some historians believe that Colombia's native population was probably no more than about 850,000 when the Spaniards

13. On the indigenous cultures of the Cauca region, see Gregario Hernández de Alba, "The Highland Tribes of Southern Colombia," in Steward, *Handbook of South American Indians*, vol. 2, pp. 915–60; see also his "Sub-Andean Tribes of the Cauca Valley" in ibid., vol. 4, pp. 297–327. On the trade, mining, and gold working of the Cauca Indians, see Herman Trimborn, *Señorío y barbarie en el Valle del Cauca* (Madrid, 1949), 167–92.

14. Melo, *Historia*, pp. 51–4.

arrived.[15] Others estimate that it was at least as high as three million, and possibly in excess of four.[16] Indeed, a recent calculation indicates a population in excess of one million for the Eastern Cordillera region alone, with another million in the Cauca Valley, at least half a million on the Caribbean coast, and with populations of between 300,000 and 400,000 for the upper and middle Magdalena Valley and its central slopes, and for the southern altiplano region around Pasto.[17] In light of these estimates, the scale of demographic decline during the century after the conquest was terrifying. Most Indian communities were to experience catastrophic reductions, and some suffered complete extinction.

Contours of the colonial economy

The decimation and destruction of indigenous societies, which was sudden and violent in some areas, and more gradual in others, was paralleled by the emergence of new forms of social and economic organization designed to meet Spanish needs and aspirations. Two basic patterns emerged. One was a rural economy in which arable farming combined with cattle raising to meet the basic needs of Spanish settlers; the other was a mining economy that extracted gold, essential for trade with Europe. These economies were established in the same general pattern that Spaniards employed throughout the Americas. To establish themselves in an area, Spaniards founded towns from which they sought to dominate and to exploit the local native population. These towns were not natural commercial centers, to which the products of rural hinterlands flowed in exchange for manufactures; they were, rather, power bases from which the Spanish coerced Indians to supply goods and labor to support settler communities.[18]

Spaniards were mainly drawn to areas with substantial native populations, for these had Indian labor that could be mobilized to meet settlers' needs, through *encomienda* and *mita urbana*.[19] Hence the Chibcha region,

15. Jaime Jaramillo Uribe, *Ensayos de historia sobre la historia colombiana* (Bogotá, 1968), p. 91.
16. Hermes Tovar Pinzón, "Estado actual de los estudios de demografía histórica en Colombia," *ACHSC*, vol. 5 (1970), pp. 65–103. For a recent comment on this debate, and an emphasis on the peculiarly destructive effects of Indian porterage, see Thomas Gomez, *L'Envers de L'Eldorado: Economie Coloniale et Travail Indigène dans la Colombie du XVIème Siècle* (Toulouse, 1984), pp. 309–24.
17. Melo, *Historia*, pp. 63–9.
18. For further comment on the role of early Spanish towns in America, see Richard Morse, "Some Characteristics of Latin American Urban History," *American Historical Review*, vol. 67 (1962), pp. 317–38.
19. On the development of colonial settler societies on the basis of these institutions in two important areas of New Granada, see German Colmenares, *Encomiendas y población en la Provincia de Pamplona, 1549–1650* (Bogotá, 1969), and *La Provincia de Tunja en el Nuevo Reino de Granada: Ensayo de Historia Social, 1539–1800* (2nd ed., Tunja, 1984).

with its dense population, well-cultivated lands, and disciplined labor force, soon became the core area for Spanish occupation of the interior, focused on Bogotá and Tunja.[20] In the south, Spaniards settled in the Upper Cauca Valley, with strongholds at Popayán and Cali; in the west, they entered the Central Cordillera and founded the province of Antioquia. Indian communities in these regions were rarely comparable to the Chibchas in their social and economic complexity; however, they had relatively large populations, well-organized agricultural systems and, most important, traditions of gold mining and gold working, all of which the Spanish were eager to exploit. Thus, the larger indigenous communities were soon harnessed to satisfy the Spaniards' two primary needs: to establish permanent settlement based on control of native agricultural societies, and to exploit deposits of precious metals.

The development of mining played a particularly important part in shaping the colonial economy. The search for gold in the region had started early in the sixteenth century, when Spaniards carried to the mainland the quest for gold that had dominated their activities in the Caribbean islands. Thus, after establishing themselves at Santa María la Antigua in Darién, Spaniards quickly set about prospecting for gold in local rivers and streams. In 1512, an expedition under Balboa's command made a first probe into the gold-producing regions of the Colombian interior, sallying southward from the Gulf of Urabá in a quest for the lands of "Dabeiba," a great cacique said to be rich in gold. They failed to find the sources of gold, however, and for another generation Spanish adventurers concentrated on ransacking the stocks of gold ornaments found among native peoples along the shores of Tierra Firme.[21]

In these early years, the search for gold involved looting rather than mining. In the 1530s, Pedro de Heredia and his companions explored and raided the Sinú country between Cartagena and Darién, ransacking the tombs of the Sinú peoples for mortuary regalia. From grave robbing on the Caribbean littoral, Spaniards from Cartagena were then drawn deeper inland in search of plunder, beyond the Lower Sinú into the Cordillera Central.[22] From 1536, several expeditions, drawn by the same stories of the gold of Dabeiba that had enticed Balboa inland many years earlier, also made their way southward from Urabá. Here men from the coast were to meet competitors from the south. When Juan de Vadillo arrived at the upper reaches of the Cauca River in 1538, he encountered an expedition

20. An account of Spanish exploitation of Indians in the areas of Santa Fe de Bogotá and Tunja, and of royal efforts to control it, is given by Esperanza Gálvez Piñal, *La visita de Monzón y Prieto de Orellana al Nuevo Reino de Granada* (Seville, 1974). On the punitive methods used to extract gold from the Indians, see pp. 7–30, 103–8.
21. Sauer, *Early Spanish Main*, pp. 220–9.   22. Melo, *Historia*, pp. 113–21.

sent by Sebastián de Belalcázar from Quito, which, under the command of
Jorge Robledo, had already discovered alluvial gold in the Upper Cauca
and was extending its search over the surrounding region. Meanwhile,
Jiménez de Quesada was entering the high basins of the Eastern Cordillera, an area that also offered the prospect of rich reserves of precious
metals.[23] It was at this juncture that looting began to be supplanted by
mining, leading to the development of a gold-mining industry that was
crucial to the formation of the colonial economy in New Granada. The
pillaging of the *cabalgadas*, the raids typical of the early years on the coast,
now gradually gave way to a more systematic exploitation of mineral
resources throughout the interior, starting the first great cycle of New
Granadan mining.

The conquest of the Chibchas yielded an impressive booty in gold, but
in the long term Quesada's Kingdom of New Granada proved richer in
land and people than in gold or silver mines. Although there were some
gold placers and rich reserves of emeralds at the mines of Somondoco and
Muzo, the highlands of the Eastern Cordillera had relatively few sources of
gold. The only substantial deposits were found some hundreds of miles to
the north of Bogotá, where, from about 1552, miners set up operations in
the regions of Vélez and Pamplona. The early *vecinos* of Bogotá and Tunja
also went farther afield, west of the River Magdalena. Around mid-
century, they founded the towns of Ibagué, Mariquita, Victoria, and
Remedios, each of which became a focus for gold mining among the
western tributaries of the Magdalena. These mining zones, together with
those of Pamplona, formed one axis of the early colonial economy, providing the towns of New Granada with gold throughout the sixteenth century. But the richest deposits of gold were found far beyond the Kingdom of
New Granada, in the south and west of Colombia. There, along the course
and slopes of the River Cauca, important mining districts developed at
Cáceres and Santa Fe de Antioquia in the north, around Arma, Anserma,
and Cartago to the south, and in the headwaters of the Cauca near Popayán. To these gold fields, others were added during the second half of the
sixteenth century when Spaniards from the upper Cauca Valley pushed
into the Pacific lowlands, where they found the gold-rich rivers of the
lower Chocó. It was principally on these districts that the sixteenth-
century gold boom in New Granada was built.[24]

New Granada's gold rush was a phenomenon of the latter half of the
century, when the mining of veins and alluvions began to gather pace in

23. Robert C. West, *Colonial Placer Mining in Colombia* (Baton Rouge, Louisiana, 1953), pp. 5–8.
24. This account of early mining is drawn from two sources: German Colmenares, *Historia económica y
    social de Colombia, 1537–1719* (Bogotá, 1973), vol. I, pp. 188–95 and West, *Colonial Placer
    Mining*, pp. 9–34.

various regions of the country.[25] Until mid-century, much of the gold
found in New Granada came from Indian hoards, mainly taken from Sinú
tombs and from the Chibchas. Then, from around 1560, mining districts
in Pamplona and on the western slopes of the Magdalena became the
primary source of gold, mostly mined by Spaniards from Bogotá. Gold
production in the south and west was also underway in these years, but it
was less stable and less valuable, partly because of the scarcity of Indian
labor. From around 1580, such scarcity also began to affect the districts
controlled from Bogotá, as the Indian workforce declined dramatically.
However, gold production recuperated from this temporary crisis as new
mines came in operation after 1580. These were mainly in Cáceres and
Zaragoza, where deposits were so rich that miners could afford to buy
black slaves to work them. Production now soared to unprecedented
levels, reaching a high point in the final decade of the sixteenth century.
The boom finished around 1620. New Granada's gold output now began
either to decline or to level off, and did not recover until new deposits
were opened up in the late seventeenth and early eighteenth centuries. By
this time, however, the major circuits of the territory's external and
internal trade had been laid down. New Granada had become a distinctive region in the empire, outside the orbit of the great, silver-based
espacio peruano to the south, and with its own commercial connections to
Spain.[26]

Beyond the shifting frontiers of the mining economy, another kind of
colonial society developed, using Indian labor for agriculture. During the
years of the mining boom, the encomenderos of New Granada and Popayán exploited trade in Indian products to obtain gold from the mining
zones.[27] Spanish settlers also created large landholdings in the core areas
of conquest, on the Caribbean coast around Cartagena, in the Kingdom of
New Granada around Bogotá and Tunja, in the vicinity of Santa Fe de
Antioquia, and in the Upper Cauca valley around Popayán and beyond,
in Pasto. These landholdings were used by their owners to cultivate
European crops and to raise livestock for sale in city markets and mining
zones.[28] Before the end of the sixteenth century, landholdings of this kind
were replacing the encomienda as a major source of wealth, as the latter

25. Colmenares, *Historia económica*, vol. I, pp. 217–50.
26. The concept of an *espacio peruano* is developed by Carlos Sempat Assadourian, "Integración y
    desintegración regional en el espacio colonial: Un enfoque histórico," in his collection of essays,
    El sistema de la economia colonial: Mercado interno, regiones y espacio económico (Lima, 1982), pp. 109–
    34.
27. Gomez, *L'Envers de L'Eldorado*, pp. 81–9, 279–87.
28. For a general discussion of the formation of landed estates in New Granada, see Juan Friede,
    "Proceso de formación de la propiedad territorial en la América intertropical," *Jahrbuch für
    Geschichte Von Staat, Wirtschaft und Gesellschaft Lateinamerikas*, vol. 2 (1965), pp. 75–87.

was undermined by falling Indian numbers.[29] However, early in the seventeenth century, the prosperity of agriculture diminished when the decline of mining stunted the growth of domestic markets. As poor whites and mestizos found it increasingly difficult to live in the dwindling economy of the encomenderos and mineowners, they drifted to rural areas where they founded farming settlements that later became Spanish parishes. Such, for example, were the origins of areas, in the San Gil and Socorro region north of Tunja, and in the Medellín areas of Antioquia, that were to become much more important in the eighteenth century.

The tendencies toward ruralization and greater domestic self-sufficiency in New Granada during the seventeenth century suggest that the region became poorer as gold mining contracted, but do not necessarily mean that the colony saw a generalized retreat into economic decline. The jeremiads of royal officials may well exaggerate the scale of New Granada's depression, since they were primarily concerned to explain falling revenues and were therefore preoccupied with the performance of taxes on gold production. Depleted though it undoubtedly was, the output of gold continued to fuel the regional interchange of foodstuffs and basic manufactures. Indeed, interregional trade was fostered after 1620 by the establishment of a mint in Santa Fe de Bogotá, and by the introduction of a silver coinage that facilitated internal trade by stimulating the circulation of money and offsetting the deflationary effects of gold exports.[30]

Information on trade within New Granada during the seventeenth century is scarce, but competition over the farming of river port revenues around mid-century suggests that internal commerce in domestic products was reasonably buoyant.[31] Merchants and landowners in the districts of Santa Fe and Tunja, Neiva, and Popayán continued to profit from sales of wheat, livestock, and sugar products in the mining regions of Antioquia, Popayán, and the upper Magdalena Valley, while the flow of gold, which came in return, consolidated the foundations of a commercial agriculture laid down in the latter sixteenth century.[32] There were also signs that the colony was developing a rudimentary manufacturing sector. In the final decade of the sixteenth century, the president of the audiencia of Santa Fe called upon the corregidors in his jurisdiction to organize Indian labor in workshops for producing woollen cloth, coarse woollen skirts, blankets, and hats.[33] By 1610, there were eight such *obrajes* in the city of

29. For a full discussion of the decline of the encomienda, see Julián B. Ruíz, *Encomienda y Mita en Nueva Granada en el siglo XVIII* (Seville, 1975), pp. 125–218.
30. On the establishment of the mint and the introduction of silver coinage, see Juan Friede, *Documentos sobre la fundación de la Casa de Moneda en Santa Fe de Bogotá* (Bogotá, 1963).
31. For these revenues, see Colmenares, *Historia económica*, vol. 1, pp. 277–9.
32. Ibid., p. 286.   33. Ibid., p. 135.

Tunja, and during the seventeenth century the city became the hub of a flourishing trade, conducted with other regions in New Granada and with neighboring Venezuela.[34] The growth of interregional trade was further reinforced during the late seventeenth century by the development of farming communities in the San Gil and Socorro regions, producing crude cotton textiles both for their own use and for markets in other areas of New Granada. Thus, during the seventeenth century, New Granada went through a long phase of change and consolidation, during which it became more self-sufficient in basic foodstuffs and crude textiles, and less dependent on gold mining and imports from Spain.

Commerce with Spain was carried by the "galeones de Tierra Firme," which supplied Spanish South America via Cartagena de Indias and Portobelo/Panama. In the early years of Spanish settlement in Colombian territory, there had been several possible routes for connecting New Granada with Spain's Atlantic trade routes. One route lay overland through Venezuela to the Gulf of Maracaibo; another possibility was for a route that would connect to the Pacific sealanes, which ran between Peru and Panama; another was through Cartagena de Indias, which was linked to the interior by the River Magdalena. In the end, the latter predominated, thanks mainly to the ascendancy of Jiménez de Quesada and his patron Fernández de Lugo. Thus, rather than being absorbed into either a Venezuelan sphere of influence or oriented toward the emerging Peruvian/Pacific economy, New Granada was to take Cartagena as its leading port and to look northward to the Caribbean for its connections with the Spanish transatlantic trading system.[35]

While gold production was in full spate, commerce with Spain flourished; it began to contract from about 1610, in a decline that apparently continued throughout the century.[36] From around mid-century, the Spanish galleons that supplied New Granada and Peru became increasingly

---

34. A report made in 1761 recalled that Tunja had been "in the past century and in part of this present century, the storehouse of commodities, not only because of the abundance of products and goods of all kinds but also because of the strength and constancy of their trade; the merchants and hacendados of Maracaibo and Mérida traded annually with the province of Tunja to supply themselves with mules, blankets, hats, linens, shirts and other so-called domestic goods, some for their haciendas and others to profit from their exchange for cacao in the cities of La Grita, Cúcuta, Salazar de las Palmas and San Faustino, carrying on this trade in *pesos fuertes*, of which there was a large number . . . " AHNC, Aduanas (Cartas), tomo 8, fol. 428. For further information on the economy of Tunja in the seventeenth century, see Luis Torres de Mendoza, *Colección de Documentos Inéditos*, 42 vols. (Madrid, 1864–84), vol. 9, p. 418; also Vicenta Cortés Alonso, "Tunja y sus vecinos," *Revista de Indias*, vol. 25 (1965), pp. 196–202.

35. See Gomez, *L'Envers de L'Eldorado*, pp. 119–39. The early development of Spanish trade with New Granada is described in Pierre and H. Chaunu, *Seville y L'Atlantique* (1504–1650), 8 vols. (Paris, 1955–60), vol. XVIII (Part I), pp. 1016–42.

36. Colmenares, *Historia económica y social*, vol. 1, p. 242.

irregular, moving from annual sailings to two- or three-year, and some-times longer, intervals. Then, between 1675 and 1700, the galleons made only six return journeys, in 1675–6, 1678–9, 1681–2, 1684–6, 1690–1, and 1695–8.[37]

Historians have usually regarded this change in the pattern of sailings, together with a decline in the value of their officially recorded cargoes of treasure, as a symptom of decline in American commerce and as a signal that the colonial economies were contracting or becoming more capable of supplying their own needs. In fact, the slower movement of transatlantic traffic did not necessarily mirror a crisis of colonial commerce. It is true that official figures show a decline in the value of treasure carried to Spain from South America, but widespread evasion of duties means that govern-ment statistics are very unreliable. If we turn to the more realistic esti-mates of treasure returns from the Americas that were made for merchants outside Spain (particularly the Dutch), it seems that, far from contract-ing, the value of treasure exported from the Indies rose considerably during the late seventeenth century. Indeed, these estimates suggest trea-sure returns reached levels in the 1670s and 1690s that exceeded the peaks achieved in the heyday of the first great American mining boom.[38] So, although the fleets sailed much less frequently in the latter half of the seventeenth century, they may well have carried a more valuable trade.

Unfortunately, we do not know how much New Granada contributed to the transatlantic trade during these years, because so much was carried in contraband. What is clear, however, is that the colony's overseas trade tended to escape into the hands of foreigners. It went through contraband both within the system of Spanish shipping and outside it, directly to foreign ports in the Caribbean. For, as the English, French, and Dutch began to use their colonies in the Caribbean as bases for illegal trade with neighboring Spanish colonies, so the coasts of New Granada became a favorite target for smugglers. Cartagena de Indias was particularly attrac-tive because imports could be exchanged for gold from New Granada's interior, and because the slave-trading contracts that the Spanish crown granted to foreign companies provided a cover for illegal importing.[39]

37. Lutgardo García Fuentes, *El comercio español con América, 1650–1700* (Seville, 1980), pp. 402–3. In his quantification of the movements of shipping during this period, García Fuentes shows that transatlantic traffic fell to only 22% of the total for the century and for fifty years scarcely recovered the levels reached in the decade from 1610 to 1619. Ibid., p. 218.

38. Michel Morineau, *Incroyables gazettes et fabuleux metaux. Les retours des trésors américains d'après les gazettes hollandaises (XVIe–XVIIIe siècles)* (Cambridge, 1985), Table 41, p. 242; Table 42, p. 250; Table 43, p. 262; Table 45, pp. 279–82.

39. Curtis Nettels, "England and the Spanish American Trade, 1680–1715," *Journal of Modern History*, vol. 3 (1931), pp. 1–33.

Thus, colonial resources were diverted to foreigners through contraband, in a pattern of illegal trade that was to present Bourbon governments with a persistent problem throughout the eighteenth century.

Colonial government: Structure and development

During the late seventeenth century, the looseness of Spanish economic control over New Granada was matched by the weakness of colonial government. In theory, government was clearly and effectively structured. At its apex stood the audiencia of New Granada, created in 1550, with its seat in Bogotá and with ultimate responsibility in matters of law and civil government.[40] The territory was further divided into units of provincial government, in a number of *gobiernos, corregimientos,* and *alcaldías mayores* of varying size, wealth, and importance. By the later seventeenth century, the most important of these were Santa Fe and Tunja at the heart of New Granada, Cartagena on the Caribbean coast, and Popayán in the south. These provinces held the largest and richest towns in the territory and, with them, the strongest components of its government. As separate *gobiernos,* they were in turn divided by the jurisdictions of fiscal, military, civil, and ecclesiastical government, each designed to uphold a specific area of authority. In practice, however, such divisions fractured rather than facilitated royal control over the territory because they splintered central authority, thereby compounding the problems of communication and command imposed by distance. Some provinces, for example, were more subordinate to the audiencia in Bogotá than others. The *gobierno* of Santa Fe was most easily controlled by the audiencia because some of the responsibilities for its government were directly exercised by the audiencia's president. At the other extreme was the *gobierno y comandancia general* of Cartagena, whose governor was appointed directly by the king and who, largely because of his military preeminence, enjoyed a high degree of independence from the audiencia judges in Bogotá. Most complicated was the position of Popayán, which came under the double jurisdiction of the audiencias of Santa Fe and of Quito. In matters of civil government and defense, most of the province fell under the authority of Quito, though this was disputed by the audiencia in Santa Fe, which retained some rights in these spheres. In the ecclesiastical sphere, there were also divisions, with the diocese of Popayán pertaining to the archdiocese of Santa Fe de Bogotá, but with some parts of the province of Popayán, such as Pasto, coming into the diocese of Quito.[41]

---

40. For comment on the early phases of government in New Granada, and the difficulties facing the audiencia, see Gomez, *L'Envers de L'Eldorado,* pp. 63–77.
41. The administrative structure of New Granada, together with comments on its history, is laid out

Seventeenth-century New Granada was not, then, a unified or coherent administrative entity. The boundaries of civil and ecclesiastical governments were far from uniform, the lines of fiscal management crossed the borders between audiencias, and the authority of New Granada's audiencia was fragmented by the jurisdictions of provincial governments, several of which functioned as virtually autonomous units under governors who paid little heed to orders from Bogotá.[42] Penetration of local interests into the tribunal of the audiencia further reduced its effectiveness, diluting the efficiency of royal control over New Granada and creating problems that, in the eighteenth century, were to persuade the Bourbons to create a new political authority, a viceroy, to preside over the audiencia and provincial governments.

Even before the accession of the Bourbon dynasty, the debility of royal authority in the region had become a matter of serious concern to the crown. One problem arose from attacks on Spanish sovereignty in the area. In 1695, the Scots attempted to implant a colony at Darién and, though the expedition proved to be so ineptly organized that it posed no great danger, it was a direct and disturbing challenge to Spanish sovereignty in the area and required a military response.[43] Even worse, the port of Cartagena de Indias was assailed in 1697 by a French fleet under the command of Admiral Pointis and, after a successful attack, delivered into French hands. Although temporary, the fall of the city caused considerable losses both to private and royal economic interests, and was a humiliating defeat for Spain.[44] Not surprisingly, it raised alarm at the center of Spanish government and led to an immediate, high-level investigation of civil and military administration in Cartagena.

The weakness revealed by the fall of Cartagena was simply one aspect of a broader problem of government in the audiencia of New Granada. During the final decade of the seventeenth century, the authority of royal administration in New Granada seems to have virtually broken down in several important respects. In 1685, Charles II's Council of the Indias commissioned a *visita general* of New Granada in response to reports of "the disorder which exists in that Kingdom in the treatment of the Indians and the collection of tributes," of the virtual enslavement of the

in Francisco Silvestre, *Descripción del Reyno de Santa Fe de Bogotá* (1789) (Bogotá, 1968). Information on the province of Popayán is also drawn from Peter Marzahl, *Town in the Empire: Government, Politics and Society in Seventeenth Century Popayán* (Austin, Texas, 1978), p. 9.

42. For a general, anecdotal account of the government in early seventeenth-century New Granada, see Manuel Lucena Salmoral, "Nuevo Reino de Granada, Real Audiencia y presidentes: Presidentes de capa y espada, 1605–1628," in *Historia Extensa de Colombia*, vol. III, tomo 2 (Bogotá, 1966).

43. For a full account of the organization of the expedition in Scotland and its fate in Darien, see John Prebble, *The Darien Disaster* (London, 1968).

44. Enrique de la Matta Rodríguez, *El Asalto de Pointis a Cartagena de Indias* (Seville, 1979).

Indians by encomenderos in the province of Popayán, and of the prevalence of fraudulent practices in the registration and exportation of gold.[45] This *visita* was not to be a success; indeed, it simply dramatized the problems that it had been commissioned to resolve. *Visitador-general* Carlos Alcedo y Sotomayor was deflected from his task by the capture of Cartagena, and the *visita* ended abruptly when he was sent to the city to investigate the reasons for its fall. For when he attempted to implement his orders, Alcedo y Sotomayor was refused entry to Cartagena by the governor, who insisted that neither Alcedo nor the audiencia had any jurisdiction over him or the military establishment in the city. The governor then arrested Alcedo and, after failing to suborn him with a large bribe, deported him aboard a small, leaky boat bound for Havana.[46] But, if the *visita* came to a sudden and ignominious end, the information that Alcedo gathered before his expulsion is worth recounting, because it throws light on the problems the Spanish government faced in New Granada at the end of the Hapsburg period.

For the Spanish crown, the central problem was one of effective government. In his investigations, Alcedo found few areas in which royal authority was not openly flouted. In the two major provinces of Popayán and Santa Fe, Indian labor was exploited without regard for the law, and revenues from tributes bore no relation to Indian numbers. The crown was also defrauded of income by widespread evasion of taxes and duties on the products of the colony's single richest resource, its gold mines. Alcedo reported that a royal decree ordering payment of 50,000 pesos that *vecinos* of Mompós owed in unpaid quintos had never been implemented; he also found that collusion between miners and officials in the province of Cartagena permitted the practice of fraud on such a grand scale that, in twenty years, the minuscule sum of 241 pesos had been paid in *quintos.* Referring to the payment of quintos into the treasury of the Tribunal de Santa Fe, Alcedo further alleged that the crown was being defrauded of the enormous sum of 20,386 castellanos each year, a sum equivalent to a gold production of some 407,700 castellanos (almost a million silver pesos). Furthermore, he affirmed that the coasts of New Granada were infested by smugglers, and that foreigners, especially the Dutch, enjoyed easy access to both New Granada's markets and its gold.[47] And, although Alcedo himself achieved nothing in his investigation of the fall of Cartagena,

45. AGI Santa Fe 357, "Copia de la comisión dada a D. Carlos de Alzedo, Oidor de la Real Audiencia de Santa Fe para la visita de la tierra del Nuevo Reino de Granada" (Madrid, 1695); ibid., "Instrucción que ha de observar el Licenciado Don Carlos de Alzedo Sotomayor."

46. AGI Santa Fe 357, "Memorial de Carlos de Alcedo y Sotomayor al Consejo de Indias" (San Lorenzo, October 31, 1699). Also see Matta Rodríguez, *El Asalto de Pointis,* pp. 135–49.

47. AGI Santa Fe 357, "Lo que resulta de las consultas hechas al Consejo por D. Carlos de Alcedo Sotomayor."

evidence gathered in subsequent inquiries indicates that the city's governor had been much more concerned with lining his own pockets than with defending the city.[48] Such corruption in one of New Granada's most important cities suggests that the malfeasance of royal funds was commonplace at the highest levels of provincial government.

Alcedo's reports are insufficiently broad in scope or specific in detail to provide a comprehensive picture of New Granada's government and economy at the end of the seventeenth century; they do nonetheless convey the unmistakable impression that Spain had lost control of the region in two interrelated ways. One was economic, and was reflected in the colony's commerce. In drawing attention to the prevalence of contraband on New Granada's Caribbean coast, Alcedo's report shows the weaknesses of Spain's commercial control over the colony in the late seventeenth century. This was, of course, part of a more serious structural deficiency in imperial economic relations bound up with Spain's inability to provide its colonies with a supply of imports that was sufficiently cheap to compete with foreign goods supplied directly from the English, Dutch, and French Caribbean. The roots of the problem were, in short, in the very structure of a Spanish transatlantic trade that, by the close of the seventeenth century, had become little more than a conduit for foreign products transshipped to America through Spain.

Foreign commercial penetration also reflected Spain's political weakness in the colony. Not only did low salaries and slack supervision of officials lead to extensive collusion in smuggling, but late seventeenth-century New Granada also seems to have fragmented into a cluster of virtually autonomous provinces that were detached from close supervision from Spain. The judges of the audiencia in Bogotá might try to assert their authority over these provinces, but it was not readily acknowledged. Indeed, when the president of New Granada sought to support Alcedo's ill-fated mission to Cartagena in 1698, the ensuing dispute between the governor and the audiencia came close to armed conflict, and ended with the governor's flight to Jamaica.[49] Behind this sharp crisis within colonial government lay another phenomenon that both reflected and accentuated the weakness of royal authority: the widespread evasion of royal taxation. The impoverished state of the royal treasuries of New Granada showed that colonial officials had been deeply corrupted, while lack of funds also undermined effective administration and defense.

The transition to Bourbon rule

So, at the start of the eighteenth century, Spanish control over New Granada's government and resources was very weak. Provincial govern-

48. Matta Rodríguez, *El Asalto de Pointis*, pp. 65–78.
49. On the dispute between the audiencia and the governor, and its outcome, see ibid., pp. 135–70.

ments operated without reference to the audiencia in Bogotá, royal finances were in a shambles, trade was largely in the hands of foreigners, and coastal defense was so flimsy that Cartagena de Indias, the colony's major port and military stronghold, failed to withstand attack by a French filibuster. In short, government in New Granada was divided and ineffective, cut off from the clear command of metropolitan Spain and without an undisputed single source of authority within its own territory.

If the government in Madrid was aware of these problems, it was in no position to remedy them. During the last decade of the seventeenth century, government in Spain drifted, awaiting the death of its crippled, childless king. Then, with the death of Charles II in 1700, Spain entered a deep political crisis. When Philip of Anjou, grandson and protegé of Louis XIV, inherited the throne to become Philip V of Spain, supported by France, his succession was challenged by England, Austria, and the Dutch Republic. Fearful of French dominance in Europe, these powers backed a rival Hapsburg claimant and formed a Grand Alliance to oppose the Bourbon succession, thereby plunging Spain into a prolonged international war. For over a decade, the future of Spain was kept in the balance, as rival powers fought on its territory in Europe and competed for commercial ascendancy in its American colonies.

At the end of the War of the Spanish Succession (1702–13), Philip V retained his throne, and Spain entered a new stage in its political history. Under a monarchy that aspired to rebuild Spanish power and prestige in Europe, a long, spasmodic, and uneven process of imperial reform and realignment took place, beginning in Spain itself but gradually extending to the Americas. In New Granada, the process started surprisingly early. During the last decade of Hapsburg rule, Spain had investigated the problems of government in the region; under the first Bourbon, action was taken to remedy them, as part of a wider program of reform in American government and commerce.

Repair of Spain's colonial system did not begin immediately. Throughout the War of the Spanish Succession, Philip V's government was preoccupied with survival, and was consequently careful to avoid any novelty that might disturb relations with the colonies.[50] As far as American government was concerned, this meant that established Hapsburg practices continued. Thus, for example, the crown continued to sell appointments to the colonial audiencias, a practice that not only raised money but also helped sustain loyalty to the new regime by allowing colonials to share in the power and perquisites of government.[51] In New Granada,

---

50. Henry Kamen, *The War of Succession in Spain, 1700–1715* (Bloomington, 1969), pp. 9–41; John Lynch, *Bourbon Spain, 1700–1808* (Oxford, 1989), pp. 22–60.

51. On the sale of office in these years, see Mark A. Burkholder and D. S. Chandler, *From Impotence to Authority: The Spanish Crown and the American Audiencias, 1697–1808* (Columbia, Mississippi, 1977), pp. 18–36.

meanwhile, there was no effort to follow up the investigations made by Alcedo y Sotomayor, nor any attempt to repair the disorders in government that he had encountered. New Granada therefore continued under the same weak, decentralized form of government that had prevailed under the last Hapsburg, without any novel intervention from the central authorities in Spain. It was only when the War of Succession was over that Philip V embarked on policies to revive Spain and its empire; then, for the first time during the eighteenth century, New Granada became the arena for reformist policies formulated in Madrid.

At first, Bourbon reorganization of the Spanish state focused on Spain itself. Counseled by his French advisors, Philip V concentrated on administrative reform at home, remodeling Spain's government along more centralized lines, stabilizing the coinage, and stimulating royal finances. His first priority was to shift power away from the traditional conciliar structure dominated by the aristocracy, toward a cabinet, or *despacho,* working through departmental ministries. Started during the War of Succession, this administrative restructuring was formalized in 1714 with the creation of four secretaries of state: war, justice, state, and navy and colonies. Despite a brief reversal in 1715, the new form of government continued to develop and to propagate reforms, and as it took root, so was more government attention given to the Americas. Between 1716 and 1723, the new Secretariat for the Navy and the Indies became active, bringing both colonial government and commerce under review, and elaborating policies designed to make the colonies more responsive to Spanish needs.[52]

From this context, the first Bourbon reforms to affect New Granada emerged. Political reform began with the establishment of the first Viceroyalty of New Granada in 1719; economic reform started in 1720 with a project for revivifying Spanish commerce with New Granada and Peru. During the course of the century, these reforms were followed by other measures which, being aimed at improving the Spanish colonial system, enhancing royal authority and increasing the flow of colonial resources from the Americas to Spain, also affected New Granada's economy and government. However, before we examine the impact of Bourbon imperialism, we must first map out the salient features of New Granada's society and economy, and trace the main trends in its demographic and economic development during the century of Bourbon rule.

52. Kamen, *The War of Succession*, pp. 83–117; John Lynch, *Bourbon Spain*, pp. 60–6.

PART I

Economy and society in eighteenth-century New Granada

2

Resources and regions

Seventeenth-century maps of New Granada show a country divided into four great administrative units, each a relic of the years of Spanish conquest. On the Caribbean coast were the two *gobiernos* of Santa Marta and Cartagena; in the interior, the *Nuevo Reino de Granada* dominated the east of the country; in the west and southwest lay the great *governación de Popayán,* extending to the borders of Ecuador. Eighteenth-century maps, by contrast, present a more detailed picture of the territory's topographical features and administrative divisions, showing all the provinces created by postconquest settlement and, in later maps, placing these provinces within the framework of the viceroyalty created by the Bourbon monarchy.[1] Greater cartographical sophistication was in part a reflection of the progress of government under Bourbon rule, and the splendidly detailed *Plan Geográfico del Vireynato de Santafé de Bogotá, Nuevo Reyno de Granada,* drawn up in 1772, mirrors the new concern with ordering and controlling colonial territory.[2] But if better maps present a more accurate definition of the land and its political boundaries, much is also concealed beneath their orderly surface. When New Granada first came under Bourbon rule, it was a mosaic of regions, each isolated from the others by long distances and difficult terrain, and distinguished by cultural differences arising from variations in the local blend of Europeans, Indians, and Africans. The area of effective settlement was, moreover, quite small. Much of the territory shown in colonial maps was only notionally controlled by the Spanish state. Between and beyond the towns marked on contemporary maps were vast tracts of land where settlement was thinly spread or nonexistent, where administrative boundaries were blurred, and where the presence of government was often limited to the occasional visits of itinerant missionaries. Indeed, by the eighteenth century, New Granada had assumed a demographic and economic configuration that did

1. For some reproductions of colonial maps of New Granada, see Eduardo Acevedo Latorre, *Atlas de mapas antiguos de Colombia, siglos XVI a XIX* (Bogotá, 1986). For further information on maps of New Granada, see Vicenta Cortés, *Catálogo de mapas de Colombia* (Madrid, 1967); Kit S. Kapp, *The Early Maps of Colombia up to 1825* (North Bend, Ohio, 1971).
2. This map is reproduced in Acevedo Latorre, *Atlas,* pp. 100–1.

not easily lend itself to Spanish exploitation. Settlement was concentrated in the interior, far from the influence of maritime trade; the population was composed largely of free people who owed neither tributes to the colonial state nor economic prestations to its elites; and, finally, the economy was fragmented into regions whose parts interacted more with each other than with the Atlantic world.

Demography and economy

A useful vantage point from which to view New Granada's economy and society in the eighteenth century is provided by the countrywide census that was taken in 1778–80.[3] In these years, New Granada had a small population. In fact, with fewer than 800,000 people, its population was smaller than it had been in the early sixteenth century, before the decimation of the natives that followed Spanish conquest and settlement. Most people lived in the countryside, clustered in the hinterlands of rustic provincial towns with between 5,000 and 15,000 people living in their jurisdictions. Bogotá, the viceregal capital and New Granada's leading city in the late eighteenth century, had a mere 20,000 or so inhabitants; the only other city of comparable size was Cartagena de Indias, New Granada's major port.[4] As Map 2.1 shows, the great majority of New Granada's population lived deep in the interior of the country, mostly in the Eastern Cordillera where the Kingdom of New Granada had first been founded. In 1780, this region was the central nucleus of New Granada. Some 360,000 people (45% of the colony's total population) lived there, in the highland plateaus and basins between Bogotá and Pamplona, with another 82,500 (10%) in the flanking *tierra caliente* areas of the slopes and adjacent plains of the Magdalena Valley, in Guaduas, Neiva, Honda, and the province of Mariquita.

Outside this central core were three other main regions of settlement. In the north, on the Caribbean littoral, some 162,000 people (20% of the total population) lived in the provinces of Cartagena, Santa Marta, and Río Hacha, most of them in the hinterland of Cartagena de Indias, the colony's principal Atlantic port. Far to the south lay the province of Popayán, with over 91,000 inhabitants, most of them in the jurisdictions of the towns that stretched southward along the Cauca Valley and into the highlands around Popayán and Pasto. Taken together, these areas in the province of Popayán had about 11.5% of New Granada's population. To the west, colonial occupation was much less substantial. In the Central

---

3. This census is outlined in Appendix A, Table I.
4. To compare New Granadan cities in the eighteenth century with those of other Spanish American countries, see Luisa Hoberman and Susan Migden Socolow (eds.), *Cities and Society in Colonial Latin America* (Albuquerque, New Mexico, 1986), p. 5.

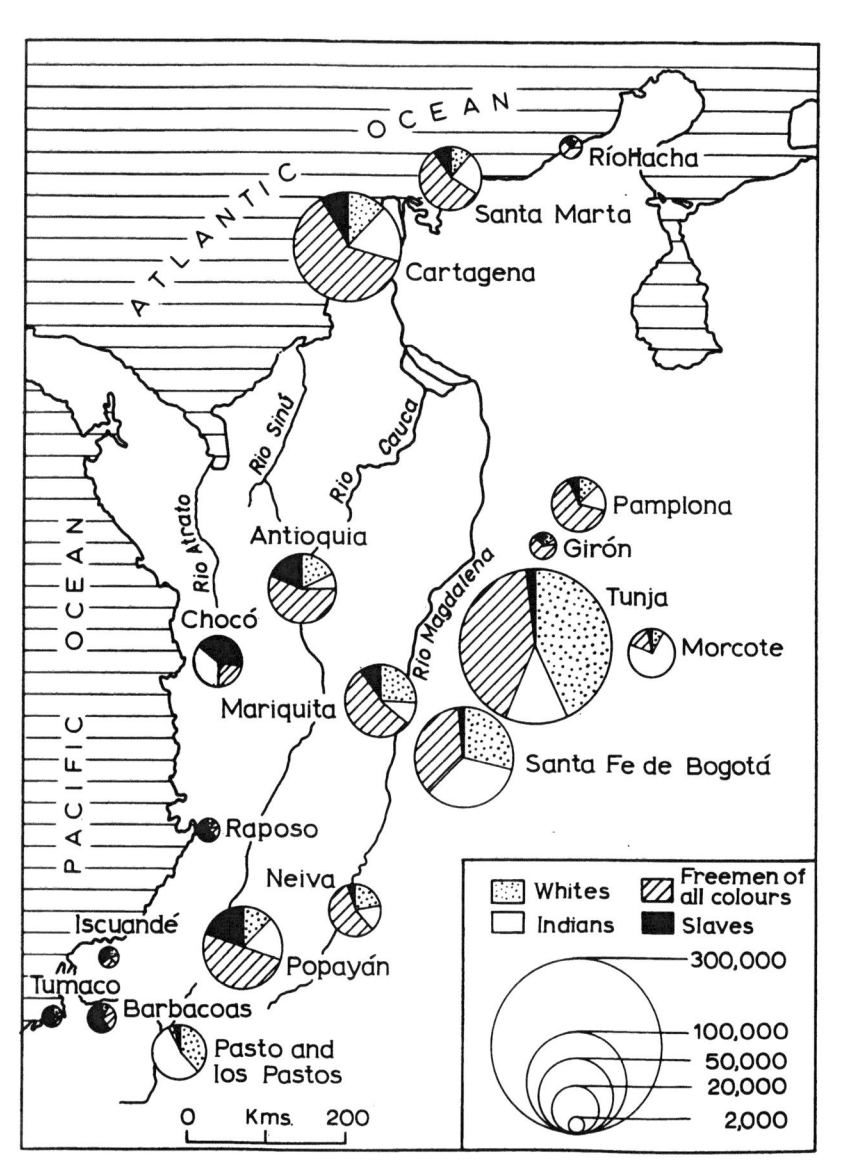

Map 2.1. Population distribution in New Granada, 1778–80. (For the census data on which this map is based, see Appendix A, Table 1.)

Cordillera, Antioquia had little more than 46,000 inhabitants (about 6% of the population), who were living from gold mining and agriculture in a region that was still scarcely colonized. Farther west and southwest, in the Pacific lowlands, were New Granada's other chief mining zones. Taken together, the gold fields of Barbacoas, Raposo, Iscuandé, and the Chocó had a population of close to 30,500 (4% of New Granada's total), of whom half were in the provinces of the Chocó.[5]

During the eighteenth century, the population was growing and changing, as New Granada became a fundamentally mestizo society, quite different from the societies of Spain's colonial heartlands in Mesoamerica and the central and southern Andes. In the 1778–80 censuses, the population was divided into the usual four racial categories: whites, blacks, Indians, and "free people of all colors" (*libres de todos colores*). Of these, by far the largest single group was that of the *libres* or mestizos. By 1780, people of mixed race made up almost half (46%) of New Granada's population. Most of the rest were classified either as white (26%) or Indian (20%), followed by a substantial minority of black slaves (8%). The preponderance of the *libres* is striking. By the end of the eighteenth century, Indian society had shrunk to a shadow of its former self, displaced by mestizos and whites. Undermined by epidemics and exploitation after the conquest, the Indian communities that were in close contact with whites were continually eroded by *mestizaje*, the process of miscegenation that drew Indians into mestizo society. At the end of the eighteenth century, the only areas in which Indians were still a local majority were in the province of Pasto, in the Llanos of Casanare, and in frontier areas along the Pacific and Caribbean coasts where Indians had successfully resisted, or evaded, white encroachments. Elsewhere, Indians had become a minority in their own land, outnumbered by whites and mestizos in a demographic structure that contrasted sharply with those of the Andean lands to the south, in Ecuador, Peru, and Bolivia.[6]

Mestizaje was the driving force behind population growth. In 1751, Basilio Vicente de Oviedo drew attention to the phenomenon of *mestizaje* and to its repercussions in rural society when he referred to population change in an area of the province of Tunja:

In the jurisdiction which today is of the town of San Gil. . . . There were three villages which in the past had 1,000 Indians; these were Guane, Chancón, and Charalá and Oiba. Today there are in all these villages 200 Indians, while of those called Spanish – which includes whites, mestizos, *cuaterones* and *cholos* – there are more than 10,000 inhabitants, of whom in truth no more than 200 have come from Spain to settle.[7]

5. Appendix A, Table 2.   6. Appendix A, Table 3 and 4.
7. Basilio Vicente de Oviedo, *Cualidades y riquezas del Nuevo Reino de Granada* (Bogotá, 1930), p. 118.

Although Oviedo was careful to point out that the Indians had not suffered the same marked tendency to decline in areas where fewer whites had settled, the process that he described was typical of most of New Granada, and reflects a general tendency for the mestizo population to expand at a far more rapid rate than that of the Indians. Indians were constantly being drawn away from their own communities into areas of white settlement where, by marriage and cohabitation with mestizos, they were being added to the half-caste population while simultaneously reducing the reproductive base of their original communities.[8]

The growth of the mestizo population was most marked in the Eastern Cordillera region, where it was clearly reflected in pressures to revise the status of the Indians' protected lands, the *resguardos de indios*. Faced with the sharp decline of the native population during the late sixteenth century, the crown had tried to regulate exploitation of the indigenous labor force and systematize the collection of tributes by concentrating Indian communities on *resguardos,* or Indian lands that were segregated from the Spanish settlements. However, in spite of strict legal proscriptions against intrusion into the *resguardos* by non-Indians, demand for land from the growing white and mestizo population, combined with the Indians' need to obtain money in order to meet their tributary obligations, encouraged the illegal leasing of resguardo lands to small white and mestizo farmers.[9] Government investigations into the condition of the Indian communities reveal that this process of assimilation and expropriation had reached an advanced stage by the latter half of the eighteenth century.[10] By 1778, invasion of Indian lands and race mixture was so advanced that the government's "protector of Indians" no longer found it feasible to distinguish between the Indian and mestizo elements of the rural population; he therefore recommended that the crown should recognize reality by formally transferring the resguardos from the communal ownership of the former to the individual proprietorship of the latter.[11]

Though less numerous than mestizos, whites too had become a substantial segment of New Granada's society. At the close of the eighteenth century, they made up a quarter of the total population. White population

---

8. Ibid. Also for a general account of the decline of the Indian population in the provinces of Tunja and Santa Fe, and its consequences, see Colmenares, *La provincia de Tunja*, pp. 85–114, and Margarita González, *El resguardo en el Nuevo Reino de Granada* (Bogotá, 1970), pp. 47–80.

9. Jaime Jaramillo Uribe, *Ensayos sobre historia social colombiana* (Bogotá, 1968), pp. 170–1; González, *El resguardo*, pp. 65–70.

10. The results of two such investigations have been published. See Andrés Verdugo y Oquendo, "Informe sobre el estado actual de la población indígena, blanca y mestiza de las provincias de Tunja y Vélez a mediados del siglo XVIII," *ACHSC*, vol. I (1963), and Francisco Antonio Moreno y Escandón, *Indios y mestizos de la Nueva Granada a finales del siglo XVIII*, ed. Jorge O. Melo (Bogotá, 1985).

11. González, *El resguardo*, pp. 71–7.

growth, like that of mestizos, was most apparent in the central region of
the Eastern Cordillera. In the huge province of Tunja and to a lesser extent
in the province of Santa Fe, poor whites (many of whom may have been
mestizos passing as whites) appear to have multiplied at a rapid rate,
particularly in the temperate areas of Socorro and San Gil where an open
land frontier had been colonized in the later seventeenth century. This
overlapping increase between the white and mestizo populations caused
some social friction. Claims to *limpieza de sangre* (pure Spanish descent)
were fiercely contested during the eighteenth century, as whites fought to
distinguish themselves from the expanding mestizo and mulatto groups.
Conflicts over the right to use the honorific title "don" (traditionally
appropriated by whites to demonstrate their superiority over the native
and half-caste masses) also multiplied, as provincial "nobles" struggled to
restrict its usage to those who, by reason of birth or office, assumed a
superiority over white as well as Indian and mestizo commoners.[12] Evidently, the growth of the white population was generalizing the use of don
to the point where it was losing its meaning as a signifier of social
standing.

The reasons for the growth of the white population lay chiefly within
New Granada. Although Spanish emigration to the Americas revived
during the eighteenth century, the peninsular Spanish component of the
population remained small. Growth in the white population therefore
stemmed from a natural increase among the American Spaniards or creoles, rather than from immigration. Of course, the growth of the creole
population did not rest solely upon the fecundity of the purely white
inhabitants. At the higher levels of society, among the wealthier landowners, mineowners, traders, and government functionaries, there were
undoubtedly prominent families who could claim unbroken white descent
and who could preserve a strictly white lineage by marrying within their
own class and with immigrant Spaniards. But among the majority of
whites, who stood outside the ranks of the social elites, marriage or
cohabitation with members of other racial groups probably served to swell
the numbers of those who might pass as white. It is not difficult to
imagine how a poor white might produce children by a mestizo or mulatto woman, allowing them to adopt the superior patrimonial racial status
and then, by mingling again with half-caste women, to produce more
offspring with a claim to whiteness.

If New Granada's population was undoubtedly increasing during the
later eighteenth century, it is difficult to measure the pace of growth or
trace its regional variations. According to Viceroy Caballero y Góngora,
the population of the whole viceroyalty, including both the audiencias of

12. Jaramillo Uribe, *Ensayos*, pp. 181–203.

Santa Fe and Quito, grew at an average annual rate of about 2.3% between 1770 and 1778, and, despite a smallpox epidemic, continued to grow substantially in the decade after 1778. He suggested that the viceroyalty's population had probably increased by about a sixth between 1778 and 1788 (the equivalent of a 1.7% annual rate of growth), to reach a total of some 1,492,680 inhabitants.[13] The viceroy's calculations must be treated with some skepticism, because, for the decade 1778–88, they are based on figures for the province of Antioquia, where social and economic conditions were not typical of those found in other, more populous regions. Nevertheless, there are good reasons for supposing that the rate of population growth in Antioquia was roughly matched in other main regions of New Granada. Pedro Fermín de Vargas, for example, drew attention to the long upward trend in the prices of basic necessities in Bogotá between 1739 and 1791 as evidence that the city's population was increasing, and his comments on the Socorro region suggest that this was a region of particularly strong demographic growth.[14] Equally, the reorganization of Indian lands in the provinces of Tunja and Santa Fe after mid-century suggests that there, too, the mestizo and poor white population was growing vigorously.

The censuses of the late eighteenth century are an imperfect instrument for measuring the rates and distribution of demographic change in late colonial Colombia, because they present too static a picture of the region's population. Nonetheless, they do at least reveal a society that had been profoundly transformed since the Spanish invasions. By the late eighteenth century, the indigenous population had evidently been greatly weakened in most areas. This was especially true of the tropical lowland areas where Spaniards had settled, both on the Caribbean coast and along the Magdalena and Cauca valleys. There the effects of postconquest exploitation and epidemics had virtually annihilated Indian peoples. In the Andean highlands, Indian communities had survived alongside white and mestizo settlements in *resguardos* that gave them an independent subsistence base; however, even in this environment they were increasingly outnumbered in rural societies dominated by whites and mestizos. Except in the southern province of Los Pastos and in areas beyond the frontiers of Spanish agricultural settlement, Indian communities had generally become mere remnants of their former selves, reduced to a point where recovery was impossible. By the end of the eighteenth century, then, New

13. Posada and Ibáñez, *Relaciones de mando*, p. 242. In letters to Spain written at the time of the smallpox epidemic, Caballero y Góngora stated that mortality in the epidemic was fairly low, due to the introduction of vaccination in many of the main towns: Caballero y Góngora to Gálvez, Bogotá, June 15, 1783, Archivo Restrepo, Correspondencia reservada del Arzobispo-Virrey (no. 48).

14. Pedro Fermín de Vargas, *Pensamientos políticos* (Bogotá, 1968), pp. 89–90, 100.

Granada had become a largely hispanicized society, where Spanish culture had spread away from its original bases in the cities, and creoles, mestizos, and mulattoes had displaced native peoples in the countryside.

The conversion of New Granada into an essentially mestizo society had important implications for its development. The dual society of Indian and Spanish "republics" envisaged by early Spanish law had been almost completely undermined by *mestizaje* in New Granada, and compared to the Andean territories to the south, Indian communities made only a small contribution to the Hispanic state and economy, whether in labor, markets, or taxes. There were of course regional variations within New Granada, but generally the absence of large native populations, based in the corporate ownership of land and standing in a special relationship to the Spanish state, had produced a different social order from regions of the Americas where Indians were in the majority. Racial divisions reinforced by economic inequalities stratified New Granadan society as they did in other parts of Spanish America, but New Granada was in many ways a less rigid society than those where Indian cultures had remained strong, such as the highlands of Quito, or the southern Andean regions of Peru and Upper Peru, or southern Mexico. In most of New Granada, colonial society was more of an ethnic hybrid, racial divisions were less important in social and political life, and, without alternative native languages and cultures, lower-class society was more thoroughly hispanicized. This did not necessarily mean that the society was better integrated or that its popular strata were more easily controlled and disciplined by the hispanic elites. It simply meant that identity had different cultural roots and associations. Without a strong sense of ethnic separateness, the mestizo and poor white population tended to identify strongly with their localities. As white and mestizo parishes and villages grew, they jealously cultivated local rights and privileges and sought official recognition as autonomous municipalities able to manage their own affairs. So, alongside the postconquest hierarchies of urban elites, great estates, and mining enterprises, some regions in New Granada had large and growing free populations of peasants and farmers who socially had more in common with the rural communities of sixteenth-century Castile than with the Indian societies of eighteenth-century Peru or Mexico. In this sense, New Granada bore little resemblance to the colonial societies of its Andean neighbors with their large Quechua and Aymara-speaking populations. Seen as a whole, it also differed markedly from the society of the adjoining province of Caracas, where creole planters dominated a society that rested on African slavery.

The growth and mestizization of New Granada's population during the eighteenth century gradually modified the spatial patterns of settlement laid down after the conquest. The demographic archipelago created by Spanish settlement in the sixteenth and seventeenth centuries was enlarged, both by the extension of settlement on mining and cattle frontiers and by the spread of peasant agriculture in highland regions. The underlying structure was unchanged, however. Toward the end of the century, New Granada remained a loose conglomeration of regions, each focused on the towns that Spaniards had long since established as bases from which to exploit the territory's human and natural resources.

The economy of eighteenth-century New Granada was also structurally similar to that created by the Spaniards during the sixteenth century. It moved around two principal axes. One was an agriculture geared to subsistence and domestic markets; the other was a mining economy supplying precious metal to pay for trade with Europe. During the eighteenth century, gold was still New Granada's *produit moteur,* and colonial agriculture had few direct connections with external markets. Some tropical commodities were exported to Spain, particularly cacao cultivated in Cúcuta and in the Magdalena Valley. But because Spain could obtain such products as sugar, tobacco, and cacao in sufficient quantity or better quality from its other colonies, European markets had little relevance to the majority of New Granada's farmers and landowners. Hence the region's commercial agriculture was largely confined to interregional and intraregional circuits of exchange. The most valuable of these linked the agricultural regions of the eastern highlands and the Cauca Valley with the mining zones in the west. The gold mining centers of the Antioquian highlands and the Pacific lowlands acted as a magnet for merchants, attracting imports of hardware, textiles, and luxuries from Spain as well as the products of New Granada's agriculture and industry, including cattle and livestock products, domestic cloth, wheat, cheese, cacao, tobacco, and sugar products. These interregional circuits were buttressed by others that linked highland and lowland areas. There were, for example, movements of cattle from lowland pastures to highland urban markets; conversely, wheat was carried from the cool uplands to consumers who required flour in the towns of the tropical lowlands. There was also a flourishing interregional trade in crude cotton cloth, known as *ropa de la tierra,* produced in Socorro and the Llanos, and tobacco and sugar products were also widely traded both within and between regions.

The economic integration fostered by such interregional trade was, however, counterbalanced by poor internal transport and communications. On the timescales of transoceanic transportation during the eighteenth century, the colony's principal port was relatively close to Spain. The voyage from Cádiz to Cartagena de Indias took around four weeks; the return journey, via Cuba and the Bahama channel, was rather longer, at about seventy days.[15] This relative ease of communication between Spain and New Granada ended abruptly on the Caribbean coast, however, and most of Colombian territory was isolated from the Atlantic economy. The River Magdalena provided a passage from the Caribbean deep into the interior, but it was a long and costly journey, particularly when moving upriver from the coast. As for overland communications, these were slow and uncomfortable when not positively dangerous. Even the trail between Bogotá and Honda, linking the capital with the Magdalena River and the outside world, became virtually impassable during certain months in the year, prompting one viceroy to warn his successor that this was "a road the very sight of which will horrify Your Excellency, especially if it is travelled in the wet season."[16] Transport between the coast and the south and west of the country was even more arduous, often requiring travel over precipitous, sometimes densely forested mountain trails.

New Granada's agrarian economy was, consequently, highly regionalized and its regions were built around the larger towns. As centers of administration and regional trade, these towns were the focal points of Hispanic culture, concentrating the relatively wealthy, privileged, and powerful members of society together with the domestic servants, artisans, lawyers, priests, and merchants who provided the services they required. These urban centers were small, however, and their capacity to stimulate agricultural production was correspondingly weak. Townsfolk were invariably supplied with basic foodstuffs from the rural jurisdictions of their towns, usually within the radius of a day or two's travel. Beyond the economic perimeters of the towns lay open frontiers of uncolonized lands that, when used, were generally given over to semiferal cattle herds, grazing the natural pastures of huge, vaguely delimited ranches. If we now examine the colony's main regions, we will find that this basic economic pattern was repeated throughout New Granada, but with marked local variations caused by differences in climate and relief, and in systems of landownership and labor organization.

Cities and regions

The Caribbean region

The first region of Spanish colonization in Colombian territory was on the Caribbean coast and, thanks to the role of Cartagena de Indias as New Granada's principal port, the area had continued to develop throughout the colonial period. The region's economy was basically shaped by networks of administrative, commercial, and agricultural activity that radi-

---

15. Ibid., p. 4.   16. Cited in R. C. West, *Colonial Placer Mining*, p. 126.

ated from Cartagena de Indias and Mompós, both of which were centers of government and entrepôts for trade with the interior. Joined by the River Magdalena, these towns were the main axis of the coastal economy, and, as Map 2.2 shows, most of the region's population was concentrated around and between them.

Of all New Granada's regions, the Caribbean coast was best placed to take advantage of external markets because of its proximity to Atlantic sea-lanes and its link to Spain through the system of fleets that called at Cartagena. In fact, however, coastal agriculture benefited little from transatlantic trade and depended instead on a web of local markets. For, without legal access to the dynamic foreign markets of the Caribbean in the burgeoning plantation economies of the English, French, and Dutch islands, maritime trade in agricultural products was confined to the neighboring Spanish ports of Portobelo and the Antilles. Such markets offered little scope for coastal agriculture. The Spanish Caribbean islands produced many of the same tropical foodstuffs and, in the case of Cuba, even exported agricultural products (mainly tobacco and beeswax) to Cartagena. Thus overseas trade affected the region's agriculture only indirectly, by sustaining the commercial and productive activity of towns that carried trade between Europe and the interior of New Granada.

The two main concentrations of demand in the region were the city of Cartagena and the town of Mompós. As the major centers for the organization and distribution of New Granada's external commerce, both supported relatively sizeable populations. Mompós had 7,000–8,000 inhabitants in the 1770s, and was the major port on the River Magdalena.[17] It received gold from Antioquia and the Chocó, tobacco from Ocaña and the upper Magdalena, cacao from Cúcuta and Neiva, and wheat from Pamplona; during the later eighteenth century, the presence of the royal tobacco and aguardiente monopolies in the town also encouraged local tobacco and sugar cultivation. Most of the land in its vicinity was used for extensive cattle ranching, producing meat, tallow, and hides for the market of Cartagena.[18] Cartagena de Indias, New Granada's major port and most important military base, was by far the largest concentration of population in the coastal region, and the epicenter of the regional economy. Toward the end of the eighteenth century, the city had a population of between 14,000 and 16,000, which included close to a third of all the

17. This figure was given by the viceroy, on the basis of information received from the city's parish priests, when the corregimientos of the province of Cartagena were being reorganized in 1776. AGI Santa Fe 586 (ramo 1), Viceroy Flóres to Gálvez, Santa Fe, August 15, 1776.

18. These and the following comments on Mompós and its region are based on the accounts of the region given in Francisco Silvestre, *Descripción*, 55; Rafael Soto, *Decenios de Mompós en la Independencia* (Barranquilla, 1960), tomo 2, pp. 20–8; and, most important, Orlando Fals Borda, *Historia Doble de la Costa, 1: Mompox y Loba* (Bogotá, 1980), passim.

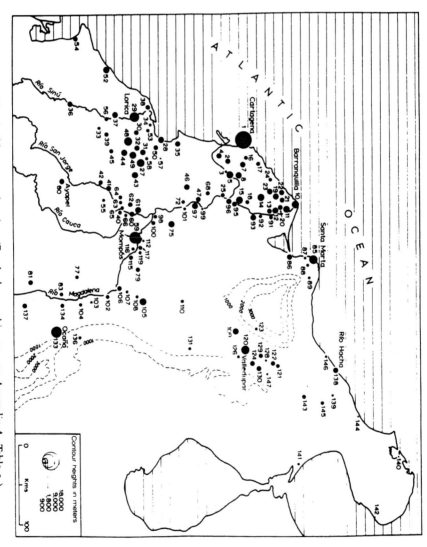

Map 2.2. The Caribbean coastal region. (For the key to this map, see Appendix A, Table 5.)

whites living in the coastal region.[19] As the largest military and naval establishment in the viceroyalty and the entrepôt for the colony's commerce with Spain, the city offered employment to a substantial specialized workforce of small traders, artisans, and laborers. A glimpse of the city's artisanate is provided in the following table, which shows the occupations of 835 artisans who were called for militia service from three of the city barrios in 1779 and 1780.[20]

The impact of the city of Cartagena on the neighboring countryside can be traced in a report made by Antonio de Arévalo in 1776, when he was commissioned to investigate the city's capacity to withstand a seige. Arévalo looked closely at Cartagena's food supply, and his report offers an unusually clear picture of the relation of a colonial city to its surrounding region.[21] To support its population, Cartagena relied partly on agricultural resources found within the area of the city itself. Much of the food consumed within the port – beans, bananas, plantains, yams, cassava, sweet potatoes, cheese, butter, and the like – was cultivated within the city and its environs, particularly in Barú, an island that shielded the Bay of Cartagena from the sea. Vegetables were provided in large part by the *huertas* or market gardens located within the city walls, and fish came in abundance from the Bay of Cartagena without need for recourse to more distant waters. The city also produced much of its own pork: Arévalo calculated that, in a wartime emergency, there would always be about 500 pigs ready for slaughtering in corrals within the city walls. As for salt, essential for both the seasoning of food and the preparation of both pork and beef, there was plenty to be had from the beaches of Barú and the nearby Ciénaga de Tesca, brought by the poor who lived in the shanties just outside the city walls. Land values in the environs of the city were too high and the soil too infertile for city landowners to concern themselves with the cultivation of other basic foodstuffs. They concentrated instead on the production of "tiles, bricks, charcoal, firewood, some cattle and the like, which offer them a yield proportionate to the value of their land and their efforts."[22]

19. A report on the province of Cartagena, made by the Bishop of Cartagena in 1772, estimated that the population living within the city walls amounted to more than 14,000 inhabitants: See Eduardo Gutiérrez de Piñeres, "Población de la Provincia de Cartagena de Indias en el año de 1772," *Boletín Historial, Año 3*, no. 29 (Cartagena, 1917), p. 2. Of this population, more than 2,000 were slaves. The 1779 census reported a population of 16,361, with 4,393 whites and 3,048 slaves: see Appendix A, Table 5.

20. AHNC Miscelanea, tomo 31, fols. 149–54, 1014–15; AHNC Milicias y Marina, tomo 48, fols. 725–34.

21. Arévalo's report is reproduced in Enrique Marco Dorta, "Cartagena de Indias: Riquezas ganaderas y problemas," *Tercer Congreso Hispanoamericano de Historia* (Cartagena, 1962), tomo 1, pp. 335–52.

22. Ibid., p. 338.

Table 2.1. *Occupational structure of Cartagena de Indias, 1779–80*

Occupation	No.	Occupation	No.
Tailors	81	Slaughtermen	4
Carpenters	79	Gunsmiths	3
Cobblers	75	Lampmakers	3
Gold- and silversmiths	30	Hacendados	3
Barbers	28	Musicians	2
Grocers	27	Confectioners	2
Masons	25	Saddlers	2
Painters	23	Packers	2
Blacksmiths	17	Tilemakers	2
Farmers	14	Keepers of weights	1
Shipwrights	14	Pilots	1
Butchers	13	Sculptors	1
Cigar makers	13	Doctors	1
Horticulturalists	10	Apothecaries	1
Fishermen	9	Carters	1
Scribes	6	Tanners	1
Quillmakers	5	Woodcarvers	1
		Architects	1

Local farming and market gardening were insufficient, however, to supply the city's markets for maize and meat, and the influence of its markets spread into neighboring areas. The maize that was used for making *pan de bollo,* the dietary staple for the city's common people, was brought from the fertile savannahs west of Cartagena, to which coastal waters offered cheap and easy access. Most of the 36,000 fanegas of maize annually consumed in the city came from the Sinú region, from the complex of settlements around the mouth of the Sinú River, centering on the town of Lorica. Wheat, on the other hand, was imported, either from the interior of New Granada, or, as increasingly happened in the eighteenth century, from overseas. Aside from maize, the urban market also offered outlets for meat and other cattle products, for sugar and its products (particularly cane brandy), and, to a lesser extent, cacao. Markets for these products were dominated by great landowners, who carved out huge estates in the savannahs of Tolú, in the hinterland of Mompós to the south, and, to a lesser extent, in the regions east of the Magdalena River in the province of Santa Marta. Cattle raising was one of the pillars of coastal agriculture. During the first half of the eighteenth century, Cartagena's meat supply seems to have depended largely on hacendados of Mompós, who drove cattle from their lands around Mompós and in the neighboring province of Santa Marta.[23] Arévalo's survey of cattle ranches in the hinterland of Cartagena de Indias indicates that meat supply from areas closer to the city was much improved by the 1770s, though the size of herds within twenty or thirty miles of the city was generally small.[24] The bulk of the meat consumed within the city still came from more distant sources: Arévalo noted that it usually required some forty days to organize the transport of cattle from the ranches that normally supplied Cartagena.

This ranching economy was largely in the hands of great proprietors. Over the course of the eighteenth century, landed proprietors based in Cartagena de Indias and Mompós built up extensive holdings by taking up frontier land and legalizing possession by payments to the crown.[25] The impulse behind this movement came partly from a group of peninsular Spaniards who arrived with a military expedition in 1698, took up permanent residence in Cartagena, and whose descendants came to constitute a new elite of landowners and officials in the city.[26] Landholding was evidently essential to both the social standing and economic stability of leading creole families, especially for those who, like the Conde de Pestagua, the Marqués de Santa Coa, and the Marqués de Valdehoyos, became sufficiently rich to secure aristocratic titles with *mayorazgos* (entailed estates) grounded in their landed properties. But the great fortunes were not built on land alone. The wealthiest creole families of Cartagena and Mompós accumulated wealth through involvement in overseas commerce, slaving, and mining, as well as agriculture, while consolidating and extending their fortunes by judicious marriages, either between themselves or with suitable peninsular immigrants.[27]

Great estates were an important element in the agrarian social structure of the coastal region. For the core of their labor force, the haciendas relied on imported black slaves, most of whom were employed in the production

---

23. Luis Navarro García, "Los regidores en el abasto de Cartagena de Indias," *AEA*. vol. 38 (1981), pp. 173–214.

24. In the environs of the city, Arévalo names four ranchers with a total of 190 cattle; within two and four leagues of the city, he listed eleven ranches with some 1,310 cattle, of which only three had herds of more than 200 head; from four to eight leagues there were fourteen ranches in which the average size of the herds was not much larger. Only when the distance from the city exceeded eight leagues did the average size of herds pertaining to a single owner tend to exceed 100 cattle; even then, the large ranch, with more than 800 or 1,000 head, was exceptional. Marco Dorta, "Cartagena de Indias," pp. 346–9.

25. Hermes Tovar Pinzón, *Grandes empresas agrícolas y ganaderas* (Bogotá, 1980), pp. 32–4.

26. Carmen Gómez Pérez, "El Consulado de Sevilla y la formación de las oligarquías en Cartagena de Indias a principios del XVIII," *IV Jornadas de Andalucía y América*, vol. 1 (Seville, 1984).

27. Tovar Pinzón, *Grandes empresas*, pp. 97–130; Fals Borda, *Historia doble de la costa*, vol. 1, pp. 75A–126A.

of sugar cane. The coastal hacienda was typically a mixed enterprise in which sugar production formed part of a range of activities, including arable farming to meet its own subsistence needs and, more important, cattle raising to supply city meat markets. Slaves were therefore not employed in large numbers. A sample of sixteen coastal haciendas suggests that it was exceptional to have more than fifty slaves working on an single hacienda. Nor were slaves used solely in the sugar economy, but they also formed a permanent, often skilled labor force of artisans and ranch hands.[28] The tendency for land to become concentrated in very large units, sometimes held in larger, multiple holdings, consisting of 20,000 to 30,000 hectares, was not necessarily a tribute to the dynamism of local markets; it was, rather, a function of the availability of land in sparsely populated areas and the related problems of recruiting free labor.[29]

The other element in the agrarian society of the coastal region was a free peasantry that survived from subsistence agriculture, combined with work in transportation along the River Magdalena. The reports made by Antonio de la Torre, a Spanish officer who traveled throughout the province in the early 1770s, and the very graphic account left by the missionary Joseph Palacios de la Vega of his journey from Cartagena to Ayapel in 1787–8, show that many, probably most, of the region's rural inhabitants lived in primitive and isolated conditions.[30] Lacking any obvious focus for their production, most of the population was thinly spread over extensive areas, often working the land in a slash-and-burn agriculture based on the household unit. It was La Torre's mission to bring these people under royal authority by gathering them into recognized communities. In the census of the 43 settlements that he founded, he estimated that some 41,133 souls had been living dispersed among the virgin plains and woodlands of the province.[31] Many, however, remained beyond the control of the state and the solace of its church. In the rest of the river region, settlement was thinly spread along the banks of the Magdalena, occasionally clustered around a small river port or customs house but generally found in tiny villages or family groups, often composed of runaway slaves or their descendants. When the French traveler Mollien sailed up the Magdalena in 1823, he was reminded of African life along the River Senegal, as the

---

28. Tovar Pinzón, *Grandes empresas*, pp. 41–57.
29. Adolfo Meisel R., "Esclavitud, mestizaje y haciendas en la provincia de Cartagena, 1531–1851," *Desarrollo y Sociedad* (Bogotá, 1980), no. 4, pp. 265–9.
30. "Noticia Individual de las poblaciones nuevamente fundadas en la Provincia de Cartagena . . . por don Antonio de la Torre Miranda," *Boletín Historial* (Cartagena, 1919), nos. 45–46, pp. 490–512; and ibid. (Cartagena, 1926), nos. 49–51, pp. 606–28. See also G. Reichel-Dolmatoff (ed.), *Diario de Viaje del Padre Joseph Palacios de la Vega* (Bogotá, 1955).
31. "Noticia Individual," p. 500.

monotony of the forests was interrupted only by the cane-houses and maize plots of the few isolated negro settlers who, far from communal existence, practiced a shifting, slash-and-burn agriculture along its margins. His final comment on the conditions encountered along New Granada's principal line of internal communication gives a vivid impression of untamed wilderness:

There is nothing more frightful than a journey along the Magdalena; even the view is no relief, because its fertile margins, which should be covered with cacao plantations, sugarcane, coffee, cotton, anil, tobacco, those banks which should offer the thirsty traveller all the delicious fruits of the tropics, which should be adorned with so many beautiful flowers are, on the contrary, bristling with weeds, lianas and thorns under towering palms of coconut and date.[32]

East of Cartagena, there was little economic activity of any importance. The province of Santa Marta had been a backwater since commerce through the port of Santa Marta had been cut short by Cartagena's development as the terminus for New Granada's trade with Spain. In the eighteenth century, the town was little more than a large village, with a population of only about 3,600; economically, it was sustained by the slow movement of goods to and from the neighboring Caribbean area, and a mostly contraband trade in European imports, which were relayed southward into the interior via Ocaña. The weakness of the port as an economic force was reflected in the fact that most of the province's population was settled inland, at some considerable distance from the coast, around Valledupar and Ocaña.[33] Parts of the coast were rich in pearl fisheries but, as these precious stones could be obtained in sufficient quantities by simply trading with the Indians, they provided no impulse for the establishment of permanent settlement.[34] And although the agricultural resources of the region included cotton, cacao, anil, coffee, sugar, and cattle, their exploitation was limited to the satisfaction of largely local needs.[35] These included the supply of cattle to the markets of Cartagena and occasional shipments of livestock to the Caribbean islands. However, the authorities' fear of contraband hindered trade with the islands, and the development of Santa Marta's ranching was severely limited by competi-

32. G. Mollien, *Viaje por la República de Colombia en 1823* (Bogotá, 1944), 50–1.
33. In 1793, the population of Valledupar was 3,781, whereas that of Ocaña was 5,679. See Appendix A, Table 5.
34. For an account of pearl fishing, written during the 1740s by the Jesuit Antonio Julián, see his *La Perla de America, Provincia de Santa Marta* (Bogotá, repr. 1951), pp. 35–7.
35. On the provinces' lack of external outlets for trade, see "Provincia de Santa Marta y Río Hacha del Virreynato de Santa Fe. Informe del Gobernador D. Antonio de Río Narváez y la Torre (Rio Hacha 1778)," in Sergio E. Ortíz, *Escritos de dos economistas coloniales: Don Antonio Narváez y la Torre y Don José Ignacio de Pombo* (Bogotá, 1965), pp. 35–8.

tion from livestock producers in the jurisdictions of Mompós and Cartagena.[36]

Beyond Santa Marta, Spanish settlement dwindled rapidly. Neighboring Río Hacha was an Indian frontier, much of which was unexplored. In 1778, the settler population of the entire province was less than 4,000, with about 1,500 in the town of Río Hacha itself.[37] The "unpacified" Indian population, on the other hand, was much larger. There may have been as many as 40,000 unconquered Indians in the provinces of Santa Marta and Río Hacha during the latter half of the eighteenth century, of whom between 12,000 and 15,000 were said to be capable of bearing arms.[38] Throughout the century, these Indians conducted intermittent and damaging raids on settlements and properties of the local frontier, eventually prompting crown-backed military retaliation during the 1770s.[39] The "pacification" campaign achieved little, however. The harsh physical environment of the Guajira Peninsula and the sustained resistance of native peoples continued to discourage Spanish settlement, which was confined to a few small clusters organized around lonely military and missionary outposts.

So, at a late stage in the eighteenth century, large tracts of the coastal region remained unpopulated and unexploited, and only the hinterlands of Cartagena and Mompós saw any substantial commercial and agricultural activity. Dominated by large landowners, agriculture expanded in response to urban demands, but without any significant external demand it was confined within narrow boundaries. A few great landowners were able to sustain an opulent life-style through their contacts with the urban market and with commerce. The mass of the population meanwhile drew little more than a bare living from the land, having been stranded in an existence barely touched by the flows of trade that passed, via the River Magdalena, between New Granada's interior and the Atlantic economy.

The Eastern Cordillera region

When the 1779 census was taken, the central reaches of the Eastern Cordillera contained the most densely settled areas in New Granada. Between them, the provinces of Santa Fe, Tunja, Girón, and Pamplona (shown in Map 2.3) held nearly half the territory's total population, which was unevenly spread over an extensive network of towns and villages in the intermontane basins and valleys of the highland area. This was the

36. Silvestre, *Descripción*, p. 55.   37. See Appendix A, Table 5.
38. AGI Santa Fe 702, "Cálculo del número de Indios Guagiros, Hombres de Armas, que se regula puede tener la Provincia del Río Hacha."
39. Allan J. Kuethe, "The Pacification Campaign on the Riohacha Frontier, 1772–1779," *HAHR*, vol. 50 (1970), pp. 467–81.

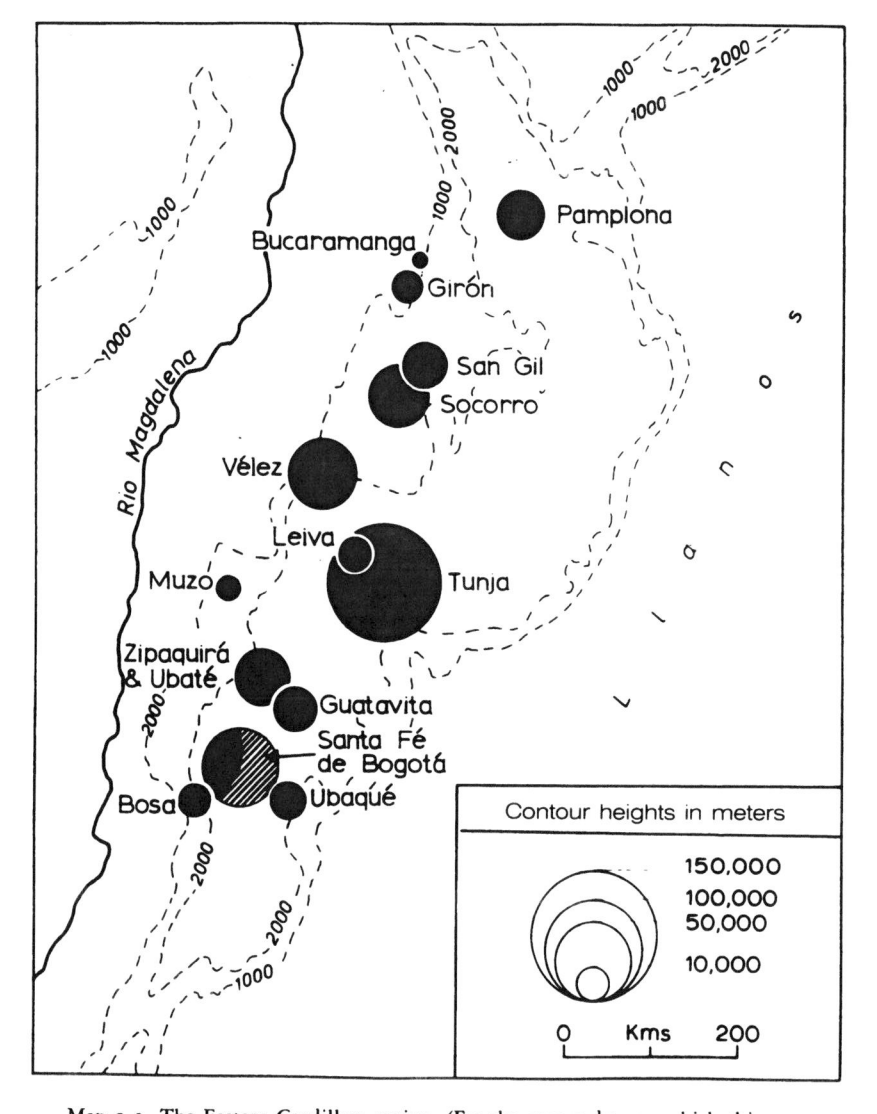

Map 2.3. The Eastern Cordillera region. (For the census data on which this map is based, see Appendix A, Table 6.)

most urbanized part of colonial New Granada, with several small towns forming links in a chain that ran northward from Santa Fe de Bogotá toward Pamplona. Associated with these towns was a series of subregions with different social and economic structures that interacted in the economic region, partly because intraregional communications were facilitated by the relative ease of movement from south to north along the cordillera.[40]

Broken down into its component parts, the region as a whole comprised three main subregions. The first had originated around Bogotá and Tunja, in the *tierra fría* areas where the Spaniards had conquered the Chibchas. Bogotá, capital of the audiencia of New Granada and seat of the viceroys during the eighteenth century, was the principal urban center in this region, and its hinterland was the most populous highland area. At the time of the census, the province of Santa Fe had a population of over 90,000, concentrated in the high plateau around Bogotá. Some 16,000 were counted as inhabitants of the city, most of them whites and mestizos; the remainder lived in or around the small towns near Bogotá, such as Zipaquirá, Facatativá, and Chiquinquirá, or spread among the numerous villages and farms of the savannah of Bogotá. At a couple of days' ride from Bogotá lay Tunja, capital of a heavily populated province of about 129,000 people. Once a close rival to Bogotá, the city was in decline by the mid-eighteenth century. In the 1760s, it had only about 3,000 inhabitants within an urban precinct whose many fine houses and richly decorated churches testified to a more prosperous past. Most of the population of the province was dispersed over the countryside, living in the villages and hamlets, and the estates and farms that dotted the highland landscape. Throughout these *tierra fría* areas, potatoes, wheat, barley, and maize were the primary crops, cattle grazed on hillside pastures and on the higher slopes, and sheep were raised to supply wool for local weavers.

North of the *tierra fría* core lay a second heavily populated area, in the *tierra templada,* which had once been dominated by the sixteenth-century town of Vélez. Here, between about 3,000 and 6,000 feet, a flourishing center for temperate agriculture had emerged among the fast-growing white and mestizo parishes created by colonization from Vélez during the seventeenth century. In addition to producing maize and other food crops for local consumption, farmers in this area cultivated sugarcane, tobacco, anis, and cotton, and their cotton production was used for artisan manufacture of crude cotton textiles. San Gil and Socorro were the main urban centers. San Gil had been granted town status in 1694, but its growth was outstripped during the eighteenth century by Socorro. By 1781, Socorro had been transformed from a parish into a flourishing and fast-growing town, with a population of about 15,000, and as many again living in the outlying parishes of its jurisdiction. Several such parishes were quite

---

40. The record that Miguel de Santiesteban made in 1741 of his journey from Bogotá into Venezuela, via Pamplona, shows that this was nonetheless a lengthy and arduous trip. It also provides a useful glimpse of the topography, society, and economy of the regions north of the capital. See David J. Robinson (ed.), *Mil leguas por América, de Lima a Caracas, 1740–1741: Diario de don Miguel de Santiesteban* (Bogotá, 1992), pp. 200–20.

large: Simacota, Oiba, and Charalá, for example, each had about 6,000 people in their jurisdictions.[41]

Farther north lay a third subregion of the Eastern Cordillera region, which itself consisted of three smaller zones. These were the *tierra caliente* around Girón and Bucaramanga, the cold country that centered on Pamplona, and the adjoining tropical plains around Cúcuta. Population in Girón and Bucaramanga was small, with only about 10,000 inhabitants. Near Bucaramanga were mines that produced a little gold; otherwise, the area relied on producing sugar, cacao, cotton, and especially good quality tobacco, both for a small export trade to the Caribbean coast and for the markets of the Eastern Cordillera region.[42] In the jurisdiction of Pamplona were some 22,000 people, most living in the *tierra fría* land around the town itself, but some also spreading into the plains around Cúcuta, where haciendas produced cacao and sugar. This formed the northern boundary of the region, and acted as a point of contact with, and transit into the Venezuelan Andes.[43]

The axis of settlement running northward from Bogotá was, then, composed of a series of local economies embracing mostly highland settlements in cold and temperate lands above 5,000 feet. These were flanked by settlements in the *tierra caliente* lands on slopes of the cordillera. To the west of Bogotá, maize and sugar were produced for the Bogotá market around Guaduas, whereas Mariquita and Neiva both produced cacao and livestock for sales in the highlands.[44] To the east of the Cordillera were the rolling plains of the Llanos of Casanare. There, cattle were raised on great ranches before being driven to the highlands to be fattened for sale in urban markets, and cotton was cultivated and manufactured into cloth by Indian communities.[45]

Throughout the region, agriculture was the basis of economic life, as there were no mining enterprises of any importance. The gold mines of Bucaramanga and Pamplona had been virtually abandoned, and attempts to revive the silver mines of Mariquita and Pamplona were continually frustrated by the inability of contemporary technology to extract the ores

41. The full census returns for the Eastern Cordillera region are in Appendix A, Table 6. Additional data on the population of Socorro and its hinterland are from John L. Phelan, *The People and the King: The Comunero Revolution in Colombia, 1781* (Madison, Wisconsin, 1978), pp. 41–2.

42. Silvestre, *Descripción*, pp. 46, 62.

43. Ibid., p. 61. A fuller account of Pamplona and Girón at the end of the colonial period is found in "Relación territorial de la provincia de Pamplona, formada por el doctor don Joaquín Camacho . . . " in Francisco José de Caldas, *Semanario del Nuevo Reino de Granada* (Bogotá, 1942), pp. 1–17.

44. Silvestre, *Descripción*, pp. 28–9, 43, 57–8.

45. Ibid., p. 44. For a full account of the development of the Llanos during the eighteenth century, see Jane Rausch, *A Tropical Plains Frontier, The Llanos of Colombia, 1531–1831* (Albuquerque, 1984), especially chaps. 3 and 4.

at less than prohibitive costs.[46] Alluvial gold was found in the province of
Neiva, as well as at Chaparral near Ibagué and at various sites along the
course of the middle Magdalena. All were too small, however, to create
any substantial market for the products of farming.[47] The main alternative to agriculture was cloth manufacture. Both the widespread use of the
ruana (a short woollen poncho) and the need for cheap woollen blankets in
the bracing climate of *tierra fría* created demands for woollen goods that
were met partly by household weaving and partly by artisans residing in
the towns. In the warmer climates, where cotton was cultivated, the
manufacture of woollens gave way to the production of cotton cloth.
According to Miguel de Santiesteban, writing in 1741, this cloth was of
coarse quality. Some of it served "for the shirts for poor people"; other
larger pieces, made by Indians to pay their tribute, were useful for making
ships' sails or tents.[48] However, given the high price of imported cloth,
there were ample markets throughout New Granada for domestic cotton
cloth, especially in the interior, and this stimulated the growth of a small
but flourishing cottage industry around Socorro and San Gil. Although
little is known about the industry's organization, contemporaries agreed
that these communities were the most prosperous and industrious in New
Granada, and that they enjoyed a significant trade not only with other
areas in the highlands, but also with the distant gold mining regions of
Antioquia and the Chocó.[49]

Bogotá had emerged as the region's leading city, due to a combination
of three factors: its role as a center for government, its position in a fertile
and populous area, and its function as the principal point for distributing
imports brought from Cartagena, in conjunction with the Magdalena
River port of Honda. After the conquest, Bogotá had competed for primacy with Tunja and Vélez, which had their own route to the Magdalena
via the port of Carare, but, helped by the audiencia, the encomenderos
and merchants of Bogotá secured the development of the *camino real* from
Honda and made this trail the main route for supplying the Eastern
highlands.[50] The establishment of the mint in Bogotá in 1620 had both
recognized and reinforced the city's role as a center for the gold trade and
for distribution of imports throughout the interior. Operating from their

46. On fruitless efforts to revive the Mariquita silver mines, see Bernardo Caicedo, *D'Elhuyar y el siglo
    XVIII neogranadino* (Bogotá, 1971).
47. Silvestre, *Descripción*, p. 59; Vicente Restrepo, *Estudio sobre las minas de oro y plata de Colombia*
    (Bogotá, 1952), pp. 132–4, 206–7.
48. Robinson (ed.), *Mil leguas por América*, p. 200.
49. Oviedo, *Cualidades y riquezas*, pp. 174–80; Silvestre, *Descripción*, p. 61; Fermín de Vargas,
    Pensamientos Políticos, pp. 14, 26, 55, 103–4; Felipe Salvador Gilij, *Ensayo de historia americana*
    (1784) (Bogotá, 1955), pp. 373–5.
50. On the development of Honda as the major river port connecting New Granada with the coast,
    see Colmenares, *Historia económica y social*, vol. I, pp. 269–76.

stores in Bogotá's *Calle Real*, or through their dependencies in Honda, the merchants of the capital maintained a network of trade that spread across the Eastern Cordillera region and throughout the length and breadth of the central and southern regions. From Honda, they managed an important trade with the mining regions of Antioquia and the Chocó; from Bogotá itself, they supplied the towns and villages of virtually the entire highland region, as far north as Pamplona and as far south as Popayán and Pasto. Thus, through the control that Bogotá's merchants held over the distribution of imported goods, the towns of the Eastern Cordillera were able to draw in gold produced by the mines of the west.

Santa Fe de Bogotá was the major town of the Eastern Cordillera, and New Granada's leading city. The population within its jurisdiction grew from around 20,000 in the first half of the eighteenth century to about 30,000 at the end. Throughout the century, Bogotá remained primarily an administrative and commercial center. As the capital of the audiencia, and later the Viceroyalty of New Granada, it was the seat of the colony's civil and fiscal administration, and housed its leading officials, together with the small contingent of lawyers, notaries, and petty functionaries who serviced government. It was also an ecclesiastical capital, being the seat of the archbishop of Bogotá and the headquarters of various regular orders. In 1778, the city had a substantial clerical population of some 800 priests, monks, and nuns, servicing thirty churches and eight monastic houses.[51] By 1800, the number of clergy had reached 1,200, so that there was one cleric to every twenty-five or thirty laypeople within the city.[52]

When he visited Bogotá in 1741, Miguel de Santiesteban found it an agreeable place, "with wide, level streets, high and low houses of stone and lime, so spacious and comfortable that almost all have a garden or orchard . . . external facades with many wooden balconies, stone portals, and sumptuous, richly-adorned churches that reflect the wealth the city once had."[53] But, despite its splendid site, spacious layout, and pleasant atmosphere, to an outsider Bogotá did not appear a wealthy or productive town. Santiesteban noted that the dress of the local people showed Bogotá and New Granada's interior to be poor compared to Peru. Among white women, fashions were a century behind the times. They dressed with great simplicity, with the hats and shawls worn by their grandmothers and none of the fine linens, laces, and silks that were common in Lima, where even servants were fashionably dressed.[54] Nor did the city show any greater signs of prosperity half a century later. In 1789, Francisco Silvestre

---

51. Pérez Ayala, *Antonio Caballero y Góngora* (Bogotá, 1951) Cuadro A..
52. A useful survey of eighteenth-century Bogotá is found in Gary A. Brubaker, "Santa Fe de Bogotá: A Study of Municipal Development in Eighteenth-Century Spanish America" (unpub. Ph.D. thesis, University of Texas, 1960). For population statistics, see pp. 56–7.
53. Robinson (ed.), *Mil leguas por América*, p. 186.   54. Ibid., p. 189.

thought the capital of the viceroyalty to be a rustic town, where dirty, unpaved streets were occupied by drunks and beggars.[55]

Certainly Bogotá was no hub of industry. The militia lists of 1783 offer a glimpse of the occupational structure of the city, providing information on the occupations of 665 men recruited into the ranks of nine militia companies. Though this group represented only about a tenth of the city's male population, it gives an idea of economic activities within the city. The occupations listed are shown in Table 2.2.[56] By far the greatest number of these artisans came from Bogotá itself. Among them were very few Spaniards, whereas of those who came from outside the city, most were from the country towns and villages within its hinterland, such as Zipaquirá, Chocontá, Chinquinquirá, Facatativá, and Tunja. Thus, although in this period contemporaries often commented on the influx of vagabonds to the city, Bogotá clearly did not attract many outsiders into its artisan workforce, which was almost wholly composed of men born and raised within the city itself.[57]

The urban workers recruited into the militia companies reflect the city's character as an administrative and commercial rather than a manufacturing center. A large number were engaged in trading and selling activities. Dealers (*tratantes*), grocers (*pulperos*), wholesale and retail merchants together numbered eighty-five, making them the third largest group, after tailors and masons. In fact, this figure understates the importance of trading activity in the city, because it did not include either the merchants of the *comercio de Santa Fe* or the *comercio de España,* who were exempt from militia service, or the many small traders who moved between the city and the surrounding area. There were few weavers in the town, probably because the weaving of cotton and woollen cloth was concentrated in Tunja and in the towns of Socorro and San Gil. But the tailors – who made up the cloth received from Europe, from Quito, and from the cottage weavers of the neighboring provinces – formed the largest single group of workers. These men, along with the masons, cobblers, carpenters, metalworkers (i.e., silver- and goldworkers, blacksmiths, and employees of the Casa de Moneda), appear to have formed the backbone of the city's artisanate.

55. Silvestre, *Descripción,* pp. 31–3.
56. This table is constructed from information given in the lists of nine militia companies established in 1783, when a regiment of ten companies with a projected complement of a thousand men was formed. The total number of recruits listed in the nine companies for which data are available is 672. Of these 665 have their occupation specified. See AHNC Milicias y Marina, tomo 18, fols. 51–71.
57. The origins of the artisans, where stated, were as follows: from Santa Fe de Bogotá, 451; from Spain, 12; from neighboring towns, 88; from other places, 12.

Table 2.2. *Occupational structure of Santa Fe de Bogotá, 1783*

Occupation	No.	Occupation	No.
Tailors	104	Millers	3
Masons	90	Lampmakers	3
Cobblers	66	Buttermakers	3
Carpenters	57	Amanuenses	3
Dealers	54	Stone cutters	3
Farmers	35	Billiard-hall keepers	2
Silverworkers	28	Boxmakers	2
Barbers	21	Jewelers	2
Grocers	20	Tanners	2
Students	15	Packers	1
Day workers	15	Schoolmasters	1
Tilemakers	13	Gardeners	1
Clerks	11	Valuers	1
Hatmakers	10	Wax chandlers	1
Saddlers	10	Employees	1
Bakers	8	Hunters	1
Musicians	7	Potters	1
Vagabonds	7	Dyers	1
Ironworkers	7	Engineers	1
Goldworkers	6	Watchmakers	1
Retail merchants	6	Druggists	1
Painters	5	Receivers	1
Mint employees	5	Upholsterers	1
Shopkeepers	1	Penmakers	1
Woodsmen	5	Agents	1
Hairdressers	5	Ropemakers	1
Weavers	4	Lumbermen	1
Wholesale merchants	4	Peons	4
Architects	1		

Comments made by Viceroy Guirior in 1777 suggest that the majority of artisans eked out a poor living from the practice of their crafts. When he tried to group the city's artisans into organized guilds, Guirior remarked that the crafts of Bogotá were in such a poor state that, in their apparel, idleness, and licentious living, artisans were barely distinguishable from beggars and vagabonds. According to Guirior, they did not even conform to a civilized European code of dress, and he particularly disliked the custom of using ponchos. "The use of *ruanas* in these Kingdoms is" he said, "a leading cause of uncleanliness: It covers the upper part of the body, and the wearer cares not whether he is clean or dirty underneath: bare of foot and knee go all the common people, with only the covering of a *ruana*, which, though in fact a very appropriate garment for travelling on horseback, should be prohibited for all other uses."[58] Nothing came of Guirior's ambitions for improving the city's artisanate, for poverty and simplicity of dress reflected the character of an isolated agrarian economy where even the relatively wealthy enjoyed only very modest standards of material life.

Most areas in the Eastern Cordillera had limited prospects for economic development. Although the region contained much fertile land and produced a wide range of products, markets for its agriculture were very restricted. In the seventeenth century, wheat producers had sold flour to Cartagena, where it provisioned both the urban market and the Spanish fleets that visited the port. During the eighteenth century, this extra-regional market was lost as Cartagena increasingly imported its flour from overseas, and external demand for foodstuffs came mainly from the distant western mining districts, which bought flour, cheese, and tobacco from the *tierra fría* areas.[59] Within the region itself, markets were highly localized, as the proximity of different climatic zones meant that a broad range of agricultural products could be obtained within small areas. Most communities could obtain basic staples such as potatoes, maize, barley, wheat, beans, onions, and other vegetables from within their immediate vicinity, and those in *tierra fría* could usually obtain sugar and tobacco from cultivators who were no more than fifty or sixty miles away. The scope for agricultural commercialization was, then, confined to small areas and small populations, and trade in foodstuffs was generally restricted to the weekly markets of local towns.[60] Even Bogotá, the largest city in the region, offered only a very limited market. Its basic foodstuffs were mostly supplied by small producers who sold their goods in the city square, leaving the larger producers to provide meat, wheat, and sugar products.

Agrarian society in the Eastern Cordillera was far from homogeneous. In the older areas of settlement, in the *tierra fría* country around Bogotá and Tunja, large landholdings created in the wake of the conquest coexisted with small farms and a peasant agriculture. Most of the large estates

---

58. AHNC Miscelanea, tomo 3, fols. 287–313. Quotation from fol. 293.
59. West, *Colonial Placer Mining*, pp. 115–22, describes this trade.
60. The best eighteenth-century description of agricultural production and markets in the highland region is found in Oviedo, *Cualidades y riquezas*, pp. 95–195. Codazzi's geography, written during the early nineteenth century, also provides a detailed description of agriculture in the area: It is reprinted in Eduardo Acevedo Latorre (ed.), *Jeografiía Física i Política de las Provincias de la Nueva Granada por la Comisión Corográfica bajo la dirección de Agustín Codazzi*, 2 vols. (Bogotá, 1957–8). A superb evocation of the landscape and society of the Eastern Cordillera region, also from the mid-nineteenth century, is Manuel Ancízar, *Peregrinación de Alpha* (Bogotá, 1970 ed.), passim. For a description of local trading systems during the early nineteenth century, see Frank Safford, "Commerce and Enterprise in Central Colombia, 1821–1870" (unpublished Ph.D. thesis, Columbia University, 1965), pp. 103–6.

had been established in the later sixteenth century, when the decline of the Indian population and the crown's multiplication of encomienda grants diminished the value of existing encomiendas and encouraged elite families to accumulate extensive multiple landholdings. The formation of large landholdings was well under way by the 1590s. By then, when Indian lands in the Sabana de Bogotá had already been reduced to about 5% of the territory they had previously held, about half the Sabana area, including the best flatlands, was taken by Spaniards, especially encomenderos. Land grants were in large units – the basic unit of distribution was the *estancia de ganado mayor* of about 6.7 square miles – that favored the formation of large private holdings. When most of the remaining half of the Sabana was distributed between the 1590s and the 1640s, the size of this unit was reduced to 0.84 square miles and this allowed the emergence of a stratum of medium- and small-sized farmers, known as *estancieros* and *labradores*.[61] Nonetheless, in the highland plains around Bogotá, the large landowner with a number of *estancias de ganado mayor* dominated the rural scene, and his power was reinforced by the system for organizing Indian labor.[62] This gave preference to the large landowner in the allocation of forced Indian labor, providing hacendados with both a permanent and a seasonal workforce through the systems of *alquiler* and *concierto*.[63] Even when forced Indian labor was abolished in 1720, the large landowner did not lose this advantage. Not only did the new system retain many of the formalities of the traditional *concierto*, but the hacendado's ownership of extensive tracts of land also gave leverage over a local labor force.[64] Indians were forced to work at low wages for most of the year in order to meet their tributary obligations; mestizos, poor whites, and Indians who had left their communities provided an additional source of labor, as they could be incorporated into the hacienda economy as tenants, paying rents in labor and services.[65] Over the course of the eighteenth century, this

61. Juan A. Villamarín, "Encomenderos and Indians in the Formation of a Colonial Society in the Sabana de Bogotá, 1537–1740," unpublished Ph.D. thesis, Brandeis University, 1973, pp. 240, 291–2.

62. Numerous examples of such haciendas, both secular and ecclesiastic, are described in Camilo Pardo Umaña, *Las Haciendas de la Sabana: Su historia, sus leyendas y sus tradiciones* (Bogotá, 1946), passim. One particularly striking example was the mayorazgo of San Jorge, which is thought to have covered about a quarter of the entire area of the Sabana de Bogotá. See ibid., p. 210. For further information on the landowners of the Sabana de Bogotá, see Tovar Pinzón, *Grandes empresas*, pp. 137–49.

63. Alquiler was "seasonal work of a few days or weeks, usually involving whole communities in planting, weeding and harvesting"; concierto was "permanent work in which one or more men, sometimes women, served in agriculture and other hacienda work for six months or more." See Villamarín, "Encomenderos and Indians," p. 197. On the preference given to large landowners in the allocation of Indian labor, see ibid., pp. 12, 206, 294.

64. Tovar Pinzón, *Grandes empresas*, pp. 63–73.

65. Villamarín, "Encomenderos and Indians," p. 237.

tendency toward concentration seems to have become more pronounced. Large agricultural enterprises made up of several haciendas became more common, mainly because peninsular Spaniards who settled in Bogotá purchased land from the older families and from the church, and infused new blood into the city's elite by intermarriage.[66]

Concentrated landownership was also found in other areas of early conquest and colonization. In the *tierra fría* areas around Tunja, estates were generally smaller than in the Sabana de Bogotá, but here too there were marked inequities in the distribution of land. The best located lands were, it seems, in the Indian *resguardos* and in the hands of large- and medium-sized proprietors, with *estancias* of between 300 and 900 hectares.[67] In the immediate vicinity of Vélez, another area of early colonization, the same problem of unequal access to land prevailed. In 1777, a colonial official commented that in Vélez "there are two classes of people: one of those who possess their own land and constitute the class of *caballeros* (gentlemen), and another of the poor who live on the lands of the former, and who are known as renters." The latter's condition he thought unenviable, as they were "born and brought up in such abject conditions that, suffering a servitude greater than that of slaves and being less independent than Polish serfs, they endure all, because of habit and in order to retain that parcel of land on which they were born and in which they possess nothing except the herbs and roots on which they sustain themselves, when the gentleman so permits."[68] Large holdings also predominated in the *tierra caliente* areas of the mountain slopes. In the Upper Magdalena pastures of the provinces of Mariquita and Neiva, Indians had long been displaced by the spread of livestock farming, and both the Jesuits and *santafereño* landlords had created extensive estates for raising cattle and cultivating sugarcane.[69]

Throughout the highlands, the economy of large estates devoted mainly to stock raising and wheat cultivation was supplemented by a peasant economy, which produced for subsistence and for local markets. As the Indian population declined, white and mestizo farmers invaded the lands that the crown had reserved for Indian communities, and during the eighteenth century these resguardo lands acted as an internal frontier that provided peasants with an opportunity to farm independently of landlords. The *visitas* (official inspections) of the province of Tunja conducted

66. Tovar Pinzón, *Grandes empresas*, pp. 140–9.
67. Colmenares, *La provincia de Tunja*, p. 175. On the structure of landownership in the province of Tunja, also see Orlando Fals Borda, *El hombre y la tierra en Boyacá* (Bogotá, 1957), especially p. 143; and, by the same author, "Indian Congregations in the New Kingdom of Granada: Land Tenure Aspects 1595–1850," *The Americas*, vol. 8 (1957), pp. 331–51, especially pp. 342–3.
68. AHNC Mejoras Materiales, tomo 7, fols. 3–4; Manuel García Olano to Viceroy, 1777.
69. Tovar Pinzón, *Grandes empresas*, pp. 149–86; Villamarín, "Encomenderos and Indians," p. 218.

between 1750 and 1778 show that it had become common for whites and mestizos to rent lands and even to live within the Indian resguardos of the Bogotá and Tunja areas.[70] Increasingly, Bourbon officials recognized that one solution to this illegal occupation of Indian land was not to try to enforce the laws that prohibited it, but to change them. This led to a break with the tradition of protecting Indian lands, and to the regrouping of Indian communities and sale of surplus resguardo land to non-Indians. The revision of policy started in 1755 with the suppression of several resguardos in the provinces of Tunja and Santa Fe, following *visitas* by Oidor Verdugo y Oquendo in the former and Oidor Joaquín de Aróstegui in the latter. It then took on new force in the 1770s when the fiscal of the audiencia, Francisco Antonio Moreno y Escandón, recommended further changes to the resguardos as part of an overhaul of the barely functioning system of *corregimientos de indios*.[71] Fresh sales of Indian community lands, some to the small farmers who worked it and some to local landowners who used it to round off their holdings, then followed.[72]

Despite the fact that the highland areas were relatively populous, agriculture in the region was poorly developed. For the large landowners, arable farming was less important than stock raising, and fertile lands suitable for maize and cereal cultivation were often given over to extensive grazing, even on the Bogotá savannah. Some contemporary observers held the system of tenure responsible for this neglect of agriculture, blaming the large landowners for failing to cultivate their lands. In 1776, for example, Viceroy Guirior denounced "the serious damage that arises from the fact that some, by reason of ancient grants or other title, consider themselves owners of immense lands which they do not cultivate . . . nor permit others to cultivate, leaving them fallow so that neither the community nor individuals can achieve the benefits offered by their usufruct . . . "[73] Pedro Fermín de Vargas echoed this argument in 1790, when he complained that the "the limitless extent of many haciendas causes a great vacuum in the population of these territories . . . turning wheat lands into pastures, and depriving the Kingdom of a great number of people who could find their livelihood on lands which now feed animals."[74] Like Viceroy Guirior, Fermín de Vargas favored reform to release these lands onto the market, and argued that only a more even distribution of land would promote prosperity and agricultural development. To support this view, he drew attention to conditions in the temperate valleys

70. A general account of the situation prevailing on the resguardos in this period is given by Margarita González, *El Resguardo*, pp. 57–64.
71. Moreno y Escandón, *Indios y mestizos de la Nueva Granada*, pp. 26–30.
72. Margarita González, *El Resguardo*, pp. 74–5; German Colmenares, *La provincia de Tunja*, p. 205.
73. Posada and Ibañez, *Relaciones de mando*, pp. 144–5.
74. Fermín de Vargas, *Pensamientos políticos*, p. 100.

around Vélez, Socorro, San Gil, and Girón, where land was more evenly distributed. Although there were some large haciendas in these areas, agricultural production was mainly in the hands of small, independent farmers, many of whom owned their own parcels of land. Fermín de Vargas observed that this encouraged the growth of population and prosperity, "because their inhabitants have divided the land into small parts which they own and cultivate with greater care, and have sufficient to support their families." This, he added admiringly, allowed them "to live like the ancient Romans, and like them to increase their population progressively."[75]

In fact, the poverty and backwardness of agrarian society in the highlands around Bogotá and Tunja cannot be entirely attributed to the structure of landownership. The landowners' preference for stock raising was a rational response to the conditions of a small market, where most foodstuffs were supplied by peasants, and it also reflected the difficulties they encountered in creating and controlling a landless labor force. Indeed, despite their privileged position, landowners had a rather poor standard of living, and were not a wealthy and powerful class. Until their expulsion in 1767, the Jesuits had been the greatest landowners of the region, and had been able to maximize their returns by sustaining an integrated complex of agrarian enterprise in which haciendas in different environments specialized within a web of mutual interdependence.[76] But even the greatest creole landowners could not approach the agricultural wealth generated by the Jesuits nor imitate their success, because they simply lacked the markets to enable them to do so. Bogotá, home of the region's social and economic elite, reflected the mediocrity of creole fortunes. The city was not distinguished for its wealth or culture, few families held aristocratic titles, and contemporary commentary suggests that, despite their large holdings, the local landowners were by contemporary European standards no more than a respectable, rather impoverished provincial gentry with a simple, rustic lifestyle.[77]

75. Ibid.
76. German Colmenares, *Las haciendas de los Jesuitas en el Nuevo Reino de Granada, siglo XVIII* (Bogotá, 1969) especially pp. 45–68.
77. Moreno y Escandón, "Estado del Vireinato de Santafe, Nuevo Reino de Granada," *BHA*, vol. 23 (1935), p. 554. The rustic style of the capital is reflected in the description left by the Jesuit Gilij; see his *Ensayo*, pp. 381–2. It is worth noting that the Archdiocese of Santa Fe was valued at between 12,000 and 14,000 pesos in the 1760s, when the dioceses of Quito, Cuzco, and La Paz all exceeded 20,000 pesos in value, and when the archdioceses of Lima and La Plata were worth 30,000 and 50,000 pesos respectively: AGI Quito 280, "Relación de los Arzobispados y Obispados . . . " The comments of foreign travelers who visited Bogotá after independence show how little this situation had changed during the 1820s and 1830s: see Safford, "Commerce and Enterprise," pp. 44–8.

The southern provinces

In the south lay another distinct macroregion, in the huge province of Popayán. Administered by a crown-appointed governor, this province had a jurisdiction that encompassed virtually the whole of southern and southwestern Colombia. Except for the northern towns of Cartago, Anserma, Caloto, and Toro, the province was part of the audiencia of Quito, and it included the subprovinces of Iscuandé, Raposo, and Barbacoas on the Pacific coast, and Pasto in the highlands to the south, all of them administered by lieutenant governors appointed in Popayán.

The region was made up of several distinct geographical and economic zones. Its original heartland lay in the city of Popayán, where the Spaniards had established themselves early in the sixteenth century. As the provincial capital, Popayán continued to be the region's main urban center, with about 14,000 inhabitants living in its vicinity and a group of wealthy vecinos who drew their fortunes from gold mining in the neighboring region, and more important, from mines in the Pacific lowlands.[78] North of Popayán, a chain of towns stretching along the high valley of the Upper Cauca River from Caloto through Cali and Buga to Anserma contained most of the region's population, as Map 2.4 shows. The northern towns were merely the decaying remnants of early mining settlements, and the more important towns of Buga, Cali, and Caloto were of modest proportions. In the 1770s, Cali had about 5,000 inhabitants in the town itself, with another 6,000 in its hinterland, and Buga and Caloto were of similar size.[79] Like Popayán, these towns connected with mining areas in the Pacific lowlands. Directly westward were the thinly populated but economically important gold mining zones of Barbacoas, Iscuandé, and Raposo in the hot lowlands of the Pacific coast; to the northwest lay the province of the Chocó, another important mining area. Administratively, the Chocó was part of the province of Popayán until 1740, when it became an independent province; economically, it retained strong ties with Popayán and the Cauca towns, because the richest miners were citizens of Popayán and Cali, and their haciendas and farms were the Chocó's main source of provisions. Finally, on the southern rim of the province lay the region of Pasto, supervised by a lieutenant of the governor of Popayán. About 11,500 people lived in and around this town, with another 15,000 living in villages scattered over the high, cold country of the surrounding Andean landscape.

78. For a view of the city at mid-century, see the observations made by Miguel de Santiesteban, in Robinson (ed.), *Mil leguas por América*, pp. 135–6.
79. See Appendix A, Table 7. On Cali, see German Colmenares, *Cali: Terratenientes, Mineros y Comerciantes, siglo XVIII* (Bogotá, 1983), p. 137.

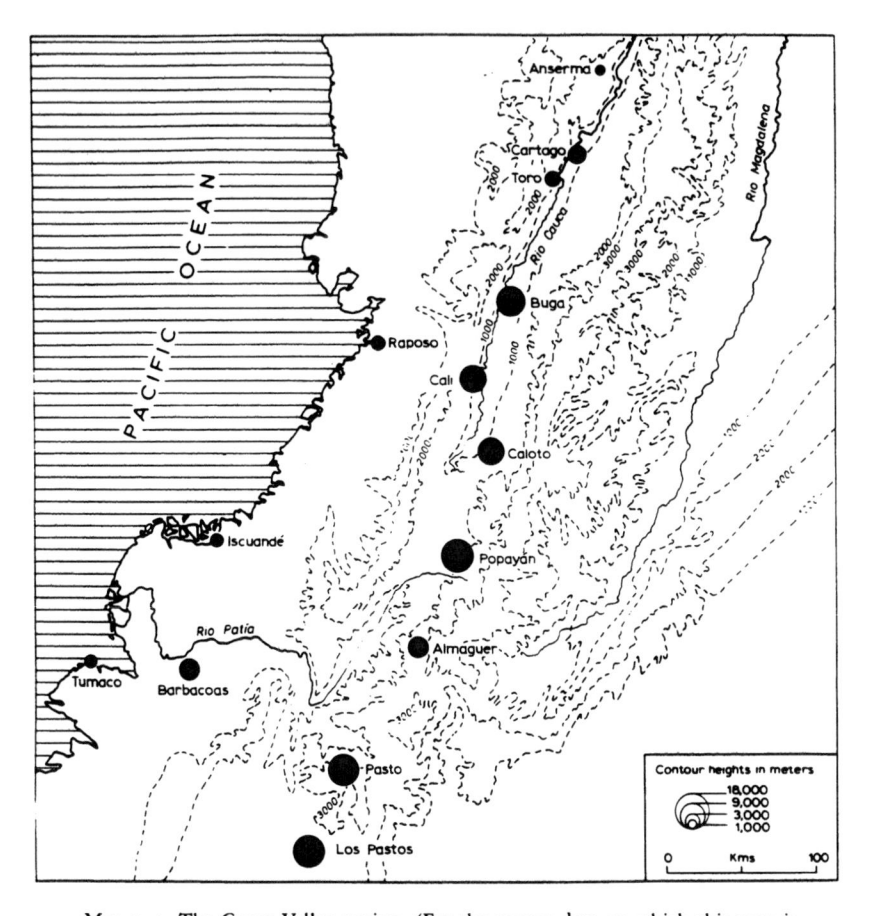

Map 2.4. The Cauca Valley region. (For the census data on which this map is based, see Appendix A, Table 7.)

Of the subregions of southern Colombia, Pasto stands apart. Socially, culturally, and economically, it had more in common with the territory of Quito than with the region that lay northward in Popayán and New Granada. Most of its population were Indians and its agriculture was similar to that of *tierra fría* in the Eastern Cordillera. It was on the whole a poor region, where only the Jesuits seem to have been able to create successful agricultural enterprises producing wool, cattle, and cereals for trade with the Popayán and Quito areas. Although the highland haciendas were able to sell wheat in both Popayán and the Quiteño towns, the high cost of transportation to such markets reduced their trade to a rather irregular traffic, vulnerable to the disturbances that frequent rainfall caused on the connecting roads.[80] The fate of the Jesuit haciendas put up for sale in the 1770s illustrates the shortcomings of the Pasto economy. The value of seven large haciendas, inclusive of their buildings, livestock, and equipment, was fixed at only 103,599 pesos, or little more than 11,000 pesos per hacienda.[81] Notwithstanding the low price and special arrangements to facilitate sales, bids were forthcoming for only five of the properties. As an official explained, Pasto landowners simply did not have the funds to make such purchases, unless they were given very extended mortgages on generous terms.[82] Even when the crown reduced the interest payable on mortgages from the standard 5% to 3%, there were still complaints that repayments could not be made because of the difficulties of exchanging agricultural produce for hard cash.[83]

The heart of the southern regional economy lay in the temperate uplands near the city of Popayán and along the broad stretch of the Upper Cauca Valley, between Cali and Buga. In these areas, gold, mostly from the Pacific lowlands, provided the basis for external exchange, fostered the development of a money economy, and eased the pressures toward subsistence induced by isolation from overseas markets. Here, gold fulfilled the function that sugar or cacao exercised in the mobilization of resources in Brazil or Venezuela. From the mines came a constant demand for meat and cattle products, for sugar products, principally aguardiente, and for tobacco, all of which were supplied from the Cauca Valley region.

Throughout the area, livestock raising was a basic form of agricultural enterprise, mainly producing cattle, but also breeding horses and mules, or sheep in highland areas. The largest livestock-producing estates were owned and run by the Jesuits until 1767, when they were expelled; they then passed into the hands of government administrators before being sold, mostly to large landowners. Sugar cultivation was also fundamental to the agrarian economy throughout the Cauca Valley. From Caloto to Cartago, landowners generally cultivated sugar on some of their lands, chiefly for the molasses used in making aguardiente. By the 1770s, many landowners in the Cauca Valley were also producing tobacco. So, too, it seems were landowners in the hinterland of Popayán, as the city's municipal council protested against the tobacco estanco in 1772 on the grounds that it would deprive them of profits from an essential commercial crop.[84] After 1778, tobacco cultivation became more concentrated, as the rules of the state monopoly restricted legal production, first to areas near Caloto

80. ACC Libro Capitular (1775), tomo 27, fol. 57.
81. ACC Colonia C II-17it 52 75, Ramón de la Barrera to Governor Joseph Ignacio Ortega, Pasto 11 October 1770.
82. Ibid.   83. Colmenares, *Las haciendas de los jesuitas*, pp. 135–6.
84. ACC Libro Cap. 1772, tomo 26, ff. 153–5.

and Buga, then, by 1795, to the area of Llanogrande (modern Palmira).[85]
In the cool, fertile lands around the city of Popayán, agriculture was more
diverse than in the Cauca Valley. Hacendados produced a range of temperate food crops, such as wheat, barley, and maize, potatoes, beans, and
onions, while also raising livestock. Like the Jesuits, large landowners
either sold their products in urban markets or to merchants who carried
them to the mining districts, whereas those who owned mines also used
their haciendas to feed the slaves they employed in mining. The hacienda
economy was, then, generally a mixture of arable and livestock farming,
producing both for the market and for the subsistence of the estate owner,
his dependents, and workers.[86] As in the Caribbean coastal region, estates
devoted to livestock were the most common form of commercial agriculture enterprise. Indeed, meat was so plentiful that it had become the
dietary staple of the common people throughout the Cauca region.[87]

The agrarian structure of the core area was dominated by large estates
that had grown up in the wake of conquest, first around the provincial
capital in the city of Popayán, and later around Cali and Buga. By the
eighteenth century, three main types of agrarian enterprise had emerged
in the province of Popayán. First, the *haciendas de campo* of the Valley of
Popayán, developed in conjunction with the early encomiendas to supply
Spanish settlers with cereals; second, the immense *hatos* (ranches) created
in lands taken up in the Cauca Valley during the wars of Indian conquest
of the late sixteenth and early seventeenth centuries, and devoted to
extensive cattle grazing; and, third, the *haciendas de trapiche* which produced sugar products for urban and mining markets. The latter were
invariably linked to cattle ranches, which provided food for the slave labor
used in the sugar economy.[88]

Though smaller than Popayán, Cali was also the focus of an agrarian
society dominated by large landowners. Here the Indian population had
been small at the time of colonization, and the great estate developed in
order to monopolize the scarce labor available. The valley's immense
fertility was, however, barely exploited during the colonial period. Little
land was cultivated, and much of it was turned over to cattle, which
roamed wild over extensive natural pastures and provided the meat that
was the main source of Cali's trade.[89] The concentration of land was

85. González, *Ensayos de historia colombiana*, pp. 123–4.
86. Zamira Díaz de Zuluaga, *Sociedad y Economía en el Valle del Cauca, vol. 2: Guerra y Economía en las Haciendas, Popayán, 1780–1830* (Bogotá, 1983), pp. 31–60.
87. Colmenares calculates that with a population of about 15,000, Popayán consumed about 4,400 *libras* of meat per day, or about a million and a half *libras* each year. On the organization of the city's meat supply, see Colmenares, *Historia económica y social II: Popayán*, pp. 218–27.
88. Ibid, pp. 199–207.
89. From early in the seventeenth century, Cali sent livestock products to the mining areas to

extraordinary: Colmenares estimates that the entire Valley of the Cauca from Cartago to Cali may have been in the hands of about 100 people, of whom 79 lived in Cali and Buga. This did not make them rich. Agriculture offered minimal returns, the price of land was extremely low, and most landowners possessed little movable property. To acquire the specie so lacking in the agrarian sector, landowners had to turn to commerce and mining, or make alliances with merchants and miners.

In the eighteenth century, the development of gold mining on the Pacific lowlands injected a new dynamism into the Cauca economy. Sugar cultivation, using slave labor and often organized by hacendados who were also involved in mining and who transferred their slaves between agricultural and mining activities, now became the most profitable aspect of the agrarian economy. The number of slaves employed on these estates rarely exceeded thirty or forty, but the number represented a high proportion of the overall investment in agriculture. And, like the landowners of Popayán and the Caribbean coast, the Cauca landowners employed their slaves in an estate economy that aimed at internal subsistence, while maximizing returns from mining and sales of sugar products.[90]

As trade with the mining areas grew during the eighteenth century, the opportunities to profit from agriculture increased accordingly. The rewards were largely taken by the great landowners, who often integrated mining and agriculture within interlocking enterprises. The ability of the great landowners to dominate commercial agriculture was due partly to the existing structure of landownership and partly to the nature of the mining economy. The mining settlements were small and scattered, often highly mobile, and usually located in the unhealthy tropical lowlands of the Pacific littoral. The high costs of hauling goods over the long and difficult trails tended to keep the small farmer from participating in interregional markets, and the mining markets were consequently controlled mainly by the small group of wealthy families whose predecessors had accumulated vast tracts of fertile and well-positioned Cauca lands. Their hold on land, reinforced by informal political power, enabled such families to dominate regional markets, and their economic power was reinforced by connections with mining and commerce that gave them access to capital and credit. During the sixteenth and seventeenth centuries, the traditional elite of Popayán encomenderos and landowners had been revivified by intermarriage with peninsular immigrants who pro-

exchange for gold, and to Quito and Popayán to exchange for manufactures from the Ecuadorian *obrajes* and from the merchants who brought imports from Spain: See Gustavo Arboleda, *Historia de Cali*, 3 vols. (Cali, 1956), vol. I, pp. 167–9, 202. The importance of such trade to the landowners of the area may be judged by the effects of the cattle plague of 1688, and by that of 1772: See ibid., vol. I, p. 317, and vol. II, p. 360.
90. Colmenares, *Cali*, pp. 21–78.

vided the wealth required to invest in mining, preserving its seigneurial values by absorbing a rational, commercial orientation.[91] During the eighteenth century, this trend continued, as successful Spaniards were integrated into Popayán's elite by intermarriage, thus reinforcing its wealth and power, while preserving its essential character.[92] The landed gentry of Cali was also eager to absorb the new rich into its ranks. Mineowners and immigrant merchants were incorporated into the patriciate by marriage, reinforcing the small group of leading families that dominated the city.[93] Thus, through the operations of an economic system that combined extensive livestock farming with highly capitalized sugar production, self-sufficient arable farming, gold mining, commercial enterprise, and office holding, the creole gentry of Popayán and Cali captured much of the wealth of the Cauca region and dominated its society.

The creation and sustenance of the gentry's economic power rested on the institution of slavery.[94] In the sixteenth century, the foundations of the interrelated agricultural and mining economy had been built on Indian labor, until the depletion of Indian numbers forced landowners and miners to buy black slaves. These slaves were mainly destined for the mines, but they were also incorporated into agricultural use. The need for a constant core of laborers to deal with the growing herds of cattle, the prohibition against employing Indian labor in the sugar mills, and the transferability of slaves between mining and agricultural work, all made slave labor an attractive proposition for those landowners with sufficient capital to make the investment.[95] Once acquired, the slaves released landowners from reliance on poor whites and coloreds who preferred to seek independence in subsistence plots or in urban work, and enabled the

91. The emergence of an important element of this landowning elite, which was based in the city of Popayán, is described in Marzahl, *Town in the Empire*, pp. 3–34.

92. Colmenares, *Historia económica y social II: Popayán*, pp. 237–47.

93. Colmenares, *Cali*, pp. 129–37.

94. The importance of slavery in agriculture can be illustrated by comparing the viceroy's estimate of the number of slaves employed in mining in 1778 with the total slave population enumerated in the 1779 census. The viceroy calculated that 6,320 slaves were employed in the province's mines in 1778; the 1779 census showed that there were more than 18,000 slaves in the province. Thus it appears that nearly two-thirds of the slave population was employed in agricultural and domestic work. See José Manuel Pérez Ayala, *Antonio Caballero y Góngora, Virrey y arzobispo de Santa Fe, 1723–1796* (Bogotá, 1951), pp. 348, 392–3.

95. A *visita* made in Cali in 1688 indicates that Indians were still used in agricultural work and that encomiendas still persisted. Rules were newly laid down for the regulation of Indian labor, and to ensure that the vecinos were able to hire the Indians as wage laborers, allowing a third of the encomienda Indians each year for this purpose. It was, however, specifically prohibited to use Indians for work within an *ingenio* (sugar refinery) or *trapiche* (sugar mill). See Arboleda, *Historia de Cali*, vol. 1, 246–51.

landowners to extract greater advantage from their resources by putting them to intensive use.

Reports on estate management made by two prominent hacendados during the last quarter of the eighteenth century show how a slave labor force might be put to maximum use in an economy that combined self-sufficiency with a strong market orientation. In 1775, José de Mosquera and Antonio de Arboleda outlined the organization of their Popayán and Caloto haciendas for the instruction of the *Junta Municipal* responsible for administering confiscated Jesuit estates. Both men described sugar mills that required large quantities of slave labor and animal power for their operation. They reported that each separate mill needed fifty slaves, both men and women, who would sow, cut, and process the cane, while cultivating maize and plantains and raising cattle for their own subsistence. In addition, fifty horses were required for the constant grinding of the cane, with four horses yoked in pairs to supply each vat of boiling sugar. Twenty mules were also required for transporting the raw cane and the slaves' food supplies to the mills, and forty oxen for the carriage of firewood to feed the ovens. These were not, José de Mosquera observed, hard and fast rules for sugar production. The number of workers, mules, and oxen used varied with the fertility of the land, the accessibility of fuel for the sugar vats, and the distance of the maize plots from the sugar mills.[96] In one respect, however, the advice was clear. It aimed to exploit the estates' commercial potential to the fullest possible extent, while minimizing their outgoings and dependence on external supplies.

The very detailed accounts kept by the administrador of the ex-Jesuit haciendas of Japio and Matarredonda for the years from 1774 to 1777 show these same principles in action. As many as possible of the commodities of everyday use, from food to furniture and tallow for candles, were provided from the estates' own resources. Certain items could be obtained only from the outside (clothing for the slaves, iron and steel for the making of tools, and specialized jobs, such as lock making), but such expenditures were rigorously checked and kept to a minimum.[97] The records of the hacienda of Coconuco (another ex-Jesuit property, bought by Francisco de Arboleda in 1770) also show how estate owners were able to buttress their autonomy by using local Indian laborers when they were available. Located in *tierra fría*, Coconuco's lands were used for cultivating various grains and for grazing sheep and cattle. Slaves provided the spe-

96. ACC Colonia, Civil II-17it, 54 04. Josef de Mosquera to Ignacio de Velasco, Popayán, February 20, 1775; Manuel Antonio de Arboleda to Junta Municipal, Popayán, March 30, 1775.
97. ACC Col. Civil II-17it, 55 29, ff. 1–68. "Libro que yo Dn. Felix Antonio Manrique, Administrador de estas haciendas de Japio y Matarredonda, pertenecientes a las Temporalidades de Regulares expulsos del Colegio de esta Ciudad de Popayán, he formado. . . ."

cialized core of the workforce (e.g., as millers, cheesemakers, and tanners), whereas the local Indian village was the source of seasonal agricultural labor. Use of Indian labor was, indeed, such an entrenched and traditional practice that when the new owner gave instructions to his administrator in 1823, he did not detail the rights and duties of the Indians as he did for the slaves, so regulated was the practice by long-standing customs of colonial origins.[98] Beyond the hinterland of Popayán, Indian labor was generally not available and landowners relied on either slaves or the labor provided by freed blacks, mulattoes, and mestizos. In the vicinity of the mining town of Caloto, for example, most of the land was owned by vecinos of Popayán who also controlled the local mines, and thereby dominated the local economy. Although these vecinos owned fifty-four *haciendas de campo* in Caloto's jurisdiction, the rest of the population, of some 10,000 people, were either employed by those hacendados or worked lands that were barely capable of supporting them. In the areas of the cities of Toro and Anserma, similar situations of poor subsistence farming prevailed, occasionally supplemented by labor in the mines.[99]

Commercial agriculture in the Cauca region was not the exclusive preserve of such great landowning families as the Caicedos, the Mosqueras, and the Arboledas. Below the upper ranks of the landowning class lay a larger grouping of more modest landowners, who worked their *hatos* and *estancias* with two or three slaves. These men also participated in commercial agriculture, and when the government aguardiente monopoly was introduced in 1765, they joined with the large landowners to protest against it.[100] The militia records of Cali, Buga, and Cartago also testify to the existence of groups of *labradores*, men who often rented their land from the large landowners of these towns.[101] In Cali, these poorer whites were known as "montañeses" (because they did not have town houses) and they constituted an intermediate social group that looked to the great landed proprietors for leadership.[102] In 1793, they were described by the procurator of Cali's town council as those who "breed their fine styles of cows, bulls, mules and horses under the protection of the owners who allow them the use of their lands for nothing or for a small rent."[103] Around

98. J. León Helguera, "Coconuco: Datos y documentos para la historia de una gran hacienda caucana, 1823, 1824, y 1876," *ACHSC*, vol. 5 (1970), pp. 189–203. On the Indians from whom the Popayán landowners drew their labor, see Joanna Rappaport, *The Politics of Memory: Native Historical Interpretation in the Colombian Andes* (Cambridge, 1990), pp. 38–56.

99. "Estado general de las ciudades y pueblos del Cauca en 1771," *Boletín Historial del Valle*, nos. 73–5 (Cali, 1941), pp. 58–96.

100. "Cali en 1765. Informe rendido al Virrey sobre la subversión del Estanco de Aguardiente y los movimientos subversivos que eso ocasionó," *Boletín Historial del Valle* (Cali, 1937), nos. 43–5, pp. 246–52; Arboleda, *Historia de Cali*, tomo 2, pp. 326–7.

101 AHNC Virreyes, tomo 5, fols. 813–31.   102. Colmenares, *Cali*, pp. 138–40.

103. Arboleda, *Historia de Cali*, vol. III, p. 227.

Buga, there were about 105 *haciendas de trapiche* in 1779, some of them owned by the same families, whereas tobacco cultivation supported small farmers who rented land from large landowners, possibly on a share-cropping basis.[104]

In the militia lists, the *labradores* were listed together with the artisans, and both considered themselves distinct from the mass of blacks and free coloreds. The French traveler Mollien observed that "pride of race is no less in the Cauca Valley than in the colonies of the Caribbean; and this reaches such a point that the poor will only cultivate the mountain lands where the cold does not allow the employment of negroes." He also noted that "even the muleteers, proud of their white blood, are ashamed to walk, so that it takes some effort to distinguish the poor (white) from the rich."[105]

Although the case of the *labradores* indicates that Cauca agriculture was not divided along two rigidly separate axes – large landowners using slave and Indian labor on the one hand, and peasant farmers engaged in subsistence and occasional day work on the other – the region's agrarian structure had a marked tendency toward dualism. On one side stood the large landowners who specialized in ranching and sugar production, and dominated the markets for meat and sugar products. On the other side stood the mass of small peasant farmers, whites, mestizos, and mulattoes, whose participation in the market economy was limited to the sale of dietary staples like maize, plantains, and vegetables. Thus, although the heavy reliance of Cauca landowners on slavery and their close relations with urban and mining markets made the region particularly responsive to external influences that affected the demand of those sectors during the eighteenth century, the tendency of the hacendados to seek autonomy in the supply of their estates and to force the small producer onto marginal lands meant that most farmers were little affected by changes in the market economy. Only those with access to large supplies of land and capital were able to avail themselves of the gains offered by trade with the mining camps and urban commercial centers.

Throughout New Granada, then, agriculture offered few opportunities for the expansion of incomes or the accumulation of capital. Neither legal trade nor contraband provided the agriculturalist with significant external outlets for his products, and farming – from the level of the large hacienda to that of the subsistence plot of the peasant family – was mainly geared to meeting domestic demands. Commercialization of agriculture within the context of the domestic economy was, moreover, restricted by

104. Tulio Enrique Tascón, *Historia de Buga en la colonia* (Bogotá, 1939), pp. 251–3; Arboleda, *Historia de Cali*, pp. 139–40.
105. Mollien, *Viaje*, p. 286.

the small scale of internal markets. Most commodities could only be traded locally, as high costs of transportation prevented them from competing with acceptable substitutes produced in other areas, and local trade served markets that were too small in terms of numbers of consumers and purchasing power to promote specialization. Ownership of extensive estates that could be used for producing sugarcane, cereals, and livestock supported regional landed elites who enjoyed above-average incomes from agriculture, but production of low-priced foodstuffs did not favor the accumulation of great fortunes. Nor, of course, did agriculture sustain economic ties with the parent power. Trade with Spain depended instead upon the gold mines that Spaniards had found and developed during the sixteenth century, and that, throughout the colonial period, provided the means to finance imports from Europe.

3

Mining frontiers and the gold economy

New Granada had quickly become renowned for its gold following the conquests of the mid-sixteenth century, and gold mining continued to be of central importance to the colonial relationship throughout the centuries of Spanish rule. Of all New Granada's resources, gold seemed the most significant to Spanish governments, because it financed trade with Spain, stimulated interregional commerce, and provided an important source of revenue to the royal exchequer. This point was forcefully expressed by a late eighteenth-century observer, when he noted that

> the principal and almost sole motive for the subsistence of this vast kingdom and its commerce with Spain . . . is the gold which is taken from the numerous mines worked in the provinces of Popayán, Chocó, and Antioquia; the other provinces, such as the Audiencias of Quito and Santa Fe, subsist upon this gold and the trade with the mining provinces. . . .[1]

Thus, insofar as both external trade and domestic markets depended on gold production, the development of the mining sector is clearly a major theme in New Granada's economic history during the eighteenth century, and one that deserves close attention. However, before we examine the progress of mining and its role in New Granada's economic life in the late colonial period, we should from the outset be careful not to exaggerate the wealth that gold generated. For in terms of its scale, organization, and technology, and the economic dynamism that it engendered, gold mining in New Granada scarcely bears comparison with the great silver-mining industries of contemporary Mexico and Peru, or with the gold fields of eighteenth-century Brazil. Indeed, compared to Mexican and Peruvian mining, it scarcely merits the name of an industry. Located mainly in sparsely populated regions, using a crude technology and employing only a very small proportion of the country's labor force, gold mining in New Granada yielded only a fraction of the wealth generated by mining in the other viceroyalties and was consequently a much less powerful stimulus to economic activity.

1. Quoted in West, *Colonial Placer Mining*, p. 112.

Mining techniques

Virtually all gold mined in eighteenth-century New Granada was found in areas of difficult access, amidst humid, forested tropical lowlands or in mountainous backlands far from the main population centers. There, mining was the work of small slave gangs or individual prospectors who operated from encampments scattered throughout the areas in which auriferous alluvions and gravels were found. The work was very labor-intensive and employed a simple technology, composed of a few standard techniques. The most widely used was that of stream placering, whereby gold-bearing sands were scooped from the riverbeds during the dry season and washed in a *batea* (a shallow clay or wooden bowl). A variation on this basic technique was provided by pit placering, by which miners dug large holes to remove auriferous sands and gravels, then sifted the extract in pans to remove the gold. Another form of alluvial mining was ground sluicing. This involved channeling water to wash gold-bearing soil placed in a sluice; the heavy material was removed by hand or run off by the force of the water, leaving a fine layer of clay that the miners sifted for gold dust. Because it required considerable preparation and depended on maintaining an adequate water supply, sluice mining was highly labor intensive and tended to be used by miners working with slave gangs. Where a reliable source of water could not be assured by diverting nearby streams, the miners were forced to work seasonally, relying on the rainwater that they could trap in small reservoirs during the wet season.[2]

Mines of a kind typical in Mexico or Peru, which produced ores by working veins that lay deep underground, were very rare in eighteenth-century New Granada. After the conquest, the Spaniards who worked the lodes found at Buriticá, Anserma, and Remedios had improved on Indian techniques of digging vertical or sloping shafts from the surface to the lodes and crushing the ores on hand-operated stone mills. By introducing European practices of timbering and draining underground shafts, they were able to reach greater depths than the Indians, whereas the introduction of water-powered stamp mills also allowed them to extract gold from harder ores.[3] However, despite attempts to revive it during the eighteenth century, vein mining made little progress in New Granada. Such mines were few in number, employed only a tiny fraction of the workforce engaged in mining, and never approached the scale or organizational complexity found in the silver mines of Mexico or Peru.

2. For a more detailed description of these methods, see West, *Colonial Placer Mining*, pp. 55–62, Vicente Restrepo, *Estudio sobre las minas*, pp. 228–48, and William F. Sharp, *Slavery on the Spanish Frontier: The Colombian Chocó, 1680–1810* (Norman, Oklahoma, 1976), pp. 46–50.
3. West, *Colonial Placer Mining*, pp. 54, 65–6.

The alluvial mines that produced most of New Granada's gold were worked by two kinds of labor: black slaves and free prospectors, known as *mazamorreros*. In the Pacific lowland mining zones, slavery was the dominant form of labor, and mine ownership was concentrated in a few hands. In Antioquia, by contrast, ownership was less concentrated and, though slaves were also used in mining, the free labor of *mazamorreros* or prospectors played a much more important part in production.[4] The scale of mining enterprises was never very large. At its simplest, mining was the work of independent prospectors, or miners working with one or two slaves. This kind of mining was most often found in Antioquia. In the Pacific lowlands, the search for gold often involved larger enterprises, but these were generally not very big. In the Chocó, a *cuadrilla* composed of more than thirty slaves was considered large; only a few of the biggest mineowners owned more than a hundred slaves.[5]

Once taken from the ground, gold-bearing ores received little further processing. Ores obtained from veins were usually crushed by hand and gold was separated from the residue by careful sifting in a *batea*. This same technique of washing was also used to separate gold dust from the auriferous concentrate taken from the placers. According to the law, all gold had to be taken to the *fundición*, or royal foundry, where it was assayed, cast into ingots, and taxed by the crown. The technical process involved in smelting was simple, requiring only rudimentary equipment, a few skilled men, and some laborers.[6]

Clearly, mining in New Granada was radically different from that of the American silver regions. The extraction of gold did not generate great enterprises based on the large fixed investments and substantial protoproletariats found in silver mining, and refining did not involve a complex or expensive technology. New Granada mining was also unimpressive when compared to the gold economy of contemporary Brazil, where new cycles of discovery during the first half of the century generated a boom of such tremendous proportions that it attracted large movements of migrants, created whole new areas of settlement, and shifted the balance of the entire economy.[7] Nevertheless, for all its simplicity, mining was a vital element in New Granada's economic life and, despite its limitations

4. "Ordenanzas formadas por el Señor Don Juan Antonio Mon y Velarde . . . " Antioquia, 23 August 1787, in Emilio Robledo, *Bosquejo Biográfico del Señor Oidor Juan Antonio Mon y Velarde, Visitador de Antioquia 1785–1788*, 2 vols. (Bogotá 1954), vol. 2, p. 50.
5. Sharp, *Slavery on the Spanish Frontier*, pp. 176, 206.
6. Even the more complex operations involved in minting gold coins used relatively simple technology and little labor. See the description of the machinery and expenses of the Santa Fe mint given in A. M. Barriga Villalba, *Historia de la Casa de Moneda*, 3 vols. (Bogotá, 1969), vol. 2, pp. 65–7.
7. A. J. R. Russell-Wood, "Colonial Brazil: The Gold Cycle, c. 1690–1750," in L. Bethell (ed.), *Cambridge History of Latin America*, vol. 3 (Cambridge, 1984), pp. 547–662.

as a pole for economic development, the resurgence of gold mining over the course of the eighteenth century had important implications both for the region's economy and its relations with Spain.

The expansion of mining frontiers

The revival of New Granadan mining began at the end of the seventeenth century, when new frontiers for gold placering opened in two regions. One frontier was in the Pacific lowlands of Western Colombia, especially in the Chocó (see Map 3.1); the other lay in the Central Cordillera, in the highlands of the province of Antioquia (see Map 3.2).

Gold fields in the Pacific lowlands had first been exploited in the late sixteenth century, around Nóvita and Toro, and by the 1580s the Chocó had become sufficiently important to be designated a separate province. Indian rebellion in the same decade had, however, forced settlers to abandon Nóvita and to reestablish their town of Toro in the Cauca Valley. With this withdrawal, the *gobernación* of the Chocó was suppressed, and the area brought under the jurisdiction of Popayán. Chocó mining revived briefly in the 1630s, when miners from Popayán returned to the area with their black slaves, until Indian resistance again forced a retreat. Toward the close of the seventeenth century, miners from the provinces of Popayán and Antioquia returned to the Chocó once more and, when Indian rebellion was overcome, extensive exploitation of the region's placers recommenced in the 1690s. The old *real de minas* at Nóvita was reestablished, many new mining camps were set up on the tributaries of the San Juan and Atrato rivers, and, by 1726, the crown recognized the economic importance and fiscal potential of the Chocó by detaching it from the jurisdiction of Popayán and making it an independent province, with a governor stationed at Quibdó.[8]

The impulse behind the retaking and expansion of the mining frontier in the Chocó had come from the province of Popayán, where influential *vecinos* of several towns secured official approval for expeditions to subjugate the Indians and to establish mines. In the course of a generation, between 1690 and 1710, these miners had achieved a control that, in the course of the eighteenth century, was to enrich a small group of families in the cities of Popayán and Cali, most of whom linked their mining enterprises in Caloto and the Chocó with large agricultural holdings in the Cauca and Popayán valleys.[9] Fresh flows of gold into the province of

---

8. West, *Colonial Placer Mining*, pp. 16–18; Enrique Ortega Ricaurte (ed.), *Historia Documental del Chocó* (Bogotá, 1954), pp. 165–9. The fullest account of colonization in the seventeenth century is found in Caroline Hansen, "Conquest and Colonization in the Colombian Chocó, 1515–1740," unpub. Ph.D. thesis, University of Warwick, 1991.

9. Colmenares, *Historia económica y social, Popayán*, vol. II, pp. 144–52.

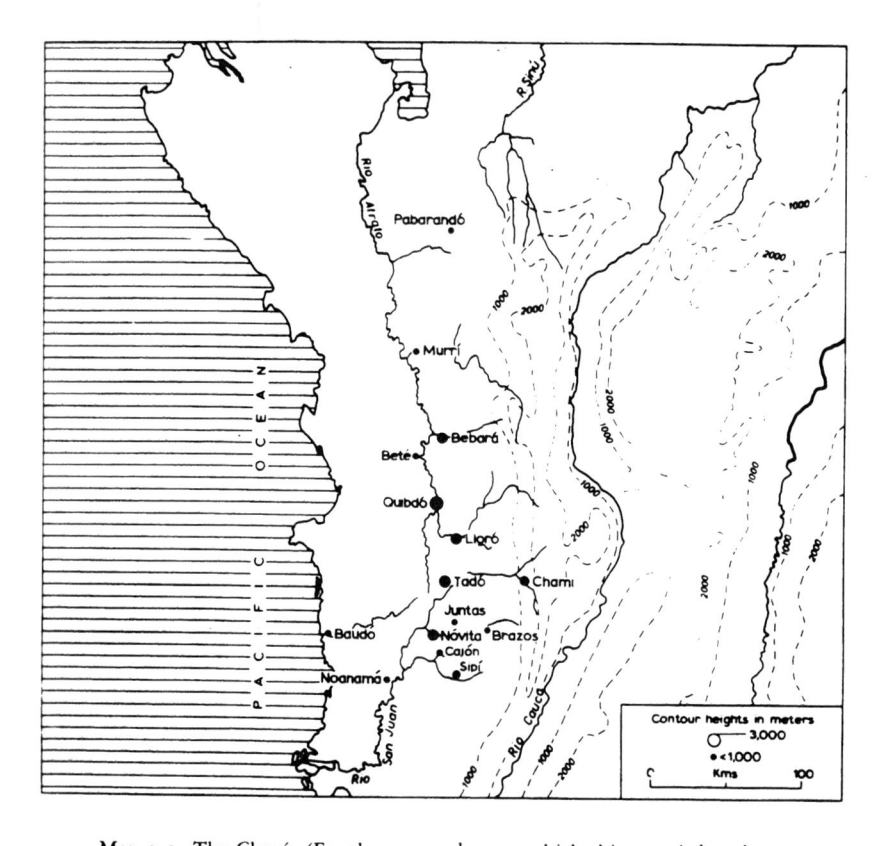

Map 3.1. The Chocó. (For the census data on which this map is based, see Appendix A, Table 8.)

Popayán from the Chocó were also supplemented by a related revival of mining in the southernmost section of the Colombian Pacific coast, in the subprovinces of Raposo, Iscuandé, and Barbacoas, where the extraction of gold was mainly organized by miners from Cali.[10]

Growth in mining activity during the first half of the eighteenth century was facilitated by an increased supply of black slave labor. During the War of the Spanish Succession, the French Guinea Company organized a substantial import of slaves through Cartagena – about 4,250 in 1703–14 – and high levels of imports were sustained after the war by the English South Sea Company, operating under the terms of the concession made at the Treaty of Utrecht in 1713. Between 1714 and 1736, the English company brought around 10,300 slaves into Cartagena, and, when the English *asiento* ended in 1736, the various Spanish licensees who

10. West, *Colonial Placer Mining*, pp. 18–20; Colmenares, *Cali*, pp. 95–102.

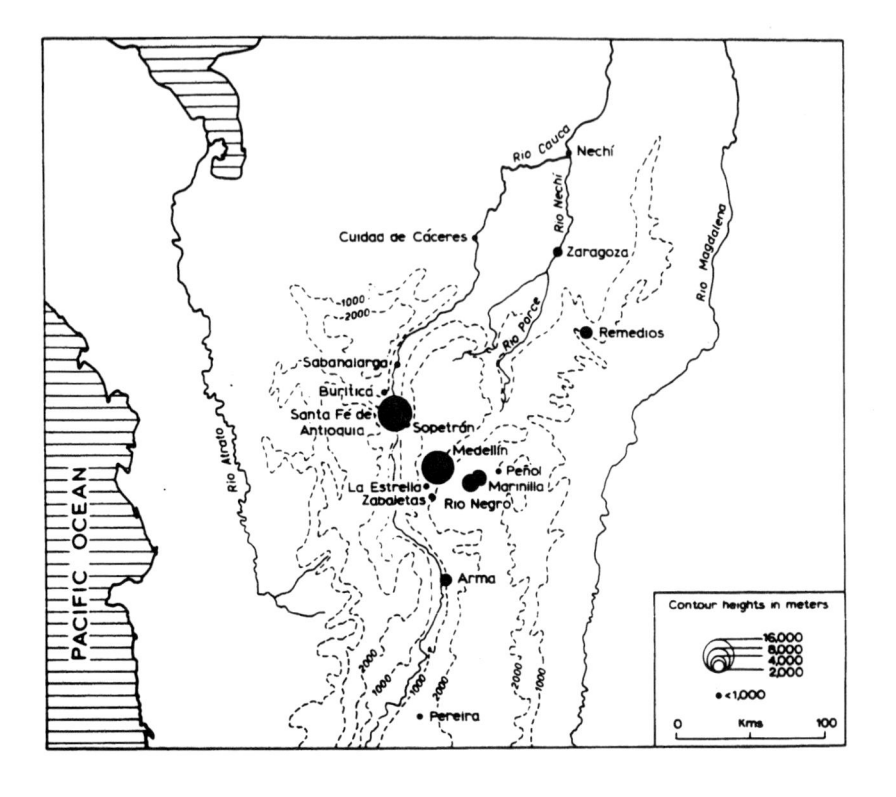

Map 3.2. Antioquia. (For the census data on which this map is based, see
Appendix A, Table 9.)

took over the English monopoly imported almost 13,000 additional slaves
between 1746 and 1757.[11] It is difficult to calculate exactly how many of
these slaves went to the mining districts, but vigorous growth in the
Chocó's slave population indicates that large numbers went to work in
Pacific lowland gold mines. Indeed, reports to the Council of the Indies
estimated that the Chocó slave population had grown at a spectacular pace
during the 1720s and 1730s, rising from only about 500 at the time of
the first viceroyalty (1719–23) to between 10,000 and 12,000 slaves in
1738.[12] This was almost certainly a great exaggeration. At no time in the
eighteenth century did the Chocó slave population reach this level. More
cautious estimates show nonetheless that there was a marked growth
throughout the century, particularly in the early years. The number of
slaves in the Chocó increased from around 600 in 1704 to around 2,000 in

11. Colmenares, *Historia económica y social, Popayán,* vol. II, pp. 41, 56.
12. AGI Santa Fe 264, Consulta del Consejo de Indias, October 20, 1738.

1724, doubled to almost 4,000 by 1759, and almost doubled again during the following two decades, reaching just over 7,000 by 1782.[13]

The extension of the mining frontier in the Pacific lowlands was based on black slave labor; in the province of Antioquia it depended largely on free labor and was associated with the natural increase of the region's population. In the late sixteenth and early seventeenth centuries, Antioquia had held the richest mining zones in New Granada, located in the broad expanse of territory formed by the northern escarpment of the Central Cordillera and drained by the River Cauca and its tributaries. When the Spaniards found substantial deposits of gold, both underground in the *cerro de Buriticá* and in the alluvions of the river banks, the region had quickly attracted one of New Granada's richest gold rushes.[14] At first, miners focused on exploiting the gold veins of Buriticá using Indian labor; this activity was then supplemented and later supplanted by placer mining among the numerous streams of the Cauca River system. Together, these underground and alluvial mines produced a boom that lasted from the 1590s until the early 1630s, when the initial surge of Spanish mining in Antioquia wavered and ended. Exhaustion of the richest deposits, combined with labor shortages and growing problems in obtaining credit and food supplies, now depressed Antioquian mining to its nadir. In 1663, an official reported that all the important mines were worked out, and the Indians available for labor were reduced to a total of sixty in the whole province; after four years of shortage, many slaves had also died from hunger.[15]

So, by the mid-seventeenth century, the remnants of Antioquia's once flourishing mining communities were working under increasingly adverse conditions. After depleting the most accessible deposits, miners were forced further afield, into remote areas where returns were less certain, essential supplies more difficult to obtain, and profits consequently lower. Without adequate returns, miners could not buy the slaves who formed the essential core of their workforce, and even when slaves were available, there were not enough Indians under Spanish control to provide basic foodstuffs for the slaves' subsistence. Thus Antioquian mining entered into a cycle of depression that induced a regression toward subsistence in the province and increasingly isolated its inhabitants from contact with neighboring regions. Those who could, evacuated the area, taking with

13. For a review of demographic change in the Chocó, and population during the eighteenth century, see Sharp, *Slavery on the Spanish Frontier*, pp. 17–24. For population in 1780, see Appendix A, Table 8.

14. For the development of mining in Antioquia during the early colonial period, see West, *Colonial Placer Mining*, pp. 20–7.

15. Cited by Tulio Ospina, "El Oidor Mon y Velarde, Regenerador de Antioquia," *Repertorio Histórico* (Medellín, 1918), vol. II, pp. 414–15.

them the remnants of their wealth and leaving the towns of the province in a state of stagnation and decadence from which many – particularly Zaragoza, Remedios, Victoria, and Cáceres – were never fully to recover.[16]

Although the crisis of the early mining centers brought a decisive end to the first phase of the gold cycle in Antioquia, the province did not sink into an irreversible decline. In the later seventeenth century, Antioquian society began gradually to refocus in new areas of settlement and, with demographic recovery and internal colonization, its inhabitants started to reopen the mining frontier. In this process, Antioquian mining changed its character. Unlike the Chocó, recovery in Antioquia was based on free rather than forced labor, and the frontier was pushed outward by prospectors who moved from stream to stream, panning river silt for gold dust. A shift of settlement toward the Aburrá Valley and the development of the highland placers of the *Tierra de los Osos* on the Antioquian Batholith underpinned and sustained renewed growth until at least the middle of the eighteenth century.[17]

There was no sudden boom of the kind experienced in Brazil's Minas Gerais during the same period, nor did the large enterprises that had functioned in Antioquia during the sixteenth century revive. Renewed growth in mining derived instead from a combination of farming and gold prospecting among those of the region's free peasantry who sought an escape from subsistence. As late as 1776, population in the entire province of Antioquia was a mere 45,000, and its largest town had no more than 14,000 to 15,000 inhabitants living in ruralized, isolated conditions.[18] Commercial agriculture was correspondingly limited, even in the populated core of the province that centered on the settlements of Medellín, Santa Fe de Antioquia, Marinilla, and Rionegro. These small towns were all within two days of each other, but transport between them was poor and each produced most of its own food. Communication with neighboring provinces was still more difficult, and, with so few outlets for the cacao, tobacco, cotton, wheat, and other crops cultivated in Antioquia, gold prospecting offered the main opportunity for obtaining money and imported goods.[19]

Escape for subsistence farming was, then, one motive for mining; the

16. James Parsons, *Antioqueño Colonisation in Western Colombia* (Berkeley and Los Angeles, 1949), pp. 41–7.

17. For general descriptions of economic and demographic trends in Antioquia during the late seventeenth and early eighteenth centuries, see ibid., p. 47; West, *Colonial Placer Mining*, pp. 27–30; Restrepo, *Estudio sobre las minas*, pp. 41–2.

18. Francisco Silvestre, "Relación que manifiesta el estado de la Provincia de Antioquia . . . (1776)," *Archivo Historial* (Manizales, 1919), vol. 12, pp. 573–85.

19. A full account of Antioquia's agriculture is given by Ann Twinam, *Miners, Merchants and Farmers in Colonial Colombia* (Austin, Texas, 1982), pp. 91–109.

unequal distribution of land around the main towns was another. During his official mission to the province in the 1780s, Oidor Mon y Velarde observed that it seemed paradoxical to attribute the misery of the mass of the populace to lack of land, because between one-half and three-quarters of the province's area was still unpopulated and uncultivated. But, he noted, the concentration of most of the growing population in the center of the province and the existence of large holdings (often held without legal title and frequently underused) deprived many of land that was necessary to support themselves and their families.[20] It seems, then, that Antioquia had a substantial peasant population that was driven into mining by lack of land, thereby underpinning the development of a gold-producing economy based on free labor rather than slavery.

If the revival of Antioquian mining depended on free labor during the early eighteenth century, in the second half of the century there were also signs of increasing investment in slaves. In the late 1750s, Governor José Baron de Chaves reported that there were only about 900 slaves working in the mines of Antioquia.[21] By 1778, this number had apparently mushroomed to between 9,000 and 13,500.[22] In 1758, one entrepreneur alone registered the establishment of thirty-nine new mines and was conceded permission to import a hundred negro slaves to work them.[23] As important new mines were also opened during the 1760s and 1770s in the Río Grande, Río Chico, and Santa Rosa de Osos areas, these new mines further increased the demand for slaves, until, during the 1780s, large miners using sluicing techniques and slave labor helped to push the province's gold production to unprecedented levels.[24]

20. Robledo, *Bosquejo Biográfico*, vol. I, p. 195; vol. II, pp. 172, 199.

21. Rodolfo Segovia, "Crown Policy and the Precious Metals in New Granada," unpub. M.A. thesis, University of California, Berkeley 1959, p. 23.

22. According to the local census, there were 13,501 slaves in Antioquia in 1777, of whom about 8,000 were located in the jurisdiction of Santa Fe de Antioquia, and 2,500 in Medellín: see Appendix A, Table 9. The general census of the viceroyalty counts 8,931 slaves, of whom 4,035 were women and 4,896 were males: see Appendix A, Table I. Francisco Silvestre, who was governor of the province between 1782 and 1785, estimated that Antioquia's slave population was close to 10,000, or about a fifth of the province's total population: see Silvestre, *Relación*, pp. 156–7. Clearly, the figure of just under 4,896 slaves in 1778, given in Twinam (*Miners, Merchants and Farmers*, p. 40) is mistaken. Taken from Restrepo's *Estudio sobre las Minas*, this figure refers only to male slaves, whom Restrepo misleadingly regarded as the workforce for the mines. In fact, it is evident from Silvestre's description of mining by slaves that women and children were also involved in searching for gold, if only because slaves were given basic subsistence by their masters and were left to earn money for clothing and other goods by working their own placers at weekends.

23. AHNC Aduanas (Cartas), tomo 8, Jose de Arce y Zavala to Crown, Santa Fe, October 2, 1760, f.452. Some further information on Quintana's mining exploration is given in Restrepo, *Estudio sobre las minas*, pp. 42–3.

24. Ibid., p. 41; also Twinam, *Miners, Merchants and Farmers*, pp. 39–41.

Gold production during the eighteenth century

Although these signs of growth in the Chocó and in Antioquia clearly indicate a revival in Colombian mining during the eighteenth century, precise measurement of gold production is impossible. Contemporary data allow us to measure the value of gold that entered official channels, whether for payment of the *quinto* (the royal severance tax), for *fundición* (smelting into ingots at the royal foundries), or for conversion into coin at the royal mints. However, because miners and merchants often evaded these official channels, the *quinto, fundición,* and coinage statistics invariably underestimate the value of gold actually mined.[25] Correlating quinto returns with gold output is further complicated by changes in tax rates. From 1696, the quinto was charged at 5%, with an additional 1.5% collected under the name of "cobos"; in 1759, taxes on gold fell to 6%, when the cobos were reduced to 1%; finally, in 1777, the quinto was cut to a uniform 3%.[26] Such tax reductions, particularly that of 1777, may well distort a production curve built on quinto returns, because miners presumably had less incentive to evade taxation when it was levied at lower rates. However, in order to indicate general trends in the scale and distribution of gold production, we will assume that the gap between registered and real production remained more or less constant over the century, and warn that our figures offer only approximate indicators of orders of magnitude and long-term trends in output.

Starting from the assumption of a constant rate of tax evasion, Jorge Orlando Melo has used two sources to estimate trends in Colombian gold production during the eighteenth century: the records of quintos paid in the principal mining regions and records of gold converted into coin at the royal mints.[27] To indicate general trends in mining production, the pattern of production that he derives from quinto payments is shown in Table 3.1.[28]

These figures are, of course, an incomplete representation of gold pro-

---

25. Sharp suggests that the quintos collected in the Chocó may reflect only between a half and two-thirds of gold actually mined; however, as his assertion that half of the gold produced did not pay tax is based on Francisco Silvestre's estimate of the amount of gold illegally exported, this may well be too high, since illegal exports might have paid quintos. See Sharp, *Slavery on the Spanish Frontier,* pp. 71–3. For Antioquia, Twinam simply argues that tax evasion was so widespread and massive that gold output is "greatly underrepresented in *fundición* statistics," but she does not attempt to estimate the size of the gap between gold smelted and that mined. Twinam, *Miners, Merchants and Farmers,* pp. 23–5.

26. Colmenares, *Historia económica y social,* vol. 1, pp. 222–34; Barriga Villalba, *Historia de la Casa de Moneda,* vol. 1, pp. 102–3, 113–4, 329–38.

27. Jorge Orlando Melo, "Producción de oro y desarrollo económico en el siglo XVIII," in his *Sobre historia y política* (Bogotá, 1979), pp. 61–84.

28. Ibid., p. 68. Melo converts gold castellanos into silver pesos at the rate of 2.72 pesos per castellano.

Table 3.1. *Gold output in New Granadan mining regions,*
according to the Quintos, 1700–99 (in thousands of silver pesos)

Years	Popayán	Barbacoas	Chocó	Antioquia
1700–4	638			
1705–9	821			
1710–14	1069			
1715–19	1039	275	716	176
1720–4	1308	163	943	
1725–9	1452		1501	
1730–4	1270		1855	
1735–9	1391	613	2366	256
1740–4	1124	317	2323	348
1745–9	792	326	2312	316
1750–4	564	243	1747	544
1755–9	944	461	1498	559
1760–4	1020	921	1687	820
1765–9	1055	952	1678	751
1770–4	1483	995	1808	1125
1775–9	1360	893	1639	1684
1780–4	1908	1361	1940	1987
1785–9	1731	1688	2158	2655
1790–4	1616	1767	2667	3281
1795–9	1541	1783	2581	3662

duction in eighteenth-century New Granada. They tell us nothing about gold that circulated illegally, and show only quinto payments made in four treasuries, not all of which have data for quinto revenues throughout the century. However, as these treasuries were in New Granada's principal gold-producing areas, their quinto revenues are worth considering, *faute de mieux*, as a rough indicator of long-term trends in mining output.

The first question to which the quinto records offer an approximate answer concerns the scale of magnitude of gold output in New Granada and its development over the course of the eighteenth century. As Table 3.1 shows, the quintos suggest that, in the average year between 1715 and 1719, New Granada's mines produced about a half-million silver pesos worth of gold (converting gold castellanos into silver pesos at the rate of 2.72 pesos per castellano). Less than twenty years later, in 1735–9, quinto records indicate that output was almost twice as large, at 925,200 pesos per average year. (This figure is confirmed by Miguel de Santiesteban who, after consulting with expert officials in Popayán and Bogotá during his travels in New Granada in 1740–1, concluded that at most the territory produced about 400,000 castellanos – over a million pesos – per year.)[29] Production then seems to have fallen back in the 1750s, to around 650,000 pesos per

29. Robinson, (ed.), *Mil Leguas por América*, pp. 137, 187.

average year, before rising again to reach nearly 900,000 pesos per year in the 1760s. The million mark was passed during the 1770s, and the climb continued in the 1780s, to around 1.5 million pesos per average year, until in 1795–9, when quintos equivalent to a production of nearly 2 million pesos were paid into the royal treasuries.

The quinto records also roughly indicate how the chronology of growth was related to trends in regional production. Growth was vigorous in Popayán and the Chocó until the 1740s, with a phase of relative decline around mid-century, and a revival during the 1760s and 1770s. Production trends in these regions then diverged markedly. After 1785, growth apparently fell off in Popayán (though not in its subprovince of Barbacoas), whereas in the Chocó mid-century stagnation was followed by strong, more or less sustained growth until the mid-1790s. The incomplete data for Antioquia, on the other hand, show a different pattern, with a surge in 1750–4, and an impressive, generally uninterrupted rising trend after 1770.

The quinto data also show how the relative weight of New Granada's gold-producing regions shifted over the course of the eighteenth century. According to Melo's figures, growth during the first half of the century was based mainly on increased output from mines in the Chocó and the province of Popayán (including its subprovinces on the Pacific coast). Then, during the second half of the century, the province of Antioquia became a leading producer, with its placer mines in the highlands of the Central Cordillera adding substantially to New Granada's total gold output and making Antioquia a mining district of greater importance than the Chocó. This shift in the balance of regional output is illustrated in Figures 3.1 and 3.2.

The accuracy of the quinto figures can be tested against another set of statistics that provide a rough index of the scale and trends in gold output during the eighteenth century. These are found in records of gold coined at New Granada's mints. Like the quintos, coinage statistics do not correlate directly with gold production, because not all gold was coined. In the mining regions of Antioquia and the Pacific lowlands, gold circulated in the form of gold dust (as there was generally no other form of money available); gold was also smelted into ingots and converted into ornaments.[30] If, however, we assume that the value of gold coined was a

---

30. In 1748, the crown approved a viceregal decree that prohibited the export of gold ingots from New Granada: see José María Ots Capdequi, *Instituciones de gobierno en el Nuevo Reino de Granada durante el siglo XVIII* (Bogotá, 1950), p. 130. However, later references to exports of "oro en pasta" suggest that this prohibition was not enforced; Viceroy Ezpeleta specifically mentions that the greater part of gold smelted at Mompós was exported to Spain in bars: see Vicente Restrepo, *Estudio sobre las minas*, pp. 195–7.

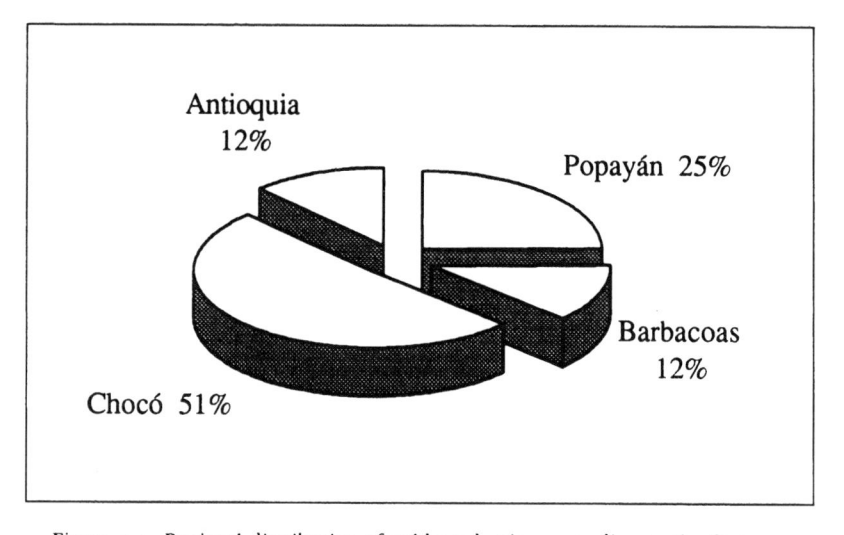

Figure 3.1. Regional distribution of gold production, according to the Quintos, 1735–64.

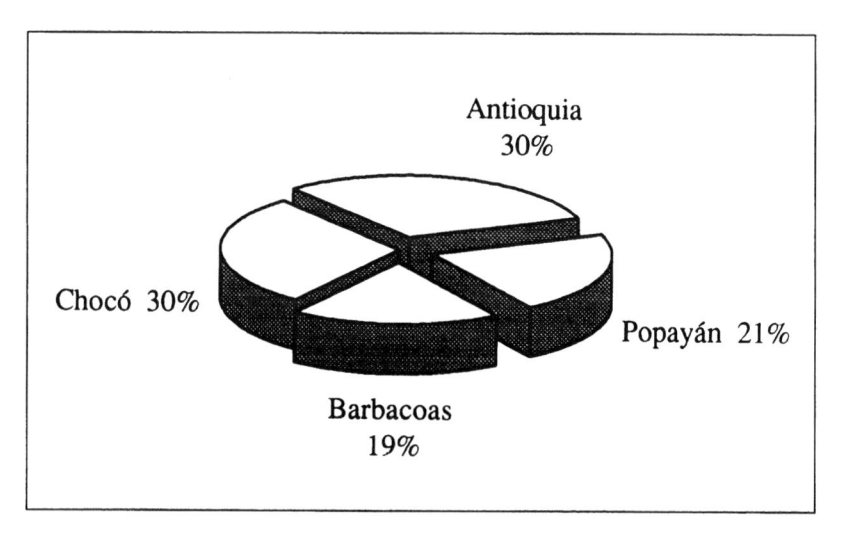

Figure 3.2. Regional distribution of gold production, according to the Quintos, 1765–99.

relatively constant proportion of that mined, then the coinage figures offer another, albeit imperfect, gauge of trends in the mining economy during the eighteenth century.

Here again, the secular trend is clear, as Figure 3.3 shows. Before the late 1750s, all gold coins were minted at the *Casa de Moneda* in Bogotá,

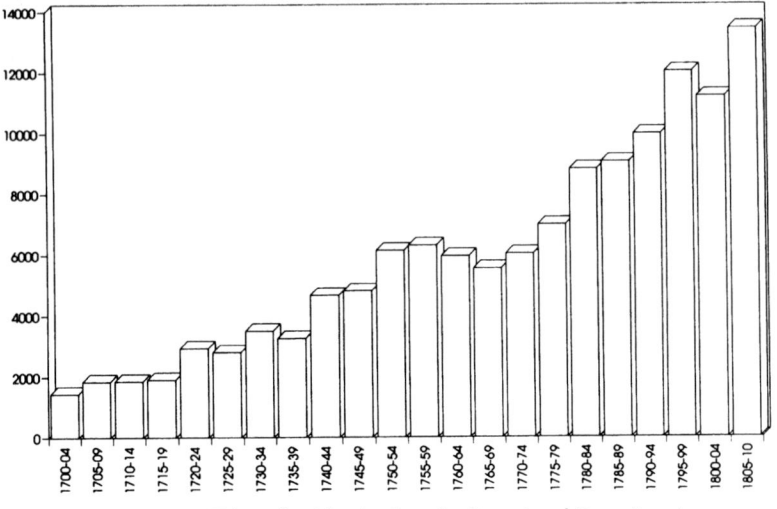

Figure 3.3. Value of gold coined at the Bogotá and Popayán mints (quinquennial totals), 1700–1810 (in thousands of silver pesos).

and from the beginning of the century until mid-century the mint's output rose continuously. By the 1730s, the value of gold coined was more than double that of the opening years of the century, and in the 1740s and early 1750s, it had doubled again.[31] Between 1758 and 1763, there was a sharp reduction in the value of gold coin issued from the Bogotá mint, but this was probably caused more by institutional changes than by real alterations in output. For, during these years, a new mint established in Popayán came into operation, diverting gold that would previously have gone to Bogotá.

The establishment of this new mint was the culmination of a protracted process that had started in the 1720s, when the cabildo of Popayán petitioned the crown for permission to establish an independent *Casa de Moneda* in the city. The Popayán miners insisted that a second mint would benefit both the crown and the mining interest. They argued that if miners could take their gold to the mint personally, then they would no longer incur the losses involved in selling gold at a heavy discount to merchants from Bogotá, and would therefore be less likely to evade taxation.[32] In 1729, the crown, beguiled no doubt by the promise of larger

---

31. See Appendix B, Table 1.
32. The miners reported that in trading gold with the Santa Fe merchants, they lost 8 to 10 *reales de plata* in every *doblón* (ACC Libro Capitular [1758], tomo 21, ff. 28–9). Assuming that they referred to the *doblón* of 2 *escudos*, the equivalent of four silver pesos, this implied a loss of roughly 25% per *doblón*. Sharp's calculations for bullion dealings in the Chocó show a similar discount on crude gold there: see his *Slavery on the Spanish Frontier*, pp. 63–5.

tax returns, granted this request. But establishing a working mint in Popayán took much longer. Not only did mineowners of Popayán prove unable to raise sufficient funds to pay the crown for the right to operate the mint, but the scheme also encountered strong opposition from the mint contractors in Bogotá, who fought a protracted legal battle to protect their traditional coining monopoly. After a delay of two decades, the project was revived in 1749, thanks largely to the initiative of Pedro Agustín de Valencia, the son of a Spanish merchant who had become a wealthy mineowner.[33] Even then, opposition from Bogotá hindered the workings of the Popayán mint. In the 1750s, its operation was complicated by a legal battle with the heir of the Bogotá mint contractor who persisted in defending his claim to a monopoly of minting in New Granada, supported by commercial interests in the capital. Faced with these legal impediments, Valencia was unable to take full advantage of his privileges for coining until they were confirmed by royal order in 1758. Following further legal battles, the mint's future was eventually secured. Operated by Valencia's family until it was taken into direct administration by the crown in 1771, it became an important secondary center for turning gold into coin for the remainder of the colonial period.[34]

Over the century as a whole, the amount of gold minted in New Granada increased impressively, particularly after mid-century, when the mints in Bogotá and Popayán were both operating. In 1700, gold coins to the value of only 267,000 silver pesos were coined in Bogotá; in 1800, nearly a million and a half pesos were produced by the same mint, with almost another million coming out of the mint in Popayán.[35] The quinquennial totals of gold minted, presented in Figure 3.3, show that gold coining grew throughout the century, with especially fast rates of growth in 1720–4, 1730–4, 1740–4, and in the decades around the end of the century.

These overall trends in the scale and regional distribution of gold production are broadly confirmed by data from specific mining regions. In his study of the Chocó, William Sharp uses quinto records to estimate the scale and trajectory of production, and although his estimates are generally lower than Melo's, the trends (see Figure 3.4) are essentially similar.

33. A new gold discovery probably provided Valencia with the means to propel the project forward. In 1743, he had discovered new deposits in Raposo, and the profits he took from the mines of Yurumanguí made him one of Popayán's leading miners. On the Yurumanguí mines, see Restrepo, *Estudio sobre las minas*, p. 84; for biographical details on Valencia, see Gustavo Arboleda, *Diccionario biográfico y genealógico del antiguo Departamento del Cauca* (Bogotá, 1962), pp. 447–50.
34. This outline of the early history of the Popayán mint is drawn from accounts given in the city's cabildo records, especially ACC Libro Capitular, vol. 21, 1758, fols. 27–31; and from Miguel Lasso de la Vega, *Los tesoreros de la Casa de Moneda de Popayán* (Madrid, 1927), pp. 1–48; and Arcesio Aragón, *Fastos payaneses* (Bogotá, 1939), pp. 97–100.
35. For annual figures, see Appendix B, Table 1.

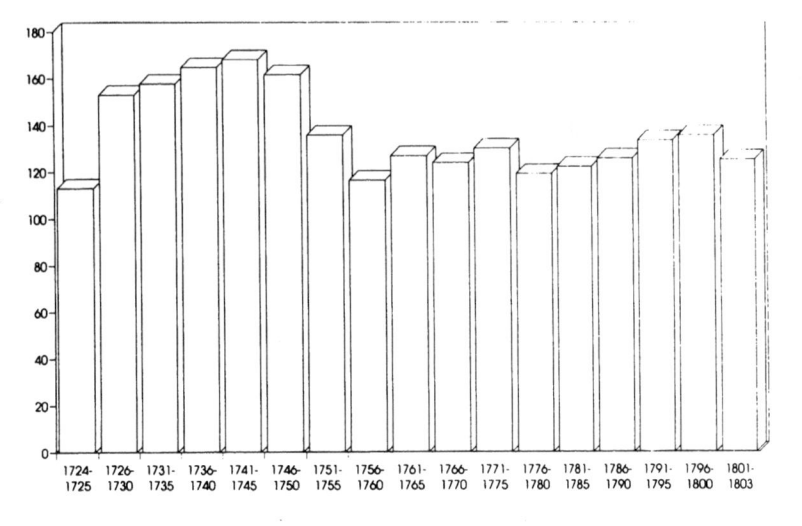

Figure 3.4. Chocó: Average annual gold production, according to the Quintos, 1724–1803 (in thousands of castellanos).

Sharp's data indicate that Chocó gold production rose throughout the period between the mid-1720s and 1750; then, after peaking in 1741–5 at over 165,000 castellanos per average year, production declined around mid-century, stagnating at annual averages that were generally under 126,000 castellanos from 1750 until 1790. During the 1790s, output moved upward again, to yearly averages of more than 134,000 castellanos, but never recovered the high levels of the first phase of growth early in the century.[36]

Quinto records from the archives of Popayán also show trends that, for most of the century, confirm those identified by Melo. Popayán quintos show a strong phase of growth during the first half of the eighteenth century. Production equivalents calculated from the quinto revenues show that annual averages rose from about 51,000 castellanos in 1700–9 to over 77,000 castellanos in 1710–19, and peaked at averages around 100,000 castellanos in the 1720s and 1730s. This upward trend was interrupted in the 1740s and early 1750s when Popayán quinto revenues contracted in a manner similar to those of the Chocó. Thus it seems that gold production in southern and southwestern Colombia fell during the 1740s to around 70,000 castellanos per average year, before slipping back to an average annual production of about 42,000 castellanos in the 1750s. After 1759, the quintos gradually recovered, until, by the late 1770s,

36. For these figures, see Appendix B, Table 2. Sharp converts gold castellanos into silver at the rate of 1:2.3 and 1:2.4.

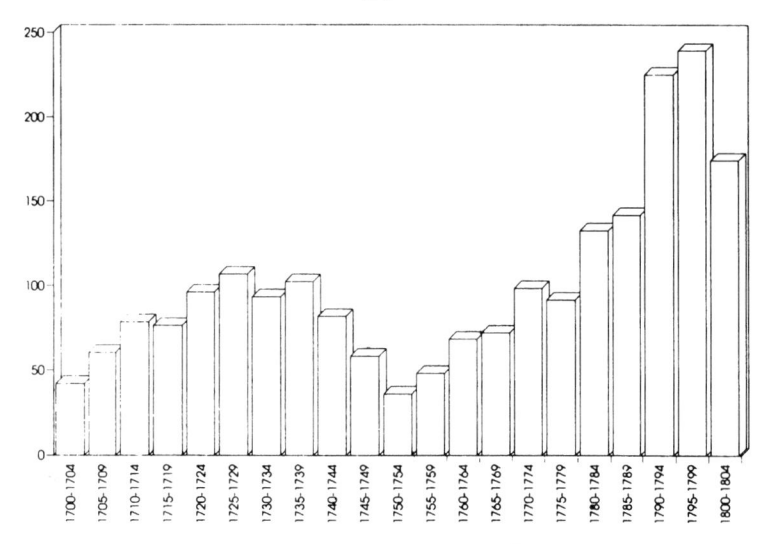

Figure 3.5. Popayán: Average annual gold production, according to the Quintos, 1700–1804 (in thousands of castellanos).

they were again averaging around 95,000 castellanos per year. Finally, as Figure 3.5 shows, the last decade of the century saw a tremendous surge in Popayán's quinto revenues, indicating an average annual output of over 230,000 castellanos per average year (around 600,000 silver pesos) in 1790–9.[37] This final burst of growth, which is not reflected in Melo's statistics, probably indicates increased production in Popayán's subprovince of Barbacoas, which, according to Melo's separate statistics for Barbacoas (shown in Table 3.1), doubled its production during the closing years of the century.

In Antioquia, gold registered for smelting (depicted in Figure 3.6) follows a trajectory of output broadly similar to that reflected in the quinto records compiled by Melo. After oscillating around an average level of about 22,600 *pesos de oro* during the first half of the century, registered production climbed steadily, decade by decade, from the 1750s into the 1790s. From averages of nearly 60,000 *pesos de oro* in 1750–9, the value of gold smelted in Antioquia doubled in 1775–9, before more than doubling again, to reach an average of over 260,000 pesos per year between 1785 and 1799.[38] The pattern of mining growth in Antioquia therefore differed from that of Popayán and the Pacific lowlands, in that

37. In converting castellanos to silver pesos, I have used the rate given by Melo, of 2.72 pesos per castellano. For the annual averages of gold produced in Popayán, estimated from quinto records, see Appendix B, Table 4.
38. See Appendix B, Table 3. The *peso de oro* was worth two silver pesos.

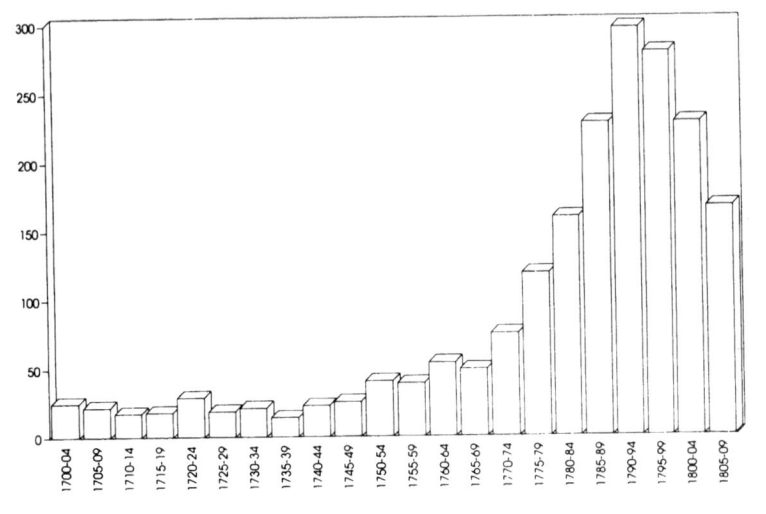

Figure 3.6. Antioquia: Annual averages of gold registered for smelting, 1700–
1809 (in thousands of *pesos de oro*).

the major phase of expansion occurred during the second rather than the
first half of the century, turning the province from a relatively minor into
the major regional source of New Granadan gold.

The figures given in this chapter are, to repeat, only roughly correlated
with real gold output, and one must remember that the pace of growth
during the closing decades of the century is very probably exaggerated by
the effects of tax changes. The reduction of the quinto to 3% in 1777 may
well have inflated gold registrations during the ensuing years by reducing
the incentive to evade tax; in Antioquia, special measures for forcing
merchants to pay the quinto probably also artificially boosted gold registrations from the mid-1780s. However, such measures certainly do not
account for growth over the period as a whole, nor do they explain the
rising trend of quinto revenues earlier in the century. Moreover, the
timing of changes in gold output shows that it is impossible to attribute
the recovery of New Granadan mining to Bourbon policies, since growth
was already well under way long before the late 1770s, when Spanish
officials took positive steps to promote mining development. Indeed, it is
fair to say that it was not Bourbon government that stimulated mining
development, but rather the reverse. Not only did the revival of gold
mining rekindle metropolitan interest in New Granada during the first
half of the eighteenth century, but by stimulating the colony's interregional trade in domestic products, growing gold output also made an important indirect contribution to the strengthening of colonial government,

by increasing returns from taxes on production, consumption, and exchange.

Despite such growth, New Granada's gold production contributed only a small part of a much larger flow of gold from the Americas to Europe during the eighteenth century. Indeed, if we compare the figures outlined in this chapter with statistics for gold imported into Europe from Iberian America, it is clear that New Granada was, for most of the century, a very minor gold producer when compared to Brazil. Imports of Brazilian gold into Europe averaged over 9 million pesos in 1722–31, more than 8 million pesos in 1732–41, around 6 million pesos in 1752–61, and about 4.5 million pesos in the 1760s and 1770s. Only at the end of the century, long after the Brazilian boom was over, did Brazilian gold exports fall to levels that were close to the peak of New Granadan output, at around 2 million pesos. New Granada's gold output was also only part of a larger gold production in Spanish America. If we compare our estimates of New Granadan production with Morineau's figures for gold imported into Spain from its colonies, it seems likely that, before the final decade of the century, New Granada's output tended to equal about half the value of gold received in Spanish ports.[39]

Mining regions and the gold trade

The mining regions themselves were generally poor and showed little sign of the wealth that they generated. Compared to the great gold-mining zone of Minas Gerais in Brazil, New Granada's gold-mining areas were backward, impoverished places, far from the main centers of settlement. What profits were made from mining went mostly to people living in other regions, particularly in such major centers of government and commerce as the cities of Popayán, Bogotá, and Cartagena. In the Pacific lowlands, there was little scope for regional development, as neither the land nor the climate favored agricultural settlement. Compared to the fertile lands and hospitable climate of the contiguous Cauca region, the humid tropical climate and heavily forested lands of the Chocó, Barbacoas, Raposo, and Iscuandé had little to entice settlers, and they long remained among the most sparsely populated and undeveloped regions of Colombia. Miners in the Pacific lowland regions were mainly outsiders who brought in slaves to search for gold and, apart from the small amounts of food that they could persuade or coerce the tiny Indian populations to produce, they relied on food and other goods imported from other regions. Investments in slaves and reliance on external supplies made mining in these areas a risky enterprise, and the profits of even well-

39. Morineau, *Incroyables gazettes et fabuleux métaux*, Table 71, pp. 478–80.

capitalized miners were not very large: Sharp calculates rates of return of between 7% and 10%, but they may well have been lower.[40] Whatever the profits they took from their mining enterprises, the miners of Popayán and Cali certainly did not invest them in the mining zones, but instead carried those profits back to the Cauca Valley where, together with slaves who were moved between mining and agriculture, they could help support family enterprises based in great haciendas. It is, moreover, probable that much of the profit from Pacific mining found its way into the hands of merchants who traded, directly or indirectly, with the mining zones.

Miners in the frontier gold fields exchanged their gold dust for supplies of food, aguardiente, tobacco, metal for tools, and manufactures that were brought by *rescatadores*. These traders then either passed the gold dust on to their wholesalers, or registered it themselves at the royal foundries for conversion into ingots and payment of the quinto.[41] Such trade obviously served the miners in one important respect. It released them from the formalities of delivering their gold dust to the royal foundries and paying the quinto, while simultaneously supplying them with the provisions that they needed to sustain their activities. But reliance on merchants also had disadvantages, because the exchange of gold between miner and merchant was generally conducted on terms that favored the latter. In the Chocó, merchants who purchased gold directly from miners paid less than its true value, and profited from the difference between the rate of exchange in the mining fields and the value of gold at the royal foundries.[42] Although miners may have found this to be an acceptable price for the gold traders' services, their dependence on merchants for all but the most basic foodstuffs made them vulnerable to exploitation of another kind. For it seems that traders who were ready to confront the hardships of trade with mining regions provided only a small supply of goods at high prices, and forced the miner to accept onerous terms, particularly if he had to rely on credit. In 1780, a visitor to the Chocó observed that, in order to dispose of all their goods, merchants forced miners to buy assortments of merchandise, including goods they did not need. Moreover, the miners usually had recourse to credit to obtain these goods, contracting to pay off the debt from future output. If they delayed in paying, they became even more dependent on the merchant, as interest on unredeemed loans accu-

---

40. For Sharp's calculations, see his *Slavery on the Colombian Frontier*, pp. 171–89; for a critique of his method and an explanation of why mining may have sustained lower rates of profit, see Colmenares, *Historia económica y social*, vol. II, pp. 153–65.
41. The fact that merchants and traders registered and paid tax on most of the gold produced in the mining zones was made plain in a report made by the fiscal of the Real Audiencia in 1703, during a controversy over the rates at which the quinto should be paid by miners and merchants; the report is reproduced in Barriga Villalba, *Historia de la Casa de Moneda*, vol. 1, pp. 335–6.
42. Sharp, *Slavery on the Colombian Frontier*, pp. 63–4.

mulated. In 1780, it was said that this situation was so common that most Chocó miners owed more than they owned.[43]

In the Antioquian region, the physical and climatic environment was much more suitable for agricultural and urban development, and the region was consequently more socially and economically developed than the Pacific mining areas. However, because its indigenous population had rapidly disappeared in the sixteenth century, Antioquia was for a long time left on the margins of colonial society, and its development during the eighteenth century had to start from a small demographic base. Mining nevertheless contributed more to regional development than it did in the Pacific lowlands, because it was very largely in the hands of local inhabitants. This helps to explain why the town of Medellín emerged as an urban center of growing importance during the late colonial period, and why Antioquia continued to develop a flourishing regional economy after independence. But, although growing yields from its mines enriched the province over the course of the eighteenth century, Antioquia depended heavily on goods imported from outside, and this trade tended to drain wealth from the region. In 1787, Oidor Mon y Velarde reported that goods imported into Antioquia were sold at prices that were between 50% and 100% higher than those of the nonmining regions. The practice of selling on credit (encouraged by the absence of small denomination silver currency) pushed prices even higher.[44] When explaining the province's relative poverty, Mon y Velarde pointed out that most of its wealth was taken by merchants from other regions. "The *comerciantes* who trade in gold," he said,

take all of it out of the province, where until now neither the slightest industry nor manufacture is known because even the crudest goods are brought in from the *Reino* (of New Granada), so that all the gold leaves without more than the slightest circulation among the inhabitants and miners. All are feudatories of the merchants, and they of their correspondents in Santa Fe, Cartagena and Santa Marta.[45]

Merchants sometimes formed companies with miners, but generally avoided direct involvement in production.[46] The merchant's role in min-

---

43. "Relacion del Chocó . . . conforme al reconocimiento del Capitan de Ingenieros don Juan Jiménez Donoso," November 15, 1780, in Ortega Ricuarte, *Historia Documental del Chocó*, pp. 227–33.

44. "Sucinta relación de lo ejecutado en la visita de Antioquia . . . ," in Robledo, *Bosquejo Biográfico*, p. 350; AHA Colonia, Hacienda tomo 747, mss. 11988. "Informe hecho por el Sr. Don Juan Antonio Mon y Velarde . . . para el uso de la moneda en esta Provincia," Antioquia, August 23, 1787.

45. AHA Colonia, Hacienda, tomo 747, mss. 11988.

46. This had not always been the case. In 1761, a treasury official recalled that in the past wealthy miners had joined with merchants of Cartagena to import slaves for mining. But, he observed,

ing was, rather, to provide advances of slaves and goods, usually on credit. Sometimes miners bought directly from wholesalers in towns like Cali, and then took supplies to their mines in the Pacific lowlands.[47] More commonly, however, small merchants took goods from wholesalers or from hacendados on credit terms of up to a year, and sold them in the mining districts for gold dust. Having acquired gold, they then used it to finance further commercial transactions through such towns as Popayán, Cali, Honda, Mompós, Cartagena, and Santa Fe de Bogotá, where they would discharge their debts and acquire fresh supplies of trade goods.

Gold mining and the New Granadan economy

Because some of this trade was in goods imported from overseas, part of New Granada's gold output was siphoned out of the country without ever touching its economy. But the gold mines were not simply enclaves, linked directly to Europe. In fact, until 1784, the mining regions of the Pacific lowlands were formally sealed off from direct contact with Atlantic maritime routes by repeated prohibitions on navigation on the Atrato River. This measure, designed to prevent illegal exports of gold to foreigners in the Caribbean, did not eliminate smuggling, but it did mean that the Chocó was largely supplied from within the domestic economy, either from the province of Popayán or from Mompós, Honda, and Santa Fe de Bogotá. This arrangement was, moreover, welcomed by merchants in Cartagena. When the viceroy consulted the merchants in 1774 about the possibility of opening the Atrato to maritime trade from the Caribbean, they firmly opposed the idea. They accepted that free navigation on the Atrato would be convenient to Spanish importers but argued that access from the sea would damage a valuable interregional commerce and, by depriving New Granadan producers of important markets for agricultural and other products, spoil the larger market for European imports.[48] In fact, when the Atrato was opened after 1784, it was used mainly for imports of iron, steel, and other European manufactures, whereas foodstuffs and other commodities continued to be supplied from neighboring provinces in New Granada.[49] So, before gold left the coun-

the merchants had become reluctant to back miners because of the losses that they had suffered, and now abstained from joining with them. "Informe de los medios utiles y convenientes a el fomento del Reino, beneficio de los vasallos, y aumento de la Real Hacienda," AHNC Aduanas (Cartas) tomo 8, f.436, José de Arce y Zavala, Santa Fe, October 2, 1760.

47. Colmenares, Cali, pp. 113–15.

48. AGI Consulados 333, Junta de los individuos del Comercio de España, Cartagena, August 6, 1774.

49. In 1774, the crown ordered the colonial authorities to investigate the question of opening the Atrato River to navigation, but, despite Viceroy Guirior's recommendation in favor, it was not

try, it irrigated and stimulated the economies of neighboring regions, generating trade in a range of agricultural and other products, and thereby enlarging the markets of the agrarian regions that lay beyond the mining zones. Such trade involved a wide variety of colonial products, including sugar and its derivatives, tobacco, salt, anis, cheese, wheat, dried and salted beef, cacao, as well as crude cotton, and linen and woollen cloth, carried over networks of trails that led from Popayán and the Cauca Valley to the Pacific lowlands, and from Bogotá and the Eastern Cordillera to Antioquia.[50]

Evidence of the stimulating effects of mining growth is found in the development of trade in the cities of Popayán and Bogotá which, judging by the revenues drawn from sales taxes, showed a strong propensity for expansion, especially after mid-century. The average annual value of alcabalas collected in Bogotá in 1700–4 was less than 6,000 pesos; in 1720–4 it was unchanged, and in 1740–5 it had grown only slightly, to just over 8,000 pesos per year. There was then a sudden surge in 1756–60, to over 28,660 pesos per average year, followed by a high and sustained rate of growth until, in 1805–8, when the average exceeded 100,000 pesos per annum.[51] Revenues from the alcabala paid on goods sold within the jurisdiction of the city of Popayán expanded at a similar pace, though on a lesser scale. In 1722–6, revenues averaged less than 900 pesos per year; in 1741–5, the annual average was 2,671 pesos. After the Popayán mint began its first coining operations in 1753, they grew rapidly in succeeding decades, reaching an average of around 20,000 pesos in 1795–1804.[52] In both cases, the surge forward in the 1750s and 1760s was partly attributable to greater administrative efficiency, as alcabala collection shifted from tax-farmers to direct royal administration.[53] But there were also clear signs of real growth, as reflected in the revenues of tithes on agricultural production.[54]

In Popayán, the economic effects of mining development were most obvious in the provincial capital, particularly after the mint began to operate at mid-century. In 1763, the procurator of the city's cabildo reported that the presence of the mint had greatly stimulated both the

actually opened until 1784. AGI Santa Fe 956, Caballero y Góngora to Gálvez, May 31, 1784; also Pérez Ayala, *Antonio Caballero y Góngora*, p. 363; and Silvestre, *Descripción*, p. 41.

50. West, *Colonial Placer Mining*, pp. 112–22.

51. I am most grateful to Professor John TePaske and Professor Alvaro Jara for this information, drawn from their unpublished research on royal revenues recorded at Bogotá. Subsequent references to their research will be acknowledged as TePaske and Jara, "Cartas cuentas de la real caja de Santa Fe de Bogotá," unpub. mss.

52. See Appendix C, Table 8.   53. ACC Colonia CII-20ea 51 38.

54. For an analysis of revenues from the diezmos in Popayán, which includes figures for Antioquia, see Jorge Orlando Melo, "La producción agricola en Popayán en el siglo XVIII, según las cuentas de diezmos," in Fedesarrollo, *Ensayos sobre historia económica colombiana* (Bogotá, 1980).

mining and commerce of the province, increasing trade with the Pacific mining regions and releasing the miners from dependence on merchants from Bogotá. Previously, the latter, by forcing miners to sell to them at low prices, had been able to "fatten like a leech on the blood and substance of these Provinces, which is gold . . . "[55] The installation of the mint changed this relation, the cabildo said, and Popayán prospered. Records of merchandise entering the city show that trade with Quito, mostly in cloth from Quito's obrajes, increased sharply around mid-century.[56] Another sign of vigorous growth in Popayán's trade was the fact that it attracted an increasing number of Spanish migrants, some of whom were merchants who married into the creole land and mineowning elite.[57] In 1756, there was a sufficient number of such Spaniards to justify the formation of a militia company of *forasteros*,[58] and by 1764, the size of the resident merchant community rivaled that of Bogotá and Cartagena.[59] In 1778, the crown recognized the city's renaissance as a commercial center by acceding to the Popayán merchants' request for an independent mercantile tribunal to deal with the affairs of "the copious number of *comerciantes* domiciled and married in the country, besides the many transient merchants from Quito, Santa Fe, Honda and Cartagena who have their factors and agents there . . . "[60] Henceforth, Popayán had a merchant delegation equal in status to those of Bogotá and Quito.[61]

Antioquia's trade, much of which came via Bogotá, showed a similar propensity for vigorous growth, which was in line with the province's

55. ACC Libro Capitular, (1763) tomo 23, ff.38–9.
56. Scattered data from the records of trade entering the city of Popayán indicate this increase in the import of Quito's textiles, described as *ropa de Quito*, as follows: 1735, 241/2 cargas; 1745, 2501/2; 1765, 2531/2; 1769, 612 (ACC Colonia C II-5a 36 24 and 40 95; ACC Colonia C II-14a 50 51 and 50 73). This development was no doubt partly influenced by the redistribution of Quiteño trade away from Peruvian markets where, following the abolition of the galleons and the opening of the Cape Horn route in the 1740s, the products of Quito's industry faced strong competition from cheaper imports of European cloth. It was facilitated by tax transfers made by the government of Quito to the authorities in Cartagena, in the form of the annual *situado* that subsidized military expenditure in that fortress-port. In the hands of the merchants who carried it from Quito into New Granada, via Popayán, the *situado* provided a useful source of capital for financing trade en route.
57. See Gustavo Arboleda, *Diccionario Biográfico y Genealógico*, for data on some of the Spanish merchants who took up residence in the city during the eighteenth century, showing how they became absorbed, through intermarriage, into the local community.
58. ACC Libro Capitular, tomo 20 (1756), no folio numbers. Unfortunately, this document names only the officers of this *compañía Española de Forasteros Miliciana*, all of whom were prominent merchants, but provides neither the number nor the names of the other members.
59. Forty individuals of the "commerce of Popayán" directed a petition to the crown, requesting that the farm of the city's alcabala and aguardiente revenues, for which they had corporately contracted in 1761, should be allowed to run its full term. See ACC Colonia C II-20ea 51 38.
60. ACC Libro Capitular, tomo 28 (1777), fol.146.
61. AHNC Consulados, tomo 3, fols. 433–5. Real Orden, July 3, 1778.

rising gold output. Whereas the value of imports was generally less than 40,000 silver pesos before 1750, after 1760 it doubled, and then doubled again in the 1770s, before finally reaching values of about half a million silver pesos between 1780 and 1810.[62] And, because most of this trade was in goods produced in New Granada, particularly the crude textiles manufactured in the Socorro region, Antioquian mining evidently contributed to energizing the economy of central New Granada in much the same way as the Pacific gold fields infused new energy into the regional economy of the province of Popayán.[63]

The economic influence of the mining sector must, however, be kept in perspective, because it certainly did not transform New Granada's economic life. Within the large territory that stretched through the plains and forests of the tropical lowlands and across the broken terrain of the Andean cordilleras, the possibilities of economic growth continued to be limited by the dispersion and small scale of settlement, the difficulties of internal transportation, and the scattered, low-intensity character of New Granadan mining. These factors remained constant throughout the eighteenth century, hindering regional economic integration and leaving New Granada as an essentially undeveloped economy. The resurgence of gold mining did nevertheless contribute something to changing the conditions that had left New Granada on the margins of the Spanish Empire in the later seventeenth century and during the eighteenth. For by stimulating the circuits of New Granada's internal trade, providing the means to buy more imports from Europe, and giving government the opportunity to raise and to spend more revenues, gold mining would provide a base for a revival of Spanish government in, and Spanish commerce with New Granada during the century of Bourbon rule.

---

62. Twinam, *Miners, Merchants and Farmers*, Table 7, pp. 51–4. At the end of his second term as governor of Antioquia, in 1785, Francisco Silvestre estimated that over 250,000 pesos, or a half million silver pesos, left the province each year, both as gold dust and gold ingots: see Silvestre, *Relación*, p. 147.

63. On the composition of Antioquia's trade, see Twinam, *Miners, Merchants and Farmers*, pp. 60–9.

PART II

The Economics of Bourbon colonialism: New Granada and the Atlantic Economy

4

New Granada and the Spanish mercantile system, 1700–1778

So far, we have examined the structures of settlement, society, and economy in eighteenth-century New Granada and have seen something of the economic links that bound the colony to Spain. However, by focusing on the character of New Granada's social and economic structures, the foregoing chapters have tended to emphasize elements of continuity and evolution within the colony, without paying much attention to the external factors that affected its development. And yet, of course, the eighteenth century saw important changes in relations between Spain and her colonies, as the Bourbon kings who inherited the Hapsburg throne sought to reverse the seemingly inexorable process of decline that Spain had suffered during the seventeenth century. Not only did the new dynasty establish a more centralized and absolutist authority within the metropolis, but, by political, military, and economic reform, it also sought to bring about what has been called the "second conquest of America."[1]

This was not a process that began immediately or proceeded smoothly. The first reforms were hesitant in tone and uneven in application, and the great age of reform did not arrive until the reign of Charles III. New Granada, however, felt the repercussions of change at the metropolitan center early in the century, when its trade and administration were touched by Madrid's earliest efforts to reassert control over the resources of its empire. Later in the century, other phases of colonial reform impinged on the region, further altering its systems of trade and administration. To assess the impact of these reforms, we will now consider changes in Spanish mercantilist policy, showing why they originated, how they were applied, and how they affected New Granada's commerce and economy. Our point of departure is at the beginning of the century, at the time of transition from Hapsburg to Bourbon rule, when the political crisis of the empire was matched by the virtual collapse of the Atlantic commercial system that linked the colonial economies to the mother country.

1. John Lynch, *The Spanish American Revolutions, 1808–1826* (2nd ed., London, 1986), p. 7.

New Granada and the Spanish commercial system

Throughout the colonial period, New Granada's external commerce was formally monopolized by Spain and regulated by the code of mercantilist legislation that covered all Spanish-American trade. From the early sixteenth century, Spain confined the commerce of its colonies within a system regulated by the metropolitan state, in order to enrich the Spanish monarchy and privileged groups within it. For most of the colonial period this mercantilist system had three essential features. First, all trade from Spain was funneled through a single entrepôt, at Seville until 1717, then at Cádiz. Second, all trade was organized by the merchant guild of the *Cargadores a Indias,* which, together with the *Casa de Contratación,* was responsible for carrying trade across the Atlantic, enforcing commercial regulation, and collecting duties on trade. All transoceanic trade was limited to authorized Spanish merchants; foreigners were, with a few exceptions, legally excluded from direct commerce with colonials, though they did participate in the trade using Spanish intermediaries. Third, colonial trade was carried in armed convoys, one of which, called the *flota,* supplied the Viceroyalty of New Spain through Veracruz, whereas the other, known as the *galeones de Tierra Firme,* supplied Spanish South America via Cartagena de Indias and Portobelo.

New Granada was directly integrated into this system of trade, thanks to its gold mines and to the fine natural harbor of Cartagena de Indias, a port that had become a major entrepôt for Spanish trade in the later sixteenth and earlier seventeenth centuries. Through Cartagena came a variety of goods from Europe, including such essential raw materials as iron and steel, a wide variety of textiles, and many agricultural commodities, especially wine, olive oil, and spices. In exchange, New Granada provided gold, either in coin, jewelery, plate, or (illegally) in gold dust; small quantities of exotic tropical commodities, such as cacao, were also exported, some to Spain and some to other colonies, such as Cuba and Mexico. Historians have long believed that this trade contracted sharply in the later seventeenth century, because the Tierra Firme fleets sailed less frequently to South America and, according to official records of their treasure cargoes, carried a smaller commerce. However, as we noted in Chapter 1, unofficial foreign reports of treasure arriving in Europe from the Americas indicate that the trade was very buoyant in the late seventeenth century, carrying larger amounts of treasure than at any previous time.

New Granada's contribution to this apparent revival is not known, because records of treasure arriving in Europe on the Tierra Firme fleets do not distinguish between bullion from Peru and bullion from New Granada. It seems likely, however, that New Granada's trade was growing in the last decades of the Hapsburg period, because new deposits of gold were being discovered and exploited, particularly in the Pacific lowlands. But if the territory's capacity to absorb imports from Europe was growing, it brought little benefit to Spain or its government. The most valuable cargoes carried to the Indies consisted of foreign re-exports, and most of the treasure that came in exchange was therefore taken by foreigners, leaving little for Spanish producers or for a Spanish state that was consistently defrauded of revenues.[2] Thus, when Charles II died, the American colonies did not depend economically upon the Spanish metropolis: the lion's share of their markets and treasure was taken by foreign traders and producers.

The underlying weakness in colonial economic relations was openly revealed when the Bourbon Philip V came to the throne. During the War of the Spanish Succession, the system of transatlantic fleets came to a virtual standstill and the growing separation between the metropolitan and colonial economies became a clear divorce. Without the fleets to channel their trade to the Indies, the foreigners who had dominated the *Carrera de Indias* now forged direct contacts with Spain's colonies. Encroachments on Spain's colonial markets came from ally and enemy alike. On one side, French merchants took advantage of Louis XIV's alliance with Bourbon Spain to organize a traffic with the Americas directly from French ports – they made particularly deep inroads into the rich Pacific markets of the Viceroyalty of Peru. On the other side, English and Dutch merchants developed a profitable contraband trade with the Spanish colonies from their trading bases in the Caribbean, from whence they established smuggling routes into Mexico through Veracruz, to Peru via the Isthmus of Panama, and into New Granada via Cartagena and Santa Marta.[3]

Such was the scale of foreign economic penetration and so serious were the losses it caused both to Spanish traders and the Bourbon state that, during the war, Philip V's ministers contemplated changing the whole system of colonial commerce. In 1705, for example, the *Junta de Comercio* discussed two proposals for reorganizing Spain's American trade. One recommended establishing a monopoly company with a capital of some 20 million pesos, to serve as a competitor to the great companies that other European nations used for their colonial trades.[4] Another proposal called for the abolition of the convoys altogether, to be replaced by "the free

---

2. Morineau, *Incroyable gazettes et fabuleux métaux*, pp. 268–9; see also Lynch, *Bourbon Spain*, p. 21.

3. On foreign, particularly French influence in Spanish American trade during the War of Succession, see Geoffrey J. Walker, *Spanish Politics and Imperial Trade, 1700–1789* (London, 1979), pp. 19–63.

4. AGI Indiferente General 2046A, "Papel segundo en que se propone la forma de establecer la navegación de las Indias," Manuel García de Bustamante, August 15, 1705.

movement of individual vessels from the ports of Spain to those of the
Indies."[5] In the event, neither reform was undertaken and Spain's transatlantic traffic continued to be severely disrupted for the duration of the
conflict. For New Granada, as for Peru, this meant that trade with Spain
was largely replaced by trade with foreigners, and, as we shall now see,
early Bourbon governments found it very difficult to rebuild Spanish
control over South American commerce.

Commerce during and after the War of the Spanish Succession, 1700–1720

Precise measurement of New Granada's trade during the early eighteenth
century is impossible, because official records of treasure carried to Spain
generally fail to distinguish between exports from Peru and exports from
New Granada. Of one thing, however, we can be certain. Both during and
after the War of Succession, Spain's trade with the colony was almost
completely undermined by foreign interlopers. Throughout the war,
Spanish merchants complained repeatedly about the competition from
foreign smugglers at Cartagena and along New Granada's Caribbean
coast, and called for measures to stem the loss of their trade. In 1702, for
example, Spanish merchants reported that the French were making large-
scale illegal imports into both Cartagena and Santa Marta, aided by
compliant local officials. They particularly complained about the activities
of French merchants who, after arriving with Admiral Ducasse's squadron,
were evidently intent upon setting up a regular commerce between France
and Cartagena. To counter this threat, Spanish merchants requested that
the crown appoint new officials to manage the port's trade, independently
of the governor of Cartagena and the audiencia of New Granada.[6] No
action was taken, however, and by 1704 a threat from another quarter had
surfaced, in the form of a large contraband trade at Santa Marta, where the
local governor colluded with English and Dutch merchants.[7] Together
with contraband through Portobelo, the value of illegal trade was huge. In
1705 it was said that "in one year with another . . . six million pesos are
taken to England, half in silver and gold and half in commodities," all
carried by smugglers from the coasts of Portobelo and Cartagena to Jamaica.[8]

Resuscitation of the Spanish convoys did not ease the problem. When
the first galleons to arrive from Spain since 1695 entered the Bay of

5. Ibid., Parecer de D. Ambrosio Daubenton, September 10, 1705.
6. AGI Consulados 314, Cristóbal de Marmol to Consulado of Seville, November 21, 1702.
7. AGI Consulados 314, Joseph Bermudez Becerra to Consulado of Seville, February 5, 1704;
   Consulado of Seville to Bermudez Becerra, October 3, 1704.
8. AGI Indiferente General 2046A, Parecer de D. Ambrosio Daubenton, September 10, 1705.

Cartagena in 1706, under the command of the Conde de Casa Alegre, they brought little respite from foreign interloping. During the six months that followed the galleons' arrival in Cartagena, thirty smuggling vessels entered the port, all loaded with merchandise that was subsequently transported into the interior of New Granada, and from there into the provinces of Peru.[9] Faced with such competition, and delayed by the failure of Peruvian merchants to arrive at Portobelo, the galleons were forced to wait for nearly two years at Cartagena, where sales of about 4 million pesos were made.[10] The fleet then sailed to Portobelo in January 1708, to meet with Peruvian merchants who had left Lima with cargoes worth more than 7 million pesos.[11] If the trade had been less than Spanish merchants had hoped, then the greatest blow fell when, on returning from Portobelo to Cartagena to prepare for the voyage home in June 1708, the galleons were attacked off Cartagena by Admiral Wagner, with terrible losses. Only two ships survived to take refuge in Cartagena, where their cargoes were unloaded to await an escort across the Atlantic. Eventually, 8 or 9 million pesos of Peruvian and New Granadan treasure remaining from Casa Alegre's lost fleet returned to Spain in 1712, carried by the French admiral Ducasse shortly before the war ended.[12]

So, the first galleons to arrive in Cartagena in over a decade had entirely failed to revive Spanish trade with New Granada, and after this failure Spain's trading links with New Granada were practically severed, leaving the colony's resources to be diverted once again into foreign hands for the duration of the war. An idea of the scale of foreign contraband was given by a Spanish resident of Cartagena in 1712; he estimated that illicit trade was probably worth about 2 million pesos a year, paid for in New Granadan gold.[13] Thus, during the entire course of the war, it seems that most of the colony's trade went to foreigners, with little more than the 4 million pesos gathered at the Cartagena fair in 1706 reaching Spain from New Granada. In economic terms, the colony had become almost completely detached from Spain, neither relying on the metropolis for the greater part of its imports, nor returning more than a relatively small proportion of its gold production.

New Granada's informal commercial freedom continued after the war, when English interloping in Spanish America assumed an even larger scale. At the Treaty of Utrecht (1713), England had secured the *asiento de*

9. Walker, *Spanish Politics and Imperial Trade*, p. 38.
10. The estimate of Cartagena's contribution is from AHN, Codices, Libro 755b, Consultas y pareceres del Consejo de Indias, tomo IV, fol. 34, "Informe de Bartolomé Tienda de Cuervo," 1734.
11. Walker, *Spanish Politics and Imperial Trade*, pp. 44, 272, note 84.
12. Morineau, *Incroyable gazettes et fabuleux métaux*, p. 312.
13. AGI Consulados 315, Leonardo Bossemarte to Consulado of Seville, October 6, 1712.

negros (the official monopoly contract to supply Spanish America with slaves), together with the extraordinary privilege of sending an "annual ship" to the American monopoly ports to trade alongside the transatlantic fleets from Spain. Prized from Spain as the price of peace, this concession jeopardized both the integrity of Spain's colonial monopoly and the crown's income from trade revenues because it gave the English a legal foothold in American trade and a cover for contraband. Worse still, the terms of the Treaty of Utrecht limited Spain's options for reforming its system of colonial commerce. The English annual ship was linked to the movement of the convoys so that, in order to meet its treaty obligations, Spain was forced to retain the outmoded and ineffective commercial system that had long shown itself incapable of resisting foreign competition. Rather than replacing the convoy system, Bourbon ministers could only attempt to revive it.[14]

Their failure to do so was reflected in the poor performance of trade during the years following the war. Between 1713 and 1721, only one small convoy of four ships sailed to Cartagena and Portobelo, and after encountering considerable difficulties in disposing of its cargoes, it was lost at sea on the return voyage in 1715.[15] The value of treasure carried by this fleet is not known, but it is unlikely that it took more than a few million pesos, gathered from both New Granada and Peru. In 1718–19, a further 750,000 pesos were carried by ships that sailed from Cartagena, but this still left New Granada's total exports to Spain in 1713–21 at a level little better than that achieved during the very disturbed years of the War of Succession. Clearly, much remained to be done if Spain was to redirect the colony's resources back into the legal channels of the *Carrera de Indias*.[16]

Spain's problems in controlling New Granada's trade were not, of course, confined to this region; they were part of a larger crisis that affected the whole system of Spanish commerce with South America. Foreign interlopers were active not only in Cartagena and Santa Marta but also in Portobelo, where they traded for silver and other goods from Peru. It was in fact the diversion to foreigners of Peruvian rather than New Granadan trade that blocked the revival of the Tierra Firme galleons. As long as they were adequately supplied with contraband, Peruvian merchants were unwilling to organize convoys to take their silver to Panama and Portobelo, and, because Peru was the galleons' major market, their reluctance to trade with Spain made it extremely difficult to restart the fleet system. Spanish trade was consequently caught in a vicious circle of decline. While foreign interlopers were filling colonial markets with ille-

---

14. Walker, *Spanish Politics and Imperial Trade*, pp. 93–4.　15. Ibid., 59–63.
16. On the Tierra Firme trade as a whole in the period 1713–20, see ibid., pp. 67–92.

gal imports, the galleons could not be easily restored to a regular timetable; when the galleons failed to arrive, illegal foreign trade flourished, making it doubly difficult to resuscitate the fleets. To break this impasse and to confront the English economic challenge, the Bourbon government attempted to revitalize the transatlantic fleets by firm intervention embodied in the *Proyecto para galeones y flotas,* which it introduced in 1720.

The aim of the *Proyecto* was to reestablish the fleet system, so that Spain could recover its colonial commerce from foreign interlopers, rebuild its merchant marine, and enlarge the crown's revenues from taxes on trade. For the Tierra Firme galleons, this meant annual sailings from Cádiz in September, with a maximum of fifty days allowed to merchants to complete their transactions in Cartagena and Portobelo, and a further fifteen days in Havana on the return journey.[17] Because the *Proyecto* did not change the traditional structure of the *Carrera de Indias,* its success was to depend heavily on the enforcement of anticontraband measures in the Indies, to ensure that markets were not saturated by smugglers before the fleets arrived. With the newly established viceregency in place in New Granada since 1719, this seemed possible, because there was a stronger authority to curb the contraband and corruption that was ruining Spanish trade. In practice, however, neither commercial reorganization nor administrative vigilance was sufficient to restore the colonial monopoly. The crucial rule of the *Proyecto* – that the galleons should move at regular, predictable intervals – was consistently broken, and the new viceroy proved a poor guard against the encroachments of foreign interlopers.

The reform of the fleet system and the New Granadan trade, 1720–1739

When first put to the test in 1721, the galleons immediately failed to comply with the new rules of the *Proyecto,* or to fulfill the hopes of its proponents. The first galleons to sail under the new regulations of the 1720 *Proyecto para Galeones y Flotas* left Spain months later than scheduled, and spent two years in American waters completing their business.[18] The delay was caused by the very problem that the galleons were supposed to prevent: foreign contraband on the shores of New Granada. Since the War of Succession, smugglers had increasingly concentrated on the Caribbean rather than the Pacific, and illegal trade on the coast of New Granada was assuming the status of a permanent traffic with well-established routes, official collusion, and steady markets. The shores of New Granada, partic-

17. For description and analysis of the *Proyecto,* see Antonio García-Baquero, *Cádiz y el Atlántico,* vol. 1, pp. 152–8, 197–208, and Walker, *Spanish Politics and Imperial Trade,* pp. 107–11.
18. On the 1721 galleons commanded by General Baltasar de Guevara, see Walker, *Spanish Politics and Imperial Trade,* pp. 137–49.

ularly at the ports of Cartagena, Santa Marta, and Río Hacha, became areas of intense smuggling activity, associated with both the activities of the English South Sea Company and the many small foreign traders who ranged freely among the Spanish islands and along the coasts of the Spanish mainlands.[19] Before the galleons arrived in 1721, foreigners were already active at Cartagena and along its coasts, and they had even established a base at Barranquilla from which to channel their goods directly into the interior.[20] From there they penetrated inland, up the Magdalena River: by 1721, Mompós had become a major staging post for contraband, where foreigners traded as openly as they had on the coast itself.[21] Deep penetration of New Granada's trade by foreigners was coupled with heavy smuggling through Portobelo, blighting Spanish trade with Peru. When the *galeonistas* sailed to meet the Peruvian merchants after spending five months at Cartagena, they found that many foreigners had arrived before them, including not only the English annual ship, but also fourteen English and Dutch ships waiting to sell their cargoes for Peruvian silver.[22] Large quantities of silver were diverted to the interlopers and when the convoy returned to Cartagena in August 1722, it contained many unsold cargoes, which were taken back to the city for storage.[23] Eventually, after spending two years in the Indies, Guevara's galleons returned to Spain in 1723 with cargoes valued at 12.3 million pesos, a small amount considering that many years had passed since the previous convoy.[24]

This was a great disappointment for the Andalusian merchants who organized the fleets and for the Spanish government, and the galleons' debacle led to bitter recriminations. These were mainly directed against the newly installed viceroy of New Granada, whose presence in Cartagena had apparently done nothing to hinder illegal trade, despite the fact that one of his principal duties was to ensure that the port and its coast were cleared of contraband before the arrival of the galleons. In practice, the viceroy completely failed to fulfill this responsibility. Although Viceroy Villalonga went to Cartagena with orders to combat fraud and contraband, smuggling continued unabated during his residence in the port. Indeed, it was said that, rather than combating contraband, Villalonga profited from it. When Patiño, the Spanish minister responsible for colonial commerce, ordered a secret investigation into the smuggling that had undermined the galleons of 1721, it confirmed that the viceroy, together

19. On contraband during the period of the English annual ship, see G. H. Nelson, "Contraband Trade under the Asiento," *American Historical Review,* vol. 51 (1945), pp. 55–67.

20. AGI Santa Fe 374, Joseph de Aguila to crown, Cartagena, March 29, 1721.

21. AGI Santa Fe 374, Francisco Baloco Leygrave to crown, May 30, 1721; August 25, 1721.

22. AGI Santa Fe 374, Joseph García de Luna to crown, September 22, 1722.

23. On Guevara's galleons, see Walker, *Spanish Politics and Imperial Trade,* p. 149.

24. Value of treasure given by Morineau, *Incroyable gazettes et fabuleux métaux,* Table 54, pp. 362–6.

with other prominent officials in Cartagena, including the governor and his wife, was involved in breaking the very rules he was supposed to enforce. Such was the extent of official corruption in Cartagena, Patiño reported, that "no ship, whether English, Dutch or French, has been stopped from arriving at the port or its coast, and disembarking all its cargoes . . ."[25] Indeed, it found that, shortly before the arrival of the galleons, two French ships had sold more than a quarter of a million pesos' worth of cargoes at Cartagena and off the coasts of Tolú. These findings, together with complaints from the Spanish merchants of the Carrera de Indias, led to the introduction of some new anticontraband measures and, more significantly, contributed to the suppression of the first Viceroyalty of New Granada in 1723. However, although the crown quickly abandoned the experiment with a viceregency in New Granada, it clung to the commercial reform of the *Proyecto* and stubbornly persisted in trying to make it work. Thus, when Guevara's galleons returned to Spain in 1723, they were shortly followed by another convoy to South America, under the command of General Grillo.

The fleet commanded by Grillo fared somewhat better than its predecessor of 1721. Shortly after they arrived at Cartagena in February 1724, the galleons had to compete with the English annual ship and consequently they spent more than two years in Cartagena before moving on to Portobelo in mid-1726. Contraband was again ubiquitous. On entering Portobelo, the *galeonistas* found that an English squadron at Portobelo had neutralized Spanish anticontraband measures and, hemmed in by English warships, the galleons were delayed for a further two years.[26] However, for all their difficulties, when they eventually returned to Spain, it was with treasure valued at about 20.3 million pesos.[27] Thus the eight-year period from 1723 to 1730 had seen an improvement in the value of Tierra Firme exports to Spain. Between them, the Guevara and Grillo galleons had returned about 32.6 million pesos from Portobelo and Cartagena, which was considerably larger than returns taken by the two convoys that had sailed during and immediately after the War of Succession.

This incipient recovery in Spanish trade with Tierra Firme was sustained during the succeeding decade. In 1730, another galleon convoy, commanded by López Pintado, sailed to Tierra Firme. There, the *galeonistas* waited six months at Cartagena before moving on to Portobelo to meet with the Peruvian flotilla, and they managed to return to Spain after only a year in American waters. The fair at Cartagena was apparently a great success, thanks to effective anticontraband measures taken by the

25. AGI Santa Fe 374, Joseph Patiño to Andrés de Pez, Cádiz, April 14, 1722.
26. Walker, *Spanish Politics and Imperial Trade*, pp. 151–5.
27. Morineau, *Incroyable gazettes et fabuleux métaux*, Table 54, pp. 362–6.

governor of Quito and by the galleons' commander. In January 1729, Dionisio Alcedo y Herrera, president of the audiencia of Quito, had placed a ban on overland trade with Cartagena for the year before and the year after the arrival of the galleons, to ensure that legal trade did not disguise smuggling, as it had in the past.[28] Moreover, when López Pintado arrived in Cartagena with the galleons in 1730, he succeeded in frustrating the plans of local officials who planned to sell off captured foreign goods before the fair, and also in breaking up a smuggling ring that operated in collusion with the coastguard.[29] As a result, galleon sales at Cartagena were extraordinarily buoyant: Alcedo y Herrera later reported a turnover of some 7 million pesos.[30] Success at Cartagena was, however, balanced by disappointment at Portobelo. When the galleons met with the Peruvian merchants at Portobelo, the presence of an English annual ship again undermined the Spanish traders. Not only did the Lima merchants bring less silver to the fair than expected, but they also spent half their 9 million pesos on merchandise supplied by the English. Thus the relatively quick turnaround of the 1730 galleons masked a serious failure in the purpose of the convoy. The fleet returned quickly to Spain, but had to leave a large part of its unsold cargoes at Portobelo.[31] Once again, the colonials' preference for trading directly with foreigners had undermined the operations of the Spanish monopoly system, and the treasure returns of the fleet were disappointingly low, at between 11 and 13 million pesos. This was, however, followed by bullion shipments of between 3.3 and 4.1 million pesos in 1734, as the *galeonistas* who remained in the Indies slowly disposed of their cargoes.[32]

After this experience, the crown finally accepted that rebuilding an efficient system of annual convoys for the trade of Peru and New Granada was a practical impossibility. Since the inauguration of the *Proyecto para galeones y flotas* in 1720, its central rule – that the galleons should be both regular and predictable in their journeys – had been consistently broken, and the few convoys that did arrive in Cartagena and Portobelo had done little to combat contraband. Faced with this reality, the crown suspended the Tierra Firme galleons in January 1735, and allowed markets to be restocked when necessary by individual registered vessels. Madrid also

28. AGI Consulados 316, Dionisio de Alcedo y Herrera to Consulado, Quito, June 30, 1730; AGI Consulados 317, Manuel López de Pintado to Dionisio Alcedo y Herrera, Cartagena de Indias, June 28, 1731.

29. Walker, *Spanish Politics and Imperial Trade*, p. 179.

30. AGI Consulados 317, Dionisio de Alcedo y Herrera to Consulado de Cádiz, Quito, November 20, 1733.

31. Walker, *Spanish Politics and Imperial Trade*, pp. 177–88.

32. These and the following figures for the Tierra Firme trade are from Morineau, *Incroyable gazettes et fabuleux métaux*, Table 54, pp. 362–6.

recognized that, to be effective, the galleon system had to be attuned to the level of demand in colonial markets. A system of *avisos* or mailboats designed to relay information about markets and galleon sailings was therefore established, so that Spanish merchants would not find prices too low and sales too slow when they arrived in the Americas.[33] Thus, for some years, trade was conducted in individual vessels licensed by the crown, and, in 1735–40, these ships took about 15.6 million pesos to Spain from Portobelo and Cartagena.

In 1737, a half-hearted effort was made to revive the Tierra Firme convoys, when the crown permitted the organization of a small fleet of merchant vessels, escorted by coastguard ships under the command of General Blas de Lezo, to sail for Cartagena and Portobelo. Given the long gap since the previous convoy, Spanish merchants hoped that colonial markets were ready for renewed trade. This was too optimistic. The fleet's success at Cartagena in 1731, combined with continuing contraband afterward, had left New Granada's markets fully stocked.[34] So, when Blas de Lezo's convoy arrived in 1737, only a million pesos arrived in the port, instead of the 4 million expected.[35] Blas de Lezo's convoy further saturated New Granada's markets and it would take many years before its cargoes were sold. Indeed, some of the Spanish merchants who came with this convoy were still in Cartagena trying to sell their goods twelve years later.[36] As for the projected fair at Portobelo, it never took place. After two years of negotiation and official pressure, the *Armada del Sur* finally arrived in Panama in July 1739 to do business with the Spanish convoy at Portobelo. But before the fair could be held, Portobelo was captured and sacked by Admiral Vernon in December 1739, marking the end of its long history as a leading entrepôt for Spanish Atlantic trade.[37] The Tierra Firme galleons never sailed again. Their suspension continued throughout the Anglo-Spanish war of 1739–48 and they were not revived after the war, despite appeals from the Cádiz consulado.

Looking back over the period between 1720 and 1739, it is clear that, as a method for reviving Spanish colonial commerce, the *Proyecto para galeones y flotas* had fallen far short of expectations, particularly in trade with South America. Instead of becoming an alternative to illicit foreign

33. Walker, *Spanish Politics and Imperial Trade*, pp. 195–200.
34. A Cartagena merchant warned that contraband was worse than he had seen it in thirty-two years of experience; it had reached such proportions that it had greatly depressed the prices of imported textiles, and scoured the provinces of New Granada, Popayán, and Quito of all the funds disposable for legal trade: AGI Consulados 318, Gervasio de Herrera to Consulado, Cartagena, October 20, 1736.
35. AGI Santa Fe 1162, Blas de Lezo to Marqués de Torrenueva, Cartagena de Indias, March 28, 1737.
36. AGI Consulados 324, Diputados del Comercio to Consulado, Cartagena, February 8, 1749.
37. Walker, *Spanish Politics and Imperial Trade*, pp. 203–9.

trade, the fairs at Portobelo and Cartagena simply provided an additional channel for smugglers, especially the English South Sea Company.[38] The magnitude of Spain's losses to foreign contrabandists can be judged by comparing the value of treasure returns from South America during the periods 1679–98 and 1721–40. Treasure shipments from South America as a whole in 1679–98 were between 146.3 and 160.3 million pesos; in 1721–40, the value of treasure carried to Spain was between 84 and 96 million pesos. This decline was due mainly to contraction in trade from Cartagena and Portobelo. In 1679–98, between 133.6 and 143.6 million pesos were carried from Cartagena and Portobelo on the Tierra Firme fleets; in 1721–40, treasure cargoes fell to between 64 and 67.1 million pesos. Thus, whereas treasure returns from Tierra Firme averaged between 6.7 and 7.1 million pesos per year at the end of the seventeenth century, in 1721–40 the average fell to between 3.2 and 3.3 million pesos per year.[39]

The *Proyecto* should not be dismissed as a total failure, however, for it did enable Spain to recover some of the trade that it had lost to foreign interlopers during the first twenty years of Bourbon government. Even on the Tierra Firme route, where contrabandists were particularly active, the period 1721–40 saw some growth in legal commerce, to which New Granada contributed. In 1700–19, treasure exports to Spain from Cartagena probably did not exceed about 7 million pesos (an average of less than a half-million pesos per year). After the reform of the galleon system in 1720, on the other hand, the scale of Spanish trade with New Granada improved considerably, despite the difficulties of regularizing the fleets. When Guevara's galleons returned to Spain in 1723, they carried 12.3 million pesos, of which about 6 million pesos were supplied by New Granada. In 1729–30, some 20.3 million pesos were returned to Spain from the sales of the Grillo galleons of 1723, of which at least 11.4 million pesos were from Lima. New Granada's contribution may therefore have been as high as 8 million pesos.[40] The López Pintado galleons of 1730–1 also traded successfully at Cartagena. Seven million pesos were reported to have arrived from New Granada for trade in the port, making a major contribution to the 11 to 13 million pesos that the galleons eventually took back to Spain. It seems, then, that New Granada supplied around 21 million pesos to the three fleets that sailed between 1723 and

---

38. Of the company, Lynch states that between 1715 and 1732, it "probably controlled at least 25% of all British exports to Spain and America, immune from the formal Spanish monopoly": Lynch, *Bourbon Spain*, p. 151.

39. Morineau, *Incroyable gazettes et fabuleux métaux*, Table 39 and Table 54, pp. 232–6 and pp. 362–6, 369.

40. For the total value of treasure returned to Spain in these galleons, see ibid., pp. 362–6. For the value of treasure loaded in Callao, see Walker, *Spanish Politics and Imperial Trade*, p. 273, note 84.

1730, so that on these convoys alone the colony exported an average of at least 1 million pesos per average year during the period 1721–40. This estimate is based on imperfect evidence, but it is strengthened by Viceroy Castelfuerte's assertion, made in 1731, that New Granada could provide 3 million pesos to the trade at three-year intervals.[41]

The buoyancy of New Granada's contribution to the galleons that sailed between 1721 and 1731 cannot, however, be wholly attributed to government intervention to revive the Tierra Firme fleets. For during the opening decades of the eighteenth century, exploitation of new placer mines was substantially increasing the value of gold mined in New Granada, thereby expanding the colony's capacity to finance overseas trade. This growth is reflected in the payment of quintos to the crown in four main mining regions of New Granada. In 1715–19, quintos paid were equivalent to an average annual output of 441,200 silver pesos per year; in 1735–9, average annual output, again estimated from the quintos, had risen to 925,200 pesos.[42] Thus, it seems that the recovery of Spanish trade with New Granada owed at least as much to the growing vigor of the colony's mining sector as it did to reform of the commercial system.

Although more gold was available to pay for trade with Spain, metropolitan merchants still had only a very slack hold on New Granada's overseas commerce. When General Blas de Lezo arrived with his small convoy of merchant ships in 1737, he reported that Cartagena was virtually blockaded by foreign smugglers and estimated that about 75% of the colony's gold output was being channeled through the province to pay for contraband imports.[43] In the same year, the governor of Cartagena confirmed that contraband was taking most of the region's gold. He observed that foreign smugglers had changed their tactics, switching from large ships to small, well-armed sloops that sailed along the whole length of the coast, and he estimated that they were taking around 2 million pesos annually from New Granada.[44] Thus, by the end of the 1730s, foreign smugglers were still taking as much of New Granada's trade as they had at the start of the century.

Evidently, neither administrative nor commercial reform had succeeded in bringing New Granada's trade under firm and constant Spanish control. The territory's economy was still only loosely attached to the metropolitan power and substantial flows of the colony's gold, together with the Peruvian silver that leaked through the holes in the monopoly at Por-

41. Walker, *Spanish Politics and Imperial Trade*, pp. 196–7.
42. Calculated from the figures given in Table 3.1: see Chapter 3.
43. Lance R. Grahn, "An Irresoluble Dilemma, Smuggling in New Granada, 1713–1783": in Fisher, Kuethe, and McFarlane, *Reform and Insurrection in Bourbon New Granada and Peru*, p. 138.
44. AGI Santa Fe 422, Report from governor of Cartagena, October 17, 1737 mentioned in Consejo de Indias, October 21, 1738.

tobelo, continued to find their way into the hands of the foreign interlopers who sailed the Caribbean coasts. In these circumstances, more
drastic reorganization was required if Spain was to recoup its commerce
and reassert its political authority. In 1739, the first steps toward these
goals were taken. When Spain reentered war with Britain, the crown
moved toward a complete restructuring of the commercial and administrative systems that had for so long governed Spanish South America. For
New Granada, this second phase of Bourbon reform brought two changes.
The first was its incorporation into a reestablished viceroyalty; the second
was a dramatic departure from the old structure of colonial commerce,
involving the final suppression of the Tierra Firme fleets and a reordering
of long-established patterns of transatlantic trade. To the political reform
and its implications, we will return later; first we must investigate the
impact of reorganization in the system of colonial commerce.

Realignments in South American commerce

In 1739, the outbreak of war with the British finally ended the English
asiento, allowing Spain to repair a serious flaw in its commercial monopoly
and providing an opportunity to depart permanently from the discredited
galleon system. Henceforth, Spanish trade with the Americas was carried
in individual merchant vessels, rather than in convoys. Known as *registros
sueltos,* or register ships, these vessels could sail to various Caribbean and
Atlantic ports. Channels for trade were further amplified by the permission given in 1740 for Spanish shipping to enter the Pacific via Cape
Horn. So for New Granada, internal political reorganization coincided
with another reform of the commercial system. Just as the establishment
of the first viceregency in 1719 had been accompanied by the *Proyecto para
Galeones* of 1720, so was the reestablishment of the viceregency in 1739
matched by the abandonment of the fleet system.

Although there was ample precedent for the employment of register
ships in the transatlantic trade, both as a supplement and occasional
substitute for the fleets, the suspension of the fleets marked a new departure in the history of Spanish trade with South America.[45] Henceforth,
Spanish merchants were freed from the competition of the English Asiento
Company and able to establish more regular contact with the markets of
America. According to Vásquez de Prada, this brought into being a new
class of merchants, composed of Spaniards who emigrated to America in

---

45. According to 1720 Proyecto regulations, licenses were granted to individuals for loading register
    ships sent to the Indies. On the register ships in the trade with the Pacific coast, see Sergio
    Villalobos R., *El comercio y la crisis colonial* (Santiago, 1968), p. 67. For a list of the register-ships
    sent to America between 1700 and 1740, see Walker, *Spanish Politics and Imperial Trade,* pp. 230–
    3.

pursuit of their business, and who, because they were not necessarily connected with Andalusian commercial houses, preferred commercial freedom to restriction.[46] The scale of colonial commerce with Spain, which García-Baquero has measured by tracing changes in the tonnage of transatlantic shipping, also showed a clear tendency to grow after the abolition of the fleets, with the register ships as the primary vehicle of that growth.[47] But it was in Spanish South America that the temporary suspension of the fleets during the 1739–48 war had its greatest effect. For, unlike the Mexican *flotas*, which were revived in 1757, the Tierra Firme galleons were permanently abandoned and the freer movements of the licensed register ships encouraged the development of trade routes outside the old artery of South American commerce that had linked Spain to Peru, via Panama and Portobelo.[48]

The supersession of the galleons, which had moved large shipments from metropolis to colonies at well-spaced intervals, by individual ships that sailed at irregular moments with small cargoes, had important implications for the entire structure of Spanish colonial trade with South America. Supply and demand were no longer concentrated at the continental fairs at Portobelo and Cartagena, but were dispersed among a number of urban centers that drew on the markets of broad hinterlands. Freed from the prescribed routes and erratic timing of the convoys, shipping could now respond to price changes in colonial markets and could gravitate toward the areas that combined the most favorable circumstances for exchange.

The ports most immediately affected by the abolition of the galleon system were those that had acted as its termini: namely, Cartagena de Indias, Portobelo, and Lima. Of these, Portobelo was the hardest hit. The end of the galleons and the opening of a direct route to Peru via Cape Horn undermined its role as the entrepôt for trade between the Atlantic and the Pacific and, because it was in a poor, sparsely populated area with little trade of its own, the port lost its raison d'être. Cartagena and Lima were much less adversely affected, as both had their own important economic hinterlands and therefore continued to attract substantial Spanish trade. Lima, however, saw its commercial importance diminish, as it no longer monopolized exchange between Spain and Peru and had to face

46. Valentín Vásquez de Prada, "Las rutas comerciales entre España y América en el siglo XVIII," *AEA*, vol. 25 (1968), pp. 206–7.

47. García-Baquero, *Cádiz y el Atlántico*, vol. 1, pp. 164–74; 541–6.

48. Guillermo Céspedes del Castillo, "Lima y Buenos Aires. Repercusiones económicas y políticas de la creación del Virreinato de la Plata," *AEA*, vol. 3 (1946), pp. 702–12. For further comment on the impact in South America of the suppression of the galleons, see Roland D. Hussey, *The Caracas Company, 1728–1784* (Cambridge, Mass., 1934), and Sergio Villalobos R., *El comercio y la crisis colonial*, pp. 69–91.

competition from Buenos Aires and Cartagena. Having persistently failed to support the galleon system, the Lima merchants suddenly rediscovered its merits and pleaded with the crown for reinstatement of the convoys.[49]

Lima's anxiety to return to the fleet system as a way of resisting competition from Buenos Aires was accentuated by the fact that its traditional commercial monopoly in the great Peruvian economic region was also challenged from Cartagena de Indias. Indeed, of the three ports that had previously been the cardinal points for the galleon system, only Cartagena made unmistakable gains from its demise. Whereas Lima had to cope with competition in its traditional markets from Buenos Aires, Cartagena's role as the principal port for its region was unchanged. It not only continued to be the focus for exchanging European merchandise for New Granadan gold, but it also began to play a larger part in Quito's trade, which had previously been controlled from Lima.

Quito's movement away from Lima's commercial orbit was already under way during the early years of the century, due to the availability of contraband at Cartagena, but it became more pronounced after the suppression of the galleons. This shift was reflected in a dispute between Lima and Cartagena merchants that began in the late 1750s, when the two groups quarreled over their respective rights to trade in the Pacific. On the one hand, Peruvian merchants sought to prevent importation into Pacific markets of goods carried via Cartagena or Panama, whereas on the other Cartagena merchants insisted that goods imported to Lima via Cape Horn should not be trans-shipped to Guayaquil. In 1758–60, the Consulado of Lima, backed by Viceroy Superunda, claimed that markets in the provinces of Quito were an integral part of Lima's trade and argued that allowing Cartagena access to these markets would damage the Peruvian economy in two ways. First, it would increase contraband trade from the Caribbean into the Pacific; second, it would undermine the shipping industry of the Pacific, since Lima's merchants used their profits from imports into Quito to maintain their ships at Guayaquil's yards.[50] The crown apparently ignored these complaints for many years, so that in 1768 the issue was reopened. Supported by Viceroy Amat, Lima's merchants again petitioned Madrid for an end to trade between Cartagena and Quito, via Portobelo, because it was undermining Lima's trade with the Quito region and damaging its shipping in the Pacific.[51] The merchants

49. This volte face was prompted by the loss of monopoly power brought about by the opening of new trade routes, via Cape Horn and Buenos Aires, and the intrusion of new merchants. See Walker, *Spanish Politics and Imperial Trade*, pp. 212–14.

50. The history of this dispute is summarized in AGI Consulados 331, Viceroy Amat to crown, Lima, April 20, 1767.

51. Ibid., Informe del Tribunal del Consulado de Lima, Madrid, January 8, 1768.

of Cartagena mounted a strong countervailing case. They argued that the trade of Quito should pertain to them and they were supported by royal officials anxious to defend the revenues raised from such trade through their port. The latter group pointed out that Quito merchants had traded through Cartagena since the end of the seventeenth century and that this trade had become customary since the suspension of the galleons, on the understanding that the Quito merchants did not interfere with the Lima monopoly by re-exporting goods from Cartagena into Peru.[52] Cartagena merchants also insisted that their whole system of trade would be upset if Lima's claim to a monopoly of Quito markets was accepted. The crown, they stated, had laid down clear lines of demarcation for trade in South America. By opening Cape Horn to navigation, the crown had provided for the supply of Peru, and thus had left the northern ports of Cartagena and Portobelo to supply the markets of the new Viceroyalty of New Granada. To ignore these demarcation lines would allow unrestrained competition that, they claimed, would ruin Spanish commerce. For Cartagena, this division had to be sustained because "the principal consideration and greatest market for Spanish trade in this Kingdom (of New Granada) is the province of Popayán, because of the links and connections which its business sustains with Quito and the Chocó, being positioned between the two . . ."[53] If this division were altered, they predicted, fewer ships would come from Cádiz to Cartagena, shortages of imports would follow and, in consequence, all the progress made against contraband would evaporate. The clock would be turned back to the time of the galleons bringing back "the old and forgotten vices of the coast, which the vigilance of the most zealous officials of those times was unable to contain, leaving Spanish commerce in complete decay, the Kingdom in total penury, and the Royal Treasury empty and unable to meet the costs of maintaining the military strongholds of this Viceroyalty."[54]

To resolve the dispute, the crown commissioned a full investigation, while in the meantime allowing the free movement of imports into Quito both by the Cape Horn/Pacific route via Lima, and the Atlantic route via Cartagena.[55] And this, eventually, was how the issue was left. The Peruvian merchants were deprived of the monopoly of Quito's markets, but control was also denied to the merchants in Cartagena. Both now had to compete in Quito's markets. This was not the perfect solution for Cartagena's merchants, who would have preferred to monopolize Quito's market for European goods. However, it worked to their advantage in the

52. Ibid., Informe de la Real Contaduría de Cartagena, 1769.
53. Ibid., Informe de los diputados del comercio, Cartagena, December 2, 1769.
54. Ibid.   55. Ibid., Real Cédula, San Lorenzo, October 17, 1768.

long term, for although supplies continued to enter Guayaquil from Lima, Cartagena strengthened its contacts both with the province of Popayán and with the populous provinces of highland Quito.

If Cartagena's role in transatlantic commerce was undamaged, even enhanced, by the end of the galleon system, how did reorganization in the *Carrera de Indias* affect the volume and value of New Granada's trade with Spain? Did the register ships create closer and more regular contacts between New Granada and Spain? Were they more capable than the galleons in combating foreign intrusion into New Granada's markets, thereby redirecting to Spain resources that had been siphoned off by contraband? Did they stimulate any new development of New Granada's resources, linking the colony more closely to the needs of the metropolitan power? To answer these questions, we must look more closely at the broad patterns of shipping and commerce between Cartagena and Cádiz in the forty years between 1739 and 1778.

New Granadan trade with Spain, 1739–1778

The effect of the new maritime system on New Granada's trade was initially delayed by the Anglo-Spanish war of 1739–48, when shipping movements between Spain and her colonies were constantly impeded by enemy action at sea. The register ships sustained links between Cádiz and Cartagena in wartime, but only at the cost of heavy losses. Of twenty-seven ships that sailed from Cádiz to Cartagena between 1739 and 1748, eleven were lost at sea, mainly to enemy capture. However, once the war was over, the register ships certainly created a more frequent and stable system of transportation for Spanish trade with New Granada. In the decade 1749–58, thirty-seven ships left Cádiz for Cartagena, followed by twenty-eight in 1759–68, and thirty-six in 1769–78. Not all of these ships were merchant vessels – they included some mailboats and naval vessels – but these numbers clearly show that replacing the galleons by licensed shipping permitted more regular contact between Spain and its colony. [56]

The new shipping system was not immediately effective in diminishing contraband. After arriving in Cartagena in 1737, General Blas de Lezo had swiftly reorganized the coastguard in order to combat foreign interloping, at considerable expense to the royal treasury, but when Vernon attacked Cartagena in mid-1740, Blas de Lezo was killed and his warships were lost, leaving the coast wide open to smugglers for the duration of the war. [57] The result was a tremendous boom in illicit foreign trade. In 1743,

---

56. See Appendix C, Table 1.
57. Grahn, "An Irresoluble Dilemma," in Fisher, Kuethe, and McFarlane, *Reform and Insurrection in Bourbon New Granada and Peru*, p. 139.

Spanish merchants in Cartagena complained that foreign interlopers were "the masters of trade on all these coasts," and the governor of Panama reported that foreigners continued to flock to the Isthmus, where they took silver from Peruvian merchants.[58] The scale of contraband in these years is reflected in the contemporary estimate that, during Viceroy Eslava's government (1739–49), more than 7 million pesos of contraband were confiscated in Cartagena alone.[59]

When peace was restored, the new system seems to have had greater success in redirecting the flow of New Granadan resources from illegal foreign traders into Spanish hands. Even before the war ended, foreign contraband in the Caribbean apparently began to decline. The English author of "Remarks on the Spanish Trade" recalled that large quantities of goods were returned unsold from the Spanish colonies between 1746 and 1748, and English officials in the West Indies reported a marked fall in the illicit trade as soon as the war was over. A French observer, commenting on the decline of St. Domingue's contraband trade with Cuba, attributed this to the efficiency of the new system of shipping adopted by the Spanish, and the evidence for New Granada suggests that the greater flexibility permitted by this system did stimulate a quick recovery of Spanish commerce with the colony.[60] A report from Cartagena in 1750 stated that the inrush of legal imports following the war had pushed prices down, and between 1748 and 1753, Spanish trade in the port seems to have flourished, reaching the unusually high level of 3 million pesos per year.[61]

The success of Spanish trade was mirrored in the decline of contraband seizures in Cartagena. In 1750–4, the value of these seizures fell to less than 10% of their wartime value, and in 1755–9, it tapered away to virtually nothing. This fall may be partly attributable to a shift in contraband trade toward Santa Marta, where contraband seizures increased in 1750–4, but insofar as contraband can be measured by the value of illicit goods captured by the authorities, there seems to have been a substantial decline in the total value of illicit trade entering New Granada.[62] Cer-

58. AGI Consulados 319, Miguel Lasso de la Vega to Virrey Eslava, Cartagena, January 9, 1743; AGI Consulados 320, Dionisio de Alcedo y Herrera, Panama, November 15, 1743.

59. Posada and Ibáñez, *Relaciones de Mando*, p. 72.

60. Richard Pares, *War and Trade in the West Indies* (Oxford, 1936), p. 114.

61. AGI Consulados 325, Marqués de Valdehoyos to Consulado, Cartagena, October 25, 1750. The estimate of trade is from Abbé Raynal's *Histoire Philosophique*. The figure given by Raynal for Cartagena's exports is 14,553,166 *livres tournois*, which, converted to pesos at a rate of 5:1, was 2,910,633 pesos. Of this, 2,817,460 pesos were in gold and silver. See Morineau, *Incroyable gazettes et fabuleux métaux*, p. 495.

62. For the value of official seizures of contraband, see Grahn, "An Irresoluble Dilemma," in Fisher, Kuethe, and McFarlane, *Reform and Insurrection in Bourbon New Granada and Peru*, Tables 3 and 5, pp. 134, 144.

tainly contemporaries believed that the register ships had ended the fla-
grant breaches of the Spanish monopoly that were common in the first half
of the eighteenth century. In 1769, the merchants of Cartagena referred to
large-scale contraband as "the old and forgotten vices of the coast," as
though they were long buried in the past.[63] In short, the new organization of commerce came closer to accomplishing the goals that the *Proyecto*
of 1720 had so obviously failed to secure: namely, a regular flow of
Spanish trade and a reduction of foreign interloping.

The achievements of the register ship system should not be exaggerated, however. Although ships from Cádiz called more frequently at
Cartagena, the scale of traffic with Spain was still very small. On average,
only about three vessels per year arrived in Cartagena from Spain between
1749 and 1778, and the postwar surge of 1748–53 was not long sustained. From an estimated 3 million pesos per year in 1748–53, officially
registered imports from Cartagena into Spain fell back to an annual average of around a million pesos in 1754–78.[64] The colonial authorities also
continued to regard contraband as a major problem requiring strong
action. Thus, in 1758, Viceroy Solís banned foreign ships from importing
flour into Cartagena, on the grounds that the trade was a cover for
smuggling, and to sustain the ban he engaged a private contractor to
supply the port with flour from the interior.[65] This brought protests
about shortages from people in Cartagena, but these protests merely
convinced the viceroy that his measures had been successful in curtailing
contraband, and he recommended that his successor should continue
them.[66] The ban on importing foreign flour was therefore retained under
the viceroys Messía de la Cerda and Guirior, and efforts to ensure that
Cartagena was supplied with wheat from New Granada were continued.[67]

In practice, foreign goods continued to enter the port illegally. Occasionally, local officials relaxed the rules on foreign shipping and this,
together with the import of slaves, combined to keep contraband channels
through Cartagena wide open during the 1760s and 1770s. Thus, for
example, a scandal arose in 1764 over the illegal entry of seven foreign
ships (two French and five English) during 1763 and 1764, and the public
sale of their cargoes of slaves, wheat, wines, and other merchandise.[68] In

63. AGI Consulados 331, Informe de los diputados del comercio, Cartagena, December 2, 1769.
64. Morineau, *Incroyable gazettes et fabuleux métaux*, p. 418, note 89; p. 420. Total bullion exports
    arriving in Spain from Cartagena between 1765 and 1778 were 12,928,174 pesos. According to
    official registrations of gold received from Cartagena, some years saw no exports at all, whereas
    others saw substantial exports; the annual average for the period is 923,441 pesos.
65. On the contract, see María Angeles Eugenio Martínez, "Reapertura de la via Carare-Vélez. El
    asiento de Blas de la Terga (1754)," *AEA*, vol. 41 (1984), pp. 513–52.
66. Posada and Ibáñéz, *Relaciones de mando*, p. 85.   67. Ibid., pp. 109, 143.
68. AHNC Aduanas (Cartas), tomo. 5, fols. 945–6.

addition, loopholes in the law were used to cover contraband. A common trick was for foreigners to feign damage to their ships in order to enter Cartagena legally and then, with the collusion of officials, to dispose of their cargoes in order to pay for repairs.[69] So, although the replacement of the fleets by register ships established firmer economic contacts between Spain and New Granada, Spain was still far from exercising a monopoly over New Granada's external commerce, or stemming a continuing flow of the colony's resources to foreigners.

The principal flaw in the reform was the fact that it did not effect a radical overhaul of the whole system of colonial commerce. Spain's trans-atlantic trade was still hedged in by many institutional restraints, such as the need to obtain licenses from the crown, the obligation to sail only to the port named in the license, and high tariffs and port charges in both Spain and America. Contraband was, furthermore, encouraged by the manner in which duties on the trade were assessed by Spanish officials. Merchandise sent to the colonies was valued by weight and volume rather than value, so that the Spanish trader favored expensive goods and ne-glected the lower end of the market, leaving space for the smuggler. In New Granada, contraband trade was also stimulated by the presence of gold, a commodity much prized in the neighboring foreign colonies of the Caribbean, island economies that were perennially short of specie. Finally, even with improvements to the coastguard, the Caribbean ports and shores of New Granada were impossible to police effectively. The authori-ties tried to seal Cartagena from smuggling by banning foreign imports of flour, but contraband continued to filter into the country, through the many gaps opened by bribery of port officials and smuggling along the extensive coastline between Río Hacha and the Isthmus of Panama.

If the reorganized commercial system could not reserve New Granadan markets for Spain, then it was even less successful in stimulating the exploitation of the colony's natural resources. In the time of the galleons, New Granada's trade involved the exchange of gold for European textiles (most of them European re-exports channeled through Spain) and a mix-ture of iron and steel hardware, foodstuffs such as olives, oil, wine, pepper, and cinnamon, plus a miscellany of other commodities, of which the most important were soap, wax, and paper. The advent of the register ships brought no fundamental change to this pattern. Imports from Spain consisted of much the same mix as before, with gold providing New Granada's major form of payment.[70] The Cádiz merchants who traded

69. AHNC Aduanas (Cartas), tomo. 12, fols. 449–51; AHNC Aduanas, tomo. 8, fols. 189–90. Also see the comments made by Viceroy Messía de la Cerda: Posada and Ibáñez, *Relaciones de mando*, pp. 109–10.

70. Information on imports into New Granada is taken from the registers of ships that arrived in Cartagena in the 1760s and 1770s, and found in AGI Contratación 1663 (ramos 1–4) and 1664

through Cartagena were primarily interested in taking gold for their imports and, apart from one or two other commodities such as small quantities of cacao, they showed scant interest in developing New Granada's potential exports.[71] Without markets in Spain, New Granadan resources had few other legitimate outlets. Cartagena had some trade with the Spanish Caribbean islands, consisting mainly of imports of tobacco, sugar, and wax from Cuba and cacao from Guayaquil (via Portobelo), in exchange for re-exports of European imports, especially to Portobelo. But this trade was of little relevance to New Granada's agriculturalists, even those in the coastal provinces, because in terms of agricultural production the Spanish islands were competing rather than complementary economies. The foreign islands with well-developed, specialized sugar plantation economies, however, were ready to take agricultural products from the Spanish mainland, including such New Granadan products as the cattle and mules bred in the provinces of Río Hacha and Santa Marta. But because such trade was prohibited unless special licenses were granted by the colonial authorities, it provided only a narrow and uncertain vent for New Granada's agricultural surplus.

On balance, it seems that the Spanish mercantilist system, as it functioned for most of the eighteenth century, inhibited the economic development of New Granada. The possibilities for development were, admittedly, not very great, because most of New Granada's population and economic activity was located far in the interior of the country, divorced from easy access to external markets by the costs imposed by distance and the difficulties of transportation. However, the restraints imposed on trade with foreigners deprived New Granadan agriculturalists of the few possibilities that did exist for selling their products overseas. Indeed, not only did mercantilist regulation block access to overseas markets for agricultural products, but the system also failed to protect producers for New Granada's domestic market. The wheat producers of the provinces of Santa Fe and Tunja repeatedly complained that, despite the official prohibition on direct trade with foreigners, Cartagena was regularly supplied with imports of foreign flour, which displaced their product from the coastal market. Thus, although the rules of the Spanish monopoly hindered exports of agricultural products to foreign markets, they did not prevent imports of such products from foreign producers.

(ramos 1–2). A general breakdown of imports for 1748–53 was made by the Abbé Raynal, showing that of nearly 1.8 million pesos of European goods imported into Cartagena in the average year, more than 1.3 million pesos consisted of foreign manufactures. See Morineau, *Incroyable gazettes et fabuleux métaux*, p. 492.

71. For a list of Cartagena's exports in 1748–53, see the account made by the Abbé Raynal, cited in ibid., p. 495.

New perspectives on economic policy

During the 1770s, colonial ministers finally began to recognize and to address these problems, as the government of Charles III sought to modify and modernize Spain's mercantilist policy. After Spain's defeat by the British in the Seven Years' War, Madrid finally embraced the idea of comprehensive reform of the colonial system. This began slowly, with a selective decree of *comercio libre* for the Caribbean islands in 1765, which allowed them to trade with Spanish ports other than Cádiz, the traditional, exclusive entrepôt. Later, in 1776 and 1777, this measure was extended to Santa Marta and Río Hacha in New Granada, on the grounds that such impoverished regions, which were outside the major trade routes, needed greater freedom to encourage their trade and development.[72] Moreover, with this shift in official attitudes in Spain, leading officers of the Spanish state in New Granada were also prompted to think about the economic development of the colony, and to propose reforms for promoting more effective exploitation of its resources.

When Viceroy Messía de la Cerda presented a final report to the crown, in his *relación de mando* of 1772, he drew Madrid's attention to the fact that the existing mercantile system underexploited the colony and, pointing to the poor condition of New Granada's economy relative to its rich potential, he called for measures to improve mining and internal transportation. Messía de la Cerda also insisted that Spain should exploit more fully the wide range of New Granada's tropical and other commodities. This, he argued, would both promote prosperity and reduce foreign interloping by removing the temptation to inhabitants of the coastal provinces of Santa Marta and Río Hacha to trade with foreigners.[73]

Other critics condemned the existing system in stronger terms, blaming it for the stagnation of the colonial economy. One such critic was Francisco Antonio Moreno y Escandón, a New Granadan who became a *fiscal* (crown attorney) and oidor of the audiencia in Bogotá. In 1772, Moreno wrote a long report in which, among other things, he pressed for new policies to develop New Granada's economy. The existing system of trade, Moreno argued, satisfied neither the interests of the crown nor its colonial subjects, because it simply failed to take advantage of the region's multiple resources. "This kingdom," he pointed out,

---

72. The extension of *comercio libre* to Santa Marta was decreed by a Royal Order of October 4, 1776; to Río Hacha by a Royal Order of August 20, 1777: AHNC, Aduanas, tomo 6, fols. 308–11; 493–5. On the introduction of *comercio libre* in Cuba, see Allan J. Kuethe and G. Douglas Inglis, "Absolutism and Enlightened Reform: Charles III, the Establishment of the Alcabala, and Commercial Reorganization in Cuba," *Past and Present*, No. 109 (1985), pp. 118–43.

73. Posada and Ibáñez, *Relaciones de mando*, pp. 105–9.

does not enjoy an active commerce. . . . Its substance consists of the gold taken from its mines, without trade, sale or export of its agricultural products and manufactures. Its supply of merchandise, textiles and other so-called Spanish goods depends on one or other register-ship sent from Cádiz to the port of Cartagena, from whence these imports are sent into the interior of the Kingdom, at high costs in duties and transport. . . . Such is the weakness of trade that those who profit from it are rare, and those who matter in the transatlantic trade are even rarer.[74]

Not only did the trade fail to offer sufficient outlets for colonial agricultural and manufactured goods, but according to Moreno y Escandón, it also depressed trade and production within the colony, either by undermining regional manufactures, as in the case of Quito's textile industry, or by draining specie in payment for imports into New Granada. Moreno y Escandón therefore called for restraints on imports from Europe and special measures to develop exports, particularly from the Caribbean littoral. He suggested that the colony's export trade could best be increased and diversified by endowing private companies with temporary monopoly privileges so that they might build up a trade in raw materials and agricultural commodities.[75]

These ideas for reform found strong support from Manuel de Guirior, who served as viceroy of New Granada in 1772–6. Like his predecessors, Guirior thought it essential to diversify and expand New Granada's exports, but, influenced by Moreno y Escandón, his proposals for achieving such change were more radical. Guirior not only recommended the removal of duties on some agricultural products, to encourage their export to Spain; he also proposed a general relaxation of the traditional restrictions on colonial exports. Spanish merchants, he observed, took only bullion and cacao from New Granada and, due to the structure of duties, preferred to take on sugar in Havana rather than carry the viceroyalty's abundant supplies of sugar, cotton, tobacco, dyewood, and hides back to Spain. Lower duties offered one means to change this, but Guirior did not consider this sufficient to promote New Granada's exports. He therefore suggested that New Granadans be allowed to export to foreign ports of the Caribbean any surplus left by Spanish traders.[76] In the past, private licenses had been granted for such trade on a strictly ad hoc basis. Now, however, Guirior was recommending that such trade be formalized and regularized.

To defend this break with the long-established rules of the Spanish monopoly, he argued that the existing pattern of Spanish trade contrib-

74. Francisco Antonio Moreno y Escandón, "Estado del Virreinato de Santafé, Nuevo Reino de Granada," p. 588.
75. Ibid., pp. 589–92.
76. AGI Santa Fe 552. Informe of Tomas Ortíz de Landázuri on Viceroy Guirior's letter of June 15, 1773, Madrid, February 28, 1774.

uted to the depression rather than the development of the colony's economy. Like Moreno y Escandón, Guirior insisted that the demand for bullion and coin to pay for imports from Spain tended to drain New Granada of the specie required to facilitate and foster internal trade. Moreno y Escandón recommended that the problem be dealt with both by stimulating gold production and by diversifying exports; Guirior followed a similar line of argument, but he took it further. He recommended freedom for colonial merchants to export to foreign colonial ports, and he wanted to restrict imports from Spain into New Granada.[77]

Curbing European imports was not an entirely unorthodox proposal, given that most of Spain's exports still consisted of foreign manufactures. Indeed, when Guirior criticized the Cádiz merchants for their failure to develop the colony's resources and their preference for importing foreign goods, and called for differential rates of duty to promote trade in Spanish manufactures, he was merely echoing ideas that were becoming increasingly fashionable among official circles in Spain. But in his *relación de mando*, Guirior went further still. There, he argued that the existing Spanish trade actually harmed the New Granadan economy by draining it of specie in exchange for luxury articles that only encouraged a "damaging frivolity" among colonial consumers. Spain's national interest would, he observed, be better served by allowing the colony greater economic autonomy: measures to promote growth in the domestic economy, including its textile industry, would strengthen Spain's administrative and military power in the colony by enriching the economic base from which it drew its revenues.[78]

Viceroy Guirior's assessment of New Granada's economic potential and his proposals for economic policy suggest that he was strongly influenced by creole opinion, and particularly by Moreno y Escandón. The Cádiz monopoly was not only blamed for failing to stimulate colonial exports; it was also portrayed as an obstacle to developing the agricultural and manufacturing potential of the region. Moreno y Escandón and Guirior also recognized that this situation could not easily be changed within the confines of the Spanish monopoly, because metropolitan markets would not absorb many of New Granada's products, and that the only way to generate export-led growth was by breaking down institutional barriers to trade with foreigners in the Caribbean. After all, Guirior pointed out, the suppression of such a natural pattern of trade did little to preserve Spain's monopoly. Where legal trade was prohibited, illegal trade arose as an irrepressible substitute. So, instead of seeking to suppress a

77. AHNC Milicias y Marina, tomo 125, fols. 1000–7: "Causas de que procede la pobreza general del Reino . . ."
78. Posada and Ibáñez, *Relaciones de mando*, pp. 143–6.

trade that the government was powerless to prevent, Guirior urged the crown to turn it to the state's advantage. The fiscal advantages were obvious. In the short term, legalization of the trade with foreign colonies would cut the costs of policing the coast, while raising revenues from customs duties; in the long term, the economic activity generated by the trade would generate still more taxable income for the royal treasury.[79]

Here, then, was a new economic policy for New Granada, designed to stimulate growth by greater freedom for exports, combined with government intervention to encourage mining and agricultural development. The first official response from Spain, framed by Tomás Ortíz de Landázuri of the *Contaduría General,* was, however, to reject it out of hand. Landázuri acknowledged the need for some change in policy, because New Granada's trade with Spain was slight in relation to its size and natural wealth, and the colony's economy was in such "a deplorable state that . . . it burdens the crown with more than 400,000 pesos per year that are sent from Peru to maintain military bases, garrisons and fortifications . . ." But he attributed New Granada's poor economic performance to the effects of foreign contraband rather than to the deficiencies of the Spanish commercial system, and he denounced Guirior's proposal for freedom to export to foreign colonies as "so scandalous that it can only be regarded with amazement."[80]

Changes in Spanish commercial policy were nevertheless put into effect in the years that followed, as part of a wholesale reform of the system of transatlantic trade. The greater freedom to trade that was extended to the New Granada ports of Santa Marta and Río Hacha in 1776 and 1777 was therefore the prelude to wider change. As Viceroy Flóres pointed out, it was extremely difficult to isolate coastal "free trade" zones from the rest of the colony; he therefore concluded that "circumstances demand recourse to a general freedom."[81] The concession of this freedom came on October 12, 1778, when the famous *Reglamento de comercio libre* extended imperial free trade to all the Spanish American colonies, leaving only some temporary restrictions on the trade of New Spain and the captaincy-general of Caracas. With the *Reglamento de comercio libre,* Viceroy Caballero y Góngora later remarked, the crown had "finally recognized the important truth that import and export duties charged by the customs are not so much a branch of the treasury as a means by which policy may enable national commerce to prevail over foreign commerce . . ."[82]

The extension of imperial free trade to New Granada in 1778 was

79. AHNC, Real Audiencia, tomo 9, fols. 256–66.
80. AGI Santa Fe 552, Tomas Ortíz de Landázuri, Madrid, February 28, 1774.
81. AGI Indiferente General, Flóres to Galvez, Bogotá, February 28, 1777 (no. 324).
82. Pérez Ayala, *Antonio Caballero y Góngora,* p. 353.

paralleled by renewed reform of government. In 1776, José de Gálvez became Minister for the Indies and immediately embarked on a grand design for restructuring colonial government. In line with Gálvez's general strategy, Juan Francisco Gutiérrez de Piñeres was appointed Regent of the audiencia of Santa Fe on April 6, 1776; by royal decree of December 23, 1776, he was also invested with the powers of visitor general of the audiencia, treasuries, and various administrations of New Granada and provinces of Tierra Firme. Gutiérrez de Piñeres arrived in Cartagena de Indias on August 20, 1777 and took up his post in Santa Fe de Bogotá in January, 1778.[83] While he embarked on his review and reform of New Granadan government, the central authorities launched *comercio libre*, finally abolishing the Cádiz monopoly and the fleet system, while Spain also went to war, once again, with Britain. Thus, in 1778, political and economic reforms in New Granada converged, just as they had in 1719–20 and in 1739. We will examine political reform and its repercussions later, in Part III. But first we will focus on the implications of Caroline economic policies for New Granada, and try to gauge the effects of *comercio libre* on the territory's trade and economic life.

83. Pablo E. Cárdenas Acosta, *El movimiento comunal de 1781 en el Nuevo Reino de Granada*, 2 vols. (Bogotá, 1960), vol. I, pp. 83–4.

5

Commerce and economy in the age of imperial free trade, 1778–1796

The lynchpin of Caroline economic reform was the *Reglamento de comercio libre* of 1778 which, by providing for greater freedom for trade within the empire, offered the prospect of unlocking the economic potential of the Hispanic world. The main provisions of the *Reglamento* may be briefly stated. First, and most important, it released colonial trade from the constraints of the old commercial system, pivoted on Cádiz and dominated by a privileged oligarchy of Andalusian merchants. In 1778, the Cádiz monopoly was formally ended and henceforth all the major Spanish and Spanish American ports were open to trade with each other. To promote colonial commerce, the *Reglamento* also reduced the many restraints that affected transatlantic shipping and trade. Thus the formalities required to ship cargoes to the Americas were relaxed, several traditional impositions on shipping and trade were abolished, and duties on trade were both standardized and reduced. Steps to enlarge the scale of Spain's trade with its colonies were, moreover, matched by measures to promote trade in Spanish products, so as to stimulate growth and development in metropolitan agriculture and industry. To this end, differential tariffs were placed on exports from Spain to its colonies, forcing foreign products to pay heavier duties than goods made in Spain. Finally, the *Reglamento* reduced tariffs on exports from the colonies to Spain, so that the metropolitan economy might receive a larger, cheaper flow of raw materials and other primary products from the Americas.[1] Under Charles III, the Madrid government also sought to encourage free movement of trade between Spain and her colonies by ending local monopolies, such as those that the *corregidores de indios* exercised over the trade of Indian communities in both Mexico and Peru. In some areas of colonial economic life, state intervention to stimulate colonial production went still further, though not always to the benefit of colonial producers. While the crown actively encouraged production of precious metals and primary commodities that could be exchanged for goods sent from Spain, American products that

---

1. The text of the *Reglamento* is published in Bibiano Torres Ramirez and Javier Ortíz de la Tabla, (eds.), *Reglamento para el comercio libre, 1778* (Seville, 1979).

competed with metropolitan goods (such as the textiles of Quito and Mexico or the wines of Peru and Argentina) were exposed to intense and unprotected competition from imports. Evidently, the aim of Bourbon government was not simply to promote colonial prosperity; it was to turn the colonies into larger, more dependent markets for metropolitan exports, and dedicated suppliers of previous metals and other natural resources.

Designed to benefit Spain by enlarging markets for its agriculture and industry and increasing flows of primary commodities from the colonies, *comercio libre* seems to have succeeded splendidly during the years when Spain avoided involvement in international war. During the long respite between Anglo-Spanish wars from 1782 to 1796, colonial commerce grew rapidly. Exports from Spain to the Americas increased by about 400%, and Spanish producers succeeded in enlarging their share of American markets from 38% in 1778 to an average of 52% for 1782–96. Exports from the American colonies to Spain increased by an even larger amount. Their annual average value in 1782–96 was ten times higher than in 1778. Much of this increase was fueled by additional exports of American treasure, which, at 56% of total American exports still supplied the greater part of colonial returns to Spain. The continuing predominance of treasure returns should not, however, obscure the fact that *comercio libre* stimulated an unprecedented diversification of colonial exports. Closer commercial contacts with Spain opened larger markets for colonial producers of such commodities as sugar, tobacco, cacao, cotton, and dyestuffs, and these trades boomed as never before. In the end, imperial free trade failed to stimulate sufficient growth in manufacturing to convert Spain from an agrarian into an industrial economy, because it favored Spain's agricultural producers more than its industries and reinforced the traditional structure of a colonial commerce in which Spain supplied its colonies with foodstuffs rather than manufactures, and funneled trade mainly through the traditionally dominant port of Cádiz.[2] Liberalization of the colonial commercial system had nonetheless encouraged a remarkable expansion that allowed Spain to take fuller advantage of the markets and resources of its American colonies.

For Spain's colonial subjects *comercio libre* offered less obvious benefits. On the one hand, greater freedom for trade within the empire offered some advantages to American consumers and producers. In the first place, the removal of restrictions on transatlantic trade and traffic opened new trade routes and reduced the power of the mercantile oligopolies that had traditionally controlled the *Carrera de Indias*. By the same token, *comercio*

2. John Fisher, *Commercial Relations between Spain and Spanish America in the Era of Free Trade*, 1778–1796 (Liverpool, 1985), pp. 87–90.

libre pushed down the prices of imports from Europe, to the benefit of the colonial consumer, while offering new opportunities for American producers, for whom freer trade with Spain opened a wider range of potential markets for their exports. This was particularly important for hitherto marginal economies like Cuba, Río de la Plata, and Venezuela, because it offered them the chance to prosper by exporting the products of their plantations and ranches.[3] On the other hand, imperial free trade also had damaging implications for American economic interests in colonies where European imports competed with domestic agriculture and manufactures. For as peninsular traders eager to take advantage of greater commercial freedom flooded American markets with imports from Europe, the consequent fall in their prices reduced local merchants' profits or even forced them out of business; it also damaged colonial agriculture and manufacture by exposing American producers to greater competition from European substitutes. Furthermore, Spanish trade offered relatively small compensating growth in markets for American exports except bullion, so that expansion in transatlantic trade offered few fresh opportunities for export-based growth, while simultaneously draining American economies of their circulating specie. Seen from this perspective, Caroline commercial reform was the effective instrument of a new imperialism that, in the words of John Lynch, "increased the colonial status of Spanish America and intensified its underdevelopment."[4]

Comercio libre and New Granadan trade

To gauge the effects of Bourbon economic policy on late colonial New Granada, we must first consider the impact of commercial reform on the volume of trade with Spain during the years that followed the introduction of *comercio libre*. Here, the repercussions of reform were far from dramatic or immediate, as, no sooner was it inaugurated than the new commercial regime was undermined by the effects of international war. Shortly after news of the reform reached Cartagena in 1778, prices of European goods in the port dropped dramatically, in anticipation of an inrush of imports through the newly deregulated *Carrera de Indias*. This effect was, however, soon reversed, when war with the British disrupted the movement of Spanish shipping in the Atlantic. So, although the prices of European imports in Cartagena fell in 1778 when news of the *Reglamento* first reached the port, the anticipated boom in trade with Spain

---

3. On commercial reform and the trade of these economies, see Allan J. Kuethe, *Cuba, 1753–1815: Crown, Military and Society* (Knoxville, Tennessee, 1986); Tulio Halperín Donghi, *Politics, Economics and Society in Argentina in the Revolutionary Period* (Cambridge, 1975); P. Michael McKinley, *Prerevolutionary Caracas: Politics, Economy and Society, 1777–1811* (Cambridge, 1985).
4. Lynch, *Spanish American Revolutions*, p. 14.

did not materialize.[5] Quite the opposite. Shortly after the war started, Spanish transatlantic trade ground to a halt and the crown had to introduce special wartime measures to keep colonial trade going, by organizing convoys for the Atlantic crossing, offering special insurance facilities through the royal treasury, and, in 1780, permitting neutrals to trade with selected ports in Spanish America.[6] These measures did not improve New Granada's overseas trade. Neutrals were not allowed to enter Cartagena or other New Granadan ports, supply by convoy provided too little, too late, and, by mid-1780, some 2 million pesos were bottled up in Cartagena awaiting shipment to Spain.[7] When Cartagena's trade was finally unblocked, it was not by commerce with Spain, but by permission to trade with foreigners. In March 1781, the crown allowed merchants in Cartagena de Indias to trade with ports of allied and neutral powers, thereby allowing contacts with North American ports and with the French and Dutch colonies in the Caribbean.[8]

It was ironic that the crown should release New Granada from the Spanish monopoly only a couple of years after *comercio libre* had been introduced to strengthen that monopoly; however, the concession to trade with friendly and neutral foreigners was intended only as a temporary deviation from Caroline commercial policy, aimed at helping New Granada's government cope with the vicissitudes of war. For as Viceroy Flóres marshaled defenses at Cartagena during 1780, government expenditures had risen steeply while revenues from trade declined, causing the viceroy serious financial problems. Flóres had therefore pressed the crown to open Cartagena's trade for fiscal reasons, in order to revive customs revenues and persuade Cartagena merchants to make loans to his government.[9] In fiscal terms, the measure quickly proved its worth. Trade with foreigners brought an influx of imports that boosted revenues from the tariff on imported European goods (the *almojarifazgo de entrada de géneros de Castilla*).[10] It also restored confidence among Cartagena merchants who, placated by permission to trade with foreign ports, provided the viceroy with a large loan of half a million pesos, repayable in Havana at the end of the

5. AGI Santa Fe 659 Gutiérrez de Piñeres to Gálvez, April 30, 1779.
6. On the effects of war on the trade of Peru and Río de la Plata, see Villalobos, *El comercio y la crisis colonial*, pp. 99–100; royal efforts to maintain the flow of colonial commerce are described by E. Rodríguez Vicente, "El comercio cubano y la guerra de emancipación norteamericana," *AEA*, vol. 11 (1954), pp. 61–106.
7. When a convoy finally arrived in American waters, it was composed mainly of ships bearing mercury for New Spain; few cargoes went to Cartagena. For its composition, see ibid., p. 81.
8. AGI Indiferente General 1955, Real cédula, March 14, 1781.
9. AGI Santa Fe 593 (ramo 2), Flóres to Gálvez, May 6, 1780; ibid., June 27, 1780.
10. See Appendix C, Table 2.

war.[11] This was, then, a sensible and realistic measure in wartime. It allowed the crown to raise revenues from a trade that would otherwise have been carried by smugglers, and it satisfied both the government and merchants in New Granada. But the measure also had disadvantages for Spain. For the duration of the war, trade between Spain and New Granada was replaced by trade with foreigners, setting a precedent that was to hinder the revival of Spanish commerce in peacetime and thus to blunt the impact of *comercio libre* on New Granada's economic relations with the metropolitan power.

Generally, Spain's colonial commerce expanded rapidly when war ended in 1783, as merchants rushed to take advantage of freer trading facilities and to exploit colonial markets depleted in wartime.[12] Not so in New Granada. Unlike other major ports in Spanish America, Cartagena did not witness a postwar boom in trade with Spain. By mid-1785, few ships had arrived from metropolitan ports, and it was not until late that year that Spanish trade with New Granada showed any sign of expansion.[13] Postwar stagnation was partly the result of the wartime trade with foreigners. In 1784, Madrid had authorized Cartagena merchants to sell off foreign goods legally imported during the war, so they might dispose of the large stocks that they had accumulated.[14] This was not the sole reason for the sluggishness of Spanish trade with the colony during the early years of *comercio libre*, however. More important was the continuation of direct trade with foreigners, a practice that projected into peacetime the patterns of trade built up in war. In 1783 and 1784, most of the shipping entering the port of Cartagena came from foreign rather than Spanish ports. Some traders were using licenses granted in wartime, which the colonial authorities continued to honor; some were specifically authorized to trade with French ports, on the grounds that Spain's ally required aid and assistance after the war; some were even permitted to trade with English ports in the Caribbean, supposedly to provide a cover for gathering military intelligence.[15] So, although the gaps in Spain's commercial monopoly opened

11. AGI Consulados 337, Francisco Simón de Miranda to Tribunal del Consulado, Cartagena, August 11, 1781.

12. Fisher, *Commercial Relations between Spain and Spanish America*, pp. 45–7, 61–2.

13. AGI Santa Fe 605, Caballero y Góngora to Gálvez, July 20, 1785.

14. The presence of these stocks was acknowledged by a royal resolution to the viceroy in 1784 – which allowed merchants to sell foreign goods acquired during the war. AGI Santa Fe 605, Caballero y Góngora to Gálvez, January 15, 1785.

15. For a more detailed consideration of the composition of shipping entering Cartagena in these years, and of the measures allowing trade with foreigners, see Anthony McFarlane, "El comercio exterior del Virreinato de la Nueva Granada: Conflictos en la política económica de los Borbones, 1783–1789," *ACHSC*, vol. 6–7 (1971–2), pp. 70–7, 95–6. An outline of the quantity of foreign shipping, relative to shipping from Spain, entering the port of Cartagena between 1783 and 1790 is given in Appendix C, Table 3.

Table 5.1. *Trade between Cartagena and Spain, 1784–93*

Year	Imports	Exports (pesos)
1784	1,543,648	1,650,525
1785	2,584,896	1,981,733
1786	2,155,797	462,098
1787	1,644,501	4,648,231
1788	3,363,957	2,074,521
1789	2,593,647	2,300,708
1790	1,233,525	2,312,101
1791	1,677,260	2,843,518
1792	1,462,840	1,859,880
1793	1,296,473	919,272
Annual Average	1,955,652	2,105,259

by emergency wartime measures were formally closed when peace returned, in practice the restoration of New Granada's trade to Spanish hands was delayed by government tolerance of legal trade with foreigners.

After 1785, these distortions created by wartime blockade and emergency measures were finally removed, and trade between New Granada and Spain began to respond more freely to the regime of *comercio libre*. The results were clearly reflected in the movement of shipping between Cartagena and the ports of the Peninsula, which increased substantially during the later 1780s and early 1790s.[16] So, too, did the value of imports and exports passing between Spain and Cartagena, as shown by the official records reproduced in Table 5.1.[17] The scale of this commercial expansion can be appreciated by simply comparing the value of imports and exports in this decade with that achieved in the years before *comercio libre*. Before 1778, imports from Spain into Cartagena de Indias were worth about 1 million pesos per year. After 1785, they surged forward, reaching a peak of 3.3 million pesos in 1788 and averaging 1.96 million pesos per year for the decade 1784–93 as a whole. The colony's exports to Spain also increased substantially, averaging 2.1 million pesos per year in 1784–93, a level roughly double that of the average year in 1754–64.

The greater freedom for trade allowed under the regime of *comercio libre* had, then, enlarged Spain's trade with New Granada, bringing a more rapid and substantial growth in the decade after 1785 than at any previous

16. See Appendix C, Table 3 and Table 9. It should be noted that a large proportion of the shipping arriving in Cartagena from Spain continued to come from Cádiz, the traditional extrepôt. For an illustration of the origins of the shipping that sailed to Cartagena from metropolitan ports, see Appendix C, Table 4.

17. AGI Santa Fe 957, Real Aduana de Cartagena de Indias, April 14, 1795.

time in the eighteenth century. How did this growth affect the colony's economy? In his economic history of Colombia, W. P. McGreevey suggests that the policies of Charles III succeeded in stimulating production for export and enlarging the size of the surplus transferred to the metropolis, thereby bringing "the advent of a truly export-oriented economy." McGreevey also argues that New Granada's economy stagnated, despite growth in output and exports, because the surplus generated by growth was taken in taxes that were transferred to Spain.[18] However, if we now examine the performance of New Granada's export and import trade during the late eighteenth century, we will find that this analysis is mistaken. Although Bourbon policy made the colony more open to imports, it did not make New Granada any more obviously export-oriented than it had previously been; moreover, if growth in New Granada's economy was slow and halting, it was not because the crown drained a surplus from the region in taxes (which it did not), but rather because Spain failed to provide markets for the colony's resources.[19]

Bourbon reform and New Granadan mining

Consider, first, the development of New Granada's exports. Did Bourbon policy divert a larger share of the region's mining, agricultural, or raw material resources from the domestic to the metropolitan economy, and did it stimulate greater production for export? Let us start with the mining sector, traditionally the country's principal means of financing external trade. Here, Bourbon policy clearly succeeded in channeling more of New Granada's gold output to Spain. This is plainly reflected in the commercial statistics shown in Table 5.1 and Table 5.2, both of which show an expansion of exports, particularly treasure exports. But, if *comercio libre* allowed Spain to take more of New Granada's gold by increasing the competitiveness of imports from the peninsula, neither Bourbon commercial reform nor direct government intervention at the point of production made any noticeable difference in the structure, scale, or output of New Granada's gold mines.

In the first place, commercial reorganization did not benefit gold mining in New Granada in the same way that it affected silver mining in Mexico. Like the silver produced in New Spain, the gold of New Granada was not marketed directly. The greater part of the colony's gold output was converted into coin, and it was from this stock of specie that Spanish merchants took most of the precious metal that they exported to the peninsula. As producers of a commodity that was processed internally

---

18. William Paul McGreevey, *An Economic History of Colombia, 1845–1930* (Cambridge, 1971), pp. 24–33; quotation from p. 30.
19. The remittance of tax revenues from New Granada to Spain is discussed in Chapter 8.

before export and priced in terms of a bimetallic ratio fixed by the crown, miners did not receive any direct stimulus from the external markets that they supplied; accordingly, changes in demand created by commercial reform had little impact on the pace of mining production. The influence of economic reform on the mining sector must therefore be sought in the effects that it had upon the conditions of production. For it was upon factors affecting the organization of supply – such as the availability of capital, the level of technical knowledge, and the condition of transportation facilities – that the output of precious metal ultimately depended.

In Mexico, the repercussions of commercial reform were transmitted to the silver mining industry indirectly through the changes that *comercio libre* induced in the merchant community. By undermining the privileged position of the merchant oligopolists of Mexico City, the trade reforms encouraged them to shift their funds into other areas of economic activity, including the extraction and processing of silver.[20] There was no comparable movement of mercantile capital into New Granada's mining sector following the *Reglamento* of 1778. Mining was rarely an attractive alternative to commerce, because it was located in frontier areas far from the main centers of colonial society, required substantial investment in slaves, and was difficult to manage successfully from a distance. In a city like Popayán, where wealthy merchants married into the local patriciate, there was probably some movement of capital between mining and commercial enterprises, but this was not typical of conditions in the industry as a whole. There were few substantial fortunes based on mining in New Granada and the rich absentee mineowner of Popayán was an exceptional figure; most gold miners were small operators, living in primitive conditions in the backland regions of the mining frontier, and taking only the small and uncertain profits of the prospector.[21] So long as the merchant was able to obtain gold through exchange and purchase on the open market, he had no good reason to risk his funds in mining itself, and the only investment that merchants put into mining was generally in the form of short-term credit, advanced in the form of goods that were paid for after a few months. In these circumstances, Bourbon officials regarded government intervention as an essential recourse, and they therefore launched a series of projects designed to inject new capital and technology into mining and to improve the conditions of its organization. It is, however,

---

20. David Brading, *Miners and Merchants in Bourbon Mexico*, pp. 116, 130, 152.
21. For contemporary comment on the low level of profits in the mining sector, see the remarks of the oidor Mon y Velarde with regard to Antioquia, in Robledo, *Bosquejo biográfico del Señor Oidor Juan Antonio Mon y Velarde*, tomo 2, p. 66. For general observations on the poverty of the miners, and estimates of the rate of profit, see Pedro Fermín de Vargas, *Pensamientos políticos*, pp. 57–60. Recent estimates of rates of profit among the large mineowners of the Chocó are given by Sharp, *Slavery on the Spanish Frontier*, pp. 171–89.

doubtful that of themselves these plans had any greater effect on mining output than the reforms of *comercio libre*.

Caroline plans to stimulate mining were first signaled in 1777, when the mining severance tax, the *quinto*, was reduced from 5% to 3%. However, leading officials in New Granada remained convinced that the performance of the mining sector lagged far behind its potential, and during the later years of Charles III's reign, they introduced a number of schemes for fostering fresh growth. Here, Archbishop-Viceroy Caballero y Góngora (1782–9) played a leading role. When he first reported to the Minister for the Indies on economic conditions in the colony, he reiterated the old official cliché, that the neglect of "its precious metals and natural riches" was the principal cause of New Granada's backwardness, and called for direct government intervention to promote and diversify mineral exploitation.[22] According to Caballero y Góngora, scarcity of capital and antiquated technology were the main obstacles to growth, and he therefore patronized several schemes for improving investment and working techniques in the mining sector. Some of his schemes – such as those he recommended for the development of iron, copper, lead, and zinc mining – came to nothing; his plans for increasing gold production, on the other hand, led to several government-sponsored projects in New Granada's major mining zones.

The least well-known of these projects was one in which Caballero y Góngora was himself directly involved, through his creation and patronage of the *Real Compañía de Minas y Plantificaciones Industriales de Popayán*. This involved a small group of wealthy citizens from the city of Popayán who, led by Pedro Agustín de Valencia, a prominent mineowner and retired treasurer of the Popayán mint, cooperated with the government in setting up a joint-stock company to exploit the defunct gold and silver mines of Almaguer. In its conception, the scheme was an ambitious one that envisaged the employment of "one or two thousand men or more, partly slaves and partly free men paid at rates appropriate to their skills." To support its mining operations, the company planned to buy pasture land for cattle grazing in the Patía Valley and for raising sheep near Almaguer, using their wool to manufacture crude textiles for the workforce, together with cotton that would also be cultivated on company land. The company also intended to organize the production of basic foodstuffs, such as plantains, maize, rice, and wheat, to feed its mineworkers.[23] To launch the enterprise, seventeen prominent citizens of Popayán gave 22,000 pesos in slaves and money for forty-four 500-peso

---

22. Archivo Restrepo, Correspondencia reservada del Arzobispo-Virrey: Caballero y Góngora to Gálvez, Santa Fe, October 15, 1782 (no. 9).
23. AGI Santa Fe 837, Caballero y Góngora to Valdes, Turbaco, April 8, 1788 (no. 227); Testimonio no. 1, fols. 1–10.

shares, with the Valencia family holding a controlling interest.[24] Pedro Agustín de Valencia held seventeen shares, while his sons Joaquín and Tomás bought another seven between them. Most of the remaining share-holders held only one share each, and the dominant role of the Valencias was strengthened by the fact that at least six of the shareholders were related to them by marriage, or had business connections with Pedro Agustín de Valencia.[25]

The company did not rely on private initiative and private capital alone. The governor of Popayán and the archbishop-viceroy both lent enthusiastic support to the venture and, in addition to four shares bought for the crown by the viceroy, the metropolitan government made an 8,000-peso loan to the company from the colonial treasury. Crown patron-age and financial support, together with a concession of monopoly rights over the minerals of Almaguer, seemed to assure the company of success. By 1789, it had increased its capital to 40,000 pesos, and Caballero y Góngora was convinced that it had a brilliant future.[26] Both the viceroy's and the investors' optimism were eventually confounded.[27] After a few years, the company abandoned the Almaguer concession and shifted its operations to the mines of the Vega de Supía and Quiebralomo, near the town of Anserma in the north of the province.[28] There it was apparently more successful, since work continued until at least 1810. Ultimately, however, the company's contribution to the development of the province's mining sector was insignificant. When the governor of Popayán inspected

24. In 1788, the shareholders and their holdings were listed as follows:

Pedro Augustin de Valencia	17
Rafael de Rebolledo	1
Joaquín de Valencia	2
Joaquín Sánchez Ramirez de Arellano	2
Tomás de Valencia	5
Manuel Bernardo Alvarez	1
Antonio Sánchez Ramírez de Arellano	1
Gregorio de Angulo	1
Ignacio Carvajal	1
Francisco Josef de Quintana	1
Andres Pérez de Arroyo	2
Luis Tadeo Jiménez	1
Juan Antonio de Ibarra	1
Eduardo Alonso de Yllera	1
Josef Martínez de Escobar	2
Augustín Nieto Polo	4

25. These were Alvarez, Angulo, Arroyo, Carvajal, Ibarra, and Rebolledo. Information on their connections with the Valencia family is found in Gustavo Arboleda, *Diccionario Biográfico*, pp. 5, 6, 27, 100, 221, 373, 447–50.
26. Pérez Ayala, *Antonio Caballero y Góngora*, pp. 347–8.
27. A general account of the company's activities is given by Segovia, "Crown Policy and the Previous Metals in New Granada," pp. 75–86.
28. AGI Santa Fe 837, governor of Popayán to crown, August 20, 1794.

his province in 1797, he made disparaging remarks about the condition of its mines generally, and specifically reported that there were few signs of any progress at the company's operations in the Supía area.[29] So, in southern and southwestern New Granada, neither government intervention nor private initiative had changed the conditions under which the mining sector operated. Starved of capital and served by a primitive technology, the growth of its output relied on the extension of the mining frontier, rather than on greater productivity in the exploitation of mineral resources.

Another government project to boost mining production is found in the scheme put forward in 1788 by Oidor Antonio Vicente de Yáñez, during his *visita* of the Chocó. Yáñez argued that exploitation of the Chocó gold mines was impeded by lack of labor and capital, and he decided that this could be alleviated only by government assistance in the provision of the black slaves. His project was very similar to, and probably copied from a scheme advocated some years earlier by the miners of Popayán. In 1781, Vicente Hurtado, an officer of the cabildo of Popayán, had argued that the mines of Popayán, Antioquia, and the Chocó were all underproducing because mineowners had neither the personal capital nor the government financial support required to buy slaves. He therefore suggested that the crown set up a government-managed investment fund for buying slaves, who would then be distributed to the miners on credit, and on terms that they could afford. To provide the capital for this fund, he recommended that the quinto should be levied at the old rate of 5%, and that half the revenues collected should be transferred to a special account for financing slave imports.[30] As the quintos were generally paid by the merchants who traded in gold rather than by the miners themselves, the scheme was evidently an attempt to force gold traders to contribute part of their returns for reinvestment in the process of production. Yáñez's project of 1788 was similar to Hurtado's in both conception and execution, as it sought to stimulate production by providing royal funds to buy 1,500 slaves for distribution to the Chocó miners on favorable credit terms. In the event, the scheme was a miserable failure, for it was launched at the time when gold output in the Chocó was falling, and mineowners were consequently reluctant to expand their enterprises.[31]

A further arena for government intervention in mining was in the province of Antioquia. There, an unusually comprehensive program for promoting exploitation of mineral and agricultural resources was planned

---

29. AGI Santa Fe 623, Informe of the governor of Popayán, December 5, 1797.

30. AGI Santa Fe 836, governor of Popayán, "Informe sobre un proyecto para el común General," Madrid, December 10, 1782.

31. A description of the project and its outcome is given by Sharp, "Slavery on the Spanish Frontier," pp. 472–4.

and partly executed during the 1780s, under the supervision of Juan Antonio Mon y Velarde, oidor of the audiencia of Santa Fe and *visitador* of Antioquia in 1786–8. Traditionally regarded as the first architect of Antioquia's extraordinary rise to economic prominence within Colombia, Mon y Velarde in fact derived many of his ideas from Francisco Silvestre who, during his initial term as governor of the province in 1775–6, drew government attention to the province's rich resources and made positive plans for their exploitation.[32]

According to Silvestre, gold was so "generally found throughout the extent of the territory, that if the population were to correspond in size to those of Peru and New Spain . . . this province alone would over-shadow . . . all the riches which have made those two powerful kingdoms famous."[33] As it was, gold output fell far short of its potential. In high-land mines such as those of Santa Rosa de Osos, lack of water and machin-ery for controlling water supplies meant that ample deposits of alluvial gold could be worked only when it rained, whereas the exhaustion of the best-known deposits meant that miners had to penetrate deeper into the backlands, where it was difficult to maintain either slave gangs or free prospectors. Worse still, the greatest reserves of gold, compared to which the alluvial deposits were mere detritus, were to be found in the "many vein mines that are untouched and neglected, although the stones found on the face of the earth display gold to dazzle the eyes."[34] The legendary mines of Buriticá, which were said to have once yielded 30,000 cas-tellanos per year solely for the upkeep of the soldiers who guarded the slave gangs, were now totally abandoned, and mining had shifted entirely to the alluvions. This Silvestre attributed to a lack of appropriate technical knowledge and to a shortage of capital sufficient to support the kind of enterprise that such mining required. He therefore recommended crown support for mining companies capable of providing both capital and technical expertise, and, as a mark of his confidence in this approach, Silvestre himself formed a company to exploit the veins of Buriticá.

The importance that Silvestre attached to the revival of the vein mines was matched by his concern to find means of stimulating the province's trade. Internally and externally, Antioquia's commerce was hindered by poor transport, by the shortage of circulating specie (reflected in the widespread reliance on credit), and by an onerous system of taxes on trade. To overcome these obstacles, Silvestre made a number of proposals. In the first place, he recognized the need to integrate Antioquia into the larger economy by improving its communications with neighboring regions. He

32. Francisco Silvestre, "Relación que manifiesta el estado de la provincia de Antioquia (1776)," *Archivo Historial* (Manizales, 1917), pp. 569–605.
33. Ibid., p. 572. 34. Ibid., p. 551.

accordingly recommended improving three main routes: to Cartagena by way of Ayapel and the San Jorge River, to give Antioquia a direct outlet to the coast; to the River Magdalena by way of Sonsón and Mariquita, to improve contacts with the main body of New Granada; and, finally, with the gold mines of the Chocó by way of Bebará, to provide links with another mining region. Second, he urged that steps be taken to encourage the inhabitants within the province to clear and maintain trails between their settlements, as this would allow the mining camps easier access to cheaper supplies and broaden the scope of the internal market for the products of agriculture. Third, he recommended that a gold and silver currency be introduced into the province to facilitate exchange and to encourage the extraction of gold from Antioquia. Finally, he suggested lowering duties on interprovincial trade so that merchants would increase their trade with the province, and have fewer incentives for smuggling.[35]

Silvestre's insistence on the need for positive government action to stimulate trade and mining in Antioquia prepared the path for reformist policies in succeeding years. During his inspection of the Viceroyalty of New Granada, *visitador-general* Gutiérrez de Piñeres drew upon Silvestre's reports and recommended that the ex-governor's projects be implemented, adding that Silvestre himself might ideally fulfill the role of the "authorized, active and zealous person who, by his policies and his example, might encourage the miners and stimulate their industry."[36] Silvestre accordingly served a second term as governor in 1782–5, and his proposal for an official inspection of the province and its mines, together with his various schemes for reform, was implemented when Juan Antonio Mon y Velarde was sent to the province in 1786.[37]

When conducting his *visita* of Antioquia between 1786 and 1788, Mon y Velarde echoed many of Silvestre's judgments. He found the inhabitants were generally very poor, agriculture rarely developed beyond subsistence, internal commerce stagnant, and government corrupt and disorganized.[38] To redeem the province from its poverty, Mon y Velarde conducted an energetic campaign to reform its mining industry. As the legal code that regulated operations within the industry was outdated and ignored, Mon y Velarde considered it essential to revise the mining ordinances in order

35. Ibid., pp. 572–99.
36. AGI Santa Fe 837, Gutiérrez de Piñeres to Gálvez, Santa Fe, August 31, 1779 (no. 145).
37. For an account of Silvestre's career, and for a transcription of the report he left at the end of his second term as governor, see Francisco Silvestre, *Relación de la Provincia de Antioquia*, ed. & trans. by David J. Robinson (Medellín, 1988).
38. Robledo, *Bosquejo biográfico del Señor Oidor Juan Antonio Mon y Velarde*, tomo I, pp. 195–196; tomo 2, pp. 143–4.

to clarify the rights and responsibilities of the mining community, and to improve the status of the miners.[39] Here, his primary aim was to control the size of mining claims so that individuals could not take rights to mineral deposits over vast tracts of land simply to prevent their exploitation by others.[40] He also considered government intervention essential for revival of the rich vein mines of Buriticá. Silvestre's company had made no progress there, and Mon y Velarde recommended that the government should transfer to Antioquia the Spanish mining experts who, paid by the crown, were working to revive the silver mines of Mariquita, so that they might restore the gold-workings of Buriticá and regenerate private interest in vein mining.[41]

The visitor's plans for revitalizing mining extended beyond intervention within the industry itself because Mon y Velarde recognized that progress in mining relied on reducing the high costs of production caused by the inflated prices of basic supplies. Antioquia depended on imports of cacao, tobacco, liquor, and textiles from neighboring regions; a high proportion of earnings from the mining sector was consequently absorbed in financing basic consumption, rather than improving production. And, as gold was drained out of the province to pay for imports, Antioquia's potentially rich agricultural resources were neglected. So, to promote the agricultural production required to support a healthy mining industry and to transform the peasantry into prosperous, tax-paying subjects of the crown, Mon y Velarde implemented several measures aimed at increasing food production and facilitating trade within the province.[42] In the major towns, such as Santa Fe de Antioquia, Medellín, and Rionegro, he established committees, called *juntas de agricultura,* composed of prominent officials and a local representative, and charged them with finding means to improve agricultural production.[43] Because much of the land around the main towns was concentrated in the hands of large landowners who left it uncultivated or forced the peasants to pay high rents, the population tended to scatter into the surrounding countryside, where they eked out their subsistence on the frontier. To increase commercial food production, he sought to regroup these outlying farmers into village communities, where production could be organized to supply the mining camps

39. AHA Minas tomo 357, mss. 6706. "Testimonio del expediente formado para el arreglo de las ordenanzas de minas compuesto de varios oficios de algunos sujetos que se hallan con conocimiento de las minas" (1788).
40. Robledo, *Bosquejo biográfico del Señor Oidor Juan Antonio Mon y Velarde,* tomo 2, pp. 65–7, 365–7.
41. Ibid., pp. 354–5.
42. For a full discussion of the province's agriculture in the eighteenth century, see Twinam, *Merchants, Miners and Farmers,* pp. 91–109.
43. Robledo, *Bosquejo biográfico del Señor Oidor Juan Antonio Mon y Velarde,* tomo 2, pp. 116–18, 126.

with essential foodstuffs; he also attempted to encourage farmers to cultivate cacao, tobacco, and cotton, to obviate the need for imports.[44]

Another key element in Mon y Velarde's plans to advance the commercialization of Antioquia's resources was his scheme for introducing a silver currency into the province, to ensure that more gold could be exported without demonetizing the region. Silver was virtually unknown in Antioquia and, because the province had no mint, gold coins were extremely scarce; the main medium for local exchange was simply the untreated gold dust taken from the region's rivers. This was, however, an unsatisfactory form of money. Gold dust was primarily used in exchanges between miners and the merchants who supplied them with imports and, because it was cheap relative to imported goods, it tended constantly to flow out of the area into surrounding regions, depriving Antioquia of a source of exchange for internal payments. Without an alternative form of currency, local wages and transactions had to be paid by barter and credit, both of which slowed the functioning of a market economy and deprived the government of tax revenues. The use of gold dust as a medium of exchange also robbed the crown of revenues by reducing the amount of gold that passed through official channels for smelting and coining.[45] Mon y Velarde therefore insisted that a silver currency was crucial both to the economic development of the province and to the fiscal interests of the crown. Consequently, an agreement was made with a group of merchants engaged in trade between Antioquia and the exterior to buy some 25,000 pesos' worth of silver money from the colonial mints for transfer to Santa Fe de Antioquia, where they would be paid an equivalent value, plus a premium, in gold.[46] By injecting a silver currency into the region, Mon y Velarde sought to overcome the problem that affected New Granada's economy as a whole, but hit the mining regions particularly hard: namely, the tendency for gold to flow out of the region, leaving it without specie and deflating the local economy.

Although Mon y Velarde's reforms in Antioquia were much more comprehensive than those used to promote mining in Popayán and the Chocó, their impact on mining output was probably equally limited. For in spite of Mon y Velarde's efforts, the mining code remained a dead letter, gold dust continued to be the main currency of Antioquia, and twenty years after the *visita* a contemporary observer found the mining sector was still

---

44. Ibid., pp. 13–25, 329–330, 350–4, 357–8.
45. AHA Colonia, Hacienda tomo 747, mss. 11988.
46. AHA Colonia, Libros tomo 466, mss. 584. "Expediente sobre elecciones de los Diputados del Comercio de esta ciudad y jurisdicción de Antioquia . . . y order del Virrey para que se establezca oro y plata acuñada en esta provincia" (1788).

short of adequate supplies, capital, and technical expertise.[47] In Antioquia, as in the other gold-bearing zones of New Granada, neither government intervention nor commercial reorganization had any substantial impact on production. Growth had begun long before the policy changes of the late eighteenth century, and its rhythms were little affected by policies for providing slave labor or improving mining technology. The real success of Bourbon policy lay not in increasing either the production or productivity of the mining industry, but in drawing on its growth to increase crown revenues and to enlarge imports from Spain. At the end of the eighteenth century, officially registered gold output in New Granada had grown enormously since the beginning of the century, but government had played a negligible role in this expansion. Mining also remained essentially unchanged at the point of supply: it was still an industry of scattered mining camps dispersed on isolated frontiers that focused almost exclusively on the production of gold. Meanwhile, attempts in the late eighteenth century to develop New Granada's other mineral resources, with crown-financed projects to revive silver mining in Mariquita, to control the Muzo emerald fields, and to exploit deposits of platinum were also costly failures.[48]

Export diversification and expansion

Government attention to developing New Granadan resources for export was not confined to mining, however, and to gauge the effects of Bourbon policy on the colony's production we must also consider the development of nonmineral exports during the years of *comercio libre*. Official interest in promoting exploitation of a wider range of New Granada's resources did not begin with *comercio libre*. During the 1770s, leading colonial officials agreed that New Granada's economic progress depended on developing an "active" trade, thus reducing reliance on gold as a means for financing imports. In 1772, for example, Moreno y Escandón had suggested that

47. José Manuel Restrepo, "Ensayo sobre la Geografía, Producciones, Industria y Población de la Provincia de Antioquia en el Nuevo Reino de Granada," in Francisco José de Caldas (ed.), *Semanario del Nuevo Reino de Granada* (1808–1810).

48. For the viceroys' accounts of these projects, see Pérez Ayala, *Antonio Caballero y Góngora*, pp. 348–52, and Posada and Ibáñez, *Relaciones de mando*, pp. 343–8, 500–4. The background to the silver mining project is discussed in Arthur Whitaker, "The Elhuyar Mining Mission and the Enlightenment," *HAHR*, vol. 31 (1951), pp. 558–83. Its results in New Granada are discussed in detail in Bernardo J. Caycedo, *D'Elhuyar y el siglo XVIII Neogranadino* (Bogotá, 1971), pp. 123–258, and in Sandra Montgomery Keelan, "The Bourbon Mining Reform in New Granada, 1784–1796," in Fisher, Kuethe, and McFarlane, *Reform and Insurrection*, pp. 41–53. For accounts of the platinum project, see Segovia, "Crown policy and the Previous Metals in New Granada," pp. 93–113; also Sharp, *Slavery on the Spanish Frontier*, pp. 51–4.

the crown should grant monopoly trading rights to a Spanish company to exploit Santa Marta's dyewood trade; in 1776, Viceroy Guirior recommended free trade with foreign colonies as a means of finding markets for New Granada's agricultural production. In the event, such schemes were superseded by the reforms of the *Reglamento de comercio libre,* but colonial officials continued to promote plans for diversifying New Granada's exports, with government projects to stimulate the development of exports in four main products: cotton, cacao, cinchona bark, and dyewood.

The export of hides also showed a slight tendency to expand, but even at its peak it was so small that it does not merit detailed examination.[49] When hides were shipped to Spain, they were generally used as ballast, and their export had no appreciable effect on the agricultural activities of the regions from whence they came. Of far greater importance was cotton, drawn mainly from the province of Cartagena.

In the 1760s and 1770s, Bourbon government became interested in developing American cotton exports to provide raw materials for Spain's cotton textile industry. Thus, in 1766, American raw cotton exports were freed from duty, while in 1768, 1770, and 1771, increasingly strict restrictions were imposed on the import into Spain of foreign cotton cloth.[50] Before 1778, none of these measures had any appreciable effect on New Granadan trade in raw cotton.[51] Then, following the introduction of *comercio libre,* the trade showed a striking increase. After 1785, average annual exports of cotton to Spain were about ten times larger than before the introduction of *comercio libre,* and in the early 1790s they were still growing.[52] Seen in perspective, however, the growth in cotton exports had little impact on New Granada's economy. The effects of the trade were mainly felt in the province of Cartagena, where cotton for export was cultivated among the small towns and villages near the coast, and where the planting, processing, and transport of the crop provided a new source of employment.[53] A report made to the governor of Cartagena in 1794 stated that cotton was the province's only export crop, giving work to "a

---

49. See Appendix C, Table 5.

50. Richard Herr, *The Eighteenth Century Revolution in Spain* (Princeton, 1958), p. 140.

51. During the 1770s, cotton exports from New Granada were very small. In 1770, for example, only 2,573 arrobas of cotton were shipped to Spain; in 1775, only 1,801 arrobas. (Figures calculated from ships' papers for those years, in AGI Contratación 2654, ramos 1–5; Contratación 2661, ramos 1–4; Contratación 2662). The response to the tariff concession of 1768 was so feeble that in 1773 the crown ordered the governor of Cartagena to bring it to the attention of agriculturalists in the province (AHNC Aduanas [Cartas] tomo 3, fol. 399).

52. See Appendix C, Table 6.

53. AHNC Aduanas, tomo 13, fol. 377; AHNC Aduanas tomo 22, fols. 617–20. See also the comments of two contemporary observers in S. E. Ortíz, *Escritos de dos economistas coloniales,* pp. 73–74, 229.

mass of poor people who have dedicated themselves to its cultivation."[54] It had not, however, engendered any great prosperity. Farmers sold their crops partly for money and partly for clothing, but their labors earned little more than a bare subsistence, punctuated by periods of deprivation between harvests. Some raw cotton from the interior, cultivated in the hot lands around Girón, also began to find a market in Spain during the 1790s.[55] Impressed by the North American example, contemporary observers frequently commented on the possibilities for developing large-scale cotton exports as a means of stimulating the New Granadan economy. However, as so often happened, expectation exceeded achievement. Although cotton became the colony's single largest export commodity after gold, and made the most important contribution toward diversifying an external balance of exchange dominated by gold, it hardly touched the surface of New Granada's agrarian economy and society. Cultivation for export temporarily varied the pattern of subsistence agriculture in the rural economy of the coastal region bordering the Caribbean, but the poor quality of the crop prevented it from establishing a firm foothold in overseas markets.[56] Meanwhile, cotton cultivation in the interior remained chiefly in the hands of peasant farmers, who produced it to manufacture crude textiles for the domestic market.

Better access to Spanish markets under the new commercial regime also appears to have encouraged expansion of the cacao trade through Cartagena during the 1780s and early 1790s.[57] But here, too, the growth of exports was relatively slight and did not stimulate any significant expansion of production. Indeed, expansion of Cartagena's cacao exports after 1785 owed more to a change in trade routes, caused by official policies in Venezuela, than it did to any substantial growth of demand for New Granada's cacao. The colony's most important cacao-producing region was located in the valleys of Cúcuta, which had long exported part of its crop through ports in Venezuela. Thus, when the intendant-general in Caracas imposed a 5,000 *fanega* ceiling on cacao exports from Maracaibo to Veracruz in 1785, New Granadan cacao producers lost a major outlet for their cacao. According to the cabildo of Pamplona, which immediately protested to the viceroy on behalf of Cúcuta producers, the Maracaibo trade was so important that the restrictions had caused a sharp fall in the

---

54. AGI Santa Fe 643, Sindico procurador general Manuel de Otoya to governor of Cartagena, May 9, 1794.
55. Pedro Fermin de Vargas, *Pensamientos Políticos*, p. 14.
56. One great difficulty was in cleaning the cotton prior to export overseas. This remained a problem during the nineteenth century, when efforts were still being made to promote the export of cotton. See Guillermo Wills, *Observaciones sobre el comercio de la Nueva Granada, con un apéndice relativo al de Bogotá (1831)* (Bogotá, 1952), pp. 19–22.
57. See Appendix C, Table 7.

price of local cacao and led to the loss of much of the season's crop. The cabildo duly warned that if the Venezuelan authorities did not rescind the measure, New Granada would lose the Mexican silver paid for cacao, and the producers would have to cut production, since Spain was incapable of taking even half of the 8,000 *fanegas* normally sent each year to Maracaibo.[58] But despite supporting recommendations from the fiscal of the audiencia in Bogotá, the restrictions were not lifted.[59] In 1788, the hacendados of the Cúcuta valleys were still trying to find an alternative outlet that would allow them to sidestep the obstacles to trade through Maracaibo. They suggested that the crown open the Orinoco and its tributaries so that they might trade with Spain and Mexico via the port of Guayana.[60] Again, officials pressed their claim with both the viceroy and with the metropolitan government, but the project was stillborn.[61] Thus, the apparent expansion of cacao exports to the metropolis during the 1780s may in fact conceal a decline in the New Granadan production of the crop, due to the loss of intercolonial markets. Certainly Pedro Fermín de Vargas, writing in 1791, was convinced that this was so. He recorded that cacao production in Cúcuta had declined directly as a result of the restrictions on trade through Maracaibo.[62] Further confirmation of the failure of *comercio libre* to expand New Granada's cacao trade is also found in comments made by Viceroy Ezpeleta in 1794, when he argued that internal duties on cacao, combined with high costs of transport, raised its price to levels that could not compete with prices of producers in other colonies.[63]

During the viceregency of Archbishop-Viceroy Caballero y Góngora, government action encouraged a brief but conspicuous expansion in the export of cinchona and dyewood, two previously neglected commodities. Of the two, cinchona was less important in terms of volume and value exported. Trade in this commodity does, however, offer an interesting example of a typically Bourbon economic intervention, in which the government sought to turn the eighteenth-century vogue for scientific inquiry to the practical advantage of both the metropolitan economy and the royal treasury. In New Granada, schemes for the development of

---

58. AHNC Aduanas tomo 1, fols. 366–99. Cabildo of Pamplona to viceroy, August 30, 1785.
59. Ibid., fols. 372–3. Fiscal to viceroy, May 31, 1786.
60. AHNC Aduanas (Cartas) tomo 9, fols. 658–60.
61. AHNC Aduanas (Cartas) tomo 4, fols. 469–73. Francisco Silvestre also recommended the scheme in his report on the viceroyalty: see Silvestre, *Descripción*, p. 61. Viceroy Caballero y Góngora thought it sufficiently worthy of royal attention to include it as a project for consideration in his *relación de mando:* see Pérez Ayala, *Antonio Caballero y Góngora*, p. 360. The fact that it was not put into operation is shown by the repetition of the recommendation in the 1790s: see Pedro Fermín de Vargas, *Pensamientos políticos*, p. 30).
62. Pedro Fermín de Vargas, *Pensamientos políticos*, p. 56.
63. AGI Santa Fe 643, Ezpeleta to Gardoqui, October 19, 1794.

cinchona exports began with research carried out by the Botanical Expedition, the natural history survey launched by Archbishop-Viceroy Caballero y Góngora and backed by royal patronage in 1783.[64] Directed by the Spanish scientist José Celestino Mutis, the expedition was commissioned to investigate the environment of New Granada and to classify its flora and fauna. Its purpose was not purely academic, however. Mutis had long been interested in discovering and developing natural resources of economic value, and the botanists under his direction showed a strong interest in plants that could be turned to profitable commercial use. Archbishop-Viceroy Caballero y Góngora shared this interest and, when the expedition found three different kinds of cinchona, he was quick to exploit botanical research for commercial and fiscal ends. Samples were sent to Spain, and the archbishop-viceroy subsequently undertook to develop a trade in the drug on behalf of the treasury, under direct management by royal officials. The archbishop-viceroy planned to develop the trade through the machinery of a state marketing monopoly that would buy the commodity in the colony at fixed prices, pay for its transport to Spain, and organize its sale in metropolitan markets. The surge of cinchona exports (27,000 *arrobas* between 1785 and 1788) was brief, however, and Caballero y Góngora's ambitions could not be fully realized.[65] Bedeviled by poor organization, lack of government interest in Spain, and the competition of cinchona exports for Guayaquil, the project slowly faded, leaving little trace on the colony's economy.[66]

Government intervention to promote exports was far more successful in stimulating the trade in *palo de tinte*, a dyewood from the provinces of Santa Marta and Río Hacha that produced a red dye akin to that of logwoods from Brazil and Central America. During the 1770s, various proposals had been made for developing these strategically important but sparsely populated provinces, but it was in 1778 that Antonio de Narváez y la Torre, then governor of Santa Marta, presented the first plan for developing an export trade in the "brasil wood" that was found in abundance in the province.[67] In 1784, the viceroy was ordered to investigate the scheme and to consider practical means of putting it into operation; as a result, a government agency was set up to develop the dyewood trade.

For the crown, the project held several advantages. First, it promised to

---

64. Florentino Vezga, *La Expedición Botánica* (Bogotá, 1936), pp. 26–33.

65. AGI Santa Fe 957, "Resumen en un Quatrenio de las embarcaciones que han salido de este Puerto de Cartagena para los de la Peninsula desde el año de 1785 hasta el de 1788."

66. For contemporary comment on the failure of the cinchona *estanco*, see Nariño's "Ensayo sobre un nuevo plan de administración en el Nuevo Reino de Granada," in Antonio Nariño, *Escritos políticos* (Bogotá, 1982), pp. 18–19. See also Wills, *Observaciones sobre el comercio de la Nueva Granada*, p. 25.

67. Ortíz, *Escritos de dos economistas coloniales*, pp. 26–7, 52.

check foreign encroachment in a strategic area and to broaden exploitation of colonial resources. Second, the development of the dyewood trade offered a means to provide the metropolis with a valuable raw material that might otherwise fall into the hands of foreign interlopers. Finally, if Narváez y la Torre's reasoning was correct, then the trade would also discourage British penetration into Spanish territory in Central America by undercutting the British logwood trade with Campeche. However, although the crown undoubtedly appreciated the long-term benefits that the metropolis might derive from the development of Santa Marta's dyewood, the most effective and immediate impulse to action came from the urgent financial needs of the colonial government in New Granada. In 1783, the archbishop-viceroy had been ordered to reaffirm Spanish sovereignty over the disputed area of the Darién coast, and, to achieve this goal, he was instructed to mount a military expedition to pacify the area and to prepare it for colonization by white settlers. The order was made at a time when there was no naval force in Cartagena, when the *situado* had been suspended, and when the colonial treasury, already strained by the expense of wartime defense incurred in the preceding years, was having to repay large loans taken from the Cartagena merchants during the war. Thus, without special provision of troops, ships, or money, the high cost of the expedition – more than 1 million pesos – and most of its manpower had to come from within the colony itself.[68]

Faced with this extraordinary fiscal burden, Archbishop-Viceroy Caballero y Góngora seized upon the scheme for developing dyewood exports as a means of financing Darién colonization. He had already licensed a Catalan merchant, Gerardo de Oligos, to export dyewood from Santa Marta to the foreign colonies of the Caribbean, and to bring in return supplies of gunpowder, flour, and other provisions for the military establishment in Cartagena.[69] In 1785, he went a step further, and recommended the organization of an *estanco de palo tinte,* or royal monopoly for the dyewood trade.[70] At first, the proposal for an *estanco* met with an

68. Pérez Ayala, *Antonio Caballero y Góngora*, pp. 366–8. An account of the expedition is given by Manuel Luengo Muñoz, "Génesis de las expediciones militares al Darién en 1785–86," *AEA,* vol. 18 (1961), pp. 333–416.

69. Gerardo de Oligos was a Barcelona merchant who had arrived in Santa Marta in 1777 and become closely involved in trading with the foreign colonies during the 1779–83 war. With the continuation of this trade after the war, he was shown special favor by the viceroy, who personally protested to the Dutch authorities when Oligos was cheated by some Curacao merchants (AGI Santa Fe 552 *Informe* of Francisco Machado on letter of Caballero y Góngora, November 20, 1787). In 1784, Oligos was granted a special license to export colonial products to the foreign colonies due to the lack of Spanish shipping in Santa Marta (AHNC Aduanas [Cartas] tomo 5, fols. 1164–5). In 1785, he received the contract to export dyewood to the colonies and when he died the business passed to his son, Pablo Oligos, who continued to trade from Santa Marta (AHNC Aduanas [Anexo], tomo 14, fols. 617–46).

70. AGI Santa Fe 603, viceroy to Gálvez, Cartagena, December 24, 1785.

unfavorable reception in Madrid, due to opposition from Spanish mercantile interests. A group of Cádiz merchants with connections in Cartagena de Indias had recently become interested in the dyewood trade and, jealous of its interests, it sought to sabotage the archbishop-viceroy's plans for government intervention. As a result of the merchants' machinations, Archbishop-Viceroy Caballero y Góngora received a royal order in 1784 rebuking him for the concessions made to the Catalan Oligos, and directing him to allow the Conde de Prasca and other Cádiz merchants to export the commodity to Spain without hindrance from the Catalan contractor.[71] Nevertheless, in the light of the new financial pressures generated by the Darién expedition, the archbishop-viceroy thought himself justified in subordinating private commercial interests to those of the crown and he simply pushed on with his scheme for establishing an *estanco de palo tinte*. In May 1786, he commissioned the fiscal of the audiencia of Santa Fe, Don Antonio Vicente de Yáñez, to visit the province of Santa Marta and Río Hacha in order to investigate the state of the local treasury, to eliminate fraud and contraband, and to set up the dyewood monopoly.[72] By October, Caballero y Góngora was able to make out a more detailed case for establishing an *estanco,* arguing that the Conde de Prasca and his associates had misinformed the crown when they presented their case against government intervention in the trade.[73] He pointed out that the extensive contraband practiced in this region, the need to pacify the Guajira Indians, and the financial requirements of the Darién expedition all made it essential that the royal treasury take advantage of the extraordinary demand of the neighboring colonies for brasil-wood. In fact, while the archbishop-viceroy was still making his case, Yáñez had already put the scheme into operation, ordering those who held dyewood within the jurisdiction of Cartagena to sell their stocks to government warehouses within fifteen days.[74] Because the leading historian of Santa Marta has mistakenly stated that the scheme never became operational, it is worth giving a brief account of its history.[75]

   In its original form, the scheme was a simple one. The colonial administration merely interposed itself between the dyewood cutters and the merchant exporters. There were no restrictions on cutting the wood, provided that it was sold to government storehouses at a fixed price of 5 pesos per *carga;* the *estanco* then sold it to merchants, at 5 pesos per

71. José María Ots Capdequí, *Nuevos aspectos del siglo XVIII español en América* (Bogotá, 1946), pp. 344–5.

72. AHNC Miscelanea (Colonia), tomo 73, fols. 527–8, Caballero y Góngora, Turbaco May 7, 1786.

73. AGI Santa Fe 957, Caballero y Góngora to Marqués de Sonora, Turbaco October 19, 1786.

74. AHNC Aduanas tomo 10, fols. 34–6.

75. Ernesto Restrepo Tirado, *Historia de la Provincia de Santa Marta,* 2 vols. (Seville, 1929), vol. 2, p. 262.

quintal. By manipulating buying and selling prices, the *estanco* was to meet its own administrative costs, while its profits were to cover the expenses of the Darién expedition.[76] Caballero y Góngora blithely assured the Minister for the Indies that the local inhabitants welcomed the new arrangement because it offered them a guaranteed market for the dyewood, while freeing them from dependence on the few rich Cartagena and Santa Marta merchants who monopolized the province's commerce. Instead of the advances of goods made by the merchants and their agents to the cutters at excessively high prices, the government monopoly made all payments in cash and this, the archbishop-viceroy argued, would provide the cutters with good wages and stimulate the province's economy by injecting it with cash.[77] Caballero y Góngora freely admitted that Spanish merchants resented the monopoly, but argued that they would eventually be reconciled, because the new system would enable them to buy at one wharf all the dyewood that they desired without having to place their funds and commercial reputations in the hands of agents and shippers. And, as the commodity sold for between 18 and 20 pesos per *quintal* in Cádiz, they were left with a reasonable profit margin.[78]

The interests of both cutters and merchants were, of course, incidental to the archbishop-viceroy's main purpose. For Caballero y Góngora, the *estanco* was crucial to his plans for financing the Darién expedition, and this led to more direct government involvement in the dyewood trade than had originally been envisaged. In 1787, the government ceased to be a mere intermediary in the trade and became an active participant in dyewood exports; in so doing, it opened a direct channel of exchange with the newly independent United States of America. Indeed, the archbishop-viceroy closely supervised the trade through an agent engaged specifically

76. According to the viceroy's plan, dyewood was to be bought at the fixed price of 5 pesos per *carga*, and then sold to merchants at 5 pesos per *quintal*. By means of this operation, the royal treasury was to receive a double profit. One *carga* equalled 10 *arrobas* and 10 *libras*, or 260 *libras*; one *quintal* equalled 4 *arrobas* or 100 *libras*. Thus, for every 2 1/2 *quintals* sold, there was a saving of 10 *libras*, which as the viceroy calculated, produced another *quintal* with every 10 *cargas* that were marketed. Thus the treasury not only made a gain of 15 pesos per *carga* from the difference between the buying and selling price, but it also received a concealed profit of 8 pesos in every ten *cargas* handled by its storehouses. Caballero y Góngora expressed the naive hope that both cutters and merchants would be deceived by this device of imposing different measures for buying and selling. Indeed, he anticipated that the profit from this maneuver would be sufficient to pay the salaries of the *estanco* employees, while leaving the ordinary profits as a clear gain for the crown.

77. In his *relación de mando*, the viceroy repeated this charge, stating that only "four or six merchants" exported dyewood from Santa Marta, and that "they pay the cutters for it at base prices in dry goods and overpriced merchandise": Pérez Ayala, *Antonio Caballero y Góngora*, p. 379. The same argument had been put forward by Yáñez during his *visita*: AHNC Milicias y Marina, tomo 131, fol. 230.

78. AGI Santa Fe 957, Caballero y Góngora to Marqués de Sonora, Turbaco October 19, 1786.

for that purpose. Salvador de los Monteros, whom the archbishop-viceroy had previously employed to export naval supplies from Jamaica to New Granada, was sent to New York to obtain both supplies and colonists for the Darién expedition.[79] In New York, Monteros organized trade with the partnership of Lynch and Stoughton, paying an interest rate of 7% on the varying periods of credit that were offered to him and a 5% commission to the American agents on the merchandise acquired.[80] Supplies from the United States were taken in North American vessels to New Granada, where the ships were loaded with colonial products for the return journey. Some cargoes of cotton and hides were taken by the North Americans, but the main export was dyewood, destined to be sold directly to the Americans by the royal administration. These commodities were carried from New Granada to New York and Philadelphia, where they were stored by Monteros while he arranged for their sale in the United States, or their shipment to London and Amsterdam.

The scheme did not always work smoothly, and Monteros's correspondence with the archbishop-viceroy illustrates some of the problems that affected the export of New Granadan products. The archbishop-viceroy's determination that the scheme should be self-financing created periodic liquidity problems for his agent, who found that New Granada's exports to the United States needed careful marketing. In 1788, Monteros acknowledged that the dyewoods, cotton, and hides that were reaching him were all profitable items, but noted that they had to be sold gradually to maintain their prices. He also encountered difficulties due to discontinuity between sales and payments. In the same year, he complained that business was often held up because he could not pay the shippers who had completed the round trip; this not only made him unpopular with the carriers but also involved extra expense, as he had to pay interest to his suppliers. He therefore requested that the archbishop-viceroy send money and goods so that he might meet outstanding debts and deal promptly with the freight charges.[81] By the end of 1788, this problem had become more acute. While awaiting a cash return from consignments of dyewood that he had sent to London and Amsterdam, Monteros was faced with the pressing demands of his creditors in New York. But, because there was an inelastic demand for dyewood in North American ports, the sudden arrival from New Granada of a batch of dyewood cargoes had seriously depressed the price of the product, thus making it even more difficult for

79. In January 1787, Salvador de los Monteros informed the viceroy that he had left Jamaica and was in Port au Price, en route to New York: AHNC Aduanas (Anexo), tomo 11, fols. 4–14.

80. Ibid., fols. 60, 70, 127, 458.

81. Ibid., tomo 14, fols. 909–11. Monteros to viceroy, New York, May 21, 1788.

Monteros to pay his debts.[82] Indeed, there were signs that the market for dyewood was approaching saturation, and Monteros warned that it was becoming increasingly difficult to obtain a good price for dyewood in any accessible market.[83] However, by this time the dyewood *estanco* and trade had served a valuable fiscal purpose for the crown. In 1788 alone, exports of approximately 86,693 *arrobas* of dyewood to North American ports were recorded, an amount that, in terms of volume, was about three times as large as the total amount of cotton (which was then New Granada's largest agricultural export) sent to Spain.[84] And, although revenues from this trade certainly did not solve all the archbishop-viceroy's financial problems, they did produce revenues at a time when, in the wake of the Comunero rebellion, government finances were in disarray.

If the archbishop-viceroy's deviation from the orthodox tenets of Spanish mercantilism demonstrated the fiscal potential of a more flexible commercial policy and appeared to vindicate those officials who argued that trade with foreigners was a means of stimulating exploitation of New Granada's agricultural resources and raw materials, it was not to be a precedent for greater commercial freedom and export growth. One problem was that, after 1788, the dyewood trade suffered a sharp contraction as it encountered the problem that so often faced primary exports from the colonies: a tendency for supply to outrun demand. By allowing voluminous exports onto the market within the short space of two years, Archbishop-Viceroy Caballero y Góngora had reduced the price of New Granadan dyewood in overseas markets and thus undermined his own *estanco* experiment. In 1789, the government's dyewood monopoly was suppressed and the trade returned to private hands.[85] It did not revive, however, as falling prices discouraged the merchants of Cartagena from taking up Archbishop-Viceroy Caballero y Góngora's state-sponsored initiative.[86]

Another, more serious problem derived from government efforts to promote exports through trade with foreigners: it opened new channels for contraband imports. Even before the dyewood trade with the ports of North America had been fully established, the merchants of Cartagena had complained that contraband through Santa Marta had become so

82. Ibid., fols. 993–4. Monteros to viceroy, New York, September 1, 1788.
83. AHNC Aduanas (Anexo), tomo 14, fols. 944–6. Monteros to viceroy, New York, September 12, 1788.
84. Ibid., fols. 417–8, 892–3, 885–6, 925, 931, 935–7, 940–1, 987. The amount of dyewood exported to North America in 1788 exceeded the total quantity sent to Spain in the four years from 1785 to 1788. In that period, some 69,348 *arrobas* of dyewood were exported to Spain, an average annual export of 17,704 arrobas (AGI Santa Fe 957, "Resumen de un Quatrenio . . .").
85. AGI Santa Fe 957, Gil y Lemus to Valdés, Cartagena, February 28, 1789.
86. AGI Santa Fe 957, Tomas Pérez de Arroyo to crown, Madrid, July 11, 1791; Agustin Gnecco to crown, Madrid, November 19, 1793.

considerable that it was undermining the market for their legal imports.[87] They therefore appealed to the crown to prohibit all contacts with foreigners, on the grounds that it was ruining legal trade. An official inquiry held in 1785 confirmed this view. For, when investigating the volume of foreign shipping that had entered Cartagena since the end of the Anglo-Spanish War in 1783, it found that the special licenses issued by the archbishop-viceroy for trade with the foreign colonies had turned a wartime expedient into a continuous traffic, and had created a substantial and growing contraband trade through the ports of Santa Marta and Río Hacha.[88] These ports, it was said, had become the focal points for contraband on the coasts of New Granada, and illicit trading had reached the point where most kinds of dry goods could be obtained more cheaply through smuggling than in Cádiz itself. Estimating that at least 3 million pesos' worth of cloth and other goods had been illegally imported through Santa Marta and Río Hacha since the end of the war, the report concluded that contact with foreigners was badly damaging metropolitan trade with the colony and should therefore be suppressed.[89] While Caballero y Góngora was in office, this advice was largely ignored; the dyewood trade sheltered contraband trading with North Americans, and licenses given for trade in slaves and provisions led to an expanding contraband commerce with the British in Jamaica. Determined to raise revenues for the Darién project, the archbishop-viceroy chose to ignore these side effects of his policies. However, among the merchants who organized New Granadan commerce with Spain they provoked increasingly vociferous protest, and after the end of the archbishop's viceregency in 1789, his successors brought commercial policy back onto a conventional path, one that was primarily directed toward protecting markets for Spanish imports.

Bourbon economic policy did not, then, succeed in making New Granada a markedly more export-oriented economy, geared to supplying metropolitan Spain with a larger, more diverse range of its resources. By 1793, the character of the colony's commerce remained substantially unchanged, showing only a slight tendency to diversify its composition. As Table 5.2 indicates, gold remittances continued to account for over 90% of the value of New Granadan exports to Spain during the late eighteenth century, and diversification in the export sector was minimal.[90] Exports of cacao, cotton, dyewoods, and similar products were larger than they had been before *comercio libre*, but they still formed only a minor part of total exports. Whereas their value was measured in thousands of pesos, that of gold taken overseas was measured in millions.

87. AHNC Aduanas tomo 2, fols. 323–31.   88. Ibid., fols. 333–9, 351–3.
89. AHNC Real Hacienda, tomo 8, fols. 412–14.
90. AGI Santa Fe 957, Real Aduana de Cartagena de Indias, April 14, 1795.

Table 5.2 *Exports from Cartagena to Spain, 1784–93*

Year	Precious metals (pesos)	Commodities (pesos)
1784	1,570,217	80,308
1785	1,817,098	164,635
1786	372,156	89,942
1787	4,424,081	224,150
1788	1,939,462	135,059
1789	2,114,290	186,418
1790	2,108,328	203,773
1791	2,558,245	285,273
1792	1,634,037	225,845
1793	671,117	248,155
Annual average	1,920,903	184,157
Percentage	91	9

The reorganization of colonial commerce by the *Reglamento de comercio libre* had evidently left unaltered the "passive" pattern that had long characterized New Granada's trade. The outflow of the colony's growing gold output to Spain had increased to pay for imports from the metropolis, but the export of agricultural products and raw materials had grown only slightly. Moreover, Caballero y Góngora's projects for developing new exports had quickly run into serious obstacles. Spanish markets for New Granadan products like cacao, cotton, hides, and cinchona bark were too small to sustain substantial new economic activity, whereas exploitation of foreign markets for dyewood damaged Spanish trade by allowing foreigners to enter New Granada's ports, and thus to conduct a contraband commerce that competed with Spanish imports into the colony. Developing New Granada's exports within the confines of the Spanish monopoly was, in short, distinctly problematical. Spain's markets offered inadequate outlets for the colony's products, and direct contact with foreign markets that could absorb its exports could not be permanently permitted because it undermined Spain's monopoly. Nor were these the only obstacles that Spain encountered in harnessing New Granada's resources for metropolitan advantage. If we now turn to the import trade, we find that there, too, *comercio libre* had only temporary and limited success.

Comercio libre and New Granada's imports

The end of the Cádiz monopoly and the relaxation of other restraints on trade undoubtedly helped to enlarge Spain's markets in New Granada, as both Tables 5.1 and 5.2 show. But *comercio libre* did not ensure dependence on Spanish suppliers. Although Spanish merchants improved their position in New Granadan markets, continuing contacts with foreigners, both legal and illegal, meant that a substantial proportion of the colony's resources continued to be diverted into foreign hands. The intrusion of foreign contraband was, as ever, a problem that affected Spanish American trade far beyond the confines of New Granada. The deficiencies of Spanish industry and high duties on foreign products meant that smuggling was widespread, both within the trade between Spain and her colonies, and directly between colonies and foreign ports. The principal stimulus to contraband came from Spain's inability to supply textiles that could compete in quality and price with those produced in other European countries. Colonial free trade undoubtedly stimulated Spanish textile manufactures, particularly Catalan silk and cotton producers, and helped Spain to reduce its previous reliance on foreign producers.[91] Nonetheless, foreigners continued to supply almost half Spain's exports to its colonies, and remained particularly strong as suppliers of manufactured goods.[92] Cádiz, which remained the entrepôt for most American trade, exported more foreign than national goods and most of its Spanish exports were agricultural goods from Andalusia. Even Barcelona's trade with the Americas contained a huge agricultural component: 31% of its exports were of aguardiente, compared to 27% for printed cottons and linens, and 16% for silks.[93] In Spain, then, the principal beneficiaries of *comercio libre* were agricultural rather than industrial producers, and foreign textile producers continued to take a major share of American markets.

The crown tried to encourage national textile production by raising tariffs on the import of foreign textiles into Spain and on their re-export to America, at times even prohibiting their introduction into Spain and its colonies. Comments from contemporary observers suggest, however, that such measures merely encouraged fraud and smuggling. One device for evading higher tariffs and prohibitions on foreign textiles was simply to disguise them as Spanish exports before they were shipped to America. In late eighteenth-century Cádiz, there was a flourishing business for disguising French stockings as Spanish products so that they might pay lower

91. On the development of the Catalan textile industry and the region's trade with the colonies, see Pierre Vilar, *La Catalogne dans l'Espagne Moderne*, 3 vols. (Paris, 1962), vol. 3, pp. 112–15, 126, 484–5, 559–66. On the expansion of the Mexican market for Spanish textiles, see Brian R. Hamnett, *Politics and Trade in Southern Mexico, 1750–1821* (Cambridge, 1971), pp. 115–16.

92. In the early nineteenth century, the Spanish statesman Canga Argüelles estimated that the foreign share of Spain's colonial trade in 1784–96 was around 50%. See J. Canga Argüelles, *Diccionario de Hacienda* (2nd ed., Madrid, 1833), tomo I, p. 43. This estimate has been confirmed by Fisher's recent statistical survey of colonial commerce, which estimates the foreign share of the American trade through Spain over the period 1778–96 at 49.1%. See Fisher, *Commercial Relations between Spain and Spanish America*, p. 46.

93. Ibid., pp. 49–52.

duties on export to the colonies.[94] Another means open to foreign merchants for reaching American markets was to avoid Spain altogether by smuggling goods directly into the colonies, usually via foreign colonies in the Caribbean. This was risky, but risks were compensated by high profits. The French observer J. F. Bourgoing calculated that direct, illegal trade from Europe enabled the smuggler to evade duties of at least 14% on importation into Spain, 7% on re-exportation from Spain, and another 7% on entering the American port. By deducting the smuggler's costs, Bourgoing reckoned that evasion of duties gave him an advantage of 22% over the Spanish fair trader, without even taking into account the additional profits he stood to take from illegal export of American products.[95] Incentives for smuggling were further increased by prohibitions on trade in such articles as foreign thread, stockings, and other fabrics. Reducing the supply of such articles from Spain merely raised their prices and increased the likelihood of contraband.[96]

Illegal trade was further encouraged by the inconsistency of anticontraband regulations. When captured, foreign contraband goods were sold to the public on behalf of the royal treasury, and so frustrated the very object of their prohibition, namely, to eliminate competition against nationally produced fabrics. Indeed, one observer argued that the consumer taste for such goods had been developed by such measures during the 1779–83 war with England, when their sale as the spoils of war had diverted demand away from Spanish substitutes.[97] Spain's ability to suppress illegal trade within the Caribbean area was also hindered by British commercial policy. In 1766, Britain established free ports in its West Indian colonies in order to strengthen their role as entrepôts for trade with French and Spanish possessions. Before the American War of Independence, most of the free port trade was with the French, but after 1783 exports of British manufactures to the Spanish colonies became the most important element of a trade that, as it expanded, attracted increasing attention from British industrial interests.[98]

94. J. F. Bourgoing, *Tableau de l'Espagne Moderne* (2nd ed., Paris, 1797), p. 446.

95. Ibid., pp. 187–8.

96. This effect was described by one commentator as follows: "How is it possible that the prohibition of foreign stockings for the commerce of the Indies – which was decreed by the Reglamento of 1778 – could fail to produce an inevitable contraband, when in Spain they are neither well-made (especially those of white silk) nor made in sufficient quantity, and when those inhabitants had to supply themselves by any means and at any risk; and still more, when, as a result of the prohibition, a pair of stockings *de la banda* or *a la limeña* . . . are priced in Lima, due to their shortage, at up to 40 and 60 pesos a pair? The merchant would be ignoring his own interest if he did not expose to the remote danger of loss a good which could assure him such an exorbitant gain, even after generous handouts to the customs officials." A. Arellano Moreno, *Documentos para la historia económica en la época colonial* (Caracas, 1970), p. 493.

97. Ibid., pp. 498–9.

98. Francis Armytage, *The Free Port System in the British West Indies* (London, 1953), pp. 68–71, 84–93.

To these general conditions favoring contraband trade, specific local factors continued to make New Granada a favorite destination for foreign smugglers. Its harbors were within close reach of foreign ports in the Caribbean, chances of detection among the many bays and inlets of its long coastline were slight, and its merchants could pay for imports in gold. Crown policies designed to promote the development of commodity exports and to improve the supply of black slave labor available to the mining sector also inadvertently assisted the contraband trade. As early as 1785, merchants and officials in Cartagena complained that the licenses issued by Archbishop-Viceroy Caballero y Góngora for trade with the foreign colonies acted as a cover for contraband activity on a large scale. However, the archbishop-viceroy persisted in permitting both Spanish and foreign ships to import provisions and naval supplies from the Caribbean islands and, as the dyewood trade with North America also grew to substantial proportions, this provoked growing opposition from both merchants on the coast and landowners in the interior.

In 1787, the representatives of the Spanish merchants in Cartagena informed the crown that the archbishop-viceroy's tolerance of trade with foreigners was seriously damaging commercial interests in both the metropolis and the colony. They argued that the export of precious metal to pay for manufactures imported directly from foreign colonies endangered the industry and commerce of Spain, while the importation of foreign wheat was ruining colonial agriculture.[99] The governor of Cartagena, disaffected by the archbishop-viceroy's refusal to consult with him over the foreign trade problem, added to this chorus of complaints about the frequency of contact with foreigners. In 1787, Governor Carrión y Andrade declared that numerous English, French, and Dutch ships made regular calls at Cartagena, while the traffic of Spanish ships sailing to the foreign colonies with viceregal licenses was steadily growing. There were, to his knowledge, more than forty such licenses and passports in the secretariat of the Cartagena government, as well as some sixty notes recording cargoes brought in from foreign ports by ships allegedly in government service. According to the governor, arms and provisions that might have been imported from Veracruz or some other Spanish colonial port were brought from the foreign colonies to provide a cover for the introduction of prohibited merchandise.[100] In 1788, the governor repeated these allegations, reporting again on "the multitude of ships which have come to this port with goods and effects from the foreign colonies."[101] He also provided detailed information both on the nature of the

99. AGI Santa Fe 955. Petition to the Consejo de Indias, July 26, 1787; ibid., "Noticias de Cartagena de Indias en fecha 16 de abril de este presente año de 1787."
100. AGI Santa Fe 1014, governor of Cartagena to Valdés, October 26, 1787.
101. Ibid., Cartagena, February 1, 1788.

illicit trade, and on the involvement in it of members of the archbishop-viceroy's entourage.[102]

Criticism of the archbishop-viceroy's policies was taken up in the following year by Carrión's successor in Cartagena, Governor Cañaveral. When requesting advice on the treatment of ships coming from the foreign colonies, Cañaveral denounced the archbishop-viceroy's transgression of royal orders prohibiting this trade and stated that, in the period between 1782 and the beginning of 1789, the latter had allowed the entry into Cartagena of more than a hundred ships from foreign ports.[103] The cabildo of Santa Fe de Bogotá also remonstrated against such trade, on the grounds that it nullified all the efforts made by the viceroys Guirior and Flóres to build up the internal wheat trade and to reduce the dependence of the coastal cities on foreign supplies. The cabildo condemned the consequences of this retrograde step with dramatic emphasis. Looking back on the viceregency of Caballero y Góngora, its spokesman denounced it as "that fatal period" in which

agriculture decayed, our commerce faltered, and that industry which was still in its infancy was totally abandoned; while our own wheat was left without a market, under cover of its import the most active contraband was conducted on the beaches of the Kingdom and along the entire coast, foreign goods being impudently sold to the detriment of our own, snatching from our hands the specie which our merchants should have taken and remitted to Spanish correspondents; in short, these provinces seemed more like English colonies than dominions of the Catholic King. . . .[104]

Such harsh criticism of the archbishop-viceroy's measures confirmed a shift in the direction of policy that was being orchestrated from above. When Caballero y Góngora's viceregency ended in 1789, Cartagena's merchants found a most effective ally for the protection of their monopoly of New Granadan trade in the person of the new viceroy, Francisco Gil y Lemus. Throughout his six months of office, Gil y Lemus stayed in Cartagena, where he was strongly influenced by the Spanish mercantile establishment in the port. Shortly after taking up office, the viceroy reported that his principal problem was curbing quasi-official trade with the foreign colonies of the Caribbean. He complained that it was difficult to estimate the full extent of the trade that had been built up on the twin foundation of dyewood exports and imports of foreign wheat, as there was no complete record of the licenses that had been issued to legalize it.[105] But Gil y Lemus was convinced that by providing a cover for contraband,

102. Ibid., Cartagena, May 30, 1788; ibid., Cartagena, August 16, 1788.
103. AGI Santa Fe 1015, governor to Valdés, Cartagena, August 31, 1789.
104. AGI Santa Fe 655, Cabildo of Santa Fe to Valdés, Santa Fe, October 26, 1789.
105. For a comparison of the recorded numbers of ships entering Cartagena from Spain and from foreign ports in the period 1783–90, see Appendix C, Table 3.

these two lines of trade constituted a serious threat to metropolitan economic control over the colony, and he resolved to end all forms of trade with foreigners. He therefore planned to end the importation of foreign flour into Cartagena, arguing that its partnership with contraband would destroy the trade with Cádiz. Second, he resolved to return the dyewood trade to private hands, allowing Spanish merchants to make contracts with the *estanco* of Santa Marta and to ship the commodity to Spain on their own account. [106]

To complete his reassertion of metropolitan control over the colony's external trade, Viceroy Gil y Lemus also recommended purging the administration in Cartagena. He alleged that it had become so corrupt that the sale of licenses to trade with foreigners was itself a business, with publicly quoted prices. Accordingly, he recommended the removal from office of all those who had conspired to protect the trade with foreigners, and called for an improvement in anticontraband measures as the only way to eliminate "the sad necessity of seeing the continued extraction of wealth with which the foreigners were enriching themselves and prospering, while the King's subjects are weakened and annihilated." [107] Thus, during the brief viceregency of Gil y Lemus, the archbishop-viceroy's informal commercial policy was reversed. Legalized trading contacts with foreigners were terminated, and the tone was set for a resumption under Viceroy José de Ezpeleta (1790–6) of practices more compatible with the orthodox canons of Spanish mercantilism.

The suppression of trade with foreigners proved impossible. So long as Spain was unable to supply the colony with all the goods that its markets required, trade with the foreign islands of the Caribbean continued. And, during the early 1790s, the contraband trade between the ports of New Granada and the Caribbean possessions of rival powers not only continued, but flourished. After 1790, ships' masters returning to Spain consistently reported poor sales in Cartagena, and the truth of their reports is reflected in official statistics that show that the value of imports from the metropolis began to fall off, dropping from an annual average of 2,439,470 pesos in 1786–9 to 1,417,524 pesos per average year in 1790–3. [108] Cartagena merchants also became still more vocal in their complaints about the contraband trade. In 1795, a group of Cartagena

---

106. AGI Santa Fe 573 (ramo 2), Gil y Lemus to crown, Cartagena, January 30, 1789.

107. Ibid., February 27, 1789. For his reform proposals, see ibid., May 14, 1789.

108. Reports from ships' masters are found in AHNC Aduanas, tomo 9, fols. 718–19, 916–17, 927; AGI Indiferente General 2449, Presidente Juez de Arribadas to Pedro de Lerena, Cádiz, February 1, 1791; ibid., February 22, 1791; ibid., "Declaración y nota de la carga que conduce de Cartagena de Indias el Bergantin la Resolución," Barcelona June 12, 1791; AGI Indiferente General 2450, Presidente Juez de Arribas to Conde de Lerena, Cádiz, June 29, 1791; Indiferente General 2451, Presidente Juez de Arribas to Gardoqui, Cádiz May 22, 1792; Indiferente General 2453, idem, April 30, 1793; ibid., May 7, 1793.

merchants reported that for the previous three years their trade with the metropolis had suffered a sharp decline due to the influence of contraband.[109] They recognized that war with France, declared in 1793, had played some part in this recession, but insisted that its primary cause was the growing influx of smuggled goods from the foreign islands of the Caribbean. Although the value of trade with the peninsula had fallen by about 50%, they alleged that contraband over the same period had reached between 3 and 4 million pesos. Woolens were in short supply, and Spanish silks and other products were sold at normal prices, but the market was saturated with linens and all kinds of cotton goods. Such was their profusion in Cartagena and throughout the colony that various sorts of German and French lawns and linens, as well as a whole range of prohibited cottons, were sold at prices lower than those currently found in Cádiz and other Spanish ports. In the city of Cartagena, trade in these goods was so open that they were peddled in the streets, and their consumption so common that everybody "from the lady to the slave-girl, from the artisan to the most respectable businessman, goes dressed in fine muslins, *musolinetas* and other prohibited fabrics of cotton and worsted."[110]

When calling for stronger measures to check the ruinous competition of contraband, the merchants argued that the slave trade, freed from traditional restrictions by the royal decree of 1791, provided a legal cover for the smuggler. Under the new legislation, colonial traders were permitted to go to the foreign colonies in their own vessels, in order to search for slaves that they could pay for in bullion and other colonial products.[111] In theory, licenses were issued for only one return journey and returns could be made only in slaves and some other listed articles. In practice, almost all the vessels employed in the traffic made several journeys under one license, imported only two or three slaves at a time, and brought instead large consignments of cloth from Jamaica and other islands. These were then often landed at the coastal village of Sabanilla or on the tiny offshore Rosario Islands, where the consignments awaited subsequent reshipment in small boats to Cartagena or directly to markets in the interior of New Granada.

The free slave trade also opened a dangerous gap in the Spanish monopoly. In 1794, Viceroy Ezpeleta informed the Minister for the Indies that since 1791, only 446 slaves had been imported into New Granada under the new regulations, and the slave trade had become little more than a

109. AHNC Aduanas (Cartas), tomo 10, fols. 996–1000.
110. AGI Indiferente General 2466, *Representación* of the Sindico of the Consulado of Cartagena.
111. For a full discussion of the new policy toward the slave trade, see J. F. King, "Evolution of the Free Slave Trade Principle in Spanish Colonial Administration," *HAHR*, vol. 22 (1942), pp. 34–56.

vehicle for the contrabandist.[112] However, the viceroy showed scant sympathy for the complaints of the Cartagena merchants, whom he accused of complicity in the traffic. In 1792, two highly detailed reports on contraband in Cartagena revealed to Ezpeleta the web of fraud and corruption that enveloped commercial activity in the port, penetrating both the mercantile establishment and the city's administration. According to his anonymous informer, smuggling had reached the point where it was viewed as completely normal both by the public and by the authorities. The customs administration, he alleged, was itself riddled with corruption. Its chief officer was a prominent smuggler, as were the commander of the Bocachica fortress (which overlooked the narrow passage into the Bay of Cartagena and was the key point for controlling the movement of shipping), their subordinate officers, and several prominent merchants. All of these individuals, it was said, were publicly involved in marketing contraband goods.[113] An incident reported in 1795 confirmed this view. When Tomás Andrés Torres, a very prominent Cartagena merchant, was arrested for selling contraband imports, he did not deny the charges against him. He simply argued that if the governor was to be justified in making a case against him, then he would have to arrest everybody in the city, because all were involved in contraband.[114]

Despite efforts to end the legal trade with foreigners, illegal trading continued unabated, helped by the official licenses that were given to private and naval vessels, authorizing them to sail to foreign colonies. In 1792, for example, a naval schooner preparing to sail for Jamaica loaded 60,000 pesos, of which only 12,000 pesos were connected with its official mission. The remaining 48,000 pesos were sent by private persons involved in illegal trading. Apart from the merchants, the officialdom of Cartagena had a substantial interest in the voyage, as many of them had borrowed from merchants in order to invest in it. None of the senior officials of the port "from the Governor to the last administrator and even the fiscal of the royal treasury" were unaware of the vessel's sailing or its purpose. When the guards were not co-opted into illegal activity by their superiors, they were powerless to act against it for fear of losing their jobs. The very fortresses, stores, and ships of the king had become deposits for contraband, centers for a large illegal traffic that permeated the commercial activity of the city and filtered through to the surrounding provinces.[115] In 1794, the crown acknowledged that the "great clandestine commerce" that passed through Cartagena, Río Hacha, Santa Marta, and

---

112. AGI Santa Fe 643, Ezpeleta to Gardoqui, October 19, 1794 (no. 614).
113. AHNC Aduanas (Cartas), tomo 10, fols. 985–7.
114. AHNC Aduanas, tomo 20, fols. 678–80.
115. AHNC Aduanas (Cartas), tomo 10, fols. 989–90.

Portobelo was undermining legal trade, but offered no antidote other than a request for greater vigilance from the viceroy, a policy that had consistently failed since the inception of the viceroyalty.[116] Clearly, the liberalization of imperial commerce had failed to secure New Granada's markets for imports, just as it had failed to develop New Granada's resources for export.

The effects of *comercio libre* on New Granada's economy

To conclude our assessment of New Granada's commerce and economy in the age of *comercio libre,* two general observations remain to be made. The first is comparative, and concerns New Granada's position and performance within the system of Spanish colonial commerce as a whole. Seen in this general context, it is clear that New Granada remained on the economic periphery of Spain's empire at the end of the eighteenth century. In 1782–96, the average annual value of Spanish exports to America increased fourfold and colonial exports to Spain increased tenfold.[117] Thus, by merely doubling its value, growth in New Granada's trade was considerably lower than the average for Spanish transatlantic trade as a whole. It was small wonder, then, that New Granada was a relatively unimportant contributor to Spanish colonial commerce, which contradicted the official belief that with commercial reform, its wealth of natural resources would make the region one of Spain's most dynamic colonies. In 1782–96 exports from Cartagena and Santa Marta represented only around 3.2% of Spanish imports from the Americas, compared to nearly 14% from Peru, 12% from Río de la Plata, and 10% from Venezuela. As a market for imports from Spain, New Granada was somewhat more important, taking 8.2% of goods shipped from Cádiz. But this also compared poorly with Peru, which took 21.6% of imports from Cádiz between 1785 and 1796, and with Venezuela and Río de la Plata, which both took over 10%.[118] The introduction of imperial free trade did little, then, to change New Granada's economic relationship with Spain. The region remained an inefficient, rather inward-looking colony that, despite its apparently rich natural resources, made only a small and slow-growing contribution to American colonial commerce.

The other general observation about New Granada in the age of *comercio libre* is specific to the region itself, and concerns the causes and conse-

---

116. AGI Santa Fe 960, Real orden, April 20, 1794.

117. Fisher, *Commercial Relations between Spain and Spanish America,* pp. 88–9.

118. Ibid., pp. 55, 77. For a comparison of New Granadan and Peruvian commerce in this period, see J. R. Fisher, "The Effects of *Comercio Libre* on the Economies of New Granada and Peru: A comparison," in Fisher, Kuethe, and McFarlane, *Reform and Insurrection of Bourbon New Granada and Peru,* pp. 147–63.

quences of its limited commercial growth. The poor performance of commerce with Spain stemmed in part from policy expedients that allowed colonial resources to be diverted into foreign hands. During the viceregency of Archbishop-Viceroy Caballero y Góngora, the growth of Spanish traffic into Cartagena was undercut by an increase in trade with foreigners, who were licensed by the viceregal government in order to secure financial support for the Darién colonization project. And although this policy was reversed under Caballero y Góngora's successors, contraband imports continued to damage markets for Spanish trade during the early 1790s, before the renewal of war with Britain. Indeed, Cartagena's merchants estimated that contraband imports to the value of more than a million pesos per year entered New Granada in the three years between 1793 and 1796, filling half the colony's markets for European goods. So, if New Granada became more open to imports in the late eighteenth century, this was as much the result of foreign interloping as the consequence of Bourbon imperialism.

While Spain failed to dominate New Granada's import markets, it also failed to generate growth in exports. Despite the loosening of restrictions on Spanish trade, neither Spain nor its colonies offered any strong demand for New Granada's agricultural products and other nonmineral products, so that the colony's producers remained largely isolated from overseas markets. It is true that there was some improvement in opportunities to export products such as cacao, cotton, hides, cinchona, and dyewoods, but these were too slight to offer any platform for general economic growth. Furthermore, any positive impact that such exports might have had on the colony's economy must be offset against the negative impact of agricultural imports from Spain that competed with colonial products. Unrestrained imports of Catalan aguardiente into Cartagena led to a fall in the sales of local aguardiente and this, in turn, diminished demand for the molasses produced by coastal hacendados. Nor was this compensated by opportunities to export sugar. As the spokesman of the coastal landowners pointed out when pleading for a ban on Spanish aguardiente imports, New Granada's sugar simply could not compete with that of the Caribbean islands.[119] Wheat producers in the interior also felt that their interests were damaged by the commercial policies of the 1780s. Foreign flour, mostly from the United States, was imported into Cartagena by both Spanish and foreign ships, preventing New Granadan wheat from recovering its lost markets on the coast. These economic effects of Spanish commercial policy may help to explain why the movement against Spain, which began in 1810, quickly attracted elite support

---

119. AGI Santa Fe 643, Sindico procurador general Manuel de Otoya to governor of Cartagena, May 9, 1794.

in Cartagena and Bogotá, both cities with a concentrated group of large landowners.

In New Granada, then, *comercio libre* proved to be doubly flawed. It failed either to secure metropolitan primacy in supplying the colony's markets for imports or to promote growth through exports. This double failure not only undermined Spain's role as an economic metropolis, but it was also politically damaging, as colonials became increasingly critical of the deficiencies of the Spanish system and outspoken in their opposition to it. In 1791, for example, Pedro Fermín de Vargas pointed out that for most of the colony's population, which was concentrated in the interior, overseas trade was an irrelevance. He accepted that *comercio libre* had given some stimulus to the economy of the coast, but observed that the interior of the country remained as it had been in the days of the galleons. Distance from the metropolis, high tariffs, and the extremely poor state of internal communications meant that the common people could not afford European imports, and that Spain's pretensions to supply them were futile. Vargas therefore advised Spain to abandon its quixotic policy of seeking to dominate the colonial market and, confining itself to supplying only "the fine merchandise which has a market among the rich," to encourage instead a colonial textile industry capable of meeting local needs.[120] His criticisms also showed creole awareness that Spanish policy had entirely failed to create the "active" trade envisaged by the reformers of the 1770s. Vargas realized that the preoccupation with gold mining and the colony's reliance on exports of specie to pay for its imports stood in the way of economic development.[121] In effect, Vargas was arguing that, though gold was one of the few articles in which New Granada had a comparative international advantage, the organization of production in mining impeded development of both the industry and the country as a whole. Based on the extensive, low-productivity labor of slaves and subsistence labor, and crippled by the high costs of basic supplies, mining was not conducive to either technical improvement or capital accumulation. To Vargas, the best means of stimulating the colony's economy was to encourage its agricultural and industrial production for both internal and external markets. To this end, he recommended that the crown should reduce the duties on overseas trade, allow the colony to trade freely with foreigners, and take steps to improve transportation facilities within the area.[122] Nor was his a lone voice. In 1797, Antonio Nariño, another creole critic of Spanish government and later a prominent leader of the movement for independence, also lamented New Granada's economic stagnation, describing its commerce as "languid" and its inhabitants as

---

120. Fermín de Vargas, *Pensamientos políticos*, pp. 102–5.
121. Ibid., pp. 57–65.   122. Ibid., pp. 96–8, 102–3, 110.

"the poorest in America." Nothing was more common in New Granada, said Nariño, than "the spectacle of a ragged family, without a *real* in its pockets, living in a miserable shack surrounded by cotton plants, cinnamon shrubs, cacao trees and other riches, including precious stones." Like Vargas, Nariño wanted greater freedom for colonial producers to trade in both internal and external markets, so that they could commercialize the territory's rich natural resources; he also favored the introduction of paper and copper currency to offset the shortage of specie caused by its export.[123]

Creole proposals to develop New Granada's economy were ignored by the Spanish government, however. In neighboring Caracas, which had no precious metals to export, de facto freedom of trade with foreigners was permitted, allowing colonial producers to enlarge and diversify their exports.[124] In New Granada, by contrast, the crown's concern to funnel gold into the Spanish trading system continued to deprive colonial producers of outlets outside this system. The development of overseas commerce was confined by the rules of the Spanish system and was left to the merchants of Cartagena de Indias, a small group of peninsulars who, through their connections with Cádiz, dominated New Granada's external trade. If we now examine their activities, it will become clear that they contributed little to developing the territory's resources, for their connections with the colonial economy that lay beyond Cartagena were always tenuous, and their commitment to domestic development correspondingly slight.

123. "Ensayo sobre un nuevo plan de administración en el Nuevo Reino de Granada," in Nariño, *Escritos políticos,* pp. 13–37; quotations from p. 14.
124. On this policy in Caracas, see McKinley, *Pre-revolutionary Caracas,* pp. 39–45.

6

Merchants and monopoly

At the beginning of the eighteenth century, New Granada lacked a substantial and influential merchant class of the kind found in Peru and Mexico. In 1695, a group of some twenty merchants in Bogotá had established a *consulado de comercio* modeled on those of Lima and Mexico City, by contracting with the crown to pay the royal tax known as the *avería*, due on goods imported by the galleons, in return for the right to a self-governing mercantile jurisdiction.[1] The Consulado of Santa Fe de Bogotá did not survive for long, however. Its members were unable to fulfill their financial obligations, and when the galleon system itself collapsed during the War of the Spanish Succession the Consulado lost its rationale. It was suppressed in 1713, reflecting the inability of New Granadan merchants to sustain an institution of this kind.[2] Many decades then passed before a *consulado de comercio* was reestablished in New Granada. When the institution was revived in 1795, it was at Cartagena de Indias, the country's leading port and home of its mercantile elite.

Cartagena de Indias and New Granada's commerce

Although Bogotá was the headquarters of New Granada's government, Cartagena was the hub of its commerce and throughout the eighteenth century the development of a mercantile elite in New Granada was primarily associated with this port. There were merchants in other cities, of course. Bogotá, Mompós, Honda, and Popayán were all important markets and redistribution centers for European imports, and there were numerous secondary regional centers for such trade in towns like Cali,

1. The merchants involved in the project were a small group. A document drawn up by their attorney, Tomás de Solórzano, named twenty *comerciantes* as its backers: AGI Consulados 68, Pretensiones de los comerciantes del Nuevo Reino de Granada . . . Madrid, March 23, 1695.
2. Robert S. Smith, "The Consulado in Santa Fe de Bogotá," *HAHR*, vol. 45 (1965), pp. 442–7. A fuller account of the origins and history of the Consulado is given in Manuel Lucena Salmoral, "Los Precedentes del Consulado de Cartagena: El Consulado de Santafé (1695–1713) y el Tribunal del Comercio Cartagenero," *Estudios de Historia Social y Económica de América*, no. 2 (Universidad de Alcalá de Henares, 1986), pp. 179–98.

Medellín, and Pasto. But the colony's highest concentration of merchants was in Cartagena, for reasons that are easy to explain. As the first port of call for the South American fleets, Cartagena had long been the principal focus for New Granada's import and export trade, to which provincial traders traveled to exchange precious metals for European merchandise. Juan and Ulloa's description of the city, made in 1735, offers a glimpse of its commercial life:

> The Bay of Cartagena is the first place in America at which the galleons are allowed to touch; and thus it enjoys the first fruits of commerce, by the public sales made there. These sales, though not accompanied by the formalities observed at Porto Bello fair, are very considerable. The traders of the inland provinces of Santa Fe, Popayán and Quito, lay out not only their own stocks, but also the monies intrusted to them by commissions, for several sorts of goods, and those species of provisions which are most wanted in their respective countries. Their traders bring gold and silver in specie, ingots and dust, and also emeralds. . . . This little fair at Cartagena, for so it may be called, occasions a great quantity of shops to be opened, and filled with all kinds of merchandise; the profit partly resulting to Spaniards who come in the galleons and are either recommended to, or in partnership with the *Cargadores,* and partly to those already settled in that city. . . . This commercial tumult lasts while the galleons continue in the bay; for they are no sooner gone, than silence and tranquillity resume their former place. This the inhabitants of Cartagena call *tiempo muerto,* the dead time; for, with regard to the trade carried on with the other governments, it is not worth notice.[3]

From this description, it is clear that New Granada's external trade was largely controlled by two groups of merchants, both of which operated in Cartagena. The first was that of the *cargadores,* the Spanish merchants who traveled with the fleets to sell goods at the Cartagena and Portobelo fairs. The second group was composed of wholesale merchants (*comerciantes*) resident in Cartagena, who bought up stocks from the galleons for resale to local retailers and redistribution within the interior. These men were peninsular Spaniards, like the *cargadores.* Juan and Ulloa referred to them as *chapetones,* or Spanish immigrants, and, noting that they "carry on the whole trade of that place, and live in opulence," distinguished them from the families of the creoles or American Spaniards who, in Cartagena, "compose the landed interest."[4]

While the fleet system functioned, the development of the merchant community in Cartagena was constrained by the privileged position enjoyed by members of the *Universidad de Cargadores a Indias* – the guild of Spanish merchants dealing with the colonies – who were the sole legal intermediaries in the transatlantic trade. Organized by the *Casa de Contra-*

3. Jorge Juan and Antonio de Ulloa, *A Voyage to South America* (John Adams translation, abridged, New York, 1964), pp. 40–4.
4. Ibid., p. 27.

tación and the *Universidad de Cargadores*, the fleet system funneled colonial trade through a single entrepôt in Spain, and ensured that commercial houses located in the Andalusian ports of Seville, Cádiz, Puerto de Santa María, and Sanlúcar controlled the oceanic trade while limiting merchants in the Americas to trade within their respective colonies.[5] Under this system, New Granada's trade with Spain was managed by the *cargadores*. They brought cargoes from Cádiz (which replaced Seville as the entrepôt for colonial commerce in 1717), sold them at the galleon fair in Cartagena, and then returned to Spain with the proceeds, taking profits from both independent commercial operations and from commission business. Meanwhile, merchants in New Granada, like merchants in other American cities, were confined to trade within the colony, acting as the distributors of imports brought by the fleets.

During the 1720s and early 1730s, wealthy merchants in Mexico and Peru tried to modify this oligopoly by creating a direct commerce with Spain. Had it succeeded, this initiative might have strengthened merchant groups throughout the Americas, including New Granada, by allowing them a larger share of the profitable import and export trades. However, pressured by the Consulado of Cádiz, the crown decreed in 1729 that all transatlantic commerce had to be carried by "the factors who embark in the fleets, galleons, and other ships."[6] American residents could not have goods consigned directly to them, nor were they permitted to send consignments other than through peninsular Spaniards of the *Universidad de Cargadores*. Despite strong opposition from the Consulados of Mexico and Peru, this order, forbidding colonial merchants from sending money to Spain to buy goods, was repeated in 1735.[7] Under these conditions, merchants in New Granada were unable to build a fully independent trade with Spain. Instead, they relied on Andalusian merchants to supply them with imports from the metropolis, while they were confined to business within the colony.

Realignments in mercantile organization

From mid-century, New Granada's merchant community became stronger, as patterns of trade changed following the suppression of the galleon system. Now that trade was carried in individual vessels rather than in periodic convoys, peninsular merchants no longer traveled in groups to meet with their colonial counterparts at a prearranged time and place, for a short, intensive exchange. Instead, overseas trade was increasingly han-

5. On the *cargadores a Indias*, see García-Baquero, *Cádiz y el Atlántico*, vol. 1, pp. 458–63.
6. Rafael Antúñez y Acevedo, *Memorias históricas sobre la legislación y gobierno del comercio de los españoles* (Madrid, 1797), p. 298.
7. J. J. Real Días, "Las Ferias de Jalapa," *AEA*, vol. 16 (1959), pp. 251–3.

dled by resident factors, who could provide a constant flow of information on local market conditions and handle the slower, more continuous flow of business brought by occasional register-ships from the metropolis. In 1749, the crown also loosened the regulations governing participation in transatlantic commerce, by allowing American citizens to ship goods to and from the metropolis without having to use the *cargadores* as intermediaries.[8]

Both reforms encouraged the growth of a merchant community in Cartagena, although liberalization of the rules concerning colonial commerce with the metropolis still did not permit merchants in the colonies to compete freely with the *cargadores*. For there was an important caveat to the 1749 decree, which was designed to prevent merchants in the Americas from dispensing entirely with the services of the Spanish merchant houses that had always organized the transatlantic trade. Any Spanish merchant sending goods to an American *vecino* had to guarantee under oath that the goods had been purchased by the resident with his own funds. Twenty years later, this means of preventing colonial merchants from supplanting the *cargadores* was still vigorously defended. The president of the *Casa de Contratación* attempted to change the rule in 1769, but his efforts met with an immediate response from the Consulado of Cádiz, which protested that such change would ruin its members' business. To allow American residents to trade as factors would make the registered *cargadores* redundant, the Consulado argued, because the owners of merchandise exported to the Americas – who were usually foreigners – would simply deal directly with American residents. The Council of the Indies readily appreciated the danger to Spanish merchants and upheld the old rule.[9] Thus, despite modifications to its structure, the *Carrera de Indias* continued to be the preserve of Spanish merchants who were registered members, or *matriculados,* of the *Universidad de Cargadores a Indias*. Nevertheless, despite the continuing tendency of the crown to protect the Andalusian monopoly from colonial competition, the end of the galleon system undoubtedly encouraged the development of a mercantile elite in New Granada, which was located chiefly in the port of Cartagena de Indias. For as the South American fleets were replaced by register-ships, the transient merchants who had dominated the colony's commerce in the age of the galleons were increasingly supplanted by factors who resided in Cartagena for years at a time and became identified with the colony and its commerce.

8. Antúñez and Acevedo, *Memorias históricas,* pp. 300–5.
9. AGI Indiferente General 801, Año de 1769, Consultas de negocios seculares: Marqués del Real Tesoro, February 28, 1769; Consulado de Cádiz, March 21, 1769; Consejo de Indias, July 10, 1769.

We can trace the evolution of Cartagena's merchant community in a series of disputes over rights of mercantile jurisdiction that began after the galleons were abolished. During the time of the galleons, the Spanish merchants who came to Cartagena were *matriculados* of the *Universidad de Cargadores a Indias,* and when they arrived on the fleets they brought with them delegates (*diputados del comercio*) chosen by their guild to deal with commercial litigation among its members while they were in America. Thus, when the last of the Tierra Firme fleets arrived in Cartagena in 1737, its merchants were accompanied by delegates empowered to deal with commercial litigation, and while they remained in the port during the next decade, trapped by war and slow sales, these delegates continued to exercise the mercantile jurisdiction. This practice changed at mid-century, when the delegates of the last fleet returned to Spain. Left without their mercantile court, Spanish merchants remaining in Cartagena first petitioned the viceroy, then the Consulado in Spain, to install two merchants chosen from their number as *diputados del comercio* in the port.[10] The Consulado in Cádiz duly agreed, no doubt recognizing that Spanish merchants required a permanent commercial court in the port now that the replacement of the galleons by register-ships encouraged merchants to remain in Cartagena as factors. Once this mercantile court was established, the *cargadores* then fought tenaciously to prevent resident merchants in Cartagena from sharing in their privileged status, a determination that provoked protracted disputes within the city's merchant community.

Trouble began in 1756, starting a series of disputes over the election of *diputados del comercio* and the extent of their powers, which provides a useful barometer of changes in the city's merchant elite. For during the next two decades, Cartagena's merchants divided into two factions, as the *cargadores* from Spain sought to preserve their exclusive status against merchants who resided in Cartagena. Both groups were composed of peninsular Spaniards. The difference was that one was made up of *matriculados* or registered members of the *Universidad de Cargadores;* the other group was composed of *comerciantes vecinos,* or those merchants who had either never been *matriculados,* or had lost their membership because they had taken up permanent residence in the port.

Conflict between the two groups started in 1756, when a group of resident merchants elected two delegates to act on their behalf in a differ-ence with the city's lieutenant governor. This immediately incited protest from the existing delegates appointed by the Consulado de Cádiz, who complained to the viceroy that only they had the right to speak on behalf

---

10. AGI Consulados 325, Diego Luis de Medina et al. to Consulado de Cádiz, Cartagena, January 30, 1750.

of the merchant community.[11] In 1757 the dispute erupted again, when a peninsular merchant refused to acknowledge the authority of the delegates appointed by the Cartagena deputies. Shortly afterward, in 1759, the *cargadores* asserted their right to control the mercantile jurisdiction by demanding a tribunal that would deal with their cases separately from those of the merchants resident in the port. To resolve this conflict, the viceroy sought compromise by giving both groups a share in the election of deputies: in 1759, he ordered that ten Cartagena merchants should join with ten Cádiz *matriculados* and that each group should select a deputy from their own members. This compromise failed to satisfy the *matriculados*, however. Harking back nostalgically to the age of the galleons as a time of lost harmony, when merchants had been clearly identified with Spain or with the colony, they insisted that the only way to avoid further discord was to redraw the traditional lines of separation. By 1760, the viceroy decided to concur with this view. He accepted that, to end conflict among the merchants of Cartagena, the *matriculados* should have their own separate tribunal, composed of two of their members and the governor of Cartagena.[12]

But competition between *cargadores* and Cartagena merchants did not end here. The *cargadores* continued to feel threatened by resident merchants who, one of the delegates explained in 1764, "have greater knowledge and connections with the Kingdom [of New Granada], [because] buyers travel regularly [to Cartagena] with orders for them, and in their houses make the first business deals. . . ."[13] The *comerciantes vecinos*, on the other hand, felt that the Cádiz merchants discriminated unfairly against them. At one stage, for example, Cartagena merchants refused to pay their shares toward a loan required by the crown, on the grounds that the burden of the loan had not been evenly distributed according to ability to pay, and they called on the viceroy to make an impartial reassessment.[14] In 1776, the Cartagena merchants also informed the viceroy that they were systematically excluded from the valuable office of *maestría de plata*, as the deputies of the Cádiz Consulado in Cartagena favored only "those who have the title of *comerciantes de España*, without allowing those of Cartagena to enjoy the same benefit."[15]

These complaints were apparently part of a campaign, led by Cartagena merchant Juan Fernández Moure, to secure for resident merchants the

---

11. AGI Consulados 326, Arrechederreta and Villanueva to Consulado, Cartagena, December 13, 1756. The deputies chosen in Cartagena were Joseph Antonio Zavala and Joseph Inocencio Morquecho.

12. AHNC, Consulados, tomo 4, fols. 530–44, 618–49, 699–708, 710–12, 717–18.

13. AGI Consulados 329, Diputados del comercio to Consulado, April 29, 1764.

14. AHNC Real Hacienda (Cartas), tomo 2, fols. 411–16.

15. AHNC Consulados, tomo 5, fols. 307–11.

same rights as those enjoyed by the Cádiz merchants. In 1771, Fernández Moure had already petitioned the viceroy either to allow the resident merchants to participate in the port's *tribunal del comercio*, or, failing this, to appoint their own deputies. For, he pointed out, although both the *cargadores* and the retailers (*mercaderes*) in the port had autonomous deputations, the resident peninsular merchants were the only group without any independent means of handling their own affairs.[16] This was forthrightly opposed by the Cádiz *matriculados*, who continued to refuse resident merchants entry to their *tribunal del comercio* for fear that it would loosen their control over the transatlantic trade.[17]

Eventually, this long-running dispute was resolved in 1776, when a viceregal order abolished the distinction between the *matriculados* and the *vecinos comerciantes* and brought them together under the jurisdiction of the same tribunal. Although this decision was delayed by opposition from Cádiz, the two groups were finally reconciled under the new commercial regime introduced by the *Reglamento de comercio libre*.[18] With the advent of imperial free trade, there was no longer any reason to maintain the distinction between Spanish merchants in the port, and in 1784 the wholesale merchants in the port came together to petition for a Consulado to oversee the business of all merchants involved in Cartagena's overseas trade.[19]

Evidently, replacement of the fleets by individual register-ships had brought adjustments in the organization of trade between Spain and New Granada, encouraging the growth of a resident community of peninsular merchants who acted as factors for businesses in Cádiz. Development of a colonial merchant class was still restricted, however, because members of the Spanish guild of *cargadores* continued to exercise a strong influence over the transatlantic trade, limiting participation to its members and restricting membership to those merchants who were active, registered *matriculados* from Spain. Before *comercio libre* was introduced, these men persistently and successfully defended their privileges, for fear that if they allowed Cartagena's resident merchants parity of status, this would clear the way for open competition from colonials. The *cargadores'* determination to avoid this danger is clearly reflected in an incident that occurred in

16. AHNC Consulados, tomo 4, fols. 749–50.
17. AGI Consulados 332, Francisco Joaquín Barroso to Consulado, Cartagena, July 31, 1771; AGI Consulados 333, Francisco Joaquín Barroso to Consulado, August 27, 1774; ibid., July 10, 1775; AGI Consulados 335, Francisco Joaquín Barroso to Consulado, June 30, 1775.
18. AGI Santa Fe 552, Informe de Francisco Machado, Madrid, May 11, 1778.
19. AHNC Consulados, tomo 4, fols. 751–2. This letter from the *comerciantes* of Cartagena to the viceroy of August 26, 1784, refers to "una armoniosa unión" of the two bodies of merchants, and reports on "lo útil y conveniente que será a este comercio el establecimiento de un formal Tribunal del Consulado a imitación y con las mismas reglas y privilegios que obtienen los de las ciudades de Mexico y Lima . . ."

1774, when a creole merchant, one Bernardo Alcázar, tried to enter the trade as a *cargador matriculado*. The Cádiz commercial delegates in the port immediately demanded that Alcázar be excluded. He was, they said, not only an American but also a mulatto, and was thus debarred from the trade by law. Colonials, they insisted, had no place in overseas trade because, if allowed to trade directly with Spain, they would ruin peninsular merchants.[20]

Some colonials were nonetheless able to take advantage of the law that allowed American residents to engage in commerce with Spain using their own resources. The registers of ships leaving Cartagena in the 1760s and 1770s, for example, include consignments made in the names of prominent local landowners of the city and province of Cartagena. Such notables as the Marquesa de Valdehoyos of Cartagena, the Marqués de Santa Coa, and the *maestre de campo* José Fernando de Mier y Guerra, both of Mompós, all made consignments of cacao, hides, and money during these years.[21] These were, however, occasional remittances rather than a regular business, and such activity fell far short of that of the great landowners of Caracas, who, in the late eighteenth century, exported agricultural products in very large quantities, sometimes in their own vessels.[22] This is hardly surprising, of course, because the properties of landowners in the coastal region were used mainly for grazing cattle and cultivating sugar for local consumption, and offered few possibilities for an export agriculture.

Spanish factors in Cartagena

Whether registered *cargadores* or resident *comerciantes vecinos*, the merchants who organized Spanish trade through Cartagena were all peninsular Spaniards, acting mainly as factors for Cádiz commercial houses and as commission agents for trade organized in Cádiz. Registers of ships voyaging between Cartagena and Spain during the 1760s and 1770s show that the bulk of the trade was handled in this manner. The old form of trade, in which men from Cádiz made return voyages to the port, was not entirely superseded, but on the whole business was conducted through middlemen in Cartagena.

Commercial records, which identify Spanish merchants in Cartagena during these years, suggest that most were the emissaries of Cádiz commercial houses, who were specifically sent to Cartagena to receive cargoes and organize returns, sometimes as members of a Spanish family firm that

20. AGI Consulados 333, Francisco Joaquín Barroso to Consulado, November 30, 1774.
21. Information on cargoes sent to Spain in these years is in AGI, Contratación 2654, 2661, 2662.
22. McKinley, *Pre-revolutionary Caracas*, p. 67.

needed factors to handle its business in the port.[23] Ships' registers show that merchants did not usually confine themselves to working for one commercial house, however. Generally, they handled goods sent "on the account and risk" of various merchants in the peninsula, sending return cargoes on the same basis. If the merchants' primary role was as factors and commission agents, the cargo registers of the 1760s and 1770s also show several instances of Cartagena-based merchants importing and exporting on their own account. This seems, however, to have been the smaller part of their business. Most trade originated in Spain, and the main activity of the Cartagena-based merchant was to sell imports and remit returns on a commission basis.

A probate dispute involving the estate of Antonio Paniza, a Spanish merchant who died in Cartagena, suggests the character and scope of such business. When the affairs of the Paniza, Guerra de Mier & Company were wound up after 1778, its accounts show a large spectrum of activities, reflected in its outstanding debts. Some were for small amounts, evidently owed by retailers who had taken goods on credit from the company stores; other, generally much larger amounts were owed by traders in Cartagena, in several towns in the interior, and overseas, in Havana, Madrid, and Portobelo. Such debts could be very large by New Granadan standards. For example, Manuel Díaz de Hoyos, a merchant in Bogotá, owed 15,000 pesos for merchandise received from the company, to be paid for over a term of three years. Interestingly, Paniza, Guerra de Mier & Company seems to have acted as a bank too, lending in cash to suitable borrowers. The Bishop of Santa Marta and other clerics were among its debtors, as was a retailer of Cartagena who had a mortgage on his house at an interest rate of 5% per year. The assets of the company also included both rural and urban property. An hacienda and its small slave force were valued at just over 8,700 pesos, and four houses in Cartagena were worth nearly 16,000 pesos. Paniza's own estate was valued at over 150,000 pesos, of which nearly 44,000 were in cash and goods, though most of the estate was in commercial debts, totaling over 74,000 pesos.[24] Another Spanish merchant, Juan Pablo Sarratea, who died in Cartagena in 1771, had a smaller, but still considerable estate. Considered by his fellow merchants as a leading importer, thanks to his firm contacts with the Cádiz house of Sáenz de Tejada, Sarratea left an estate that was thought to have been worth as much as 100,000 pesos.[25] By the standards of eighteenth-century New Granada, these were very considerable assets and they suggest that Cartagena's leading importers made good profits.

23. For examples, see Anthony McFarlane, "Comerciantes y Monopolio en la Nueva Granada: El Consulado de Cartagena de Indias," *ACHSC*, vol. 11 (1983), pp. 49–52.

24. AHNC, Testamentarias de Bolívar, tomo 26, fols. 917–95.

25. Ibid., tomo 52, fols. 980–3.

Although their presence in Cartagena strengthened commercial ties with the mother country, the number of Spanish *comerciantes* in the port was small. A petition presented to the viceroy in 1763 named thirty-three such individuals, of whom twenty-six were listed as members of the "comercio de España" and seven as merchants of Cartagena.[26] A record of merchant contributions to a royal loan lists forty-two *comerciantes* in 1771, but makes no distinction between registered members of the *cargadores* and long-term residents.[27] A few years later, in 1774, a royal order stated that there was only a "small number" of about fifty *matriculados en la Universidad de Cargadores* in Cartagena. The mercantile community of Buenos Aires, to take one comparison, experienced far more vigorous growth in this period, rising from around forty-four comerciantes in 1744 to 145 in 1778.[28]

Merchants and trade in the interior

The relationship of merchants in the interior of New Granada to those of Cartagena was similar to that which existed between the latter and the merchants of Cádiz. As the main source for imported European goods, the Cartagena merchants occupied an advantageous position in the most valuable sector of the colonial market. The merchants of the principal centers for internal trade depended on them for a supply of foreign imports and generally also relied on the credit extended by the Cartagena merchants for the exercise of their business. At times they traveled to the coast to buy imports for cash, but it was more usual for them to obtain imported merchandise by remittance from Cartagena merchants, taking it on extended credit terms on the promise to pay the Cartagena supplier within a given period of time and at a specified rate of interest.[29]

Imports were distributed by several routes that connected Cartagena to the interior.[30] Some led directly to mining zones, and the traders who supplied both the Chocó area and the province of Antioquia sometimes did so by means of direct communication with merchants in Cartagena.

26. AGI Consulados 321, Diputados del Comercio to Consulado, Cartagena, April 30, 1745; AGI Consulados 328, Joseph Antonio de Zavala to Consulado, Cartagena, June 20, 1763.

27. AHNC Real Hacienda (Cartas), tomo 2, fols. 408–9.

28. Susan M. Socolow, *The Merchants of Buenos Aires, 1778–1810: Family and Commerce* (Cambridge, 1978), p. 13.

29. The absence of colonial notarial records for Cartagena during this period makes it impossible to use mercantile contracts as a means of tracking commercial relations between the port and the interior. There are, however, occasional indications of their nature in merchant contracts found in other sources. See for example AHNC Consulados, tomo 4, fols. 962–4; Biblioteca Luis Angel Arango (Bogotá), *Documentos relativos a amonedación y fisco en la Colonia*, Ms. 118.

30. The best survey of inland transport routes is provided by West, *Colonial Placer Mining*, pp. 112–30.

Either they traveled to the port to purchase imports from its wholesalers, or the Cartagena merchants sent representatives to the mining towns and settlements to trade on their behalf, or remitted consignments of merchandise to the provincial traders who acted as their agents. This trade could be carried via the Cauca River by way of Cáceres, but by the early 1770s the more usual route was via the Magdalena River port of Nare and then overland to Medellín and Santa Fe de Antioquia, an arduous journey of some twenty days. Nare also provided the point of entry for traders journeying to Antioquia from the Eastern Cordillera cities of Bogotá, Tunja, and so on, again at considerable cost and effort.[31] Merchants from Popayán also had contacts with the business community in Cartagena, despite the great distance between them. They conducted trade through Honda and along the Magdalena River, or via the *camino real,* which led through Bogotá, Tunja, Pamplona, and thence to the coast. However, the most important point for the internal distribution of imported goods and the major mercantile center in New Granada's interior was Bogotá, which was strategically placed in the most populated region of the colony.[32]

Merchants in Bogotá, like those of other cities in the interior, generally relied on wholesalers in Cartagena for remittances of imports from Europe. Acting as traders on their own account or as agents for Cartagena merchants, they received imported merchandise from the port, usually on credit for periods of between six and twelve months, and arranged for the transfer of gold bullion or specie to the port when payment fell due. They then disposed of the merchandise by both wholesale and retail sale from their stores in the capital, and by the transfer of smaller consignments to traders in other towns in the interior, often extending the chain of credit that usually started from Cádiz. No study of the Bogotá merchants exists, but the nature of the business in which they were involved, and the manner in which they conducted this business can be illustrated by some examples drawn from the records of contracts that prominent merchants registered with the city's notaries.

Manuel Díaz de Hoyos, a Spaniard related to aristocratic families in Cartagena, was an outstanding member of Bogotá's merchant community during the latter half of the eighteenth century. For nearly fifty years, Díaz de Hoyos carried on his trade in the capital, and by the 1790s he had

31. For a contemporary description of Antioquia's trade routes in 1786, see Silvestre, *Relación*, pp. 116–26; a graphic account of the difficulties affecting transport into Antioquia is also found in Twinam, *Miners, Merchants and Farmers*, pp. 82–6.

32. An indication of the size and resources of the capital's merchant community, compared with those of other major towns can be seen from the contributions that they made to the *donativo* (royal fund) of 1793. See *Papel Periódico de Santafé de Bogotá*, no. 99, pp. 371–2, no. 116, pp. 505–6, no. 102, pp. 395–6, no. 158, p. 844, for the contributions of merchants from Santa Fe, Popayán, Honda, and Mompós.

become a highly respected citizen in its community, and captain in the Cavalry Militia of Bogotá.[33] In his early days in the city, he acted as the agent for the Marquesa de Valdehoyos, a resident of Cartagena, owner of large estates, and speculator in the slave trade. In 1760, Díaz de Hoyos appears in the notarial records, declaring a loan of 6,000 gold pesos made to a Venezuelan merchant on the Marquesa's behalf, and repayable to her in large quantities of cacao.[34] In 1770, his contracts show that, in addition to disposing of more than 20,000 pesos' worth of European merchandise from his store in Bogotá, he also lent 300 gold pesos to the newly appointed governor of the Llanos province to cover his expenses.[35] Later, money lending figures more prominently in the notarial records: in 1780, his debtors included other merchants and members of the viceregal administration who, between them, acknowledged loans that totaled more than 5,000 pesos, given at an interest rate of 6%.[36] In 1784 he also lent 5,300 pesos to a Chocó mine and slaveowner, money that, it was stipulated, was to be repaid in gold from the Chocó.[37] During the 1790s, he was investing large sums in direct trade with Cádiz. In 1791, Díaz de Hoyos made over 300,000 pesos available to two merchants, Bernardo Gutiérrez and Luis Merino, so that they would organize imports from Cádiz on his behalf. By 1797, he was claiming that they had defrauded him, and that he was on the verge of complete ruin.[38] However, his days as a merchant were not over: in 1800, traders in the capital acknowledged receiving goods worth nearly 300,000 pesos from Díaz de Hoyos.[39]

Notarial documents also record the activities of other Bogotá-based merchants who were involved in business at a more modest level, distributing imported merchandise among provincial traders who came to the city as well as to other merchants in the city itself. Thus, for example, in 1770 Ventura de la Peña recorded credits that he had given in imported goods to traders from the towns of Vélez and Ibagué. These debts were to be repaid within nine months, partly in gold coin, and partly in local cloth that he could resell in the capital.[40] This was only a fraction of his business. By 1780, he claimed to be worth 30,000 pesos, of which 25,000 pesos were owed to him in outstanding commercial debts. Of the remainder, he held 4,000 pesos in coin, and 1,000 pesos in gold and silver plate.[41] Other contracts record the names of many other men who were

33. AHNC Consulados, tomo 3, fols. 171.
34. AHNC Notaría Primera, tomo 191 (1760), fol. 772.
35. Ibid., tomo 201 (1770), fols. 248–9, 297, 300, 308–9.
36. Ibid., tomo 205 (1780), fols. 99–100, 175–6, 233–4.
37. Ibid. (1790), fols. 84–5. 38. AHNC Consulados, tomo 3, fols. 171–5.
39. AHNC Notaría Segunda, tomo 198 (1800), fols. 228–32, 285–7.
40. AHNC Notaría Primera, tomo 201 (1770), fols. 289–90, 413.
41. AHNC Notaría Segunda, tomo 161 (1780), fol. 163.

similarly involved in distributing European imports within the interior, generally by giving consignments to provincial merchants on the promise of future payment (usually a year later) in gold or silver money, or in goods from the region from which the trader came.[42] Among the other Spanish merchants who were prominent in the capital were Vicente Rojo and Pedro Ugarte, both of whom became aldermen in the cabildo of Bogotá in the years before 1810. In addition to their business in imported goods, both men were, like Díaz de Hoyos, involved in lending large sums of money to other merchants and to officials.[43]

Trade in imports from Europe was, however, only part of the volume of commerce that entered Bogotá. An official report on the capital's alcabala administration and revenue in 1761 shows that by far the largest quantity of goods paying sales tax was composed of "géneros del Reino," or products of the domestic economy. Imports from Europe amounted to 400 *cargas* of goods, together with more than 2,000 jars of wine, fish, olives, and olive oil, and 395 iron bars. Of these, 261 *cargas* consisted of "géneros nobles" and textiles, mostly linens, woolens, silks, and hats; the other 139 *cargas* were an assortment of goods, mostly different types of haberdashery, wax, paper, Castilian and tabasco pepper, cinnamon, cumin, and hardware. The volume of domestic products entering the city was more than seventy times larger, amounting to 19,300 *cargas*. Nearly three-quarters of this volume consisted of molasses, which alone accounted for nearly 13,900 *cargas*. The rest consisted of sugar, tobacco, cacao, and anis (over 2,500 *cargas*), domestic linens, Tunja shirts and blankets, and woolens from Quito (over 500 *cargas*), miscellaneous items such as soap, leather, leather sandals, tallow, candlewicks, and many different foodstuffs, (rice, conserves, cheeses, cheese and honey cakes, chickpeas, garlic, and salt fish). In 1761, nearly 1,600 cattle and 4,500 pigs met the city's demand for meat.

The large traffic in domestic products was, no doubt, carried by a host of small traders, who sold their goods in the city market or through the small retail stores known as *pulperías*, or who simply peddled them in the streets. Of their lives and activities, we know virtually nothing: the small traders of colonial New Granada await their historian. One thing is obvious, however. The profits from these trades were much smaller than those from European imports. In fact, although imports formed only a fraction

42. The notarial archives are replete with contracts concerning this kind of business. The examples on which the above statement is based are drawn from AHNC Notaría Primera, tomo 191 (1760), fols. 298–9, 358–9; tomo 201 (1770), fols. 5–6, 21–2, 68, 90–1, 143, 201, 218, 220, 294; tomo 205 (1780), fols. 70–1, 80–1, 304, 421–2; tomo 228 (1810), fols. 26, 27, 38, 62, 156, 172–3, 188, 199, 232, 252, 267–70, 375–6.
43. AHNC Notaría Primera, tomo 201, fols. 147, tomo 161, fol. 86 (1790), fols. 26–34, 253–4, tomo 228 (1810), fols. 131, 208, 251; Notaría Segunda, tomo 198 (1800), fols. 5–6.

of the volume of goods sold in Bogotá, their total value was higher than that of domestic products. Of more than half a million pesos of goods paying the sales tax, imports were valued at over 281,000 pesos, and domestic products at 240,000 pesos.[44]

According to the administrator of customs in Bogotá, writing in 1789, there was no clear demarcation between wholesalers and retailers in the city. Complaining of the difficulties he experienced in collecting the *alcabala,* the administrator observed that "even the *comerciantes* of the best class sell small quantities of goods from their warehouses, down to the quantity or value of a *cuartillo,* the lowest denomination in the currency of this country."[45] However, although even the merchants of the "best class" may have been ready to deal at a very petty level, during the early 1780s merchants in Bogotá began to press claims for parity of opportunity and status with their counterparts in Cartagena.

Initially, the claims of the merchants in the capital were modest. In 1785, the representative appointed by the "deputies and other individuals of the commerce of Santa Fe" pointed out that his clients were in constant contact with Cádiz and other Spanish ports authorized for colonial trade, from which they ordered merchandise for resale in the city of Bogotá, the place of their residence. For this reason, he petitioned the viceroy to permit such imports to come directly to the capital without delay or interference by the customs house in Cartagena. The viceroy, who was disposed to take any step that might encourage trade, acceded to the request.[46] However, the number of merchants who signed the petition suggests that these independent *comerciantes* were as yet a very small group. Only eleven merchants, mostly peninsular Spaniards, signed the petition, identifying themselves as "individuals of the commerce of this city with that of Cartagena, Cádiz, and the other ports of the Spanish Kingdoms."[47] Evidently most merchants in the interior still relied on Cartagena to supply them with imports that they could then resell in the interior, rather than dealing directly with suppliers in metropolitan Spain.

The relative weakness of the Bogotá merchant community was further emphasized in 1796 when, in response to the creation of a Consulado in Cartagena, the merchants in the capital petitioned for the establishment of a separate consular institution in the capital that would be wholly independent of Cartagena and have jurisdiction over the provinces of the interior. As some thirty-four merchants "who employ their capital in trade with Spain" and an equal number of merchants "who buy here and in

44. AHNC Impuestos varios (Cartas), tomo 26, fols. 237–42.
45. AHNC Aduanas (Cartas), tomo 3, fols. 921–7. Quotation from fol. 921.
46. AHNC Aduanas, tomo 20, fol. 779.   47. Ibid., fol. 779.

Cartagena" supported the petition, the mercantile community in Bogotá was evidently growing larger and stronger.[48] Nonetheless, Viceroy Ezpeleta refused to accept that they were the peers of the Cartagena merchants. "It is well known," he bluntly observed,

> that the trade of the Kingdom of New Granada with the metropolis and with the other colonies of America is carried mainly through the port of Cartagena, in which are gathered the true *comerciantes* who receive merchandise on their own account, and from there distribute it to the interior provinces, where there are generally only factors and retailers who deal at second and third hand.[49]

Cartagena merchants in the age of *comercio libre*

Following the introduction of *comercio libre*, greater freedom for trade with Spain brought some new men into New Granadan commerce, mainly into the merchant community of Cartagena. The most obvious change in the mercantile community of the port was the entry of Catalans, who arrived immediately after the decree of *comercio libre* with large imports of aguardiente.[50] A decade later, in 1789, Catalans "who traffic and trade in this city" organized their own contribution to the celebrations for the accession of Charles IV, suggesting that they had become a distinct and well-established group.[51] Their specialty continued to be the aguardiente trade, and contemporaries attributed their economic success to the fact that they were prepared to extend their business from importing into directly retailing liquor from shops and stalls in the city.[52]

Catalan participation in Cartagena's trade was part of larger growth in the port's merchant community. A list of debts accumulated by the port's customs administration in the two years of 1789–90 includes 175 names, of whom 49 had either disappeared, died, or become insolvent.[53] Not all these debtors were necessarily merchants, but even if we allow for a margin of error, this figure suggests a considerable increase in the number of merchants operating in the port. However, other evidence indicates that the number of resident *comerciantes por mayor*, the wholesale merchants who handled the bulk of the import trade, remained small. Lists of merchants attending the meetings of the *comerciantes* in 1780 and 1786

48. AHNC Consulados, tomo 2, fols. 1004–27.
49. AGI Santa Fe 957, Viceroy Ezpeleta to Diego de Gardoqui, Santafé, July 19, 1796.
50. AGI Santa Fe 659, Gutiérrez de Piñeres to Gálvez, April 30, 1779.
51. AHNC Historia Civil, tomo 18, fols. 346–9, 357–8.
52. A general account of the Catalan aguardiente trade is found in Gilma Mora de Tovar, "El comercio de aguardientes catalanes en la Nueva Granada (siglo XVIII)," *Boletín Americanista*, no. 38 (1988), pp. 209–26.
53. AHNC Aduanas, tomo 12, fols. 733–42.

name only about fifty individuals.[54] During the early 1790s the number of such merchants residing in Cartagena was much the same. Lists of contributors donating to the crown in 1793 identify forty-six merchants who, as members of the *comercio de Cartagena* and of the city's cabildo, made payments appropriate to their standing.[55] A census of 1795 recorded the names of some fifty-three *comerciantes* in Cartagena, together with fifty-nine associates or employees who were registered at the same addresses, and who were either the relatives of their patron, or were related to some other member of the merchant community.[56]

Within this community of merchants engaged in trade with Spain, there appears to have been a high turnover of personnel. Of the forty-two *comerciantes* named in 1771, only eleven were still in Cartagena by 1786. Similarly, of the fifty-three merchants listed in the 1795 census, only eighteen were men who had been trading in the port ten years earlier. This pattern persisted during the next decade. By 1808, less than half of the *comerciantes* named in the census of 1795 still resided in the port and figured as members of its trading community.[57] But the merchants evidently occupied high standing in the city, which was reflected in their domination of the cabildo. In 1793, for example, at least nine of fourteen cabildo officers were merchants.[58]

Under the terms of the *Reglamento de comercio libre,* the American-born Spaniard or creole was allowed to trade with Spain on the same footing as the peninsular Spaniard. Not only was he accorded the same right to import goods from Spain on his own account, but he might also fit out ships for independent trading ventures between colonial ports and the authorized ports of the metropolis.[59] But in practice, creole participation in the overseas trade of New Granada was discouraged; while José de Gálvez was Minister for the Indies, official policy sought to confine the creole merchant to internal commerce, whereas peninsulars organized the transatlantic traffic.[60] Some creoles nevertheless did enter the mercantile elite: Ignacio de Pombo, for example, was a native of Popayán who joined the ranks of the *comercio de España* and became a prominent figure in Cartagena's merchant community during the final years of colonial rule.

54. AHNC Consulados, tomo 5, fols. 68–9, 84–6, 91–3; AHNC Comercio, tomo 1, fol. 39.
55. *Papel Periódico de Santafé de Bogotá,* no. 107, fols. 435–6 (September 13, 1793); no. 186, fol. 1068 (April 3, 1795).
56. AHNC Censos de varios departamentos, tomo 6, fols. 73–6.
57. Information on the merchant community in 1808 is taken from a list of contributors to a royal "donation" of that year. AHNC Abastos, tomo 9, fols. 613–17.
58. *Papel Periódico de Santafé de Bogotá,* no. 186, April 3, 1795, p. 1068.
59. For the rules governing American involvement in trade with Spain, see Antúnez and Acevedo, *Memorias históricas,* pp. 296–305.
60. For the direct statement of this policy by José de Gálvez, see Luis Ospina Vásquez, *Industria y protección en Colombia 1810–1930* (Medellín, 1958), pp. 44–5.

But he was an exceptional figure. In Cartagena as elsewhere in the Americas, the practices of transatlantic trade underpinned peninsular domination. With its emphasis on credit transactions that were arranged over long distances in an age of slow communications and involved long periods of gestation, the colonial trade relied heavily on personal relationships and mutual trust between merchants. Any commercial house that sent merchandise from Spain to a factor in the colony depended heavily on his judgment, efficiency, and honesty. A default by the factor could ruin his patron, because debt recovery in the colony entailed protracted and expensive legal procedures that might damage a merchant's reputation and liquidity. Spanish merchants therefore had strong reasons for employing family members and fellow countrymen as their partners and agents in the trade.[61] Not only were such *paisanos* more likely to inspire confidence than Americans, but Spanish law also offered better safeguards against dishonesty. All merchants who left Spain as factors, taking goods on commission to credit, had to present bonds from guarantors who each put up 500 *ducados de vellón,* which was to be forfeited if the former did not return to Spain to discharge their debts within a prescribed period.[62] The merchant community of Cartagena was, then, a body of mainly peninsular immigrants who retained close contacts with Spain and whose business ties were frequently reinforced by those of kinship.

The basic practices of the trade were also largely unchanged by *comercio libre.* Although there may have been an increase in the number of shippers and merchants who visited the port to sell imports or to buy New Granadan products, the core of Cartagena's *comerciantes* continued to act mainly as factors and commission agents for Spanish firms. The letters that Juan Antonio Valdés recorded in his copy book for 1796–7 contain many examples of both these and other kinds of business.[63] Valdés acted as a factor for Spanish firms, receiving goods sent from the peninsula and remitting returns for commissions of between 5% and 6%. He also conducted an independent trade, and this combination of roles was no doubt the rule among the larger merchants of Cartagena. Independent business yielded larger profits, but it also entailed greater risks. So, by maintaining regular or occasional employment as factors for Cádiz houses, Cartagena's merchants earned commissions that would both supplement their personal capital and provide some protection against total loss. Meanwhile, the old trade routes linking Cartagena to Cádiz, via Havana, remained in place. The richer *comerciantes* of Cartagena conducted their import/export business through a mercantile network that routinely used

61. See Brading, *Miners and Merchants in Bourbon Mexico*, p. 111.
62. In 1778 this period was fixed at three years. See AGI Indiferente General 2412, Presidente de Contratación to Gálvez, Cádiz, July 7, 1778.
63. Archivo de la Academia Colombiana de Historia (Bogotá): Borrador de cartas, no. 4.

bills of exchange to facilitate trade, backed by a stream of gold from New Granada. Payment in gold was not, however, the sole form of return made by the merchants. If they relied mainly on the import trade, then Cartagena merchants also took an interest in commodity exports that offered the chance of profit in overseas markets.[64] However, as we have seen, trade in agricultural products and raw materials continued to be only a small element in New Granada's balance of trade, which still depended largely on remittances in gold. Cartagena's merchant community thus continued to be small, focused on imports rather than the exports, and with consequently limited involvement in the economy of New Granada at large. It was nonetheless still the preeminent force in organizing the colony's external trade, a fact that was acknowledged in 1795, when a *Consulado de Comercio* was established in Cartagena.

The Consulado of Cartagena

The process that led to the Consulado's foundation started in 1789, when representatives of Cartagena's merchants first petitioned for the right to an independent Consulado. They advanced two main reasons for establishing such an institution: first, that the volume of business through Cartagena had grown to the point where the port needed an independent mercantile court to deal with increasing commercial litigation; second, supported by the viceroy, they argued that a Consulado would play an important part in promoting the colony's economic development and in assisting the authorities to counteract the growing contraband trade.[65] This initiative did not necessarily reflect any fresh dynamism among Cartagena's merchant community. The Cartagena merchants, like their counterparts elsewhere, acted with the knowledge that the crown intended to implement the plans stated in the *Reglamento* of 1778 to form a series of new Consulados, and their proposal was simply one among several similar proposals that were put forward by merchant groups in American ports during the 1780s. In 1785 and 1786, the Spanish ports of Málaga, Alicante, La Coruña, and Santander were permitted to establish Consulados and, as merchants in the Americas anticipated similar creations in the colonies,[66] the Cartagena merchants were eager to ensure that they were not passed over. In 1792, shortly after the appointment of Diego de Gardoqui as Minister for the Indies, they, like the merchants of Havana, Caracas, and Buenos Aires,

---

64. René de la Pedraja Toman, "Aspectos del comercio de Cartagena en el Siglo XVIII," *ACHSC*, vol. 8 (1976), pp. 107–25.
65. AGI Santa Fe 957, "Reglas que se proponen por los Diputados de Cartagena," February 28, 1789; ibid., Gil y Lemus to Valdés, Cartagena, March 15, 1789.
66. Manuel Nuñes Dias, *El Real Consulado de Caracas* (Caracas, 1971), pp. 202–5.

repeated their petition.[67] This time it was granted and, in 1795, a royal order was issued to prescribe the rules for governing a Consulado of Cartagena.[68]

By the end of 1795, the Consulado was in operation, functioning under the same basic rules that governed the other recently created consulados in Spanish America.[69] Those connected with the colony's overseas trade became entitled annually to elect representatives to a governing body that was invested with legal jurisdiction over mercantile affairs throughout New Granada, including the audiencia of Quito. In the first year of its existence, the officers of the Consulado were selected by the crown. In subsequent years, the leading officials were to convoke a *junta general* composed of all current wholesalers and retailers engaged in overseas trade, together with shippers who paid the *avería* tax on their own account, captains and masters of ships, and all those qualified traders who had lived for at least five years in any town or city where a deputation of the Consulado was established.[70] These men were then to elect individuals to the vacant posts in the governing body of the Consulado, offices that included a prior, two consuls, a syndic, and nine councillors. The fulltime officials of the Consulado – the secretary, treasurer, and accountant – were appointed by the crown.

The founding statutes of the Consulado required that officers of the Consulado should be merchants of known wealth and sound financial standing, respected and recognized as prominent members of the trading community. Representatives of the Cartagena merchants were more specific. They recommended that eligibility for elected offices be confined to wholesale merchants with working capital of more than 16,000 pesos, retail merchants with a minimum working capital of 10,000 pesos, and shipowners with vessels of not less than 100 tons, capable of overseas navigation.[71]

The officers of the Consulado had two main functions. First, the prior and two consuls were to act as the court responsible for dealing with commercial affairs and mercantile litigation. This *tribunal de justicia* met at regular intervals to hear cases brought before it by merchants regarding commercial transactions, bankruptcies, administration of the wills of its

67. German Tjarks, *El Consulado de Buenos Aires*, 2 vols. (Buenos Aires, 1962), vol. I, p. 56; AGI Santa Fe 957, Manuel de Rodrigo y Espinosa to crown, July 16, 1792.
68. AGI Santa Fe 957, Real cédula de erección del Consulado de Cartagena de Indias, June 14, 1795.
69. These rules are explained in detail in Nuñes Dias, *El Real Consulado de Caracas*, pp. 234–77, and in Ralph Lee Woodward, *Class Privilege and Economic Development, The Consulado de Comercio de Guatemala 1793–1871* (Chapel Hill, 1966), pp. 9–20.
70. AGI Santa Fe 957, Real cédula de erección del Consulado de Cartagena de Indias, article XLV.
71. AGI Santa Fe 957, Extracto de las reglas formadas por los comerciantes de Cartagena . . . para gobierno del Consulado que pretenden establecer. Article I.

members, formation and liquidation of companies, and so on. For the judges, this was a time-consuming responsibility, and not all merchants were prepared to give their time. The merchant Juan Antonio Valdés, for instance, appealed for exemption from office in the Consulado because, he said, half of any week would be taken up by the meetings of the tribunal and the juntas, forcing him to neglect his private business.[72] To expedite the processing of commercial litigation outside the port itself, the Consulado was also empowered to appoint deputies in the towns of the interior and, in 1796, it submitted to the crown a list of twenty-one officers located in all the main towns of New Granada, including the Isthmus of Panamá and Guayaquil, the principal port of the audiencia of Quito.[73] These men were the representatives of the Consulado in the provinces, and they were responsible for the same duties that the tribunal discharged in Cartagena. Neither the tribunal nor its deputies had the right to hear appeals. These were heard before the *Tribunal del Alzadas,* a court organized by the provincial governor in Cartagena, and by a judge of the audiencia in Bogotá, in consultation with the litigants involved in any case of appeal.

The second general function of the Consulado was to form a *junta de gobierno,* composed of elected and full-time officials who met two or three times a month to consider the most appropriate means of stimulating economic activity within the colony.[74] In particular, the Consulado was made responsible for building and maintaining a sound trail from the capital to the river port of Opón, for building boats suitable for navigation on the Magdalena and Cauca rivers, and for improving the channels in those rivers. In addition, it was charged with opening all-year navigation through the Canal del Dique, a tributary channel of the Magdalena that provided direct communication between the main channel of the river and the port of Cartagena.[75] To finance this and other projects, the Consulado was given the privilege of collecting an *avería,* a tax of 1/2% on all goods imported and exported through the ports of its jurisdiction.

Launched on a wave of optimistic rhetoric and worthy intentions, the Consulado failed to generate within the merchant body any enthusiastic commitment to its wider aims. In practice, it was an institution that was narrowly based in a small group of predominantly Spanish merchants who simply rotated Consulado offices among themselves. In the rules laid down by the crown, precautions had been taken to ensure that the Consulado did not fall into the hands of a small and self-perpetuating clique that might use it solely for its own advantage. Officers were therefore selected

---

72. AGI Santa Fe 957, Juan Antonio Valdés to Diego de Gardoqui, October 31, 1795.
73. AGI Santa Fe 957, Consulado to Gardoqui, April 30, 1796.
74. AGI Santa Fe 957, Real cédula de Erección del Consulado, articles XXI, XXII.
75. Ibid., article XXIII.

by a complicated procedure, under rules designed to ensure that they were not closely related to one another. However, by 1799, the Consulado petitioned the crown for a loosening of these rules, on the grounds that the network of relationships that bound together the principal *comerciantes* of Cartagena made it difficult to observe the existing regulations.[76] Serving in the Consulado therefore became something of a family affair, in which identity of economic interest was reinforced by relationships of blood and marriage. In the ten years for which election records are available, 116 posts became available within the Consulado.[77] These were held by seventy different individuals, of whom thirty-six men served once, whereas the remaining eighty positions were held by thirty-four men who served in various positions and on different occasions. It was, then, common for a man to serve twice, sometimes three times, in the offices of the Consulado, reflecting the tendency for overseas trade to concentrate in the hands of Cartagena's small group of peninsular merchants.

This clique of merchants was not entirely isolated from colonial society, despite its overwhelmingly peninsular composition, because Spaniards did marry into creole society, particularly in Cartagena, where they formed links with the local landed elite. But the merchants of Cartagena had no strong ties with the creole elites of the interior. Heavily identified with and dependent upon the fortunes of Spain's transatlantic trade, Cartagena's merchant class was essentially an enclave community composed chiefly of peninsulars who were inactive in, and largely disconnected from the politics of the country that lay beyond the confines of Cartagena de Indias. Closer in traveling time to Spain than to many places in the interior of New Granada, their position was on the fringes of colonial society, where they profited from their role as commercial intermediaries but contributed little to the territory's economic and political life. When the system of Spanish colonial commerce began to break down under the strain of international war between 1796 and 1808, this divorce from the wider society of New Granada and from the interests of creoles in the interior was to expose them to growing criticism and enmity.

76. AGI Santa Fe 959, Consulado to Secretario del Estado, Cartagena, November 1, 1799.
77. These ten years were 1795, 1797 to 1801, and 1804 to 1808. The results of elections in these years are recorded in AGI Santa Fe 958, 959, 960.

PART III

The politics of Bourbon colonialism: Reconstructing the colonial state

7

Renovation: The establishment of the viceroyalty

From the foregoing account of New Granada's commerce during the eighteenth century, it is obvious that Bourbon economic reform failed to transform New Granada's trade or to reshape its economy. For most of the century, trade grew very slowly and the region's economy continued to be oriented more toward self-sufficiency than export. Even after the introduction of *comercio libre,* which permitted commerce with Spain to expand during the 1780s, growth in exports was slight and foreigners still effectively competed with Spaniards in the import trades. Bourbon mercantilism did not, then, significantly enhance Spain's economic exploitation of the region, nor did it bind New Granada's economy much closer to that of the metropolis.

Adjustments to economic policy were, however, only one way in which a reviving Spanish imperialism impinged on New Granada during the eighteenth century. Following the Bourbon succession, the region's administration came under closer scrutiny from Madrid, and Philip V's government started a series of reforms that, over the course of the century, sought to strengthen the crown's authority over the region, to improve its defenses against external attack, and to force colonials to pay more toward the costs of empire. To trace the genesis of such reforms and to gauge their impact, we must return to the beginning of the eighteenth century, when the government of Philip V took the first step toward reorganizing the territory's government, by incorporating it within a new political entity, the Viceroyalty of New Granada.

The rise and fall of the first viceroyalty

Of all the early Bourbon measures to revitalize Spain's hold over its colonies, the foundation of the Viceroyalty of New Granada was the most striking, because it created the first new American viceroyalty since the mid-sixteenth century. To understand why New Granada was the object of such special attention, several factors must be taken into account. Most important was the occurrence, in 1715, of an unusual crisis at the center of government in New Granada, an event that delivered a sharp reminder to the authorities in Madrid that this was a troubled and troublesome area of the empire. Alcedo y Sotomayor's *visita* of 1695–8, together with the fall of Cartagena to the French in 1697 and the subsequent failure of Alcedo's inspection, had already revealed widespread laxity and disorder in the colonial administration and worrying weaknesses in its defenses. Left unresolved during the War of the Spanish Succession, these problems soon resurfaced to confront the Bourbon monarchy.

In September 1715, three oidors of the audiencia of Bogotá deposed the president and captain-general of New Granada, Francisco de Meneses, in an extraordinary coup d'état, placing him under arrest, seizing his property, and dispatching him from his palace in the capital to a prison in Cartagena.[1] To justify their actions, the oidors claimed that Meneses had created a species of police state in Bogotá. They alleged that he had raised the common soldiers of his palace guard "almost to a par with the royal ministers, by the authority he has conferred upon them . . ." and had engendered such an atmosphere of fear and suspicion that there was nobody who "on seeing a soldier does not feel fearful of being summoned or taken by order of the said President."[2] To legitimate their coup, the oidors also spread the rumor that they had "some highly secret and special order from Your Majesty," empowering them to proceed against Meneses.[3] On investigation, however, the conflict between the president and his fellow audiencia judges showed how far the authority of the crown had been subordinated to local and personal interests. When he first arrived in New Granada in 1711, Meneses had been heavily indebted to the French *asiento* company, because of payments made to him when his appointment to the presidency of New Granada was originally announced in 1707. Under pressure to repay his debts, he took part in a trading business, in company with a couple of Spanish merchants in Cartagena, while using his authority in Bogotá to extort payments in return for political favors. This might have passed unnoticed, had it not been for Meneses's irascible character, his failure to cultivate his fellow judges, and his involvement in a dispute with a leading creole family over access to government posts. The Flórez family of Bogotá, long entrenched at the center of patronage, used its

1. Brief accounts of the overthrow of Meneses are found in José Antonio de Plaza, *Memorias para la historia de la Nueva Granada, desde su descubrimiento hasta el 20 de julio de 1810* (Bogotá, 1850), p. 287; José Manuel Groot, *Historia eclesiástica y civil de Nueva Granada*, 2 vols. (Bogotá, 1956 ed.), vol. 2, pp. 11–21; Sergio Elias Ortíz, *Nuevo Reino de Granada: Real Audiencia y Presidentes de Capa y Espada, 1654–1719, Historia Extensa de Colombia*, vol. III, tomo 3 (Bogotá, 1966), pp. 229–32.
2. AGI Escribanía de Cámara 818A, "Quaderno principal de los autos obrados sobre el retiro y prisión del señor Don Francisco de Meneses," fols. 1–2, September 25, 1715.
3. AGI Santa Fe 367, "Copia del informe que hace al Rey . . . la parte del clero de la ciudad de Santafé sobre la deposición de D. Francisco de Meneses."

influence to manipulate rivalries within the audiencia and to engineer Meneses's fall.[4]

The palace coup of 1715 played an important part in persuading the crown of the need to reform New Granada's government. The first response from Madrid came in 1716, when the Council of the Indies commissioned Antonio Cobían Valdés, as oidor-elect of the Bogotá audiencia, to investigate the matter and, within two months, to prepare any necessary indictments. If he found that the deposed president was guilty of any grave crime, such as "sedition, treason, or something similar," then Meneses was to be left in prison; if not, the oidors who had removed him were to be arrested and replaced by two senior lawyers, and Meneses restored to his post.[5] Cobían did not complete his mission within the allotted time: indeed, Meneses was still in prison in 1718 and had not yet even been formally questioned. However, by this time, the crown had already decided to redefine New Granada's government. In 1717, Don Antonio de la Pedrosa y Guerrero – a Minister of the Council of the Indies who had served as fiscal in the audiencia of Santa Fe during the 1680s and 1690s – was sent to New Granada, empowered with the authority to establish a viceregency based in Bogotá.[6]

When Pedrosa arrived in New Granada in mid-1718, he assumed authority over the government as president of the audiencia and captain-general, rather than as viceroy, but in practice his instructions allowed him to exercise an authority that in many ways exceeded that of a viceroy. This included the power to suppress the audiencias of Panama and Quito, to act without interference from the audiencia of Santa Fe or any other official in New Granada, and to investigate all aspects of government, reforming it where necessary.[7] True to his brief, Pedrosa launched a full review of the colony's administration and reaffirmed the need to implant a firm authority at its center. The reports he received soon made it clear that the Real Hacienda in New Granada was all but bankrupt. The local treasuries were often empty and, in place of funds, simply held lists of debts owed to them by both private persons and officers of the crown. For Pedrosa, the restoration of the Real Hacienda and the remission of funds to

4. German Colmenares, "Factores de la vida política: el Nuevo Reino de Granada en el siglo XVIII (1713–1740)," in *Manual de Historia de Colombia*, vol. 1, pp. 397–402. The overthrow of Meneses may also have been part of a larger conflict over the profits of the contraband trade in New Granada, which had precipitated a conflict between the governor of Cartagena and leading citizens of Mompós in 1711: see Fals Borda, *Historia Doble de la Costa*, vol. I, pp. 88A–92A.

5. AGI Escribanía de Cámara, tomo 818B, "Autos de Cobián," fols. 23–6.

6. This account of the first viceroyalty is based on María Teresa Garrido Conde, "La primera creación del Virreinato de Nueva Granada," *AEA*, vol. 21 (1964), pp. 25–144.

7. Ibid., pp. 47–52.

Spain were his most urgent task, and he addressed himself to them with energy and efficiency.

To revive royal finances, Pedrosa did not impose new taxes but sought to enforce existing ones. He demanded payment of duties on black slaves who had been imported illegally, ordered all the provincial treasuries to collect their debts and to send their surpluses to the capital, and sought to increase revenues from the quintos paid in Bogotá by more efficient collection. By 1719, Pedrosa reported positive results. He not only stabilized the finances of Cartagena and Santa Marta, the principal military strongholds on New Granada's Caribbean coast, but had also accumulated some 50,000 pesos for remittance to the peninsula. Pedrosa had, moreover, intervened in many other areas of government, in matters large and small, and he appears to have gone some way toward reestablishing a degree of order and seriousness in the conduct of public business.[8] By mid-1719, the preparations for the new government were complete and Don Jorge de Villalonga, Conde de la Cueva, arrived in the capital to take command as first viceroy of New Granada.

During these years, renovation of New Granada's government was shored up by other, wider reforms to the colonial regime, which affected both administration and commerce in the Americas. When peace was restored following the War of Succession, Spanish ministers began to focus on anomalies of government in the colonies and, in 1717, spurred perhaps by the crisis in New Granada, Philip's government created a special committee to investigate and improve the workings of the American audiencias. After deciding that the quality of colonial administration was undermined by the poor caliber of many American oidors, the Council of the Indies determined to purge the audiencias of unqualified or superfluous judges, and, in 1718, suppressed completely the audiencia of Panama.[9] With political reform, a new determination to defend Spain's monopoly of colonial resources also took shape in these years. The earliest signs of Bourbon intentions to restructure colonial commerce appeared in 1714, when the crown created the new posts of *Oidor* and *Alcalde Visitador de la Veeduría General del Comercio entre Castilla y las Indias,* and sent two officials to America with wide powers to investigate and prosecute smugglers, to counter fraud in the royal treasury, and to suggest ways in which to improve Spain's colonial trade. Two years later, this initiative was carried a stage further, when, in May 1716, Philip's ministers contemplated more permanent solutions to the problems of American trade. From their meetings in 1716 and 1717 came several important reforms. One was the creation of the new ministerial post of *Intendente General de la*

---

8. Ibid., pp. 63–84.
9. Burkholder and Chandler, *From Impotence to Authority,* pp. 37–9.

Marina in January 1717, a post to which José Patiño was appointed and which he held concurrently with that of president of the tribunal of the *Casa de la Contratación*. Another reform transferred the *Casa de Contratación* and its monopoly of American trade from Seville to Cádiz in May 1717; a third established a regular mail service between Spain and the colonies, designed to improve communication between merchants and markets. These measures also prepared the way for the general reform of colonial commerce, which was embodied in the *Proyecto para Galeones y Flotas* of 1720.[10]

Reform of government in New Granada was, then, part of a general effort to increase the efficiency of colonial administration and commerce during the years between 1717 and 1720. It was, however, much more radical than the simple purge of personnel that took place in other American audiencias, where judges were simply removed or replaced. This was partly because the audiencia of New Granada presented a political problem of an unusual and specific kind, arising from an extraordinary dispute at the very heart of its government, and partly because of Madrid's desire to improve the region's impoverished finances and to protect its vulnerable Caribbean ports from foreign attack.[11] But these were not the sole motives for installing a viceroy in Bogotá. As the Bourbon monarchy responded to foreign commercial penetration in its colonies, the establishment of the viceroyalty was also connected with moves to rebuild Spain's commerce both with the region and with South America as a whole. Tighter administrative discipline and more effective government were not only required to improve the fiscal yield of colonial treasuries; they were also needed to restart Spain's transatlantic trade and to rebuff the commercial aggression of its European rivals. Thus, the arrival of the first viceroy in 1719 was shortly followed by the 1720 project for restarting the transatlantic fleets, and one of the main duties of the new viceroy was to stop foreign penetration of Spain's commercial monopoly.

Refashioning Spain's political and economic control over New Granada was, however, easier than sustaining it, and this first major conjuncture of Bourbon reform in New Granada, with its plans for improving both government and commerce with Spain, soon came to grief. Failure was partly the fault of the first viceroy, Don Jorge de Villalonga. Intent on displaying his status, Villalonga insisted on mounting an expensive and elaborate reception in Bogotá against the advice of Antonio de Pedrosa, the official who had prepared the new form of government and who had been de facto viceroy for the previous two years. After Pedrosa had de-

10. The background to the Proyecto between 1716 and 1720 is analyzed in Walker, *Spanish Politics and Imperial Trade*, pp. 88, 100–7.
11. Garrido Conde, "La primera creación del Virreinato," pp. 41–2.

parted for Spain, Villalonga caused further disputes by removing Pedrosa's appointees from office and undoing some of his measures, first in Bogotá and then in Cartagena. [12] If Villalonga's extravagance compared ill with the spartan efficiency of Pedrosa and his behavior gave cause for complaint to Spain, it was however his failure to stem the tide of contraband that finally brought him down, and ended the experiment with viceregal government in New Granada. His presence in the port between December 1720 and May 1721 did nothing to prevent contraband from undermining the trade of the Tierra Firme galleons of 1721 and frustrating the objectives of the 1720 *Proyecto*, and, worse still, the viceroy and his retinue were accused of complicity in contraband. Incensed at the prospect that the very minister charged with stopping smuggling had himself engaged in it, ministers in Madrid demanded action against him. In May, 1722, the fiscal of the Council of the Indies called for a specially commissioned minister to remove Viceroy Villalonga from office, pending investigation of his involvement in contraband. Should he be found guilty, the viceroy was to be arrested and imprisoned in a suitable place, twenty leagues from Santa Fe de Bogotá, and his property, credits, cash, books, and papers impounded. Similar tough action was to be taken against the governor of Cartagena and other officials suspected of smuggling. [13]

In the event, the Council of the Indies stopped short of such drastic measures. It simply reprimanded Villalonga for his inadequate reports of conditions in New Granada and postponed any further action until his residencia. [14] When that residencia was eventually held, Villalonga emerged unscathed, cleared of the many charges of contraband laid against him. [15] However, although this issue was resolved in Villalonga's favor, the disappointing performance of the 1721 galleons had shown his inability to shield Spanish commerce, and his conflicts with the governors of Cartagena and difficulties in organizing the city's defenses also reflected his failure to enforce authority on the colony's administration. [16] Thus, as doubts about the probity and efficiency of the viceroy multiplied, the new framework of New Granadan government was itself called into question. In 1723, the crown concluded that the costs of maintaining a viceregal court outweighed the benefits. The viceroyalty was duly suppressed, after a life of only five years. [17]

12. Ibid., pp. 91–118.
13. AGI Santa Fe 374, Fiscal del Consejo de Indias, Madrid, May 11, 1722.
14. Ibid., October 22, 1722.
15. Garrido Conde, "La primera creación del virreinato," pp. 127–33.
16. On Villalonga in Cartagena, see Juan Marchena Fernández, *La Institución Militar en Cartagena de Indias en el Siglo XVIII* (Seville, 1982), pp. 216–20.
17. Garrido Conde, "La primera creación del virreinato," pp. 119–25, for an account of the suppression of the viceroyalty.

With the departure of the viceroy, the colony's government reverted to its old form. The audiencia of Santa Fe again became the leading institution of royal authority in the territory, under a president who was also governor and captain-general of New Granada. In 1723, Don Antonio Manso Maldonado was appointed to the presidency and, in 1724, arrived in Bogotá to take up his office. At this point, after the abortive experiment with viceregal government, Madrid lost interest in New Granada. This lapse was, no doubt, connected to the fact that metropolitan government itself lost direction during the mid-1720s, with the temporary abdication of Philip V in 1724 and the brief ascendancy of Baron Ripperdá, a Dutch adventurer, as chief minister. Even when the government regained some stability following Ripperdá's fall in mid-1726, the development of colonial policy was overshadowed by the need of government ministers to satisfy Elizabeth Farnese's dynastic ambitions in Europe.[18] José de Patiño, a leading proponent of colonial reform, emerged as a pivotal minister in Philip's government, but apparently he was more preoccupied with using the Indies trade to improve the monarchy's finances than with creating a coherent colonial policy. Thus the early Bourbon impulse to reform government in the Americas faded.[19]

Confusion in Spain's government brought stasis in New Granada, and nothing new was accomplished for more than a decade after the suppression of the viceroyalty. When the first experiment with political reform in New Granada ended, the territory simply reverted to the old form of government, with all its attendant flaws. Interest in reform did not entirely disappear, however. When Antonio Manso, president of the audiencia between 1724 and 1729, reported to the crown at the end of his term of office, he sharply criticized the inefficiency of the region's government both at central and local levels. According to Manso, the principal obstacle to good government was at the very heart of the administration, in the audiencia. The oidors, he argued, were either insufficiently qualified or inexperienced, or they had become too involved with local interests to provide impartial and effective government on behalf of the crown. At the local level, government was also feeble and corrupt, due to the poverty of corregimientos, the poor quality of corregidors, and the widespread neglect of municipal administration. To improve the situation, Manso recommended that either the president should have more power to control his fellow judges, or that the oidors should be more carefully chosen from candidates who had experience in other audiencias or were expert lawyers. He also recommended that the oidors should be men who were less closely tied to local society, and suggested that the influence of colonial interests could be reduced by more rapid rotation of the oidors, so that they should

18. Lynch, *Bourbon Spain*, pp. 81–98.   19. Ibid., pp. 145–6.

not become permanent residents. For, he noted, even if the oidors did not personally marry into local society, the relatives who accompanied them did, leading to partiality in the dispatch of public affairs. To his recommendations for changes at the top level, Manso added suggestions for improving local government. He called for the recruitment of corregidors of better quality, and for closer regulation of the sale of cabildo offices to ensure that "persons of quality" served in municipal government.[20] It seems, then, that after three decades of Bourbon monarchy, the crown's efforts to reassert its political authority over New Granada had been largely frustrated.

The reestablishment of the viceroyalty

Although the first viceroyalty had collapsed, borne down by the incompetence of Villalonga, the machinations of his enemies, and the unsteady resolve of the authorities in Madrid, the experiment nevertheless left an enduring impression. Manso's remarks in 1729 indicate that reform of New Granada's government continued to be an object of Bourbon policy, and, by the mid-1730s, official anxiety about the British economic and military threat in the Caribbean Basin encouraged moves to revive the viceroyalty. The first step was taken in 1734, when Patiño convoked a committee of ministers to examine the reasons for the earlier suppression of the viceroyalty of New Granada and to decide if it should be reestablished. Among those consulted was Bartolomé Tienda de Cuervo, who had acquired first-hand experience of New Granada as an official in Cartagena during the first viceregency, and who now gave an important stimulus to its reestablishment.

In August 1734, Tienda de Cuervo presented a report on the colony that described its resources, surveyed its recent history, and reached clear conclusions concerning its future needs.[21] New Granada, Tienda de Cuervo insisted, was extremely rich in natural resources and had great economic potential. He assured the crown that the gold mines of both the provinces of Antioquia and the Chocó were increasing their production considerably, that the mines of the Chocó alone produced precious metal on a scale comparable to that of Peru, and that the territory contained a rich variety of other resources that were neglected to the detriment of both metropolis and colony. To prevent the loss of much of this wealth to foreigners through contraband, Tienda de Cuervo enthusiastically advo-

20. For these and other criticisms and recommendations made by Manso, see his final report, in Posada and Ibáñez, *Relaciones de mando*, pp. 9–14.
21. Tienda de Cuervo's report is found in AGI Santa Fe 385. It is reproduced in Jerónimo Becker and José María Rivas Groot, *El Nuevo Reino de Granada en el siglo XVIII* (Madrid, 1921), pp. 203–30.

cated reviving the viceroyalty. In his view, the authority of a viceroy was essential, for both fiscal and for political reasons. First, he drew attention to the fiscal advantages of a renewed viceroyalty, noting that fiscal returns had increased considerably during the first viceregency. Second, Tienda de Cuervo insisted that only a viceroy could impose a command capable of ensuring the enforcement of anticontraband measures by provincial governors. With the appropriate form of government, he concluded, New Granada could realize its tremendous economic and fiscal potential, and become "richer, more prosperous and powerful than all the rest of His Majesty's dominions in America."[22]

Such assertions in themselves were unlikely to lead to reform. It was, however, a propitious moment for restoring the viceroyalty because, in 1737–9, the Council of the Indies again became preoccupied with reforming colonial government, and persuaded the crown to take action against abuses in the American audiencias.[23] Once more, fresh thinking about New Granadan government took place in the context of a general review of colonial administration, just as it had two decades earlier. In 1737, the king sent Tienda de Cuervo's report to three prominent officials for urgent consideration and recommendation. Their response was unequivocal. In January 1738, Jorge Villalonga (Conde de la Cueva and ex-viceroy of New Granada), the Marqués de Torreblanca (Teniente General de la Marina), and Francisco de Varas (president of the Casa de Contratación) agreed that the viceroyalty should be reestablished. Three major reasons were given: to improve Spanish trade with New Granada by preventing foreign contraband, to fortify the territory against possible Dutch and English attacks, and to install a central authority capable of taking measures required to reform and control government in New Granada.[24] On receiving these reports, the king ordered the Council of the Indies to reach a quick decision on the matter.[25] In March 1738, the fiscal of the council committed his support to the proposal, stressing that a viceroy in New Granada would contain the "excesses and outrages" of provincial governors who routinely resisted the authority of the audiencia, and exercised "absolute and despotic" power over the king's subjects.[26] Finally, in October

22. Ibid., p. 229.
23. On the renewed campaign to reform the audiencias, see Burkholder and Chandler, *From Impotence to Authority*, pp. 46–8.
24. AGI Santa Fe 385, Informe sobre consulta que da D. Jorge de Villalonga, Madrid, January 29, 1738; Don Francisco de Varas to Marqués de Torrenueva, Cádiz, January 26, 1738; the Marqués de Torreblanca's report, also submitted in January 1738, is in AGI Santa Fe 264, Consejo de Indias, Consulta de 20 de octubre de 1738.
25. AGI Santa Fe 572, king to Conde del Montijo, Buen Retiro, February 1738.
26. AGI Santa Fe 385, Respuesta del Fiscal en vista de varios informes sobre el restablecimiento del Virreynato de Santa Fe, Madrid, March 12, 1738.

1738, the last hurdle was crossed; in a full and formal report to the king, the Council of the Indies gave its assent to the proposal.[27]

Its decision was not unanimous. Four ministers of the council submitted a dissenting *voto particular*, or minority report, which insisted that the viceroyalty's resurrection would generate more costs than benefits. They argued, not unreasonably, that the development of mines in Popayán and the Chocó would continue regardless of the presence or absence of a viceroy, whereas the regions without mineral wealth would continue to be impoverished because of their isolation from overseas trade. They also pointed out that, if the main reason for resurrecting the viceroyalty was to prevent contraband, the crown should be aware that this could be achieved by other means.[28] Preference for positive action carried the day, however. Persuaded that the audiencia of New Granada was insufficiently equipped to maintain royal authority throughout its jurisdiction and that the royal will could be effectively enforced only by the presence of a single powerful and authoritative figure, Philip V duly reestablished the viceroyalty. In April 1739, he appointed the Mariscal de Campo Sebastián de Eslava as viceroy of New Granada, while simultaneously promoting him to the rank of Teniente General in the royal army.[29]

The decision to reerect the viceroyalty, taken after years of consultation, not to say vacillation, was precipitated by the imminent outbreak of international war. In December 1738, news of Dutch attacks on shipping in the Caribbean was already reaching Spain from Cartagena and Havana, and in the following year, Bourbon ministers began to draw up plans for defending Caribbean ports against English attack.[30] Suspecting that Cartagena was a prime target, in July 1739 the crown ordered Viceroy Eslava to depart promptly for New Granada to take command of its defenses.[31] That the issue of defense was a major motive for reviving the viceroyalty was, moreover, underlined by the fact that the new viceroy was an experienced soldier, the first in a line of military men to hold office as the New Granadan viceroy. It would be misleading, however, to present military matters as the sole reason for reconstructing the viceroyalty; the discussions that preceded Eslava's appointment show that Spanish government was also concerned with broader issues of colonial development. If one of the viceroy's first tasks was to fortify the colony against military assault, then he was also expected to impose greater royal authority over New

27. AGI Santa Fe 264, Consejo de Indias, consulta de 20 de octubre de 1738.
28. Ibid., Voto particular of Manuel de Silva, Antonio de Sopena, Joseph de Lasequilla and Antonio de Pineda.
29. AGI Santa Fe 265, king to Conde del Montijo, Aranjuez, April 24, 1739.
30. AGi Santa Fe 572, Marqués de Torrenueva to Sebastián de la Quadra, Buen Retiro, December 26, 1738.
31. AGI Santa Fe 572, Buen Retiro, July 11 and July 13, 1739.

Granada's government and people, to bend its commerce into the orbit of Spanish trade, and to increase the colony's fiscal and economic yield. As president of the audiencia, the viceroy was invested with full authority over its judges, who were instructed to cooperate fully with him and to obey his dictates in all matters of government, war, and finance. As captain-general and governor of New Granada, he enjoyed supreme military authority and was responsible for both external defense and internal order. On the fiscal side, the viceroy was given sweeping powers to assure the efficient functioning of the royal treasury.[32]

The reestablishment of the viceroyalty marked the second major conjuncture in Bourbon reform of New Granada and a new departure in the region's administrative and political history. Unlike its predecessor, the revived viceregency endured, and between 1739 and 1810 twelve viceroys succeeded each other in the colony's highest political office. But what did this change mean in practice? Did the viceroyalty fulfill the functions envisaged by the king and his ministers? To assess the achievements and limitations of viceregal government, we will now examine its first forty years, before the third and final conjuncture of Bourbon reform began in 1778.

Viceregal government: Consolidation and achievement

New Granada had of course long been nominally subject to a viceroy, as its audiencia came within the overarching jurisdiction of the viceroyalty of Peru. In practice, however, viceroys in Lima had little effective influence over New Granada. Cushioned by distance and poor communications, the audiencia and provinces of New Granada had come to enjoy a high degree of autonomy. The problems associated with such autonomy were forcefully described by Francisco Silvestre in 1789, when he recalled conditions in the government during the early years of the century. "Because the distance from Lima was so great," said Silvestre

each oidor believed himself to be a sovereign; each wanted to command and enforce his will; each marshalled his clients, and the powers which should have been united in pursuit of peace and good government were given over to disorder and discord, or united only to subdue or overthrow he who wished to command. . . . The Royal Treasury was caught between the meddlesome and the powerful, and defrauded by all; justice was only pretence, or was used against the weak; commerce fattened the foreigners on the coast.[33]

In Silvestre's view, the reestablishment of the viceroyalty in 1739 had transformed this situation, bringing New Granada under firmer control,

---

32. These, and other facets of viceregal power are outlined in José María Ots Capdequí, *Instituciones de gobierno del Nuevo Reinio de Granada*, pp. 176–254.
33. Silvestre, *Descripción*, pp. 10.

so that "from then onwards, slackness in all areas of government began to be amended and corrected."[34]

These comments must be treated with some caution, as Francisco Silvestre was a man whose respect for viceregal government had been shaped by his experience as governor of Antioquia and as secretary to a viceroy. Nonetheless, in retrospect his emphasis on the positive results of the viceregency is plausible enough. For in the long term, the assignment of supreme authority to a viceroy redistributed power from regional to central government in New Granada, bringing its provinces under much firmer command than had prevailed under the Hapsburg regime, while also increasing the revenues that colonials paid to the royal treasury.

This redistribution of power was not accomplished without difficulty, however, and New Granada continued to enjoy a considerable de facto autonomy despite the presence of the viceroys. For although the viceroys had considerable powers, their orders still had to be transmitted through the existing networks of government, with all their inherited legal rules and regulations, their jurisdictional demarcations, and their capacity to resist change.[35] Not only did the viceroys encounter opposition from the audiencia and from governors over specific issues, but the inefficient and corrupt routines of local government also acted as a general check on initiatives from the viceregal capital.[36] Indeed, by 1743, only a few years after his appointment and triumphant defense of Cartagena, Viceroy Eslava was so frustrated by the recalcitrance of local officials that he requested permission to retire from his post.[37] His letters reveal the reasons for his disillusion. He was, in the first place, greatly irritated by the scant respect for government that he found in New Granada. "These colonials," Eslava testily remarked, "love disorder more than good government and administration (and) Spaniards and creoles, including clerics and officials, regard the viceregency as a very heavy burden . . . the total opposite of the freedom which they have enjoyed for their disorders in the past."[38] Eslava also complained that government officials were untrustworthy, and alleged that his orders were often altered or simply ignored by the officials who should have implemented them, especially in fiscal matters. Some years later, in 1746, Eslava reiterated his complaint that the viceroyalty was virtually ungovernable. "Each one of these provinces," he observed,

---

34. Ibid., p. 77.
35. The duties of viceroys and their relationship with the other leading agencies of the colonial government are outlined in Clarence H. Haring, *The Spanish Empire in America* (New York, 1963 repr.), pp. 110–27.
36. For examples of resistance from the audiencia and from the provincial government, see José María Ots Capdequí, *Instituciones de gobierno del Nuevo Reino de Granada*, pp. 121–38, 150–66, 339–41.
37. AGI Santa Fe 572, Eslava to Marqués de la Ensenada, November 11, 1743.
38. Ibid.

"needs its own viceroy, and each Audiencia a supreme council to examine the conduct of ministers."[39] And, once again, he singled out as a special problem the challenge to the viceroy's authority that came from within government, particularly from audiencia judges. If his successor was to achieve anything, Eslava argued, it was essential that the audiencias should not interfere in matters of government and finance, except where they had specific legal authority.

Complaints of this kind did not end with Eslava; his successors all commented on the way in which their plans were hindered by bureaucratic disregard for royal orders, and by the poor character of official personnel.[40] But if New Granada remained a difficult place to govern, the viceregency was a much more effective instrument of royal authority than the audiencia, and it had a noticeable impact on the political life of eighteenth-century New Granada. Of the four viceroys appointed after 1739 – Eslava (1739–49), Pizarro (1749–53), Solís (1753–61), and Messía de la Cerda (1761–72) – three served between ten and twelve years, and their long terms in office undoubtedly helped to impress a stronger royal authority on New Granada's administration. The fact that the viceroys were high-ranking army officers no doubt reinforced their authority with provincial governors who held military appointments, thereby curbing the autonomy of provincial governors, which had previously been such a flaw in royal government. Most important, however, was the fact that between 1739 and 1778, the viceroys succeeded in squeezing from colonials larger revenues that were put toward the costs of the region's defense and government.

From the moment of its restoration, a primary purpose of the viceregency was to improve royal finances. In the instructions given to Viceroy Eslava when he took office in 1739, the urgent need to reform the fiscal apparatus was strongly emphasized, and in the years that followed Eslava and his successors sought to broaden the range of taxation and to extend the administrative network for collecting taxes.[41] Fiscal reorganization was slow to begin, since Eslava remained in Cartagena de Indias throughout his viceregency, preoccupied with the defense of the city against British attack.[42] In this, he was highly successful, repelling Vernon's assault on

---

39. AGI Santa Fe 572, Eslava to Marqués de la Ensenada, Cartagena, September 15, 1746.

40. For examples, see the reports left by the three viceroys who followed Eslava, published in Posada and Ibáñez, *Relaciones de mando*, pp. 77–8, 99–100, 150–4.

41. For Eslava's instructions from the crown, see AGI Santa Fe 572, "Copia de la Instrucción que por el Consejo se ha de dar al nuevo Virrey de Santa Fe . . ."

42. Eslava's most notable success as viceroy was the defense of Cartagena against attack by Admiral Vernon in 1741, a victory that was to guarantee his promotion. On the attack on Cartagena and its defense, see James A. Robertson, "The English Attack on Cartagena in 1741," *HAHR*, vol. 2

Cartagena in 1740 and thereby dealing a heavy blow against British arms in the Caribbean. Although his military duties distracted him from the task of fiscal reform, Eslava nevertheless took some important steps toward improving returns to the royal treasury. He began by seeking to enlarge returns from existing taxes, starting with measures to reduce tax evasion and to facilitate tribute collection in the city and province of Cartagena.[43] His successor, José de Solís (1753–61), pursued the same approach, seeking to improve tax returns by establishing an official presence in neglected areas and trying to overcome ingrained habits of tax evasion. New branches of the royal treasury were accordingly established at Ocaña, at Cartago, and in Barbacoas, and a *teniente real* was appointed to oversee administration in Medellín, in the province of Antioquia.[44] However, the impact of viceregal government on tax yields was most significant in the establishment of a new area of taxation, based on the *estanco de aguardiente,* or royal monopoly over the sale of cane brandy, which was put into operation under Viceroy Eslava.

Plans to introduce an aguardiente monopoly had a long pedigree. They began shortly after the Bourbon succession, when, after fruitless attempts to prohibit the manufacture and sale of cane brandy during the late seventeenth century, the crown decided to control sales through a royal monopoly.[45] The first order to establish an estanco was made in 1700, but some time elapsed before it was put into practice.[46] The royal directive had to be repeated in 1704, and then disputes within the royal administration, which reflected conflicts between private interests involved in aguardiente importation and sales, continued to delay its operation before 1710. In that year, revenues from the estanco finally figured in the general accounts of the royal treasury, where they continued to appear in substantial amounts until 1716–17. Revenues from this source then declined dramatically, falling from an average of several thousand pesos per year to derisory sums of no more than a few hundred pesos.[47] The interruption of aguardiente revenues reflected the reversal of the new policy, and showed

(1919), pp. 62–71, and Marchena Fernández, *La Institución Militar en Cartagena,* pp. 121–44. For Eslava's subsequent career and role in making colonial policy, see Lynch, *Bourbon Spain,* pp. 175–6, 190.

43. AGI Santa Fe 288, Eslava to crown, Cartagena, March 6, 1744; ibid., March 12, 1744; ibid., March 23, 1744.
44. Posada and Ibáñez, *Relaciones de mando,* pp. 78–9.
45. AGI Santa Fe 366, Real Cédula, August 10, 1714, El Pardo in "Testimonio de autos sobre la prohibición del aguardiente de caña."
46. This account of the early years of the estanco draws partly on information found in Gilma Mora de Tovar, *Aguardiente y conflictos sociales en la Nueva Granada, siglo XVIII* (Bogotá, 1988), pp. 20–40. Where addition or correction is necessary, I have drawn on the primary sources indicated in footnotes.
47. TePaske and Jara, *Cartas cuentas de la real caja de Santa Fe,* unpub. ms.

how effective local opposition could be against a feeble government. In 1714, the debate over prohibition was reopened and, while it took place, the aguardiente estanco was suspended.[48] This brought a long hiatus in its development. More than a decade passed before the audiencia reported to the Council of the Indies on the estanco issue in 1726, and another decade passed before it was finally reinstated, in 1736. These long delays suggest that colonial interests were very active in opposing economic measures that they disliked. But in the end, the Council of the Indies was persuaded to push forward with plans for the monopoly when, in 1732, the audiencia in Bogotá stated that it offered the only solution to the colony's deep financial problems.[49] After yet another delay, a royal directive finally ordered the reestablishment of the government's monopoly over cane brandy sales in 1736, and issued regulations for its administration. By 1738, substantial revenues from this source started to flow into the royal treasury once more, for the first time since 1716.

The decisive advance in the development of aguardiente revenues came after the restoration of the viceregency, when Viceroy Eslava extended the scope of the estanco's operations to areas that had previously been exempt.[50] The results were startling. From the early 1740s, revenues from the aguardiente estanco took off, doubling average receipts between 1741 and 1746, then increasing fourfold during the 1750s and early 1760s.[51] In the crucial area of colonial finances, the viceroys were evidently earning their keep. Equally important was the fact that the viceroys brought a more interventionist approach to colonial affairs. During his viceregency, Eslava tried to impose direct royal administration on the aguardiente monopoly in the town of Honda, and was only frustrated by opposition from the audiencia and the *Tribunal de Cuentas* (Court of Audit) in Bogotá.[52] A decade later, his successor brought the estanco in Mompós under direct administration and, as revenues there more than doubled in consequence, this was a powerful precedent both for further extension of the monopoly and for replacement of private contractors by royal officials.[53]

So, in the quarter-century that followed the re-creation of the viceroyalty, the renovation of government in New Granada brought clear rewards in the vital area of royal finances. This was not entirely the work of the viceroys, as some basic groundwork had been carried out before 1739; it was, after all, the audiencia that had revived the aguardiente monopoly project in 1732. But it was under the viceregency in the 1740s,

---

48. AGI Santa Fe 366, Consulta del Consejo de Indias, July 19, 1732.
49. Ibid.   50. Mora de Tovar, *Aguardiente y conflictos*, pp. 30–3.
51. TePaske and Jara, *Cartas cuentas de la real caja de Santa Fe de Bogotá*, unpub. ms.
52. AGI Santa Fe 288, Eslava to crown, March 18, 1744.
53. Posada and Ibáñez, *Relaciones de mando*, p. 80.

and especially in the 1750s and early 1760s, that the project began to develop fully, bringing significant growth in royal revenue and shifting the colony's fiscal system to a new footing.[54] Traditional fiscal measures were not entirely abandoned, of course: Indians continued to pay tribute and the inherited apparatus of taxation remained formally intact. The old system of direct contribution to the royal treasury was relegated to a position of secondary importance, however, as the crown focused on intensifying indirect taxation on economic activity within New Granada's domestic economy. Taxes of this sort were not new: the alcabala, the quinto, and the diezmo – taxing sales, mining, and agricultural production respectively – had been in place since the sixteenth century. But during the first half of the eighteenth century, the crown opened a new fiscal frontier by taxing the sales of aguardiente derived from the colony's sugar production. In this, the viceroys unquestionably played a key role. When introduced, the aguardiente monopoly had foundered amidst opposition from colonial economic interests and uncertainty in colonial government; after the reestablishment of the viceroyalty, it prospered. Revenues from aguardiente grew substantially, then soared, until by the mid-1760s they had become an indispensable element in the budget of the colony's government. The principle of the royal monopoly, administered directly by officers of the crown, had become a keystone for further fiscal reorganization and reform during the reign of Charles III.

Caroline reform of New Granadan administration: First initiatives

The reassertion of closer political control and fiscal regulation made further progress during the years immediately after the accession of Charles III in 1759, when a new drive to increase the efficiency of government in the Americas arose in the wake of Spain's humiliating defeat in the Seven Years' War. The first forays in Caroline reformism were in Cuba, where, after Havana had been restored to Spain by Britain in 1763, the king ordered a review of Cuba's government, leading to a sweeping reorganization of the island's defenses, finances, and commerce. This was shortly followed by the initiation of a *visita general* in New Spain where, in 1765–71, José de Gálvez made the most determined and effective efforts to reform colonial administration yet seen under Bourbon rule.[55] New Gra-

---

54. The fiscal initiative in New Granada coincides with Ensenada's ascendancy in the first government of Fernando VI, a time when policy was particularly oriented toward fiscal innovation and improvement. For an account of Ensenada and his government, see Lynch, *Bourbon Spain*, pp. 164–86.

55. On reform in Cuba, see Kuethe, *Cuba, 1753–1815: Crown, Military and Society*, pp. 3–49; on Mexico, see Brading, *Miners and Merchants in Bourbon Mexico*, pp. 34–63.

nada was spared such direct intervention until 1778; nonetheless, Caroline reformism made its first appearance after the end of the Seven Years' War in 1763, when the viceroys implemented several adjustments to military and fiscal policy.

Concern with defense problems was reflected in sharp increases of expenditure on forces at strategic points. During the viceregency of Pedro Messía de la Cerda (1761–72), large investments were made in coastal fortifications and naval forces. More than a million and a half pesos were spent on closing the Bocagrande Channel into the Bay of Cartagena, in addition to large sums spent on repairing the Castle of San Lázaro and the city's northern wall, and improving fortifications at Panama. New Granada's treasury also supplied more than 700,000 pesos to the navy for coastguard defenses, and a campaign against the Guajira Indians in Río Hacha also absorbed large funds.[56] Finally, from 1771, the visitor general of the Spanish army in the Americas started a broad reorganization of the army in New Granada, beginning with an expansion of regular forces in Cartagena and Portobelo and extending to the establishment of disciplined militia forces at key points throughout the viceroyalty during the 1770s.[57]

While New Granada was being placed on a higher state of military readiness, the crown also began to seek ways of enlarging revenue returns by developing state monopolies as sources of government income. This took place on two main fronts. First, the viceroys sought to increase the yield of the existing aguardiente monopoly by transferring area administrations from private contractors to direct management by royal officials. Viceroy Solís had taken a tentative step in this direction before 1761, when he placed the Mompós estanco under direct administration, and more than doubled its revenues.[58] His successor, Viceroy Pedro Messía de la Cerda, attempted to apply this policy more generally, starting in 1764 with orders to bring the distillation and sale of aguardiente in Popayán and the city of Quito under direct royal management. This policy was not immediately successful, because it provoked widespread disturbances in the province of Popayán and its neighboring areas, and helped precipitate a major urban insurrection in Quito.[59] However, the crown signaled its determination to press forward with its fiscal demands by increasing

56. Silvestre, *Descripción*, p. 79; Marchena Fernández, *La Institución Militar en Cartagena*, pp. 161–75; 310–19.

57. Allan J. Kuethe, *Military Reform and Society in New Granada, 1773–1808* (Gainesville, 1978), pp. 10–24.

58. Posada and Ibáñez, *Relaciones de mando*, p. 80.

59. Anthony McFarlane, "Civil Disorders and Popular Protests in Late Colonial New Granada," *HAHR*, vol. 64 (1984), pp. 22–7; also "The 'Rebellion of the Barrios': Urban Insurrection in Bourbon Quito," *HAHR*, vol. 69 (1989), p. 286.

military forces in Quito and the neighboring province of Popayán.[60] Thus, though briefly slowed by colonial opposition, the crown remained firmly committed to extending the aguardiente monopoly geographically while increasing its efficiency by bringing it under direct royal administration. While Manuel de Guirior was viceroy (1772–6), the *estanco de aguardiente* was enlarged and improved in various regions of New Granada, preparing a way for Guirior's successor, Manuel Antonio de Flóres, to plan direct administration of the aguardiente monopoly throughout the colony.[61]

Another important development in fiscal policy was the extension of crown monopoly administration to the production and sale of leaf tobacco. The creation of the tobacco estanco dated back to the days of Viceroy Eslava in the 1740s, but despite repeated royal orders, it had never been put into operation.[62] The first real effort to activate the laws for a crown tobacco monopoly came in 1764, when Viceroy Messía de la Cerda cautiously created a privately administered tobacco monopoly in Honda. In return for fixed payments to the royal treasury, the viceroy empowered a single contractor to buy all the tobacco leaf produced in the jurisdiction of Honda, and gave him exclusive rights to sell it in the provinces of Santa Fe, Antioquia, Mompós, Santa Marta, and in the cities of Panama and Cartagena. Once established, the tobacco estanco developed along lines similar to those previously followed by the aguardiente monopoly. In 1772, Viceroy Messía de la Cerda attempted to extend its territorial scope, establishing a privately managed monopoly in the provinces of Popayán and the Chocó. The cabildo of Popayán blocked the contract but, by offering to manage the estanco itself for a comparable fee, accepted the principle of monopolization.[63] The next step was to bring the estanco under direct royal administration. In 1774, Viceroy Guirior ordered the Honda monopoly to be administered directly, and introduced closer control over the production of tobacco. Then, on leaving office in 1776, he suggested that this direct administration of tobacco production and sale should be extended throughout New Granada, limiting cultivation to designated zones and creating two regional administrations for its distribution in Mompós and Medellín.[64] Guirior's successor, Viceroy Manuel Antonio Flóres, took up the proposal and introduced yet another reorganization of the tobacco monopoly in October 1776. To avoid continuing

60. Kuethe, *Military Reform and Society*, pp. 48–78.

61. Posada and Ibáñez, *Relaciones de mando*, pp. 163–5; Mora de Tovar, *Aguardiente*, pp. 42–3.

62. An account of the colonial tobacco monopoly is found in Margarita González, "El estanco colonial del tabaco," in her *Ensayos de Historia Colombiana* (Bogotá, 1974), pp. 67–181. On the first attempt to implant an estanco in New Granada, see pp. 91–2.

63. Posada and Ibáñez, *Relactiones de mando*, pp. 102–4; González, *Ensayos*, pp. 92–9.

64. Posada and Ibáñez, *Relaciones de mando*, pp. 166–7; González, *Ensayos*, pp. 102–10.

overproduction, the Flóres plan aimed to restrict cultivation to areas that produced high-quality tobacco, while preventing sales of contraband tobacco by reorganizing administration. In practice, the plan seems to have accomplished little before another, much more sweeping reform of the tobacco monopoly began in late 1778.[65]

Reform was not confined to fiscal reorganization in the years before 1778. During the 1760s and 1770s, crown officials sought actively to promote development of New Granada's economy in order to expand its taxable base. One facet of this drive to mobilize resources affected the Indian population of the provinces of Santa Fe and Tunja, where officials modified the traditional policy of segregation designed to protect Indian communities, depriving Indian communities of their inherited rights and privileges. This realignment of Indian policy started in the mid-1750s, when, as a result of the inspection conducted by Oidor Verdugo y Oquendo, Indian community lands (resguardos) were sold to whites and mestizos who had illegally rented them.[66] During the 1760s, pressures on Indian resguardos continued to mount, and there were further attempts to extinguish small corregimientos, to sell resguardo lands, and to resettle dispossessed Indians in other areas. Finally, during the later 1770s, a definite strategy for more general reform took shape, directed by Francisco Antonio Moreno y Escandón, who was then *fiscal protector de indios* (crown attorney for Indians).

In many ways, Moreno y Escandón embodied both the new climate of opinion in Caroline Spain and the new type of civil servant who was ready to translate it into policy.[67] Born in New Granada of a Spanish father and a creole mother, Moreno was educated in New Granada and, upon completing his university studies in Bogotá, embarked on a promising administrative career. After marrying a Spanish woman, Moreno y Escandón visited Spain in 1764–5, and, following a brief but distinguished sojourn at the court in Madrid, returned to New Granada as the bearer of the ideas that were beginning to transform political thinking and policy at the center of imperial government. Fresh from his experience in Madrid, Moreno was involved both in the organization of the Jesuits' expulsion from New Granada and in the reorganization of the university that they left in Bogotá. From this post, he launched a project for the general overhaul of higher education in the viceregal capital. Attacking the content and quality of teaching in the city's universities, he called for the creation of a public university that would offer a modern, "scientific" alternative to clerical obscurantism, financed from the property of the

---

65. Phelan, *The People and the King*, p. 21.
66. On this next stage of reform, see Margarita González, *Ensayos*, pp. 111–36.
67. On the changing intellectual and political climate in Spain under Charles III, see Lynch, *Bourbon Spain*, pp. 256–61.

expelled Jesuits. In the end, after a decade of bureaucratic wrangling, the public university project was dropped. Moreno's insistence on reforms to university curricula and teaching had, however, injected new life into the colony's centers of learning. During the 1770s, he introduced the teaching of mathematics and physics, the reading of "modern authors," and the study of politics and government. In short, he created a form of training designed, Moreno y Escandón said, to be "useful to the State and valuable to the public."[68]

Moreno is best known, however, for his energetic pursuit of policies for rationalizing government and taxation, particularly through reform of the Hapsburg system of Indian governance. In 1772, he presented an extensive critique of this system and proposed a fundamental reorganization of the old system of protecting Indian lands and communities. With the decline in the size of their communities, Moreno y Escandón contended, Indians had surplus lands that they did not work, but rented to whites and mestizos; meanwhile, income from Indian tributes was too small to pay for corregidores to oversee their government. Moreno y Escandón accordingly proposed that the system of corregimientos and resguardos be modernized, eliminating the smaller ones and concentrating them in fewer, larger units, which would be managed by corregidors who would be responsible for collecting tributes proportionate to the real number of Indian inhabitants.[69] Between 1776 and 1778, these proposals became policy. Moreno y Escandón and his successor as *visitador*, José María Campuzano, extinguished several resguardos in the provinces of Santa Fe and Tunja, and began to redraw the boundaries of the old corregimientos. In 1779, further implementation of the policy was stopped, but the resguardo lands that had already been sold were left in the hands of their new owners, and Indians who had been moved remained in their new settlements. Thus, an important principle had been conceded. Hapsburg paternalism toward the Indians had withered before the imperatives of Bourbon political economy, as historic indigenous community rights were subordinated to crown fiscal needs and the pursuit of economic efficiency.

Ironically, Moreno y Escandón's influence in promoting reform in colonial government and society was cut short in 1778, when he himself was displaced from his post by the very drive to rationalize colonial government that he, as a zealous reformer, had favored. In 1778, New Granadan government was exposed to the final major phase of Bourbon reform, inspired by Charles III's Minister for the Indies, José de Gálvez, and

68. An account of Moreno y Escandón and his career, together with a bibliography of past work on Moreno, is given in Jorge Orlando Melo's introduction to Moreno y Escandón, *Indios y Mestizos de la Nueva Granada*, pp. 1–36. On his efforts to bring about educational reform, see pp. 15–18; the quotation is from page 15.
69. For the reports of Moreno y Escandón, see ibid., pp. 269–585.

signaled by the onset of a *visita general*, or general administrative inspection, aimed at overhauling its whole system of bureaucratic organization and management. For Moreno y Escandón, this meant transfer to another region, as he fell foul of Gálvez's policy of purging creoles from the upper tiers of colonial government, particularly creoles who held office in the land of their birth.[70] For other New Granadans, the advent of the *visita general* was to pose more serious problems, as the incoming visitor general sought to bring colonial government under firmer central control and to draw larger revenues from taxation.

The advent of the general inspection marked a definite shift in the style and techniques of government. Until 1778, the demands that the Bourbon state made on New Granada had undoubtedly grown since the undisciplined days of the last Hapsburg, but change had been modest and gradual, and had provoked little violent opposition. Although new fiscal demands had been imposed by successive viceroys, mainly through extension of the principles of state monopoly and direct administration, these reforms had been introduced slowly and in piecemeal fashion, so that they rarely aroused the opposition of more than small groups in disparate areas. Indeed, the absence of significant popular protest against taxes until the mid-1760s reflects the low impact of administrative reorganization and fiscal reform. Installation of a viceregal regime in Bogotá had, it seems, made little difference to the lives of most people in New Granada, or at least to the way in which they perceived government. However, when the *visita general* began in 1778, the mode of government was suddenly and distinctly altered. After tolerant government by a succession of pliant viceroys, harnessed to inefficient audiencia ministers, New Granada came under the command of a zealous and efficient career bureaucrat who was empowered to strengthen the colonial state by changing the long-established institutions, procedures, and practices of government. The methods used and the results achieved by his *visita general* are the subject of the next chapter.

---

70. Moreno himself was to continue his successful career, rising to become Regent of the Audiencia of Chile in 1788. See Jacques A. Barbier, *Reform and Politics in Bourbon Chile, 1755–1796* (Ottawa, 1980), pp. 185–6.

8

Innovation: The *visita general* and its impact

In New Granada, the overhaul of colonial government instigated by José de Gálvez began in January 1778, when Juan Francisco Gutiérrez de Piñeres arrived in Santa Fe de Bogotá to take up his post as regent and visitor general of the audiencia of New Granada. The *visita general* entrusted to Gutiérrez de Piñeres involved a major review of colonial government in all of the important areas of administration. In some respects, the visitor general's objectives were familiar ones. Like the viceroys, he was expected to make colonial government more receptive to central command, to increase revenues, and to harden military defenses. There were, however, important differences. As visitor general, Gutiérrez de Piñeres was enjoined and empowered to act quickly, he sought to bring about rapid change over a broad front, and he was ready to employ forceful methods. Nor was his mission limited to reform within the existing framework of government. As was common with the general inspectors sent to Peru and Chile, Gutiérrez de Piñeres was required to report on the most appropriate means of introducing the system of intendancies, which was the key to Gálvez's plans for the regeneration of royal government in the Americas.

The immediate task for the visitor general was laid out in the instructions he received before leaving Spain.[1] The opening paragraph of those orders made his basic priority clear: to augment royal income from the colony, by all means possible. This did not necessarily mean new taxation. Indeed, the royal instructions explicitly ruled this out. The king's order stated that costs should be cut where possible and revenues from existing sources augmented so that "the need may not arise for my beloved subjects to suffer the burden of new impositions."[2] Gutiérrez de Piñeres was expected to start work immediately. On his arrival in Cartagena de Indias, and on his subsequent overland journey to Bogotá, Gutiérrez was to take

---

1. AGI Santa Fe 658, "Vuestra Majestad da a D. Juan Francisco Gutiérrez de Piñeres la Instrucción que deve observar para la Visita y arreglo del Tribunal de Cuentas, Cajas, y Ramos de Real Hacienda en el Nuevo Reino de Granada y Provincias de Tierra Firme." El Pardo, February 17, 1777.
2. Ibid.

any measures conducive to combating foreign contraband; once in Bogotá, he was to examine the condition of the Tribunal de Cuentas, collecting any debts that might be owing to it, adjusting its personnel to suit his needs, and subjecting each element of the taxes that it administered to detailed, individual scrutiny. In addition, the visitor general was charged with promoting the development of mining, while stopping illegal exports of gold to foreigners from the Chocó by way of the Atrato River.[3]

Political reform

To achieve his objectives, Gutiérrez de Piñeres attempted to overhaul the government at various levels. His primary concern, expressed during the early stages of the inspection in 1778, was to implement Gálvez's policy of purging creoles from the American audiencias and treasury administrations. Indeed, the appointment of Gutiérrez de Piñeres was itself a first step in this direction, because by making him regent of the Santa Fe audiencia, Gálvez had pushed aside the two creole candidates favored by the Council of the Indies. This marked the beginning of a new wave of appointments to the audiencia that was to diminish creole influence from the high point that it had reached in the early 1770s. For although only two creoles were appointed to the audiencia after the accession of Charles III, these two creoles had joined a third, the *limeño* oidor Antonio de Verástegui who served in Bogotá between 1743 until his death in 1776. Thus, of the five ministers who constituted the audiencia in the early 1770s – four oidors and a fiscal – three were creoles and two were peninsulars. Seen in this context, the shift in the composition of the audiencia that took place after 1776 is striking. First, the balance shifted decisively from creoles toward peninsulars. When Gutiérrez de Piñeres was made regent in 1776, the peninsular Manuel Silvestre Martínez was appointed as *fiscal del crimen;* in 1777, the Spaniard Joaquin Vasco y Vargas replaced the creole Verástegui; in 1778, the *quiteño* Romualdo Navarro was transferred to the audiencia of Guadalajara, and in September 1779 the Catalan Pedro Catani took office as an oidor in Bogotá. This "Europeanization" of the audiencia was then further consolidated in 1780, when fiscal Moreno y Escandón was transferred to Lima, and in January 1781, when the long-serving Benito Casals was replaced by a new peninsular oidor, José de Osorio.[4] Thus, by 1781, all creoles had been eliminated from the audiencia and of the ministers who had been appointed before 1776 only one remained, the Spaniard Juan Francisco Pey y Ruíz. The

---

3. Ibid.
4. For these new appointments to the audiencia, see Pablo E. Cárdenas Acosta, *El movimiento comunal de 1781 en el Nuevo Reino de Granada, con copiosa documentación inédita*, 2 vols. (Bogotá, 1960), vol. 2, pp. 313–19.

purge of creoles was therefore matched by another, equally important change: the introduction to the audiencia bench of new men, who had no previous contacts with creole society in Bogotá and who were therefore free of the local ties that had bound peninsular oidors in the past. The intention was, moreover, to ensure that in the future audiencia ministers should not be allowed to settle in Bogotá, or to build ties with local society. To this end, Gutiérrez de Piñeres recommended that dispensations to oidors allowing them to marry into local society should henceforth be given much less freely.[5]

While participating in the reconstruction of the audiencia, the visitor general also attacked the position of leading *santafereño* families in the treasury administration, another area where the crown wished to diminish creole influence. Recalling that the *Real Cédula* of January 20, 1775 had expressly forbidden the employment in any exchequer office or treasury of individuals related to each other "up to the fourth grade of consanguinity or the second of affinity," Gutiérrez de Piñeres found that the rule was largely ignored in Santa Fe.[6] Vicente Nariño and Joseph López Duro, accountants of the *Tribunal de Cuentas* (Court of Audit) in the capital, Manuel de Revilla, another high-ranking treasury officer, Benito Casals, oidor of the audiencia, and several other crown employees in government offices in the capital, were all related to each other in various ways, mainly through their ties to the Alvarez family.[7] Gutiérrez de Piñeres was particularly critical of this family, observing that "the house of Alvarez is powerful here through the connections which it has in the principal posts, through the large numbers of individuals which make up the family, and through other connections." The Alvarez clan was, in short, a prime example of the permeation of colonial administration by an interlocking family network of the kind that José de Gálvez wished to eliminate from government. The treasury officials Vicente Nariño, Jose López Duro, and Manuel de Revilla, the oidor Benito Casals, were all related through their marriages to Alvarez sisters, together with Francisco Robledo, *asesor* to the viceroy, and Manuel García Olano, administrator of the tobacco revenues in Socorro. They thus formed a veritable family network at the center of government. Gutiérrez de Piñeres was, moreover, particularly preoccupied with the Alvarez connections because the viceroy's personal advisor and his secretary were so closely associated with the family as to create public suspicion that the viceroy's government was controlled by a faction.[8]

Gutiérrez de Piñeres's concern to reduce local influence in government

5. AGI Santa Fe 659, Gutiérrez de Piñeres to Gálvez, March 31, 1778, reservada no. 29.
6. Ibid., March 30, 1778, reservada no. 26.
7. Ibid., also May 15, 1778, reservada no. 38.   8. Ibid., March 31, 1778, no. 29.

went beyond the Alvarez family. Indeed, his stance evidently threatened several leading members of the *santafereño* patriciate, because Viceroy Flóres felt it necessary to come to their defense. If the 1775 law was rigorously enforced, the viceroy argued, then "all the first families of this city are going to suffer, for, being limited to three or four of the superior rank – the Prietos, Ricaurtes, Caycedos and Alvarez – they are connected among themselves and with the officers of the tribunal of the royal exchequer." To the viceroy, it appeared unjust that these people, "who have no wealth for their maintenance nor other career to give their sons than the few posts which their country offers, should be dispossessed of these posts . . ." In responding to the viceroy's comments, Gutiérrez de Piñeres accepted that attention should be given to the local patriciate in the distribution of government jobs, but opposed giving any special favor to these leading families above "the many other honourable and deserving subjects," both European and creole, who were eligible for service. He also insisted that the *Real Cédula* of 1775 be enforced to the letter, that recruitment should draw on a wider group of candidates, and that employees should be prevented from serving in the place of their birth.[9] Clearly, Gutiérrez de Piñeres was determined to dilute, if not destroy, the influence that the *santafereño* patriciate enjoyed in official circles.[10]

Fiscal innovation

After recommending changes of personnel in the higher levels of the colony's bureaucracy, the visitor general turned his attention to the general reorganization of the machinery for managing and collecting royal taxes.[11] In the instructions issued by the crown, Gutiérrez de Piñeres was enjoined to devote special care to the organization of monopolies that controlled the sale of tobacco and aguardiente. Because the latter was already one of the most productive sources of revenue in the colony, it was hoped that the former would, with competent administration, achieve comparable importance. Accordingly, the visitor general's examination of fiscal structure focused first on the condition of the state's monopolies, its estancos.

Before the arrival of the visitor general, Viceroy Flóres had started to curb tobacco production in New Granada by restricting cultivation to certain areas, and he had put forward plans for establishing two centers for processing and distributing the tobacco grown in New Granada. Gutiérrez de Piñeres found these plans inadequate, however, because tobacco was illegally cultivated throughout the colony and its wholesale and retail sale

---

9. Ibid., July 31, 1778.
10. For an analysis that reaches a similar conclusion, see Phelan, *The People and the King*, pp. 14–17.
11. For a general review of Charles III's reforms as they affected New Granada, see ibid., pp. 18–27.

generally continued without restriction, in complete disregard of royal directives. Although the crown had ordered that the tobacco monopoly established in New Granada should observe the same rules that governed the operation of the estanco in metropolitan Spain, in practice it consisted of no more than a few factories where tobacco was processed and sold, without rules to govern either prices or supply. Consequently, Gutiérrez de Piñeres drew up a general plan for the proper organization of the estanco. To control the distribution of tobacco in the provinces, he set up five *administraciones principales* under the direction of a central authority in the capital, worked out detailed instructions for estanco employees, and created a special force of guards to root out illegal cultivation.[12] Similar plans were made for reorganizing the aguardiente estanco.[13] The drive to increase revenues by more efficient collection was reinforced by a rationalization of management designed to hold down administrative costs. Thus, the visitor general merged the crown monopoly of playing cards (the *estanco de naipes*) with that of tobacco, while unifying the management of all the estancos under a new central office that would oversee the accounts and revenues collected by the four main monopolies.[14]

Determination to enlarge fiscal yields by administrative rationalization and rigorous enforcement also formed the principal themes of Gutiérrez de Piñeres's reform in other important areas of royal taxation in New Granada. Bureaucratic laxity was not confined to the aguardiente and tobacco monopolies: the visitor general found that abuses had crept into all aspects of tax collection.[15] Consequently, between 1778 and 1781, he formed and introduced comprehensive new plans for reorganizing all branches of the royal exchequer. These plans aimed to reduce the total number of taxes that had accumulated, and frequently fallen into disuse, during the centuries of Spanish rule, while rigorously enforcing the most important levies on colonial production and consumption. The alcabala (the sales tax that covered all transactions except those specifically exempt) was singled out for special attention. On discovering that the alcabala was not imposed on all those items that were liable to the tax, and that the official price lists on which estimates of duty were calculated had become outdated, Gutiérrez de Piñeres produced a detailed review of all aspects of the regulations governing alcabala payments for the guidance of its ad-

12. AGI Santa Fe 659, Gutiérrez de Piñeres to Gálvez, August 31, 1778 (no. 52); ibid., November 30, 1778 (no. 60, 61, 63, 64).

13. AGI Santa Fe 660, Gutiérrez de Piñeres to Gálvez, December 31, 1780 (no. 223).

14. AGI Santa Fe 659, Gutiérrez de Piñeres to Gálvez, June 30, 1779 (no. 124); AGI Santa Fe 660, "Nuevo Plan e Instrucción para el gobierno de la Dirección General de las quatro rentas unidas del tabaco, aguardiente, naipes y pólvora mandada establecer en esta Capital por Real Orden de 14 de octubre de 1779," May 27, 1780.

15. AGI Santa Fe 660, Gutiérrez de Piñeres to Gálvez, September 30, 1780 (no. 209).

ministrators.[16] Furthermore, he cut through the tangle of local accretions and exemptions that had grown up around the alcabala, and clearly separated the old tax of the *Armada de Barlovento,* which, by dint of local custom, had become unofficially subsumed within the sales tax. Clarification and classification was the prelude to reorganization. Gutiérrez de Piñeres proceeded, as he had with the monopolies, to form a general plan for the management of the alcabala and *Armada de Barlovento.* A new central administration was set up in Bogotá to direct, coordinate, and account for the colony's revenues from these taxes,[17] and satellite administrations were established in the principal towns for their provincial enforcement and collection.[18]

Separation of the *Armada de Barlovento* tax from the alcabala did not constitute a new tax, but simply revived a category that had become confused with the alcabala. In practice, however, the revival of the *Armada de Barlovento* was popularly perceived as a new tax, and reform of the alcabala increased the tax burden on transactions in the domestic market by adding another 2% to the existing sales tax. Furthermore, sales taxes were henceforth payable on a schedule fixed in accord with local prices and collected by a more efficient, government-controlled administration.[19] The resentment that this inevitably caused was then aggravated by making the sales tax payable on a range of articles that, due to administrative inertia and local custom, had long been treated as exempt.[20] Tax pressures were also increased in more obvious ways. In 1780, the visitor general implemented royal orders to raise the price of tobacco and aguardiente sold to the public by the estancos.[21] In the same year, the crown also decided to subsidize the expenses of war with England by requiring its colonial subjects to pay a *donativo,* a "donation" that was in fact a temporary capitation tax on the adult male population.[22]

Modifications and additions to the pattern of fiscalization were not new to the colony. Previous viceroys had attempted to enhance revenue yields

16. Ibid., "Instrucción General para al más exacto y arreglado manejo de las Reales Rentas," October 12, 1780. An outline of these provisions is given in Pablo E. Cárdenas Acosta, *Del Vassalaje a la Insurrección de los Comuneros* (Tunja, 1947), pp. 227–81.

17. AGI Santa Fe 660, Gutiérrez de Piñeres to Gálvez, January 31, 1781, nos. 228, 229, 230, 231.

18. Ibid., no. 223.   19. Cárdenas Acosta, *Del Vassalaje,* p. 281.

20. Following the reforms of the visitor general, all the articles and staple foods used by the rural and urban poor became subject to tax; only bread remained free. See David P. Leonard, "The Comunero Rebellion in 1781. A Chapter in the Spanish Quest for Social Justice," unpub. Ph.D. thesis, University of Michigan, 1951, p. 78.

21. Cárdenas Acosta, *Del Vassalaje,* pp. 342, 351.

22. AGI Santa Fe 660, Gutiérrez de Piñeres to Gálvez, March 3, 1781 (no. 245), informing Gálvez of the instructions issued for its collection in New Granada. Indians and *castas* paid 1 peso per head; Spaniards and nobles, 2 pesos per head. Women, slaves, the indigent and oversixties, and certain categories of minors were exempt. See Pablo E. Cárdenas Acosta, *Del Vassalaje,* p. 329.

by means of new imposts on aguardiente and tobacco, and more efficient retrieval of older taxes, such as the alcabala and the quinto. However, although the measures introduced by the visitor general simply continued an existing process, his measures were unprecedented in both their scope and in the offense that they gave to a wide spectrum of traders, farmers, and consumers. First, Gutiérrez de Piñeres created new problems for the trader by introducing a system of official registration for all goods entering internal channels of trade. His scheme was a simple one. Merchants transporting goods across the colony had at all times to carry *guías* or officially stamped invoices that listed their merchandise and its provenance, showed that they had paid appropriate duties at its place of origin, and stated its destination. When the goods were sold, the merchants then had to obtain a *tornaguía*, an official receipt that indicated they had reached their destination and there paid the alcabala due at the time of resale.[23] In its conception, the scheme was not original: Viceroy Guirior had recommended its introduction some years earlier.[24] But its practical application was new to the colony and aroused strong antipathy. Not only did the new scheme increase the risks of smuggling but, by adding to the bureaucratic formalities imposed on the trader, it probably also increased the opportunities for extortion and peculation by the minor officials with whom the trader dealt. The sudden implementation of new rules for the cultivation, processing, and sale of tobacco dealt a similarly swift blow to the interests of peasant farmers in areas where tobacco growing was banned by the visitor general's reorganization of the monopoly. Previously, the regulations of the tobacco monopoly were observed mainly in the breach; now the countryside was suddenly swept by the officers and guards of the newly established administrations, who uprooted and burned tobacco plants and crops in areas where cultivation was prohibited. Third, the visitor general's measures were inimical to many consumers, because increases in the prices of aguardiente and tobacco, combined with higher sales taxes, pushed up the cost of basic goods.

Colonial responses to reform

Fiscal innovation aroused widespread popular resentment, and produced a reaction that was eloquent testimony to its impact. As a wave of directives and orders issued from the visitor general in Bogotá, an opposite wave was unleashed in the form of popular commotions that spread across the region of Socorro, igniting flashpoints in both town and countryside and conjuring up the visitor general's nemesis, the great Comunero insurrection of

23. AGI Santa Fe 660, Gutiérrez de Piñeres to Gálvez, August 26, 1780 (no. 211).
24. Posada and Ibáñez, *Relaciones de mando*, p. 169.

1781. The epicenter of the rebellion was in the towns of Socorro and San Gil which, as tobacco and cotton producing areas, felt particularly afflicted by the new fiscal measures. In some towns and villages, crowds that gathered for market day, or assembled following Sunday Mass joined in spontaneous demonstrations against the local tax administrations; in others, opposition to the tax commissioners took the form of preplanned attacks by bands of armed men, who were often spurred on by delegates from the centers of rebellion. In both cases, restraint and discipline governed popular action. Under the slogan, "Long live the King and down with bad government," the rebels committed remarkably little violence against either persons or private property. They invariably confined their actions to protest against the measures of the visitor general, usually by sacking estanco offices and by selling their tobacco and aguardiente stocks. The orderly character of the rebellion was further reflected in the organization built up by the participants to press their demands and conserve their purpose. To unite the forces of protest and to consolidate their gains, the Comuneros, led by Francisco Berbeo, *vecino* of Socorro, created a "Supreme Council of War." Composed of the "captains-general" who represented the rebel towns, the council took over the functions of government in rebel areas and sent out representatives to neighboring towns, inviting them to join the cause. Thus, as resistance continued to spread across the province of Tunja, a coherent movement gradually emerged and, united under a common leadership and with a definite program of demands, it hardened into an organized and large-scale rebellion against the ministers of the crown.[25]

With the viceroy in Cartagena, marshaling the colony's forces in defense against external attack during the war with England, and with only the viceregal palace guard for protection, the colonial government was in a poor position to defend itself. At first, an attempt was made to oppose the rebels with force, but the tiny contingent of troops sent to check their advance was both outnumbered and outmaneuvered. The rebels drew strength and confidence from the ignominious collapse of royalist military tactics, and by May 1781 a Comunero force of some 15,000 to 20,000 people assembled in the vicinity of the town of Zipaquirá, ready to march on the capital. Unprepared to resist such an attack, the royal authorities in Bogotá sought to forestall the rebel force by conciliation. While hasty preparations were made to defend the city, a commission was sent to parley with the rebel leaders in Zipaquirá.

With the prospect of official recognition, the Comuneros' leaders now formulated the rebels' grievances into a *plan de capitulaciones,* an outline of terms for presentation to the commission. Many of the terms were, given

25. An excellent narrative of the rebellion is given by Phelan, *The People and the King,* chaps. 9–12.

the origins of the revolt, entirely predictable, demanding the expulsion of the visitor general, the abolition of the estancos, an end to the *Armada de Barlovento* and the *guías,* and a return of the alcabala to its old form: in short, a general reversion to the fiscal status quo. Facing the threat that the capital might be invaded, the government's negotiators agreed to the terms laid out in the *capitulaciones.* They publicly accepted the Comunero demands in their entirety, while secretly abjuring the pact. Following this acquiescence to their demands, which were sealed by the oaths of the king's ministers and consecrated at a service conducted by Archbishop Caballero y Góngora, the majority of the rebels dispersed and returned to their homes. Although resistance continued to flare up in the form of local rioting in different parts of the country until the end of 1781, the arrival of troops from Cartagena and the gradual disintegration of the core of the Comunero movement under a divided leadership enabled the royal administration slowly to regain control. Satisfied that their demands had been met and their protest vindicated, most of the Comuneros were happy to accept the general pardon extended to those who had participated in the rebellion and to resume the rhythms of their rural life. Remaining pockets of resistance were gradually extinguished until, by March 1782, the audiencia felt sufficiently strong to renounce openly the concessions that the commission had made during the previous year.[26]

Continuity and change in colonial government

The Comunero rebellion of 1781 administered a shock to the Spanish government in New Granada from which it took some time to recover. The program of reforms planned by the visitor general was restarted when Gutiérrez de Piñeres returned to Bogotá in February 1782, but it was to be modified and eventually reduced. For during his nine-month absence in Cartagena, the visitor general had lost the political initiative and found it difficult to resume his work. The appointment of Archbishop Caballero y Góngora to the viceregency further diminished the visitor general's authority because, after his role in dealing with the Comuneros, the archbishop had the ear of a grateful monarch. Thus, although Gutiérrez de Piñeres was convinced that the last vestiges of revolt had been swept away and although he was determined to restart his reform program, he no longer enjoyed his old ascendancy and had to deal with a viceroy and audiencia judges who were reluctant to risk any further disturbance. Gradually, Gutiérrez de Piñeres became convinced that he could no longer properly fulfill his function. In January 1783, he reported to Gálvez that oidors Pey y Ruíz, Vasco y Vargas, Catani, and fiscal Silvestre Martínez

26. On the end of the rebellion and its aftermath, see ibid., chaps. 15–18.

had formed a faction against him, and he recommended that they all be removed. A month later, he reported that the viceroy was making official appointments without his consultation and stated that, if he could not act effectively, he should be given another post.[27] This attempt to reestablish his authority backfired. In late 1783, Gutiérrez de Piñeres was transferred back to Spain, where he took up a position on the Council of the Indies.

Despite the visitor general's rather ignominious retreat from New Granada, his reforms were not abandoned. At the end of 1782, the archbishop-viceroy reported that the population had lapsed back into docility, and that the revenues of the colonial exchequer were beginning to recover.[28] Then, at intervals during the first six months of 1783, he informed the crown that the tax changes and the restrictions on tobacco production that had precipitated the rebellion were being successfully implemented. Some modifications had been made to avoid any risk of a popular outcry, but the archbishop-viceroy boasted that the essential purpose of fiscal reform had been fulfilled.[29] There was, however, one major point of the reformist program inspired by Gálvez and implemented by his officials in other parts of Spanish America that was completely unhinged by the Comunero rebellion. In 1782, Gutiérrez de Piñeres had strongly reaffirmed his belief that the installation of intendants in New Granada should go forward as planned.[30] The archbishop-viceroy took the opposite view, however, and his opinion prevailed. Throughout his term in office, from 1782 to 1789, Archbishop-Viceroy Caballero y Góngora steadfastly opposed such major administrative reform because of the political dangers that would be involved so soon after the Comunero rebellion. Thus, although action was taken to implant the intendancy system in the audiencia of Quito, where an intendant was appointed for the province of Cuenca, in New Granada it was not put into effect.[31] This was partly due to the archbishop-viceroy's opposition, but other factors also obstructed change in the government. During the 1780s, the colonial treasury was deep in debt and would have been hard pressed to support a new class of salaried officials. Then, with the death of José de Gálvez in 1787, the architect and principal proponent of the *Ordenanzas de Intendentes* disappeared, and the issue of government reform in New Granada simply fell into abeyance. It was not resurrected until many years later, when, in

27. AGI Santa Fe 661, Gutiérrez de Piñeres to Gálvez, December 31, 1782; March 31, 1782 (reservada no. 2); January 31, 1783 (reservada no. 9); February 6, 1783 (reservada no. 10).
28. Archivo Restrepo, Correspondencia reservada del Arzobispo Virrey, Caballero y Góngora to Gálvez, October 15, 1782 (no. 2).
29. Ibid., Caballero y Góngora to Gálvez, January 31, 1783 (no. 15); April 30, 1783 (no. 33); June 15, 1783 (no. 46).
30. AGI Santa Fe 658, Gutiérrez de Piñeres to Gálvez, August 31, 1782 (no. 50).
31. Luis Garcia Navarro, *Intendencias de Indias* (Seville, 1959), pp. 46–8.

1807, *Contador General* Francisco Viana secured royal approval for the appointment of four intendants in New Granada.[32] In the event, however, the scheme was again aborted, this time by the imperial crisis caused by Napoleon's invasion of Spain.

Without an intendancy system, structural reform of New Granada's government proved impossible. Before the Comunero rebellion, there had been attempts to reorganize local government: Fiscal Moreno y Escandón had been commissioned to rationalize district government by regrouping corregimientos so that they might better conform to the contemporary distribution of the population, and Viceroy Flóres had created three new corregimientos to facilitate government in the province of Cartagena. However, in the wake of the rebellion, such reorganization was simply shelved.[33] So, too, was Viceroy Flóres's plan for placing a corregidor in the capital to preside over its cabildo and to take steps essential to improving law and order in the wake of the Comunero rebellion. The archbishop-viceroy had proposed financing the appointment, with a large salary of 5,000 pesos, by dismembering the corregimientos of Mariquita and Tunja, both of which he thought could be ruled from Bogotá; he also insisted that the post should always go to an army officer, to ensure efficiency and to prevent the office from falling into local hands.[34] This proposal was ignored, however, on the grounds that the imminent introduction of intendants rendered it redundant. So, when plans for introducing intendants were dropped, the government of the city and its jurisdiction was unchanged, remaining the responsibility of the viceroy and audiencia.

The sole change to local government was found in Socorro, where a new corregimiento was established in September 1781, with Francisco Berbeo as the first corregidor. This was, however, merely a temporary expedient designed to placate the *socorranos* and to use Berbeo as an instrument of mediation. Within a year, Berbeo was sacked and the corregimiento was suppressed.[35] It did not resurface until years later, in 1795, when the crown approved a plan put forward by Juan Rodríguez de Lago of Tunja for a corregimiento to oversee government in the region of Vélez, San Gil, and Socorro, and appointed Rodríguez de Lago to the post.[36] This, it seems, was the only significant reform of local government during the late

32. AGI Santa Fe 552, "El Virrey de Santa Fe: sobre que se observe en aquel Virreynato en lo posible la Ordenanza de Intendentes," Francisco Viana, June 1807.
33. On these measures, see the *relación de mando* of the archbishop-viceroy in Pérez Ayala, *Caballero y Góngora*, pp. 301, 324–7.
34. AGI Santa Fe 552, "Borrador de lo que pensó el Señor Virrey representar a la Corte sobre elección de Corregidor de Santa Fe . . ."
35. Phelan, *The People and the King*, pp. 175, 200–1.
36. Ulíses Rojas, *Corregidores y Justicias Mayores de Tunja y su Provincia desde la fundación de la ciudad hasta 1817* (Tunja, 1962), pp. 606–15.

eighteenth century, and although successive viceroys reaffirmed the need
for further reorganization, the task always proved too troublesome and
costly. Virtually all viceroys referred to the corrupt practices of the corregidores and urged their replacement by paid officials, but, without
additional funds for salaries, the administration of justice at the local level
continued to be distorted by the abuses of unpaid officials.[37]

The failure to effect Gálvez's plans for a "revolution in government"
through the establishment of provincial intendancies was mirrored at the
center of government by the viceroys' retention of a dominant role. In
their tripartite capacity as supreme military commander, superintendent
of the *Real Hacienda,* and president of the audiencia of Santa Fe, the
viceroys took on broad responsibilities for developing colonial resources,
overseeing fiscal affairs, and ensuring that the law was effectively administered at both central and local levels. Although there were occasional
complaints that they did not exercise sufficient control over appointments
to the governorship of the colony's provinces, there are no signs that their
power or prestige diminished during the late eighteenth century.[38] Indeed, the viceroys were the principal agents for the more active style of
government favored by the later Bourbons, and they continued to play an
important part in regulating financial and economic affairs in New Granada.

That other great institution of Habsburg colonial government, the
audiencia, also preserved its position in the colony's administration, where
it remained the focal point for the administration of civil and criminal
justice, and continued to discharge important duties within the vital
sphere of government finance. There are, however, signs that it became a
more efficient instrument of the state during the late eighteenth century,
and that Gálvez's plan to curtail local influence at the highest level was
successfully implemented. Expanded in 1776 to include a regent and a
fiscal del crimen, and with another oidor attached to its bench by royal
order in 1778, the audiencia received an infusion of new blood during the
visita general, with three new men taking up places between 1779 and
1781.[39] As the *visita general* came to an end, the composition of the
audiencia underwent further alteration, with four new appointments
made in 1781–3.[40] Moreover, during the *visita general* and in the years
that followed, the audiencia was firmly placed in the hands of bureaucrats
recruited in the peninsula, and contacts between its members and the

---

37. For the comments of successive viceroys on the problems of local government, see Posada and
    Ibáñez, *Relaciones de mando,* pp. 150, 315–21, 453–5.
38. See, for example, the remarks of Viceroy Pedro Mendinueta. Ibid., p. 452.
39. Restrepo Sáenz, *Biografías de los mandatarios,* pp. 368, 382–4.
40. Archivo Restrepo, Correspondencia reservada del Arzobispo Virrey, Caballero y Góngora to
    Gálvez, January 31, 1783 (no. 21).

families of *santafereño* patriciate were reduced. In 1778–1810, twenty-four new men served in the Bogotá audiencia, four as regents, fourteen as oidors, and six as fiscals. Of these eighteen were peninsular Spaniards and seven were creoles. Only three creoles were from New Granada itself: Francisco Moreno y Escandón briefly held the post of fiscal until he was removed in 1782; in 1787, Joaquín de Mosquera y Figueroa, a creole from an opulent landed and mineowning family in Popayán, was made an oidor in Bogotá, whereas the *santafereño* José Antonio Berrio served ten years as fiscal after his appointment in 1790. The other creoles were men from elsewhere in the Americas.

Local men were, then, a small minority of appointees who served on the audiencia in the years between 1778 and 1810. Equally important, however, was the fact that audiencia officials served for shorter periods after 1778. Between 1738 and 1777, audiencia officials had usually served for very long spells of between twenty and thirty-five years; between 1778 and 1810, the period in office became much shorter, rarely exceeding ten years. This more rapid turnover of judges indicates that the visitor general's strictures concerning relations between oidors and the local community had been enforced. After 1778, audiencia officials were transferred more often and were less frequently married to the daughters of the local creole patriciate.[41] Here, at least, the revolution in government planned by José de Gálvez had made its mark.

The efficiency of government is harder to gauge, but there were signs of closer cooperation between viceroys and the audiencia after 1778 and greater professionalism among the tribunal's judges. Successive viceroys remarked on the heavy burden of work placed on the oidors and recommended various expedients to relieve the pressure. Archbishop-Viceroy Caballero y Góngora approved the regent's appointment of three auxiliary judges to deal with the backlog of civil and criminal appeals, and provided the financial means to expedite the processing of audiencia cases. He also recommended the establishment of a separate *Sala del Crimen,* or court of criminal appeal, so that the audiencia might dispose of a larger staff to fulfill its functions.[42] However, although succeeding viceroys supported this proposal, the Madrid government persistently ignored these requests and the audiencia still had to cope with an excessive work load.[43]

At the apex of the fiscal bureaucracy the viceroy continued to occupy the leading position, with the audiencia in an important supporting role. Although it had been Gálvez's intention to curtail the fiscal functions of

---

41. These comments on the composition of the audiencia are based on data given by Burkholder and Chandler, *From Impotence to Authority,* Appendix X, pp. 221–4, and by Restrepo Sáenz, *Biografías de los Mandatarios,* pp. 295–427.
42. Pérez Ayala, *Caballero y Góngora,* pp. 323–4.
43. Posada and Ibáñez, *Relaciones de mando,* pp. 314, 447–8.

the viceroys and to replace them with *superintendentes subdelegados de Real Hacienda,* in New Granada the viceroy remained firmly in control of treasury affairs. As superintendent of the *Real Hacienda,* the viceroys bore final responsibility for the fiscal matters in the colony and exercised an important influence over financial administration. The fiscal bureaucracy had been considerably modified by the introduction of new departments to administer the state monopolies of tobacco, playing cards, aguardiente, and gunpowder. Organized in provincial administrations, these departments were responsible to directors installed in central offices of management in the capital. Those of Bogotá seem to have been consistently well managed from the time of their establishment by the visitor general and, unlike those in the audiencia of Quito, required no modification to their form of operation.[44] Alongside these new departments stood the older structure of fiscal organization, in which the provincial treasuries were supervised by the *Tribunal de Cuentas* in Bogotá, the central court of audit that scrutinized the accounts and collected the net products of the main provincial treasuries.[45] Comprised of only two aging ministers with a few subordinates, the court was immersed in a continuous backlog of accounts until the 1790s. Then, during the viceregency of José de Ezpeleta, it was made more active and efficient. By order of the viceroy, the staff of the court was expanded to the point where it was not only able to catch up on its accounts, but it was also prepared to take on new work.[46]

In addition to these two main departments for the administration, collection, and disposal of royal revenues in New Granada, the audiencia judges organized various committees for managing special funds, such as those that derived from sequestered Jesuit property, tithes, and the Monte Pío, or official pension fund.[47] They also shared with the viceroy some of the responsibility that fell upon him in his capacity as general superintendent of the colonial treasure: all the oidors sat on the *junta general de tribunales,* together with the ministers of the court of audit, the directors of the monopolies, and various treasury officials.[48] According to a royal order of 1778, the audiencia had no competence to intrude on the viceroy's jurisdiction as superintendent. But it became customary to allow it to do so, both for the sake of administrative convenience and to avoid disputes with the judges.[49] After 1797, the participation of the audiencia in central discussion of fiscal affairs was somewhat curtailed. In that year, a *junta superior de real hacienda* was established, and only selected oidors were included in its membership. Authorized to examine all the extraordi-

---

44. Ibid., p. 372.   45. For a list of these treasuries, see Silvestre, *Descripción,* p. 63.
46. Posado and Ibáñez, *Relaciones de mando,* pp. 369–70.
47. Ibid., p. 314; Silvestre, *Descripción,* pp. 65–6.
48. Posada and Ibáñez, *Relaciones de mando,* p. 376.   49. Ibid., p. 367.

nary expenditures, supplements, and advance payments made by the treasury, this body took decisions by majority vote. However, the viceroy retained his overall power for the decisions of the *junta superior* which, like those of the *junta general de tribunales* that it replaced, could not be implemented without his approval.[50]

Thus, after the Comunero rebellion, government in New Granada was reinstated largely in its old form, without the system of intendants interposing a new layer of peninsular bureaucrats between creoles and the centers of power. But if a complete overhaul of government was frustrated, creole influence in the audiencia had been reduced by the introduction of new men from Spain, and, through more efficient government, the pressures of Caroline reformism were sustained.

Government finances after the *visita general*

The results of tighter administration were most clearly demonstrated in the crucial area of finance. Since the reestablishment of the viceroyalty in 1739, the costs of internal administration and defense against external attack had constantly outrun the income available from colonial revenues. Military expenditure was the largest single item in the colonial budget, and any surplus acquired by the Bogotá treasury from its provincial subsidiaries was automatically committed to supporting the garrison and fortifications of Cartagena de Indias. During the 1770s, the financial strains involved in maintaining the military establishment became particularly obvious, when enormous sums were spent on improving the fortifications of Cartagena. Such expenditure had placed a heavy strain on the colonial exchequer. Not only was it impossible to remit any surplus to Spain, but the viceroys also required large annual subsidies from Quito, Lima, and Veracruz to maintain the garrisons of Cartagena, Portobelo, and Panama. For this reason, Gutiérrez de Piñeres's main objective during his *visita* had been to find a means to enable the viceroyalty to meet the expanding costs of government and defense, to eliminate the deficits of its treasury, and ultimately to convert the deficit into a surplus that might be transferred to Spain.

His main contribution in this area was to augment government income by more effective exploitation of the colonial consumer. The principal instrument for such exploitation were the monopolies of tobacco and liquor, and the alcabala. In 1772, the sales from aguardiente in the audiencia of Santa Fe yielded revenues of about 200,000 pesos per annum; tobacco sales produced about 100,000 pesos.[51] From the early 1780s,

---

50. Ibid., p. 517.
51. BL Additional Mss., 13,987. "Notas relativas al Plan Geográfico del Virreynato de Santa Fe, que formó el Dr. Don Francisco Antonio Moreno y Escandón," fol. 66.

revenues from both of these sources increased considerably. By the end of the century, the net yield of the tobacco monopoly reached an average annual value that was more than three times higher than the 1772 level. The growth of aguardiente revenues, though less impressive, was also striking. Expansion of returns from this source was checked in the early 1790s by the importation of a competing product from Spain, but growth was resumed when war provided protection from imported aguardiente.[52] Closer administration of the alcabala also proved profitable for the colonial treasury. In the 1750s the replacement of tax farmers by direct administration in Bogotá had provided a basis for growth. The administrator of the alcabala reported that revenues immediately rose from an annual average of 8,000 pesos to an annual average of more than 19,000 pesos.[53] By the 1790s, the yield was far higher and was still growing. In 1791, it stood at nearly 72,000 pesos; in 1795 it was at nearly 76,000 pesos.[54] The increase in the flow of income to the colonial exchequer did not immediately resolve the financial problems of the viceroyalty, however. When Archbishop-Viceroy Caballero y Góngora came into office in 1782, he inherited a debt of nearly 900,000 pesos from his predecessor, and throughout the decade 1779–88, growth of income was counterbalanced by a disproportionate increase in government expenditures.[55] Thus, when Caballero y Góngora relinquished his post in 1789, the colonial deficit had more than doubled.[56]

The weakness of government finances cannot be attributed to a lack of pressure on New Granadan taxpayers. It was, rather, the result of growing expenditures, which were due partly to the extraordinary costs incurred during the 1779–83 war with the British, when large sums were required to support the naval station in Cartagena, and partly to the postwar Darién colonization project, which absorbed more than a million pesos.[57] In the short term, the colonial treasury could meet these high costs only by running into debt. In the long term, however, the fiscal reforms of the visitor general helped to ensure that the budget was balanced. By the 1790s, the colony yielded an income that was sufficient not only to cover its routine peacetime expenditure on the maintenance of administration and defense, but also to repay its debts and even to make available a small surplus for remittance to Spain.

Although the reforms introduced by Gutiérrez de Piñeres must take most of the credit for stabilizing colonial finances, the attainment of fiscal

52. For aguardiente revenues, see Mora de Tovar, *Aguardientes y conflictos*, Grafico 13, p. 172.
53. AGI Santa Fe 264, Consejo de Indias to Joaquín Joseph Vásquez, July 28, 1756.
54. Posada and Ibáñez, *Relaciones de mando*, pp. 381, 528.
55. Pérez Ayala, *Caballero y Góngora*, p. 376.
56. Santa Fe 573, Gil y Lemus to Valdés, January 30, 1789 (reservada no. 4).
57. Pérez Ayala, *Caballero y Góngora*, pp. 375, 383–5.

equilibrium also owed much to careful financial management by the later viceroys. When Francisco Gil y Lemus took over command of the viceroyalty in 1789, he immediately turned his attention to rectifying the effects of heavy government spending by his predecessor, Archbishop-Viceroy Caballero y Góngora. Caballero y Góngora had employed *visitadores* to inspect the provinces of Antioquia and Popayán, but the reports made by Gil y Lemus suggest that there was still considerable scope for improving fiscal administration at both the central and provincial levels. He recommended action in two main areas. First, he attempted to reduce the costs of government by pruning the viceregal secretariat, reducing military expenditures, removing financial support from the recently established colonies of Darién, and suspending government projects that were running at a loss. Second, he formed plans to inspect all the provincial treasuries, and to tighten up the control of these treasuries from the capital. To eliminate the long delays involved in processing the accounts of provincial treasuries and monopoly administrations, Gil y Lemus established weekly meetings for the *Tribunal de Cuentas* and the directors of the monopolies, and enlarged the staff of the former so that it might conduct its business with greater expedition.[58]

Gil y Lemus was promoted to the viceregency of Lima after only six months in New Granada, but his successor, José de Ezpeleta, took up the recommendations he had made. Under Ezpeleta's watchful supervision, there was a marked recuperation in government finances. After little more than a year in office, Ezpeleta concluded that the condition of the colonial treasury was even worse than Gil y Lemus had supposed. Not only was it still burdened with debts of about 2 million pesos, but the costs of the naval station in Cartagena had also risen far above their anticipated ceiling. As for the remittance of revenues to Spain, he noted that this had never been accomplished by any of his predecessors. For in spite of repeated royal orders that profits from the tobacco and playing card monopolies and returns from the Jesuit properties sequestered in 1767 should be earmarked for transfer to the metropolis, they had continually been used to defray costs within the viceroyalty.[59] Moreover, the treasury still had an outstanding debt of 1 million pesos, borrowed at 5%, which it was quite unable to repay. To deal with the debt problem, Ezpeleta suggested that it should be funded by an issue of bonds, paying interest at 4%. This, the viceroy argued, would have the dual advantage of both saving the treasury 1% per annum in interest payments, and of stimulating the economy by

---

58. Gil y Lemus presented a summary of his recommendations in a report that he made shortly before leaving New Granada. A copy of the report is printed in E. Sánchez Pedrote, "Gil y Lemus y su memoria sobre el Nuevo Reino de Granada," *AEA*, vol. 8 (1951), pp. 185–204.

59. AGI Santa Fe 638, Ezpeleta to Valdés, November 19, 1789 (no. 79).

increasing the volume of money in circulation.[60] Funding the colonial debt by such a method was rejected by the crown, however, and Ezpeleta was forced to find more orthodox means of solving the government's financial problems. He was remarkably successful. By the end of 1795, he was able to claim that the treasury yielded sufficient revenues both to meet its commitments within the viceroyalty and, for the first time, to send a surplus to Spain.[61] According to Ezpeleta, this had been achieved simply by vigilant administration and stringent economy. Under his guidance, he boasted, the *Tribunal de Cuentas* in Bogotá had been converted into a more effective instrument for financial control. It had not only cleared its backlog of delayed accounts but had also exercised closer scrutiny over the practices of the provincial treasuries.[62] Savings had also been made by reducing military expenditures, and cutting back the militias of the interior.[63]

Although fiscal reorganization had finally produced the desired results, the stability of colonial finances was still precarious. No sooner had Ezpeleta accumulated a small surplus than a return to war with the British in 1796 diverted it to military uses in Cartagena, so that it never reached Spain. Nevertheless, the colonial treasury did not immediately fall into deficit under the pressures of war. On the contrary, by the time that the Peace of Amiens was concluded in 1802, Viceroy Pedro de Mendinueta had accumulated a million and a half pesos for remittance to Spain, and, in addition, had supplied nearly half a million pesos in subsidies to the treasuries in Caracas and Maracaibo, and to the French commander in St. Domingue. Mendinueta attributed his achievement to the measures taken by Ezpeleta, to his own zeal in enforcing them, and to the care that he had taken to ensure that extraordinary expenditures did not go beyond tolerable limits. His main task had been to maintain a rigorous check on the expenditure of the colonial treasury, for its income did not suffer unduly as a result of war. Disruption of commerce with Spain reduced customs revenues, but did not seriously damage the treasury's total receipts because the fall in returns from duties was almost exactly balanced by the expansion of revenues from the sale of domestically produced aguardiente.[64] But, if the finances of the viceroyalty initially withstood the strains of war, in the longer term the colonial government found it increasingly difficult to meet its obligations. Indeed, by 1808, its treasury was so drained that it was unable to pay the salaries of some of its employees.[65] By then, however, the financial difficulties of the colonial

---

60. AGI Santa Fe 639, Ezpeleta to Valdés, June 19, 1790 (no 266).
61. Posada and Ibáñez, *Relaciones de mando*, pp. 379, 384.
62. Ibid., p. 369.   63. Ibid., pp. 393–4.
64. For Mendinueta's account of colonial finances during his period of office, see ibid., pp. 525–31.
65. AHNC Consulados, tomo 4, fol. 797.

administration were only one aspect of a crisis of far greater dimensions, for when the Bourbon monarchy was captured by Napoleon in 1808, the very legitimacy of the colonial government was called into question, heralding its fall.

The boundaries of Bourbon reform

Over the whole century of Bourbon rule, Spanish government had undoubtedly achieved much in New Granada. Under viceregal administration, the weak and attenuated authority inherited from the late Hapsburgs had been replaced by a firmer, more centralized system of government; an exhausted treasury had been restored to health by cumulative reconstruction of the fiscal system, and enlargement of state revenues had financed improvements in the colony's administration and its defenses against foreign attack. But although New Granada was more firmly governed and its subjects were forced to contribute more to financing their government and defense, we should not overestimate the efficacy of Bourbon reform.

In the first place, reform of colonial government stopped short of the stage reached in other colonies, because the Comunero rebellion of 1781 prevented implementation of the intendancy system, the key point of José de Gálvez's plans for restructuring government in the Americas. Thus, at the turn of the century, New Granada's government still retained the form that it had taken more than half a century earlier, when the viceroyalty was reestablished in 1739. Bourbon achievement of reform in the spheres of economy and government finance was also mixed. Overseas commerce had expanded, but on a scale lower than that found in other colonies; government interventions in the economy had done little to stimulate production for export, and Spanish trade, challenged by foreign interlopers, was still unable to monopolize the colony's markets. And, finally, growth in government finances stopped short of fulfilling Madrid's goals. Revenues had grown tremendously from around mid-century, with a particularly fast pace of growth after the reforms of the *visita general*. But reform did not produce a fiscal surplus, available for transfer to Spain. Until the *visita general* of 1778–83, New Granada imported more tax revenues than it exported. In 1774, according to Tomás Ortíz de Landázuri of the Spanish *Contaduría General*, the defense of Cartagena was still subsidized from Quito with a subsidy worth some 400,000 pesos per year.[66] After the *visita*, the viceroyalty became more financially independent and its revenues grew steadily, but it still did not send treasure to Spain in remitted tax revenues.

---

66. AGI Santa Fe 552, Tomas Ortíz de Landázuri, Madrid, February 28, 1774.

When he looked back on the history of the viceroyalty in 1789, Francisco Silvestre observed that most of the main sources of revenue had increased their yields, especially the royal monopolies; however, he also noted that larger expenditures on soldiers and employees of the fiscal administration within the country meant that income barely covered costs.[67] The viceroys' own reports also show that no tax transfers were made until the very end of the eighteenth century, and then only on the rare occasion when fiscal emergency in the metropolis prompted intense efforts to squeeze the colonies for funds. It is therefore impossible to sustain the hypothesis that Bourbon tax transfers distorted the economic development of late colonial Colombia by making the country a capital exporter and draining it of specie.[68] In fact, the viceroys failed to extract a fiscal surplus for transfer to the mother country, so that after a century of Bourbon rule the territory was still far from becoming a profitable colony, efficiently exploited for the benefit of the monarchy. Worse still was the fact that the relatively modest results of Bourbon reform in New Granada were achieved at considerable political cost. For as we shall see in the next section, the crown's most determined efforts at reform, during the late 1770s, disturbed the equilibrium of New Granada's political society, and ultimately damaged the very authority that they were designed to promote.

67. Silvestre, *Descripción,* pp. 64–5.
68. For this hypothesis, see McGreevey, *Economic History of Colombia,* pp. 26–7.

PART IV

Government and politics

9

Power, politics, and protest

Of all the influences on the development of New Granada's political life during the eighteenth century, Bourbon policies are the most obvious. We have seen how, throughout the century, ministers of Bourbon monarchs sought to enhance royal authority and improve Spain's command of the region's resources, with varying degrees of intensity and success. The first conjuncture of Bourbon reform in New Granada, in 1717–23, was ineffectual, if not entirely futile. It did, however, clear the ground for a second conjuncture of administrative and commercial reorganization in 1739–40, from which New Granada emerged with a new framework for government, under the command of the viceroys, and a new framework for its overseas trade, carried by individual register-ships. Then, after a long phase of piecemeal, incremental reform, the government of Charles III inaugurated Bourbon New Granada's third and most radical reformist conjuncture in 1778, when Gálvez's new colonial program was applied to the region in the *visita general* of 1778–83.

New Granada's political system was therefore affected by three major moments of reform during the eighteenth century. In the first, the crown reasserted royal authority, but failed to sustain its reorganization of New Granada's system of government. In the second, Madrid established a permanent viceregal government, which strengthened the networks of royal command in New Granada by installing a strong authority at the heart of the territory. In the third, Charles III's government pushed forward the Bourbons' most radical program of colonial reform, with projects for enlarging colonial commerce, overhauling viceregal administration, restraining creole influence in government, and creating a larger, more efficient apparatus for exploiting the territory's fiscal potential. We have seen that these reforms accomplished basic Bourbon goals: they improved commerce with Spain, strengthened defense and administration, and enlarged the finances upon which Spanish rule depended. But what of their political repercussions within New Granada itself? Did Bourbon administrative and financial rationalization policy produce a more absolutist, authoritarian style of government, disrupting traditional patterns of politics and depriving colonials of freedoms and rights that they had hitherto enjoyed? What were the most important causes and sources of opposition to Bourbon policy, and how did they interact with tensions and conflicts in colonial society? And what, finally, was the meaning of the rebellion against Bourbon policy that convulsed central New Granada in 1781, when the Comuneros rose against the reforms of the visitor general? To explore these issues, we will begin by examining the context of New Granada's politics before the *visita general,* showing how changes in the boundaries and institutions of government affected political life, outlining the distribution of power in the political system, and defining the procedures and activities through which colonials understood and defined their relationships to the state. Then, in the remainder of this chapter, we will examine the eruption of political crisis during the Comunero rebellion of 1781, and consider its implications for colonial rule.

The structures of power

The major alteration to the formal structure of government in New Granada during the eighteenth century was the establishment of the second, permanent viceroyalty in 1739. This seems to have submerged New Granada within a larger system of administration, because in theory, the viceroys' jurisdiction was extremely large, encompassing the territories now occupied by the republics of Colombia, Venezuela, Panama, and Ecuador. In practice, however, the viceroys' power did not extend evenly over all these regions, and New Granada was the area that felt the effects of viceregal government most strongly. In the first place, most of Venezuela came under a separate authority, vested in a captain-general in Caracas who answered directly to Madrid. The area's autonomy and separate identity were further reinforced by a separate ecclesiastical government, with a bishop in Caracas, and after 1786, a separate audiencia, again based in Caracas. Quito also retained a high degree of autonomy and a distinctive identity, despite formal subordination to the viceroys of New Granada. It kept an audiencia with a president (later, a regent) who was also commander in chief of military forces within its jurisdiction; it had an independent fiscal administration from the mid-1770s, and in ecclesiastical matters it formed part of the Archdiocese of Lima, rather than that of Santa Fe.

Clearly, then, the establishment of the viceroyalty did not submerge New Granada into a larger political unit, where it lost its own identity. On the contrary, the old administrative boundaries remained largely unchanged, and so too did the identities and loyalties that they had nurtured. Quito and Venezuela both continued as distinctive and largely autonomous entities of government, still quite distinct from each other and from New Granada, even though they came under the overarching authority of the viceroy in Santa Fe de Bogotá. As for the audiencia of New Granada, it was also much the same after the establishment of the viceroyalty as before. The audiencia was enlarged somewhat, through the addition to its jurisdiction of three provinces of Venezuela, and the provinces that had hitherto been within the jurisdiction of the audiencia of Panama, which was suppressed in 1752. But, as these were sparsely populated areas with little economic or political weight, their incorporation into New Granada did not provoke any noticeable change to the region's socioeconomic character or balance of political power. At most, it meant that the responsibilities of provincial treasuries in the audiencia of New Granada became greater, because they were now burdened with the costs of defending the frontier territories of the Orinoco. So, the creation of the viceroyalty did not substantially alter the lines of administrative division, nor much disturb the systems of government in the countries that it brought together under the nominal, overarching authority of the viceroy in Santa Fe de Bogotá.

Though the viceregency made little difference to political boundaries, the presence of a viceroy in Santa Fe did bring the audiencias of Quito and New Granada under a stronger authority, because the viceroys wielded greater powers and enjoyed higher prestige than the audiencia presidents who had previously held the highest posts in government. In the words of a Bourbon official, the viceroy in Santa Fe filled the role of "a chief who would represent the person of the Sovereign . . . be superior to all, and watch over all other magistrates and governors, as has happened in Peru and New Spain since the beginning of the conquest, allowing both those Kingdoms to flourish. . . ."[1]

In discharging these functions, the viceroys had a greater impact in New Granada than in Quito. For although the audiencia tribunal in Quito was answerable to the viceroy in Bogotá, Quito was not easily controlled from Bogotá. This was partly a matter of distance, and partly a question of economic and social difference. Traditionally, Quito had looked more to Peru than to New Granada and, although its economic linkages with New Granada became stronger in the eighteenth century, neither the highland economy of Quito nor the coastal economy of Guayaquil depended on New Granada's commercial circuits. Highland Quiteño society was also quite different, resting on a base of Indian communities and cultures far stronger than any found in the predominantly mestizo society of New Granada. And, finally, Quito continued to look to Lima as it always had, as a center of Hispanic society and government within easier access (by sea from Guayaquil) than the mountainous inland capital of Bogotá. New Granada, by contrast, felt the presence of the viceroy much more imme-

1. Silvestre, *Descripción*, pp. 9–10.

diately, because he resided in the territory and had direct responsibilities for the government, finance, and defense over the area that stretched between Pasto and Cartagena. The presence of the viceroy was important for New Granadan political development in two respects. First, it enhanced the importance of Bogotá relative to other cities in the region by strengthening its role as the center of an administrative network; second, the existence of this administrative network, focused on Bogotá, encouraged officials and creole elites to think of the territory that embraced the provinces of the audiencia of New Granada and the province of Popayán as one country, governed from a single capital.

Change was slow, however. Aside from the adjustments to the pattern of audiencias, other administrative divisions were untouched. So, too, were the old institutions of government inherited from the Hapsburgs. At the top level of government stood the audiencias of New Granada and Quito, which acted as the supreme judicial authority for all provinces between Panama and Quito, and shared some of the viceroy's responsibilities for civil government. After 1739, New Granada became the "pretorial" audiencia of the viceroyalty, with the viceroy as ex officio president and the oidors acting as the viceroy's consultative council. The audiencia was composed of four oidors and a fiscal, and its principal function was judicial. Its judges were the colony's leading law officers, providing both the highest appellate court for civil and criminal cases in the entire jurisdiction of the audiencia, and acting as a tribunal of first instance for *casos de corte,* or criminal cases in the city of Bogotá and its jurisdiction. Judicial matters were, then, entirely the prerogative of the audiencia. Viceroys did, however, have the right to supervise the oidors' activities in order to ensure that justice was properly administered, and, until Gálvez became Minister of the Indies, they could also suspend oidors who caused public scandal or behaved in a manner that threatened public order.

Below this first tier of government, two major administrative networks came under the viceroys' command. One was the web of provincial government, composed of territorial units generally known as *gobiernos,* most of which had been created by Spanish conquerers during the sixteenth century. During the eighteenth century, there were eleven such provinces in the territory of Colombia, of greatly varying size, population, and political importance. The Caribbean coast and its hinterland were divided between the *gobierno* of Cartagena, which was strategically important for the defense and commerce of New Granada, and the lesser province of Santa Marta, which, with its subprovince of Río Hacha, covered a large but sparsely populated area, much of it an Indian frontier. The western half of the country was composed of two main colonial provinces, that of the Chocó on the Pacific coast, and the province of Antioquia inland. Both of them were rich in minerals and poor in people; indeed, the Chocó was simply a series of frontier settlements on the outer margins of New Granada's social and political life. In the center of Colombia was the heart of its society and political life, which was focused primarily on the *gobiernos* of Santa Fe and Girón and the large *corregimiento* of Tunja. These were the most populated provinces of New Granada, and, as the viceregal capital, Santa Fe was the core of its government. Flanking these highland provinces were the lowland provinces of Mariquita and Neiva, which straddled the Middle and Upper Magdalena Valleys, while to the east lay the vast, lightly populated province of the Llanos. Finally, most of the southern half of the country came within the huge *gobierno* of Popayán, which included subprovinces in Pasto, and in Barbacoas, Iscuandé, and Raposo on the Pacific mining frontier.

Mostly inherited from the processes of conquest during the sixteenth century, these provinces were highly heterogeneous; nonetheless, the economic linkages created by internal commerce (which we noted in Part II) had been reinforced by political connections. All these provinces came under the jurisdiction of the audiencia of New Granada, except Popayán, which continued to be part of the audiencia of Quito. All, except Santa Fe, were ruled by governors who were the highest political and judicial authorities in their respective regions; if they ranked as *capitán general,* then they also held overall command of local military forces. In Santa Fe, the position of governor and captain-general was held by the president of the audiencia until 1739, when it was taken over by the viceroys. Most governors were appointed directly by the king, and, with rights of appointment to only three governorships, the viceroys had limited power and patronage in this secondary tier of government. The viceroys did, however, have the right to approve appointments of the lieutenant governors who represented the governors in subprovinces, as well as the corregidores who supervised Indian government.[2] Thus, with the exception of Popayán, the provinces of New Granada had been brought together in a loose entity, as parts of the audiencia of New Granada, and this unity was reinforced by the viceroys. Furthermore, during the eighteenth century, Popayán became more closely tied to New Granada's economic and political networks, as its gold trade enlarged commerce with New Granada's provinces and its military governor came under the command of the viceroy in Bogotá.

The other principal network of government commanded by the viceroys was that of the *Real Hacienda,* or colonial exchequer. The heart of this fiscal administration lay in Bogotá, in the *Tribunal de Cuentas,* or supreme court of audit. This court supervised the provincial *cajas reales,* the region-

2. Ibid., pp. 12–63.

al royal treasuries that were invariably located in provincial capitals, and were usually the responsibility of two *oficiales reales*, one a treasurer, the other an accountant. From the provincial capitals, these officials were responsible for gathering taxes and accounts from all the subtreasuries (*cajas sufragáneas*) in their jurisdiction, which usually, though not always, corresponded with the boundaries of the provincial government.[3] The network of fiscal administration created another basis for integrating the provinces into a larger whole, because all the provincial treasuries within Colombian territory were supervised from Bogotá. Overall responsibility for this entire system of fiscal administration was charged to the viceroy, who presided over the *Junta Superior de Real Hacienda*, a committee composed of the accountant of the *Tribunal de Cuentas* and the *oficiales reales* of Bogotá, together with the senior oidor and fiscal of the audiencia. The viceroys also took responsibility during the eighteenth century for another, growing element of treasury activity: that of the royal monopolies, which, during the later eighteenth century, provided a growing proportion of crown income. This, too, tended to bring the provinces together under the government from Bogotá, because all nine "principal administrations" of the tobacco monopoly, and all twelve of those for managing the aguardiente estanco, were responsible to a central management in the capital.[4]

At the district level, in cities, towns, and villages, civil government was shared between various agencies. When a governor or his deputy was present, they played a leading part in local government, implementing orders from superior authorities, maintaining order and dispensing justice. But in the towns that formed the building blocks of Hispanic society, civil government was also exercised by colonials themselves, through the institution of the cabildo, or municipal corporation.

Cabildos were found only in cities or *villas,* and their officers held jurisdiction over large hinterlands around the urban area. Several of the early cities of New Granada, especially those in old mining zones, such as Zaragoza and Cáceres, were much decayed by the eighteenth century, and their correspondingly feeble town councils governed only small and declining populations. New towns were founded, such as San Gil and Medellín in the late seventeenth century and Socorro in the late eighteenth, thereby bringing new areas under the local government of town councils. Generally, however, the development of town government had not kept pace with population growth and shifts in settlement, and this,

3. Oscar Rodríguez, "Anotaciones al funcionamiento de la Real Hacienda en el Nuevo Reino de Granada," *ACHSC,* vol. 11 (1983), pp. 83–5.
4. Silvestre, *Descripción,* pp. 63–4.

together with the dispersion of rural habitation, meant that the writ of government often ran thin in large areas of New Granada's countryside.[5]

Hispanic town government included two kinds of officials: the *regidores* or town councillors, and the *alcaldes ordinarios* or magistrates of first instance.[6] The number of municipal officers varied with the size of the town, but generally consisted of between four and twelve regidores, with one or two alcaldes. The former were appointed by the crown and were usually proprietary offices acquired by purchase; the latter were elected officers, chosen each year by the regidores. The alcaldes were the most active element in local government, because theirs was the basic function of maintaining law and order. Where the urban jurisdiction was large, they might in turn appoint deputies to act on their behalf in the villages and parishes of surrounding rural areas.[7]

The system of government vested in royal and municipal officials depended to a considerable degree on the compliance of citizens, because the crown did not have substantial military forces to enforce its will in the region. Regular armed forces were concentrated on the Caribbean coast, where detachments of infantry and artillery from the Spanish army were deployed to defend Cartagena, Panama, Santa Marta, and Río Hacha against foreign attack. Of these, Cartagena held the biggest concentration of professional soldiers. Before the viceroyalty was reestablished in 1739, its garrison was rarely fully manned, and the number of soldiers fluctuated around 300. During the 1750s, the garrison was strengthened to between 500 and 600 men, and by 1772 consisted of around 800 infantry and artillery men.[8] Santa Marta, meanwhile, had fewer than 200 regular troops and Río Hacha was an even smaller military outpost. In the interior, regular military forces were negligible. Before 1785, the nearest approach to regular military forces inland consisted of a company of some fifty infantrymen in Popayán and a detachment of fifty cavalry and seventy-five halberdiers in Bogotá, acting as the viceregal guard.[9] So, for most of the eighteenth century, troop concentrations in New Granada were relatively small, and, as all troops were many days distant from New

5. This is amply demonstrated by reports made by parish priests in the early 1800s, summarized in Virginia Gutiérrez de Pineda, *La Familia en Colombia*, vol. 1 (Bogotá, 1963), pp. 307–59.

6. The fullest description of the Spanish American cabildo as an institution, with an outline of the character and responsibilities of its officers, is found in Constantino Bayle, *Los Cabildos Seculares en la América Española* (Madrid, 1952), especially pp. 101–324; John Preston Moore, *The Cabildo in Peru under the Hapsburgs* (Durham, North Carolina, 1954), pp. 77–114, provides a more succinct outline. There is no comparable work on the cabildo in New Granada.

7. J. M. Ots Capdequí, *Nuevos Aspectos del Siglo XVIII en América* (Bogotá, 1946), pp. 9–37; Marzahl, *Town in the Empire*, pp. 35–73.

8. Marchena Fernández, *La Institución Militar*, pp. 71, 82–98, 145–58.

9. Kuethe, *Military Reform and Society in New Granada*, pp. 11, 191–2.

Granada's main centers of population, the government could not rely on any rapid or substantial mobilization of professional military forces to support its authority in the interior. The viceroy could call out local militias, either for defense against foreign assault or for maintaining local order. But militia units were so disorganized and poorly equipped that, in the late 1770s, they were "far more shadow than substance."[10] The use of militias depended in any case on the loyalty of the king's subjects, particularly on the local notables who supplied militia leadership. If they chose to ignore or disobey an official summons to action, the authorities had no means to coerce them. The allegiance of creole elites was, therefore, an indispensable support of the colonial government, and, to understand the workings of that government, we must look beyond its purely bureaucratic machinery to the informal networks of influence that functioned at the regional and local level. For in each of the regional economies of New Granada there were small groups of landed, mining, and mercantile families that had accumulated wealth over successive generations and that, by reason of their social status and economic power, exercised a powerful influence over the affairs of their local communities.

Government and elites

In the Spanish system of government, power was theoretically concentrated in the hands of the crown, which appointed officials to govern through a bureaucratic hierarchy. Colonials had no representative institutions beyond that provided by the cabildo, the municipal corporation chosen by *vecinos* to represent their interests and manage the affairs of their towns. In theory, the distinction between these two forms of civil government was clear. Early settlers had been left to manage their everyday affairs in town councils run by prominent *vecinos,* whereas royal government was superimposed on this network of local government, and, through a bureaucratic corps appointed by the king, provided justice, claimed and collected taxes, and arbitrated between competing claims. The crown, could, however, intervene directly in town government when it chose to do so. In law, the king's governors and corregidors presided over the cabildo and could choose its officials, while the crown also had the power, which it increasingly used, to bestow proprietary posts in the cabildo on favored individuals. But if the design of colonial government was absolutist in conception, in practice royal power was constrained by the difficulties of controlling and financing the administrative apparatus of its vast empire. Lacking both a fully professional corps of bureaucrats and large standing armies, the Hapsburgs sustained their authority more

10. Ibid., p. 43.

by conciliation than coercion. Theoretically powerful, the Hapsburg state was weak in practice. The crown left government in the hands of officials who were concerned primarily with their own interests and who, by settling and marrying in the Americas, integrated into colonial society; at the same time, successive kings ceded authority to creoles by selling offices in return for cash. The framework of colonial government was therefore occupied by crown officials who pursued private interests and who, by building local alliances with creoles, became as responsive to colonial interests as they were to those of the crown. Colonial government was, in essence, a compromise between the absolute sovereignty claimed by the Spanish crown and the interests of the creole elites that dominated local and regional societies.

In late colonial New Granada, the influence of creole elites in the colonial state is most clearly reflected in Santa Fe de Bogotá. The city had played an important role in New Granada's government since it became the capital of the audiencia de Santa Fe in 1550, and in the eighteenth century it took on a higher political profile when it was converted into the capital of the Viceroyalty of Santa Fe. As the seat of the viceroy and audiencia, Bogotá was at once the headquarters of Spanish executive power and the core of judicial and fiscal administration; as the residence of the archbishops of Santa Fe and the colony's main center of learning, it also housed the colony's largest clerical establishment and its leading educational establishments. Both roles provided the families of the *santafereño* elite with chances to participate in the affairs of government, taking up opportunities that they regarded as their birthright.

The capital's elite was based on a nucleus of landowning families who claimed descent from the conquistadors of New Granada, held large estates in the hinterland of Bogotá, took up offices in the colonial church and state, and intermarried with leading peninsular officials. Though they lacked great wealth or aristocratic titles, the members of this creole elite regarded themselves as "nobles" who, by reason of their lineage and social standing, deserved a privileged position in the patronage and activities of government. Their conception of the social order and of their place within it are reflected in the *Historia y Genealogías deste Nuevo Reino de Granada* of Flórez de Ocáriz, a text published in 1672. Its author, a peninsular immigrant who claimed membership of the *santafereño* upper class due to his descent from a conquistador of New Granada, sought to establish the identity of the colonial nobility in Bogotá, its origins and attributes, and its responsibilities and rights in the colonial state.[11]

---

11. These observations are drawn from Juan A. and Judith E. Villamarin, "The Concept of Nobility in Colonial Santa Fe de Bogotá," in Karen Spalding (ed.), *Essays in the Political, Economic and Social History of Colonial Latin America* (Newark, Delaware, 1982), pp. 125–50.

At the heart of Flórez de Ocáriz's treatise lay three basic propositions: First, that society was divided into nobles and plebeians; second, that the nobility in Bogotá was composed of those who had descended from the conquistadors and nobles who had married into their families; third, that nobles should occupy the primary position in society and provide the dignatories and officers of state, through the patronage of the crown. These propositions presented an entirely orthodox picture of the social order as it was conceived in Spain, and they seem to have reflected practice in New Granada. During the sixteenth and seventeenth centuries, the status of the *santafereño* nobility was, at least in part, sustained by rewards from the crown, in the shape of privileged positions before the law, and in the institutions and ceremonial activities of church and state. [12] However, although the nobility expected the crown to support its status and to reward its services, it was not simply a passive recipient of patronage. Nobility was incompatible with poverty, and, to be recognized, noble families had to be sufficiently wealthy to display their status.

Governed by the desire to preserve and demonstrate their noble status, members of leading families had to develop economic and political strategies for conserving and increasing their wealth. This required strategic investment of resources in various ways. Wealth in agricultural, mining, and commercial enterprises had to be accumulated to form capital, not in the modern sense of wealth used to create more wealth, but as a means of demonstrating and underpinning status. Wealth also facilitated other, equally vital forms of investment in the social and political spheres. Marriage with other leading families or with appropriate peninsular immigrants required dowries for daughters; donations to the church were also an essential part of a family strategy, because they not only reinforced the standing of the family, but helped give sons access to ecclesiastical benefices. An equally essential element in a family strategy was an ability to demonstrate service to the crown, whether in military expeditions, in developing colonial resources, or in straightforward cash contributions; this was necessary as a means for seeking future rewards for family members. [13] Thus elite politics was informed by a belief that crown and nobility were mutually dependent, with reciprocal claims on each other, and political activity revolved around competition for access to the rewards offered by the patrimonial state and its church. Politics in Bogotá therefore had a parochial, nepotistic character, with the patrician family as a prime unit of organization and the occupation of offices in church and state as its primary goal.

The highest levels of government in New Granada were staffed by peninsular Spaniards. The viceregency always went to peninsulars, and

---

12. Ibid., pp. 140–1. 13. Ibid., pp. 143–4.

between 1700 and 1758 most of the men appointed to the posts of oidor and fiscal of the audiencia were born in Spain. Of thirty such appointments made during this period, seventeen were given to peninsular Spaniards, and only nine to American Spaniards (the origins of the remaining four are unknown). After the accession of Charles III, new appointments of creoles to New Granada's audiencia became rare. Between 1759 and 1776, only two creoles were given posts in Bogotá. One was the Quiteño oidor Romualdo Navarro, who was transferred to Bogotá from Quito; the other was the New Granadan Francisco Antonio Moreno y Escandón, who was appointed as fiscal in 1771. So, unlike the audiencias of Mexico, Lima, and Santiago de Chile, where creoles took most of the appointments and even established creole majorities through the purchase of audiencia judgeships, posts in the New Granadan court were more commonly taken by peninsulars.[14]

This did not prevent creole families in the capital from contributing to their own government. Creoles occupied many lesser posts and, through their contacts with peninsular officials, exercised considerable informal political influence. We know, for example, that early in the eighteenth century, the Flórez family stood at the center of a network of informal power in the capital, through the posts that family members held in the audiencia, the royal treasury, and the cathedral.[15] After the coup against President Meneses in 1715, the revelation that two of its members had played a prominent role in his deposition cost the family its position at the center of government, and after the arrival of the first viceroy in 1719 the Flórez family never recovered its place. Indeed, the coming of the first viceroy disrupted local politics considerably, because Viceroy Villalonga brought a retinue of relatives and dependents for whom jobs had to be found within the bureaucracy. However, neither this nor the reestablishment of the viceroyalty in 1739 seems to have seriously curtailed creole influence in Bogotá. For although New Granadan creoles did not succeed in penetrating the audiencia in the manner achieved by creoles in the viceregal capitals of Mexico and Peru, their alliances with Spanish officials gave them a voice at the heart of government and a share in its important posts. Many of the peninsulars who served in the audiencia of New Granada during 1700–58 resided in Bogotá for more than ten years and, as a result, were probably co-opted into local society. Indeed, if we accept John Phelan's assumption that service for more than ten years tended to make peninsulars into "procreoles," then New Granada conforms more closely to the pattern found in other American audiencias. Over the period

14. Burkholder and Chandler, *From Impotence to Authority*, pp. 221–7.
15. German Colmenares, "Factores de la vida política: el Nuevo Reino de Granada en el siglo XVIII (1730–1740)," in *Manual de Historia de Colombia*, vol. I, pp. 395, 400.

1700–58, eighteen of twenty-six ministers whose origins are known were either creoles or Spaniards whose lengthy residence in Bogotá made them procreole.[16]

The manner in which a political elite was formed from marriages between peninsular officials and creole families is reflected in two *santafereño* families founded in the eighteenth century. The first of these was the Lozanos, a family that stemmed from the Spaniard Jorge Miguel Lozano de Peralta, oidor of the Bogotá audiencia between 1722 and 1729. Lozano's eldest son married into the wealthy creole family of the Caicedos and, from this union, inherited the largest landed estate on the savannah of Bogotá. These lands gave a solid economic foundation to the Lozanos' social pretensions: they later became the basis of the entail that supported the Marquisate of San Jorge, a title that confirmed the family's position in the front rank of the *santafereño* patriciate. And, of course, the Lozanos married their social peers, so that through marriages with other creole nobles and Spanish officials, they confirmed and reinforced their position at the center of the capital's social and political elite.[17]

The renovation of the elite by marriages between peninsular officials and creole families is also clearly demonstrated in the case of the Alvarez family. The family was founded on the marriage of the peninsular Spaniard Manuel de Bernardo Alvarez, fiscal of the audiencia from 1736 to 1755, to María Josepha del Casal y Freiria, the daughter of a Galician official who had served as corregidor of Tunja and as *teniente* to the captain-general of Santa Fe during the 1730s.[18] From this marriage, consecrated in Bogotá in 1738, fourteen children survived, and through their marriages they forged close links with prominent members of the peninsular and creole upper class in the capital. The first-born son, Manuel Bernardo Alvarez y Casal, became accountant of the *Tribunal y Real Audiencia de Cuentas* in Bogotá, and married into the family of Lozano y Manrique, marquises of San Jorge and prominent creole landowners.[19] Another son, Ignacio Alvarez y Casal, became lieutenant governor of Pamplona, whereas his brother, José, married into another important creole family, the Suescún.[20] Of the nine daughters of the Alvarez–Casals marriage, six married Spanish officials serving in Santa Fe. Indeed, by 1778, these marriages meant that five highly placed officials in the audiencia and treasury of Bogotá had relations of affinity and consanguinity that contra-

---

16. Phelan, *The People and the King*, pp. 12–13; also Phelan, "El auge y la caida de los criollos en la Audiencia de Nueva Granada, 1700–1781," *BHA*, vol. 59 (1972), pp. 597–618.

17. Phelan, *The People and the King*, pp. 70–1.

18. José Restrepo Sáenz, *Biografías de los mandatarios y ministros de la Real Audiencia, 1671–1819* (Bogotá, 1952), pp. 460–1. On the Casals y Freiria and Alvarez families, see José M. Restrepo Sáenz and Raimundo Rivas, *Genealogías de Santafé de Bogotá* (Bogotá, 1928), pp. 17–23, 225–6.

19. Ibid., pp. 20–1.   20. Ibid., p. 19.

vened the laws governing ties of blood and marriage between fiscal officers. So, although the viceroys tended to dispense patronage among members of their own retinues brought from Spain, creole opportunities for
gaining access to office and influence were evidently undamaged by the
establishment of the viceroyalty. Indeed, when Charles III's *visitador general* arrived at Bogotá in 1778, the complex of relationships created by
marriage between creole nobles and officials in the audiencia and fiscal
bureaucracy had placed leading *santafereño* families in a position of considerable influence at the heart of government.

The other means by which urban elites exercised local power was by
holding office in town councils. In Bogotá, the cabildo seems to have been
a moribund institution at mid-century. In 1749, Viceroy Eslava complained that it was so difficult to sell *regimientos* (councillorships) in the
capital's cabildo that it was usually necessary to appoint interim councillors
to fill the gaps.[21] This, however, did not stop the cabildo from becoming
an important vehicle for creole interests in the years that followed. Indeed, according to Archbishop-Viceroy Caballero y Góngora, by the early
1780s the Santa Fe cabildo was the instrument of a local oligarchy and, as
such, had become an obstacle to good government in the capital. The
alcaldes, he observed, were always chosen from among the leading families of the city, and, during their year of office, their main preoccupation
was to avoid any action that might injure their personal interests and local
standing, rather than "to govern the republic" in the general interest.
And, he added, "the party of hacendados . . . who control the cabildo of
this capital . . . contribute to this disorder, since in their own interests
they obstruct order, perpetuate ignorance and shortage, and in their official decisions, reject reforms in favour of private profit . . ."[22]

In other major regional urban centers, local political life was similarly
dominated by elites formed from the alliances of creole landed families
with royal officials and immigrant merchants. Marzahl's study of
seventeenth-century Popayán clearly shows how such alliances created an
urban patriciate formed around a ruling group, which not only monopolized positions in the cabildo but, through alliances with the provincial
governor and with treasury officials, also acquired jobs and influence in
the provincial administration.[23] Here, as elsewhere, the cabildo became a
vehicle for leading families to pursue their private interests, rather than an
institution whose members had any pretension to represent the interests of
local society as a whole.[24] During the eighteenth century, some wealthy
peninsular merchants joined the cabildo, but the city's government re-

21. AGI Santa Fe 422, Consejo de Indias, July 15, 1749.
22. AGI Santa Fe 552, Borrador de lo que pensó el Sr. Virrey representar a la Corte sobre elección de
    Corregidor de Santa Fe . . ."
23. Marzahl, *Town in the Empire*, pp. 85–121.   24. Ibid., pp. 159–67.

mained largely in the hands of a narrow local oligarchy dominated by five interrelated families whose wealth was based in mining.[25] Colmenares's study of Cali, the other major urban center of the province of Popayán, also shows how leading families sought to control the cabildo's posts both as a sign of civic status, reflecting the wealth and social standing of their holders, and as a lever for influence within the provincial administration. Thus the Caicedo family used wealth acquired from mining in the Chocó to secure a dominant role on the cabildo in the opening years of the eighteenth century and, once entrenched, its political efforts were focused on combating competition from new wealth by filling cabildo posts with relatives and dependents.[26] In Medellín, wealth and office holding in the cabildo were also strongly correlated, with the wealthiest miners and merchants filling the most prestigious posts. According to Ann Twinam, local notables took office rather reluctantly, because municipal offices offered no economic benefit, and they did so only to display their social status.[27] Even so, office holding undoubtedly held attractions, if only in the negative sense that, by serving on the cabildo, the town's wealthiest miners and merchants could at least ensure that the local government did not fall into other, potentially hostile, hands. And there were of course always the benefits of local political influence for furthering private interests, as Francisco Silvestre, twice governor of Antioquia, well understood. As he pointed out in his 1785 report on Antioquia, the control of the local magistracy by creole patricians and their peninsular relatives meant that there was one law for the rich and another for the poor.[28]

When conflict arose in local politics, it was invariably based on family and personalistic factions, rather than on social or ideological divisions. In eighteenth-century Cali, miners and merchants clashed in pursuit of cabildo posts and, as many of the merchants were immigrant Spaniards, their disputes often took on the aspect of a political duel between creoles and peninsulars. However, as in Popayán and Medellín, these local conflicts did not mean that creoles rejected peninsular participation in politics. In these towns, peninsulars were readily absorbed into creole society, and when rivalries arose, they stemmed more from the clash of family clans than from any fundamental antagonism between creoles and Spaniards. The same was true of Cartagena, where Spanish officers who arrived with the military expedition of 1698 laid the foundations of a new creole administrative, commercial, and social elite by marrying into local creole landed families, and where Spanish merchants and creole hacendados

25. Colmenares, *Historia económica y social de Colombia: Popayán*, vol. 2, pp. 259–65.
26. Colmenares, *Cali*, pp. 143–54.
27. Twinam, *Miners, Merchants, and Farmers in Colonial Colombia*, pp. 113–46.
28. Silvestre, *Relación*, p. 188.

served together in the city's cabildo.[29] Elite politics in New Granada is, then, best understood in regional terms. There was no single creole "ruling class" or "oligarchy," conscious of common interests or capable of united action; there were instead local family networks, often incorporating peninsular Spaniards, which sought office and influence in their towns as the best means of preserving and extending their family enterprises and fortunes.

Popular politics

If the activities of the urban elites formed the main aspect of political life in eighteenth-century New Granada, they did not fill the boundaries of the political terrain. Outside New Granada's major cities and towns was a host of small towns and villages in which poor whites, mestizos, and Indians also participated in local politics. Much of this politics overlapped and interacted with the struggle of individuals and families to advance their fortunes by monopolizing municipal office. For, although cabildo posts did not necessarily confer any immediate economic rewards, the alcaldes' powers of law enforcement and policing could certainly be used for personal and family advantage. Indeed, such influence could extend beyond the urban precinct, because alcaldes not only dispensed justice in the town itself, but they also annually appointed *tenientes* in the outlying parishes and villages of their jurisdiction, enabling them to build a network of clients and dependents in rural areas. It is, then, easy to imagine how local communities might become politicized around factions that competed for leadership at the district level. If a faction was able to secure control of a town's cabildo, it could then position its followers as officeholders in the hamlets and parishes of the town's jurisdiction, thereby creating a network of clients that could be used to further personal ambitions.

The post of alcalde ordinario was particularly important in this respect, because alcaldes chose deputies to act on their behalf in the rural hinterland of the town. In theory, candidates for such offices had to satisfy certain criteria designed to ensure that government appointments went only to respectable whites who enjoyed social and economic standing in the community, and to prevent the concentration of local offices in the hands of a single family. A report on the province of Vélez in 1751 suggests, however, that provincial alcaldes disregarded these criteria when selecting *tenientes* to act for them in rural parishes, because they chose

29. Carmen Gómez Pérez, "El Consulado de Sevilla y la formación de las oligarquías en Cartagena de Indias a principios del XVIII," pp. 330–48; Hermes Tovar Pinzón, "El estado colonial frente al poder local y regional," *Nova Americana* (Turin, 1982), no. 5, pp. 49–52.

"persons so wretched that they have no spirit or authority for anything."[30]
In reality, this probably meant that the alcaldes delegated authority to
their kin and clients, so that they might be used for personal and family
advantage. This was certainly the implication of a proposal made in 1773
that viceroys should play a part in choosing local magistrates, to curtail
"the corruption of municipal justices by the partisanship which governs
their elections in all the cities of the viceroyalty."[31]

Contestation over municipal posts is a significant dimension of colonial
politics because it provided the primary arena in which the ordinary
citizen experienced government and formed political attitudes. Selecting
municipal officials generated a lively tradition of political action, in which
common people became involved with government, learned how to act
collectively, and both expressed and developed ideas about their rights.
Using evidence drawn from a variety of local settings, Margarita Garrido
has shown that, although rich creoles might manipulate elections for their
own purposes, ordinary *vecinos* were by no means the passive instruments
of local elites. Indeed, they were often ready to use the law to combat
monopolization of power and oppression by cliques, to reject officials who
did not have local approval, and to express disapproval of priests who
charged excessive fees, behaved immorally, or otherwise neglected their
responsibilities. Ordinary *vecinos* also entered local politics by joining in
efforts to improve the standing of their communities, usually by seeking
to convert a parish into a *villa* or a town into a *ciudad,* and through such
activity, experienced a sense of local identity and community that crossed
class lines and allowed them to think and act in the defense of collective
interests.[32]

Another element in the public life of New Granada, and a further sign
of an active popular political culture, is found in the various civil disorders
that, as a result of criminal proceedings, come to light in judicial records,
labeled as "tumultos," "levantamientos," "sublevaciones," "motines," and
"rebeliones." Research into such incidents suggests that they were invariably brief, highly localized events without significance beyond the places
in which they occurred. Nevertheless, because they were characterized by
discriminating forms of behavior, were informed by conceptions of community interest, and were underpinned by a sense that forceful illegal
action was justifiable under certain conditions, they should be seen as
elements in a tradition of popular politics.[33]

30. Ots Capdequí, *Nuevos Aspectos del Siglo XVIII,* p. 34.   31. Ibid., p. 34.

32. Margarita Garrido de Payan, "La política local en la Nueva Granada, 1750–1810," *ACHSC,* vol.
15 (1987), pp. 37–56; also, by the same author, "The Political Culture of New Granada, 1770–
1815," unpublished D. Phil. thesis, University of Oxford, 1990, pp. 76–180.

33. A more detailed presentation of this argument is found in McFarlane, "Civil Disorders and
Popular Protests in Late Colonial New Granada," pp. 17–54.

Civil disorders took several forms. The imposition and collection of taxes was one motive for collective protest. When, for example, the corregidor of Tunja tried to raise an emergency wartime loan from Vélez in 1740, he was expelled by rioters who refused the loan and acclaimed the town's *alférez real* as their leader. In the 1750s and early 1760s, the town of Ocaña also saw a series of local riots when an overzealous treasury official disputed with the local clergy and community over the collection of the sales tax. In the mid-1760s, the fiscal demands of the state provoked resistance over a wider region. The greatest public protest against this policy was in Quito, where city people mounted a resistance that lasted for several months, brought royal government to a standstill, and virtually constructed an autonomous government of their own.[34] Popular unrest also occurred in southern and western Colombia between 1764 and 1766, in the province of Popayán and the neighboring province of the Chocó. Other occasions for rioting arose in Indian and mestizo settlements when local officials and clergy exploited their positions for personal gain by imposing abnormal demands on the resources of communities, whether for labor, money, or goods. Community hostility toward local officials could also produce violent collective responses, which aimed at preventing them from taking or holding office. This unrest sometimes took the form of rioting by crowds that openly demonstrated their rejection of officials, or was sometimes carried out by small groups operating in a semiclandestine manner. Mob challenges to local authority also occasionally resulted when magistrates behaved unfairly, either by not enforcing the law or using it selectively.[35]

Collective protests of these kinds sometimes expressed factional divisions within communities; at other times, they reflected social resentments and ethnic conflicts. But what is most interesting about them is that they were invariably structured actions, underpinned by a sense of community and a belief that forceful collective protest was a legitimate form of action. In this sense, acts of rioting and rebellion were part of a wider repertoire of practical politics, reflecting assumptions that authority should take regard of local interests and opinion. If they were illegal, then they were not anti-institutional. They did not attack the machinery of the state, but they sought to control and manipulate its agents, showing a popular awareness of justice and the law that did not tolerate the unrestrained exercise of power by representatives of the state. Thus, although such civil disorders were neither inspired nor guided by any specific or explicitly elaborated political thought, they were not entirely innocent of

34. McFarlane, "The 'Rebellion of the Barrios': Urban Insurrection in Bourbon Quito," pp. 283–330; Kenneth J. Andrien, "Economic Crisis, Taxes and the Quito Insurrection of 1765," *Past and Present*, no. 129 (1990), pp. 104–31.

35. McFarlane, "Civil Disorders and Popular Protests in Late Colonial New Granada," pp. 22–44.

political ideas or significance. In the structured forms of collective protest and acts of defiance against government and its agents, we may dimly detect attitudes and beliefs that were normally unstated, and rarely expressed in written or explicit form. In their reactions to the fiscal and economic impositions of government, to the appointment of officials opposed by members of a local community, or to perceived abuses of authority by incumbent officials, these small, highly localized disturbances are reflections of popular attitudes and values, especially with respect to the relations of government to its subjects. Such attitudes are similar to those encountered in other agrarian societies: a belief in a right to land and the use of its products; a belief in the right to produce and consume essential items of consumption (foodstuffs, tobacco, and aguardiente) without arbitrary taxation; the idea that local customs should be respected and that justice be fairly administered. These attitudes implicitly defined a basic notion of freedom: the right to resist arbitrary intrusions by government and its agents. This minimal, residual notion of freedom was nurtured by the colonial experience of government, for despite its imposing structure of law and bureaucracy, Spanish government in New Granada held only loose control over the mass of the population. In this sense, the society of New Granada shared in that freedom that Mario Góngora has described as "peculiar to the Americas – a form of liberty existing outside the framework of the state . . . not based on any well-defined notion or any new concept of the state . . . [but] . . . rooted in laxity."[36]

Thus, in the provincial society of small towns and villages that proliferated in New Granada, there are signs of a lively political life, in which the official representatives of church and state found that authority depended on respect for local interests and opinion, rather than unconditional acceptance from a docile or repressed population. Political participation at the local level, whether legal or extralegal, showed that the system of justice and administration depended on public support, and that ordinary people expected their voices to be heard. Normally, such politics were highly localized, focused around men rather than ideas or programs, and represented no threat to the stability of the colonial order. Popular politics and protest were, in short, as integral a part of colonial political culture as the maneuvers of the leading creole families who occupied the front ranks of New Granadan society and government.

Political equilibrium and its rupture

For most of the eighteenth century, Bourbon policy did not induce serious strains in the colonial system of government; competition between the

36. Mario Góngora, *Studies in the Colonial History of Spanish America*, trans. by Richard Southern (Cambridge, 1975), p. 125.

various groups that constituted colonial society was contained and expressed with the localized circuits of politics that we have just described. The reasons for this are not difficult to find. In the first place, the pace of economic change was slow and disputes over resources were insufficiently acute or widespread to cause any significant conflict. Demographic growth undoubtedly generated social tensions in some regions, notably in areas where a growing mestizo population pressed on the lands of declining Indian communities, as in parts of the province of Tunja, or where Indian communities occasionally rose in self-defense against predatory officials or clerics, as in Pasto, or where nascent urban communities competed for precedence amongst themselves, as in the Socorro area. But because demographic and commercial change had only a very limited impact on the economic and social structures of regional life, such discontents were purely local affairs that lacked any resonance among wider sectors of the population.

Stability in colonial political life also owed much to the fact that institutional reform had only a modest impact on New Granada before the *visita general* of 1778–83. The first viceroyalty was simply too transient to effect any lasting change, and for most of the first half of the eighteenth century New Granada remained under the same form of administration that it had known under the Hapsburgs. When Philip V restored the Viceroyalty of New Granada in 1739, colonial administration did become noticeably more effective in some areas, as the stiffening of colonial defenses and the growth of revenues attest. But the rate of change was slow and halting, fiscal reform was applied only in some provinces, and the viceroys worked pragmatically, dealing with specific problems rather than applying innovative policies over wide areas. Meanwhile, the audiencia retained much of its old and inefficient character, despite having the viceroys in its presidency. As late as 1776, we find Viceroy Flóres complaining that in the audiencia in Santa Fe there were only two serving oidors, both of whom suffered from chronic ill health that impaired their work.[37] But perhaps most important was the fact that the form and tenor of government had been only slightly modified by the introduction of the viceregency, which left colonials with a strong sense of local autonomy.

So, although New Granada was brought under a stronger authority, exercised from the viceregal capital in Santa Fe de Bogotá, the purposes, practices, and procedures of government were still those of the old political order inherited from the Hapsburgs. For though the viceroys were installed to enhance the authority of royal government in New Granada, they still enjoyed the political latitude in interpreting and implementing the royal will that the Hapsburg regime had traditionally allowed, and, rather than blindly enforcing royal orders, viceroys and other high officials

---

37. AGI Santa Fe 585 (ramo 6), Flóres to Gálvez, Santa Fe, May 15, 1776 (no. 50).

continued to take colonial interests into account when applying metropolitan legislation. Indeed, according to Francisco Silvestre, writing in 1789, the autonomy of the viceroys and their willingness to adapt the maxims of Bourbon policy to local circumstances was the touchstone of sound government and the guarantee of political harmony before 1778. Thus, he noted with approval the fact that when Viceroy Pizarro discharged his responsibilities to improve administration in the colonial treasury, he implemented some crown policies while omitting others, "which the condition of the Kingdom did not permit, or for which the moment had not yet arrived."[38] Silvestre also praised Pizarro's successors for the same reason, portraying them as men committed to a pragmatic and conciliatory style of government, who were willing to learn from experience and ready to adapt policy to local circumstances and interests. Thus, despite installing viceroys in New Granada in order to augment royal authority, the Bourbon monarchy left them to function in the political style inherited from the Hapsburgs, preferring government by consensus rather than confrontation.

If peace was preserved under this political system, then its change was, by the same token, to promote discord. Thus, when José de Gálvez, Charles III's Minister for the Indies, abandoned compromise in favor of the more rigorous and inflexible approach introduced to New Granada by his reforming visitor general in 1778, this change was to precipitate the greatest political crisis faced by the Spanish authorities in eighteenth-century New Granada. Indeed, for Francisco Silvestre, a peninsular official with long experience of New Granada and close connections with its political elite, the attack on the traditional system of government by the visitor general (who, like his counterparts in other regions, "blindly followed the orders of Sr. Gálvez")[39] was the main cause of the Comunero rebellion of 1781, the greatest challenge to Spanish government in Colombian territory since the accession of the Bourbon dynasty in 1700.

The Comunero rebellion was an extraordinary event. At its height, the insurrection mobilized a force that was said to have numbered as many as 20,000 people, and, as this force swept toward the capital, it presented an opposition so formidable that the royal authorities were forced into a humiliating reversal of Caroline policies. It is, therefore, hardly surprising that historians have long regarded the rebellion as an event of special significance. In its scale, duration, and scope, the rebellion was not only without parallel in the history of colonial New Granada, but, because it coincided with the massive uprising of Túpac Amaru in the southern Andes, it was also part of a larger conjuncture of opposition to Spanish government, sparked by the new colonial program of Charles III. What,

38. Ibid., p. 78.   39. Ibid., p. 88.

then, was its meaning? Did the rebellion mark a turning point in the political development of the region, reflecting anticolonial, protonationalist sentiments of the kind that, after 1810, were to begin New Granada's transformation into the independent republic of Colombia? What were the political ideas and attitudes that informed the rebellion, and to what extent did they represent a challenge to Spanish rule? And what of its social content? Did popular insurrection stem solely from opposition to Bourbon fiscal policies, or was it spurred by internal, domestic conflicts arising from tension and competition between groups within colonial society? To take up these questions, we must first disentangle the grievances and groups involved in the rebellion, show how disparate discontents merged into a regional movement, and trace the dynamics of its development. Then, having set the rebellion in its social and political context, we can return to the larger issue of its place in the political development of late colonial New Granada and its implications for relations with the parent power.

Origins of the Comunero rebellion

The immediate causes of the rebellion are easily identified. Popular tumults were triggered by the fiscal measures introduced by visitor general Gutiérrez de Piñeres in 1780 and 1781, when his reforms affecting the cultivation and sale of tobacco, the sale of aguardiente, and the rate and collection of the sales tax were implemented in quick succession. The first signs of popular resistance can be traced to small disturbances that occurred, during the last months of 1780, in or near the villages of Simacota, Mogotes, and Charalá, all areas where peasant farmers were prohibited from tobacco cultivation by the new regulations of the crown tobacco monopoly.[40] These incidents were, however, simply the prelude to a larger eruption of popular rioting, activated by the introduction of the new sales tax regulations in March 1781. Resistance again took the form of local riots, but as popular resistance widened to include settlements over a larger area, it soon acquired an organized and coherent form.

The shift from sporadic acts of defiance against officials in country parishes to large-scale resistance started in the town of Socorro on March 16, 1781, when the public announcement of new sales tax regulations triggered a riot among the crowds gathered for the town's weekly market. In the days that followed, rioting broke out in the nearby parishes of Simacota and Pinchote and the town of San Gil, where restrictions on tobacco cultivation directly affected small farmers. As protests against the

40. Pablo E. Cárdenas Acosta, *Los Comuneros. (Reivindicaciones históricas y juicios críticos documentalmente justificados)* (Bogotá, 1945), pp. 210–12; 275–80.

tobacco estanco combined with resistance to the alcabala, the constituency of protest broadened. After Socorro rioted again, on March 30, a surge of discontent swept through neighboring settlements in early April, in a chain of riots against the personnel and property of the local tobacco and aguardiente monopoly administrations. Then, in mid-April, people in the town of Socorro again seized the initiative. They staged a third major riot and, from this commotion, there emerged a leadership dedicated to forming a concerted regional movement against the visitor general and his policies.[41]

The birth of the rebellion among the common people of Socorro and its hinterland, rather than in some other area of New Granada, is explained by specific local economic and political factors. First, Socorro had suffered heavy mortality from a smallpox epidemic in 1776, and the town's prosperity had been further damaged by a series of poor harvests that had pushed up food prices. Thus its citizens, particularly the poorer ones, had good reason to feel aggrieved by new taxes and higher prices for tobacco and aguardiente. A second peculiarity of the Socorro area was the distinctive structure of its local economy. This was a region where small peasant producers had long cultivated tobacco, and frequently produced other crops, particularly cotton, for sale in local and regional markets. Therefore restrictions on tobacco farming, higher prices for tobacco and aguardiente, increases in the sales tax, and closer control of trade meant that few of the region's small producers, consumers, and traders were unaffected by fiscal reform. Hence the combination of tax changes had a maximum impact.

Socorro was, moreover, the center of a region where relatively recent colonization had stimulated a lively political life, which was grounded in local issues associated with the foundation of new parishes and aspirations to gain town status.[42] During the 1760s, leading *vecinos* of Socorro had campaigned vigorously for town status, and, after a prolonged campaign, they had succeeded in detaching themselves from the jurisdiction of neighboring San Gil in 1771. With its recently acquired cabildo and fresh sense of local autonomy, Socorro was particularly sensitive to fiscal measures that affected the new town's prosperity and, with the feelings of communal identity engendered in the campaign for town status and a cabildo to provide links of clientage, it was perhaps more than usually prepared for a political mobilization involving a cross section of the local population.[43]

41. This account of the events of the rebellion is based on the reconstruction given by Cárdenas Acosta, *El movimiento comunal de 1781 en el Nuevo Reino de Granada*, passim. A chronology of events in 1781 is given in vol. 2, pp. 321–60.

42. Gary W. Graff, "Spanish Parishes in Colonial New Granada: Their Role in Town-Building on the Spanish American Frontier," *The Americas*, vol. 33 (1976–7), pp. 336–51.

43. For a list of parishes founded in the eighteenth century, see Mario Aguilera Peña, *Los Comuneros:*

Finally, tensions in agrarian society may have also caused discontent in this area, because of the combined effects of demographic growth, commercialization of agriculture, and a tendency for land to become concentrated in fewer hands.[44] This factor (which we shall examine later) is difficult to specify, but it is reasonable to suppose that, as a growing population made access to free land more difficult, a peasant society based on free ownership felt a stronger sense of relative deprivation than did the peasantry in areas where fertile, well-positioned land had long been taken up by large estates.

There are, then, a number of factors that help to explain the willingness of the *socorrano* peasants and townspeople to oppose the Caroline tax reforms. But if the location and timing of the first acts of popular protest are relatively easy to understand, then the reasons why a cluster of small local protests swiftly became a polyclass, multiethnic, and transregional movement are less apparent. Popular resentment at the fiscal demands of the state was nothing new; nor, no doubt were grievances over the distribution of land. So, why and how was popular rioting transformed into one of the great regional rebellions of eighteenth-century Spanish America?

Transformation of localized popular protests into a full-scale regional rebellion was made possible by a number of factors. One that deserves more prominence than it is usually given was the authorities' hesitant and equivocal response to early manifestations of protest. On first receiving news of local riots and disorders, the government in Bogotá left municipal authorities to restore order, and it was only after Socorro's second riot on March 30 that the visitor general intervened directly. On April 2, he sought to placate the rebels with a conciliatory gesture exempting cotton thread from the *Armada de Barlovento*. The following day, he took steps to suppress them, ordering Corregidor Campuzano of Tunja to travel personally to Socorro to restore order. Meanwhile, the visitor general continued with his program. Indeed, he further inflamed public opinion when, on April 6, the audiencia published an edict ordering citizens to contribute to the *donativo*. Although this was a single emergency levy, it was widely rumored to be a permanent head-tax, and thus it only aroused further opposition. So, having first ignored the rioters, the authorities then mixed concession with repression, and finally compounded their initial political error by allowing the movement to develop purpose and momentum. This was partly the fault of the provincial governor, the corregidor of Tunja, who, whether from fear, complacency, or a desire to embarrass the visitor general, remained inactive, leaving popular disorder to continue and spread, with fresh tumults in country parishes. This must have encouraged protestors. Upon meeting with little or no opposition from the authorities, the rioters not only found time and space to test their strength and spread their message, thereby allowing localized protests to become a coordinated network, but they were also able to sense the weakness of government forces.

Another factor that facilitated the growth of the movement was the unification of the people of Socorro under an ordered command, made possible by an alliance between the town's plebeians and patricians. If government hesitation had left a space for rebellion to develop, then this alliance canalized the torrents of local protest into one forceful stream. The point of convergence came on Easter Monday, April 16, when the waves of rioting that had spread through Socorro's district returned to the town itself. On that day, a third major riot not only put the town's alcalde and two excise officials to flight; it also launched a new phase of insurrection, with a written statement of grievances and the formal induction of members of Socorro's creole patriciate as leaders of the "común." Now the rioters acquired ideology and leadership, which molded them into a regional movement of formidable potential.

The rioters' explicit ideology was simple, and it came in the easily communicable form of a satirical poem, probably written by a Dominican friar of Bogotá. Composed of roughly rhyming stanzas, its verses expressed the outrage aroused by new taxes, and, by conjuring up images of tyranny and official impiety, it appealed to emotions of local patriotism and dislike of Spaniards. The poem evidently captured the popular mood beautifully. When read to the crowds that rioted in Socorro on April 16, its blend of invective and ridicule, political rhetoric and political gossip had an immediate popular appeal. It was swiftly adopted as a popular manifesto for the Comuneros, dubbed (apparently in humorous mimicry of bureaucratic procedures), as "our royal order" (*nuestra real cédula*), "the holy gazette" (*la santísima gaceta*), or "the official message" (*el superior despacho*). This pasquinade did not of course create ideas where none had previously existed. It spoke in colloquial language, and, by referring to local issues and hated officials, it captured and crystallized popular resentments; it also endowed popular rebellion with the dignity of a wider political meaning, defining the *socorreños* in quasi-Biblical terms as a "chosen people" whose "enterprise" was a romantic and shining inspiration for all opposed to tyranny in New Granada. Furthermore, it issued a call to action, inviting the Socorro rebels to march on Bogotá, to aid their sympathizers in the capital.[45]

45. For the full text of the poem, see Cárdenas Acosta, *El movimiento comunal*, vol. 1, pp. 121–30. For further discussion of its meaning, see Phelan, *The People and the King*, pp. 71–8.

With ideology, came leadership. On April 18, the Socorro crowds acclaimed four prominent citizens as their captains general, chosen to represent and defend the interests of the común. Now members of different social groups came together in one alliance, united under the slogan, "Long live the King, and death to bad government." The fusion of plebeians and patricians in Socorro marked a vital turning point in the development of the Comunero rebellion. For in a hierarchical society, the assumption of leadership by local notables was an important confirmation of the rioters' aims, and it strengthened their claim to be acting in benefit of the *común,* or common interest. Furthermore, in purely practical terms, it provided the rebels with an ideological and organizational capacity that was essential both for unifying the movement and giving it a clear sense of direction.

The conditions that allowed this alliance to be formed have been clearly explained by John Phelan, whose research shows that it was facilitated by ties of kin and clientage, which brought leading plebeian agitators in touch with the town's prominent citizens and municipal officials. The notary of Socorro's cabildo, Mateo Ardila, was a crucial bridge between them. On the plebeian side, Ardila was connected by family relations to the clan of butchers who orchestrated lower-class protest in the streets. On the patrician side, he had influence with members of the town's elite through both his role as town clerk and through his family relationships. Thus the leaders of the urban crowd, who came from the ranks of petty tradesmen, were linked to the town's patriciate through a single family that acted as a medium for forming the cross-class alliance vital to organized rebellion.[46] In this way, the impulse to resistance that sprang from below was transmitted to the creole patriciate, allowing popular protest to interact with elite grievances and creating a coalition that could act in the name of the community.

Comunero leadership and strategy

Creoles involved in the leadership later protested that they took up their positions because of popular intimidation. The first creole "captains" claimed that they had unwillingly accepted their appointments under pressure from a violent crowd, and, at the time, they anticipated accusations of treason by taking a secret oath of loyalty to the king, stating that they were acting under duress. In fact, only one of their number, the local magnate Don Salvador Plata, displayed an obvious and consistent reluctance to act as a leader. The others – Francisco Berbeo, Antonio José

---

46. On the character of the creole patriciate, its links with the plebeians, and the first four captains chosen in Socorro, see Phelan, *The People and the King,* pp. 50–66.

Monsalve, and Francisco Rosillo – evidently sympathized with the rioters, and took advantage of popular discontent to express their own dislike of the reforms. Berbeo was especially important, because he soon emerged as the caudillo of the Comunero movement and made a leading contribution to its organization. He assumed the title of *superintendente y comandante,* and, with Monsalve and Rosillo, quickly set about constructing a structure of command in which other men of similar social rank were placed in a supporting role as captains throughout the surrounding region.

Berbeo exemplified the social character of the Comunero leadership. Although he was only a modest landowner, his family was firmly rooted in the regional elite. Berbeo's grandfather, a Spanish immigrant from Asturias, had been *alguacil mayor* in San Gil in 1709 and *maestro de campo* in Socorro, where he took up residence. His father, who was also born in Spain, had held the post of notary in the parish of Socorro, and two of his brothers held municipal posts in Socorro. Juan Francisco Berbeo did not himself hold a municipal office, but he had traveled widely in New Granada and had acquired military experience in campaigns on the Indian frontier. He also had contacts in influential creole circles in Bogotá, particularly with Francisco de Vergara, the chief administrator of the *Tribunal de Cuentas* in Bogotá, and these contacts were later to be used in negotiations with the viceregal authorities. Of the other thirty-four captains in the Socorro region, the great majority – some twenty-eight of them – were of similar social standing. Most were literate whites who, as relatively wealthy landowners and members of the local "municipal aristocracies" of office holders and tax farmers, jealously guarded the local social and political preeminence of their families.[47]

The entry of the local notables into the movement was a development of critical importance. First, it neutralized gentry opposition to lower-class rioters; second, it broadened the social base of the rebellion and reinforced the Comuneros' claim to represent the *común;* third, the creole leadership that emerged in Socorro played a key role in canalizing popular protest into a clearly directed movement capable of organized defense and offense. Once initiated, this coalition was further strengthened by the government's ineffective efforts to intimidate and overcome the rebels. On April 9, the visitor general and audiencia were determined to take military action to quell the disturbances: they sent supplies and munitions to the corregidor in Tunja and appointed the oidor José Pardo de Osorio to lead a military force to the rebel zone. Action was slow in coming, however. Corregidor Campuzano of Tunja sent out orders but did nothing to enforce them, while news of the expedition being mustered against them encour-

47. Aguilera Peña, *Los Comuneros,* pp. 52–68. On Berbeo's background, see Restrepo Sáenz and Rivas, *Genealogías de Santa Fe,* vol. 1, pp. 108–9.

aged the Socorro rebels to organize their own forces. Oidor Osorio did not finally leave Bogotá until April 18, and he was followed by the rest of his small expedition — a total of seventy-two lightly armed soldiers — on April 21. On April 28, when Osorio's expedition finally arrived at Puente Real, midway along the road from Bogotá to Socorro, the rebels had sufficient time to prepare their defenses. On May 2, a "Supreme Council of War" was established from the captains-general of the Comuneros, to coordinate a military campaign against royalist forces under the overall command of Juan Francisco Berbeo. Meanwhile, the ranks of the rebellion swelled as more towns and villages signaled their allegiance to the Comuneros by rioting against the estancos, aligning themselves under local captains and making formal arrangements to unite under Berbeo's generalship.

The government's ill-prepared attempt to crush the Comuneros was entirely counterproductive, doing more to stimulate the rebellion than to impede it. Oidor Osorio and his soldiers were surrounded by Comunero forces at Puente Real, and, on May 8, they surrendered without a single loss of life, yielding up their arms and a large amount of treasury money that Osorio had apparently intended to use as bribes. This was a heavy blow to government prestige, and consequently boosted the rebel cause. With a military success to its credit, the patrician–plebeian alliance in Socorro gained both confidence and fresh recruits, and extended its links to form a still more formidable network of regional opposition to the government.

After their success at Puente Real, the rebel leaders added two significant new forces to their movement. First, they forced Ambrosio Pisco, the mestizo cacique who was titular leader of the Indian villagers of Santa Fe, Tunja, Vélez, and Sogamoso, to accept a position as a captain of the Comuneros. Pisco was a very reluctant recruit to the rebel cause — he even tried to escape to Bogotá in order to avoid commitment to the Comuneros — but while en route to the capital he was acclaimed by Indian villagers as their lord, and forced to become their leader and representative. Even more important was the adhesion of the city of Tunja and neighboring Sogamoso to the Comunero movement. The entry of Tunja was especially significant, because it both removed a potential threat on the eastern flank of the *socorrano* rebellion, while also adding several thousand men to the rebel forces.

Once its weakness was exposed by Osorio's futile attempts to curb the rebellion by force, the Bogotá government reversed its strategy, and turned from aggression to defense. On May 12, Gutiérrez de Piñeres left the capital for Honda, hoping to deflect the rebels from Bogotá while he escaped down the Magdalena River to Cartagena. In his absence, Gutiérrez de Piñeres left the *junta general de tribunales,* the committee of audiencia judges, senior officials, clerics, and representatives of the Bogotá cabildo that he hastily convoked to handle the crisis, to deal with the rebels as best it could, while awaiting the arrival of forces from Cartagena. The junta's first step was to try to check the advance of the Comuneros by suspending the visitor general's fiscal measures and by undertaking negotiations with rebel leaders. A negotiating committee, composed of the Archbishop of Santa Fe Antonio Caballero y Góngora, the oidor Vasco y Vargas, and, representing the capital's municipal government and creole elite, the Bogotá alcalde Eustaquio Galavis y Hurtado, was duly formed. Led by Archbishop Caballero y Góngora, this commission sought to intercede with the rebels before they marched on the capital, while the audiencia prepared the capital's defenses.

If the defeat of Osorio's forces at Puente Real was a great stimulus to the Comuneros, measures taken in May to preserve internal order in Bogotá were equally important for sustaining royal government in the capital. After the military humiliation suffered by the government, the initiative passed to the rebels and the authorities could do little to stem their advance. Nevertheless, the junta at least secured a defensive position in Bogotá by preventing rebel sympathizers from subverting order in the capital. This was to prove critically important, for although the junta lacked military means to prevent a rebel march on Bogotá, it managed to sustain a government that could present itself as a bulwark of order and enter into negotiations with the Comuneros' leaders.

The Comuneros, meanwhile, went from strength to strength. Support for the rebellion continued to spread, even reaching some settlements in the distant Llanos, where, from mid-May, a group of creoles raised an Indian rebellion and allied themselves with the Socorro movement by taking titles and commissions from Berbeo's Supreme Council of War.[48] Although growing numbers mobilized in defiance of the government, the rebel advance was also sustained by sound military leadership. Here, Francisco Berbeo, the Comunero commander in chief, played a key role. While preparing to parley with the royal authorities, he also implemented an astute military strategy designed to extend the area under rebel control, to protect it from attack, and to isolate the capital from communication or military rescue from the viceroy's forces on the Caribbean coast.

This strategy unfolded in late May, as Berbeo moved his forces in several directions. First, he turned on the town of Girón, which had refused allegiance to the Comuneros and threatened to provide an opening for royal forces sent up the Magdalena from Cartagena. After a short campaign, Girón was taken and the strategic gap to the north was closed. At the same time, Berbeo also took steps to cut Bogotá from communica-

---

48. Jane Loy, "Forgotten Comuneros: The 1781 Revolt in the Llanos of Casanare," *HAHR*, vol. 61 (1981), pp. 235–57. On the beginnings of the rebellion, see pp. 238–41.

tion and reinforcement by way of the Magdalena River. In late May, he entrusted the plebeian José Antonio Galán with a small force, and dispatched him on an expedition designed to cut the mails between Bogotá and the Magdalena River, to seek out and capture the fleeing visitor general, and to neutralize the strategic river port of Honda. This force quickly achieved its main goals. Although Galán did not capture the visitor general, he raised support for the rebellion in the Upper Magdalena Valley and, by placing a barrier between Bogotá and the coast, allowed Berbeo to pursue his major objectives in the interior. There, Berbeo retained the initiative. By shifting the Comunero vanguard southward to Nemocón, he encouraged the populace of Zipaquirá to enter the rebel coalition; second, he maneuvered the mass of his forces toward Nemocón, putting them within easy reach of the capital. On May 26, the rebel leaders entered into preliminary communications with Caballero y Góngora and his commission at Nemocón, but Berbeo sensibly played a waiting game, allowing rebel contingents from the Socorro and Tunja areas to concentrate a force of some 20,000 people nearby, at Mortiño. At the end of May, when his forces were taking up position, Berbeo also sent a force of Indians from nearby villages to guard the entry to the capital. Under protest from the authorities, the Indian forces were withdrawn, but the tactic was a clever one. By displaying his Indian allies, Berbeo exploited racial fears, thereby heightening tensions in the capital and forcing the government to consider his terms. It was in these circumstances that the rebellion moved toward its climax during the first week of June 1781.

The culmination of the Comunero rebellion

As the rebels gathered near Zipaquirá, the stage was set for the seizure of Bogotá and the overthrow of the audiencia. In the event, several factors impeded an attack on the capital. One was disagreement over tactics. The plebeians from the Socorro area had defined Bogotá as their goal, and they regarded capture of the capital as the best means to ensure that their demands were honored. Leaders from Tunja and Sogamoso, who represented the conservative creole gentry of these traditional societies, were anxious to avoid any further disturbance of the social and political order, and thus preferred to seek a negotiated conclusion at Zipaquirá.[49] Social divisions were compounded by interregional rivalries, stemming from long-standing competition between the towns of Tunja, San Gil, and Socorro. San Gil's position on tactics was equivocal, but leaders from Tunja and Sogamoso were so opposed to an advance on Bogotá that they

---

49. The character of Tunja society and its relation to the political position of leaders are discussed by Aguilera Peña, *Los Comuneros*, pp. 69–72.

threatened to use their 6,000-strong forces to prevent it. Thus, at the moment when it was poised for victory, the Comunero movement began to fracture along regional lines.

Despite this incipient split, the rebellion was sustained, thanks largely to Berbeo's skill in finding a formula to hold the coalition together. On the one hand, he satisfied Tunja leaders by opting for negotiation at Zipaquirá and drawing them into these negotiations; on the other, he calmed plebeian demands for an advance on Bogotá by co-opting five members of the *santafereño* elite to take part in Comunero negotiations with the authorities, together with the city's cabildo. Linking the capital and its elite to the Comuneros in this manner allowed Berbeo to achieve two important objectives simultaneously. First, he was able to tell his plebeian followers that the capture of Bogotá was no longer necessary, since the capital now adhered to the movement; second, he spread responsibility for the rebellion to the political establishment in Bogotá by directly involving its municipal government and some of its most prominent citizens in the negotiation of terms between the rebels and the government. Thus the internal split over tactics was resolved and, on June 5, 1781, Berbeo and his companions were able to reopen negotiations and, from a position of strength, to move toward a successful conclusion.

The terms the Comunero leaders presented to the government's peace commission at Zipaquirá were drawn up in a *plan de capitulaciones* that laid out their demands in thirty-five clauses. These terms were an extraordinary mixture, assembled in an apparently random manner, but they provide a deep sounding into the grievances and aspirations of the various groups that participated in the rebellion. Not surprisingly, many of the demands concerned the fiscal issues that had given rise to the insurrection.[50] These included abolition of the *Armada de Barlovento* tax, abolition of the *guías* or receipts showing payment of tax on goods entering trade, and abolition of the tobacco monopoly, allowing complete freedom to cultivate and sell tobacco, subject only to the alcabala. In a similar vein were demands for suspension of the *donativo,* for aguardiente prices to be returned to their old levels, and for the alcabala to be reduced from 4% to 2%, together with complete exemption of cotton – a poor man's crop – from any liability for sales tax payment. These dealt with the Comuneros' main complaints. As the final clause of the plan stated, the rebels' "principal object" had been "to free ourselves from the Barlovento charges and other taxes imposed by the Regent Visitor general."[51]

Rebel demands also extended beyond repudiation of recent fiscal inno-

---

50. The full text of the *capitulaciones* is transcribed in Cárdenas Acosta, *El movimiento comunal,* vol. 2, pp. 18–29.
51. Ibid., p. 28.

vations. The *plan de capitulaciones* was suffused with a generalized antagonism toward the fiscal demands of the colonial government, and it contained demands for alleviating the burden of taxes over a wide front. Included were demands for suppression of the state monopoly on playing cards, for lower prices for official printed paper, *bulas de cruzada,* gunpowder, and salt. In addition, various clauses called for fairer regulation of postal charges, abolition of the *media anata* tax paid by urban and rural magistrates on taking their posts, and reduction in the charges made by the scribes who drew up official documents. The economic burdens imposed by the church and clergy also came under attack, with calls for a reduction in the charges made by clerics and clerical inspectors, and for abolition or at least fairer regulation of charges made by tithe collectors.

Indian grievances over taxes and land also found a place in the Comunero demands. There were calls for the tribute payable by Indians and free blacks to be reduced by half, for alleviation of Indian exploitation by corregidors and clergy, and for the restoration of community lands, or *resguardos,* in the form of individual properties. A specific grievance of Indians in Zipaquirá was also addressed in a clause advocating that the local salt mines be returned to the native communities that had controlled them before they were taken over by the crown. Such demands partly reflect Indian participation in the rebellion, and, perhaps, partly a concern for social justice. But, like other clauses in the Comunero program of demands, they primarily reflect the economic concerns of the free peasantry. Restoring the Indians to their community lands as individual rather than corporate owners meant that, in the future, their lands might come onto the market, where they could be purchased by non-Indians who were legally debarred from buying, renting, or even residing on *resguardo* lands. Equally, concern with the Indians' right to own and operate the salt mines was not purely altruistic; it meant that all consumers could buy salt more cheaply, without interference and control by royal officials. The interests of small producers and traders also surfaced in calls for improving roads and bridges, ending private tolls, allowing freedom to pasture animals on roadsides, and ensuring fairer regulation of weights and measures by town councils.

Most interesting are the political grievances and aspirations revealed by the Comuneros' terms. Like the economic demands, these were aimed at modifying the practices of government rather than fundamentally altering its structure. The Socorro elite pressed for an extension of the town's local government by demanding that the town should have a greater degree of self-government, with its own corregidor, independent of the corregimiento of Tunja. On the other hand, calls for an end to payment of the *media anata* tax by local magistrates and for control of weights and measures by elective rather than proprietary officials, seem to reflect an interest in broadening the social base of municipal government. Measures to relieve the oppression of the poor also found a place in the rebels' terms for negotiation, particularly in demands that people who were arrested should be released on payment of a small bail fee, rather than held without trial.

These specific demands were supplemented by others with much wider political implications. The rebels not only called for the expulsion of the regent visitor general, but also demanded a government promise that no such official should ever again be sent to the colony, and that the practice of holding *residencias* on local officials should end forthwith. Even more striking was the statement that "in offices of first, second and third levels, the nationals of this America should be given preference and privilege over Europeans," because the latter lacked sufficient knowledge of and sympathy with local concerns, and because "as we are all subject to the same King and Lord, we should live together in fraternal harmony."[52] This idealized harmony was not to be disturbed by foreigners, all of whom, the Comuneros thought, should be expelled from New Granada within a term of two months. Finally, to ensure that the aims of the rebellion were observed, the Comuneros insisted that the royal government should confirm all appointments in the rebel command structure and allow the Comunero forces to be maintained as militias. A general pardon was also demanded, to seal the pact and to restore normal relations between government and citizens.

At first, the rebel demands were refused by the junta in Bogotá, which demanded revision of clauses prejudicial to the crown's fiscal interests. But, although some minor revisions were accepted by the Comunero leaders, the peace commissioners at Zipaquirá warned the junta that no further negotiation was possible and advised full acceptance of the rebel terms. On June 7, the junta concurred, while secretly disavowing the pact as one obtained by *force majeure*. The following day, Archbishop Caballero y Góngora and his commissioners solemnly swore to uphold the agreement and, with this act, the rebellion formally ended.

Following the pact at Zipaquirá, the main force of the Comuneros dissolved and the great majority of the rebels dispersed and returned to their homes. Defiance of the colonial government was not entirely over, however. José Antonio Galán, Berbeo's commander in the Upper Magdalena Valley, refused to surrender his arms, and from his base in the tobacco country of Ambalema he encouraged the extension of the rebellion into previously undisturbed areas in Mariquita, Neiva, and to the west in the province of Antioquia. Resistance to the authorities also continued in the Llanos, and from July until October, rioting against officials occurred in widely dispersed settings throughout New Granada, as far south as

52. Ibid., p. 26.

Pasto. But, if these local riots and revolts were inspired by the example of the Comuneros, they were of a very different social character than the original movement, and never achieved the degree of regional mobilization or cross-class organization found in the Comunero rebellion itself.[53]

In the original core of the rebellion, disaffection was not entirely stilled by the pact at Zipaquirá. While the population awaited royal confirmation of the terms agreed with the audiencia, peace was disturbed in early September by Indian rioting at Nemocón, and threatened by the refusal of Viceroy Flóres in Cartagena to accept the capitulations. Renewed conflict was avoided, however, by the diplomatic machinations of Archbishop Caballero y Góngora. Between June and late December, Caballero y Góngora, accompanied by a Capuchin mission, remained in Socorro on a pastoral visit, preaching peace, obedience, and reconciliation. Together they did much to restore calm, and when José Antonio Galán arrived back in the region in early September, he found very little popular support for his plans to raise a second march against Bogotá. Eventually, on October 10, Galán and his small band of followers were hunted down, arrested, and consigned in chains to the capital. There, they were tried in November 1781, and sentenced in January 30, 1782. A vindictive audiencia condemned Galán and three close companions to death and dismemberment; others among his supporters were consigned to imprisonment or exile. In the meantime, Socorro and Tunja remained quiet. On October 20 1781, Viceroy Flóres had accepted Archbishop Caballero y Góngora's advice and, by granting a general pardon and reaffirming the key fiscal concessions made at Zipaquirá, fulfilled the crown's side of the bargain made with the rebels.

In the following year, Flóres was replaced by a new viceroy. The crown's first choice was Juan de Torreázar Díaz Pimienta, the governor of Cartagena, but he died only days after arriving in Bogotá. The viceregency then passed to Archbishop Caballero y Góngora, the principal pacifier of the Comuneros, who took office in June 1782. This cleared the way for a fresh start under a viceroy who was anxious to rebuild confidence in government. To do so, he confirmed the key concessions made to the Comuneros. In August 1782, the *Armada de Barlovento* was abolished, the alcabala was returned to its previous level of 2% in the interior provinces of New Granada, the prices of tobacco and aguardiente were reduced,

---

53. On continuing rebellion in the Llanos after Zipaquirá, and for an analysis of the social character of the movement, see Jane Loy, "Forgotten Comuneros," pp. 241–56. On rebellion in Antioquia, see Universidad de Antioquia, *Documentos para la historia de la insurrección comunera en la provincia de Antioquia, 1765–1785* (Medellín, 1982), passim. On Pasto, Rebecca A. Earle, "Indian Rebellion and Bourbon Reform in New Granada: Riots in Pasto, 1780–1800," *HAHR* vol. 73 (1993), pp. 105–110. For a good general account of disturbances that occurred after the accord at Zipaquirá, see Aguilera Peña, *Los Comuneros*, pp. 127–97.

and a definitive general pardon was extended to all who had taken part in the rebellion.[54] Furthermore, in the edict that announced this pardon, the archbishop-viceroy pledged to promote a lasting reconciliation under the benign hand of absolutist monarchy. "Industry, mining, the arts, and above all agriculture and internal trade," he promised, would soon be brought "to the highest degree of prosperity."[55] Thus, Caballero y Góngora pledged a new colonial pact, in which the crown offered the fruits of economic progress in return for unquestioning obedience to royal authority.

The meaning of the Comunero rebellion

Despite the Comunero rebellion's rapid dissolution when rebel terms were accepted by the authorities, some historians have regarded it as a protonationalist movement in which leading creoles aspired for the first time to independence from Spain.[56] In fact, this view is unsupported by convincing evidence. Although it is true that the rebels mounted a great challenge to the Spanish government, their slogan was "Long live the King and down with bad government" and at no stage in the rebellion do we find either mention or sign of any determination to separate from Spain. The idea that leading New Granadan creoles sought British military and political support for independence in the years immediately after the rebellion is also without foundation. Reports of approaches to the British government emerge from an opaque world of international espionage and are not to be trusted. At most, the reports refer to the activities of a Venezuelan sympathizer of the Comuneros rather than to the creole patriciate of New Granada.[57] If such rumors were taken seriously by the Spanish government, this owed more to Madrid's fears of British intentions in the aftermath of the American War of Independence than to any imminent threat of colonial revolution. However, if the Comunero rebellion was not an independence movement, it nevertheless caused a very severe political crisis, for it had shown that the crown could not depend on the unconditional obedience of its subjects in New Granada and had revealed the vulnerability of colonial government to a concerted challenge. What, then, was the character of this crisis, and why did a cluster

54. Phelan, *The People and the King*, pp. 200–29.
55. Cárdenas Acosta, *El Movimiento Comunal*, p. 209.
56. Works of this kind are Manuel Briceño Perozo, *Los Comuneros* (Bogotá, 1880); Pablo Cárdenas Acosta, *El movimiento comunal de 1781 en el Nuevo Reino de Granada;* Francisco Posada Zárate, *El movimiento revolucionario de los comuneros* (Mexico City, 1971).
57. The slender and inconclusive evidence for assertions that Comunero leaders sought foreign support can be judged from contemporary documents printed in Manuel Briceño, *Los Comuneros* (2nd. ed., Bogotá, 1979), pp. 132–48, and Aguilera Peña, *Los Comuneros*, pp. 211–50.

of local antitax riots become a cross-class, polyethnic regional rebellion capable of humiliating the royal authorities?

According to John Phelan, "the crisis of 1781 was essentially political and constitutional in nature. . . . The central issue was . . . who had the authority to levy new fiscal exactions."[58] Seen from this perspective, the Comunero rebellion in late colonial Colombia has more in common with the Comunero rebellion of early sixteenth-century Castile than it shares with the revolutions of the eighteenth- and early nineteenth-century Atlantic world. Not only were New Granada's Comuneros seeking to defend existing administrative and fiscal arrangements against the encroachments of an absolutist monarchy that was intent on strengthening the state, but their ideology was also deeply traditional, echoing the old doctrine of a contract between sovereign and subjects and a concomitant right to resist tyranny.[59] In Comunero rhetoric and in the slogans of the rebels, Phelan finds political ideas drawn from the Spanish Golden Age and transmitted to New Granada through the practices of the Hapsburg government. Indeed, he suggests that they had become so deeply rooted that they constituted an "unwritten constitution," a set of conventions and procedures that symbolized a pact between the monarch and his subjects, a pact that the king's subjects would defend by force if necessary.[60] Thus, when these procedures were flouted by the visitor general, the Comunero movement arose as a reaction to the violation of customary arrangements and practices, with plebeian rioters and patrician leaders drawn together by a shared belief in "a *corpus mysticum politicum*, with its own traditions and procedures designed to achieve the common good of the whole community."[61]

This view has much to recommend it. For under the Hapsburgs colonial government had a substantial measure of autonomy and colonials had evidently become accustomed to a relaxed rule that was attentive to elite interests and resistant to externally imposed changes. Royal officials were not appointed simply to enforce orders from the metropolitan center, but they also governed the colonies through processes of consultation and negotiation that allowed for representation of colonial interests within the royal bureaucracy. Furthermore, under the Hapsburgs creole patricians had increasingly easy access to important government posts and co-opted peninsular officials through marriage and other relationships. This was, as Lynch observes, a system of government in which "the metropolis looked

58. Phelan, *The People and the King*, p. xviii.

59. These arguments were first developed by Rafael Gómez Hoyos, who argues that these ideas came primarily from the Spanish philosopher Suárez and were transmitted to New Granada by the Jesuits. See *La revolución granadina de 1810. Ideario de una generación y de una época, 1781–1821*, 2 vols. (Bogotá, 1962), vol. I, pp. 133–204.

60. Phelan, *The People and the King*, esp. pp. 79–88.   61. Ibid., p. xvii.

for collaborating elites, the colonies for conniving officials."[62] By reforming government and taxation without consulting the creole elites and by threatening to replace creoles with peninsulars in the royal administration, Charles III disturbed this traditional political equilibrium, with its emphasis on routine and cautious change, and its traditions of mediation and compromise.

Although Phelan's interpretation of the ideological dimension of the rebellion rightly stresses its conservative character as a defense of an established, traditional political order, we should not, however, conclude that the Comunero leadership was moved simply by an abstract "constitutional" issue. In fact, the provincial creoles who led the Comuneros had very tangible motives for entering into an alliance with the plebeian rioters who sparked the rebellion. One motive was economic. Changes in the management of royal monopolies pushed up the costs of tax farming and thus threatened a form of business that offered both monetary gains and local influence.[63] A second reason arose from local politics. The reforms of the visitor general not only altered relations between the creole elite and government in the capital, but, by bringing a more intrusive government into the provinces, they also threatened to undermine the political influence that local notables enjoyed in their home areas. Creoles involved in the rebellion did not of course complain directly about their central government's encroachment on local power. However, a lengthy memorandum sent to the crown by Salvador Plata, a leading member of the Socorro patriciate and a co-opted Comunero leader, clearly shows how the reforms aroused creole resentment by intruding into provincial political life, to the detriment of both plebeians and patricians.

In his statement, Plata said that the rebellion had two causes.[64] One, of course, was new taxes, which were widely regarded as unfair and which provoked the popular uprising. But a more important cause of the rebellion, Plata argued, sprang from another kind of injustice: that committed by the officials who managed and enforced the visitor general's fiscal reforms at the local level. The "tyrannical" behavior of the estanco guards, Plata suggests, not only stirred popular rebellion, but it also alienated creoles by damaging the dignity and authority of municipal government. For under the new regulations for the royal monopolies, Gutiérrez de Piñeres had deprived the ordinary magistrates of jurisdiction in cases involving estanco employees, thereby allowing the unscrupulous among them to behave as though they were exempt from the law. As a result, Plata argued, they lived "a libertine existence in evil entertainments

---

62. Lynch, *Bourbon Spain*, p. 332.   63. Aguilera Peña, *Los Comuneros*, pp. 82–3.

64. This document has been published in full. See Manuel Lucena Salmoral (ed.), *El Memorial de Don Salvador Plata: Los Comuneros y los Movimientos Antireformistas* (Bogotá, 1982).

disrespectful to God, to some poor husbands, and to good manners . . . ."
Worse still, they showed no respect for local judges, "treating them as
inferiors and . . . convincing all that there was no judge who could correct them, punish them, or interfere in their affairs."[65]

Plata's account must be regarded with caution; it was, after all, a self-
serving document designed to exculpate the author from implication in
the rebellion. Nevertheless, his emphatic condemnation of the behavior of
the new excise officials does give a plausible explanation of the local
gentry's readiness to enter the rebellion and take up positions of leadership. In denouncing violations of law and custom, Plata draws attention
to the fact that the ways in which the visitor general's reforms impinged
on the authority of local political authorities. By placing power in the
hands of intrusive officials who did not belong to local political factions,
these measures damaged ties of clientage and thereby diminished the
standing of local authorities. For the local notables, this was in itself a
powerful motive for involvement in the rebellion. The insolence and
depredations of excise men not only harmed peasants and plebeians, but
also struck at the authority of the gentry. Here, then, we see the crucial
cause of creole intervention in the Comunero rebellion and the reason why
popular revolt extended into a wider coalition, incorporating the leading
sectors of provincial society. While peasants and plebeians protested
against new taxes and defended their community, the provincial gentry
sought to defend its local political prestige and authority, also in the name
of the community. Such a defense of the status quo naturally limited the
political reach of the rebellion. Creole patricians wanted local autonomy
within the Spanish monarchy; their goal was simply to restore and preserve the traditional order, not to bring about its revolutionary overthrow,
and, having much to lose from prolonged political upheaval, they curbed
its potential for radicalization into a movement against the Spanish government itself.

An alternative view of the Comunero rebellion finds its origins and
importance in social rather than purely political crisis. For Indalecio Liévano Aguirre, an early exponent of this thesis, the rebellion was rooted
among an oppressed "people" composed of poor mestizos and Indians
who, in reacting against economic exploitation, formed an alliance with
the creole gentry in the hope of achieving social change, only to be
betrayed by a "creole oligarchy" that manipulated popular insurrection for
its own narrow purposes.[66] According to Mario Aguilera Peña's recent
analysis, this thesis is flawed by its oversimplified political sociology. For

65. Ibid., p. 49.
66. Indalecio Liévano Aguirre, *Los grandes conflictos sociales y económicos de nuestra historia* (3rd ed.,
    Bogotá, 1968), pp. 439–502.

by opposing an undifferentiated people to a creole oligarchy, it overlooks the diversity of social groups and interests involved in the rebellion. Nevertheless, Aguilera Peña concurs with the interpretation of the rebellion as an "anticolonial struggle" and a "social war" that "went far beyond a purely anti-fiscal conflict with the Crown and was rooted in the dynamic of the internal contradictions of New Granadan society."[67] Aguilera Peña also proposes a new periodization of the rebellion, arguing that a key moment in its development was the emergence of a "revolutionary wing," associated with José Antonio Galán's insurrectionary activities in the Magdalena Valley, where social divisions and tensions were acute.[68] However, although Aguilera Peña's disaggregation of the social groups involved in the rebellion clearly shows it to have been a loose coalition rather than a unified movement, his argument that the rebellion was driven by class conflict within New Granadan society and rooted in an agrarian social crisis is also ultimately unconvincing.

It is certainly reasonable to argue that discontent over land and resentment of landowners contributed to popular restiveness, because we know that there were deep inequalities in the distribution of land in New Granada, in both highlands and lowlands. Indeed, the *fiscal* Moreno y Escandón wrote a forceful denunciation of such inequalities in the core areas of New Granada shortly before the rebellion, following his inspection of Indian *resguardos* in the provinces of Santa Fe and Tunja. From his experience in these areas during the 1770s, Moreno y Escandón saw that access to land in settled areas was becoming more difficult for the peasantry: he observed that the best of the *realengos* (unappropriated royal lands) were bought up by the wealthy, to the detriment of those who could not afford the legal and administrative costs of purchase. Those without land consequently had "to live at the mercy of the landowners, under the painful threat of being dismissed or, because they have no income of their own with which to establish themselves, suffering whatever yoke was placed upon them. . ." Moreno y Escandón also pointed out that the poor could only find land distant from settled areas, because the towns' *ejidos*, or municipal lands, had invariably been sold off. Thus, the landless were left to squat on marginal lands, and had to bear all the costs and labor of settlement without help or encouragement. Concerned to promote a more productive agriculture, Moreno y Escandón wanted a more rational use of resources. He therefore argued that the authorities should intervene by advising local magistrates to pressure large landowners into either cultivating their unused lands or allowing others to do so.[69] And it was, of course, for these same reasons Moreno y Escandón advocated that govern-

67. Mario Aguilera Peña, *Los Comuneros*, pp. 6–7.   68. Ibid., pp. 127–46.
69. Ots Capdequí, *Nuevos aspectos*, pp. 256–8.

ment should remove lands from the corporate ownership of dwindling Indian communities and sell them off to farmers from the growing creole and mestizo population, who would use them productively.

Although grievances over land probably predisposed some of the rural poor to strike out against the authorities in 1781, it nevertheless strains credulity to suggest that the Comunero movement arose from a deep structural crisis in agrarian society, or expressed a revolutionary impulse from below. Inequality in land distribution was neither peculiar to the Socorro and Tunja areas, nor was it a sufficient cause for peasant rebellion; after all, there were deep inequalities in land ownership in other Colombian regions that did not become involved in the Comunero insurrection. Peasant land deprivation may well have generated sharper discontents in the Socorro region than in other areas because of the peculiar history and social structure of the region. As we noted above, Socorro was a recently colonized area, where there was a strong tradition of small proprietorship and family commercial farming, where demographic growth was apparently recent and vigorous, and where, consequently, the peasantry probably had expectations and aspirations different from those of Indian and mestizo peasants in areas where large landholdings had been entrenched since the sixteenth century. But, although it is likely that discontents over land contributed to popular mobilization in the rebellion, this does not mean that the Comunero movement arose from an agrarian social crisis.

If the Socorro peasantry was more disposed to rebellion than their counterparts in other regions, then this was primarily because the new tax regime introduced by the visitor general directly threatened peasant economic autonomy in a society of small farming communities. In a region where small producers were actively and directly engaged in producing and selling agricultural goods in regional markets, changes to the sales tax and royal monopolies had a particularly strong impact on peasant farmers and small traders, and were therefore an especially potent source of discontent. So, as is often the case in peasant rebellions, the Comunero movement probably drew its rural strength from a "middle peasantry" of small independent farmers who were defending their position and gains within a local market economy, rather than from a landless peasantry driven by impoverishment and landlord oppression.

Certainly there are few signs that the poorest elements in society had any major voice in the Comunero movement. Even if the discontents of the poorest sectors in rural society inspired a radical vision among those few plebeian agitators who followed José Antonio Galán, and played a part in the disturbances that Galán promoted in the Magdalena Valley, where he recruited support among landless laborers and slaves, there was evidently little potential for transforming antigovernment protest into a radical social movement in the Comunero heartlands. The plebeians of

Socorro whose protests launched the movements readily accepted, indeed demanded, leadership from the provincial creole elite, most of whom were landowners from local municipal oligarchies, and plebeian behavior during the rebellion does not display any obvious animosity toward the wealthy. In fact, a collection of petitions presented to Berbeo, the Comuneros' supreme commander, reveals plebeian and peasant preoccupation with personal and local matters, rather than with any larger social change.

These representations, which have passed unnoticed by historians of the Comuneros, were concerned with purely personal and "parish-pump" issues, ranging from individual pleas against wrongful imprisonment to the requests of Indian and mestizo communities for redress of grievances arising from taxes, oppression by local officials and clerics, and loss of resguardo lands. Of course, such petitions do not convey a complete or unclouded view of plebeian ideas and aims, but they do offer a unique sounding into the mentality of the Comunero rank and file. Directed at Berbeo while he was preparing the Comuneros' list of demands for the royal authorities, the petitions are expressed in the legal phraseology of their time and treat Berbeo as if he were an official representative of the government rather than its opponent.[70] Their content is, moreover, as conservative as their form and tone. Concerned primarily with the same issues that invariably stood behind the localized riots that occurred in New Granada's small towns and villages throughout the eighteenth century, these petitions suggest that, at its social base as well as in its leadership, the Comunero movement was framed within, and limited by, those traditional attitudes toward power and politics found in the many, lesser incidents of civil disorder that occurred in eighteenth-century New Granada.

So, although the Comunero rebellion was an uprising of singular importance in New Granada's late colonial history, distinguished by the scale of its popular mobilization and character as a polyclass, polyethnic coalition, its revolutionary potential was always very limited, and it did not induce a shift in popular political consciousness. Both the Comunero leaders and their followers were basically concerned to defend local autonomy against external interference, not to overthrow the colonial regime. They wanted freedom from political change, rather than freedom to bring about political change, and they were held together by vertical alliances between gentry and plebeians, rather than grouped in horizontal alliances based on social class or ethnic group. We should therefore avoid treating the Comunero rebellion either as a dress rehearsal for independence, or as a forerunner of the agrarian social conflicts of a later age. It makes more

---

70. AGI, Indiferente General 410, "Testimonio del quaderno de varias representaciones hechas ante el Comandante Don Juan Francisco Berbeo . . ."

sense to see the Comuneros as essentially a regional movement structured around the local politics of small towns and villages in the Socorro area, where alliances bonded by kin and clientage gave form and substance to political life in a ruralized world. Such politics reflected a sense of local identity and separateness, expressed in the claim that "nationals of this America" should have preference in the disposition of local office. This was, however, still an idea of "nation" within the Spanish monarchy, a call to defend the informal home rule nurtured under the Hapsburgs and continued under the first Bourbon kings, not a rallying cry for independence. The Comunero rebellion was, then, a protest within the political system, not a movement for its overthrow, and, despite its scale and potency, such protest left Spanish power intact.

10

Science and sedition

If the Comunero rebellion did not reflect the appearance of new ideas or principles, nor mirror changes in the political consciousness of New Granadans, it did nevertheless alter the political climate in New Granada in one important respect. Henceforth, leading peninsular officials were more sensitive about issues of public order and more alert for signs of subversion. Not surprisingly, government fear of sedition was greatest in the years immediately after 1781, when unprecedented measures were taken to provide the authorities with effective policing power. These were started by Archbishop-Viceroy Caballero y Góngora, who persuaded the crown of the need to redeploy military power in the region, both by enlarging the presence of regular troops in the capital and by raising a large disciplined militia in the towns of the interior. Consequently, between 1783 and 1789, New Granada saw the most rapid and far-reaching reorganization of military forces yet undertaken on its territory, mainly to ensure that government had the means to enforce its authority.[1]

Political order after the Comunero rebellion

In addition to mobilizing military muscle, Archbishop-Viceroy Caballero y Góngora also called for tighter control on a colonial populace that he considered to be inherently disorderly and insolent. According to Caballero y Góngora, much of the population lived in a deplorable state of idleness and debauchery, scattered over the countryside, and isolated from sufficiently rigorous religious or social discipline. New Granada's mestizos, he remarked, had almost lost "the two principal sentiments which Nature inspires in rational man – belief in one God, whom he should love, and in one King, whom it is just to obey"; he dismissed Indians and blacks as people of even more debased character. In all, the prelate concluded, the people at large were "an indomitable monster" whose indiscipline was the cause of all the colony's ills.[2] To tame these unruly rustics,

1. For a full account of the reform, see Kuethe, *Military Reform and Society*, pp. 93–101.
2. Archivo Restrepo, Correspondencia reservada del Arzobispo-Virrey, Caballero y Góngora to Gálvez, October 15, 1782 (no. 11).

he recommended that they be grouped in ordered settlements and sub-jected to the discipline of law and religion, whereas vagabonds and beg-gars should be rounded up and forced to work.[3]

In practice, little was done. During his *visita* of Antioquia in 1786–8, Oidor Mon y Velarde showed concern to bring scattered peasant farmers into an ordered network of hamlets and villages; otherwise, measures to deal with vagrants were probably confined to the viceroys' immediate range of action, in the capital and its district. There, the viceroys José de Ezpeleta and Pedro Mendinueta continued with the archbishop-viceroy's policing policy, enforced through measures to reduce the number of va-grants in the area around Bogotá, new procedures for rounding up beggars who appeared in the city, and periodic action to protect urban property against thieves.[4]

The growing population of a region where land ownership was heavily concentrated, as in the hinterland of Bogotá, may have increased the number of itinerant and seasonal laborers, vagrants, and beggars, thereby creating a restive underclass that was less amenable to social control than the peasantry and the urban artisanate. But there are few signs of any serious threat to public order from the lower classes in the closing decades of the eighteenth century. Although New Granada's populace may have been insufficiently deferential and disciplined for a peninsular Spaniard like Archbishop-Viceroy Caballero y Góngora, this certainly does not mean that the political system was in danger. Indeed, popular challenges to government authority during the late eighteenth century were easily contained within that system. The extension of the aguardiente monopoly to the mining districts of Barbacoas provoked revolt in 1791, and in 1800, Indian villagers in Túquerres, near Pasto, killed their corregidor and destroyed the property of the local estancos.[5] These were, however, purely localized disturbances in territories distant from the capital, and they did not involve widespread disorder of the kind experienced in 1781.

As for other forms of social conflict, it is difficult to find evidence of any significant threat to the stability of the colonial order. Jaramillo Uribe has argued that communities of runaway slaves, known as *palenques,* became so widespread during the late eighteenth century that it seemed there was "an agreement between the different nuclei of slaves to carry out a general rebellion," and he even detects a pattern of slave revolt that assumed the characteristics of a civil war.[6] In fact, the evidence that slave rebellion was

---

3. Pérez Ayala, *Caballero y Góngora,* pp. 328–30.

4. Posada and Ibáñez, *Relaciones de mando,* pp. 323–4, 449–50, 474–7.

5. On Barbacoas, see Kuethe, *Military Reform and Society,* p. 169; on Túquerres, see Javier Laviña, "La sublevación de Túquerres de 1800: Una revuelta antifiscal," *Boletín Americanista,* 20:28 (1978), pp. 189–96; see also Sergio E. Ortíz, *Agustín Agualongo y su tiempo* (Bogotá, 1958), pp. 46–53.

6. Jaime Jaramillo Uribe, *Ensayos sobre Historia Social Colombiana,* p. 60.

a sign of deepening social conflict is slight. Records of slave resistance show that large-scale slave revolts were extremely rare, and that slave *palenques* were small, often transient, and few in number. Many factors inhibited slave rebelliousness. The geographical dispersion of the slave population within and between regions, the fact that most slaves lived in societies where they were outnumbered by whites and free people and thus faced uneven odds in any conflict with slaveowners, and the tendency for increasing numbers of blacks to be born into slavery and socialized in its ways, all stood in the way of generalized slave revolt. Indeed, recent research suggests that slaves were more disposed to flee from their masters or to seek redress of grievances from the authorities than to launch any broader attack on slave society.[7]

Less than a decade after the Comunero rebellion, officials discounted the threat of large-scale rebellion. In 1789, Viceroy Gil y Lemus recommended dismantling the disciplined militias, on the grounds that their policing potential did not justify the burden they placed on the colonial treasury. First, he doubted that local militias were an appropriate instrument for defending government, because they provided arms and military training that could be turned against the authorities and might therefore prove more harmful than helpful in an emergency. More immediately, he felt that the expense of maintaining militias was simply not justified by threats to public order. According to Gil y Lemus, the threat of sedition in the interior had been greatly exaggerated, and he confidently prevailed upon the crown to save money by demobilizing the militia units established under his predecessor. His successor, Viceroy José de Ezpeleta, was also determined to reduce government spending, but he was more cautious about reducing the government's policing capacity through cuts to military expenditure. He preferred a milder approach to cost cutting – through a reorganization of the military to reduce costs – and by 1794, he had convinced the crown to retain a militia program in modified form. Ezpeleta wanted to keep the militias because they provided the only effective means of coercion in the interior, but, like Gil y Lemus, he did not fear any widespread revolt. In fact, Ezpeleta justified arming colonials partly on the grounds that any rebellion would not affect the whole country, and that the authorities could exploit regional differences when mobilizing forces for use against local uprisings.[8]

The dangers of political disaffection certainly did not disappear, however. In the generation after the rebellion, Spanish government in New Granada again faced the specter of sedition, this time in a different,

---

7. Anthony McFarlane, "*Cimarrones* and *Palenques:* Runaways and Resistance in Colonial Colombia," in Gad Heuman, (ed.), *Out of the House of Bondage: Runaways, Resistance and Marronage in Africa and the New World* (London, 1986), pp. 131–51.
8. Kuethe, *Military Reform and Society,* pp. 150–64.

potentially more dangerous guise. For unlike the Comunero leaders, who had rebelled in defense of a traditional order and called upon the king's name to legitimate their attack on "bad government," a younger generation of creoles embraced ideas from the philosophy and science of the European Enlightenment, and some, seeing science as a symbol of progress and finding progress in the examples of the American and French Revolutions, also came to contemplate a new political order. How, then, did this alteration in outlook take shape, and what were its repercussions in New Granada's political life?

The politics of conciliation and the cultivation of reform

Immediately after the Comunero rebellion, Viceroy Caballero y Góngora prevailed upon the crown to appease the creoles, using the example of the North American War of Independence to warn of the potential consequences of draconian retaliation. In a confidential letter to Gálvez, he observed that, had Governor Gage of Boston offered conciliations to such men as Samuel Adams and John Hancock, the British might have preserved their colonial possessions.[9] The implication was quite clear. Unless Spain learned this lesson and cultivated the loyalty of leading citizens in New Granada, it risked losing the colony. The visitor general, on the other hand, was more sanguine, expressing skepticism about the threat of separatist revolt raised by the viceroy. Gutiérrez de Piñeres argued that the reform of abuses in the government would always arouse the antagonism of individuals in all classes of society and need not be equated with ambitions for independence.[10] In his view, the dominant group in colonial society was closely identified with Spain and, for reasons of both class and color, was the natural ally of the metropolitan government. But, by recommending that the crown take care to bolster the privileged position of the creole elite, Gutiérrez de Piñeres nonetheless acknowledged that there was a conditional element in creole loyalty that required diligent cultivation.[11]

During his viceregency, Archbishop Caballero y Góngora carefully courted creole allegiance. In the first place, he ensured that the general amnesty offered to the Comuneros was honored. A few *santafereños* suspected of complicity with the rebels were quietly transferred out of the capital, but the archbishop-viceroy avoided a political witch-hunt and sought to reassure creoles of his confidence in their loyalty. Thus, he insisted that provincial creoles who had been caught up in the Comunero

---

9. Archivo Restrepo, Correspondencia reservada del Arzobispo-Virrey, Caballero y Góngora to Gálvez, February 6, 1783 (no. 26).
10. AGI Santa Fe 661, Gutiérrez de Piñeres to Gálvez, February 28, 1782 (no. 32).
11. AGI Santa Fe 660, Gutiérrez de Piñeres to Gálvez, March 31, 1780 (reservada no. 181).

movement should be permitted to hold local office, and, with the expansion of the crown monopoly administrations, he had new jobs to offer to creoles seeking government posts. Such conciliatory gestures were coupled with a positive policy for winning creole confidence with a progressive program of "enlightened" reform. On becoming viceroy, Caballero y Góngora quickly embarked on projects designed to secure support among the younger generation of creoles by introducing and disseminating modern educational, scientific, and economic ideas. In so doing, he had a dual purpose. On the one hand, the archbishop-viceroy's commitment to enlightened ideas rested partly on the practical, economic reasons commonly found among the Spanish and Spanish American advocates of the Enlightenment. In short, he saw the "useful sciences" as a means of promoting the development of colonial economic resources, and thereby serving the interests of the Spanish state. On the other hand, his interest in educational reform also involved a political calculation. After the Comunero rebellion, Caballero y Góngora was acutely aware of the need to justify Bourbon policy and political practice to the creole elites, and his support for educational reform suggests a recognition that reinvigorating political respect for Spain required fresh intellectual and cultural leadership.

In the various economic projects launched during the archbishop's viceregency, we have already seen clear evidence of official efforts to bend the techniques of the natural sciences and the tenets of enlightened political economy to the task of mobilizing New Granada's material and human resources. The *visitas* of mining districts, the project for developing the Almaguer gold mines through joint-stock business methods, the introduction of modern metallurgical techniques to revive Mariquita's silver mines, and the schemes for promoting exports of cinchona and dyewood, all reflected Caballero y Góngora's determination to use the useful sciences to foster economic activity and, by extension, to improve social discipline by providing productive employment. But the greatest impact of the new approach was found, not in the economy, but in the spheres of culture and politics, where scientific innovation altered the outlook of educated creoles in a way that ultimately was to confound the purposes of its patrons.

Archbishop-Viceroy Caballero y Góngora, the "pacifier" of the Comuneros, played an important part in promoting this change in the climate of creole opinion. His contribution to intellectual change in New Granada consisted, first, in resurrecting scientific projects and plans for educational reform that had initially been considered during the 1760s and 1770s. These reforms had been associated with two men, the Spanish scientist José Celestino Mutis, and the creole official Francisco Moreno y Escandón. Mutis had arrived in New Granada in 1761, with the post of personal physician to Viceroy Messía de la Cerda, but with the intention, after working in the recently founded royal botanical garden at Madrid, of studying natural history in an American environment. Failure to secure royal support for botanical study caused Mutis to turn to teaching mathematics and astronomy in Bogotá's Colegio del Rosario, where, as an outspoken advocate of the new sciences and critic of clerical obscurantism, he drew angry attention from the Dominicans of the Universidad de Santo Tomás. In 1774, they denounced his Copernican cosmology as contrary to faith and morals, and reported him to the Inquisition. Mutis was, however, defended by Viceroy Guirior, who at the same time patronized the plan put forward by Francisco Moreno y Escandón for a public university in which scholastic doctrines and teaching methods were to be superseded by the study of mathematics and the natural sciences. In the event, the traditionalists triumphed and the plan, which included a chair of mathematics for which Mutis was the obvious candidate, was abandoned by 1779. It was, however, to provide a basis for Caballero y Góngora's plans to realign higher education around the natural and applied sciences; he also called for new teaching methods that employed Spanish rather than Latin and provided ways to arouse and develop student interest.[12] Once again, a combination of conservative opposition from the religious orders and stinginess on the part of the crown obstructed changes in the curricula of existing institutions, and thwarted the establishment of a new public university oriented toward the theoretical and applied sciences. Some change had, nonetheless, entered the system. Mathematics and physics were taught in Bogotá's Colegio del Rosario, and José Félix Restrepo carried the study of science to Popayán, where his influence over a generation of students produced men who subsequently became some of New Granada's leading scientists.[13]

Caballero y Góngora's other, more significant contribution to the advance of the Enlightenment in New Granada was his support for a natural history survey of the kind that Mutis had envisaged in the 1760s. He launched the survey in 1782 after meeting Mutis at Ibagué, where the Spanish scientist was working in a mining project.[14] Thanks to the viceroy's support, Mutis was rescued from relative obscurity and swiftly received royal patronage. In 1783, he became director of the famous Botanical Expedition, which was to continue functioning until 1810. Details of the scientific work of the Botanical Expedition need not concern us here. Suffice to say that it produced an impressive body of information on Colombia's flora, fauna, and environment, and initiated further scientific

12. On the university reform, see the *relación de mando* of the archbishop-viceroy in Pérez Ayala, *Caballero y Góngora*, pp. 339–41. For the plan of study drawn up by the viceroy, see pp. 267–84.

13. Frank Safford, *The Ideal of the Practical: Colombia's Struggle to Form a Technical Elite* (Austin, Texas London, 1976), pp. 85–91.

14. On Mutis's work in mining, see Francisco Pelayo, "Las actividades mineras de J. C. Mutis y Juan José Elhuyar en Nueva Granada," *Revista de Indias*, 50:189, pp. 455–72.

research by spawning another permanent scientific institution, the Royal Astronomical Observatory in Bogotá.[15] For the present purpose, the significance of the Botanical Expedition lies in its cultural and political repercussions rather than in its actual scientific work. For, like the attempts to reform higher education, the activities of the expedition acted as a catalyst for introducing new elements into creole social and political thinking, and fostered attitudes that, though confined to a small elite, were more corrosive of authority than the autonomist traditions that had surfaced during the Comunero rebellion. In this sense, Caballero y Góngora's cultivation of useful knowledge had the opposite of the intended effect. Instead of winning creoles over to the Bourbon spirit of reform and innovation, it helped to disseminate ideas and to promote contacts that made creoles more aware of their own identity and interests, and concomitantly more critical of Spain and its policies.

The limits of creole citizenship

To understand the impact of enlightened ideas on New Granada's political life, we must first appreciate the fact that the tensions between creoles and the government revealed by the Comunero rebellion were never fully repaired. Despite the conciliatory gestures made after the rebellion, the governments of Caballero y Góngora and his successors could not conceal their reluctance to trust the creole elites with a dignified and equal role in administering their own society. This quickly became obvious during the internal military reorganization that was launched in 1783. At the outset, Archbishop-Viceroy Caballero y Góngora explicitly stated that, although trustworthy creoles might become subordinate officers, peninsular Spaniards must occupy the leading ranks.[16] His successors were equally determined to ensure that the army of the interior should be controlled by Spanish officers, and positions of command were accordingly dominated by peninsulars, as were the ranks of sergeant and unit commander.[17] Creoles were therefore left in no doubt that they were regarded as insufficiently reliable to control an army whose role was to police their society. Conciliating creoles by absorbing them into the new military structure was thus undermined by the viceroys' understandable unwillingness to

15. On the Botanical Expedition, see Florentino Vezga, *La Expedición Botánica* (Bogotá, 1936); Frederico Gredilla, *Biografía de José Celestino Mutis con relación de su viaje y estudios practicados en el Nuevo Reino de Granada* (Madrid, 1909); Guillermo Hernández de Alba (ed.), *Escritos científicos de don José Celestino Mutis*, 2 vols. (Bogotá, 1983); Gabriel Fonnegra, *Mutis y la Expedición Botánica: Documentos* (Bogotá, 1983).

16. Archivo Restrepo, Correspondencia reservada del Arzobispo-Virrey, Caballero y Góngora to Gálvez, June 15, 1783 (no. 45).

17. Kuethe, *Military Reform and Society*, Table 10, pp. 206–9; Marchena, "The Social World of the Military," Table 17, p. 87.

confide completely in their loyalty. Indeed, Allan Kuethe suggests that the armed forces of the interior came to appear to many New Granadans as "a foreign army of occupation," run by arrogant military men who provoked antagonism by their tendency to disregard local authority under cover of the *fuero militar.*[18]

The sensitivity of members of the creole elite to government policy after the Comunero rebellion was first demonstrated in a dispute that arose in 1785, when the *santafereño* aristocrat, Jorge Miguel Lozano, Marqués de San Jorge, was excluded from the officer corps of Bogotá's disciplined militia. Stung by this imputation of disloyalty and affront to his social standing, Lozano sent two petitions complaining about New Granada's government directly to the crown. The act itself was illegal, because such direct petitions were prohibited, but it was the accusations Lozano made that caused a major scandal. In his first petition, Lozano denounced the "deplorable state" of New Granada, which he attributed to the failure of the government and the "relaxation of good customs." He also argued that, because bad government prevented the king from knowing the true state of the colony, it was his duty to appeal directly for redress of its peoples' grievances.[19] His critique of the colonial government was extensive, and reached back to the very establishment of the viceroyalty itself.

The creation of the viceroyalty, Lozano argued, had had a number of adverse consequences. It had provided the viceroys with powers of patronage that they showered on their own retinues of relatives and dependents, to the exclusion of "honorable" citizens; this had in turn led to an undesirable influx of foreigners and peninsular Spaniards, ignoble men who engaged in petty business to the detriment of the lower classes and who were not worthy of the advancement accorded them by the viceroys. The viceroys had also failed to reward local merit, preferring to distribute offices for the profit of their own retainers "though they be only wigmakers, barbers, or footmen."[20] From condemning viceregal nepotism and discrimination against deserving creoles, Lozano went on to deliver a blistering attack on the audiencia in Bogotá, as "the most visible spectacle of tyranny" and the center of political corruption.[21] Having denounced the oidors, Lozano then turned, in an increasingly intemperate tone, to criticize Archbishop-Viceroy Caballero y Góngora and to defend the Comuneros. Lozano did not even hesitate to vilify the clergy, whom he accused of simony for their routine sale of spiritual services and sacraments at

18. Kuethe, *Military Reform and Society,* p. 102. Also see the discussion of disruption caused by the extension of military jurisdiction, pp. 102–11.
19. AHNM, Consejos, legajo 20,452, "Quaderno numero 1 y principal del sumario contra D. Jorge Lozano de Peralta," fols. 1–34, Lozano de Peralta to king, April 30, 1785.
20. Ibid., fol. 12.   21. Ibid., fols. 21–2.

excessive rates.[22] His second petition, sent some months later, was less
explicit but reiterated similar themes, stressing the government's failure
to reward the descendants of the conquistadors, its relegation of creole
nobles to minor posts (in which, he alleged, they were treated by peninsular officials as little more than servants), and its lack of respect for the
capital's cabildo.[23] Despite his social eminence, Lozano's action was to
cost him dearly. The oidor charged with investigating the case sent him to
prison in Cartagena, where he remained in custody while the Council of
the Indies considered his case. The council finally absolved him of all
charges in 1793, on the grounds that he had been sufficiently punished for
his transgression, and his case was then definitively closed by his death in
the same year.[24]

Lozano was a quarrelsome individual, whose unaccommodating views
did not necessarily represent those of the *santafereño* elite as a whole, nor
signal any general creole dissent. If the authorities singled him out for
harsh treatment, then it was largely because his loyalty had been im-
peached during the Comunero rebellion, when he had been co-opted as
one of the *santafereño* "captains" during the negotiations between the
government and the rebels at Zipaquirá. Indeed, in the investigations that
followed his arrest, witnesses were repeatedly asked about this connection,
about Lozano's ideas, and about the threat of further sedition. The witnesses generally agreed that no such threat existed and unanimously attributed Lozano's behavior to his own personal sense of grievance and lack of
tact.[25] The case is nevertheless not without significance. The very fact
that the viceroy and audiencia took such draconian action against Lozano
reveals their continuing suspicion of the *santafereño* elite and shows that,
for all the talk of conciliation, the authorities had failed fully to convince
creoles of their parity with the peninsulars. The affair also showed that
creole frustration with discrimination continued to breed discontent and
division, a fact that Francisco Silvestre frankly acknowledged in 1789. A
keen and experienced observer of New Granadan life, Silvestre thought
that eradicating rivalry between European and American Spaniards was a
political priority. Without positive discrimination designed to give creoles an equal share of military, ecclesiastical, and administrative posts,
Silvestre argued, the government would always be in fear of disturbances
that might eventually lead to the loss of the colony.[26] This prediction was
to prove uncomfortably close to the truth. A mere five years later, in
1794, the colonial authorities uncovered activities among a small group of

---

22. Ibid., fols. 31–2.   23. Ibid., Lozano de Peralta to king, October 28, 1785.

24. Ibid., "Quaderno suelto reservado que tiene el sumario sobre indagación de los designios que
    pudo tener D. Jorge Lozano Peralta," fols. 156–7.

25. Ibid., fols. 4–15.   26. Silvestre, *Descripción*, p. 116.

creole intellectuals revealing that the new ideas associated with education-al reform and scientific innovation had tended to aggravate rather than alleviate creole dissatisfactions, thereby encouraging forms of dissent that were prejudicial to the state, perhaps even threatening to its survival.

The Enlightenment in New Granada

If Archbishop-Viceroy Caballero y Góngora had imagined that promoting the scientific and economic ideas of the Enlightenment would harness creoles to the service of the state, then he miscalculated badly. By encour-aging the dissemination of "useful science" the authorities hoped to ad-vance the material progress of New Granadan society and to affirm Spain's authority. Thus, it promoted the foundation of a periodical press, sanc-tioned the establishment of "Economic Societies" to promote the develop-ment of agriculture, industry, and commerce, and allowed open discus-sion of economic issues in the press.[27] All this, no doubt, seemed harmless enough. But, in fact, the efforts of the colonial government to stimulate economic development by sponsoring such activities had the unwelcome consequence of encouraging educated creoles to view Spanish policy toward New Granada with a more critical eye. Thus, although the dissemination of new ideas was stripped of explicitly dubious political content, propagation of "useful knowledge" was to prove subtly corrosive of Spanish dominance.

In the first place, the dissemination of new ideas produced disputes over intellectual issues and academic positions which tended to accentuate divisions between creoles and peninsulars. The small intellectual world of New Granada, concentrated mainly in the capital, became broadly di-vided into two camps. On one side stood a conservative academic estab-lishment that defended scholasticism and opposed modern philosophy; on the other stood those who sought university posts and favored curricular reform and the advancement of science. This division was charged with political significance because most in the former camp were peninsulars and most in the latter were creoles, so that intellectual differences over-lapped and interacted with social rivalries. Moreover, the content of con-temporary scientific debate did nothing to diminish this division, because it exposed Americans to the racist ideas of De Pauw and Buffon, who presented the environment and peoples of the Americas as biologically inferior to those of the Old World. Supported by Humboldt, New Gra-nadan scientists joined other Americans in seeking to show the absurdity of these theories, and so they entered into a polemic which, by its very

27. For comment on the Economic Societies, which were set up briefly in Mompós and projected for Bogotá, see R. J. Shafer, *The Economic Societies in the Spanish World, 1763–1821* (Syracuse, 1958), pp. 154–6, 235–9.

content, tended to align Americans against Europeans. In so doing, they were also to reduce their cultural isolation from Europe, and concomitantly to experience growing confidence in their own scientific endeavors, identified with their American homeland.[28]

Another sign of assertiveness among the cultured creole minority in New Granada is found in the weekly journal known as the *Papel Periódico de Santafé*, which was published with official approval between 1791 and 1797. Apparently bland politically, this periodical in fact made an important contribution to the elaboration and diffusion of new attitudes and ideas. For in both content and tone, the *Papel Periódico* reflected a more critical attitude toward colonial government and an incipient sense of nationhood.[29] First, editors and authors assumed there was a "public good" that might rationally be pursued and reforms that should be undertaken to promote this good; they also addressed an enlightened public in the belief that it shared this conviction and could play a leading and reforming part in improving New Granada's economy and society. Second, the journal introduced a new, "modern" style of criticism, which stressed the superiority of empirical investigation of nature over the repetition of texts invested with only traditional authority. Third, and no less important, it created a "public," a forum for debate and discussion, which not only linked like-minded men in the capital, but also aspired to spread its notion of the general good to creoles in the provinces.[30]

Contributors to the *Papel Periódico* also reformulated the claims of creoles to participate in the government by stressing the need for educated men to shape and dictate policy. This argument is reflected in explicit attacks on the principles of "nobility" and family honor, conferred by birth, that stood at the heart of traditional elite political culture. Instead, creole writers proposed an alternative form of nobility, one based on merit and the exercise of talent for the public good.[31] The idea of replacing an "aristocracy" with a species of "meritocracy" was, in effect, a modernization of creole claims to exercise influence and power in their own land, restated in the language of the Enlightenment. This reflected the aspirations of the trained and educated creole elite who had emerged from New Granada's own educational institutions, particularly the Colegio del Ro-

---

28. Thomas F. Glick, "Science and Independence in Latin America (with Special Reference to New Granada)," *HAHR*, 71:2 (1991), pp. 307–34; Jeanne Chenu, "De la Terre aux Etoiles: Quête Scientifique el Identité Culturelle en Nouvelle Granade," in Centre National de la Recherche Scientifique, *L'Amérique Espagnole a l'Epoque des Lumiéres* (Paris, 1987), pp. 247–60.

29. This discussion draws on the study of the *Papel Periódico* in Renan Silva, *Prensa y revolución a finales del siglo XVIII: Contribución a un análisis de la formación de la ideología de independencia nacional* (Bogotá, 1988), and on Garrido de Payán, "Political Culture of New Granada," pp. 12–27. See also the stimulating discussion in Benedict Anderson, *Imagined Communities: Reflections on the Origin and Spread of Nationalism* (London, 1987), pp. 50–65.

30. Silva, *Prensa y revolución*, pp. 28–51.   31. Ibid., pp. 104–6.

sario; it may also have reflected the specific concerns of creoles who lacked a lineage derived from the conquerors and first colonists of New Granada. In fact, years later, the Spanish priest José Antonio de Torres y Peña argued that rivalry between peninsulars and creoles became increasingly acute and divisive in the last years of Spanish rule precisely because first-generation creoles, who were often the sons of Spanish officials, expected to pursue professions and to exercise influence commensurate with their education and social rank.[32]

Creole absorption of new intellectual influences was not necessarily subversive of the colonial regime. The struggle to overhaul university curricula, the influence of Mutis and the Botanical Expedition in promoting empiricist and scientific thinking, the introduction of the printing press, and the freer dissemination of information through the medium of books, newspapers, and literary salons (tertulias), were all encouraged by the viceroys during the 1780s and early 1790s, and the government could thus be regarded as an agency for transforming colonial society under the aegis of an enlightened monarchy. But if some creoles put their faith in reform from above, there are also clear signs that interest in "useful knowledge" also provided both an inspiration and a medium for questioning the legitimacy and necessity of the colonial connection.

An early, celebrated instance of the subversive potential of Enlightened science and philosophy is found in the career of Pedro Fermín de Vargas. A young and clever provincial, born in the Comunero town of San Gil, Vargas was associated with Mutis and the Botanical Expedition in the 1780s, while he was still in his twenties, and after working in the viceroy's secretariat and finding favor with Caballero y Góngora, was given the post of corregidor of Zipaquirá in 1789. Exposure to scientific thinking through contact with Mutis, coupled with a desire to advance his own career, apparently encouraged Fermín de Vargas to undertake a critical analysis of his own society, and in 1790 he wrote two perceptive reports on socioeconomic conditions in New Granada. While so engaged, Vargas also secretly nursed the idea of independence. In 1791, he abandoned his wife and family, renounced his government career, and fled the country with his mistress. Traveling to the British West Indies, to the United States, and to England, Fermín de Vargas joined the small group of Spanish American revolutionaries who plotted against Spain in Europe. In England, he became involved with the Venezuelan revolutionary Francisco de Miranda and with the latter's schemes for liberating Spanish America; in 1799 and 1803, he presented memoranda to the British government to

---

32. José Antonio de Torres y Peña, "Memorias sobre la revolución y sucesos de Santafé de Bogotá en el trastorno de la Nueva Granada y Venezuela," in Guillermo Hernández de Alba (ed.), *Memorias sobre los origenes de la independencia nacional* (Bogotá, 1960), pp. 39–42.

persuade the cabinet that New Granada would, if given the opportunity, rise against Spanish domination.[33]

Vargas was an exceptional figure, but he was not alone in his convictions. His ideas about independence had developed early, possibly as early as 1782, immediately following the Comunero rebellion, and were almost certainly discussed with his friends among the capital's creole intelligentsia.[34] Among these friends was Antonio Nariño, the creole son of a prominent Spanish official who, as treasurer of the tithes in Bogotá, was a leading member of the capital's business and administrative cliques. Although not trained in science, Nariño was an ardent bibliophile who was evidently fascinated by the scientific and political ideas of his time, and eager to discuss and propagate them among his peers.[35] In 1793, he founded a printing press, known as "La Patriótica," which was licensed by the government and authorized to print the weekly *Papel Periódico de Santafé de Bogotá* that was edited by Manuel del Socorro Rodríguez, Viceroy Ezpeleta's Cuban retainer, the city's official librarian, and the founder of a *tertulia* known as "La Eutropélica." Nariño's house, meanwhile, became a center for another *tertulia*, known as "El Casino," where members of Bogotá's aspiring intelligentsia met to read and to discuss their ideas. Within this *tertulia*, Nariño and his French friend, the physician Luis de Rieux, established an inner group known as "El Santuario," and within that there was a still more secret grouping called the "Arcano Sublíme de la Filantropía."[36] The exact purpose of these inner groupings, which were surrounded by secrecy, is not known. However, there can be little doubt that events in Europe during the early 1790s encouraged armchair revolutionaries to think that the moment had come to put their ideas into practice. For this was a period of sudden, almost unimaginable change in Europe, marked by the deposition of Louis XVI, the imprisonment of the French royal family in August 1792, and the execution of the French king in January 1793. And, while revolution swept France, the Spanish mon-

33. Gómez Hoyos, *La Revolución Granadina*, vol. 1, pp. 275–312.

34. These ideas took their clearest form in a manuscript, which describes an imaginary dialogue between Lord North and a philosopher, concerning British colonialism in North America and implicitly denouncing Spanish colonialism and authoritarianism. This manuscript is published in Gómez Hoyos, *La Revolución Granadina*, vol. 1, pp. 290–9. The influence of Robertson's *History of America* is analyzed in an unpublished paper by D. A. G. Waddell, "Britain and Late Colonial Spanish America: Some Intellectual Connections," given at the 46th International Congress of Americanists.

35. On Nariño's background, see J. M. Restrepo and R. Rivas, "Genealogía de Don Antonio Nariño," in Oswaldo Díaz y Díaz, *Segundo Centenario del Nacimiento de Don Antonio Nariño* (Bogotá, 1965), pp. 11–18. A good short summary of Nariño's life, ideas, and political activities is found in Gómez Hoyos, *La Revolución Granadina*, vol. 1, pp. 205–74.

36. Thomas Blossom, *Antonio Nariño, Hero of Colombian Independence* (Tucson, Arizona, 1967), pp. 6–8.

archy suddenly seemed vulnerable. Its old ally had become its major enemy, Spain was threatened by French subversion and invasion, and, after a frightened Charles IV purged the liberal reformers who had influenced his predecessor, Spain was forced into counterrevolutionary war against France in March 1793.

News of the great revolution in Europe and the start of an international revolutionary war evidently caused a frisson of excitement among freethinking creoles in Bogotá. In December 1793, Antonio Nariño decided to print a hundred copies of the French Assembly's "Declaration of the Rights of Man," which he had personally translated, for dissemination in the capital and the provinces. The copies did not reach their intended readers, however, for Nariño, warned of the possible consequences of publishing a prohibited document, burned all but two of them and swore his printer, Diego de Espinosa, to secrecy. There the matter might have ended, had it not been for an incident that occurred eight months later, when, on the night of August 19, 1794, some seditious pasquinades were posted in the streets of Bogotá. Already under orders to watch for seditious propaganda and suspicious Frenchmen, the government took immediate action to counter a possible threat of rebellion. Alarmed by the prospect that the incubus of revolution had entered New Granada, the regent of the audiencia, Luis de Chaves, immediately recalled Viceroy Ezpeleta from his excursion to Guaduas and promptly started an intensive search for the culprits.[37]

Creole conspiracy and its consequences

The authors of the pasquinades, six satirical, mildly seditious lampoons that called for an end to the estancos and made derogatory allusions to the oidors of the audiencia, were quickly discovered. On August 20, Francisco Carrasco, a peninsular who was a minor official in the royal treasury, reported to Chaves that, from a conversation with another Spaniard, José Fernández de Arellano, he had learned that the purpose of the pasquinades was to arouse the plebeians of the city. Secret meetings, he said, had been held by leading creole citizens with the aim of "raising an insurrection in the Kingdom and adopting the form of government presently established in France," backed by money and men supplied by five of the conspirators.[38] Arellano in turn admitted to devising the pasquinades with three creole students and, in return for a promise of clemency, he denounced

37. Two major collections of documents chart the political upheaval of 1794: E. Posada and P. M. Ibañez (eds.), *El Precursor: Documentos sobre la vida pública y privada del General Antonio Nariño* (Bogotá, 1903), and José Manuel Pérez Sarmiento (ed.), *Causas Célebres a los Precursores*, 2 vols. (Bogotá, 1929).

38. Pérez Sarmiento, *Causas Célebres*, vol. 1, pp. 229–31.

José María Durán, Pablo Uribe, and Luis Gómez as his associates. He alleged that the purpose of the pasquinades was to give an example to other provinces in New Granada and to arouse the common people in rebellion. Their action was, he said, founded in "the creoles' general and shared hatred of the *chapetones.*"[39]

Convinced that it had uncovered a serious revolutionary conspiracy, the viceroy and audiencia launched a three-pronged investigation to discover all of its ramifications. Oidor Joaquín de Inclan took charge of the case of the pasquinades and, after questioning the students at length (even torturing Durán), he extracted confessions from the three. They admitted only to writing and posting the pasquinades to annoy the oidors, however, and for all the investigating magistrate's efforts, no evidence emerged to support the audiencia's belief that their action was part of a conspiracy to overthrow the colonial government.[40] This did not save them from harsh punishment. In January 1796, the audiencia sentenced Gómez to eight years, Uribe and Durán to six years, and Arellano to four, all to be served in overseas penitentiaries; the creoles were also condemned to lifelong exile from their country. All were sent to Spain in March 1796, and subsequently completed their sentences.[41]

While Oidor Inclan pursued the matter of the pasquinades, Oidor Juan Hernández de Alba investigated the alleged plot against the government, and Oidor Joaquín de Mosquera focused on Antonio Nariño, who had been denounced for publishing the "Rights of Man." By September 1794, the judges reported to Spain that they had uncovered a serious subversive conspiracy. They alleged that the conspirators had promised large amounts of money, together with 200 or 300 armed men, in support of a plan to seize the Bogotá barracks and its arms while the troops were attending a feast-day church service. To spread their rebellion, the conspirators had printed and distributed the "Rights of Man" throughout the provinces, together with a statement that "of the four parts of Santa Fe, three were ready to cry out for liberty." The purpose of the pasquinades, the judges added, was to spread the idea that the aim of the conspirators was to end the estancos, so that plebeians would be persuaded to support "those who call themselves Republicans."[42]

As the investigating judges widened their net, many arrests were made. Mosquera arrested Nariño and his printer, Diego de Espinosa, in August,

39. Ibid., vol. 2, pp. 9–10.
40. The confessions of Gómez, Uribe, and Durán are found in ANHM, Consejos 21,249, Testimonio del Sumario y pesquisa general contra los autores del los pasquines sediciosos, fols. 26–60; Quaderno no. 4: Testimonio de Autos, fols. 29–34; 112–38.
41. Pérez Sarmiento, *Causas Célebres*, vol. I, pp. 5–7, 13–45; also Eduardo Posada, "El proceso de los pasquines," *BHA*, vol. 8 (1913), pp. 721–8.
42. Perez Sarmiento, *Causas Célebres*, vol. I, pp. 262–3.

and by the end of October 1794, Hernández de Alba had at least twenty-two suspects in prison. The viceroy and audiencia had also taken strong measures to counter the threat of rebellion. They stepped up patrols in Bogotá, placed the military on alert, and sought reinforcements from outside. Viceroy Ezpeleta also called on the clergy to preach obedience to the king, and sent warnings to officials in Venezuela and Quito to be vigilant for any signs of subversion, particularly among French residents and visitors.[43]

In Bogotá, the cabildo reacted indignantly to the measures taken in the city, with their obvious imputation of disloyalty. By October 1794, its members were protesting directly to the king in very aggrieved terms. They complained that his ministers in New Granada were creating scandal and confusion by ignoring proper legal procedures, that they were mistreating their prisoners (whom they held incommunicado and without formal charge), and were casting calumny on the city by spreading unfounded fears and suspicions that divided Europeans and creoles.[44] In January 1795, the already strained relations between the government and the municipal corporation deteriorated still further. Shortly after the annual elections of alcaldes, Viceroy Ezpeleta suddenly decided to suspend the two recently elected alcaldes, on the suspicion that one of them, José María Lozano (a son of the deceased Marqués de San Jorge), had been involved in the antigovernment conspiracy.[45] The audiencia went further. It denounced the whole cabildo for its "spirit of partiality, complicity and monopoly," its effort to exclude Europeans in the recent elections, and for its choice of Lozano, a man known for his "notorious aversion to royal Ministers and public reputation for disaffection against His Majesty's mild government." Lozano, the audiencia insisted, had inherited a hatred of government from his father, was an enthusiast for "the republican constitution in general, and especially for that of Philadelphia," and was suspected of involvement in the recent conspiracy. José Caicedo, the senior regidor of the cabildo, was regarded with equal suspicion.[46]

After the cabildo's protests had been peremptorily swept aside, the audiencia continued to hold its prisoners and, during the opening months of 1795, proceeded with their prosecution. In July, the oidors decided to send Nariño to Spain, together with the ten other prisoners regarded as prime movers in the conspiracy. These were the creoles Joseph Ayala, Ignacio Sandino, Pedro Pradilla, Francisco Zea, Bernardo Cifuentes, Enrique Umaña, Miguel Froes, José María Cabal, Sinforoso Mutis, and the Frenchman Luis de Rieux; in Spain, their cases were to be reviewed by the central government, prior to sentencing. When the prisoners had been

43. Ibid., pp. 246–61.   44. Ibid., pp. 274–82, 285–9.   45. Ibid., vol. II, pp. 147–51.
46. Ibid., vol. I, pp. 369–74.

dispatched to Cartagena in November, en route to Havana and Cádiz, the audiencia finally began to relax. In December, it released six prisoners who were still held in Bogotá on bail, and allowed another six to be freed completely.[47] For the men sent to Spain, however, the matter was far from over. When Nariño arrived in Cádiz, he seized a chance to escape and made his own way to Madrid to plead his case in the court. In March 1796, he learned that his appeal had been rejected, and he fled to Paris. From there, he moved on to England, and in London became involved with Spanish American revolutionaries who were plotting to destroy the Spanish colonial regime, with British backing. By March 1797, Nariño was back in America, embroiled in the British plan for starting a revolution for independence in Venezuela and New Granada, supported from the recently captured island of Trinidad.[48] His ten companions were less fortunate. They suffered the loss of their liberty, positions, and property until 1799, when the Council of the Indies finally decided to close the case and to pardon the alleged conspirators.[49] Even then, for some of the men rounded up by the audiencia in 1794 the consequences of their arrests dragged on for years, as they sought restitution of lost property and employment and were dogged by suspicious officials.

In fact, the audiencia's conviction that there had been a conspiracy to overthrow the government in 1794 was never proven. The students arrested for posting the pasquinades admitted their guilt, Nariño accepted that he had translated and printed the "Rights of Man," and the various interrogations of suspects showed that there was a small group of young creoles in Bogotá who had discussed the possibilities of political change in New Granada. But the investigating magistrates did not succeed in conclusively demonstrating that creole conspirators had conceived or were ready to act upon a plan to overthrow the government and to replace it with a republic.[50] Among those arrested, there were undoubtedly men who disliked the colonial government and hoped that it would be weakened by the repercussions of revolution in France. This was not definitive evidence of plans to launch a revolution, however, and in seeking to show that it was, the audiencia trespassed beyond the bounds of political reality. Indeed, the viceroy himself had swiftly accepted that fears of an imminent revolution were unfounded. In September 1794, Ezpeleta informed Madrid that he "did not believe that the common people are discontented with His Majesty's rule, nor that the unfortunate manner of thinking of a few individuals is capable of overturning good order and established gov-

47. Ibid., vol. II, pp. 59–61.   48. Blossom, *Nariño*, pp. 26–38.

49. Perez, *Causas célebres*, vol. I, pp. 513–15.

50. The interrogations of the ten prisoners sent to Spain to be sentenced for conspiracy are found in AHNM, Consejos 21,249.

ernment . . ."[51] A year later, the viceroy reaffirmed his doubts. He stated that "not the slightest preparation for a formal insurrection has been discovered or observed," and he dismissed most of the individuals rounded up for the conspiracy as "poor young men from different provinces, without the connections, influence or facilities for such a scheme." He therefore joined with the archbishop of Santa Fe to recommend clemency and reconciliation.[52]

What, then, was the political significance of the 1794 conspiracy? On balance, it seems that the audiencia's vision of an impending revolution was a hallucination induced by a potent confection of memories of the Comunero rebellion and fears that France was using subversion as an instrument of war. But if the audiencia's fears were exaggerated, the investigations of 1794 nonetheless reveal underlying tensions between creoles and colonial government, and show how politically corrosive new ideas from Europe had been, particularly in these years when excitement over the events of the French Revolution reached a peak.

At one level, tensions arose from personal and institutional rivalries between members of the audiencia, which was dominated by peninsulars, and the municipal corporation, which was dominated by creoles. According to the cabildo of Bogotá, the audiencia's behavior showed that its judges were intent on blackening the city's name and ruining its leading citizens, in pursuit of a vendetta against the municipal corporation and its members. In 1789, Antonio Nariño had clashed with the audiencia when he was *alcalde ordinario* over a refusal to overlook a breach of official protocol. This, the cabildo affirmed, had made oidor Mosquera an implacable enemy of Nariño, and had fueled the oidors' desire for revenge against the cabildo. Thus, in 1792, the audiencia decided to harass municipal officials by activating a defunct law that allowed them to hold *residencias* of town council members. Then, in 1793, Oidor Mosquera and Fiscal Blaya again clashed with the cabildo by publicly insulting an alcalde. When the cabildo made an official complaint to the Council of the Indies, these two ministers had been severely reprimanded, together with others involved in the affair. After this setback, the cabildo alleged, these judges seized upon the testimony of unreliable witnesses in 1794 solely for the purpose of revenge against creoles. In so doing, they were able to rely on support from Luis de Chaves, regent of the audiencia, because he too wished to displace creoles from the cabildo and replace them with his peninsular friends, partly to cover his illegal commercial dealings. As for Viceroy Ezpeleta, the cabildo accused him of weakness. It even alleged that the ascendancy and arrogance of the oidors was so great that the viceroy was in danger of suffering the same fate as President Meneses, who

51. Pérez Sarmiento, *Causas Célebres*, vol. I, p. 219. 52. Ibid., p. 383.

was deposed by an audiencia coup in 1715.[53] Another, more plausible reason for the viceroy's commitment to root out possible subversion was his indirect but embarrassing connection with Nariño's publication of the "Rights of Man." In his defense, Nariño revealed that the source of this document had been a book sent to the viceroy, and lent to him by the captain of the viceregal guard. Ezpeleta was, then, understandably concerned to distance himself from his creole acquaintances and to show his firmness of purpose once they had been arraigned on suspicion of treason.

The disputes between the creole elite and the government that surfaced in 1794–5 cannot, however, be reduced solely to personal rancours and institutional rivalries. Behind them lay a broader shift of attitudes among a cultured creole minority that found in the writings of the European Enlightenment and events in revolutionary France a foil for its rivalry with peninsular officials. In the case of Antonio Nariño and some of his companions (several of whom were connected to each other through their involvement with the activities of the Botanical Expedition or through academic institutions), the cultivation of useful knowledge clearly encouraged behavior that, if not necessarily seditious, was certainly of doubtful legality at a time when Madrid was seeking to stamp out all traces of French political influence.

During his lengthy interrogations, Nariño tried to convince his judges that he had not been conscious of any wrongdoing, but had simply pursued ideas that were commonplace in Spain itself. He insisted that the information and ideas contained in the document he had printed were already freely available within the colony, and that the liberal precepts he espoused were found in the writings of many Spanish authors (including an essay that Manuel de Blaya, fiscal of the Santa Fe audiencia, had published in Madrid), as well as in the constitutions of the Spanish "Sociedades patrióticas," respectable institutions that were encouraged by the government for their dedication to social and economic improvement.[54] This was, of course, a disingenuous plea. Nariño must have known of Floridablanca's indictments on the import of French political news and writing into Spain and its dominions, a censorship that, starting in 1789, culminated in the complete closure of the Spanish press in 1791.[55] He must also have been conscious that conspiratorial talk of republicanism was hardly likely to enjoy official approval at a time when the Spanish Bourbons were contemplating with horror the overthrow of their French relatives. Yet searches of Nariño's property revealed a library

53. Ibid., pp. 430–4.
54. For Nariño's interrogation and defense, see Guillermo Hernández de Alba, *El Proceso de Nariño a la luz de documentos inéditos* (Bogotá, 1958), pp. 177–225; also Pérez Sarmiento, *Causas célebres*, vol. 1, pp. 93–144.
55. Herr, *The Eighteenth Century Revolution in Spain*, pp. 239–68.

of some 2,000 books that included a substantial amount of proscribed political material. His papers left even fewer doubts as to his political interests and sympathies. They included, for example, the design for Nariño's study in which busts and portraits of classical contemporary figures were evocatively paired: Tacitus with Raynal; Socrates with Rousseau; Pliny with Buffon; Cicero with Demosthenes and William Pitt, Xenophon with Washington, and Solon with Montesquieu; a picture of Newton stood alone, facing a portrait of Nariño on the opposite wall. Much more suspicious, from the judges' point of view, was the motto, "He snatched the lightning from the skies and the sceptre from the tyrant's hand," which accompanied the bust of Franklin.[56] Moreover, Nariño's attempt to conceal his books and to destroy his copies of the "Rights of Man" shows that he was fully aware of their incriminating potential. And, even if he was merely toying with radical ideas before his arrest, his inclination toward revolution was fully revealed afterward, when, in 1796, he left Spain to become a dedicated revolutionist in France and England.

The significance of creole sedition

New Granada had, then, proved to be infertile ground for revolution. For although the conspiracy of 1794 shows that ideas hostile to the colonial order circulated among an educated creole minority, enthusiasm for republican ideals far outdistanced the bounds of effective political action. The documentation amassed by the investigating magistrates in 1794–5 reveals an impractical, poorly organized political adventure, concocted by a tiny group of idealists who were politically inexperienced and politically isolated. There is little reason to believe that the conspirators had seriously considered how to proceed from contemplating revolution to implementing it, and they had no reason to suppose that Bogotá or any other city would have rallied to their cause. This premature spark of creole radicalism was nevertheless significant in two major respects. First, it showed that, though Spain's command of New Granada appeared firm, the ideological foundations of Spanish rule had been weakened by the very forces that sought to revitalize the empire through "enlightened" reform. In Spain itself, the new learning of the "ilustrados" had become markedly more influential in intellectual and political circles during the 1780s, due largely to encouragement from the modernizing monarchy of Charles III; this change in the cultural climate had swiftly spread to the Americas.

---

56. This design is reproduced in Hernandez de Alba, *El Proceso de Nariño*, p. 160. Nariño's papers also included a parody of the "Marseillaise," which the investigating magistrates failed to recognize, possibly because it was in French. See ibid., pp. 135–6.

Transmitted through scientific and educational institutions and by the circulation of books and the periodical press, enlightened ideas not only invigorated intellectual discourse among educated creoles, but also offered them a fresh perspective on their condition. In the main American cities, a younger generation of creoles found a new medium of expression in the scientific discourse of the Enlightenment, through which they could form and voice opinions that scorned the Old World while exalting the New.[57] In New Granada, creole exposure to the Enlightenment led rapidly from the intellectual and institutional reformism favored by Moreno y Escandón in the late 1770s, to the political radicalism espoused by Fermín de Vargas, Nariño, and their circle in the early 1790s. Such radicalism was undoubtedly less dangerous to the established government than the authorities supposed, because it was neither sufficiently widespread nor organized to mount the kind of revolution that the government feared. It did, however, show that among some creoles, interest in the useful sciences had undermined respect for Spanish rule and nurtured a commitment to a regional, protonational *patria*. In science, creoles found a means to praise the environment of the New World, and by developing an interest in the resources of their country they also found a way of understanding and identifying with a distinctive *patria*. In the long term, this was to be a dangerous development. For although the revolutionary conspiracy of 1794 was rapidly dissolved by energetic executive action and remained invisible to the mass of the population, the New Granadan "Enlightenment" had nurtured an incipient sense of creole nationhood that was not so easily dispelled.

The conspiracy of 1794 was also politically significant for the damage it inflicted on relations between the creole patriciate and the colonial government. By crushing the conspiracy with a disproportionate display of reactionary zeal, born in fears of external subversion in wartime, the authorities left a residue of recrimination and suspicion that was to contaminate political relations between *santafereño* creoles and their government for years to come. Nariño and his upper-class companions were subjected to arbitrary if not brutal treatment by the Spanish authorities after their arrest; their relatives were also handled in a heartless manner, as their pathetic petitions for clemency were repeatedly scorned during years of uncertainty. This undoubtedly caused deep resentment among Bogotá's creoles and, though such bitterness may have been directed against the officials involved in the arrests rather than against Spanish colonial rule, dislike and distrust of leading officials blighted relations between a maturing generation of educated creoles and their government.

---

57. Mario Góngora, *Studies in the Colonial History of Spanish America*, trans. Richard Southern (Cambridge, 1975), pp. 177–93.

Such tensions were not of themselves sufficiently severe to endanger the stability of the colonial government. So far, internal conflicts within New Granada, whether in the form of popular rebellion or elite conspiracy, had failed to act as catalysts for wider challenges to the Spanish colonial regime. However, at the turn of the century, political conditions began to change within the empire as a whole and, though New Granada's government had withstood threats from within, it was to become increasingly vulnerable when war imposed intolerable strains on the power that stood behind it. After Spain embarked on war with Great Britain in 1796, the commercial system, military power, and political authority built by the Bourbons gradually succumbed to attacks from the British until the House of Bourbon suffocated in the deadly embrace of its ally, when Napoleon invaded Spain and usurped the Spanish throne in 1808.

This great crisis at the heart of the empire created the revolutionary situation that was absent from the Hispanic world of the 1790s; when Spaniards fought against a French takeover, the colonies followed, translating the rhetoric of Spain's resistance to France into the language of an American autonomy. Thus the catalyst for political change in New Granada was to come from outside the territory, from the decay and eventual collapse of the Bourbon monarchy under the pressures of international war. By tracing the reverberations in New Granada of Spain's wars and political crises, we shall now see how the territory's mutation from Spanish dominion into independent republic finally became possible.

PART V

Crisis in the colonial order

11

War and the weakening of the colonial order

When the government of Charles IV went to war with revolutionary France in March 1793, it launched Spain into a cycle of conflict that was to last, with only brief interruptions, for the next two decades. Almost from the first, Spain proved unable to hold its own among the great European powers. Following the execution of Louis XVI in 1793 and the rupture of the Family Compact, Spain's long-standing alliance with France was abandoned and, to combat the rising revolutionary power north of the Pyrenees, Charles IV joined with Britain, Spain's traditional enemy, to fight its traditional ally. This was an unhappy and unsuccessful alliance. After some early successes against France in 1793, the tide of war quickly turned against Spain and, after suffering heavy losses, Madrid was forced to renew the Franco–Spanish alliance in order to resist the rising power of Britain, the old enemy. This led to an immediate renewal of conflict between Spain and Britain. In August 1796, the Treaty of San Ildefonso joined Spain and France in an offensive and defensive alliance against Britain; in October 1796, Spain declared war on Britain. The decision was to prove a disaster for the Bourbon monarchy. Britain now turned the full might of its seapower against Spain, defeating the Spanish navy at Cape St. Vincent in 1787, thereby depriving Spain of commerce and revenue by cutting essential trade routes between Spain and its American colonies, and, in 1798, seizing Trinidad for use as a platform for attacks on Spain's South American territories. And worse, much worse, was to come. The Peace of Amiens allowed Spain a brief breathing space between 1802 and 1804, when there was an armed truce between the powers. But when Spain returned to war with Britain in December 1804, disaster shortly followed. The Spanish navy was cut apart at the Battle of Trafalgar in October 1805, British forces briefly invaded Buenos Aires in 1806, and the disruption of Spanish Atlantic commerce became an unstoppable decline, draining Spain's economy and treasury. Under Charles IV, the resurgent Spain of Charles III became a crippled power until, in 1808, Napoleon delivered the coup de grâce by toppling the Bourbon monarchy and placing his brother Joseph on the Spanish throne.

Against this background, Spain's hold on its colonies became increasingly tenuous. First, transatlantic communications were severed and economic ties between the metropolis and colonies were progressively weakened, as Spanish colonial commerce was torn apart by British naval power; second, the power and prestige of the monarchy diminished as military reverses multiplied, especially during the war of 1804–8; finally, after the reverberations of war had loosened the colonial connection, the metropolitan power collapsed in 1808, engulfing Spain in a deep internal crisis that sent shock waves throughout the empire. Taken together, these events were to change the course of Spanish American history; it now remains to examine their repercussions in New Granada.

The impact of war on New Granadan trade

In New Granada, the destructive effects of war began with the dislocation of transatlantic commerce. In 1795, trade with the metropolis appeared to be unusually strong, as about 3.3 million pesos in treasure left Cartagena for Spain.[1] In fact, the high value of exports was a sign of weakness, not strength, because it merely reflected the disturbances of the preceding two years, when merchants had retained their bullion rather than risk loss to French privateers during the Franco-Spanish war of 1793–5. Thus, the decay of Spain's commerce with the colony had already started in 1793, and, despite the outflow of bullion in 1795, showed no sign of improving, as the threat of war with Britain discouraged Spain's merchants from investing in any substantial business.[2] When news of the outbreak of war with the British reached the port at the end of 1796, the pessimism of the mercantile community was confirmed, and the low level of trade with Spain over the previous few years gave way to a much longer and deeper recession. Between 1796 and 1801, Spanish traffic into Cartagena fell to its lowest point since the time of the previous Anglo-Spanish war in 1779–83, bringing a concomitant contraction in imports from the metropolis. The depth of this recession is reflected in an official listing of Spanish merchant and naval shipping and imports into Cartagena, as shown in Table 11.1.[3]

The collapse of Spanish commerce with New Granada took place in spite of emergency measures taken by Madrid to sustain the transatlantic trade. After Nelson began his blockade of Cádiz in 1797, Charles IV's government had responded to the distress of Spanish merchants by legalizing trade with America in neutral ships and through neutral ports, in the

---

1. Posada and Ibáñez, *Relaciones de mando*, p. 342.
2. AGI Santa Fe 958, Junta de Gobierno, Cartagena, January 11, 1797.
3. AHNC Aduanas, tomo 13, fols. 268–73. "Razón de los Buques y Registros Españoles que han entrado en este Puerto de los de la Peninsula de España desde 28 de Noviembre de 1796 . . . hasta 30 de Septiembre inclusive del presente año de 1801."

Table 11.1. *Ships and imports from Spain to Cartagena,*
1796–1801

Year	Ships	Imports (pesos)
1796 (December)	2	41,982
1797	1	16,418
1798	1	77,984
1799	3	54,783
1800	—	—
1801	1	31,396

expectation that such a *comercio neutral* would allow Spanish merchants to sustain essential supplies to and from the colonies.[4] This news was enthusiastically received in Cartagena, and in 1798 merchants in both Cartagena and Santa Marta hurriedly prepared trading expeditions for dispatch to the Caribbean colonies of friendly and neutral nations.[5] However, in New Granada the benefits of neutral commerce were frustrated by Viceroy Pedro de Mendinueta, who adamantly refused to admit that trade with foreign colonies was permitted by the terms of the 1797 decree, despite repeated pleas from Cartagena's merchants.

Throughout 1797, the Consulado of Cartagena had persistently pressed the viceroy to open trade with the colonies of friendly and neutral powers, arguing that the crown had created a precedent for such trade during the 1779–83 war.[6] But, backed by his treasury ministers, Mendinueta resisted Cartagena's pressure, on the grounds that such a concession would merely provide a cover for contraband.[7] To support his position, he informed Madrid in December 1797 that after nearly two years of war the provinces of the interior were still well stocked with European imports and that Cartagena merchants regularly dispatched large consignments of such goods inland. With such an abundance of linens, cottons, and other textiles in the interior, the viceroy concluded, there was certainly no case

4. This measure and its context are described in Antonio García-Baquero Gonzalez, *Comercio colonial y guerras revolucionarias* (Seville, 1972), pp. 133–8.

5. AGI Indiferente General 2466, Mendinueta to Saavedra, Santa Fe, July 19, 1798 (no. 200).

6. AGI Indiferente General 2466: Petition from the Sindico Procurador General before the Cartagena Consulado (countersigned by the governor of Cartagena and a number of prominent merchants), Cartagena, May 13, 1797. Ibid., Consulado to Secretario del Estado, enclosure with Mendinueta to Secretario del Estado, Santa Fe, December 19, 1797; and ibid., Ildefonso Ruíz del Río and Manuel García del Río, Cádiz, October 27, 1797.

7. AGI Indiferente General 2466, Mendinueta to Gardoqui, Santa Fe, June 19, 1797 (no. 47); ibid., Junta de Tribunales, Santa Fe, December 15, 1797; ibid., Mendinueta to Marqués de las Hormazas, December 19, 1797 (no. 127).

for opening Cartagena to trade with the foreign colonies.[8] Following the decree allowing *comercio neutral* in late 1797, Mendinueta saw no reason to change his opinion. He insisted that the royal order did not apply to trade with foreign colonies, even if those colonies were the possessions of neutral powers. According to Mendinueta, only ships sailing from Spain or coming directly from the ports of neutral powers could be allowed to sell their cargoes in the viceroyalty. He also insisted that all exports from Spanish dominions had to be consigned to a peninsular port and, although they might pass through a neutral port, neutral markets and foreign buyers could not legally be their final destination.[9] Mendinueta's interpretation of the royal decree was legally correct. Strictly speaking, the concession did not allow trade with neutrals; it merely allowed Spanish and American merchants to use neutrals sailing out of Spanish or neutral ports as intermediaries for trade with Spain.[10] However, in Caracas, Cuba, and other Spanish colonies, colonial officials interpreted the 1797 decree more leniently, allowing trade with the colonies of neutral powers while Viceroy Mendinueta resolutely refused to do so.[11]

By sticking to the letter of the law, Mendinueta ensured that *comercio neutral* brought no relief to Cartagena. New Granada's ports remained firmly closed to trade with the colonies of friendly and neutral powers, and Cartagena's merchants were left to rely on direct contacts with Spain and neutral nations. Such contacts simply did not materialize. In the first place, trade in Spanish vessels coming from the peninsula virtually disappeared. In the second place, the British pursued a policy that discouraged the carriage of Spanish colonial trade by neutrals. British naval and privateering vessels simply stopped neutral vessels on the high seas, seized cargoes destined for Spain, and then allowed the neutral vessels to continue their voyages after compensating their masters for freight charges lost on embargoed goods.[12]

Another hindrance to the development of trade between New Granadan and neutral ports stemmed from restrictions on what neutrals might legally import into Cartagena. Under the terms of the Royal Order of 1797, only those goods that the North Americans had sent to Spain before

---

8. AGI Indiferente General 2466, Junta de Tribunales, Santa Fe, December 15, 1797; Mendinueta to Marqués de las Hormazas, December 19, 1797 (no. 127).

9. In New Granada this was made clear by an early test case involving a vessel from the Danish island of Saint Thomas into Santa Marta. Viceroy Mendinueta reported this decision in a lengthy discussion of his interpretation of the Royal Order of 1797. Ibid., Mendinueta to Cayetano Soler, Santa Fe, July 19, 1798 (no. 356).

10. Villalobos, *El comercio y la crisis colonial*, 115–17.

11. See "Informe del Real Tribunal del Consulado de Cartagena . . . extendido por Don José Ignacio de Pombo," June 2, 1800, in José Ignacio de Pombo, *Comercio y contrabando en Cartagena de Indias* (Bogotá, 1986), p. 32.

12. Ibid., pp. 33–6.

the war could be legally imported into the colonies. Because this prewar trade between Spain and North America had consisted mainly of agricultural products, this meant that neutral North American traders could not provide New Granadan merchants with the manufactured goods, especially textiles, that they most required. By 1799, Viceroy Mendinueta recognized that this was stopping trade with the United States, and informed Spain that he had tried to encourage the trade by lifting the restrictions.[13] Even so, New Granadan merchants still found trading with the United States problematic, because of difficulties encountered in disposing of the colony's exports through North American neutrals. They found that if, on the one hand, a merchant wanted to send exports to Spain through U.S. intermediaries, he was unable to obtain cash or credit from neutral traders to finance a return trade.[14] If, on the other hand, he took cash from North American intermediaries, he was forced to accept far lower prices than those that could be obtained in Europe.[15] Consequently, trade with North America was slight. In 1798, a small group of Cartagena merchants secured permission from the viceroy to buy ships in the prize markets of Cuba and Santo Domingo, so that they could export large stocks of corruptible commodities stored in Cartagena – some of these exports were subsequently sent to U.S. ports.[16] These ventures were not, however, a commercial success. For when they returned to Cartagena from the United States, carrying manufactured imports authorized by the viceroy, the merchants had to compete with contraband imports that did not pay the usual heavy duties, of 32.5%, which they incurred.[17] Not surprisingly, trade with U.S. ports did not become an effective substitute for trade with the metropolis. In the four years between 1797 and 1800, only four ships entered New Granadan ports from neutral North America

---

13. AGI Santa Fe 958, Mendinueta to Cayetano Soler, Santa Fe, June 19, 1799 (no. 345); ibid., March 19, 1800; and AGI Indiferente General 2466, Mendinueta to Cayetano Soler, Santa Fe, September 19, 1799 (no. 387). In this correspondence the viceroy explains the difficulties and impracticalities of enforcing this rule and justifies his deviation from it.

14. Andrés de León y Segovia to viceroy, 1798, AHNC Aduanas, tomo 16, fols. 500–1. For the viceroy's opinions on this problem, see Mendinueta to Cayetano Soler, Santa Fe, July 19, 1799, AGI Indiferente General 2466 (no. 357).

15. AHNC Aduanas, tomo 16, fols. 515–17. José Antonio Ugarte y José Andrés de Urquinaona, Snata Fe, June 18, 1798.

16. In 1798, Juan de Francisco Martín, Mateo Arroyo, and Andrés de León y Segovia, Esteban Balthasar de Amador, Andrés de Urquinoana, Francisco Martín de Bustamente, and Agustín Gnecco made such requests. See AHNC Aduana, tomo 10, fols. 956–9, 962–5; tomo 18, fols. 282–96. Voyages to North American ports were organized by Manuel García del Río (AGI Santa Fe 958, May 18, 1799), and by Juan Francisco Martín and Manuel Arroyo (AHNC, Aduanas [Cartas], tomo 9, fols. 197–205). Their return to Cartagena in 1800 is reported in AHNC Aduanas, tomo 11, fols. 130–8, Ignacio Cavero to viceroy, Cartagena, December 19, 1801.

17. Pombo, *Comercio y contrabando en Cartagena de Indias*, p. 35.

(three at Cartagena, and one at Santa Marta), and the trade through U.S. ports completely failed to replace prewar commerce with Spain.

The inadequacies of Spanish commercial legislation in coping with the effects of war, coupled with Viceroy Mendinueta's refusal to compromise over trade with foreign colonies, ensured that New Granada's legal trade was reduced to a fraction of its former size. It did not cease completely. Merchants were, for example, allowed to buy cargoes from foreign vessels, which, for various special reasons, received permission to enter colonial ports and to sell all or part of their cargoes.[18] There was also trade with other Spanish American colonies, and in 1799, the administrator of the Cartagena customs argued that the bulk of the port's trade was legally obtained from other Spanish territories. He stated that, of 159 vessels that had entered Cartagena between the start of the war until September 1799, most had come from Spanish colonial ports.[19] However, neither of these practices compensated for the loss of Cartagena's normal commerce. Indeed, trade with other Hispanic colonies was more a cover for smuggling than a route for legal traffic, as ships that were apparently plying to and from Spanish American ports frequently used forged or falsified papers to disguise a contraband trade with the British in Jamaica. In these circumstances, contraband grew enormously. At the end of 1797, after only a year of war, the Consulado of Cartagena complained that contraband had inverted the normal pattern of trade with the interior. Rather than buying their imports from Cartagena, the internal provinces were supplying the port with imports from the contraband trade that they obtained from the ports of Santa Marta and Río Hacha.[20] When reporting to the crown on behalf of the Consulado in 1800, José Ignacio de Pombo reaffirmed the fact that the interior of New Granada was plentifully stocked with imports, and he estimated that during the previous four years at least 3 million pesos in specie had been spent in illegal trade with Jamaica.[21] So, although the merchants of Cartagena continued to call for the right to trade with friendly and neutral foreign colonies, their trade remained at a virtual standstill until the Peace of Amiens temporarily ended war with the British in 1802.

Between 1802 and 1804, the Peace of Amiens gave Spain a breathing

---

18. Damaged foreign ships could enter the port and sell their goods if they obtained permission from the local governor, and there are numerous instances of this practice. See, for example, the cases recorded in AHNC Aduanas, tomo 8, fols. 208–32; tomo 22, fols. 49–71; tomo 24, fols. 463–82. Friendly vessels might also enter to escape enemy pursuit. AHNC Aduanas, tomo 9, fols. 474–91.

19. AHNC Aduanas, tomo 24, fols. 983–92, Ignacio Cavero to viceroy, October 30, 1799.

20. AGI Indiferente General 2466, Consulado of Cartagena to Secretario del Estado, November 20, 1797.

21. Pombo, *Comercio y contrabando en Cartagena de Indias*, pp. 22–3.

space in which to revive maritime links with the markets of the Indies and rebuild its colonial commerce. However, in New Granada the peace did not give sufficient time for Spanish merchants to recover markets that had been filled with contraband. According to the Consulado of Cartagena in 1803, the colony's markets were simply saturated by the "vast and silent circulation of contraband in the interior of this Kingdom."[22] The proof of this was that, while scarcely more than 2 million pesos' worth of imports had entered the viceroyalty by legal channels between 1796 and 1802, New Granada had

such prodigious supplies, or is so over-supplied, that what one would never have been able to imagine has come to pass: that is, that the internal provinces which have always received what they needed from this port, have succoured it with consignments valued at more than a million pesos which, despite the enormous costs of a double journey, have been retailed at a profit by speculators. . . .[23]

Textiles were the main item of this illegal trade and were allegedly sold at prices lower than those found in Spain itself; indeed, the Consulado warned that the trade of New Granada was on the point of being taken over entirely by the British. During the same year, the Royal Treasurer in Portobelo echoed this warning. He alleged that all kinds of colonial products, including gold and silver, were routinely shipped to the island of San Andrés, there to be exchanged for merchandise that was redistributed throughout New Granada as well as being shipped onward to Peru, by way of Panama. Spanish, English, French, and Dutch vessels all took part in this clandestine commerce, which was not only rife in San Andrés, but was funneled through Bahía Honda on the Guajira coast, the Gayra cove in the vicinity of Santa Marta, the inlet called "Garrote" near Portobelo, and "all the anchorages adjacent to Cartagena."[24] In these conditions, Spanish trade with Cartagena could not recuperate, and its continuing weakness is reflected in the statistics shown in Table 11.2, compiled from estimates of Cartagena's trade made by Antonio Narváez y la Torre in 1805.[25]

Clearly, Spain's trade with New Granada did not undergo a full recovery during the Amiens truce: between 1802 and 1804, the yearly value of imports was well below its average annual value in 1785–93. The recu-

22. AHNC Consulados, tomo 2, fols. 947–51, Tomás Andrés de Torres, Manuel Martínez de Aparicio, José García del Toledo to viceroy, Cartagena, October 20, 1803.

23. Ibid., fol. 948.

24. AGI Santa Fe 959, Tesorero de las Cajas de Portovelo to Cayetano Soler, Cartagena de Indias, November 21, 1803.

25. "Discurso del Mariscal del Campo . . . D. Antonio de Narváez y la Torre . . . a petición del R. Consulado de esta Ciudad . . ." (Cartagena de Indias, June 30, 1805), published in Ortíz (ed.), *Escritos de dos economistas coloniales*, pp. 96, 98.

Table 11.2. *Spanish trade with Cartagena*
1802–4

Year	Imports	Exports (pesos)
1802	983,881	3,082,828
1803	970,952	1,554,381
1804	903,637	2,468,579

peration that did occur was due largely to restocking with Spanish products that had been in short supply during the war, rather than to the recovery of markets for European goods in general. Indeed, during the period of peace, the contraband trade that had become customary in wartime continued, and many foreign products continued to come directly from Jamaica. The performance of New Granada's exports to Spain was rather better. A breakdown of their composition, shown in Table 11.3, indicates both a substantial outflow of treasure and, more striking, a considerable growth in commodity exports.[26] The former was of course largely an outrush of specie that had been detained by war, some of which may well have been going in payment for contraband imports purchased with bills of exchange redeemable in Europe. The boom in commodity exports, which were substantially more valuable than in any of the previous peacetime years, also resulted from the release of stocks accumulated in wartime. Both were ephemeral. As soon as the truce ended, English privateers blockaded Cartagena, stationing themselves offshore for most of 1805.[27] Trade with Spain consequently slumped again in 1805, when the value of imports fell to around 275,534 pesos, and exports dropped even lower, to about 192,968 pesos.[28]

This was merely the prelude to a final collapse. Following Nelson's defeat of the Spanish navy at Trafalgar in October 1805, Spain's colonial commerce entered into its terminal phase. At Cádiz, imports and exports fell off sharply until, by 1807, trade with the Americas had reached its lowest point in a decade.[29] Meanwhile, the British, faced with the loss of European markets due to Napoleon's continental blockade, intensified their already determined efforts to penetrate Spanish American markets.[30]

26. Ibid., p. 98.
27. Amar y Borbón to governor of Popayán, October 17, 1805, "Archivo del Virrey Amar," *BHA*, vol. 32 (1945), p. 352.
28. AGI Santa Fe 960, "Estado General que manifiesta el Comercio de esta Plaza de Cartagena de Indias, correspondiente al año de 1805."
29. García-Baquero, *Comercio colonial y guerras revolucionarias*, pp. 175–83.
30. For a full account of these efforts, see Dorothy Goebel, "British Trade to the Spanish Colonies, 1796–1823," *American Historical Review*, vol. 43 (1938), pp. 288–320.

Table 11.3. *Exports from Cartagena, 1802–4*

Year	Gold and silver	Commodities (pesos)
1802	2,142,692	940,136
1803	935,800	618,581
1804	1,673,747	794,832
Total	4,752,239	2,353,552

From 1806, the British government devoted increasing attention to enlarging British trade with the colonies of its Spanish enemy, and, if pressures for military action against the Spanish Empire in America lost some of their force in these years, it was partly because, even while still dominated by Spain, the Spanish American market provided an increasingly valuable outlet for British trade and an essential source of bullion.[31]

In New Granada, the crown allowed a commerce with European neutrals to restart in 1805, but, although this allowed some exports of tropical products from Cartagena, *comercio neutral* was of no more significance than it had been during the previous war with Britain. In fact, contraband trade assumed even more formidable proportions when war restarted, and the colony's external commerce became still more firmly linked to British ports in the Caribbean, principally Jamaica. The extent of this clandestine commerce with the enemy is of course impossible to measure accurately, but in a confidential report of 1807 Viceroy Amar y Borbón freely admitted that it had become a large and well-organized traffic, facilitated by the involvement of merchants, the connivance of corrupt officials, and the provision of British naval protection. Amar y Borbón based his conclusions on intelligence received from a Spanish sea captain who had been captured by the British and taken to Jamaica, where he was briefly held prisoner. On returning to New Granada, the captain informed the authorities that the British ship that had seized his vessel had at the time been escorting two Spanish schooners to Sabanilla, a small port at the mouth of the River Magdalena, where they spent three days unloading their cargoes and taking on at least 800,000 pesos in gold. On returning to Jamaica with his captors, the Spaniard was held for a further five weeks, and during this time he had seen at least another eight Spanish vessels set sail for Sabanilla with contraband cargoes. The conclusion was plain. Regular cargoes of contraband were exported to Cartagena from an enemy colony, paid for by large amounts of bullion that were sent by merchants of the port in collusion with local officials.[32]

31. John Lynch, "British Policy and Spanish America 1783–1808," *JLAS*, vol. 1 (1969), pp. 1–30.
32. AGI Santa Fe 960, Amar y Borbón to Cayetano Soler, December 7, 1806 (reservado no. 10).

Viceroy Amar y Borbón, who had taken office in 1803, had no solution to the problem. He briefly closed the ports of New Granada in 1805, distributed a few licenses to individuals in Cartagena for trade with Cuba, and recommended stricter methods of policing the coast.[33] The licenses solved nothing. Those who did not get them resented those who did, and in 1805, the Consulado of Cartagena appealed directly to Spain for more tolerance of trade with foreigners, so that all its members could salvage their businesses.[34] Madrid was unsympathetic to the Consulado's petition. Indeed, in 1805, the Spanish government gave control of New Granada's commerce with neutrals to agents of the *Caja de Consolidación de Vales Reales,* the body set up to find new ways of financing war. Between 1805 and 1808, these agents dominated the small residue of New Granada's legal trade, trading with German merchants until 1807; later the British firm of Gordon-Murphy and Company was brought in to export bullion from Cartagena to Spain.[35] Neither of these expedients stopped the flow of contraband, however, and in 1807, *Contador General* Francisco Viana called for a radical rethinking of Spain's policy on New Granadan commerce. Viana pressed the Minister for the Indies to recognize that contraband was simply unavoidable while Spain prohibited importation from foreign sources of goods that the colonial consumer wanted but that Spain could not itself provide, and while Spain was unable to absorb all of New Granada's exports. He accordingly advised that the only means of reducing contraband was to permit a free commerce with the ports of neutral powers, organized by Spanish subjects and carried by national shipping.[36] Opening New Granada's trade to foreigners was, however, still unacceptable to the Council of the Indies. Fearful for the future of Spain's monopoly, it preferred to cling to the shreds of an unworkable policy, supporting the anticontraband measures that Viceroy Amar y Borbón had advocated the previous year.[37] Thus the interests of Cartagena's merchants and of New Granadan exporters were ignored by a Spanish government determined to defend a commercial system that had become demonstrably untenable.

For all the damage it did to Spanish commercial ties with New Granada, the derangement of Spain's mercantile system did not of itself endanger the stability of the colonial government, nor did it necessarily prefigure a deeper crisis in the colonial relationship. This was, after all, not the first time that war had cut New Granada's trade with Spain, and

33. Ibid.
34. AGI Santa Fe 960, Consulado to Secretario de Estado, October 20, 1805 (no. 27).
35. Jacques Barbier, "Commercial Reform and *Comercio Neutral* in Cartagena de Indias, 1788–1808," in Fisher, Kuethe, and McFarlane (eds.), *Reform and Insurrection,* pp. 116–20.
36. AGI Santa Fe 553. Viana to Cayetano Soler, Madrid, April 16, 1807.
37. AGI Santa Fe 960, Nota de la Mesa; ibid., Amar y Borbón to Cayetano Soler, December 17, 1806 (no. 489).

even the prolonged disruption that came after 1796 did not cause economic hardship in the colony as a whole. Unlike neighboring Venezuela, which depended heavily on exports of cacao and indigo, New Granada was not crippled by the loss of overseas export markets, because the export of agricultural commodities made a relatively small contribution to the overall balance of trade. Nor was the economy deprived of essential imports. Contraband was easily obtained in return for specie and consumers did not go short of European goods, which were abundantly provided by smugglers. Thus the economic costs inflicted by war did not induce widespread disaffection toward the colonial regime. Those who bore the brunt of commercial dislocation were in the small circle of merchants and producers who engaged in the import/export business, and they directed their complaints against metropolitan policy, not Spanish rule.

If the divergence between crown policy and colonial economic interests was insufficiently deep to destabilize the colonial regime, the reverberations of war nevertheless gradually weakened Spanish authority. For as Spain's strength was sapped by successive British victories, both at sea and on American territory (at Santo Domingo and Trinidad in the 1790s and at Buenos Aires in 1806), relations with Spain looked increasingly open to change; this in turn encouraged elements in New Granada's elite to see the colonial connection in a new light and to ponder the prospects for their own country in an uncertain world. Formulation of new views about the colonial system was, however, very gradual, and was not necessarily inimical to Spanish sovereignty. Indeed, although the economic connection with the metropolis was weakened by war, the political connection remained strong throughout the years of Anglo-Spanish war. War did of course resurrect the threat of subversion from secret adversaries of the colonial system but, as we shall now see, the threat proved slight. In the end, it was to be Spain's vertiginous collapse in 1808 that would create the conditions for New Granada's separation from the parent power, rather than the ideas and projects of heroic or far-sighted creole "precursors."

Wartime subversion and creole opinion

The absence of any significant internal threat to Spanish rule was clearly demonstrated early in the war in an episode involving Antonio Nariño, the *santafereño* creole who had been outlawed for his involvement with the supposed republican conspiracy of 1794. In 1797, the viceregal authorities were warned that Britain was backing exiled creoles, led by Francisco de Miranda and including Pedro Fermín de Vargas and Antonio Nariño, to instigate local revolts in Venezuela and New Granada, prior to a British attack.[38] In the event, the threat proved illusory. After landing in Ven-

---

38. Blossom, *Nariño*, pp. 36–40. A contemporary view of the danger to New Granada, given by an

ezuela, Antonio Nariño did indeed return to New Granada, where he reconnoitered the area of Tunja, Vélez, and Girón with a view to raising a revolution against Spain. However, he quickly came to the conclusion that, though the common people were discontented with taxation, they were unable to conceive of a general assault on the government. Hunted by his old enemies, who were led by Oidor Hernández de Alba, Nariño finally despaired of his plans and, in mid-July 1797, surrendered to the authorities.[39]

The authorities feared that Nariño's incursion was part of a wider plan, and Hernández de Alba accordingly continued to search for the slightest sign of subversion. Official suspicions were heightened in August 1797, when the authorities in Tunja discovered some seditious papers, including a pasquinade against Spaniards and the colony's government. Oidor Hernández de Alba quickly organized an intensive pursuit of their supposed author, Manuel Vicente Prieto, a native of Caloto and erstwhile acquaintance of Pedro Fermín de Vargas. Prieto took flight to avoid arrest, but was eventually captured in the province of Neiva in mid-September and subsequently imprisoned in Bogotá. When interrogated by Hernández de Alba, he admitted writing the pasquinade but he did not confess to complicity in Nariño's project. Prieto seems to have heard rumors of Nariño's movements and knew of his arrest, but no direct link between them was proved, nor was it likely. Prieto was nevertheless arraigned for treason, as well as for unconnected crimes of robbery and attempted murder, and as late as 1804 he was still imprisoned in Bogotá, awaiting judgment from the Council of the Indies.[40]

With the capture of Nariño and Prieto, New Granada's authorities eliminated the threat of insurrection. As in 1794, when Spain was at war with France, government anxiety about internal subversion in 1797 had been magnified by fears that a foreign power, this time Britain, was using American revolutionaries as a vanguard for attacking the empire. But, if the authorities' apprehension concerning British intentions was justified, (the British governor of Trinidad did support a conspiracy to subvert Venezuela in 1798–9), in reality the prospects of an anti-Spanish uprising in New Granada were slight. Nariño quickly discovered that New Granada was not ripe for revolution and, although the authorities remained vigilant, they had no further cause for alarm.

oidor of the audiencia de Santa Fe, is found in the report of the Conde de Torre Velarde (Santa Fe, July 19, 1797), included in S. E. Ortíz (ed.), *Colección de Documentos para la Historia de Colombia* (Bogotá, 1965), pp. 13–23. On British plans, see John Lynch, "British Policy and Spanish America, 1783–1808," pp. 11–14.

39. Gómez Hoyos, *La Revolución Granadina*, vol. 1, pp. 238–9: Blossom, *Nariño*, pp. 39–45.

40. AHNM, Consejos 21,228. Criminales contra Don Manuel Vicente Prieto por un papel sedicioso contra el Estado y Gobierno, Quadernos 1–5.

As for Nariño, he was completely neutralized. Indeed, having failed to bring about change through revolution, Nariño turned back to the crown as an instrument for material and political progress. Once arrested, he made his peace with the authorities by candidly confessing to his activities in Europe and abjuring his revolutionary convictions, and, encouraged by Viceroy Mendinueta, attempted to speed his rehabilitation with an account of administrative reforms that he thought necessary to secure public confidence in the monarchy. In this report, written in hope of receiving clemency from the government, he advocated the suppression of the alcabala, the reform of the tobacco and aguardiente monopolies, the introduction of a capitation tax levied at a standard rate, and the introduction of tariffs that would favor agricultural exports, all of which he presented as measures essential for the development of New Granada.[41] The promise of political rehabilitation was unfulfilled, however. For another six years, Madrid insisted that the authorities keep Nariño in prison, until his declining health finally persuaded Viceroy Mendinueta to override royal orders and allow him a conditional freedom.[42]

Clearly, New Granada was not ready for revolutionary insurrection in the late 1790s, nor were there any further signs of internal sedition during the decade after the imprisonment of Nariño and Prieto. The fate of these men no doubt served as a deterrent to dissent, but it is unlikely that many creoles had as yet cast off loyalty to the Spanish monarchy. Nevertheless, if Spanish sovereignty was still an apparently unshakable axiom of New Granada's political culture, acceptance of the colonial political system did not prevent an educated minority from exploring and expressing ideas that contained the germs of an alternative. For although the *Papel Periódico* ceased publication in 1797, the creole spirit of criticism that it had embodied remained alive in other forms of association and publication.

Shortly after Humboldt's visit to New Granada in 1801, the *Tertulia del Buen Gusto* was established in Bogotá under the patronage of Manuela Sanz Santamaría de Manrique, a wealthy *santafereña* who had an interest in science and literature, and who was the mother of Angel Manrique, a youth who had been implicated in the conspiracy of 1794. The young creoles who attended the *tertulia* were ostensibly concerned with literature and the cultivation of artistic taste, in imitation of the aristocratic salons of Paris and Lima. Although there were "prudent men" who suspected the *tertulia* dealt in subversive political ideas, the government of the day saw no harm in such activity.[43] It is nonetheless worth noting that this asso-

41. Antonio Nariño, "Ensayo sobre un nuevo plan de administración en el Neuvo Reino de Granada," in José María Vergara y Vergara, *Vida y escritos del General Antonio Nariño* (Bogotá, 1946), pp. 67–92.

42. Blossom, *Nariño*, pp. 45–64.

43. The allusion to "prudent men" and doubts about the true purpose of the tertulia were made by

ciation attracted men like Camilo Torres, José Montalvo, José María Salazar, José Fernández Madrid, and the brothers Frutos and José María Gutiérrez, all of whom were later involved in the movement toward independence.

The revival of creole cultural and scientific association was also reflected in the foundation, in 1801, of the *Correo Curioso, Erudito, Económico y Mercantil*. This journal, which was dedicated to discussions of scientific, literary, and economic matters, was created by Jorge Tadeo Lozano and the priest José Luis de Azuola y Lozano, both of whom were from elite *santafereño* families that had long been prominent in public affairs. The former was the son of José María Lozano, who had been suspected of subversion in 1794, and grandson of Jorge Miguel Lozano de Peralta, the Marqués de San Jorge who had fallen foul of the authorities during the 1780s. The latter was connected through his mother to the Lozano and Caicedo clans and through his father to the main branch of the Azuola family, which was in turn connected through marriage to other leading *santafereña* families.[44] In its content, the *Correo Curioso* seems politically anodyne. However, behind essays such as those that stated "the need for a currency," or extolled on "that which is needed and not needed in New Granada," or called for means to stimulate colonial commerce, or pressed for the establishment of a "Patriotic Commercial Company" and an Economic Society, stood a concern to define and propagate issues from a New Granadan perspective and to assert a social and intellectual identity separate from that of Spain.[45]

In 1806, another journal added to the sources of information available to creoles, when Manuel del Socorro Rodríguez, previously editor of the *Papel Periódico*, started to publish the fortnightly *El Redactor Americano*, together with a monthly supplement. Again, the content was mainly of a general and literary kind, but the paper also disseminated news of events in Europe and eulogized Napoleon in a manner that enraged Spanish conservatives like José Antonio de Torres y Peña.[46] Finally, in January 1808, the creole Francisco José de Caldas, the most brilliant and distinguished of New Granadan scientists to emerge from Mutis's circle, started publication of the *Semanario del Nuevo Reino de Granada*, yet another journal dedicated to diffusing "useful knowledge" for the common good. Its long discourses on economic, demographic, geographical, and climatic

the Spanish cleric, José Antonio de Torres y Peña. See his *Memorias sobre los orígenes de la independencia nacional*, p. 77.

44. On the Azuola family and its connections, see Restrepo Saenz and Rivas, *Genealogías de Santa Fe de Bogotá*, vol. 1, pp. 74–9.

45. Biblioteca Nacional de Colombia, Fondo Quijano Otero, no. 58. *Correo Curioso*, nos. 17, 18, 22, 39, 40, 41, 42.

46. Torres y Peña, *Memorias*, p. 77.

matters were also less politically innocent than they seem, for in such concerns we can again detect the outlines of a nascent creole patriotism identified with the provinces of New Granada.[47] Indeed, when the editor commented on an article by Joaquín Camacho describing the province of Pamplona, he clearly alluded to New Granada's future as a nation. Reflecting on Camacho's dictum that "nothing is great when born," Caldas asserted that "all nations have had their infancy and their epoch of stupidity and barbarity. We have just been born. . . ."; he then proceeded to call upon "our compatriots, those who truly love their country, those who long for the enlightenment and happiness of the Kingdom of New Granada . . . to keep alight the sparks and the dim lights which we have so far acquired . . ." In another coded remark, the writer observed that "if an imprudent father . . . demands of a child the firm step of an adult, if he punishes it harshly and severely for each badly-pronounced syllable, he will ruin it in the cradle, and far from forming a man useful to his country, will make a timid and useless citizen."[48] For the politically attuned creole reader, the analogy with Spanish government can hardly have passed unnoticed. Furthermore, the notion of the New Granadan as "citizen," rather than subject, suggests that in the years when Spain realigned itself alongside France and became embroiled in a war that steadily undermined the Spanish Atlantic economy, analysis of the condition of New Granada, with its related emphasis on the need to advance science, to reform education, and to promote the material prosperity of the country, had taken on an increasingly obvious political connotation. This did not mean that creoles were preparing for independence, but it does show that the maturing generation of educated creoles was developing views that, by providing a critical perspective on the traditional colonial order, were to help them repudiate that order when it crumbled under the pressures of war.

Creole criticism of the Spanish commercial system

Another current of criticism that developed during these years stemmed from economic, particularly commercial, interests in New Granada. It came first from Cartagena, where members of the city's mercantile establishment clashed with the authorities over commercial policy. Initially, mercantile complaints about the damage done by war was limited to a demand for palliatives, in the form of special licenses for trade with neutral and foreign colonies. However, from 1800, José Ignacio de Pom-

---

47. For these examples, see Francisco José de Caldas, *Semanario del Nuevo de Granada*, vol. 2 (Bogotá, 1942 ed.).

48. Ibid., pp. 18–19.

bo, a prominent merchant of Cartagena, voiced more open criticisms of
government economic policy, criticisms that eventually led him to advocate radical and wide-ranging change of Spain's increasingly decrepit colonial system.

At first, his proposals for changing the system were modest enough. In
a report that he submitted to Madrid on behalf of the Consulado in 1800,
Pombo described the dramatic decline of Cartagena's trade with Spain
during wartime, and urged the crown to allow unrestricted commerce
with neutral and friendly nations as the only effective means of preventing
a complete takeover by British contraband. This unexceptional proposal
was, however, accompanied by strong criticism of the viceroy for his
failure to allow such trade, and by the suggestion of a contractual basis to
Spain's monopoly. "The metropolis," Pombo argued, "is responsible for
supplying its colonies with all they need . . . and exporting all the fruits
and products of its soil . . . (and) only by discharging completely this
duty . . . should it enjoy the privilege of an exclusive commerce."[49]

A few years later, when trade failed to recover during the Peace of
Amiens, Pombo widened his attack from criticism of the imperfections of
royal policy into a more generalized critique of Spanish economic policy.
In 1804, he wrote a long and detailed denunciation of the institutional
demoralization and economic distortions caused by contraband.[50] Pombo
bluntly blamed the advance of contraband on a corrupt government,
observing that measures to prevent contraband were practically useless in
a land where "the laws and rights of the citizen are so little respected."[51]
From this premise, he then proceeded to analyze New Granada's trade
with a barrage of statistics, and to suggest measures for removing the
obstacles that "nature, government and ignorance" placed in the way of
developing New Granada, "the richest in all kinds of natural products of
all the American possessions of the Spanish Monarchy."[52] His proposals
attacked the very core of the traditional Spanish colonial system. To
stimulate the economy, he called for investment by the Royal Treasury to
improve transport and communication in New Granada, and he advocated
reducing fiscal impositions on trade and abolishing the royal monopolies
of aguardiente and tobacco. To advance agriculture, he favored ending
Indian tribute, distributing land among the Indians, redistributing unused lands among those who had none, and encouraging immigration of
foreign Catholics to establish new rural settlements. Pombo's suggestions
for political reform were even more radical. He wanted abolition of the
slave trade, an end to slavery and measures to promote the union and

49. Pombo, *Comercio y contrabando en Cartagena de Indias*, p. 32.
50. For this document, dated March 12, 1804, see ibid., pp. 49–122.
51. Ibid., p. 50.   52. Ibid., p. 56.

mixture of all the "castes," to create a single class of citizens. His espousal of the economic doctrines of the Spanish Enlightenment also shines through his insistence on the need to reform the church, by limiting the property that it held in mortmain, regulating the parish clergy, and reforming, even extinguishing, monastic institutions. Educational reform was another priority learned from the Enlightenment. Pombo called for the establishment of printing presses, public newspapers, and patriotic societies in the capital and provinces; he recommended establishing primary and agricultural schools, schools of drawing, mathematics, biology, medicine, and so on, together with a public university to teach the "divine and human sciences."[53]

Summarizing his plans, Pombo enumerated eight points for the immediate attention of government. These were, first, a purge of governors and officials in the maritime provinces to combat contraband and corruption; second, a reduction of duties on imports of foreign manufactures and the use of tariffs as an instrument of economic rather than fiscal policy; third, an end to the slave trade, which simply enriched the British at Spain's expense, and the replacement of slavery by free immigration of European Catholics. Then, with three proposals designed specifically to tackle the problem of smuggling, Pombo ended his report with a recommendation that government by intendants and subdelegates be introduced into New Granada, particularly in the ports, where these officials might provide a fair and efficient alternative to the military governors.[54]

Pombo's extraordinary program for reform, a program that clearly reflected the influence of liberal Spanish and foreign political economists, was of course disregarded by Madrid. It is, nonetheless, very interesting because it suggests that by the early 1800s leading creoles were becoming deeply disillusioned with the traditional colonial system. For such men, Spain was no longer a source of ideas or a model for imperial rule. When Pombo submitted a shorter version of this report to the crown in 1807, reiterating many of the points made in his 1804 broadside, he referred to his wide reading of books by foreign as well as Spanish economists in his search for a means to awaken New Granadan agriculture from "the deep lethargy in which it is buried."[55] He even suggested that the United States was an example of economic development that New Granada might follow, should royal policy permit. "In the United States of North America," he pointedly observed, "there are no monopolies, no sales taxes, no tithes, nor any tax on agriculture, either when sown, harvested, sold, consumed or exported abroad; and yet the revenues of the public treasury

53. Ibid., pp. 57–8.   54. Ibid., pp. 71–101.
55. This document, dated April 18, 1807, is printed in Ortíz (ed.), *Escritos de dos economistas coloniales*, pp. 123–34. Quotation from p. 134.

are currently in excess of 12 million pesos."[56] But if Pombo was influenced by economic liberalism, his commitment to it was not complete nor unreserved, and the crown was evidently still regarded as the essential agency for promoting change. Thus, though Pombo was drawing up an agenda for reform that would later provide the economic ideology of a new political order after 1810, while Spain continued to function as a metropolitan state, such ideas reflected desire for change within the imperial system, rather than an ambition to break away from it.

The campaign against Spanish mercantile privilege

José Ignacio de Pombo's commitment to reform, which he voiced in the name of the Consulado, was not shared by all the merchant community in Cartagena. Although he had become a wealthy merchant in Cartagena and, through his marriage into the rich and influential Dios Amador family, had entered the Cartagena patriciate, Pombo was in many ways an exceptional figure among the merchants of Cartagena. The son of a prominent creole family of Popayán, he had been educated at the Colegio del Rosario in Bogotá and had subsequently become an aficionado of modern science and a devotee of economic progress, and was closely connected to Mutis and his protegés in Bogotá. He not only maintained contact with Mutis and his circle (acting as patron to Francisco José de Caldas, among others); in 1801, he also befriended Humboldt on the latter's visit to Cartagena and, as a member of Cartagena's Consulado, became an assiduous advocate of policies for advancing New Granada's material and cultural life.[57] His ideas therefore probably had more in common with the "enlightened" creole minority of the capital than with the peninsular businessmen of the *cartagenero* mercantile elite. Certainly, the internal affairs of the Consulado, which can be reconstructed from its archive, suggest that the merchant guild was deeply divided, particularly during its formative years, when Pombo's brother Manuel was treasurer.

Early signs of tension are found in an apparently trivial dispute started by José de Arrazola y Ugarte, a Spanish merchant who was employed as the Consulado's accountant. In 1797, Arrazola y Ugarte complained that he was inadequately paid for his work, and that the prior and consuls did not accord to him or his fellow officers, the secretary and the treasurer, the treatment that their positions merited.[58] He also alleged that the paid officers were excluded from their rightful role in decision making and

56. Ibid., p. 125.
57. On José Ignacio de Pombo, see Gómez Hoyos, *La Revolución Granadina*, vol. 2, pp. 250–300. His most important writings on commercial policy are printed in Pombo, *Comercio y Contrabando en Cartagena de Indias*, and S. E. Ortíz (ed.), *Escritos de dos economistas coloniales*, pp. 121–269.
58. AGI Santa Fe 958, Contador to Secretario del Estado, May 1, 1797.

prevented from participating with the governing junta in the Consulado's financial affairs.[59] Whatever the original cause of this dispute, it took on a new complexion when the treasurer, Manuel de Pombo, joined with Arrazola y Ugarte in opposing the prior and governing junta. Pombo not only accused them of avaricious self-regard in the payment of salaries from Consulado funds, but he also deplored their apathetic and unenlightened attitude to the Consulado's responsibilities in the field of economic development. According to Pombo, the prior represented a faction that was concerned only with its own self-interest, and he blamed them for the signal lack of progress that the institution had made toward its prescribed goals of promoting the colony's commerce and economic development.[60]

With this trenchant attack on the ruling circle, Pombo emerged as its most vocal and persistent critic. During his six years as treasurer, up to the time that he was sacked in 1804, Manuel de Pombo constantly drew attention to the junta's apathetic attitude and its mismanagement of consular funds; more important, he also tried to increase creole influence within the Consulado by bringing in hacendados to represent the local landed interest, and by seeking to secure preference for the full-time officials in the *junta de gobierno*, together with voting rights in the annual elections.[61] In the end, Pombo's determination to shift power from the peninsular mercantile establishment came to nothing. His colleague, Arrazola y Ugarte, was removed from office amidst bitter recrimination in 1799, and Pombo's attempts to bring local landowners into active participation in the Consulado were frustrated by the governing junta.[62] And, finally, Manuel de Pombo was defeated by his opponents in 1804, when he refused to accept bills for routine expenses on the grounds that he had been excluded from the decisions that had approved them.[63] Faced with this defiance, the elected officers and consuls of the Consulado accused Pombo of undermining order by spreading "perverse ideas," creating disturbances, carrying arms at meetings, and victimizing certain merchants. Pombo vigorously denied these accusations and, contrasting his own devotion to duty with the indifferent records of his accusers, asserted it was his very zeal and efficiency that offended the hide-bound clique that ran the

59. Ibid.; and AGI Santa Fe 959, Conde de Casavalencia to Consulado, January 9, 1801.
60. AGI Santa Fe 958, Manuel de Pombo to Secretario del Estado, May 7, 1797.
61. AGI Santa Fe 958, Consulado to Secretario del Estado, March 31, 1798. By the Royal Order of November 21, 1797, the Consulado had been required to elect three hacendados (as a consul and two councillors), but it pleaded that not only were there few hacendados of sufficient social stature for these posts, but those who resided on their haciendas could not properly discharge their duties: AGI Santa Fe 959, Consulado to Secretario del Estado, November 1, 1799.
62. AGI Santa Fe 958, Consulado to Secretario del Estado, March 4, 1799; Consejo de Indias, July 23, 1799.
63. AGI Santa Fe 959, Consulado to Ministro de Hacienda, June 30, 1803; ibid., Manuel de Pombo to Cayetano Soler, July 2, 1803.

Consulado.[64] By now, however, Pombo was labeled as a troublemaker by the governor of Cartagena and, at the governor's insistence, he was forced to leave the city for a politically less sensitive post as an official of the Casa de Moneda in Bogotá, where he could also be more closely supervised by the viceregal authorities.[65]

Tranquility did not immediately return to the Consulado with Pombo's departure for the capital, because an acrimonious dispute broke out over the choice of his successor.[66] However, it seems that the peninsular mercantile establishment had regained the upper hand, as the Consulado relapsed into a quiet period, characterized by apathy among its members and absenteeism among its officials. In 1804, the first attempt to hold an election for offices vacant in the Consulado failed to attract the necessary quorum of sixteen voters.[67] When elected, members attended to their duties infrequently and subsequently treated the Consulado with little respect.[68] In 1809, the prior noted that absenteeism had become such an entrenched problem that only disciplinary measures against certain individuals could compel them to attend to their duties.[69]

In these circumstances, the Consulado failed to become a beacon for promoting economic development in New Granada. Although it investigated and discussed schemes designed to improve transport and communication, its projects either came to nothing or were so minor that they had no significant effect on New Granada's economic life. In 1802, the Consulado reported that it had improved a channel at the mouth of the Magdalena River but, as the work cost a mere 500 pesos, it was obviously not of much consequence.[70] In 1804, the Consulado reported that it had concluded improvements to the wharf in Cartagena, but again the minimal cost of the operation indicates that it was of marginal importance.[71] More typical of the Consulado's approach to public works was its attitude to a scheme for the improvement of port facilities in Guayaquil. Although the Consulado gave verbal support to the project, it was not prepared to finance it, and recommended instead that a special tax be raised in Guayaquil for that purpose.[72] Other proposals from the provinces of the interior met with a similar response. The Consulado invariably pleaded that it

64. Ibid., Manuel de Pombo to Secretario del Estado, March 12, 1804.
65. AGI Santa Fe 1016, Governor Cejudo to Cayetano Soler, June 30, 1802.
66. AGI Santa Fe 959, Consulado to Secretario del Estado, August 20, 1804.
67. AGI Santa Fe 1016, Governor Cejudo to Cayetano Soler, February 5, 1804.
68. AGI Santa Fe 958, Joseph Antonio Mosquera, October 2, 1799; AGI Santa Fe 1016, governor of Cartagena to Cayetano Soler, June 30, 1802; ibid., February 5, 1804; AGI Santa Fe 657, Joseph Antonio Mosquera, September 1, 1809.
69. AGI Santa Fe 657, Joseph Antonio Mosquera, September 1, 1809.
70. AGI Santa Fe 959, Consulado to Secretario del Estado, September 1, 1802.
71. Ibid., December 20, 1804.   72. Ibid., July 31, 1802.

lacked the funds necessary to undertake the schemes put before it, however practical and useful they might appear. Indeed, the cabildo of Santa Marta found it so difficult to enlist the Consulado's cooperation that it petitioned the crown for the right to assume control of the duty levied to support the mercantile guild, so that the cabildo might undertake the work proposed on its own initiative.[73]

The Consulado's reluctance to act as an agency for economic development also led it to neglect other projects for which it had been given specific responsibility in its charter. Work on the routes connecting Bogotá and its neighboring towns with the River Magdalena – via the trails of Opón, Carare, and Otro Mundo – was never even started. After more than a decade of inactivity, the Consulado continued to ignore or resist proposals for opening and improving these routes, continually quibbling over the costs entailed.[74] Even in the case of the Canal del Dique, the Consulado was slow to act, despite the fact that navigation by this channel lowered costs of transportation between Cartagena and the main course of the River Magdalena. Only after the cabildo of Cartagena agreed to provide 20,000 pesos of the 100,000 pesos required for work on the Dique did the Consulado accept its responsibilities in this area.[75] It then used the costs of this task as an excuse for neglecting others.[76]

Dilatoriness in discharging its duties was partly due to the Consulado's poor financial condition. When reviewing its performance in 1808, Consulado officers insisted that the disruption of trade by war had restricted its income and thereby inhibited expenditure on public works.[77] This was not an unreasonable excuse because, as we have seen, Spain's trade with New Granada contracted dramatically during the two Anglo-Spanish wars of 1796–1802 and 1804–8. This excuse was, however, viewed with considerable skepticism in some quarters. Not only did internal critics like Manuel de Pombo denounce the leadership of the Consulado for its lack of public spirit, but after the turn of the century commercial interests in the interior of New Granada also criticized its indolent and unimaginative attitude toward the economic needs of the colony. These were in part simply jurisdictional disputes of a kind common to colonial politics; however, taken together, they reflect a widening creole dissatisfaction with Spain's system of trade and its economic policies.

The center for opposition to Cartagena was in Bogotá, where, after 1796, a small group of merchants campaigned for an independent consul-

73. AGI Santa Fe 552, Informe on petition of Cabildo of Santa Marta, December 4, 1804.
74. AGI Santa Fe 960, Consulado to Secretario del Estado, June 30, 1808.
75. Antonio Ybot León, *La artería histórica del Nuevo Reino de Granada* (Bogotá, 1952), pp. 227–8.
76. AGI Santa Fe 960, Consulado to Secretario del Estado, June 30, 1808.
77. Ibid.

ado, which would represent the interests of the interior.[78] Several concessions were made to them over matters of jurisdiction and rights of appeal
in mercantile cases, but in 1804 the pressures for the establishment of a
consulado in Santa Fe, either in addition to or in place of that in Cartagena, were revived in a strong and coordinated series of petitions from
merchants in various towns of the interior. In March 1804, the merchants
of Antioquia informed the viceroy that their trade was being damaged by
the Consulado's failure to take any action to stimulate trade within the
interior, and by unfair treatment in the port's commercial court. Most of
the Antioquian merchants engaged in the redistribution of imports were,
they said, creditors of businessmen in Cartagena and therefore could not
expect an unbiased hearing in its mercantile courts. The Antioquians
argued that such conflicts of interest were less likely to arise if cases were
brought before the *Tribunal de Alzadas* in Bogotá, and they accordingly
appealed for inclusion within the jurisdiction of the tribunal in the capital. Support for their request came from Viceroy Amar y Borbón, from the
merchants of Santa Fe, and from the *Tribunal de Alzadas* itself, for they all
accepted that the traders of the interior should not have to depend on the
distant and potentially biased court of Cartagena.[79] Within a short time,
these claims were incorporated into a broader campaign for the transfer of
the Consulado from Cartagena to Santa Fe de Bogotá.

The leader of this campaign was the creole merchant José Acevedo y
Gómez, a native of Charalá in the Socorro region and a man who was later
to achieve political prominence in the overthrow of the royal government
in Bogotá in 1810. Supported by the petitions of merchants and cabildos
in surrounding towns, Acevedo y Gómez vigorously denounced the Cartagena Consulado for failing to promote the colony's economic and commercial development, and he suggested that Cartagena's domination of
New Granada's external trade actively impeded that development. Referring first to the growth of population over the previous fifty years and to
the increase in internal trade and production that this had stimulated,
Acevedo y Gómez stressed the need to establish a consulado in the capital
in order to encourage exploitation of internal resources. It was essential,
he argued, that some means be found for promoting the development of "a
useful and continuous communication between the Metropolis and its
colony, and between the colony's ports and the towns of the interior." In
his view, the merchants of Cartagena had proved entirely unsuited to the
achievement of this end. First, their Consulado had continually neglected
public works that would have improved links between the interior of the

---

78. See AHNC Miscelanea, tomo 13, fols. 1–58; AGI Santa Fe 959, Los diputados del Comercio de
    Santafé, Madrid, January 17, 1801.
79. Ibid., fols. 892, 894; AGI Santa Fe 959, Amar y Borbón to Cayetano Soler, Santafé, May 19,
    1804.

colony and the markets of the metropolis; second, its revenues had been squandered on the construction of a road that served no other purpose than to connect the homes of rich merchants in Cartagena with their country homes and "pleasure houses" in the resort of Turbaco. Meanwhile, the areas of Socorro, Tunja, and Pamplona, areas rich in agricultural and mineral resources, were deprived of the assistance essential to the development of an export trade in their products.[80]

The report presented by the town of Socorro supported Bogotá's petition for an independent Consulado with a strongly worded attack on the monopoly accorded to the port by the Spanish mercantile system. According to the cabildo of Socorro, Cartagena merchants had no reason to promote an active trade or to encourage agriculture, because "their fortunes [are] assured by possession of the exclusive privilege of supplying the internal provinces of the Kingdom with the European merchandise which they require, at whatever price they care to ask. . . ."[81] The cabildos of both Santa Fe de Bogotá and San Gil repeated similar complaints about the Cartagena merchants' lack of interest in the products, internal trade, and communications of the interior of New Granada. The former observed, with a touch of sarcasm, that for ten years the Cartagena Consulado had not given any thought to fulfilling the duties placed upon it by the king, and had displayed a propensity for neglect that, in men who were particularly involved in commerce, could hardly be excused by ignorance of the problems of the interior of the colony.[82]

These arguments were given added impetus by representations from the towns of Tunja, Pamplona, and Purificación, and the whole campaign was supported by the viceroy. Viceroy Amar y Borbón, a man who tended to bend to strong opinion, not only confirmed complaints about the Consulado's inaction in the area of transportation improvements; he also airily suggested that the geographical and climatic disadvantages of the port of Cartagena made it an inappropriate site for a consulado, particularly because the port was a mere entrepôt "limited to a commission business in imports and exports to the metropolis."[83] In a later communication to the royal authorities, Acevedo y Gómez repeated these arguments and added that the character of the port's mercantile community precluded it from exercising an effective function in the colony's economic development. Because almost all the members of the Consulado were factors of commer-

80. AGI Santa Fe 960, El diputado de comercio de Santafé de Bogotá to Cayetano Soler, November 19, 1804.

81. Ibid., Viceroy Amar y Borbón to Cayetano Soler, Santa Fe, September 19, 1805, enclosure no. 2, Informe del Villa del Socorro. See also AHNC Consulados, tomo 1, fols. 624–7.

82. AHNC Consulados, tomo 1, fol. 628. For the petition of San Gil, see AGI Santa Fe 960, representación del Cabildo de San Gil, Sala Capitular de la Villa de San Gil, July 6, 1804.

83. Ibid., Viceroy Amar y Borbón to Miguel Cayetano Soler, Santa Fe, September 19, 1805.

cial houses in Cádiz, Acevedo y Gómez argued, they remained only for the time needed to make sufficient money to escape from the disagreeable climate of Cartagena. For the same reason, they were totally divorced from interest in, or attachment to the country, lacked either the physical or moral motives that were required to fulfill the aims of the Consulado, and merely used the offices of the Consulado to distribute the salaries attached to its appointments.[84]

Such expressions of dissatisfaction did not succeed in changing crown policy, despite support from the viceroy. This is hardly surprising, because while Spain was at war, adjustments to commercial institutions in New Granada were of minor concern to metropolitan governments preoccupied with larger, more pressing military and financial problems. However, we should not overlook the significance of the issue within New Granada itself. Criticism of Cartagena's merchants and Consulado reflected a growing awareness that Spanish mercantile organization failed to meet the needs of economic interests in the interior and, more important, it also voiced the creole opinion that Spanish merchants and institutions were responsible for that failure.

Seen in retrospect, the failure of Cartagena's merchants to promote colonial interests by expanding the colony's commerce is perfectly understandable. Located at considerable distance from the major population centers and agricultural zones of the interior, Cartagena's merchants simply had no strong reasons for breaking away from the traditional "passive" commerce based on exploiting New Granada's markets for European imports in exchange for gold. The sheer distance between producers and ports, combined with high internal transport costs, put New Granada at a competitive disadvantage compared to other areas in the Americas. Tropical commodities such as sugar, cacao, tobacco, and cotton could all be more easily exported from places that were better positioned to connect with maritime trade routes, such as Cuba or Caracas, not to mention the foreign colonies that also supplied Spain with agricultural exports. Small wonder, then, that Cartagena's merchants continued to take their profits primarily from selling imported European merchandise, for which New Granada's mines and mints provided a perfectly adequate return in the form of gold. Nevertheless, the passivity of Cartagena's merchants and the inertia of their Consulado made them easy targets for creole criticism, and this criticism, combined with aspirations for an autonomous merchant guild, suggests that the breakdown of legal trade during wartime had heightened creole perceptions of the underlying divisions between colonial and metropolitan economic interests. Indeed, in deploring the Cartagena merchants' lack of commitment to the colony, Acevedo y Gómez

84. Ibid., El diputado consular de Santafé to Miguel Cayetano Soler, Santafé, October 7, 1805.

expressed the view, found in other creole commentators of the period, that New Granada was a community with an interest and identity of its own, different from that of Spain and her merchants.

The complaints about Cartagena's merchants and Consulado that emanated from the towns and regions of the interior are therefore significant in several respects. By berating the Consulado, its detractors expressed dislike of the domination of New Granada's overseas trade by peninsulars, and thus voiced their dissatisfaction with the Spanish commercial system. By emphasizing the need to develop the resources of the interior, the campaign for a consulado in Bogotá echoed views expressed in the circles of enlightened creole intellectuals and spread these ideas beyond the *tertulias* of the capital. By drawing together towns in the interior against Cartagena, the campaign also showed that creoles in Bogotá could build a network for practical political action that spread beyond the capital into neighboring provinces. None of this meant that creoles who criticized Spanish policy and institutions were contemplating, let alone planning, independence from Spain. The decay of Spanish mercantilism encouraged some New Granadans to entertain ideas that were later to help them perceive a life outside the Spanish empire, but while the monarchy remained intact, such critics remained firmly within the boundaries of the existing political system, framing their claims in terms of the institutional procedures and practices of the colonial order, and appealing to the authority of the king as arbiter. The emergence of a community of creole opinion concerned with changing the Spanish mercantile system should not, therefore, be confused with the creation of a subterranean political network dedicated to independence. What, then, was the overall effect of Spain's wartime reverses on the political situation in New Granada?

The damage of war

On balance, war weakened Spanish authority in New Granada in two ways. While British naval and commercial assault progressively ruined the Spanish economic system during the Anglo-Spanish war of 1805–8, the fiscal demands and military reverses of war also inflicted political damage on the prestige of the monarchy, both at home and abroad. In Spain itself, the alliance with France forced the government into a deepening fiscal and political crisis that added to the problems caused by Charles IV's inertia and Godoy's venality. And, if the Spanish priest José Antonio de Torres y Peña is to be believed, Spain's war in alliance with France also undermined respect for government in New Granada. According to Torres y Peña, the alliance with revolutionary France was from the outset an aberration that undermined Spain's stature and authority. First, he argued, it helped to sow discord by allowing Frenchmen and French ideas to enter New Granada, thereby promoting interest in "unjust ideas" inimical to royal authority; second, it caused dismay among "all men of honour, whether Europeans or Americans," by giving rise to the amortization decree that attacked church property; third, the unhappy state of the monarchy under the influence of Godoy and France undermined confidence in the representatives sent from Spain, tainting them with the scent of corruption. In New Granada, said Torres y Peña, this had directly damaged the authority of the viceroy, lending weight to pernicious rumors that Viceroy Amar y Borbón, a Godoy appointee, was a venal and self-serving vendor of public office, who was unconcerned with the interests of the country he governed. Torres y Peña also asserted that the loss of Santo Domingo, caused by Spain's involvement with France, had exposed the vulnerability of the empire; after this event, he recalled that, in New Granada, "all men of good judgment feared that as the island of Española was the first stone dislodged from this vast edifice [of empire] to satisfy French ambition, it would not be long before the same happened to the *Nuevo Reino.* . . . "[85]

Looking back over the period between 1796 and 1808, there are good reasons for believing that Torres y Peña was right when, in 1814, he detected the symptoms of underlying crisis in events that took place years before the overthrow of the royal government in New Granada. For although there were no serious challenges to the colonial government from its subjects in New Granada (Nariño's adventure of 1797 being merely a quixotic gamble), the standing of the colonial regime had been steadily and subtly eroded by the reverberations of international war. When war destroyed the colony's economic connection to Spain, the metropolitan government further undermined its credibility by failing to find means to protect the colonial interests injured by the collapse of transatlantic commerce. Indeed, by sustaining the irrelevant rules of a mercantilist monopoly shattered by contraband, it simply encouraged colonials to turn to the enemy for a contraband trade that, by corrupting officials, further undermined respect for the government. During the prolonged alliance with France, New Granada's creole enlightenment was also able to flourish. Between 1792 and 1808, Madrid revived the reform projects of leading Spanish liberals in an effort to strengthen the Spanish economy for war, thereby giving renewed respectability to ideas that had been fiercely suppressed in the counterrevolutionary struggle with France during the first years of the decade. And as liberalism revived in Spain, so it gathered fresh force in New Granada. Not only did the events of war stimulate creole interest in international affairs (an interest fed by the circulation of both Spanish and foreign newspapers and gazettes), but it also allowed

85. Torres y Peña, *Memorias*, pp. 77–80.

creoles to revive their interest in the enlightened ideas that they had been encouraged to adopt by Archbishop-Viceroy Caballero y Góngora during the 1780s. Thus, the small educated elite that had imbibed the influences of modern science and philosophy through their associations with the Colegio del Rosario and educational reforms in the late 1770s and 1780s, and through connections to the Botanical Expedition during the 1780s and 1790s, were able openly to resume discussion of ideas that were implicitly critical of the established Hispanic political and economic order.

Such ideas did not of course make revolutionaries, let alone a revolution. They did, however, sharpen creole perceptions of the flaws in the colonial order, so that when the monarchy was engulfed by the great political storm that broke over the empire during and after 1808, there was a creole intellectual leadership ready to conceive an alternative to that order. Committed to the cause of economic and social progress in their patria, conscious of themselves as an intellectual elite, and linked by family ties to the urban patriciate that held royal and municipal office, a small grouping of creole patricians was ready to translate its cultural aspirations into political action amidst the confusion that followed the eclipse of the Bourbon monarchy. The context for their action, the means that they used, and the consequent collapse of Spanish rule in New Granada, are examined in the next chapter.

12

The fall of royal government

When Don Antonio de Amar y Borbón arrived at Bogotá in September 1803 to take up his post as viceroy, he took command of a territory that, in spite of all Spain's difficulties following the resumption of war with the British in 1804, was apparently secure under the government of the metropolitan power. The celebrations surrounding Amar y Borbón's inauguration were lavish and good humored, and his predecessor, Viceroy Pedro de Mendinueta, handed over office with a *relación de mando* that was positive and reassuring in its tone. Mendinueta warned Amar y Borbón to sustain vigilance against foreign subversion, to prevent the entry of foreign books and papers that might be harmful to religion and the state, and to be alert for "a philosophical fanaticism, and above all a spirit of novelty, (which) might turn a few heads, inducing them to accept notions which they indiscreetly profess as their own ideas." But he concluded his *relación de mando* on a heartening note, stating that, despite some minor disturbances to public order, he had the satisfaction to hand over a territory in a "state of tranquillity, so that Your Excellency might discharge his responsibilities for the common good."[1] And Amar y Borbón did indeed pass a few uneventful years as viceroy, in which none of his experience as a high-ranking military commander in Spain was needed to manage the affairs of a land that, whatever the underlying disaffections of elements in its population, showed no obvious signs of unrest or political instability.[2] However, after less than four years of dedicating himself to the routines of government business, Amar y Borbón was suddenly faced with an unprecedented crisis in 1808, when the Spanish monarchy suddenly collapsed. Within two years, he was not only unceremoniously drummed out of his high office by a creole opposition, but, in losing his command, he also saw the very system of viceregal government thrown to the ground.

To explain the fall of the royal government in New Granada we must

---

1. Posada and Ibáñez, *Relaciones de mando*, pp. 585–6.
2. On Amar y Borbón's background, and his appointment and early years as viceroy, see Mario Herrán Baquero, *El Virrey Don Antonio Amar y Borbón: La Crisis del Regimen Colonial en la Nueva Granada* (Bogotá, 1988), pp. 32–42.

first look beyond the colony itself, to the disintegration of authority in metropolitan Spain. This started in 1808, when the embattled Spanish state, which was already enfeebled by war and palace intrigues, was plunged into a grave and prolonged crisis. After the entry of French armies into Spain in 1807, the Ancien Régime entered its terminal agony. In March 1808, a party of malcontent nobles associated with Prince Ferdinand, the heir to the throne, organized the overthrow of the favorite Godoy and the abdication of Charles IV in favor of his son. In April, Napoleon, impatient to make Spain a more effective and reliable ally, decided to deal with the disarray in its government by a bold maneuver: the imposition of his brother Joseph on the Spanish throne, backed by an army of occupation. Despite collaboration from a substantial element of the Spanish nobility, clergy, and political class, the plan misfired. Popular antagonism to the French occupation exploded in an insurrection in Madrid in May, and Madrid's example was followed throughout Spain in a series of provincial risings against the French intruder. A war of national liberation with undertones of social revolution now began in provincial Spain. On one side stood Napoleon, his army, and his allies among the Spanish political class. Confronting the French was an extraordinary popular movement that spread from region to region, carrying the propertied classes and the clergy in its wake and creating a network of town and provincial juntas that sprang up in areas not occupied by France. Thus, the fall of Ferdinand and the struggle against the French caused political authority in Spain to fragment, as local power devolved onto juntas that acted like independent states, mobilizing their own armies and even pursuing their own foreign policies.[3]

The first response to imperial crisis in New Granada

While the Spanish juntas concentrated on resistance to Napoleon in the opening months of the crisis, New Granada, like other American colonies, was cushioned from the immediate impact of that crisis by distance and the slow passage of news. The first official word of events in Spain reached the Americas from the two leading provincial juntas, those of Oviedo and Seville, which, in June and July, hastened to contact colonial governments and to secure their allegiance. Oviedo sent emissaries to Mexico, while the Junta of Seville, which titled itself "Supreme Junta of Spain and the Indies," dispatched commissioners to all the main American dominions. In June 1808, one of these commissioners, José de Pando y

---

3. For accounts of events in Spain in these years, see Raymond Carr, *Spain, 1808–1939* (Oxford, 1966), pp. 79–119; Timothy Anna, *Spain and the Loss of America* (Lincoln, Nebraska, and London, 1983), pp. 15–63.

Sanllorente, left Cádiz for New Granada. After consulting with the governor of Cartagena following his arrival in the port in early August, he arrived at Bogotá on September 2 for talks with Viceroy Amar y Borbón. There was, it seems, some disagreement between Sanllorente and the viceroy, but this was concealed behind a public front of undivided support for Spain. On September 5, Viceroy Amar y Borbón convoked a gathering of leading officials, military men, clerics, and some prominent citizens and, after proclaiming Ferdinand king and declaring war on France, promised to support the Seville Junta and to provide funds from the royal treasury for its war effort in Spain. A Spanish officer was sent to Popayán to organize a similar event, while in Bogotá, Sanllorente collected half a million pesos from the government and private subscription before returning to Spain.

As yet, there was no open opposition to Spain, although behind the facade of unity the first murmurings of doubt and dissent were heard among the ranks of the creole patricians whom Seville was seeking to rally in aid of the stricken mother country. In Cartagena, Sanllorente's mission aroused ill-feeling because the governor of the province, when consulting with the Seville agent, ignored the cabildo entirely and simply ordered compliance with his recognition of the interim government in Seville.[4] In Bogotá, creoles were included in discussions with Sanllorente, but this did not prevent complaints. There was, one contemporary recalled, "some annoyance among a few participants, because they had not been given time to explain themselves as they wished."[5] These disagreements apparently arose from creole resentment at the arrogant behavior of Sanllorente, and at the pretensions of the Seville government in abrogating to itself the title of "Supreme Government of Spain and the Indies," without any prior consultation with the colonies.[6] However, the New Granadan government, bolstered by professions of public sympathy and support for the mother country, held firm. Indeed, José de Torres y Peña remembered these early months of the crisis as an interlude of solidarity among "men of the better sort" who "celebrated and appreciated the action of the Seville Junta, with which they were at once united without any other purpose than that of cooperating in the common cause of the monarchy . . ."[7] This sense of common cause did not last for long, however. During the ensuing year, the peninsular government entered into an increasingly desperate struggle for survival against advancing French forces and, as

4. Gabriel Jiménez Molinares, *Los Mártires de Cartagena de 1816*, 2 vols. (Cartagena, 1948–50), vol. I, pp. 44–5.
5. Torres y Peña, *Memorias*, p. 81.
6. José Manuel Restrepo, *Historia de la Revolución de Colombia*, 5 vols. (Bogotá, repr. 1969), vol. I, pp. 100–3.
7. Torres y Peña, *Memorias*, p. 80.

Spain staggered through successive crises, the accumulated resentments and developing aspirations of New Granada's educated elites were rapidly transmuted into antagonism toward the viceregal government and a claim for political autonomy.

The realignment of political forces within New Granada echoed the changing relationship between Spain and its colonies, as the future of the empire became increasingly uncertain. After the initial months of confusion in Spain, the metropolitan government briefly stabilized in September 1808, when delegates from provincial juntas came together at Aranjuez in a Supreme Central Junta, which was authorized to coordinate the war against Napoleon's armies and provide a focus for the government of Spain and the Indies. However, it did not become an effective central government, capable of binding Spain's provinces into a force for defeating the French. For some months, the Seville Junta continued to claim autonomy and to insist that it had a special right to manage colonial affairs; it also favored allowing colonials who did not want to accept Seville's authority to establish their own juntas, modeled on those of Spain. By the beginning of 1809 the Central Junta finally emerged as the dominant force, and it was widely recognized by provincial juntas in Spain and by governing officials in the colonies. But it was still left with the problem of securing creole allegiance in the Americas. To do so, it issued political promises that, in New Granada, were to encourage creoles to demand that the viceregal government share its power with the citizens of the colony's leading towns.

In January 1809, the Central Junta proclaimed that "the vast and precious dominions that Spain possesses in the Indies are not properly colonies or factories as are those of other nations, but an essential and integral part of the Spanish monarchy," and, as such, "should constitute part of the Central Junta."[8] To this end, colonial officials were ordered to send to Spain delegates elected to represent the colonies in the Central Junta, alongside the representatives of the Spanish provinces. In New Granada, selection of a delegate was duly organized in May and June 1809, and the elections gave the creole patriciate its first taste of participation in the political order that had arisen as a substitute for the traditional monarchical regime. Such participation was limited to the small creole elites of New Granada's main urban centers, who were mobilized through the traditional institution of the cabildo. The procedure for electing a delegate was very simple. The cabildo of the leading city in each province was called upon to nominate two or three candidates, one of whom was chosen by lot to go forward to a next electoral round. In this second round, a single delegate was then chosen, again by lot, to act as the

8. Quoted in Anna, *Spain and the Loss of America*, pp. 51-2.

viceroyalty's delegate to the junta. Conveniently for the viceroy, the man who emerged as the delegate was Don Antonio Narváez y la Torre, an ex-governor of Santa Marta who was acceptable to the authorities and widely respected among the creole elites, particularly in the three provinces of the Caribbean coast, for which he had been a joint candidate. There was some resentment that the delegation had not fallen to the *santafereño* patrician Camilo Torres, but the election was accepted as fair and Narváez y la Torre's name went forward without opposition.[9]

The emergence of a creole opposition

Like most other delegates chosen to join the Central Junta as colonial representatives, Narváez y la Torre did not go to Spain to take up his office, probably because the future of the Junta was so uncertain. The election is, however, significant in two respects. First, it shows that during the early months of 1809 the first instinct of leading creoles was to remain loyal to Spain and to await a political accommodation with the metropolis. Equally of interest was that the election showed the ability of a network of creoles to organize themselves as a loose political force, capable of coordinated action.

By scrutinizing the backgrounds and links of the candidates put forward in the elections, Margarita Garrido shows that, of the candidates chosen in the New Granadan provinces (leaving aside those of Quito and Panama, both of which stood outside New Granadan political society), most were members of a network of creoles linked by family, professional, and business ties, and especially by intellectual and political outlook.[10] Bogotá's two leading nominees were Camilo Torres and Joaquín Camacho, both of whom were the chosen candidates of five provinces. Torres was the son of a distinguished Popayán creole family, but he had become a permanent resident in Bogotá, where he was educated at the Colegio del Rosario and practiced at the bar of the Royal audiencia. In 1794, he defended Francisco Antonio Zea, then accused of sedition, and was himself briefly suspected of involvement in the creole conspiracy of that year. By marrying into the prominent and wealthy creole clan of Prieto y Ricaurte, Torres also entered the web of the *santafereño* patriciate, which connected him with those very families whose political influence Gutiérrez de Piñeres had tried to reduce during his *visita general* of 1779–83.[11] Joaquín Camacho, who was born in Tunja, was from another important provincial family,

9. Restrepo, *Historia de la Revolución*, p. 106; Manuel José Forero, *Camilo Torres* (Bogotá, 1960), pp. 79–80.
10. Garrido de Payán, "Political Culture of New Granada," pp. 63–6.
11. Manuel José Forero, *Camilo Torres*, pp. 354–6; Gómez Hoyos, *La Revolución Granadina*, vol. 2, pp. 7–10.

and, following his education at the Colegio del Rosario, he became a leading lawyer and professor of law at the university. He was connected to Mutis and his circle, and, like Torres, had been involved in defending an individual involved in the conspiracy of 1794; he subsequently held political office, however, when Ezpeleta made him lieutenant governor of Tocaima.[12] Other men connected with this network of lawyers and "ilustrados" were chosen in more than one province. Father Eloy Valenzuela, who was connected with the Botanical Expedition and whom Torres had defended when he was accused of preaching a revolutionary sermon in 1797, was nominated in two provinces; so, too, was Frutos Joaquín Gutiérrez de Caviedes, a creole lawyer who was originally from Cucutá, and had become a member of the *santafereño* intelligentsia. Luis Eduardo Azuola, a leading Bogotá patrician who had held several important offices in the colonial administration, was another candidate with votes in two provinces, thanks probably to his wide administrative and political experience.[13] Among those with single nominations were others connected to the intelligentsia of Bogotá, such as Ignacio de Pombo, José María Lozano, the lawyers José María Toledo, José Munive, and Antonio Ayos, and, indeed, the successful candidate Antonio Narváez y la Torre, who had written reports recommending reforms of the commercial system.

The selection of these men is not surprising. As lawyers and men of administrative experience, all were eminently qualified to serve as delegate. But, as Garrido argues, the multiple nominations secured by some individuals and the connections between many of those who appeared on the list of nominees suggest that a network of educated creoles ran a coordinated campaign to ensure the election of a candidate acceptable to creole reformers. It seems, then, that the small group of enlightened creoles from the generation that had formulated and advanced reformist views over the previous two decades was beginning to organize and coalesce into a political force, united around the plan to create political equality between peninsulars and creoles, a principle which Frutos Joaquín Gutiérrez ardently recommended in his private correspondence of February and March 1809.[14]

Although creoles were presented with the tantalizing prospect that Spain would recognize white Americans as citizens equal to Spaniards, with rights to participate in the government of the empire, colonial officials were very reluctant to relinquish their monopoly of power. On the contrary, now that their government had been made insecure by the

12. Restrepo Sáenz and Rivas, *Genealogías de Santafé de Bogotá,* pp. 192–4; Gómez Hoyos, *La Revolución Granadina,* vol. 2, pp. 45–6.

13. Restrepo Sáenz and Rivas, *Genealogías de Santafé de Bogotá,* pp. 76–7.

14. See the "Cartas de Suba" of Frutos Joaquín Gutiérrez, in Eduardo Posada, *Bibliografía Bogotana,* 2 vols. (Bogotá, 1917–25), tomo 1, pp. 209–19.

confusing events in Spain and by the threat of French-inspired subversion in the colonies, they tended to regard colonials with suspicion and to treat disagreement as sedition. This was apparent at an early stage in the crisis, when, in October 1808, Viceroy Amar y Borbón took advice on measures to defend the royal government. The fiscal of the audiencia, Manuel Mariano de Blaya, reflected official distrust of colonials in all his recommendations. First, he called for a propaganda campaign to denigrate Napoleon as an impious tyrant who was in league with the Jews, so that New Granadans would not be politically seduced by the French pretender; he also pointed to possible subversive connections within the creole elite, through Francisco Zea (of the Botanical Expedition and the conspiracy of 1794) and Ignacio Sánchez de Tejada (an ex-secretary to the viceroy), both of whom had gone over to Napoleon's side. Blaya's instinct was to isolate New Granada from the world, punishing anyone who received correspondence without reporting it to the authorities, and censoring the mails to destroy correspondence with all persons who were "in any way suspect." To this end, he recommended that Amar y Borbón institute a secret network of intelligence in all provincial capitals, in order to root out anyone "of whatever rank or condition, who might promote, disseminate or publicize propositions or maxims subversive of our present Government, our legitimate monarch and our established authorities . . ."[15] Viceroy Amar y Borbón concurred with this advice insofar as was practical, and, while publicly exhorting New Granadans to reject the tyrant Bonaparte and to contribute funds to the Spanish cause, he was also prepared to repress any critics of the established order.[16] Here lay the seeds of a conflict that was increasingly to divide creoles from the established authorities during 1809, when leading creoles intensified demands for the formation of a junta modeled on those of the Spanish provinces.

This division, which was to lead creoles from cooperation to confrontation with the government, began in mid-1809. In August the creole patriciate of the city of Quito deposed the president of the Quito audiencia and set up an autonomous junta that declared loyalty to Ferdinand VII; this junta also denounced peninsular officials as the creatures of a corrupt, pro-French regime, and called upon the other cities of the viceroyalty to follow Quito's example. When news of the coup reached Bogotá in September, it had a catalytic effect on politics in the city, by injecting courage into a previously cautious creole patriciate and confirming the fears of government ministers. Viceroy Amar y Borbón tried to counter the threat

15. "Informe del Fiscal D. Manuel Mariano de Blaya, Cartagena, October 20, 1808," Banco de la República, *Proceso histórico del 20 de julio de 1810. Documentos* (Bogotá, 1960), pp. 49–54; quotations from pp. 52 and 53.

16. S. E. Ortíz, *Genesis de la Revolución de 20 de Julio de 1810* (Bogotá, 1960), pp. 25–6.

to his authority and to rally support by convoking a *junta de notables* composed of members of the government, the Bogotá cabildo, the upper echelons of the clergy and military, and leading citizens.[17] However, this gesture had the opposite of its intended effect, since the two sessions of the junta, held on September 6 and 11, allowed marked differences to surface.

The proceedings began badly because the viceroy surrounded his palace, where the meetings were held, with armed guards. Some creoles saw this as a deliberate act of intimidation intended to discourage the free expression of opinion and to flush out opponents of the government; they therefore insisted that the meeting should guarantee their persons and property against arrest and embargo before they made their opinions known.[18] Once the sessions were under way, the majority, or at least the most vocal opinion was in favor of appeasing Quito and bringing creoles into the viceregal government. There is no official record of the proceedings, but according to Oidor Carrión y Moreno, "almost all the cabildo, supported by a clutch of pretentious lawyers who were determined to take over, declared their desire for a junta similar to those established in Spain." And, Carrión y Moreno added, this faction orchestrated speeches and organized support for "the old ideas of independence which have repeatedly arisen in that country."[19] Viceroy Amar y Borbón and his ministers tried simply to ignore these demands. Camilo Torres and Frutos Gutiérrez later recalled that there were twenty-eight votes in favor of creating a *junta provincial* in order to negotiate peacefully with the Quiteños, but, amidst creole indignation, the viceroy "dissolved the meeting without counting votes, and its resolutions were neither drawn up nor signed, in spite of having been repeatedly reaffirmed by the cabildo . . ."[20]

Viceroy Amar y Borbón did, nonetheless, seek compromise. Whereas prominent creoles argued that the Quiteños had acted in good faith and pressed for a conciliatory policy toward them, the judges of the audiencia of New Granada took the opposite view, denouncing the Quiteños for treason and calling for firm military action. The viceroy tried to satisfy both sides. He sent the *santafereño* aristocrat Don José María Lozano, Marqués de San Jorge, to Quito to negotiate, while also dispatching troops to restore royal authority should conciliation fail. In the event, the

17. The best account of the effects of the Quito rebellion in New Granada, on which the following remarks are largely based, is Robert L. Gilmore, "The Imperial Crisis, Rebellion and the Viceroy: Nueva Granada in 1809," *HAHR*, vol. 40 (1960), pp. 2–24.

18. "Informe de la Audiencia de Santafé al Consejo de Regencia," February 19, 1810, Banco de la República, *Proceso histórico*, p. 141.

19. "Informe del Oider D. Joaquín Carrión y Moreno al Consejo de Regencia," August 31, 1810, in Banco de la República, *Proceso histórico*, pp. 199–200.

20. "Exposición de motivos que han obligado al Nuevo Reino de Granada a reasumir los derechos de la soberanía . . . " September 25, 1810, in Banco de la República, *Proceso histórico*, p. 219.

revolt was summarily crushed by an army sent from Peru and, in its aftermath, the rift between the government and politically active creoles in the capital became steadily harder to bridge.[21] So, far from drawing the elite together, the September meetings simply accentuated differences, setting the cabildo against the audiencia and pitting creoles against peninsulars. The *santafereño* elite, particularly the educated creole patriciate that saw itself as a trained and enlightened political class, now openly resented the authorities' stubborn refusal to regard them as trusted compatriots worthy of sharing power in the hour of imperial emergency. Thus, amidst an atmosphere of deepening crisis, the creoles' pent-up resentment against peninsular privilege found expression in political opposition, which was further magnified by personal animosity toward certain of the audiencia judges.

The September confrontation between peninsular officials and creoles who aspired to participate in the government was, then, a critical conjuncture in New Granada's political development, for it simplified political differences and created a coherent set of oppositions in the minds of political actors. When the viceroy and his ministers refused to accede to demands that creoles regarded both as completely legal and politically legitimate, the viceroy's critics labeled his government as despotic and unpatriotic. Thus the rhetoric of resistance against foreign despotism that Spain had used to rally patriotic support now began to turn against the colonial government. And, as creole opposition surfaced, government ministers' suspicions of creole disloyalty were confirmed, thus persuading them to turn to repression. Differences of opinion hardened into uncompromising antagonisms, and political choices were reduced to the struggle of "tyranny" against "sedition."

Radicals and repression

In late September 1809, a process of radicalization began, as political differences became more sharply defined. Opposition against the government began with attempts to drive a wedge between the viceroy and the audiencia. Rumors that the oidors intended to seize control of the government circulated, and pasquinades accusing the viceroy and his ministers of plotting to hand over the country to the French were disseminated both in the capital and provinces.[22] The government, on the other hand, took steps to strengthen its capacity for repression and to intimidate the opposition by deploying its forces. Troops were brought to the capital from Cartagena, the military establishment in Bogotá was reorganized, and the

21. Gilmore, "The Imperial Crisis, Rebellion and the Viceroy," pp. 15–18.
22. "Informe de la Audiencia de Santafé," Banco de la República, *Proceso histórico*, p. 142.

viceregal guard was doubled. At the end of September, the viceroy also tried to stop the circulation of political manifestos and news of events in Europe by forbidding the writing, copying, dissemination, and reading of literature defined as seditious by the authorities.[23] The oidors began to lead patrols around the streets, and were believed to be secretly preparing legal procedures against those who had dissented from official opinion during the September meetings.[24]

Policing measures did not discourage creole opposition, however. Indeed, after the viceroy's refusal to institute a junta in Bogotá, some creoles turned to plotting the overthrow of government. The first individual accused of such sedition was Andrés María Rosillo y Meruelo, a dean from the Santa Fe cathedral chapter. In October 1809, Pedro Salgar, a parish priest from Girón who resided in Bogotá, denounced Rosillo y Meruelo to the viceroy, who passed the information to the audiencia. Rosillo y Meruelo was allegedly planning to seize the viceroy, take control of the arms and treasury of the capital, and create an independent junta governed by creoles and supported by forces composed of some slaves freed from an hacienda, together with a couple of thousand men from Zipaquirá and Socorro. This plot was, in Viceroy Amar y Borbón's opinion, all "rather complicated, remote and improbable," but he nonetheless took appropriate policing measures and advised the audiencia to deal with Rosillo y Meruelo. He also put the lawyers Ignacio Herrera and Joaquín Camacho under suspicion by reporting that Rosillo y Meruelo had been seen in secret consultations with them.[25] The audiencia judges duly undertook to investigate Rosillo y Meruelo's activities. Their interrogation of the viceroy's informer, Pedro Salgar, confirmed the viceroy's story, with some additional details. Rosillo y Meruelo's coconspirators, it seems, included such prominent creoles as Antonio Nariño, Luis Caicedo, Sinforoso Mutis, Pedro Groot, Antonio Baraya, Ignacio Herrera, and Balthasar Minaño, an oidor from the Quito audiencia. Their plan allegedly embraced a number of ambitious aims. These included raising a force of some 2,000 men in the provinces and raising a simultaneous revolt in Cartagena, whereas in the capital, the troops were to be bribed, the viceroy kidnapped, and two of the oidors executed, prior to establishing an independent junta to be presided over by Luis Caicedo for two years and by Antonio Nariño or Pedro Groot for the following two years.[26] Apparently, prominent members of the creole elite in the capital, led by men long suspected of

23. For this order see "Providencias del Virrey Amar in 1809," in ibid., pp. 68–71.

24. Ortíz, *Genesis de la Revolución*, p. 33.

25. See "Oficio del Virrey a la Real Audiencia, October 15, 1809," in Banco de la República, *Proceso histórico*, pp. 74–6.

26. For the testimony of the informant describing the plot, see "Declaración del Doctor Pedro Salgar," in ibid., pp. 77–80.

subversive leanings, were now intent on the seizure of power by revolutionary means. The audiencia judges also reported that, during their investigations, they had discovered that, at the end of September 1809, Rosillo y Meruelo had secretly suggested to the vicereine that she and her husband should lend support to a plan for the formation of an independent government in the colony. It was said that Rosillo y Meruelo promised the viceroy would become king of the new state in place of Ferdinand VII, if he supported an armed putsch against the audiencia.[27]

It is not clear whether this conspiracy actually existed; the oidors may well have exaggerated Salgar's allegations in order to persuade the viceroy to take harsher repressive measures.[28] However, the unveiling of the alleged conspiracy and the arrests that followed helped to keep up the political tension aroused by the Quito revolt, and heightened creole fears of repression. At the end of October and during November 1809, various arrests were made, including Antonio Nariño and Balthasar Minaño; Rosillo y Meruelo fled from the capital to his native Socorro where, after an extensive hunt, he was finally arrested in the following year. The audiencia favored a firm crackdown on dissidents and urged the imprisonment of all those suspected of complicity in the conspiracy.[29] The viceroy, however, dealt cautiously with prominent citizens suspected of involvement. Thus, the alcalde Luis Caicedo, his fellow *cabildante* Acevedo y Gómez, the lawyers Joaquín Camacho and Ignacio de Herrera, the royal official Pedro Groot, and the army officer Antonio Baraya, were all left at liberty and in their posts in spite of their apparent implication in the plot.

The viceroy's lenience probably stemmed not only from his doubts about the reality of the conspiracy, but also from his reluctance to alienate the creole patriciate of the capital. He apparently saw the arrest of a few radicals as sufficient indication of his determination to defend royal authority and he may have hoped that moderation would allow a rapprochement with the creole establishment in Bogotá. By this time, however, the audiencia and the cabildo were becoming the foci of distinct factions in the capital, with the cabildo acting as a forum for stating creole grievances and demands. In November 1809, the cabildo issued the strongest and

---

27. "Real Acuerdo," in ibid., pp. 82–3; also Horacio Rodríguez Plata, *Andrés María Rosillo y Meruelo* (Bogotá, 1964), pp. 85–91.

28. Historians have yet to dispel the mystery that surrounds the conspiracy. Ortíz describes the plot but offers no convincing judgment on the extent to which prominent creoles were involved. (See Ortíz, *Genesis de la Revolución*, pp. 75–89.) Blossom, concerned with the involvement of Nariño, also refers to the plot but provides no evidence that it really existed or that Nariño was involved. (See Blossom, *Nariño*, pp. 65–74.) Beyond a protest of innocence at the time of his arrest, Nariño's correspondence reveals nothing. (See E. Posada and P. M. Ibáñez (eds.), *El Precursor*, vol. 2, pp. 289–94.)

29. "Informe del Oidor D. Joaquín Carrión y Moreno," in Banco de la República, *Proceso histórico*, p. 201.

most unequivocal statement of its position in a report to the Central Junta, written by its *asesor,* the lawyer Camilo Torres. This "Representación del Cabildo de Santafé," known to historians as the "Memorial de Agravios," presented a classic statement of creole resentment at peninsular domination of colonial government, and reflects the advance of creole political aspirations since the start of the Spanish crisis in 1808.

Confrontation and the escalation of crisis

In the Memorial de Agravios, Torres elaborated on three principal themes. First, he denounced the discrimination against creoles that had deprived them of office, and condemned the unenlightened policies by which the old regime had hindered economic progress. Second, Torres demanded equal representation for the colonies alongside the provinces of Spain in the Supreme Central Junta, warning that Spanish intransigence might lead to an independence movement comparable to the one that had cost Britain its colonies. Third, he affirmed the loyalty of the cabildo to Ferdinand VII, and called for the establishment in New Granada of provincial juntas composed of representatives from the colony's cabildos. In his view, these were the essential requirements for preserving New Granada's loyalty to the metropolis.[30] Torres's statement was strongly supported by the Bogotá cabildo, eleven of whose members, a clear majority, signed the document and authorized its dispatch to Spain. It was, however, completely unacceptable to Viceroy Amar y Borbón, who prevented the statement from being sent to Spain. The audiencia also sought to attack its creole opponents in their stronghold by urging the viceroy to appoint six new councillors to the cabildo to ensure that, in the forthcoming elections of the cabildo, the key posts of *alcaldes ordinarios, síndico procurador,* and *asesor* went to "persons who merit the full confidence of the government."[31]

Designed to intimidate and neutralize the creole faction that aspired to participate in New Granada's government, this maneuver did not achieve the desired effect. Viceroy Amar y Borbón was reluctant to use his power to exclude troublemakers from the cabildo's elective offices and, ignoring the new councillors, he allowed "the party of the innovators" to retain control of the elective offices.[32] But the viceroy's attempt to fill the proprietary posts with his nominees nonetheless aggravated tensions by intruding on the rights of the creoles to manage the city council. For although the cabildo had traditionally included a number of peninsulars

30. "Representación del Cabildo de Santafé, Capital del Nuevo Reino de Granada a la Supreme Junta Central de España, en el año de 1809," in ibid., pp. 85–109.
31. "Informe del Oidor D. Joaquín Carrión y Moreno," in ibid., p. 200.   32. Ibid.

among its members, the *santafereño* upper class regarded the town council as its preserve and resented the encroachment of outsiders. This had been made plain in the mid-1790s, when the cabildo repeatedly protested to the crown about disrespect and interference from the audiencia. Then, the cabildo had complained bitterly about Viceroy Ezpeleta's behavior toward the creoles in 1794, when he had refused them entry to the barracks and placed guards on the houses of Europeans, and it also denounced his subsequent attempts to fill the municipal offices with peninsular Spaniards.[33] Under pressure, the cabildo grudgingly accepted that the elective posts of alcalde should alternate between creoles and peninsulars, but it continued to fight against such intrusion by objecting to the peninsulars chosen by the viceroy. In the eyes of the *santafereño* elite, such men were mere parvenus, mere "tramps and stowaways" who had no place alongside the "nobility" of Bogotá, and it insisted that preference should be given to the descendants of the conquerors and to men who had been born in the colony, in accord with the Laws of the Indies. Such, the cabildo stated, "have always been the rules by which the city council of Santa Fe has governed its operations, without there ever having been factions of Europeans or those native inhabitants who are odiously called creoles."[34] So, when Viceroy Amar y Borbón thrust six new regidores, all peninsulars, into the cabildo in 1810 and forced a Spaniard into the office of *alférez real*, he opened old wounds. Indeed, by setting peninsular against creole, Amar y Borbón made the cabildo a symbol of creole rights against the viceregal government, and his interference was later to be given as a prime example of the "tyrannical" government that caused his downfall.[35]

Conflict between the cabildo and the government was kept alive by a dispute over the office of *alférez real,* in which the creole Luis Caicedo was replaced by the Spanish merchant Bernardo Gutiérrez. Gutiérrez had first bid for this post in 1807, but had been rejected by the cabildo as unsuitable because he was accused of misappropriating the funds of another Spanish merchant.[36] When Gutiérrez again sought the office in December 1809, this time with the viceroy's support, a majority of the cabildo repeated its earlier rebuff and only accepted Gutiérrez when forced to do so.[37] But opposition to Gutiérrez – and thus to the viceroy – continued

33. British Library, Egerton 1809, fols. 734–55; "Representación del Cabildo y Regimiento de la Ciudad de Santa Fe contra el Virrey D. José de Ezpeleta."
34. Ibid., fols. 734, 737, 738.
35. See "Motives que han obligado al Nuevo Reino de Granada a reasumir los derechos de la soberanía . . . Santa Fe, September 25, 1810," in Banco de la República, *Proceso histórico*, p. 220.
36. The documents tracing cabildo opposition to Gutiérrez have been compiled by Enrique Ortega Ricaurte, *Documentos sobre el 20 de julio de 1810* (Bogotá, 1965). For the cabildo's deliberations on the first attempt by Gutiérrez to secure the office within it, see pp. 26–8.
37. Ibid., pp. 29–36.

within the cabildo, where personal grudges reinforced political differences and exacerbated the confrontation between the viceregal administration and its opponents. The campaign against Gutiérrez was led by Ignacio de Herrera, a creole lawyer who already stood in the forefront of creole opposition to the viceroy and audiencia. In January 1810, Herrera launched a stinging, defamatory attack on leading officials in a paper presented to the cabildo for dispatch to the government in Spain. He denounced the viceroy and oidors as the corrupt creatures of Godoy, represented them as an avaricious, pro-French fifth column, and called, in the strongest terms yet seen, for the formation of a patriotic junta committed to the defense of the sovereign rights of Ferdinand VII.[38] Moreover, faced with an intrusive *alférez real* who was little more than the viceroy's spy, Herrera passionately opposed his presence. Conflict between the two men came to a head in April 1810, when Gutiérrez demanded copies of the instructions that Herrera had drawn up in January for the Central Junta, including those sections that had been deleted by moderate members of the cabildo. The two men came to blows in a clangorous public incident, and through the conflicting testimonies of the protagonists and witnesses to their brawl come clear echoes of the political tensions that suffused Bogotá's society.[39] These tensions were, moreover, heightened by news of the deteriorating situation in Spain, where the Central Junta had collapsed at the end of 1809.

As the conflict between the cabildo and government deepened during the opening months of 1810, government repression intensified. In Bogotá, Herrera was subjected to increasing harassment by the audiencia, thereby feeding fears of impending arrest among the government's opponents.[40] Even more ominous was the treatment meted out to three youthful acolytes of Rosillo y Meruelo who, in February 1810, had attempted to raise rebellion in the Llanos. The men were summarily executed, on the express orders of the viceroy and audiencia, and their heads were sent to Bogotá for public display.[41] This caused great outrage in the capital. To Camilo Torres, this episode showed that government ministers were "cruel satraps," and he applauded the two youths as "martyrs for the liberty of the Reino."[42] Political polarization was, moreover, widened by news from

---

38. For the text of this paper, see "Memorial del Síndico Procurador de Santafé, Doctor Ignacio de Herrera, January 15, 1810" in S. E. Ortíz (ed.), *Colección de Documentos para la Historia de Colombia* (Bogotá, 1965), pp. 93–100.

39. These testimonies are collected in Enrique Ortega Ricaurte, *Documentos*, pp. 40–112.

40. "Memorial del Doctor Herrera'," pp. 113–18.

41. On this rebellion, see Rausch, *A Tropical Plains Frontier*, pp. 131–4; Ortíz, *Genesis de la Revolución*, pp. 98–102.

42. Camilo Torres to Ignacio Tenorio, May 29, 1810, Banco de la República, *Proceso histórico*, pp. 56–7.

Spain. In November 1809, Napoleon's armies had inflicted a crushing defeat on Spanish forces at Ocaña, and, pursued by French forces, the discredited Junta Central was forced to retreat to Cádiz and the island of León where, in January 1810, it was replaced by the conservative Council of Regency. Napoleon's offer of independence to Spain's dominions in the Americas, made in December 1809, also forced an increasingly isolated Spanish government to make unprecedented concessions to the colonies. In February 1810, it issued a proclamation that decreed equality for Americans in vivid terms:

> From this moment, American Spaniards, you see yourselves elevated to the dignity of free men. . . . Take into account that, on pronouncing the name of he who will represent you in the National Congress, your destinies no longer depend on Ministers, Viceroys or Governors; they are in your hands. . . .[43]

This was dangerous rhetoric. To secure its recognition in America, the Council of Regency now openly acknowledged that the colonies had been oppressed in the past; moreover, by conceding political rights to colonials, it increased the difficulties facing crown officials who were seeking to sustain their authority against creole pressure. In New Granada, this repudiation of the old regime, with its explicit recognition of colonial claims to self-government, gave the viceroy's opponents the chance to seize the political initiative. The arrival of Antonio Villavicencio and Carlos Montúfar, the Regency's representatives to New Granada and Quito, also gave them their moment to mobilize against viceregal government.

Conflict in Cartagena

In New Granada, the first repercussions of the Regency's actions were felt in Cartagena de Indias. When Villavicencio and Montúfar arrived in the city in May 1810, their presence had an immediate, catalytic effect on its politics, forcing resolution of a conflict between the governor of Cartagena and his military subordinates on the one side, and the city's cabildo and those who favored autonomy on the other.

Throughout 1808 and most of 1809, Cartagena had remained politically quiet. On receiving news of the crisis in Spain, the first concern of Cartagena's merchant community was to recover its commerce. In October 1808, the Consulado pressed Viceroy Amar y Borbón to legalize trade with foreign colonies in the Caribbean, on the grounds that now that the metropolis was in such difficulties, there was no hope of reviving trade

---

43. J. D. Monsalve, *Antonio de Villavicencio y la Revolución de Independencia*, 2 vols. (Bogotá, 1920), vol. 1, p. 70.

with Spain. Indeed, the Consulado observed, even if Spain were able to send ships to the colony, it could not provide more than a third part of the goods consumed there, "the other two parts being the product of alien hand or manufacture . . . received from the foreigner." As for New Granadan exports,

the substance of this State or Kingdom has for years been taken by outsiders through Trinidad, Cuba, Puerto Rico and Maracaibo, by the foreigners of Saint Thomas and the Anglo-Americans who traffic in those ports, or by the clandestine commerce which has been carried on and will inevitably be carried on, on a progressively larger scale, with Jamaica.[44]

Leading officials in Cartagena supported merchant pressure to legalize trade with foreigners, on the grounds that only commercial revenues could save a depleted colonial treasury from imminent financial collapse. They pointed out that the financial situation was desperate, as customs revenues had fallen to a minimum, the local tobacco and aguardiente monopolies hardly covered their costs, and the Quito subsidy for the previous year had still failed to arrive. Efforts to raise a loan of 200,000 pesos from Cartagena's merchants had yielded only 10,000 pesos and, as the merchants could not cover the shortfall in government income, the administration had been forced to place its officials on half-pay.[45] The viceroy duly acceded to these pressures and, at the end of 1808, legalized trade with foreigners.[46]

At the beginning of 1809, legal trade with the English started in earnest, when a number of English ships arrived in Cartagena laden with goods, thus signifying that, after the armistice with Spain, trade between the two nations was now permitted.[47] Viceroy Amar y Borbón accepted this, and sanctioned trade between the ports of New Granada and the English colonies, while awaiting confirmation from Spain.[48] Spain did not, in fact, approve: in March 1809, a directive from Spain ordered the suspension of all trade with the British.[49] The viceroy and his advisors sensibly decided to ignore this order. In October 1809, Viceroy Amar y Borbón decided to allow the trade to continue, on the grounds that it was essential both to the economic well-being of the colony and the financial survival of the government.[50] However, by this time, the condition of Cartagena's trade was no longer a vital issue in the city's politics. For as

44. AHNC Consulados, tomo 4, fols. 776–81. Junta de Gobierno del Consulado to governor of Cartagena, October 11, 1808.
45. Ibid., fols. 781–93, 797.   46. Ibid., fols. 800–6.
47. AHNC Aduanas, tomo 22, fols. 7–19; tomo 23, fols. 307–18.
48. AHNC Consulados, tomo 4, fols. 814–18.   49. AHNC Aduanas, tomo 20, fols. 448.
50. AHNC Aduanas, tomo 13, fols. 842–7.

developments in Spain increasingly threatened the survival of the metropolitan government, the governor of Cartagena faced growing pressures to
share power with the local elite.

At the time of the Quito revolt, the cabildo of Cartagena was dominated by conservative opinion and had shown no inclination to side with
the rebels. It rejected overtures from Quito, and declared its adherence to
the Central Junta as the representative of Ferdinand VII. But, as the
Spanish crisis deepened in the last months of 1809, loyalism gave way to
demands for autonomy. Now the cabildo insisted that the governor should
establish a junta in which cabildo members had a voice and a chance to
determine their own affairs. In late 1809, pressure for a junta came from a
small group of creoles who met regularly in the houses of the city's *alcaldes
ordinarios,* the lawyers José María García del Toledo and Domingo Díaz
Granados, and who maintained contact with a faction of like-minded
kinsmen in Mompós. To achieve their goal, this group developed a political strategy similar to that of their counterparts in Bogotá: they sought to
influence the cabildo and to use it as a base upon which to build a junta.

The governor, Francisco Montes, was keenly aware of his adversaries'
tactics and, like the audiencia judges in Bogotá, he tried to neutralize the
cabildo by packing it with his supporters and sympathizers. Thus, when
cabildo elections were held in December 1809, he presented his own
nominees, drawn from the ranks of the military in the port. This maneuver failed, however, and in the months that followed, Montes's position at
the head of the provincial government became increasingly vulnerable.
Not only did he face the antagonism of a cabildo dominated by his
opponents, but Montes also found that he was unable to count on the
support of the substantial peninsular community resident in the city.
Politically, his position was weakened by his very recent appointment to
the governorship and his arrival at Cartagena when the French were advancing into Spain; this made him vulnerable to the charge that he was an
afrancesado, a Bonapartist collaborator ready to accept French rule. Such
rumors would have been less damaging if the Spanish merchants in Cartagena had been convinced that his government was acting in their best
interests. But alliance with Governor Montes did not offer them the most
promising means of securing political stability in the port. When the
Central Junta collapsed and power devolved upon the Regency in January
1810, Montes was placed in an increasingly difficult position. Appointed
under the old regime, he was reluctant to recognize the Regency and
seemed intent on provoking open conflict with his creole opponents in
Cartagena. On the other hand, the Spanish merchants in the port, many
of whom were closely tied to Cádiz interests, were eager to embrace the
cause of the Regency and were anxious to avoid antagonizing the creoles in
Cartagena. Thus, not only did Spanish members of the cabildo support

action against Montes, but a prominent peninsular merchant and ex-prior of the Consulado joined in public condemnation of his methods of government.

The arrival of Villavicencio in early May 1810 brought matters to a head. While Villavicencio appealed for unity between Europeans and Americans, the cabildo maneuvered the governor into accepting the Regency and forced him to accept two deputies to share his command. The cabildo also increased its numbers, taking in four new councillors of its own choosing. Thus fortified, it accused the governor of obstruction and, aided by popular demonstrations instigated by leading creoles, decreed his removal from office on June 14, 1810. To replace him – and presumably to neutralize military opposition – the cabildo called upon his second-in-command, the peninsular lieutenant governor Blas de Soria, who was installed under the same power-sharing arrangement previously imposed on Montes.[51] This was a conservative coup. The men who shared power with Blas de Soria were both leading members of the Cartagena patriciate – one was Tomás Andrés de Torres, a peninsular merchant, the other Antonio de Narváez y la Torre, the elective deputy to the Central Junta. Thus power was shared between creoles and Spaniards. The peninsular merchants in the port had joined with conservative creoles, not to effect a break with Spain, but to strengthen ties with the remnants of the Spanish government in Cádiz. Their aim was to support the Regency and, as Nariño later recognized, to protect their commerce with the metropolis.[52] Cartagena was, however, soon to come under the control of creoles who were determined to break with Spain and, a little more than a year later, in November 1811, a Supreme Junta was to make Cartagena the first province in New Granada to declare its complete independence from Spain.

The overthrow of viceregal government

Following the fall of Montes at Cartagena, the viceroy and audiencia in Bogotá were increasingly isolated. The viceroy, alarmed by the encouragement that Villavicencio had given to the cabildo of Cartagena and fearful that his impending arrival in Santa Fe would precipitate a similar process there, prepared to neutralize his opponents before Villavicencio set foot in Bogotá, and rumors circulated that the authorities had prepared a list of nineteen prominent creoles who were to be arrested and executed.[53] Al-

51. This account of politics in Cartagena in 1809 and 1810 draws on Jiménez Molinares, *Los Martires de Cartagena*, vol. 1, pp. 38–120.

52. *La Bagatela*, no. 18, November 3, 1811.

53. Monsalve, *Antonio Villavicencio*, vol. 1, p. 87; José Acevedo y Gómez to Miguel Tadeo Gómez, July 1810, in Adolfo Leon Gómez, *El Tribuno de 1810* (Bogotá, 1910), p. 46.

though this was probably an astute piece of antigovernment propaganda spread by the viceroy's enemies to discredit him, the rumor of imminent repression reflects the highly charged state of the capital and the deep division that now separated the peninsular administration from its creole antagonists. And, as the city awaited the arrival of Villavicencio, news from the provinces intensified the mood of impending crisis. The deposition of the governor of Cartagena in mid-June was followed by cabildo-led revolts against local officials in Cali on July 3, Pamplona on July 4, and, closer to the capital, in Socorro on July 9 and 10. Of these, the rebellion of Socorro was the most potent regional threat to the government, due to its violent, popular, and anti-Spanish character. The citizens of the town of Socorro, led by members of local creole clans, had risen against their corregidor (a peninsular appointed by Viceroy Amar y Borbón in place of the creole incumbent), and after a riot in which a number of people were killed, the corregidor and the local military were defeated and local government placed in the hands of the town's cabildo. On July 11, that body, posing as the defender of holy religion and the sovereign Ferdinand VII, declared its independence from the viceroy's government and called on the cabildos in the neighboring towns of San Gil and Vélez to join them in an independent government.[54]

It was, then, against a background of growing agitation and open rebellion in the provinces that the *santafereño* dissidents contemplated their position and deliberated on their next move. At a secret meeting on July 19, a small group of prominent creoles – including Camilo Torres, José Miguel Pey, Jorge Tadeo Lozano, Ignacio de Herrera, Joaquín Camacho, and José Acevedo y Gómez – agreed to stage a disturbance in the city during the following day in order to force the viceroy to convoke a junta. Their plan was to spark a popular riot in the central square of the city on market day by involving the rich Spanish merchant José Llorente in a dispute with one of their number, Antonio Morales. The plan was duly executed on July 20, and although the conspirators came close to failure, the threat of violent disorder in the streets persuaded the viceroy first to negotiate and then to accept the cabildo's demand for a supreme junta. Viceroy Amar y Borbón recorded the event in a few hurried lines that he added to a letter he had been writing to Viceroy Abascal of Peru: "I cannot continue," he hastily scribbled, "because all has been in turmoil last night and they have demanded their rights and erected a *junta de vigilancia* like the one recently established in Cádiz; I hope your grace will have a happier time with the government at your command."[55] Amar y

---

54. Horacio Rodríguez Plata, *La Antigua Provincia del Socorro y la Independencia* (Bogotá, 1963), pp. 17–38.
55. AGI, Diversos, legajo 1 (Ramo 1, no. 4), Amar y Borbón to Abascal, July 21, 1810.

Borbón had not yet been completely forced out, however, because it was agreed that he should act as president of the new junta, with José Miguel Pey, the senior alcalde of the cabildo, as vice president. On the following day, the junta, presided over by the viceroy, held its first session and its members swore to accept the Regency and to rule in the name of Ferdinand VII.[56]

The overthrow of the viceregal government in Bogotá was, then, essentially a coup d'état carried out by a clique of patrician creoles who, faced with the disintegration of government in Spain, seized their chance to take power from the hands of royal officials who had effectively lost their authority to govern during the protracted crisis in Spain. Unlike the Comunero rebellion of 1781, the movement against the government in 1810 did not originate in popular discontent and rebellion; it was engineered by a faction within the *santafereño* urban patriciate that, as it saw the outworks of royal government collapsing in the provinces, forced a confused and demoralized viceroy to cede a share of power. This was not accomplished by the creoles alone. The willingness of crowds drawn from the urban lower classes to support the *juntistas* on the night of July 20 made a crucial contribution to their success. Most important, however, was the creoles' success in neutralizing military forces in the capital through negotiation with the government and co-optation of army officers. They were also helped by the character of the viceroy. Old, deaf, and demoralized by the progressive collapse of the government in Spain, Amar y Borbón's will to continue must have been further sapped by the news, brought by Villavicencio, that the Council of Regency had replaced him. In the moment of crisis, he chose to abdicate responsibility to Oidor Jurado, a man who had only recently arrived in Bogotá, and he accepted Jurado's judgment that the best way to avoid violence was to eschew resistance. Troops were consequently placed at the disposal of the cabildo, rather than used against it.[57] The ability of the conspirators to act without interference from the army was, moreover, strengthened by the cooperation that they received from Antonio Baraya, a creole officer who helped undermine the Bogotá garrison from within.

The junta in Bogotá was evidently not intent on independence from Spain and its members clearly wished to avoid any social disorder. Thus,

---

56. For detailed accounts of the events of July 20, see Ortíz, *Genesis de la revolución*, pp. 135–203, and Liévano Aguirre, *Los Grandes Conflictos*, pp. 557–87. Both draw heavily on the graphic contemporary narratives given in "La Constitución Feliz: Periódico Político de la Capital del Nuevo Reino de Granada" and the "Diario Político de Santafé de Bogotá," periodicals that started in August 1810 and that published the first histories of the revolution in the capital. These are reprinted in Luis Martínez Delgado and Sergio Elías Ortíz (eds.), *El Periodismo en la Nueva Granada, 1810–1811* (Bogotá, 1960).

57. See the remarks of Oidor Carrión, in Banco de la República, *Proceso histórico*, pp. 203–4.

they sought at first to share power with the viceroy and selected members of the colonial bureaucracy. It was only when a group of young radicals, led by José María Carbonell, mobilized popular support against the remnants of the old regime that the leading creoles in the junta repudiated their links with colonial officials. Carbonell, who had been a minor functionary in the Botanical Expedition, played a key part in bringing crowds into the streets on the night of July 20, and he and his followers subsequently organized people from the city's popular quarters to bring about the imprisonment of Oidor Hernández de Alba and Fiscal Frías. Their incarceration was swiftly followed by that of other oidors and European Spaniards; on July 25, Viceroy Amar y Borbón was himself placed under arrest, and a struggle for control of the government now started. Suddenly, the cautious maneuvers of the creole patriciate were overshadowed by popular tumult, fed by lower-class antagonism toward privileged peninsulars and led by a radical who evidently wished to break decisively with the Spanish colonial regime. Popular mobilization was brief, however. It did not extend beyond the practice of attacking officials, seen in so many popular disturbances in late colonial New Granada, and the creole junta successfully sustained its authority in Bogotá.

To assert their authority, the patricians in the Bogotá junta set up departments of government and mobilized armed support. First, the junta divided its thirty-seven members into sections charged with overseeing matters of government, finance, trade, war, and ecclesiastical affairs; second, to control radicals in the city, the junta organized a military force, calling on the landowners of the savannah of Bogotá to marshall their retainers into companies of cavalry. Carbonell and his followers continued to agitate, and subsequently established a popular junta to support their political ideals of popular sovereignty and equality. On August 13, they again stirred the populace, this time staging riots that forced the junta to transfer the viceroy and vicereine from house arrest to the city's public prisons. This radicalization of the rebellion was ephemeral. Horrified by the rough and insulting treatment that the crowds inflicted on Amar y Borbón and his wife, the creole elite of Bogotá secured their release and quietly transferred them out of the city on August 15, 1810. The junta then made its first move to repress the popular activity that threatened the stability of its government and, on August 16, arrested Carbonell and some of his companions.[58] Like their counterparts in Cartagena, the creole patricians of Bogotá had accomplished a swift transfer of power to a privileged coterie, and, after withstanding the challenge of a few individuals who favored popular revolution, the junta turned its attention during the remaining months of 1810 to establishing a wider authority in New Granada.

58. Liévano Aguirre, *Los Grandes Conflictos*, pp. 591–615.

At its first session on July 21, the junta had declared itself the provisional supreme government of New Granada, and called upon cabildos throughout the territory to send delegates to the capital to form a federal form of government "on the bases of the freedom and respective independence" of the provinces.[59] This proclamation reflected the views of the enlightened reformist elite, which wanted political change to be firmly directed from above and was anxious to avoid any disruption of the existing social order. Such men were not necessarily averse to widening political participation, but they intended future government in New Granada to be based on the association of respectable, educated, and propertied citizens who, by reason of their social rank and education, saw themselves as the natural leaders of their society. Thus, when the Bogotá junta laid down rules for elections of provincial delegates on December 10, 1810, it ordered that the suffrage should be limited to householders and property owners, and explicitly excluded servants and dependents. The junta also avoided a clear call for independence. Although it repudiated the Regency, the Bogotá junta preferred to await the outcome of events in Spain before breaking completely with the metropolis. It was, accordingly, ready to accept delegates both from provinces that recognized the Regency and from those that, like Popayán and Santa Marta, were still controlled by royal officials.

The collapse of central authority

If the junta had succeeded in imposing its authority within Bogotá by late 1810, its pretensions to leadership of the rest of New Granada were soon shattered. Opposition came first from the junta of Cartagena, which issued a manifesto declaring that the congress of provinces should meet at Medellín rather than in Bogotá. Regional differences then quickly multiplied, as the provinces broke into competing areas. Sogamoso split from Tunja, Mompós from Cartagena, Vélez from Socorro, Quibdó from Nóvita, and Ibagué and Tocaima from Mariquita. The determination of local elites to take control of their own areas also created divisions in the south, in the province of Popayán. In the city of Popayán itself, the Spanish army officer Miguel Tacón remained in his post as governor, and, when he sought to maintain his authority over the whole province, Cali and the towns of the Cauca Valley formed the opposing alliance of the "Confederated Cities of the Valley." When the first Congress of New Granada's provinces finally met at Bogotá, on December 22, 1810, it was attended by only six deputies, drawn from Bogotá, Socorro, Pamplona, Neiva, Nóvita, and Mariquita. But even this small group failed to achieve har-

---

59. Cited in Restrepo, *Historia de la Revolución*, vol. 1, p. 134.

mony. For although the Bogotá junta refused to accept delegates from areas that had broken from their provinces, the majority in the Congress favored the incorporation of deputies from Sogamoso and Mompós. When the Junta used censorship and military intimidation to enforce its will, the Congress dissolved itself in February 1811, having achieved nothing.[60]

After the dissolution of the first, abortive provincial Congress, regional division and disunity became steadily more entrenched. By March 1811, Bogotá formed its own Republic of Cundinamarca, which, by continuing to recognize the rights of Ferdinand VII, became "a monarchy in republican form." Indeed, its first president, Jorge Tadeo Lozano, was satirized as "His Majesty King Jorge the First." When Nariño replaced Lozano later that year, Bogotá again became a focus for centralism, but during the ensuing years the majority of the provinces refused to accept the city's leadership. Now that Spain's authority and power was gone, the cabildos of the provinces regarded independence from the erstwhile viceregal capital as more important than independence from the metropolitan power. Thus New Granada fractured into contending cities and regions, some of which were themselves further divided by opposing local factions.

So, once New Granada was released from the magnetic field of Spanish authority, the regional economic differences and highly localized factional politics that had been contained in the framework of the colonial order came to the surface, splintering the country into autonomous units. In the years after 1810, the administrative unity that Bourbon viceregal governments had striven to impose on the territory of New Granada during the eighteenth century collapsed amidst a welter of competing forces. Now that power had devolved upon the "pueblo," there was no consensus about who should hold that power or how it should be exercised. If the vision of an American *patria,* nurtured during the final decades of Spanish rule, had provided a focus for opposition to Spain, it soon proved insufficient to counteract the centrifugal forces embedded in New Granada's pattern of disparate regions. For the next few years, regional elites stubbornly pursued their own interests and, by failing to build a coherent national polity, eventually laid New Granada open to Spanish reconquest in 1815.

60. Ibid., vol. 1, pp. 142–54; Liévano Aguirre, *Los Grandes Conflictos,* pp. 641–70.

Epilogue

After the fall of the viceregal government in 1810, New Granada's provinces enjoyed only a brief freedom. Obsessed by local affairs, the provinces failed to unite against a resurgent Spanish monarchy, and after General Morillo's expeditionary army landed at Santa Marta in 1815 the forces of metropolitan counterrevolution swiftly reconquered New Granada for Spain. Permanent reconstruction of the colonial order was more difficult. If weariness with civil conflict and regional disunion facilitated Spanish reconquest in 1815–16, then the savage repression that followed helped rekindle opposition to the renascent colonial regime.[1]

In some regions, a popular resistance rooted in the freedom enjoyed between 1810 and 1815 mounted an anti-Spanish insurgency that, if it could not create a nation, kept alive the idea of independence and prepared a way for liberation.[2] In 1819, Bolívar brought his irregular army across the Andes from the Venezuelan plains and, by defeating Spanish forces at the Battle of Boyacá, began the final liberation of the country from Spanish rule. At this point, New Granada was brought under republican government, but subsumed, together with Venezuela and Ecuador, within the great tripartite state known to historians as Gran Colombia. This arrangement endured until 1830 when, after a succession of local revolts against the Bolivarian government, Venezuela and Ecuador seceded from the union and became separate republics. In 1832, the Republic of New Granada was established under a central government in Bogotá, forming the basis for the state that, after further constitutional mutations, became the Republic of Colombia in 1886.

Independence did not usher in an age of economic transformation. At first, New Granada's leaders foresaw a bright future for the nascent state, which was now free to offer its rich resources in the markets of the world. Freed from the trammels of Spanish domination, they assumed that the

---

1. Hermes Tovar Pinzón, "Guerras de Opinión y Represión en Colombia durante la Independencia," *ACHSC*, vol. 11 (1983), pp. 187–233.
2. Oswaldo Díaz Díaz, *La reconquista española*, 2 vols. (Bogotá, 1964–7), passim; Brian R. Hamnett, "Popular Insurrection and Royalist Reaction: Colombian Regions, 1810–1823," in Fisher, Kuethe, and McFarlane (eds.), *Reform and Insurrection*, pp. 292–326.

return of peace, the opening of free contacts with other nations, and the removal of Spanish institutional controls would provide sufficient conditions for developing New Granada's economy. But release from the entanglements of the Spanish past was not so easily achieved. Although the burdens of Spanish commercial and fiscal impositions were removed, the economic and social structures that evolved during centuries of colonial rule presented more enduring obstacles to change. In economic terms, separation from Spain had important implications. As an independent nation, New Granada had direct access to foreign markets and capital, economic policy was brought under national direction, and local entrepreneurs could participate more fully in the country's external commerce. In the long term, the significance of these changes was considerable, permitting alterations in both the direction and composition of external trade, strengthening domestic mercantile groups, and modifying the relative importance of groups and regions within the economy. But during the early decades of republican government, the New Granadan economy saw only minor adjustments to the patterns of activity that were characteristic of the colonial period.

During the 1820s, politicians commonly attributed the country's economic backwardness to the effects of Spanish mercantilism, and assumed that the removal of institutional obstacles to private initiative was sufficient both to promote economic recovery and to lay the foundations of future prosperity. Accordingly, among the first acts of the legislature of the Republic of Colombia at the 1821 Congress of Cúcuta were measures to abolish fiscal and corporative restrictions on production and commerce, to promote freedom for foreign trade, and to encourage free markets for land and labor.[3] Economic progress failed to measure up to political expectations in these years, however, largely because New Granada's position within the international economy remained fundamentally unchanged. Foreign trade continued to rest on gold exports, and the country therefore retained a position in the world economy that was essentially similar to that of the colonial period. Like other Latin American countries, New Granada was exposed to a brief and intense burst of British trade and investment in the 1820s, but the boom soon ended. With British loans to the government of Gran Colombia in 1820, 1822, and 1824 went an upsurge in trade with Great Britain, as the loans provided foreign exchange. When the government defaulted in 1826, the inflow of investment was stemmed and the country became unattractive to British enterprise and capital. Without external finance, overseas trade sank back into colonial patterns in the 1830s and 1840s, as imports were forced into

3. For an account of economic policy during the period of Gran Colombia, see David Bushnell, *The Santander Regime in Gran Colombia* (Newark, 1954), pp. 127–150.

line with the country's ability to provide gold in exchange.[4] British capital now turned away from Latin America, toward better opportunities in Europe and the United States; in these conditions, New Granada was left to vegetate on the "old periphery" of Hispanic American precious metal producers, awaiting the redirection of European capital and commerce.[5]

When new opportunities in international markets failed to materialize, there was no alternative basis for growth. Although politicians recognized the need to promote economic development, they were incapable of framing policies that might effectively meet this need. With the failure of the laissez-faire approach that was followed during the 1820s, economic stasis weakened the political commitment to liberal policies. During the 1820s, there had been a strong conservative minority in the legislature which, by opposing liberal policies toward mortmain and by resisting liberal efforts to free interest rates from colonial restrictions, had voiced the dissent of those who still retained an attachment to the social organization and moral attitudes of the old order.[6] After the collapse of Gran Colombia in 1830, such conservative approaches to economic policy were to play an increasingly influential part in shaping government action.

Under the conservative administrations of the Republic of New Granada, the Bourbon example of reform from above, by government fiat, was still relevant. During the eighteenth century, Bourbon administrators had introduced schemes to advance exploitation of the colony's economic resources by the introduction of modern mining technology and the dissemination of scientific, practical knowledge. Although none of these schemes was very successful, the belief that government was a crucial agency for reform and rationalization, and that scientific education and innovation were vital to economic progress, left an enduring imprint on the attitudes of the Colombian ruling elite. In the decade after independence, these attitudes were reflected in schemes to contract European scientists to work in New Granada, and in plans for channeling university students into the study of applied science.[7] During the 1830s and 1840s, government intervention to promote economic development also spread

4. On foreign loans, see ibid., pp. 112–26; on British and U.S. trade with Colombia, see McGreevey, *Economic History of Colombia, 1845–1930*, pp. 35–6.
5. The phrase "old periphery" is Wallerstein's: see Immanuel Wallerstein, *The Modern World System II: Mercantilism and the Consolidation of the European World-Economy, 1600–1750* (New York, 1980), pp. 166–7; on trends in British investment in Latin America in this period, see P. L. Cottrell, *British Overseas Investment in the Nineteenth Century* (London, 1975), pp. 19–25.
6. Bushnell, *The Santander Regime*, pp. 52–4.
7. For an account of the main strands in politics and society in postindependence Colombia, see Jaime Jaramillo Uribe, *El pensamiento colombiano en el siglo XIX* (Bogotá, 1974), pp. 119–49. On attitudes toward science and education, see Frank R. Safford, *The Ideal of the Practical* (Austin, Texas, 1976), pp. 99–123.

into other areas, as conservative statesmen flirted with neomercantilist solutions to the problems of economic depression and political disorder.

From their policies, two distinct, interrelated tendencies emerged. First, steps were taken to encourage the development of a domestic industry through the extension of government aid to entrepreneurs. The concession of monopoly or partial monopoly privileges made during Santander's government of Gran Colombia were extended under the governments of the Republic of New Granada. Between 1832 and 1844, exclusive rights for the application of new techniques were granted to enterprises producing china and porcelain, paper, glass, cotton cloth, and iron. The government also offered long-term loans at low rates of interest to new enterprises, though the financial state of the treasury probably meant that few, if any, such loans were actually made.[8] In addition, it sought to encourage training in industrial skills by setting up workshops, creating apprenticeship schemes, and undertaking to instill industrious habits among the lower classes through both material incentives and coercion.[9] The second major strand of government policy designed to promote industrial growth involved tariff protection. In 1831, the *Secretario de Hacienda*, José Ignacio de Márquez, presented a series of arguments for adopting a protectionist policy that would prohibit the importation of foreign goods, to encourage the development of industry that had been held back by the colonial system.[10]

The pursuit of industrialization was chimerical, however, and the colonial pattern of buying manufactured imports with gold remained intact. Mining and the import business that it supported continued to constitute the most profitable sectors of the economy, and scarce capital was either drained abroad in exchange payments or tied up in imports or financing government borrowing. Under these circumstances, it was politically impossible to provide effective protection for national industry, or to create the monetary institutions required to remedy the shortage of capital. To promote an autonomous national industry demanded much more than the panaceas of conservative politicians. It required support from a financially stable and prosperous government, backed and influenced by groups with a stake in manufacturing. Both were conspicuously absent, and the diluted, fiscally oriented protectionism of conservative adminis-

---

8. These projects and their outcomes are described in Safford, "Commerce and Enterprise," pp. 150–75, 179–86.

9. Safford, *The Ideal of the Practical*, pp. 55–72.

10. These arguments were put forward in an address to the Convention of 1831. For a lengthy quotation from this address showing the principal ideas of Márquez, see Ospina Vásquez, *Industria y protección en Colombia*, pp. 194–8. Also Aníbal Galindo, "Apuntamientos para la historia económica y fiscal del país" (1874), chap. 3, in Galindo, *Estudios económicos y fiscales* (Bogotá, 1978), pp. 142–50.

trations, with their penchant for projects and monopoly contracts, and their concern with useful knowledge, education and technical training, were feeble essays in economic and social reform that eventually satisfied no one. By the late 1840s, disillusionment within the political and economic elites and among urban artisans provoked a period of political ferment and confrontation. Between 1849 and 1854, a new coalition of interests, firmly committed to laissez-faire, came to the forefront of national politics, marking the start of a liberal hegemony that was to endure almost to the end of the nineteenth century.[11]

In the first decades of independence, then, there had been no strong basis for autonomous economic development, and republican governments were no more successful in promoting growth than their Bourbon predecessors. Colombia remained a cluster of unevenly developed regions, only loosely connected by a primitive network of transport by river and mountain trails, and the national state was not coterminous with a national economy. Instead, the republic straddled an archipelago of thinly populated, largely self-sufficient regions with distinctive local cultures and little economic interdependence. Nor, until the development of tobacco exports at mid-century, did Colombia find a product that was capable of generating the active trade that could stimulate its economy. In this environment, there was no firm basis for autonomous development or political stability. Attempts to promote national manufactures during the 1830s were essentially an improvised response to stagnation and depression, and, though some Colombian statesmen entertained ideas for domestic industrialization, their ability to attain it was continually curtailed by the debility of the government and divisions among regional elites, both corollaries of a fragmented economy. Devoid of adequate financial resources and unable to impose a stable authority over the whole national territory, early republican governments lacked the means to meet basic obligations, much less to play a leading role in promoting an economic transformation.

Unable to conjure up national unity amidst regional diversity and growing social divisions, a sector of the Colombian elites turned to new solutions at mid-century. Determined to overcome the legacy of colonialism, liberals demanded radical reform in both political and economic

---

11. For a brief survey of Colombian politics in these years, see J. León Helguera, "The Problem of Liberalism versus Conservatism in Colombia, 1849–1885" in Frederick B. Pike (ed.), *Latin American History: Select Problems* (New York, 1969), pp. 226–32. Also Jaime Jaramillo Uribe, "Las sociedades democráticas de artesanos y la coyuntura política y social colombiana en 1848," in *ACHSC*, vol. 8 (1976), pp. 5–18, and, on the influence of French ideas, R. L. Gilmore, "Nueva Granada's Socialist Mirage," *HAHR*, vol. 34 (1956). For a more detailed study of the emergence of the Liberal party and the period of its ascendancy, see Helen Delpar, *Red against Blue: The Liberal Party in Colombian Politics, 1863–1899* (University of Alabama, 1981), passim.

spheres. This brought a commitment to free trade, and from around 1850 until the early 1880s, the Colombian economy entered a new phase of development based on cycles of commodity exports, and became more closely attuned to external markets. The vague and ineffective notions of industrialization present in the 1830s were now swept aside, and replaced by a vision of Colombia as an integral and complementary part of the international economy. However, in their eagerness to purge the country of the residues of colonialism and to set it upon a new path, the liberals tended to ignore the enduring influences of the colonial past, and the capacity of those influences to hinder and alter innovation. Assuming that the free pursuit of individual gain was synonymous with public welfare, liberal governments followed policies that tended to accentuate rather than heal social divisions.[12] Thus, when looking back over the experience of Colombia during the nineteenth century, one liberal politician was to recall that "in Colombia the first, if not the only industries of national, popular character have been civil war and politics."[13]

12. This is the thesis argued by McGreevey, *Economic History of Colombia*, pp. 67–181.

13. José María Quijano Wallis, cited by Charles W. Bergquist, *Coffee and Conflict in Colombia, 1886–1910* (Durham, North Carolina, 1978).

Appendix A: The population of New Granada

Table 1. *Distribution of population in New Granada, 1778–80*

Province	Whites	Indians	Freemen of all colours	Slaves	Total
Santa Fe (incl.Guaduas)	28,057	32,054	35,573	1,463	97,147
Tunja	101,658	32,107	97,897	4,767	236,429
Pamplonaª	3,399	4,475	17,980	1,471	27,125
Mariquita	12,336	4,436	26,313	4,083	47,168
Neiva	5,908	3,850	15,810	888	26,456
Antioquia	7,866	2,034	27,535	8,931	46,366
Chocóᵇ	332	5,414	3,160	5,756	14,662
Popayán	9,768	11,363	29,949	13,380	64,460
Tumaco	512	156	490	1,981	3,139
Raposo	99	290	549	2,259	3,197
Iscuandé	612	363	855	921	2,751
Pasto & los Pastos	10,075	15,592	922	184	26,773
Barbacoasᶜ	521	512	1,678	3,907	6,618
Cartagena	13,850	19,416	75,490	9,626	118,382
Santa Marta	4,566	8,504	22,882	3,988	39,940
Riohacha	351	633	2,513	453	3,950
Girón	1,470	126	4,593	804	6,993
Los Llanosᵈ	1,558	15,189	4,046	119	20,912

ªIn the censuses of 1778–80, the city of Pamplona is treated as part of the province of Tunja. Here, Pamplona has been treated as a separate province by including its population with that of the Alcaldía de Betas de Pamplona and the old mining town of Salazar de las Palmas. Data on these are from AHNC, Censos de varios departamentos, vol. 6, fol. 273. Because Pamplona and its neighboring area have been separated from Tunja, the population figures for that area have been reduced accordingly.
ᵇThe figure given by the Padrón General for the Chocó is inaccurate. These figures are from the provincial census taken in the Chocó in 1778, and are from AHNC, Censos de varios departamentos, vol. 6, fol. 377.
ᶜThere is no data for Barbacoas in the 1778–80 census. This figure is taken from a census of 1797, found in AGI Santa Fe 623, governor of Popayán, December 5, 1797.
ᵈFor the sake of clarity, the population of the Llanos has been concentrated on the town of Morcote in Map 2.1. In reality, the population was dispersed over a larger area.
Source: Unless otherwise stated, these data are from the "Padrón General del Virreinato del Nuevo Reino de Granada," reproduced in Perez Ayala, *Antonio Caballero y Góngora*, Cuadro A. Other sources are listed above.

353

Table 2. *Settlement in the late eighteenth century*

Region	Population	% of Total
1. Caribbean Region		
Cartagena	118,382	14.93
Santa Marta	39,940	5.04
Rio Hacha	3,950	0.50
Regional Total	162,272	20.47
2. Eastern Cordillera		
Santa Fe	88,348	11.15
Tunja	236,429	29.81
Girón	6,993	0.88
Pamplona	27,325	3.45
Regional Total	359,095	45.29
3. Upper Magdalena Valley	47,168	
Mariquita		5.95
Guaduas	8,799	1.11
Neiva	26,456	3.34
Regional Total	82,423	10.40
4. Central Cordillera		
Antioquia	46,366	5.85
5. Upper Cauca Valley	64,460	
Popayán		8.13
6. Southern Highlands		
Pasto y los Pastos	26,773	3.38
7. Pacific Lowlands		
Raposo	3,197	0.40
Iscuandé	2,751	0.35
Tumaco	3,139	0.40
Barbacoas	6,618	0.83
Chocó	14,662	1.85
Regional Total	30,367	3.83
8. Eastern Plains		
Llanos	20,912	2.64
TOTAL	792,668	100%

Table 3. *Ethnic distribution in New Granada*[a]

	Whites	Indians	Freemen of all colors	Slaves
1. Caribbean Region				
Cartagena	6.82	12.41	20.50	14.81
Santa Marta	2.25	5.43	6.21	6.14
Rio Hacha	0.17	0.40	0.68	0.70
Regional Total	9.24	18.24	27.39	21.65
2. Eastern Cordillera				
Santa Fe	12.50	20.16	8.21	1.81
Tunja	50.09	20.51	26.59	7.34
Girón	0.72	0.08	1.25	1.24
Pamplona	1.67	2.86	4.86	2.26
Regional Total	64.98	43.61	40.91	12.65
3. Upper Magdalena Valley				
Mariquita	6.08	2.83	7.15	6.28
Guaduas	1.32	0.31	1.45	0.44
Neiva	2.91	2.46	4.29	1.37
Regional Total	10.31	5.60	12.89	8.09
4. Central Cordillera				
Antioquia	3.88	1.30	7.48	13.74
5. Upper Cauca Valley				
Popayán	4.81	7.26	8.13	20.59
6. Southern Highlands				
Pasto y los Pastos	4.96	9.96	0.25	0.28
7. Pacific Lowlands				
Raposo	0.05	0.19	0.15	3.48
Iscuandé	0.30	0.23	0.23	1.42
Tumaco	0.25	0.10	0.13	3.05
Barbacoas	0.26	0.33	0.46	6.01
Chocó	0.16	3.46	0.86	8.86
Regional Total	1.02	4.31	1.83	22.82
8. Eastern Plains				
Llanos	0.77	9.70	1.10	0.18
TOTAL	100%	100%	100%	100%

[a]Expressed as percentages of total population.

Table 4. *Ethnic composition of major regions*

	% White	% Indian	% Freemen of all colors	% Slave
1. Caribbean Region				
Cartagena	11.70	16.40	63.77	8.13
Santa Marta	11.43	21.29	57.29	9.98
Rio Hacha	8.89	16.03	63.62	11.47
Regional Total	11.57	17.60	62.17	8.67
2. Eastern Cordillera				
Santa Fe	28.27	35.72	34.23	1.33
Tunja	43.00	13.58	41.41	2.02
Girón	21.02	1.80	65.68	11.50
Pamplona	12.53	16.50	66.29	5.42
Regional Total	36.73	19.01	41.97	2.29
3. Upper Magdalena Valley				
Mariquita	26.15	9.40	55.79	8.66
Guaduas	30.49	5.60	60.62	3.28
Neiva	22.33	14.55	59.76	3.36
Regional Total	25.39	10.65	57.58	6.38
4. Central Cordillera				
Antioquia	16.97	4.39	59.39	19.26
5. Upper Cauca Valley				
Popayán	15.15	17.63	46.46	20.76
6. Southern Highlands				
Pasto y los Pastos	37.63	58.24	3.44	0.69
7. Pacific Lowlands				
Raposo	3.10	9.07	17.17	70.66
Iscuandé	22.25	13.20	31.08	33.48
Tumaco	16.31	4.97	15.61	63.11
Barbacoas	7.87	7.74	25.36	59.04
Chocó	2.26	36.93	21.55	39.26
Regional Total	6.84	22.18	22.17	48.82
8. Eastern Plains				
Llanos	7.45	72.63	19.35	0.57

Table 5. *Distribution of population in the Caribbean coastal region*

Place	Whites	Indians	Freemen of all colours	Slaves	Total
Province of Cartagena					
1. Cartagena de Indias, (including Parroquias de San Lázaro, Bocachica & Barú.)	4,393	88	8,832	3,048	16,361
2. Turbaco	71	512	549	181	1,313
3. Truana	1	285			286
4. Arjona	106		1,105	190	1,401
5. Mahates	109		2,035	229	2,373
6. Palenque	2		314	394	710
7. María y Flamencos	2		710	636	1,348
8. San Estanislao	168		1,674	101	1,943
9. Timiriguaco	43		482	7	532
10. Barranquilla	52		2,580	44	2,676
11. Soledad	73		1,940	67	2,080
12. Sabanagrande	62		1,719	28	1,809
13. SantoTomás	26		1,062	29	1,117
14. Sabanalarga	38		2,282	92	2,412
15. Real de la Cruz	58		2,332	84	2,474
16. Santa Rosa	16		600	84	700
17. Santa Catalina	15		678	17	710
18. Palmar de Candelaria	1		688	24	713
19. Baranoa	43		1,610	28	1,681
20. Malambo	3	828	35	3	869
21. Galapa	1	539	344	26	910
22. Tubara	1	957	16	1	975
23. Usacuri	3	894	375	2	1,274
24. Pijón	18	431	79	57	585
25. Barranca	75		676	81	832
26. Yucal	1	247		5	253
27. Corozal	609		2,104	110	2,823
28. Tolú	232		1,254	189	1,675
29. Lorica	1,056		3,447	216	4,719
30. Momil	235	44	683	78	1,040
31. Sincelejo	382		983	19	1,384
32. Pinchorroy	371		750	3	1,124
33. San Carlos	2		487		489
34. San Tero	53		28	250	331
35. San Onofre	18	59	550	609	1,236
36. San Gerónimo	236		930	19	1,185
37. San Pelayo	343		1,343	38	1,724
38. San Bernardo	28		970	30	1,028
39. Ciénaga de Oro	27		805	20	852
40. San Antonio Abad	101		526		627

Table 5. (cont.)

41. San Benito Abad	64		1,251	115	1,430
42. Caymito	91		537	221	849
43. Cince	281		1,316	103	1,701
44. Chinú	92	121	1,652	61	1,926
45. San Juan Sahagún	67		953	37	1,057
46. San Jacinto, San Carmen & San Francisco	88		1,475	8	1,571
47. San Juan , San Cayetano & San Agustín	70		1,090	21	1,181
48. San Andrés	16	3,407	11		3,434
49. Sampues	25	1,946	34	36	2,041
50. Tolú Viejo	1	1,118			1,119
51. Nicolás	1	817			818
52. San Juan de las Palmas	783	389	762	29	1,963
53. Sabaneta	1	541			542
54. Urabá	1	1,141			1,142
55. Gegua	1	484			485
56. Serete	1	817			818
57. Coloro	8	181			189
58. Morroa	11	301			312
59. Mompox	876	94	5,201	832	7,003
60. El Retiro	91		918	168	1,117
61. Magangué	220		1,321	67	1,608
62. San Sebastián	23		805	15	843
63. Santiago	38		401	4	443
64. Tacasaluma	88		637	18	743
65. Cascajal	33		495	14	542
66. Tacaloa	160		357	59	426
67. Tacamocha	11		888		899
68. Guasso	1	881			822
69. Yaty	1	525			526
70. Talaygua	1	702			703
71. Teton	341				341
72. Zambrano	541				541
73. San Josef de la Vittoria	89	184	784	27	1,084
74. Ojolargo	38		325	76	439
75. Algarrobo	73	51	1,673	62	1,859
76. Loba	7	78	661	25	771
77. Norosí	9	10	402	123	544
78. Peñon	1	227	58		286
79. Menchiguejo & Chilloa	54	296	856	8	1,214
80. Ayapel	63	85	1,125	251	1,524
81. Simití	289		757	82	1,128
82. Tablada	57	124	287	6	474
83. Morales	44		577	59	680
84. Guamoyo	17		284	37	338

Table 5. *(cont.)*

Province of Santa Marta

85.	Santa Marta	525	21	2,490	571	3,607
86.	San Juan de la Ciénaga	38	1,235	212	1	1,486
87.	San Jacinto de la Guayra	1	299	8	1	309
88.	San Gerónimo de Mamatoca	1	389			390
89.	Santa Ana de Bonda & Mazinga	1	317	1		319
90.	San Carlos de San Sebastián	84				84
91.	Sitionuevo	29	12	633	3	677
92.	Remolino	52	7	577	21	657
93.	Guaymara	30	8	1,551	105	1,694
94.	Puntagorda	1	10	25		37
95.	Pinon	76	13	991	27	1,107
96.	San Antonio	14	9	1,313	61	1,397
97.	Tenerife	72	59	1,442	77	1,650
98.	Pinto	43	178	267	3	491
99.	Morro	2	209	5		216
100.	Banco	31		873	71	975
101.	Plato	3	1	334	3	341
102.	Tamalameque	35	2	663	100	800
103.	San Bernardo	1		263	26	289
104.	Simana	8		546	22	576
105.	Chiriguana	61		2,109	93	2,263
106.	Candelaria del Banco	27		861	34	922
107.	Tamalequito	15		201	12	228
108.	Saloa	7		331	45	383
109.	Valencia de Jesus	271	8	1,412	242	1,923
110.	El Paso	6		289	153	448
111.	Ariguani	1	127	35	7	170
112.	San Sebastián	1	151	15		167
113.	Tuerto	1		600		601
114.	Pernambuco			307	26	333
115.	Guamal	19		822	31	872
116.	San Fernando	10		284		294
117.	Santa Ana	26	581	83		690
118.	Venero	1	18	77	1	97
119.	San Zenon	1	240	103		344
120.	Valledupar	841		2,144	796	3,781
121.	San José de Barranca	136	5	566	170	877
122.	Fonseca	267		526	161	954
123.	Atanques	1	346	18	1	366

Table 5. *(cont.)*

124. San Tomás de Villanueva	124	842	104	4	1,074
125. El Rosario & Marocasa	1	448		4	453
126. El Espíritu Santo	1	144	4		149
127. San Juan de César	304	19	725	115	1,163
128. Vadillo	77		715	30	822
129. El Molino	34	870	277	11	1,192
130. Becerril	44	86	154	66	350
131. Tabo	112		305	38	455
132. Ocaña	1,746	60	2,950	923	5,679
133. Agua Chica	29		766	18	813
134. San Jacinto y Fernanda	6	1	352	8	367
135. Buenavista & San Andrés	2	353	95		450
136. La Loma & Borotare	34	552	231	30	847

Province of Río Hacha

137. Río Hacha	192	17	943	363	1,515
138. Pedraza	10		275	30	305
139. Bahiahonda	1		61		62
140. Sinamaica	118		182		300
141. Sabana del Valle	8	1	15	1	25
142. Moreno	18		691	70	779
143. Arroya Cardón	1	132	1		134
144. Boroncita	1	183	239	14	437
145. Camarones	1	126	104	5	236
146. San Pedro de Cototama	1	174	2		177

Sources: AHNC, Censos de varios departamentos, vol. 6. "Padrón hecho en el año de 1778 . . . en esta Provincia . . ." Cartagena de Indias, November 26, 1778; AGI Indiferente General 1537, "Padrón General que manifiesta el número de personas havitantes en esta Provincia de Santa Marta. . . ." Santa Marta, June 21, 1793; AHNC, Censos de varios departamentos, vol. 6, fol. 369, "Padrón hecho en el año de 1778 . . . en esta Provincia de Río Hacha. . . ."

Table 6. *Distribution of population in the Eastern Cordillera region*

Place	Whites	Indians	Freemen of all colors	Slaves	Total
Province of Santa Fe					
Santa Fe de Bogotá	6,585	1,753	7,428	654	16,420
Corregimiento of Bogotá	798	4,777	6,269	51	11,895
Corregimiento of Bosa	1,926	2,578	3,505	290	8,299
Corregimiento of Ubaqué	3,570	3,754	3,519	92	10,935
Corregimiento of Zipaquirá and Ubaté	7,575	12,247	8,294	46	28,163
Corregimiento of Guatavita	3,793	6,366	6,142	38	16,399
Province of Tunja					
Tunja	53,936	29,882	44,163	737	128,718
Vélez	18,274	2,298	26,981	1,386	48,939
Muzo	2,749	621	1,711	65	5,416
Pamplona	1,385	3,659	16,018	1,430	22,492
Socorro	16,775	440	17,735	883	35,849
San Gil	4,466	225	9,884	559	15,134
Leiva	3,749	1,288	2,942	53	8,032
Province of San Juan Girón					
San Juan Girón	971	120	3,436	584	5,111
Parish of San Francisco Xavier	350	34	1,162	292	1,838
Parish of Puerto de Botijas	15		292	10	317
Parish of Puerto del Pedral	11	19	246	2	278
Alcaldía mayor de betas de Pamplona					
Parish of Bucaramanga	268		1,218	59	1,545
Sitio de Cácota	15		327	4	346
Real de la Baja	11		380	2	393
Betas	4		25		29

Sources: AHNC, Censos, Caja 1, "Padrón hecho en el año de 1779 . . . en esta ciudad de Santa Fe de Bogotá . . . y en toda su jurisdicción. . . ."; Censos de varios departamentos, vol. 6, fols. 271, 385, 389.

Table 7. *Distribution of population in the province of Popayán*

Place	Whites	Indian	Freemen of all colours	Slaves	Total
Popayán	5,220	2,789	2,509	2,923	3,702
Cali	934	330	7,120	2,606	10,990
Buga	2,547	112	6,896	2,679	12,234
Pasto	4,682	5,861	893	131	11,567
Cartago	1,169	134	2,257	763	4,323
Caloto	3,057	1,803	1,493	4,492	10,845
Almaguer	316	2,480	2,540	570	5,906
Anserma	216	63	868	365	1,512
Toro	1,232	88	1,639	167	3,126
Iscuandé	612	363	855	921	2,751
Provincia de Raposo	99	290	549	2,259	3,197
Provincia de los Pastos	5,393	9,731	59	53	15,236
Tumaco	162	490	1,981	36	2,669
Barbacoas					6,618

Source: AHNC, Censos de varios departamentos, vol. 6, fol. 375. Figures for Barbacoas are from the 1797 census in AGI, Santa Fe 623, governor of Popayán, December 5, 1797.

Table 8. *Distribution of population in the Chocó*

Place	Whites	Indians	Freemen of all colours	Slaves	Total
Nóvita	39		460	1,129	1,628
Tadó	67	457	440	1,157	2,121
Noanama	7	640	232	27	906
Brazos	14	176	328	397	915
Sipí	11	123	273	685	1,092
Juntas	6	141	29	84	260
Baudó	11	122	79		212
Cajón	1		134	238	373
Quibdó	50	1,077	400	714	2,241
Lloró	25	1,140	176	343	1,684
Chami	10	993		10	1,013
Beté	7	119	122	23	271
Bebará	36	103	296	613	1,048
Murrí	4	237	66	28	335
Pabarando	41	86	125	308	560

Source: Censos de varios departamentos, vol. 6, fol. 377.

Table 9. *Distribution of population in Antioquia*

Place	Whites	Indians	Freemen of all colours	Slaves	Total
Santa Fe de Antioquia	1,235		6,360	8,121	15,716
Medellín	2,653		9,100	2,501	14,254
Rionegro	551		2,953	686	4,190
Marinilla	1,173		2,037	372	3,852
Remedios	294		1,155	721	2,170
Arma	388		932	495	1,815
Cáceres	20		78	215	313
Peñol	1	696			697
Pereira		400			400
Zabaleras	1	116			117
La Estrella	1	228			229
Sopetrán	1	364			365
Buriticá	1	368			369
Sabanalarga	1	547			548
Zaragoza	73		654	359	1,086
Sitio de la Llana	10	5	102	24	141
Nechi	15		190	6	211

Sources: AHNC, Censos de varios departamentos, vol. 6, fols. 483, 485.

Appendix B: Gold production

Table I. *Gold coined in New Granada, 1700–1810*

Year	Value (Pesos)	Year	Value (Pesos)	Year	Value (Pesos)
1700	267240	1734	707744	1777	676736
1701	302600	1735	764048	1778	793328
1702	234328	1736	634984	1779	794240
1703	237320	1737	595952	1780	710192
1704	410448	1738	577048	1781	558280
1705	401200	1739	694960	1782	1029656
1706	394944	1740	671704	1783	1395496
1707	407592	1741	1156136	1784	744192
1708	204544	1742	981376	1785	954448
1709	436832	1743-48 average: 933345	1786	767584
1710	319328	1749-53 average: 1084022	1787	981104
1711	409904	1754	958392	1788	900320
1712	390456	1755	1145800	1789	971040
1713	452200	1756	1027208	1790	998648
1714	286240	1757	923032	1791	1131248
1715	432208	1758	635936	1792	1109488
1716	303280	1759	467568	1793	1177624
1717	424728	1760	420104	1794	993752
1718	398344	1761	479672	1795	1266160
1719	351344	1762	593776	1796	1075624
1720	1086504	1763	784584	1797	2048432
1721	746912	1764	1568624	1798	1694016
1722	524960	1765	876248	1799	1238824
1723	166600	1766	1083376	1800	1428816
1724	413440	1767	612136	1801	1504568
1725	622880	1768	475184	1802	1239096
1726	482528	1769	393720	1803	1109760
1727	315112	1770	371144	1804	1273096
1728	727736	1771	491776	1805	1463768
1729	657560	1772	926568	1806	1456968
1730	867816	1773	756840	1807	1490968
1731	658376	1774	700672	1808	1109760
1732	690064	1775	508232	1809	1225632
1733	582928	1776	619208	1810	1109624

Table 1. *(cont.)*

Value of Gold Coined in the Popayan Mint, 1753-1810

Year	Value (Pesos)	Year	Value (Pesos)
1753-70	average: 422928	1788	932552
1771-76	average: 592571	1789	801312
1777	858452	1790	885768
1778	745820	1791	824296
1779	814368	1792	951320
1780	787848	1793	920176
1781	909160	1794	984096
1782	898688	1795	947648
1783	820624	1796	947784
1784	956760	1797	948328
1785	973670	1798	924256
1786	879104	1799	939488
1787	894744	1800	926432
		1801-10	average: 931464

Sources: For Bogotá, A. M. Barriga Villalba, *Historia de la Casa de Moneda,* tomo 3, pp. 509–15, 517–20. For Popayán, J. M. Restrepo, *Memoria sobre la amonedación de oro y plata en la Nueva Granada,* Cuadro 2, p. 28.

Table 2. *Chocó: Average annual gold production, according to quintos, 1724–1803 (castellanos)*

Year	Annual Average	Year	Annual Average
1724-1725	113064	1761-1765	126948
1726-1730	152980	1766-1770	123975
1731-1735	157650	1771-1775	130134
1736-1740	164671	1776-1780	119216
1741-1745	165022	1781-1785	122239
1746-1750	161604	1786-1790	125824
1751-1755	135840	1791-1795	133567
1756-1760	116486	1796-1800	135696
		1801-1803	125366

Source: W. F. Sharp, *Slavery on the Spanish Frontier*, p. 201.

Table 3. *Antioquia: Annual averages of gold registered for smelting (in pesos de oro), 1700–1809*

Year	Annual Average	Year	Annual Average
1700-1704	24999	1755-1759	39133
1705-1709	22080	1760-1764	53971
1710-1714	17615	1765-1769	48987
1715-1719	18308	1770-1774	75136
1720-1724	29103	1775-1779	119177
1725-1729	19007	1780-1784	159608
1730-1734	21454	1785-1789	227877
1735-1739	14367	1790-1794	296755
1740-1744	23136	1795-1799	279194
1745-1749	25805	1800-1804	228164
1750-1754	40632	1805-1809	166777

Source: Data for 1700–60 are from Ann Twinam, *Miners, Merchants and Farmers*, p. 28. Data for 1760–1809 are from AHA Minas, tomo 459, ms. 453; tomo 460, mss. 462, 467; tomo 461, mss. 480, 487, 491; tomo 462, mss. 493, 506, 517; tomo 463, mss. 519, 530, 546; tomo 464, mss. 559, 567; tomo 474, ms. 2; tomo 479, ms. 54; tomo 480, ms. 81; tomo 481, ms. 92; tomo 483, ms. 126; tomo 484, ms. 155; tomo 486, ms. 173; tomo 488, ms. 205; tomo 497, ms. 290; tomo 499, ms. 309; tomo 501, ms. 340; tomo 506, ms. 405; tomo 508, ms. 430; tomo 512, ms. 493; tomo 514, ms. 513; tomo 519, ms. 597; tomo 524, ms. 651; tomo 634, mss. 10058, 10044, 10059; tomo 470, mss. 662, 621, 627, 634. (The order of the volume and manuscript numbers given above conforms to the chronological order of the figures given in the table.)

Table 4. *Popayán: Average annual gold production, according to quintos, 1700–1804 (castellanos)*

Year	Annual Average	Year	Annual Average
1700-1704	42047	1750-1754	35938
1705-1709	60352	1755-1759	48120
1710-1714	78597	1760-1764	68271
1715-1719	76377	1765-1769	72028
1720-1724	96154	1770-1774	98277
1725-1729	106742	1775-1779	91585
1730-1734	93399	1780-1784	132600
1735-1739	102278	1785-1789	141617
1740-1744	81893	1790-1794	224867
1745-1749	58277	1795-1799	239147
		1800-1804	174200

Sources: The figures for gold declared in 1700–49 are from German Colmenares, *Historia económica y social de Colombia*, vol. 1, p. 235. Figures for the quintos paid from 1752 are from the Caja Real de Popayán, Archivo Central del Cauca, Colonia, CII-18rc 5387, 5314; CII-23rc 5787, 5837, 5874; CIII-6rc 6030; CIII-4rc 5978; CIII-8rc 6290; CII-6rc 6143-44; CII-84c 6371; CIII-9rc 6429, 6496, 6512; CIII-10rc 6531, 6557, 6572, 6589, 6616, 6630, 6654, 6660; CII-15rc 6700, 6723, 6738, 6769.

Appendix C: Shipping and commerce

Table 1. *Shipping from Spain to*
Cartagena de Indias, 1731–79

Year	Ships	(Observations)
1731	2	1 aviso.
1732	-	-
1733	2	1 aviso.
1734	1	1 aviso.
1735		2 Royal Service (R.S.)
1736	3	3 avisos.
1737	5	Convoy (Blas de Lezo).
1738`	2	2 avisos.
1739	1	1 aviso.
1740	-	-
1741	3	2 avisos.
1742	-	-
1743	8	2 captured, 1 shipwreck.
1744	3	-
1745	3	-
1746	1	-
1747	2	-
1748	5	2 captured.
1749	5	2 R.S.
1750	3	-
1751	4	-
1752	6	2 avisos.
1753	6	2 R.S.
1754	-	-
1755	2	-
1756	5	1 R.S.
1757	6	2 R.S.
1758	3	1 R.S.
1759	1	-
1760	5	1 R.S.
1761	7	4 R.S.
1762	3	3 avisos (all captured).
1763	6	-
1764	2	-
1765	4	1 R.S.
1766	6	1 R.S.
1767	4	2 R.S.
1768	4	-
1769	5	2 R.S.
1770	6	2 R.S

Table 1. (cont.)

Year	Ships	(Observations)
1771	1	1 R.S.
1772	4	1 R.S., 1 shipwreck.
1773	4	1 R.S.
1774	4	1 R.S.
1775	4	1 R.S.
1776	5	-
1777	6	-
1778	4	-
1779	3	-

Source: AGI Consulados, libro 358, "Libros donde se relacionan todas las Armadas y Navios sueltos de Registros que se despachen a la Amrica desde principio de este presente aÊo de 1730 . . ."

Table 2. *Cartagena: Almojarifazgo de entrada de generos de Castilla, 1781–1800*

Year	Revenues (Pesos)
1781	3,041
1782	140,692
1783	202,440
1784	49,874
1785	142,270
1786	124,476
1787	81,433
1788	181,614
1789	135,211
1790	64,375
1791	45,630
1792	42,309
1793	18,533
1794	102,183
1795	28,020
1796	45,817
1797	48,579
1798	28,374
1799	47,473
1800	35,597

Sources: 1781–84: "Estado general de los productos que ha tenido la Real Aduana de Cartagena de Indias," Pérez Ayala, *Antonio Caballero y Góngora*, Table E. For 1785–1800: AGI Santa Fe 1116–1119, Cuentas de Alcabala.

Table 3. Shipping from Spain and foreign ports entering Cartagena, 1783–90

Year	From Spain	From foreign ports.
1783	8	43
1784	6	11
1785	24	9
1786	20	21
1787	12	29
1788	30	30
1789	32	11
1790	16	2

Table 4. Shipping from Spanish ports to Cartagena de Indias, 1783–1790

Year	Cádiz	Barcelona	Barcelona & Málaga	Málaga	Other
1783	7	-	1	-	-
1784	3	1	1	-	1
1785	13	-	9	2	-
1786	11	-	5	2	2
1787	5	1	3	2	1
1788	16	-	9	2	3
1789	14	4	9	2	3
1790	6	3	7	-	-

Sources: 1783: AHNC Aduanas (Anexo), tomo 5, fols. 250–539, Almojarifazgo de entrada de géneros de Castilla.
1784: Ibid., tomo 7, fols. 6–317.
1785: Ibid., tomo 8, fols. 195–210: Libro de Visitas y Registros . . . de las embarcaciones que entran y salen. . . . de Cartagena.
1786: Ibid., tomo 12, fols. 733–740: Almojarifazgo de entrada de géneros de Castilla.
1787: Ibid., tomo 15, fols. 2–81.
1788: AGI Santa Fe 1116, Cuentas de alcabala, (Pliego 2, almojarifazgo de entrada de géneros de Castilla).
1789: AHNC, Aduanas (Anexo) tomo 16, fols. 1010–1029: Libro de visitas y registros.
1790: AGI Santa Fe 1117, Cuentas de alcabala, (Pliego 2, almojarifazgo de entrada de géneros de Castilla).

Table 5. *Exports of hides from Cartagena to Spain*

Year	No. of hides.
1785	3,024
1786	4,792
1787	5,378
1788	4,510
1789	3,881
1790	2,039
1791	2,553
1792	7,916
1793	6,773
1794	7,476
1795	4,230
1796	5,537

Sources: Figures for 1785–89: AGI Santa Fe 957, Resumen de un Quatrenio de las embarciones y su carga que han salido de este Puerto de Cartagena para los de la Peninsula; figures for 1789–94: AGI Indiferente General 2447–2459.

Table 6. *Cotton exports from Cartagena to Spain*

Year	Cotton (arrobas)
1785	23,720
1786	20,740
1787	15,424
1788	27,656
1789	31,373
1790	30,351
1791	34,756
1792	64,791
1793	46,041
1794	75,534
1795	32,042
1796	47,786

Sources: Figures for 1785–89: AGI Santa Fe 957, Resumen de un Quatrenio de las embarciones y su carga que han salido de este Puerto de Cartagena para los de la Peninsula; figures for 1789–94: AGI Indiferente General 2447–2459.

Table 7. *Cacao exports from Cartagena to Spain*

Year	Cacao (arrobas)
1785	984
1786	5,036
1787	5,754
1788	3,950
1789	5,650
1790	7,599
1791	5,081
1792	4,743
1793	4,452
1794	17,391

Sources: Figures for 1785–89: AGI Santa Fe 957, Resumen de un Quatrenio de las embarciones y su carga que han salido de este Puerto de Cartagena para los de la Peninsula; figures for 1789–94: AGI Indiferente General 2447–2459.

Table 8. *Alcabala revenues: Popayán, 1722–1807*

Year	Revenues (pesos)
1722	1,089
1723	989
1724	951
1725	744
1726	924
1727	
1728	
1729	
1730	
1731	1,005
1732	1,209
1733	1,547
1734	1,039
1735	729
1736	
1737	
1738	
1739	
1740	
1741	4,445
1742	2,052
1743	1,994
1744	3,369
1745	1,498
1746	
1747	
1748	
1749	
1750	4,430
1751	
1752	2,994
1753	5,601
1754	6,862
1755	4,456
1756	5,909
1757	8,265
1758	6,844
1759	5,937
1760	4,752
1761	5,336
1762	5,223
1763	7,001
1764	4,551
1765	3,447
1766	4,114
1767	8,053
1768	13,717
1769	10,243
1770	9,036

Table 8. *(cont.)*

Year	Revenues (pesos)
1771	6,936
1772	7,494
1773	12,665
1774	3,654
1775	6,453
1776	10,020
1777	8,388
1778	7,431
1779	7,819
1780	7,513
1781	9,644
1782	
1783	7,096
1784	6,791
1785	8,616
1786	8,338
1787	6,632
1788	
1789	11,507
1790	12,118
1791	21,344
1792	18,370
1793	23,084
1794	
1795	21,079
1796	22,643
1797	27,243
1798	20,285
1799	17,693
1800	20,395
1801	26,907
1802	18,063
1803	9,854
1804	14,650
1805	17,325
1806	12,032
1807	11,731
1808	11,605

Sources: Archivo Central del Cauca, Colonia, CI-1a 3079, 3105, 3129, 3143, 3304; CI-5a 3477; CI-1a 3221; CII-5a 3512, 3546, 3624, 3984, 3870, 3980, 4012, 4095; CII-9rc 4275; CII-18rc 5059; CII-14a 5592, 5708; CII-23rc 5787; CIII-4rc 5837, 5874, 5978; CIII-6rc 6030, 6143, 6144; CIII-5a 6084; CIII-8rc 6290, 6371; CIII-9rc 6429, 6496, 6512; CIII-10rc 6531, 6557, 6572, 6589, 6616, 6630, 6654, 6660; CIII-15rc 6700, 6723, 6738, 6769.

Table 9. *Shipping from Cartagena to Spain, 1750–96*

Year	Ships	Ships via Havana
1750	10	7
1751	3	-
1752	5	4
1753	7	1
1754	6	1
1755	8	1
1756	1	1
1757	4	3
1758	6	4
1759	2	2
1760	3	3
1761	1	1
1762	1	1
1763	-	-
1764	5	1
1765	5	3
1766	3	1
1767	5	5
1768	6	3
1769	10	7
1770	4	1
1771	14	14
1772	5	4
1773	4	1
1774	6	5
1775	5	2
1776	3	1
1777	4	-
1778	4	2
1779	1	-
1780	1	-
1781	-	-
1782	-	-
1783	-	-
1784	3	2
1785	6	3
1786	12	-
1787	13	-
1788	14	-
1789	12	-
1790	12	2
1791	14	2
1792	20	5
1793	13	7
1794	31	8
1795	18	2
1796	13	3

Sources: For 1750–83, AGI Contratación 2902A, "Libros de la Contaduría de reglamentos de asientos de venida a Cadiz de la embarcaciones . . ." For 1784–96, AGI, Santa Fe 957, Expedientes del Consulado y Comericio.

Bibliography

Primary sources: Archives

Archivo General de Indias, Seville (AGI)

Audiencia de Quito: Legajos 126, 280
Audiencia de Santa Fe: Legajos 264, 265, 288, 357, 366, 374, 385, 552, 553, 572, 573, 585, 586, 588, 593, 603, 605, 623, 638–41, 643, 655, 659–61, 702, 836, 837, 955, 957–60, 1014–16, 1116–17, 1161, 1162, 2313, 2314, 2316.
Consulados: Legajos 314–45
Contratación: Legajos 1663–5, 2654, 2661, 2662, 2902A
Escribanía de Cámara: Legajos 818a–18b
Indiferente General: Legajos 1162, 1527, 1955, 2046A, 2209–56, 2310, 2315, 2316, 2318, 2412, 2447–59, 2466

Archivo Histórico Nacional, Madrid (AHNM)

Codices, Libro 7556
Consejos, Legajo 20,452

Archivo Histórico Nacional de Colombia, Bogotá (AHNC)

Abastos: vol. 9
Aduanas: vols. 1, 2, 6, 8, 9–11, 13, 16, 17, 19, 22, 24
Aduanas, Anexo: vols. 5, 7, 8, 11–16, 21
Aduanas, Cartas: vols. 3–5, 7–12
Asuntos Importantes: vol. 3
Censos de varios departamentos: vol. 6
Comercio: vol. 1
Consulados: vols. 1–5
Historia Civil: vols. 7bis, 18
Mejoras Materiales: vol. 7
Milicias y Marina: vols. 17, 18, 48, 125, 131
Miscelanea: vols. 3, 13, 31, 73
Notaría Primera: vols. 91, 191, 198, 201, 205, 228
Notaría Segunda: vols. 161, 198
Real Audiencia: vol. 9
Real Hacienda: vol. 8
Real Hacienda, Cartas: vols. 2–9
Virreyes: vols. 5–6

Archivo Restrepo, Bogotá

Correspondencia reservada del Arzobispo-Virrey Cabellero y Góngora

Biblioteca Nacional de Colombia, Bogotá (BNC)

Fondo Quijano Otero: *Correo Curioso*
                    Papel Periódico de Santafé de Bogotá
                    La Bagatela
                    Manuscrito 184

Biblioteca Luis Angel Arango (Bogotá)

Documentos relativos a amonedación y fisco en la colonia, ms. 118

Academic Colombiana de Historia (Bogotá)

Archivo: Borrador de Cartas, no. 4

Archivo Central del Cauca (Popayán), (ACC)

Libros capitulares: vols. 21–3, 26–8
Colonia civil I–III

Archivo Histórico de Antioquia (Medellín), (AHA)

Colonia: Documentos: vol. 558
          Hacienda: vol. 747
          Minas: vols. 357, 459–64, 470, 474, 479–81, 483, 484, 486, 488, 497, 499,
          501, 506, 508, 512, 514, 519, 524, 634
          Libros: vols. 454, 455, 457, 459, 462, 481, 502, 681

Archivo del Cabildo (Medellín) (ACM)

Libros del Cabildo: vol. 15

British Library (BL)

Additional manuscripts 13974, 13987
Egerton manuscripts 1807

Published primary sources

Acevedo Latorre, Eduardo (ed.), *Jeografía física i política de las Provincias de la Nueva Granada por la Comisión Corográfica bajo la dirección de Agustín Codazzi*, 3 vols. (Bogotá, 1957–8).
  Atlas de mapas antiguos de Colombia, siglos XVI a XIX (Bogotá, 1986).
Amar, Antonio de, "Archivo del Virrey Amar," *Boletín de Historia y Antigüedades*, vol. 32 (Bogotá, 1945), pp. 341–54.
Ancízar, Manuel, *Peregrinación de Alpha* (Bogotá, 1970 ed.).

Antúñez y Acevedo, R., *Memorias históricas sobre la legislación y gobierno del comercio de las españoles en sus colonias en las Indias occidentales* (Madrid, 1797).

Banco de la República, *Proceso histórico del 20 de julio de 1810. Documentos* (Bogotá, 1960).

Bourgoing, J. F., *Tableau de l'Espagne Moderne* (2nd. ed., Paris, 1779).

Caldas, Francisco José de (ed.), *Semanario del Nuevo Reino de Granada*, 3 vols. (repr. Bogotá, 1942).

Canga Argüelles, J., *Diccionario de Hacienda* (2nd ed., Madrid, 1833).

Fermín de Vargas, Pedro, *Pensamientos políticos* (Universidad Nacional, Bogotá, 1968).

Fonnegra, Gabriel (ed.), *Mutis y la Expedición Botánica: Documentos* (Bogotá, 1983).

Friede, Juan (ed.), *Documentos sobre la fundación de la Casa de Moneda en Santa Fe de Bogotá* (Bogotá 1963).

Documentos inéditos para la historia de Colombia, 5 vols. (Bogotá, 1955–7).

Rebelión Comunera de 1781. Documentos, 2 vols. (Bogotá, 1981).

Galindo, Aníbal, *Estudios económicos y fiscales* (Bogotá, 1978).

Gilij, Felipe Salvador, *Ensayo de historia americana* (Bogotá, 1955).

Gutiérrez de Piñeres, Eduardo, "Población de la provincia de Cartagena de Indias en al ano de 1772," *Boletín Historial*, vol. 3, no. 29 (Cartagena, 1917).

Hernández de Alba, Guillermo (ed.), *Escritos científicos de don José Celestino Mutis*, 2 vols. (Bogotá, 1983).

El proceso de Nariño a la luz de documentos inéditos (Bogotá, 1958).

Juan, Jorge y Antonio de Ulloa, *Relación histórica del Viage hecho de orden de Su Magestad a la América Meriodional* (Madrid, 1748).

A Voyage to South America (John Adams translation, abridged, New York, 1964).

Noticias secretas de America, 2 vols. (Madrid, 1918).

Julian, Antonio, *La Perla de la America. Provincia de Santa Marta reconocida, observada y expuesta en discursos históricos* (Bogotá, 1951).

Lucena Salmoral, Manuel (ed.), *El Memorial de Don Salvador Plata, Los Comuneros y los Movimientos Antirreformistas* (Bogotá, 1982).

Marco Dorta, Enrique, "Cartagena de Indias. Riquezas ganaderas y problemas," *Tercer Congreso Hispanoamericano de Historia*, vol. 1 (Cartagena, 1962), pp. 327–52.

Martínez Delgado, Luis, and Sergio Elías Ortíz (eds.), *El Periodismo en la Nueva Granada, 1810–1811* (Bogotá, 1960).

Mollien, Gustavo, *Viaje por la República de Colombia en 1823* (Bogotá, 1944).

Moreno y Escandón, Francisco Antonio, "Estado del Virreinato de Santa Fe, Nuevo Reino de Granada," *Boletín de Historia y Antigüedades*, vol. 23 (Bogotá, 1935), pp. 547–616.

Indios y mestizos de la Nueva Granada a finales del siglo XVIII (ed. Jorge O. Melo) (Bogotá, 1985).

Nariño, Antonio, *Escritos Políticos* (Bogotá, 1982).

La Bagatela (facsimile ed., Bogotá, 1982).

Ortega Ricaurte, Enrique (ed.), *Historia documental del Chocó* (Bogotá, 1954).

Documentos sobre el 20 de julio de 1810 (Bogotá, 1965).

Ortíz, Sergio Elías (ed.), *Colección de documentos para la historia de Colombia (Epoca de la Independencia)* (Bogotá, 1965).

Escritos de dos economistas coloniales (Bogotá, 1960).

Oviedo, Basilio Vicente de, *Cualidades y riquezas del Nuevo Reino de Granada* (Biblioteca de historia nacional, vol. 45, Bogotá, 1930).

Pérez Ayala, José Manuel, *Antonio Caballero y Góngora, Virrey y arzobispo de Santa Fe 1723–1796* (Bogotá, 1951).

Pérez Sarmiento, J. M., *Causas célebres a los Precursores* (Bogotá, 1929).

Pombo, José Ignacio de, *Comercio y contrabando en Cartagena de Indias* (Bogotá, 1986).

Posada, Eduardo, *Bibliografía bogotana*, 2 vols. (Bogotá, 1917–25).

Posada, Eduardo, and P. M. Ibáñez (eds.), *Relaciones de mando. Memorias presentadas por los gobernantes del Nuevo Reino de Granada* (Bogotá, 1910).

El Precursor: Documentos sobre la vida pública y privada del General Antonio Nariño (Bogotá, 1903).

Reichel-Dolmatoff, Gerardo (ed.), *Diario de viaje del P. Joseph Palacios de la Vega entre los indios y negros de la Provincia de Cartagena de Indias en el Nuevo Reino de Granada, 1787–1788* (Bogotá, 1955).

Restrepo, José Manuel, *Memoria sobre la amonedación de oro i plata en la Nueva Granada* (Bogotá, 1860).

Historia de la Revolución de Colombia, 5 vols. (repr., Bogotá, 1969).

Robinson, David J. (ed.), *Mil Leguas por América, de Lima a Caracas, 1740–1741: Diario de Miguel de Santiesteban* (Bogotá, 1992).

Robledo, Emilio (ed.), *Bosquejo biográfico del señor oidor Juan Antonio Mon y Velarde, visitador de Antioquia, 1785–1788*, 2 vols. (Bogotá, 1954).

Silvestre, Francisco, *Descripción del Reyno de Santa Fe de Bogotá* (repr., Bogotá, 1968).

Relación de la Provincia de Antioquia (ed. David J. Robinson, Medellín, 1988).

"Relación que manifesta el estado de la provincia de Antioquia" (1776), *Archivo Historíal*, vol. 12 (Manizales, 1917), pp. 569–605.

"Informe sobre la apertura del camino desde Antioquia hasta Ayapel" (1776), *Archivo Historíal*, vol. 12 (Manizales, 1917), pp. 560–8.

Torres de Mendoza, Luis (ed.) *Coleción de documentos inéditos*, 42 vols. (Madrid, 1864–84).

Torre Miranda, Antonio de la, "Noticia individual de las poblaciones nuevamente fundadas en la provincia de Cartagena" (1789), *Boletín Historíal*, nos. 45–6, 49–51 (Cartagena, 1919).

Torres y Peña, José Antonio de, "Memorias sobre la revolución y sucesos de Santafé de Bogotá en el trastorno de la Nueva Granada y Venezuela," in Guillermo Hernández de Alba (ed.), *Memorias sobre los origenes de la independencia nacional* (Bogotá, 1960).

Wills, Guillermo, *Observaciones sobre el comercio de la Nueva Granada, con un apéndice relativo al de Bogotá* (Bogotá, 1952 ed.).

Books and articles

Aguilera Peña, Mario, *Los Comuneros: Guerra Social y Lucha Anticolonial* (Bogotá, 1985).

Aiton, Arthur S., "Spanish colonial reorganisation under the Family Compact," *Hispanic American Historical Review*, vol. 12 (1932), pp. 269–80.

"The Asiento Treaty as Reflected in the Papers of Lord Shelburne," *Hispanic American Historical Review*, vol. 8 (1928), pp. 167–77.

Anderson, Benedict., *Imagined Communities: Reflections on the Origin and Spread of Nationalism* (London, 1987).

Andrien, Kenneth J., "Economic Crisis, Taxes and the Quito Insurrection of 1765," *Past and Present*, no. 129 (1990), pp. 104–31.

Anna, Timothy E., *Spain and the Loss of America* (Lincoln and London, 1983).

Aragon, Arcesio, *Fastos payaneses* (Bogotá, 1939).

Arboleda, Gustavo, *Diccionario biográfico y genealógico del antiguo departamento del Cauca* (Cali, 1910).

Historia de Cali, 3 vols. (Cali, 1956).

Arciniegas, German, *Los Comuneros* (Mexico City, 1951).

Arellano, Moreno A., *Documentos para la historia de la época colonial* (Caracas, 1970).

Armytage, Francis, *The Free Port System in the British West Indies* (London, 1953).

Barbier, Jacques A., *Reform and Politics in Bourbon Chile, 1755–1796* (Ottawa, 1980).

Barriga Villalba, A. M., *Historia de la Casa de Moneda*, 3 vols. (Bogotá, 1969).

Bayle, Constantino, *Los Cabildos Seculares en la América Española* (Madrid, 1952).

Becker, Jéronimo, and José María Rivas Groot, *El Nuevo Reino de Granada en el siglo XVIII* (Madrid, 1921).

Bergquist, Charles, *Coffee and Conflict in Colombia, 1886–1910* (Durham, North Carolina, 1978).

Bethell, Leslie (ed.), *Cambridge History of Latin America*, vols. 1–2 (Cambridge, 1984).

Blossom, Thomas, *Nariño, Hero of Colombian Independence* (Tucson, Arizona, 1967).

Borrego Plá, María del Carmen, *Cartagena de Indias en el Siglo XVI* (Seville, 1983).

Brading, David, *Miners and Merchants in Bourbon Mexico* (Cambridge, 1971).

Briceño Perozo, Manuel, *Los Comuneros* (Bogotá, 1880).

Brown, Vera Lee, "The South Sea Company and Contraband Trade," *American Historical Review*, vol. 31 (1926), pp. 662–78.

"Contraband Trade. A Factor in the Decline of the Spanish Empire in America," *Hispanic American Historical Review*, vol. 8 (1928), pp. 178–89.

Burkholder, Mark, and D. S. Chandler, *From Impotence to Authority: The Spanish Crown and the American Audiencias, 1697–1808* (Columbia, Mississippi, 1977).

Bushnell, David, *The Santander Regime in Gran Colombia* (Newark, Delaware, 1954).

Caicedo, Bernardo, *D'Elhuyar y el siglo XVIII neogranadino* (Bogotá, 1971).

Canga Argüelles, J., *Diccionario de Hacienda* (2nd ed., Madrid, 1833).

Cárdenas Acosta, Pablo E., *Del vasallaje a la insurrección de los Comuneros. La provincia de Tunja en el virreinato* (Tunja, 1947).

Los Comuneros. (Reinvindicaciones históricas y juicios críticos documentalmente justificados) (Bogotá, 1945).

El movimiento comunal de 1781 en el Nuevo Reino de Granada, con copiosa documentación inédita, 2 vols. (Bogotá, 1960).

Carr, Raymond, *Spain, 1808–1939* (Oxford, 1966).

Carrera Pujal, Jaime, *Historia de la economía espanola*, 5 vols. (Barcelona, 1943–7).

Céspedes del Castillo, Guillermo, *La avería en el comercio de Indias* (Seville, 1945).

"Lima y Buenos Aires. Repercusiones económicas y políticas de la creación del Virreinato del Plata," *Anuario de Estudios Americanos* (Seville, 1946), pp. 673–878.

Chaunu, Pierre y Huguette, *Seville et L'Atlantique, (1504–1650)*, 8 vols. (Paris, 1955–60).

Chenu, Jeanne, "De la Terre aux Etoiles: Quète Scientifique el Identité Culturelle en Nouvelle Granade," in *Centre National de la Recherche Scientifique, L'Amérique Espagnole à l'Epoque des Lumières* (Paris, 1987), pp. 247–60.

Christelow, Alan, "Contraband Trade between Jamaica and the Spanish Main and the Free Port Act of 1766," *Hispanic American Historical Review*, vol. 22 (1942), pp. 309–43.

"Economic Background of the Anglo-Spanish War of 1762," *Journal of Modern History*, vol. 18 (1946), pp. 22–36.

"French Interest in the Spanish Empire during the Ministry of the Duc de Choiseul 1759–1771," *Hispanic American Historical Review*, vol. 21 (1941), pp. 515–37.

Colmenares, German, *Encomienda y población en la provincia de Pamplona* (Universidad de los Andes, Bogotá, 1969).

Historia económica y social de Colombia, 1537–1719, I (Bogotá, 1973).

Las Haciendas de los Jesuitas en el Nuevo Reino de Granada (Universidad Nacional, Bogotá, 1969).

La Provincia de Tunja en el Nuevo Reino de Granada. Ensayo de historia social 1539–1800 (Universidad de los Andes, Bogotá, 1970).

Historia económica y social de Colombia, II: Popayán: una sociedad esclavista, 1680–1800 (Bogotá, 1979).

Cali: Terratenientes, Mineros y Comerciantes, Siglo XVIII (Cali, 1983).

"Factores de la vida política: el Nuevo Reino de Granada en el siglo XVIII (1713–1740)," *Manual de Historia de Colombia*, vol. 1, pp. 386–415.

Cortés, Vicenta, *Catálogo de mapas de Colombia* (Madrid, 1967).

Delpar, Helen, *Red against Blue: The Liberal Party in Colombian Politics, 1863–1899* (University of Alabama, 1981).

Díaz y Díaz, Oswaldo, *Segundo Centenario del Nacimiento de Don Antonio Nariño* (Bogotá, 1965).

La reconquista española, 2 vols. (Bogotá, 1964–7).

Díaz de Zuluaga, Zamira, *Sociedad y economía en el Valle del Cauca, vol. 2: Guerra y economía en las haciendas, Popayán, 1780–1830* (Bogotá, 1983).

Earle, Rebecca, "Indian Rebellion and Bourbon Reform in New Granada: Riots in Pasto, 1780–1800," *Hispanic American Historical Review*, vol. 73 (1993), pp. 99–124.

Eugenio Martínez, María Angeles, "Reapertura de la vía Carare-Vélez. El asiento de Blas de Terga (1754)," *Anuario de Estudios Americanos*, vol. 41 (1984), pp. 513–52.

Fals Borda, Orlando, *El hombre y la tierra en Boyacá* (Bogotá, 1957).

Historia Doble de la Costa, vol. 1: Mompox y Loba (Bogotá, 1980).

"Indian Land Congregations in the New Kingdom of Granada: Land Tenure Aspects 1595–1850," *The Americas*, vol. 13 (1957), pp. 331–51.

Fisher, John, *Commercial Relations between Spain and Spanish America in the Era of Free Trade, 1778–1796* (Liverpool, 1985).

Fisher, John, Allan Kuethe, and Anthony McFarlane (eds.), *Reform and Insurrection in Bourbon New Granada and Peru* (Baton Rouge, Louisiana and London, 1990).

Fontana, Josep, and Miguel Antonio Bernal, *El Comercio Libre entre España y América Latina, 1765–1824* (Madrid, 1987).

Forero, José Manuel, *Camilo Torres* (Bogotá, 1960).

Friede, Juan, "Proceso de formación de la propiedad territorial en la América intertropical," *Jahrbuch fur Geschichte von Staat, Wirtschaft und Gelleschaft Lateinamerikas*, vol. 2 (1965), pp. 76–87.

"Demographic Changes in the Mining Community of Muzo after the Plague of 1629," *Hispanic American Historical Review*, vol. 47 (1967), pp. 338–43.

Invasión al país de los Chibchas, conquista del Nuevo Reino de Granada y fundación de Santa Fe de Bogotá (Bogotá, 1966).

Galindo, Aníbal, *Estudios económicos y fiscales* (Bogotá, 1978 ed).

Gálvez Pinal, Esperanza, *La visita de Monzón y Prieto de Orellano al Nuevo Reino de Granada* (Seville, 1974).

García Baquero González, Antonio, *Comercio colonial y guerras revolucionarias* (Seville, 1972).

Cádiz y el Atlántico, 1717–1778: El comercio español bajo el monopolio gaditano, 2 vols. (Seville, 1976).

García Fuentes, Lutgardo, *El comercio español con América, 1650–1700* (Seville, 1980).

Garrido Conde, María Teresa, "La primera creación del virreinato de Nueva Granada," *Anuario de Estudios Americanos*, vol. 21 (1964), pp. 25–144.

Garrido de Payán, Margarita, "La política local en la Nueva Granada, 1750–1810," *Anuario colombiano de historia social y de la cultura*, vol. 15 (1987), pp. 37–56.

"The Political Culture of New Granada, 1770–1815" (unpublished D. Phil. thesis, University of Oxford, 1990).

Gilmore, Robert L., "The Imperial Crisis, Rebellion and the Viceroy: Nueva Granada in 1809," *Hispanic American Historical Review*, vol. 40, (1960), pp. 1–24.

"New Granada's Socialist Mirage," *Hispanic American Historical Review*, vol. 36 (1956).

Glick, Thomas, "Science and Independence in Latin America (with Special Reference to New Granada)," *Hispanic American Historical Review*, 71:2 (1991), pp. 307–34.

Goebel, Dorothy B., "British Trade to the Spanish Colonies 1798–1823," *American Historical Review*, vol. 43 (1938), pp. 288–320.

Gomez, Thomas, *L'Envers de L'Eldorado: Economie Coloniale et Travail Indigéne dans la Colombie du XVIéme siecle*, (Toulouse, 1984).

Gómez Hoyos, Rafael, *La Revolución Granadina de 1810: Ideario de una generación y de una época, 1781–1821*, 2 vols. (Bogotá, 1962).

Gómez Latorre, Armando, *Enfoque social de la revolucíon comunera* (Bogotá, 1973).

Gómez Pérez, Carmen, *Pedro de Heredia y Cartagena de Indias* (Seville, 1984).

"Los extranjeros de la América colonial: su expulsión de Cartagena de Indias en 1750," *Anuario de Estudios Americanos*, tomo 37 (1980), pp. 279–300.

"El Consulado de Sevilla y la formación de las oligarquías en Cartagena de Indias a principios del siglo XVIII," *IV Jornadas de Andalucáa y América*, vol. 1 (Seville, 1984).

Góngora, Mario, *Los grupos de conquistadores en Tierra Firme, 1509–1530* (Santiago de Chile, 1962).

González, Margarita, *El resguardo en el Nuevo Reino de Granada* (Universidad Nacional, Bogotá, 1970).

Ensayos de historia social colombiana (Bogotá, 1974).

Gordon, B. Le Roy, *Human Geography and Ecology in the Sinú Country of Colombia* (Berkeley and Los Angeles, 1957).

Graff, Gary W., "Spanish Parishes in Colonial New Granada: Their Role in Town-Building on the Spanish American Frontier," *The Americas*, vol. 33 (1976–7), pp. 336–51.

Gredilla, Federico, *Biografía de José Celestino Mutis con relación de su viaje y estudios practicados en el Nuevo Reino de Granada* (Madrid, 1909).

Groot, José Manuel, *Historia ecclesiástica y civil de Nueva Granada*. 5 vols. (2nd ed., Bogotá, 1889).

Gutiérrez de Pineda, Virginia, *La Familia en Colombia* (Bogotá, 1963).

Halperín Donghi, Tulio, *Politics, Economics and Society in Argentina in the Revolutionary Period* (Cambridge, 1975).

Hamnett, Brian, *Politics and Trade in Southern Mexico, 1750–1821* (Cambridge, 1971).

Hansen, Caroline A., "Conquest and Colonization in the Colombian Chocó, 1510–1740" (unpublished Ph.D. thesis, University of Warwick, 1991).

Haring, C. H., *Trade and Navigation between Spain and the Indies* (Cambridge, Massachusetts, 1918).

Helguera, J. León, "The Problem of Liberalism versus Conservatism in Colombia, 1849–1885," in Frederick B. Pike (ed.), *Latin American History: Select Problems* (New York, 1969).

"Coconuco: Datos y documentos para la historia de una gran hacienda caucana, 1823, 1824, y 1876," *Anuario colombiano de historia social y de la cultura*, vol. 5 (1970), pp. 189–203.

Hernández Rodriguez, Gregorio, *De los Chibchas a la Colonia y a la República* (Bogotá, 1978).

Herr, Richard, *The Eighteenth Century Revolution in Spain* (Princeton, 1958).

Herrán Baquero, Mario, *El Virrey Don Antonio Amar y Borbón: La Crisis del Regimen Colonial en la Nueva Granada* (Bogotá, 1988).

Hoberman, Luisa, and Susan Migden Socolow (eds.), *Cities and Society in Colonial Latin America* (Albuquerque, New Mexico, 1986).

Hussey, Roland D., *The Caracas Company 1728–1784* (Cambridge, Massachusetts, 1934).

Ibáñez, P. M., *Crónicas de Bogotá*, 2 vols. (Bogotá, 1915).

Jaramillo Uribe, Jaime, *Ensayos sobre la historia social colombiana* (Bogotá, 1968).

El pensamiento colombiano en el siglo XIX (Bogotá, 1974).

"Las Sociedades Democráticas de artesanos y la coyuntura política y social colombiana de 1848," *Anuario colombiano de historia social y de la cultura*, vol. 8 (1976).

Jiménez Molinares, Gabriel, *Los martires de Cartagena de 1816*, 2 vols. (Cartagena, 1948–50).

Kalmanovitz, Salomón, *Economía y nación: Una breve historia de Colombia* (2nd ed., Bogotá, 1986).

Kamen, Henry, *The War of Succession in Spain* (London, 1969).

King, James F., "Evolution of the Free Slave Trade Principle in Spanish Colonial Administration," *Hispanic American Historical Review*, vol. 22 (1942), pp. 34–56.

"Admiral Vernon at Portobelo, 1739. Documents," *Hispanic American Historical Review*, vol. 23 (1943), pp. 258–82.

Kuethe, Allan J., *Military Reform and Society in New Granada 1773–1808* (Gainesville, Florida, 1978).

Cuba, 1753–1815: Crown, Military and Society (Knoxville, Tennessee, 1986).

"The Pacification Campaign on the Riohacha Frontier 1772–1779," *Hispanic American Historical Review*, vol. 50 (1970), pp. 467–81.

Kuethe, Allan J., and G. Douglas Inglis, "Absolutism and Enlightened Reform: Charles III, the Establishment of the Alcabala, and Commercial Reorganization in Cuba," *Past and Present*, no. 109 (1985), pp. 118–43.

La Force, James C., *The Development of the Spanish Textile Industry* (Berkeley, 1965).

Lasso de la Vega, Miguel de, *Los Tesoreros de la Casa de Moneda de Popayán* (Madrid, 1927).

Laviña, Javier, "La sublevación de Túquerres de 1800: Una revuelta antifiscal," *Boletín Americanista*, 20:28 (1978), pp. 189–96.

León Gómez, Adolfo, *El Tribuno de 1810* (Bogotá, 1910).

Leonard, David P., "The Comunero Rebellion of 1781: A Chapter in the Spanish Quest for Social Justice" (Ph.D. thesis, University of Michigan, 1951).

Liévano Aguirre, Indalecio, *Los grandes conflictos sociales y económicos de nuestra historia* (3rd. ed, Bogotá, 1968).

Loosley, A. C., "The Puerto Bello Fairs," *Hispanic American Historical Review*, vol. 13 (1933), pp. 314–35.

Lorenzo Sanz, Eufemio, *Comercio de España en la época de Felipe II*, 2 tomos (Simancas, 1986).

Loy, Jane, "Forgotten Comuneros: The 1781 Revolt in the Llanos of Casanare," *Hispanic American Historical Review*, vol. 61 (1981), pp. 235–57.

Lucena Salmoral, Manuel, *Nuevo Reino de Granada, Real Audiencia y Presidentes: Presidentes de Capa y Espada, 1605–1628, Historia Extensa de Colombia*, vol. III, tomo 2 (Academia Colombiana de Historia, Bogotá, 1966).

"Los Precedentes del Consulado de Cartagena: El Consulado de Santafé y el Tribunal del Comercio Cartagenero," *Anuario de Historia Social y Económica de América* (Universidad de Alcalá de Henares, 1986), pp. 179–98.

Luengo Muñoz, Manuel, "Genesis de las expediciones militares al Darien en 1785–1786," *Anuario de Estudios Americanos*, vol. 18 (1961), pp. 333–416.

Lynch, John, *Spain under the Hapsburgs*, 2 vols. (Oxford 1965–9).

Bourbon Spain, 1700–1808 (Oxford, 1989).

The Spanish American Revolutions, 1808–1826 (2nd ed., London, 1986).

Spanish Colonial Administration. The Intendant System in the Viceroyalty of Rio de la Plata (London, 1958).

"British Policy and Spanish America 1783–1808," *Journal of Latin American Studies*, vol. 1 (1969), pp. 1–30.

McFarlane, Anthony, "El comercio del Virreinato de la Nueva, Granada. Conflictos en la política económica de los Borbones 1783–1789," *Anuario colombiano de historia social y de la cultura*, vol. 6–7 (1971–2), pp. 69–116.

"Comerciantes y monopolio en la Nueva Granada: El Consulado de Cartagena de Indias," *Anuario colombiano de historia social y de la cultura*, vol. 11 (1983), pp. 43–70.

"Civil Disorders and Popular Protests in Late Colonial New Granada," *Hispanic American Historical Review*, vol. 65 (1984), pp. 17–54.

"The 'Rebellion of the Barrios': Urban Insurrection in Bourbon Quito," *Hispanic American Historical Review*, vol. 69 (1989), pp. 283–330.

"Cimarrones and Palenques: Runaways and Resistance in Colonial Colombia," in Gad Heuman (ed.), *Out of the House of Bondage: Runaways, Resistance and Marronage in Africa and the New World* (London, 1985).

"Economía política y política económica en Colombia, 1819–1850," in Antonio Annino et al. (eds.), *America Latina: Dallo Stato Coloniale allo Stato Nazione*, 2 vols. (Milano, 1987), vol. I, pp. 187–208.

McGreevey, William P., *An Economic History of Colombia, 1854–1930* (Cambridge, 1971).

McKinley, Michael P., *Pre-Revolutionary Caracas: Politics, Economy and Society, 1777–1811* (Cambridge, 1985).

Marchena Fernández, Juan, *La Institución Militar en Cartagena de Indias, 1700–1810* (Seville, 1982).

Martínez Delgado, Luis, and S. E. Ortíz, *El Periodismo en la Nueva Granada* (Bogotá, 1960).

Martínez Shaw, Carlos, *Cataluña en la Carrera de Indias, 1680–1756* (Barcelona, 1981).

Marzahl, Peter, "Creoles and Government: The Cabildo of Popayán," *Hispanic American Historical Review*, vol. 54 (1974), pp. 636–56.

Town in the Empire: Government, Politics and Society in Seventeenth Century Popayán (Austin, Texas, 1978).

Matta Rodríguez, Enrique de la, *El Asalto de Pointis a Cartagena de Indias* (Seville, 1979).

Melo, Jorge Orlando, *Historia de Colombia: La Dominación Española* (Bogotá, 2nd ed., 1978).

Sobre Historia y Política (Bogotá, 1979).

Meisel R., Adolfo, "Esclavitud, mestizaje y haciendas en la provincia de Cartagena, 1531–1851," *Desarrollo y Sociedad* (Bogotá, 1980), vol. 4, pp. 227–78.

Monsalve, J. D., *Antonio de Villavicencio*, 2 vols. (Bogotá, 1920).

Moore, John Preston, *The Cabildo in Peru under the Hapsburgs* (Durham, North Carolina, 1954).

Mora de Tovar, Gilma, *Aguardiente y conflictos sociales en la Nueva Granada, siglo XVIII* (Bogotá, 1988).

"El comercio de aguardientes catalanes en la Nueva Granada (siglo XVIII)," *Boletín Americanista*, no. 38 (1988), pp. 209–26.

Morineau, Michel, *Incroyables gazettes y fabuleux métaux. Les retours del trésors américains d'après les gazettes hollandaises (XVIe-XVIIIe siècles)* (Cambridge, 1985).

Morse, Richard, "Some characteristics of Latin American Urban History," *American Historical Review*, vol. 67 (1962), pp. 317–38.

Muñoz Pérez, J., "La publación del Reglamento de comercio libre a Indias de 1778," *Anuario de Estudios Americanos*, vol. 4 (1947), pp. 615–64.

Navarro García, Luis, *Intendencias de Indias* (Seville, 1959).

"Los regidores en el abasto de Cartagena de Indias," *Anuario de Estudios Americanos*, vol. 38 (1981), pp. 174–214.

Nelson, George H., "Contraband Trade under the Asiento 1730–1739," *American Historical Review*, vol. 51 (1945), pp. 55–67.

Nettels, C., "England and the Spanish American Trade, 1680–1715," *Journal of Modern History*, vol. 3 (1931), pp. 1–33.

Nieto Arteta, Luis, *Economía y cultura en la historia de Colombia* (6th ed., Bogotá, 1962).

Núñes Díaz, Manuel, *El Real Consulado de Caracas* (Caracas, 1971).

Olano, Antonio, *Popayán en la colonia en los siglos XVII y XVIII* (Bogotá, 1910).

Olano, Antonio, and Miguel Díaz Arroyo (eds.), *Historia de la gobernación de Popayán por Antonio Arroyo* (Popayán, 1907).

Ortíz, Sergio Elías, *Génesis de la revolución de 20 de julio de 1810* (Bogotá, 1960).

Agustín Agualongo y su tiempo (Bogotá, 1958).

Real Audiencia y Presidentes de Capa y Espada, 1654–1719, Historia Extensa de Colombia, vol. III, tomo 3 (Bogotá, 1966).

Ospina Vásquez, Luis, *Industria y protección en Colombia, 1810–1930* (Medellín, 1955).

Ots Capdequi, José María, *Nuevos aspectos del siglo XVIII español en América* (Bogotá, 1946).

Instituciones de gobierno del Nuevo Reino de Granada durante el siglo XVIII (Bogotá, 1950).

Las instituciones del Nuevo Reino de Granada al tiempo de la independencia (Madrid, 1958).

Padilla, Silvia, M. L. López Arellano, and A. González, *La encomienda en Popayán: Tres estudios* (Seville, 1977).

Pardo Umaña, Camilo, *Las haciendas de la Sabana: su historia, sus leyendas y sus tradiciones* (Bogotá, 1946).

Pares, Richard, *War and Trade in the West Indies* (Oxford, 1936).

Parsons, James J., *Antioqueño Colonisation in Western Colombia*, Ibero-Americana no. 32 (Berkeley and Los Angeles, 1949).

Pedraja Toman, René, "Aspectos del comercio de Cartagena de Indias en el siglo XVIII," *Anuario colombiano de historia social y de la cultura*, vol. 8 (1976), pp. 107–25.

Pelayo, Francisco, "Las actividades mineras de J. C. Mutis y Juan José Elhuyar en Nueva Granada," *Revista de Indias*, vol. 50 (1989), pp. 455–72.

Pérez-Mallaina, Pablo E., and Bibiano Torres Ramírez, *La Armada del Sur* (Seville, 1987).

Phelan, John Leddy, *The People and the King: The Comunero Revolution in Colombia, 1781* (Madison, Wisconsin, 1978).

The Kingdom of Quito in the Seventeenth Century: Bureaucratic Politics in the Spanish Empire (Madison, Wisconsin, 1967).

"El auge y la caida de los criollos en la Audiencia de Nueva Granada, 1700–1781," *Boletín de Historia y Antigüedades*, vol. 59 (1972), pp. 597–618.

Pinto Escobar, Inés, *La Rebelión del Común* (Tunja, 1976).

Plaza, José Antonio de, *Memorias para la historia de la Nueva Granada* (Bogotá, 1850).

Posada, Eduardo, *El Precursor* (Bogotá, 1903).

Posada, Zárate, *El movimiento revolucionario de los Comuneros* (Mexico City, 1971).

Prebble, John, *The Darien Disaster* (London, 1968).

Rappaport, Joanna, *The Politics of Memory: Native Historical Interpretation in the Colombian Andes* (Cambridge, 1990).

Rausch, Jane, *A Tropical Plains Frontier: The Llanos of Colombia, 1531–1831* (Albuquerque, New Mexico, 1984).

Real Díaz, J. J., "Las ferias de Jalapa," *Anuario de Estudios Americanos*, vol. 16 (1959), pp. 167–314.

Restrepo, Pastor, "Genealogías de Cartagena de Indias," *Boletín Historial* (Cartagena, 1945–6), nos. 89–91, 95.

Restrepo, Vicente, *Estudio sobre las minas de oro y plata de Colombia* (Bogotá, 1952).

Restrepo Sáenz, José M., *Biografías de los mandatorios y ministros de la Real Audiencia, 1671–1819* (Bogotá, 1952).

Restrepo Sáenz, José M., and Raimundo Rivas, *Genealogías de Santafé de Bogotá* (Bogotá, 1928).

Restrepo Tirado, Ernesto, *Historia de la provincia de Santa Marta en el Nuevo Reino de Granada*, 2 vols. (Seville, 1930).

Rivas, Raimundo, *El andante caballero don Antonio Nariño. La juventud (1765–1803)* (Bogotá, 1938).

Robertson, James A., "The English Attack on Cartagena in 1741, *and Plans for an Attack on Panama" Hispanic American Historical Review*, vol. 2 (1919), pp. 62–71.

Rodríguez M., Fidel, *Monografía de Santa Rosa de Osos* (Medellín, no date).

Rodríguez, Oscar, "Anotaciones al funcionamiento de la Real Hacienda en el Nuevo Reino de Granada," *Anuario colombiano de historia social y de la cultura*, vol. 11 (1983), pp. 71–88.

Rodríguez Plata, Horacio, *Andrés María Rosillo y Meruelo* (Bogotá, 1964).

La Antigua Provincia del Socorro en la Independencia (Bogotá, 1963).

Rodríguez Vicente, E., "El comercio cubano y la guerra de emancipación norteamericana," *Anuario de Estudios Americanos*, vol. 11 (Seville, 1954), pp. 61–106.

Rojas, Ulíses, *Corregidores y Justicias Mayores en la Provinci.: de Tunja desde la fundación de la ciudad hasta 1817* (Tunja, 1962).

Ruíz Rivera, Julián B., *Encomienda y mita en Nueva Granada en el siglo XVII* (Seville, 1975).

"Remesas de caudales del Nuevo Reino de Granada," *Anuario de Estudios Americanos*, vol. 34 (1977), pp. 242–70.

Safford, Frank S., "Commerce and Enterprise in Central Colombia, 1821–1870" (Ph.D. thesis, Columbia University, 1965).

The Ideal of the Practical: Colombia's Struggle to Form a Technical Elite (Austin, Texas, 1976).

"Social Aspects of Politics: New Granada, 1825–1850," *Journal of Social History*, vol. 5 (1972).

Sánchez Pedrote, Enrique, "Gil y Lemus y su memoria sobre el Nuevo Reino de Granada," *Anuario de Estudios Americanos*, vol. 8 (1951), pp. 169–212.

Sauer, Carl O., *The Early Spanish Main* (Berkeley and Los Angeles, 1966).

Schumpeter, E. B., *English Overseas Trade Statistics 1697–1800* (Oxford, 1960).

Segovia, Rodolfo, "Crown Policy and the Precious Metals in New Granada 1760–1810" (unpublished M.A. thesis, University of California, Berkeley, 1959).

Sempat, Assadourian, *El Sistema de la Economía Colonial: Mercado Interno, Regiones y Espacio Económico* (Lima, 1982).

Shafer, R. S., *The Economic Societies in the Spanish World 1763–1821* (Syracuse, New York, 1958).

Sharp, William F., *Slavery on the Spanish Frontier. The Colombian Chocó, 1680–1810* (Norman, Oklahoma, 1976).

"The Profitability of Slavery in the Colombian Chocó 1680–1810," *Hispanic American Historical Review*, vol. 55 (1975), pp. 468–95.

Silva, Renan, *Prensa y Revolución a finales del siglo XVIII: contribución a una análisis de la formación de la ideología de independencia nacional* (Bogotá, 1988).

Smith, R. S., *The Spanish Guild Merchant. A History of the Consulado 1250–1700* (Durham, North Carolina, 1950).

"The Consulado in Santa Fe de Bogotá," *Hispanic American Historical Review*, vol. 45 (1965), pp. 442–7.

Socolow, Susan Migden, *The Merchants of Buenos Aires, 1778–1810. Family and Commerce* (Cambridge, 1978).

Soto, Rafael, *Decenios de Mompós en la Independencia* (Barranquilla, 1960).

Spalding, Karen (ed.), *Essays in the Political, Economic and Social History of Colonial Latin America* (Newark, Delaware, 1982).

Stein, Stanley, and Barbara Stein, *The Colonial Heritage of Latin America: Essays on Economic Dependence in Perspective* (New York, 1970).

Steward, Julian H., *Handbook of South American Indians*, 7 vols. (New York, 1963).

Tascón, Tulio Enrique, *Historia de Buga en la colonia* (Bogotá, 1989).

Tjarks, German, *El Consulado de Buenos Aires* (Buenos Aires, 1962).

Torres Almeyda, Luis, *La rebelión de Galán, el comunero* (Bucaramanga, 1961).

Torres Ramírez, Bibiano, *La Compañía Gaditana de Negros* (Seville, 1973).

Tovar Pinzón, Hermes, *Grandes empresas agrícolas y ganaderas*, (Bogotá, 1980).

"El estado colonial frente al poder local y regional," *Nova Americana*, no. 5, (Turin, 1982), pp. 39–77.

"Estado actual de los estudios de demografía histórica en Colombia," *Anuario Colombiano de Historia Social y de la Cultura*, vol. 5 (1970), pp. 65–103.

"Guerras de opinión y represión en Colombia durante la Independencia," *Anuario colombiano de historia social y de la cultura*, vol. 11 (1983), pp. 187–233.

Trimborn, Hermann, *Señorío y barbarie en el Valle del Cauca* (Madrid, 1949).

Twinam, Ann, *Miners, Merchants and Farmers in Colonial Colombia* (Austin, Texas, 1982).

Vásquez de Prada, Valentín, "Las rutas comerciales entre España y América en el siglo XVIII," *Anuario de Estudios Americanos*, vol. 25 (1968), pp. 197–241.

Vergara y Vergara, José María, *Vida y escritos del General Antonio Nariño* (Bogotá, 1946).

Vergara y Velasco, F. J., *Capítulos de una historia civil y militar de Colombia* (Bogotá, 1905).

Vezga, Florentino, *La expedición botánica* (Bogotá, 1936).

Vila Vilar, Enriqueta, "Las Ferias de Portobelo: Apariencia y Realidad del Comercio con Indias," *Anuario de Estudios Americanos*, vol. 39 (1982), pp. 275–340.

Vilar, Pierre, *La Catalogne dans l'Espagne moderne*, 3 vols. (Paris, 1965).

A History of Gold and Money (London, 1975).

Villalobos R., Sergio, *El comercio y la crisis colonial* (Santiago de Chile, 1968).

Villamarín, Juan A., "Encomenderos and Indians in the Formation of a Colonial Society in the Sabana de Bogotá, 1537–1740" (Ph.D. thesis, Brandeis University, 1973).

Villamarín, Juan, and Judith Villamarín, "The Concept of Nobility in Colonial Santa Fe de Bogotá," in Karen Spalding (ed.), *Essays in the Political, Economic and Social History of Colonial Latin America* (Newark, Delaware, 1982), pp. 125–50.

Walker, Geoffrey J., *Spanish Politics and Imperial Trade, 1700–1789* (London, 1979).

West, Robert C., *Colonial Placer Mining in Colombia* (Baton Rouge, Louisiana, 1952).

The Pacific Lowlands of Colombia (Baton Rouge, Louisiana, 1957).

Whitaker, Arthur P., "The Elhuyar Mining Mission and the Enlightenment," *Hispanic American Historical Review*, vol. 31 (1951), pp. 558–83.

Woodward, Ralph Lee, *Class Privilege and Economic Development; The Consulado de Comercio de Guatemala 1793–1871* (Chapel Hill, North Carolina, 1966).

Ybot León, Antonio, *La artería histórica del Nuevo Reino de Granada* (Bogotá, 1952).

Index

CAMBRIDGE LATIN AMERICAN STUDIES

CPSIA information can be obtained at www.ICGtesting.com
Printed in the USA
BVOW07s1200220215

388784BV00001B/91/P